LATIN AMERICA IN THE INTERNATIONAL POLITICAL SYSTEM

■

About the Book and Author

More than a decade has passed since the publication of the first edition of *Latin America in the International Political System*. Since then, significant events have occurred in the region, and the nature of Latin America's international relations has changed considerably. Although the purpose of this text is unchanged—that of providing students with a topical, current, and analytically integrated survey of Latin America's role in international politics—it has been completely updated and revised to reflect Latin American relations in all their modern complexity.

Organizing the discussion around the idea of the region as a separate subsystem within the global international political system, Dr. Atkins gives special emphasis to subregions within Latin America, especially Mexico, Central America, the Caribbean, Brazil, and the Southern Cone. Within this framework he focuses on the foreign policies of the Latin American states themselves and on the policies of other powers toward Latin America. In addition, Dr. Atkins looks closely at the nature and role of transnational actors in the region, including the Catholic Church, multinational corporations, international labor, transnational political parties, and guerrilla organizations. Latin American participation in international institutions—including the Inter-American System, the United Nations, and the Nonaligned Movement—is also given special attention. Finally, Dr. Atkins examines the international distribution of power and influence among states and actors, noting in particular how that balance is reflected in cooperative and conflictual interactions in the political, cultural, economic, and military arenas.

G. Pope Atkins is professor of political science at the United States Naval Academy. He has lived and worked in Argentina and Ecuador and has been a visiting scholar at the Brookings Institution, the Institute of Latin American Studies at the University of London, the *Fondo para el Avance de las Ciencias Sociales* in Santo Domingo, and the international relations department at the London School of Economics and Political Science. He has also been a senior associate at the Center for Strategic and International Studies in Washington, D.C. Dr. Atkins has written extensively on Latin American international and comparative politics, including two books on the Dominican Republic.

LATIN AMERICA IN THE INTERNATIONAL POLITICAL SYSTEM

Second Edition
Revised and Updated

———————■———————

G. POPE ATKINS

WESTVIEW PRESS
Boulder, San Francisco, & London

Copyright © 1989 by Westview Press, Inc.

Published in 1989 in the United States of America by Westview Press, Inc., 5500 Central Avenue, Boulder, Colorado 80301, and in the United Kingdom by Westview Press, Inc., 13 Brunswick Centre, London WC1N 1AF, England

First edition published in 1977 by The Free Press

Library of Congress Cataloging-in-Publication Data
Atkins, G. Pope, 1934–
    Latin America in the international political system.
    Bibliography: p.
    Includes index.
    1. Latin America—Foreign relations. I. Title.
JX1393.L3A88 1989   327'.098   88-37863
ISBN 0-8133-0526-8
ISBN 0-8133-0527-6 (pbk.)

Printed and bound in the United States of America

The paper used in this publication meets the requirements of the American National Standard for Permanence of Paper for Printed Library Materials Z39.48-1984.

10   9   8   7   6   5   4   3   2   1

To my mother,
Louise Long Atkins

Contents

List of Tables and Maps   xiii
Preface to the Second Edition   xv
Preface to the First Edition   xix

PART ONE
A FRAMEWORK FOR ANALYSIS

1 The International Political System   3

   A Systems Perspective, 3
   The Units (Actors) in International Politics, 6
   The Integrated International System, 13
   International Subsystems, 20
   Bibliographic Comment, 22

2 The Latin American Regional Subsystem   23

   Identifying Regional Subsystems, 23
   The Latin American Regional Level, 25
   Further Subsystems, 30
   Subsystem Change, 34
   Extraregional Subsystems, 47
   Bibliographic Comment, 49

PART TWO
THE ACTORS

3 The Latin American States   53

   Capability, 53
   Nationalism, 64
   Foreign Policy Decision Making, 70
   Foreign Policy Orientations, 77
   Bibliographic Comment, 83

CONTENTS

4 Nonhemispheric States 85

European Perspectives of Latin America, 85
The Soviet Union, 97
Other States, 103
Bibliographic Comment, 107

5 The United States 108

The Latin American Position in U.S. Policy, 108
Evolution of Policy, 112
Bibliographic Comment, 133

6 Nonstate Actors 135

The Roman Catholic Church, 135
Business Enterprise, 143
Labor Organizations, 150
Transnational Political Parties, 154
Guerrilla Groups, 159
Bibliographic Comment, 170

**PART THREE
INTERNATIONAL INSTITUTIONS**

7 Latin American Integration and Association 175

The Movement for Spanish American Union, 175
Integration Movements After World War II, 180
Central American Integration, 184
Caribbean Integration, 188
Transregional Integration, 192
South American Arrangements, 197
Region-Wide Associations, 198
Bibliographic Comment, 200

8 The Inter-American System 202

Regional Organization and Law, 202
Organizational Structures, 205
Inter-American Policies, 214
Bibliographic Comment, 235

9 Global and Extraregional Arrangements 237

Global Organization to World War II, 237
The United Nations System, 241
Commodity Agreements, 250

The Nonaligned Movement, 251
Bibliographic Comment, 254

PART FOUR
INSTRUMENTS AND INTERACTION

10 Bargaining   257

Economic Relations, 257
Military Relations, 276
Diplomatic and Cultural Relations, 288
Bibliographic Comment, 293

11 Violence and Accommodation   295

Some General Considerations, 295
Nineteenth-Century Patterns and Cases, 297
Twentieth-Century Patterns and Cases
  to World War II, 302
Post–World War II Patterns and Cases, 306
Central American Crisis, 320
Bibliographic Comment, 326

12 International Regimes   328

The Panama Canal, 328
Mexican-U.S. Riverine Agreements, 335
Arms Control, 335
The Antarctic Treaty, 340
Law of the Sea, 342
The New International Economic Order, 346
Bibliographic Comment, 347

PART FIVE
CONCLUSION

13 Explanations and Prescriptions   351

The Theoretical Enterprise, 351
Realism, Idealism, and Marxism, 353
Liberal Developmentalism, 359
Dependency Theories, 363
Bibliographic Comment, 370

References   371
List of Acronyms   397
Index   401

Tables and Maps

Tables

3.1	Some Capability Indicators	56
8.1	Principal Inter-American Conferences, 1889–1988	206
10.1	U.S. Export-Import Bank Loans	264
10.2	U.S. Economic Assistance: Loans and Grants	265
10.3	Assistance from International Organizations, 1946–1986	266
10.4	U.S. Military Assistance: Loans and Grants	282

Maps

Latin America	26
The Caribbean Area	27

Preface
to the Second Edition

SIGNIFICANT EVENTS and momentous changes have taken place in Latin America's international relations since the publication of the first edition of this book in 1977. Central American crisis has captured the headlines, with social revolution in Nicaragua, civil war in El Salvador, the rekindling of Soviet-Cuban activity, the greatly increased U.S. presence calculated in terms of East-West conflict, the associated military invasion of the island of Grenada, and the "declaration of independence" of local Latin American states reflected in the Contadora process and the Arias plan for negotiated settlements of the Central American conflict. Just as striking have been the human rights policies of the Carter administration, the new Panama Canal treaties, the debilitating foreign debt crisis, the Anglo-Argentine war in the South Atlantic, the end of military regimes and restoration of democratic forms in most of Latin America, the immobility of the Inter-American System, the rise of "narcotraffic" as a high-priority problem, and much more.

With this array of critical developments, U.S. policymakers have focused on Latin America as an area of primary concern. They speak of Mexico as second only to the Soviet Union as the most important bilateral concern and again view the Circum-Caribbean as a critical strategic area. One suspects, however, that the new attention has been undertaken reluctantly and unsympathetically, and, despite considerable effort, fundamental U.S. goals have not been achieved. At the same time, Latin America has had significant dealings with the Soviet Union, individual European states and the European Community, Japan, the Roman Catholic Church and other churches, transnational political parties and labor organizations, and others.

The past dozen years have also seen a heightened and more sustained scholarly interest in Latin America's role in world affairs. The first edition of this book was issued at the beginning of a surge of serious analytic attention. A large number of studies have appeared of widely varying purposes and quality. They have addressed both general and specific aspects of Latin American international relations, including, especially, U.S. policy and Latin American foreign policies. Particularly notable has been the great increase in scholarship among Latin Americans themselves. Nevertheless, the need still seems to exist for the kind of work this book attempts to be: a topically complete and analytically integrated political science survey.

The broad purposes and approach of this book remain the same as in the first edition. It is intended to introduce the reader to Latin American international relations, especially to serve as a classroom text at the upper undergraduate or beginning graduate level and as a general reference tool for anyone seeking description and analysis of the subject. The treatment is still organized around the idea of the region as a separate subsystem within the global international political system; hence, the emphasis is on the structures and processes associated with the region's international politics and with the foreign policies of the many states and other actors within and outside the region. Issues are subsumed under these primary foci. I am still persuaded of the utility and validity of this device around which to organize an introduction to the analysis of such a complex subject. I have tried to integrate the theory of political systems throughout the text while avoiding irrelevant jargon.

Certain assumptions also remain. I asserted in the first edition that Latin America should be the subject and not the object of study. This essential point of reference remains the same and is reflected in a determined effort to focus primarily on Latin America, with U.S.–Latin American relations, current issues, and other considerations subsumed under that overall objective.

The book goes far beyond the obvious necessity of updating. It is a different version in a number of essential ways and has incorporated extensive changes designed to improve the original. The revisions reflect a response to reviews, comments from professional colleagues, my own continued classroom experience and student responses, events and changes in Latin America such as those mentioned above, and developments in the academic study of the region and general international relations. The text has been carefully reviewed and much of it rewritten. Certain topics have been rearranged, the number of chapters increased, and chapter sequence reordered, all aimed at clarifying the conceptual progression of topical analysis and reducing repetitive discussion. Even greater emphasis has been placed on the importance of subregions in Latin America, on the increasing globalization of the entire region, and on Latin American foreign policy initiatives. A new concluding chapter has been written for this edition in an effort to draw the entire work together in theoretical terms; the result is admittedly a largely iconoclastic and perhaps impatient critique of extant explanations of Latin America's international relations by scholars and practitioners. The Bibliographic Comment sections have been revised (they are more selective than before) and brought as up-to-date as possible.

I wish to extend my profound gratitude to colleagues in the United States, Latin America, and Europe who offered help in the form of encouragement, advice, suggestions, comments, criticism, and information during the life of the first edition and for this revision. I also acknowledge my debt to the students who have come under my guidance during many years of teaching the subject. The list is too extensive for all of those who contributed to be mentioned individually. Nevertheless, special acknowledgment must be made to Morris Blachman, Harold Blakemore, Jack Child, Jorge Domínguez, Esperanza Duran, Fred Halliday, Edward Jamison, Luis Esteben Julia, John Lovell, the late Thomas McGann, John Martz, Helen Purkitt, Roberto Russell, Lars Schoultz, Allison Temple, Howard Wiarda, Charles Wilson, and Larman Wilson. Finally, I again pay special tribute to my wife, Joan, for her continuing professional and personal support. I am, as before, fully responsible for all that follows.

G. Pope Atkins

Preface
to the First Edition

THIS BOOK IS CONCERNED with the international politics of Latin America. The subject is analyzed with a view to introducing the foreign policies of various "actors" (both states and nonstate entities) and the political patterns and institutions resulting from their interaction. Special attention is given to the problems confronted by the Latin American states, and to their relations with each other and with other actors. An attempt is made to keep the work on a level meaningful to undergraduate students and comprehensible to the general reader by stressing the fundamentals of politics throughout.

I intend this study to partially fill a gap in the scholarly literature dealing with the international relations of Latin America. The standard works broadly surveying the subject have traditionally been diplomatic histories focusing primarily on United States–Latin American relations, or institutional-legal treatments of Pan Americanism and the Organization of American States. Other books have appeared applying political analysis with a broad topical compass, but all have suffered from at least one of several weaknesses. Among the shortcomings have been unsystematic methodology, little concern with foreign policy processes, inadequate attention to inter–Latin American relations, and failure to deal with the roles of the nonhemispheric states of Europe and Asia in Latin America. While some treatment of all of these and other themes may be found in books, monographs, and journal articles, no single basic general survey draws them all together. In sum, a number of valuable studies of sound scholarship have dealt with the international relations of Latin America, but a need exists for a topically complete, factually current, introductory level general survey using political science concepts.

The subject of this book and the method employed reflect my personal interest in Latin America and professional commitment to political science. A political systems approach is used as an organizational and analytic framework, viewing the Latin American region (defined as that portion of the western hemisphere south of the United States) as a subsystem of the international (global) system. This allows the specific Latin American subject to be pursued in such a way that adds to general rather than parochial

xix

knowledge. But this is not a book on methodology; rather, extant theories of international and comparative politics are applied to aid in the understanding of Latin America, and the need for concepts to refer to the world of experience is stressed.

The application of a systems perspective to an introductory work such as this raises certain difficulties, especially the problem of technical discussion versus understanding. I attempt to strike a compromise by employing the language of systems theory but keeping technical terms at a minimum. Important terms necessary to communicating the method are defined and used throughout, but the bulk of the analysis is purposely kept as nontechnical as possible. I further attempt to avoid levels of abstract discussion that may lead to methodological debates largely irrelevant to the concrete topic being analyzed.

I am fully aware of the risk involved in attempting to produce a study that aims for comprehensive coverage in a relatively brief space. A survey text should be topically complete, especially one that aspires to delineate the Latin American regional subsystem; but this need not require an overly long book. The text has been kept short enough to allow teachers sufficient flexibility in their own approaches by supplementing it with other materials. As a result the treatment of some subjects is necessarily sketchy. Readers are alerted to the structures, processes, and issues relevant to the Latin American subsystem, but with some sacrifice of detail in order to present a conceptually complete systemic "overview." This deficiency is partially compensated by the inclusion of bibliographic comment at the end of each chapter guiding readers to additional materials for deeper delving into areas of special interest to them.

Limits of space seem to dictate that general treatments of Latin American politics either adopt a regional perspective or be a collection of studies of individual states. Both approaches are appropriate and necessary to our understanding of the subject. This book recognizes the uniqueness of the individual Latin American states as well as their commonalities, and I have, to a degree, contrasted as well as likened them in several contexts. But the stress here is on Latin America as a regional entity, emphasizing regional power configurations, associations, relations, and other themes that seem to characterize the entire area.

General surveys such as this necessarily cover more areas of knowledge than one person can master. Three scholars must be given special mention for their substantial assistance to this project. First I want to express my gratitude to and admiration and affection for Harold Eugene Davis, my teacher in graduate school beginning some fifteen years ago, and a friend and colleague since that time. Professor Davis has been a continuing source of encouragement and assistance over the years. He commented on much of the present manuscript with keen insight and a profound knowledge of Latin America reflecting his many years of dedicated scholarship. I owe further debts to Larman C. Wilson and Larry V. Thompson, with whom I have enjoyed rewarding collaborative efforts; they also critiqued parts of the present work. So much of their work and so many of their ideas are mixed with my own in this book that I am unable to sort them out for proper attribution, and I am reduced to merely stating my obligation to them.

Valuable assistance of several kinds was rendered by D. Patrick Curry, John A. Hutchins, and John R. Probert. I am most grateful for their support.

Special tribute is paid to my wife, Joan, for her good nature, forbearance, and penetrating criticism, and for sharing the seemingly interminable typing chores.

Acknowledgment of my debt and gratitude to all of these people does not imply that they concur in this study. I alone assume responsibility for the final product—its conception, content, and presentation—as well as for all procedural and substantive errors.

G.P.A.

PART ONE

■

A Framework for Analysis

The first two chapters of this book establish the framework within which the entire study is cast. Chapter 1 discusses systems theory as an organizing device for analyzing international relations in general. Chapter 2 applies these abstract concepts to Latin America and identifies assumptions and problems in viewing Latin America as a regional subsystem of the global political system. Together these chapters provide a way to integrate the vast data concerning Latin America's international relations. Using this framework for analysis, the rest of the book provides a detailed examination of the various elements of the Latin American political system.

CHAPTER ONE

■

The International
Political System

POLITICAL SCIENTISTS CONSTRUCT organizing devices designed to assist in the understanding of political data by ordering seemingly disparate facts and events into some meaningful pattern that can be analyzed. An organizing device may be called an *approach,* a *paradigm,* a *quasi-theory,* a *conceptual framework,* or an *analytic framework.* All of these terms are roughly synonymous; regardless of which one is used, such devices have three specific purposes. First, an analytic framework (the term I prefer) provides a method of systematically determining which facts are pertinent and which should be ignored. Second, it enables one to methodically present the selected data in a coherent and logical manner. Finally, it facilitates the orderly comparison of related sets of phenomena. This chapter discusses international systems theory, which provides the analytic framework used in this book for selecting, organizing, and comparing data relating to Latin American international relations. The chapter begins with a discussion of how the approach applies to the study of international relations in general as well as Latin America's international relations in particular.

A SYSTEMS PERSPECTIVE

The Approach to This Study

A number of characteristics have evolved in the academic study of IR (as specialists tend to refer to the field of international relations). Whether specialists prefer IR to be considered an autonomous discipline or, more likely, as a field of political science, the core concepts they deal with are rooted in the study of politics. In fact, the sharp decline of interest in diplomatic or international history on the part of historians, and economists' restricted definition of politics, have further lodged the study of IR into the discipline of political science. Furthermore, within the political science emphasis, IR no longer constitutes a single field. It has grown into three separate but related areas of study: the international political system and its

3

array of subfields; foreign policy analysis and comparative foreign policy; and international political economy.

This book seeks to provide a general survey of Latin American international relations. Thus it seems appropriate for it to begin with an overview of the field of international political systems and its constituent parts and processes. Within this primary focus, this book integrates basic foreign policy analysis, including comparative aspects. International political economy is referred to as a crucial consideration, but it does not provide the primary paradigm. Likewise, historical and legal-institutional descriptions and interpretations and analyses of ideologies are pursued inasmuch as they enhance the basic approach. Finally, policy evaluations flow from these prior conceptualizations, descriptions, and analyses.

The study of any field of politics involves the problem of how an analyst handles values—not only as a detached observer but in making interpretations and defining personal preferences as well. Objectivity is an appropriate goal; however, "value-free" analysis is not only difficult to achieve but is also not necessarily desirable. The resolution of this problem depends on the position taken toward evidence and inference. I have attempted to identify issues and summarize competing arguments first, and to postpone normative conclusions and policy prescriptions until after analyzing a variety of political structures and processes.

Systems Theory as an Analytic Framework

Systems theory emphasizes structures and processes in the study of politics. A "system" fundamentally consists of the interaction between two or more distinct units and the consequences of that interaction. Put another way, a system is characterized by differentiation (the presence and workings of separate units) and by integration (the overall structure of the system and the interaction of its units in order to perform system functions). Integration implies regularity of relations, mutual dependence, and some measure of coordination among the units.

A systems approach offers distinct advantages for organizing, integrating, and analyzing the subject matter. It provides a broad overview of politics and facilitates the analysis of a wide range of relationships in the political process. Systems theory helps us to integrate political knowledge because we can apply its fundamental concepts to any level of political activity, including subnational systems, national politics, various groupings of nation-states (such as in a geographic region), and the entire international political system.

Systemic concepts of differentiation and integration can be applied by contemporary political scientists specializing in international relations to the separate but related foci of foreign policy and international politics. Foreign policy analysis (also known as "action theory") deals with the nature and actions, either singly or in comparison, of the nation-state as it functions in the international political system. The analysis of international politics (also referred to as "interaction theory") is concerned with the international system itself and the relations of states as they interact with each other. Scholars have also studied the actions of non-nation-state actors—such as multinational corporations, guerrilla groups, political parties, and others—that are units in the system. As they have increasingly directed attention to this array of actors, scholars have had to adjust their notions of foreign policy and international politics to account for the presence, characteristics, decisions, and activities of nonstate actors.

In foreign policy analysis, inquiry is focused on the attributes of the states and the way they, through their decision makers, respond to motivations and aspirations, formulate interests, analyze situations, select objectives, and decide upon and execute courses of action. Foreign policy becomes international politics when action is taken and other states or nonstate entities react, thereby commencing interaction. The study of international politics shifts from unit identification and policy formulation and execution to the structures and processes of the international political system itself, including the patterns of interaction among the units and the ways in which the system is regulated.

An area of inquiry may focus on either the individual actor or the global system; it may also focus on a region or area of the world, such as Latin America. Regional international relations can be viewed as international subsystems, defined as groupings of some of the units (nation-states and other actors) that interact on a regular basis distinct from the total process but not autonomous from the global system. A regional perspective offers analytic advantages. For example, it avoids overemphasis on the roles of great powers and superpowers and their interrelations, which, understandably, engages most IR analysts. It recognizes that lesser powers play significant international roles.

Nature of the International System

When applied to international politics, systems theory presents some methodological problems. Some critics argue that an international system does not exist and, therefore, that international politics are not susceptible to systems theorizing. This view assumes that IR should deal only with the flux of changing concrete situations that are not amenable to systemic generalization or theoretical explanation, and that students in the field must be satisfied with describing specific past events. More specifically, it assumes that international politics are anarchic—because no centralized international decision-making authority exists and a system, by definition, requires regularity. This view is similar to the position taken by some historians who view history as a series of new and unique events and who deny the existence of behavioral patterns. A similar perspective is also expressed by some sociologists who find individual psychological patterns of behavior but no social system as such.

One can hardly claim, in reply, that international events fall into immutable patterns, and one must acknowledge that the international system clearly differs in fundamental ways from domestic processes. The essential problem with a systems approach is that of regulation: The international arena, unlike the domestic arena, lacks higher authoritative decision-making agencies able to make and enforce rules and reconcile conflicting parties. Furthermore, virtually no feeling of loyalty or legitimacy exists above the level of the nation-state. The nation-state continues to be the central structural feature and decisional source in the system. Moreover, certain other actors also occupy important positions, which serves to further decentralize the system.

International politics, however, do not merely consist of anarchic competition. A degree of integration is found; however, it is considerably less than in most domestic (nation-state) systems. In reality, state independence is far from absolute, whether in the domestic or the international realm, and interdependence is increasingly a fact as well as a theory of international life. The distribution of power and influence among states and other actors has always had a primary structural influence; the "balance of power" has been recognized by strategists for centuries as an informal regulatory device. Formal regulatory institutions are embodied in international law, organizations, and other interstate regimes; various forms of informal consensus also exist. Although any authoritative activity of such institutions is ultimately limited by the sovereign autonomy of the member states, many formal and informal rules are voluntarily accepted and followed. In addition, the variety of regularized and sustained patterns of interaction is significant and, in some instances, predictable.

In sum, regular (but not in the sense of unchanging) patterns of international activities are common enough to warrant the claim that an international political system exists and that systems theory may be usefully applied to an analysis of international politics. Most thoughtful historians recognize that even unique events take place within some (perhaps changing) structure. If we view a system, at the very least, as a group of related units that interact with and affect each other, then interstate relations constitute a system. Today's international system may be characterized as primitive, undeveloped, rudimentary, and decentralized; but it is nevertheless a real system and a viable target for systems theory. A good argument may be made that it is inefficient and dangerous, but whether it is good or bad depends on the analyst's point of view and has little to do with whether or not an international system exists.

THE UNITS (ACTORS)
IN INTERNATIONAL POLITICS

Nation-States

The most important differentiated units in international politics today, as in the past three centuries, are sovereign nation-states. At present they number more than 160 and are located in all parts of the world. Although the nation-state has never been and is not now the only unit or actor in the international political system, it is and will continue for the foreseeable future to be the most prominent one. As such, it is the central concept in world politics and provides the starting point for an understanding of the international political system.

The modern state system evolved after the collapse of feudalism and the dual empire-papacy system in Europe at the end of the Middle Ages. The new system developed throughout the fifteenth and sixteenth centuries and was legally institutionalized by the Peace of Westphalia (1648), which settled the Thirty Years War among kings, pope, and emperor (supported by feudal lords). The peace arrangement recognized the independence of secular nation-states from the Holy Roman Empire and the papacy. This system subsequently spread from Europe to all parts of the world. The process was not completed in Europe until the late nineteenth century, when Italy and Germany each were finally consolidated. In the meantime, after their own emergence, the new European states began to expand their power around the globe through colonization and trade. This movement was led first by Portugal in the early fifteenth century and Spain beginning in the 1490s, followed by France, Holland, and Great Britain in the sixteenth century. Eventually, almost all European states adopted imperialist policies, and overseas empires were established in most of the non-European world.

Independent nation-states of the European type did not appear outside of Europe until the United States of America was established in 1776. Latin America followed suit between 1804 and 1824 and Japan in the late nineteenth century (through a nonrevolutionary process of "opening" to the outside world). China did not effectively become a nation-state in the Western sense until after 1911, the year of Sun Yat Sen's revolution. The European empires in Asia, Africa, and the Caribbean have largely broken up in the twentieth century, although the process still continues. Most of the new states in those areas were born after World War II, including two of the most populous nations in the world, India and Indonesia. Thus, what originated as a European system became a global one through several kinds of change; the political values of the West, in the sense of organizing human affairs at the most fundamental level into something called the nation-state, now extend virtually to the entire world.

The modern state is endowed with two unique characteristics that it shares with no other entity—the attribute of sovereignty and the relationship of nationalism to statehood. Sovereignty and nationalism are distinct concepts, but they are related in their complex evolution over the past three centuries.

Introduced in sixteenth-century international law, sovereignty is traditionally defined as the state's supreme authority over its citizens, which is absolute and indivisible, making it the final arbiter in their lives. Whether sovereignty is, indeed, indivisible has long been a matter of debate. The idea was the product of the times that witnessed the rise of the nation-state under absolute monarchs. It replaced the medieval concept of limited sovereignty under natural (divine) law embodied in the contractual relationship of the feudal system. The concept of sovereignty stressed the superiority of the territorial state to both imperial universalism and feudal localism and reflected the need for central government authority, embodied in the monarch ("the sovereign"), in order to create domestic order and stability in a given territory.

States and nations had existed throughout recorded history, but only after the consolidation of feudal units into kingdoms in Western Europe were the two elements combined. Since then, a principal theme of system development has been the search by multicultural states for a single nationhood and by homogeneous nations for statehood. These processes involve the melding of distinct entities that are not necessarily coterminous—the state (a legal-political entity defined in terms of territory, population, and effective autonomous government) and the nation (a social-cultural entity defined in terms of people who, for whatever reasons, share a sense of sameness and uniqueness). From the rise of the modern state until the late eighteenth century, dynastic states worked to create nations of their domains, with the "sovereign" serving as the symbol of national identity among the people living within the state borders. With the American and French revolutions (1776/1789) and the subsequent development of republicanism, nationalism came to be identified with "the people." Thereafter, national groups sought to create states that conformed to national boundaries, and the idea of "national self-determination" was born. Since then, a tension has existed over the nature and relationship of nations and states.

A major change in the concept of sovereignty occurred with the development of republicanism in the late eighteenth century. The locus of state sovereignty shifted from the tangible person of the monarch to the abstraction of "we the people." This transition required the doctrine of popular sovereignty to emerge, in which the voice of the people (*vox populi*) replaced the voice of God (*vox Dei*) as the ultimate base of authority.

The notion of popular sovereignty suggests this question: Can the state realistically be personified? That is, can a nonhuman abstraction act, or should one look instead to individual persons as the real actors in the system? Social psychologists have raised a parallel problem: Is there such a thing as group behavior, or is it merely the behavior of individuals in groups? Analysts tend to attribute action to states as a convenient expression, but they recognize that human beings in fact make decisions and act on behalf of states and their societies. The personification of the state is both a legal and convenient way of referring to the behavior of an identifiable collection of human beings.

State Action

Foreign Policy Orientations. The analysis of state action begins with observations of foreign policy behavior. Behavior—the actual substance of policy—depends on several dimensions of a state's orientation. "Orientation" refers to a state's evaluation of its place in the international system and its choice of methods for coping with the external world. Some analysts equate orientation with a state's tendencies regarding alignment. I, however, prefer to adopt a broader perspective and describe policy orientations in terms of four different factors: ends and means, alignment, national roles, and status-quo or revisionist commitments.

Ends-means analysis is helpful in analyzing specific policy decisions. It inquires into a state's calculation of interests and goals and the relations between the policy objectives and the policy instruments and techniques. It may also include reference to ethical and moral considerations. Ultimate state objectives are usually those identified with the age-old concept of "national interest," often referred to as a nation's "vital interests." Decision makers formulate policies in order to promote the national interest, whatever it is conceived to be. Most states conclude most of the time that their vital interests are self-preservation, security, and social and economic well-being. In any event, ultimate objectives are expressed in the most general and often symbolic or even mythical terms, which makes the idea of "national interest" highly ambiguous. Such interests may be made more specific by translating them into proximate goals of varying "distance" (long, medium, or short range). Proximate goals become tactical means leading to long-range goals and serve as springboards for ultimate objectives.

A state's choice of instruments and tactics can involve varying degrees of multilateral or unilateral and active or passive policies. The more multilateralist a state, the greater its tendency to seek joint solutions to problems through international organizations, alliances, and coalitions rather than bilateral (state to state) approaches. The more active a state, the more likely it is to initiate international actions rather than only respond to or resist the initiatives taken by others. An important aspect of activism is the degree of willingness to use coercion—to intervene in the domestic affairs of other states (through diplomatic, economic, or paramilitary means) or to use armed force to resolve conflicts. Some states quickly resort to intervention, some emphasize cooperative approaches, and others passively choose not to compete.

A second dimension of state orientation concerns tendencies regarding alignment. Does a state choose military alliance and economic or political coalition with other states? Or does it prefer some form of neutrality or nonalignment? "Neutrality" is a foreign policy orientation whereby a state will not commit its military, diplomatic, or other capabilities in an alliance or coalition with another state or bloc or is prohibited by outsiders from doing so. There are three different types of neutrality. First, neutrality may refer to the legal status chosen by a state during armed hostilities; such a choice entails defined rights and responsibilities that distinguish neutrals from belligerents. The second meaning, also recognized in international law, refers to a state that has been neutralized through the actions of others, usually through agreement among the great powers to impose and guarantee the neutrality. Finally, neutrality can also mean nonalignment—a voluntary rejection of alliance, a refusal to align with the great powers or their blocs—without reference to legal status. Certain European and Third World states today, for example, reject commitment to one side or the other in East-West bloc conflicts. Nonalignment may also serve as the practical means for obtaining economic concessions from the contending blocs. An isolationist strategy is indicated by a low level of involvement in most aspects of the international political system, few diplomatic or commercial transactions, or attempts to seal off the country against various forms of external penetration.

The third dimension of state orientation is defined in terms of "national roles." This term refers to policymakers' views of what the nation-state should do in the world based on their perceptions of both the outside world and their own societies. Role conceptions define the kinds of actions appropriate to national values. They are associated only with states that are actively involved in global or regional affairs. National role analysis, following the lead of K. J. Holsti (1988), focuses on the general types of decisions, rules, norms, guidelines, standards, commitments, and international functions that decision makers translate into various kinds of actions to be taken when confronted with geographic and issue challenges. For example, Holsti posits some typical national roles that are suggestive of U.S. perceptions of its functions in the Caribbean Basin: the role of "regional defender/leader/ policeman," protecting other states in a defined area; of "mediator," assisting in international conflict resolution; and of "protector of the faith," urging, in recent decades, anticommunism and democratic development.

Finally, foreign policy orientations may be understood in terms of a state's commitment either to the status quo or to revisionism. A state may pursue a policy of the status quo if it is satisfied with its lot in the international system, or at least is willing to accept it. A state with a revisionist commitment is dissatisfied with the status quo and desires to change the distribution of the rewards of the system in a way more to its advantage. A status quo state is likely to pursue policies aimed at keeping things the way they are and thus will usually be defensive in nature, oriented toward the preservation of peace and stability. Contrarily, the revisionist state is more likely to be on the offensive; it is less interested in peaceful and stable processes, considering that they work to its disadvantage.

Capability Analysis. Capability analysis is crucial to foreign policy formulation at several stages of the process. A broad range of "situational factors" give rise to or help shape policy decisions. These factors—the real world settings or conditions that impinge on a state's actions—either limit the state's freedom or offer opportunities. Analysts attempt to identify the relevant factors and determine how and why they influence the decisions leaders make. These influences on policymakers may stem from the intrasocietal or international environment, or they may arise in the political system as such or among the decision-making agents themselves. In given situations, several factors may operate simultaneously. Among the factors are the requirements imposed by external situations or events; in some cases states may find their decisions largely determined for them. In any case, special attention must be directed toward trends that shape the environment in which policy must operate.

The factors that influence policy decisions are complex. Policymakers must determine the capabilities and the actual or anticipated actions of other states, decide whether threats are real or imagined, anticipate the actions of other states as accurately as possible, and then cope with moves made by other states by resisting, cooperating, or accommodating them. A state's geographic setting influences such variables as world position, the presence of more or less powerful neighbors, and whether climate, terrain, and natural resources are favorable or unfavorable. The social setting of other states must also be considered, not only in terms of their strength in potential conflict but also in terms of their ability to cooperate in mutual enterprises.

Intrasocietal sociocultural and economic influences also condition the behavior and affect the actions of foreign policy officials and may be important sources for their decisions. From the intrasocietal environment come such influences as nationalism, ideology, religion, the state of the economy, and the nature of social stability. Inside the political system, interest groups, political parties, and elites may interact with decision makers, and public opinion, public relations activities, the communications media, and elections also influence policy decisions.

But a state does not simply choose a policy objective and move toward it at will. Decision makers must take into account their own national capability to implement policy and must hold realistic expectations (perhaps in the form of educated guesses) of realizing their goals. They must also consider their relative capability compared with that of other states with which they are interacting. Goals are partly a function of the process through which they are formulated, and the form of action is partly determined by the goals; but both ends and means are also largely determined by the resources available to sustain them. The concept of capability is partly synonymous with that of power—the power of the state to influence the behavior of other actors or convince them to accede to its own position. Capability analysis, in this sense, is an inventory of relative strengths and weaknesses as measured by a state's military, economic, political, and other resources. Thus, a state's capabilities influence its ends-means orientations; capabilities may provide a means to achieve other ends, or the pursuit of power may be an end in itself.

Decision Theory. The identification of the intellectual, psychological, and institutional factors that affect the reasoning processes by which leaders arrive at decisions is a difficult area of foreign policy analysis. Capability analysis may indicate what a state can do, but not what it will do, nor, necessarily, why it acted in a particular manner in the past. "Intent analysis" may be pursued with three basic decision-making models.

Many foreign policy analysts adhere to the "rational model," or "ideal model," of decision making. According to this model, when faced with a problem that requires solution, rational individuals ideally follow a certain process. They define the situation; solicit as much information as possible; specify the goal or goals to be achieved; rank priorities; consider possible alternative means for achieving the goals; select the best (most rational) alternative to be pursued; take the necessary steps to implement the decision; and evaluate the consequences of the actions so as to learn from the experience.

Other decision-making theories focus on the human decision makers themselves as they respond to stimuli from both the external and domestic environments. These theories are based on the assumption that the psychological characteristics of policymakers may depart from rational model processes. Determining these characteristics is more than a matter of detecting inefficiencies in the ideal decisional process; it requires identifying certain additional psychological factors that may intrude. Such theories may be grouped into two general categories: the perceptual and the bureaucratic models.

The perceptual model focuses on perceptions that state leaders hold of the world and of themselves. Thus, when they formulate foreign policy, their views about their environment, other actors, and national roles in the international system form part of the basis for policies and actions. Theorists distinguish between the decision maker's objective environment (reality) and psychological environment (the perception or image of reality) and the difficulty of reconciling the two. Pearson and Rochester (1988) note that images are required for decision makers to construct reality but that they can also bias their perceptions. They emphasize the phenomena of selective attention (seeing only what one wants to see) and rationalization (dismissing that which does not conform to one's images), and the importance of historical experience as a source of images.

The bureaucratic model applies to foreign policy decisions made by groups and organizations. Theorists argue that groups have their own dynamics that go beyond the collective application of rational policy-making and in addition to collective perceptions. This model involves two ideas: bureaucratic politics and organizational process. Bureaucratic biases may subconsciously or overtly shape the definition of the problem and the prescription for its solution. In organizational processes, pressures for group conformity may lead individual members to compromise or even abandon their doubts or preferences—that is, group dynamics may transcend the rational process.

Non-Nation-State Actors

Although the state is the prime actor in international politics, other entities have also played important roles and continue to do so. Any analysis focusing exclusively on the policies of nation-states ignores the important impact of other kinds of international actors. The state has never been the sole actor in the modern international political system; nor is politics only the result of state interaction. Many nonstate entities are capable of initiating cross-national interaction with other entities, and such nonstate actors can play important roles. The state-centric model of the international system (a misnomer), by focusing exclusively on the nation-state, precludes an analysis of actors that affect politics in profound ways.

The basic state units have changed over time. Chinese states, Greek city-states, Egyptian and Indian civilizations, pre-Columbian American entities such as the Aztec and Inca empires and others, as well as European empires and feudal realms, all preceded the nation-state and, in some cases, paralleled for a time or even survived along with the nation-state's ultimate spread around the globe. During the three centuries of nation-state dominance, additional actors have also appeared in the system. The Roman Catholic Church is an example of an actor predating the nation-state and today formally recognized by many nation-states. At times individual persons who were not government officials or representatives of other groups have been international actors. A variety of subnational entities have been actors: tribal groupings, leaders of breakaway provinces, sides in a civil war, rebel and revolutionary forces, governments in exile, and political parties and labor unions that do not act exclusively within state boundaries. International governmental organizations (IGOs) may sometimes be considered actors (the United Nations, the European Community, the Organization of American States, and so on). Nongovernmental international organizations (NGOs), such as the International Red Cross, also act on their own in the system. Business enterprises have also been prominent actors, especially since their accelerated development as part of nineteenth-century capitalist economies. Today they are structured as multinational corporations.

THE INTEGRATED INTERNATIONAL SYSTEM

The international political system has been integrated through the informal means of power distribution and through formal international institutions. Whereas the balance of power provides an informal mechanism for regulating international conflict, international law and IGOs represent formal attempts to control power politics and even to offer alternatives to the balance of power.

Distribution of Power and Influence

Balance-of-power theories imply equilibrium and stability within a system composed of several largely autonomous political forces. The equilibrium concept in systems theory, as well as the traditional view of the balance of power, assume that when stability or equilibrium is disturbed, either by an outside force or by internal change in one of the system components, the system itself exhibits a tendency either to reestablish the original equilibrium or to adopt a new one. According to this theory, the various states in the international political system, each with a different level of capability, group themselves in such a way that no single state or group of states is strong enough to dominate the system; power is balanced by opposing power. If equilibrium is maintained, then aggression is deterred, peace assured, and the independence of small states guaranteed. Conversely, war indicates disequilibrium, or a breakdown of the balance of power (dysfunction of the balance mechanism).

The theory of power balance is not universally accepted by scholars. Some reject it outright as an artifice, while others note that it may be exploited by states to justify their pursuit of policies aimed not at equilibrium but at a power imbalance in their favor. Still others deny the assumption that equilibrium is the normal or natural state of a system and actually view balance as abnormal. Political leaders have often pursued balance-of-power policies, however, usually aimed at achieving a "favorable" balance of power, and an international "pecking order" based on power considerations does seem to exist, whether power distribution is balanced or random. Thus, insofar as the balance of power is defined as "distribution of power" rather than "power equilibrium," I believe that the theory correctly, if roughly, describes patterns of state relationships. I further assume that an excessive shift in the balance of power tends to generate forceful reactions from those principal states adversely affected, whether or not that reaction is automatic.

The basic types of balance that have existed in the nation-state system are multiple balance and simple balance. In multiple balance, several nations balance each other on a global scale with further balances perhaps found in certain regional areas. Multiple balance was the controlling pattern of international politics from the birth of the nation-state until World War II; during that time between five and seven great powers dominated the scene, with widespread dispersal of power among them. Such a pattern may contain a "balancer," or one state that remains aloof from alliance until the balance seems to be shifting, whereupon the balancer intervenes in favor of the weaker side in order to reestablish equilibrium (said to be the role frequently played by Great Britain). In this connection, a favorable balance of power may give one state the freedom of action necessary to play this role.

Simple balance involves the concentration of power around two poles of roughly equal strength. Such a bipolar system existed after World War II, with the United States and the Soviet Union leading two sides composed of large groups of states. Bipolarity began to break up in the early 1960s with the rise of new centers of political and economic, if not military, power. Perceptible centers of such dispersed power today exist not only in the United States and the Soviet Union but also in Western Europe and Japan; perhaps in China, India, certain Arab states, and Brazil; and at times in the United Nations General Assembly. Military bipolarity may still exist, but politically and economically the world again is multipolar.

A variety of techniques exist for balancing power. The classic methods, aimed at either increasing the power of one pole or diminishing that of another, include shifting alliances, increasing armaments, seizing territory, creating buffer zones, intervening in the affairs of others, and setting states against each other in accordance with the principle of divide and conquer. Power balancing also involves creating spheres of influence or control, such as the Soviet Union's influence in Eastern Europe, the United States's influence in the Circum-Caribbean, and, potentially, the influence of Japan, China, and India in parts of Asia; Egypt and Israel in the Middle East; and Brazil in South America.

An aspect of balance-of-power theory particularly relevant to this study is the fundamental principle that proximate geographic areas are linked to a state's vital core interests. Thus, powerful states react to unfavorable events in proximate states or to actions of external states that may compete for influence in those adjacent areas. This principle accounts, for example, for U.S. opposition to other foreign influences in the Caribbean zone. Spheres of influence are essentially nonnegotiable for great powers; they are particularly important when the geographic interests of great powers overlap or when more remote powers challenge the primacy of another great power's sphere of influence.

International Institutions

A number of international institutions serve as formal regulatory instruments in the international system. International law dates from the very beginnings of the nation-state system and has been an integral part of its evolution over time. Regulation is also achieved through the activities of international organizations—which began to develop in the nineteenth century and expanded and accelerated in the twentieth—as well as other specialized interstate regimes.

International law is a body of formal regulatory rules. The concept of sovereignty is a central idea of international law but also poses a central problem: If the state is the supreme authority within its territorial bounds, are there any international laws to which the state itself is subservient? This difficulty has forced international law to rely on consent, with states reserving to themselves legal interpretation and the nature and application of law. This decentralized legal system in the international sphere was effective when the great powers generally agreed to uphold certain rules of conduct. Such was the case for almost three centuries, until the outbreak of World War I, when European powers agreed upon and enforced the law. Since then, however, no such agreement has existed. Despite these problems, a huge amount of day-to-day international business is facilitated and guided by legal agreement.

Weaker states, including older small powers and the newer developing nations, have had an ambivalent attitude toward international law. On the one hand, they see the need for legal restraint of the larger powers, but on the other hand they recognize that law tends to reflect the interests of those powers. They are suspicious of international law, viewing it as the codification of the international power structure in which violators among the weaker states are punished by the stronger ones. At the same time, their own impact on law has been significant. Their interpretation of law differs in several respects from the traditional postulates, which they view as inimical to their own interests. They stress the development of law to reflect their concerns in such areas as nationalization of foreign enterprise, territorial sea limits, and nonintervention of one state in the affairs of another.

Intergovernmental organizations (IGOs) are created and directed by governments on the general and regional levels as well as other functional levels. The leaders of most nations recognize a difficult dilemma: The nature of the system is conflictual, and yet mutual interdependence also requires cooperation. IGOs are creations of the nation-states themselves, developed by leaders in response to the practical necessities of international life and as attempts to make international politics function more smoothly. IGOs are the result of state agreements to engage in regularized consultation, to follow mutually agreed upon rules of behavior, and to establish administrative machinery to implement joint decisions.

Regional organizations, as the name implies, regulate international politics within defined geographic areas. They date from the latter half of the nineteenth century, when European Public Unions and the Inter-American System were organized. Regional organization may be classified according to their basic purposes. Some are concerned essentially with mutual defense, such as the North Atlantic Treaty Organization and the Warsaw Pact; these alliances represent formal organizational aspects of balance-of-power structures. Others are primarily concerned with specific fields of cooperation, such as the integration schemes in Europe and Latin America. Multipurpose organizations have also been created, such as the Commonwealth of Nations, the Arab League, the French Community, the Organization of African Unity, and the Inter-American System.

General international organizations are a product of the twentieth century and have been fundamentally, though not exclusively, responses to the problems of war. Global organizations such as the Hague Conferences, the League of Nations, and the United Nations (UN) have used a variety of approaches to promoting peace by attacking what their advocates have assumed to be the causes of war. Those who originated the concept of collective security, the primary rationale of both the League and the UN, have thought of it as the integration of power as opposed to the balance of power. They have assumed that war should be prevented, no matter what the issues involved, and that most of the powers of the world should come together in a global organization to deter aggression. In a sense, collective security was a "new" balance of power or a variant of the multiple balance. Inasmuch as both the new balance and collective security represented the status quo, they were not opposed. If collective security is inherently status quo oriented, as it seems to be, then a status quo situation conceivably could mean a balance of power based on collective security. Thus, collective security, originally viewed as a substitute for the balance of power, actually functions along the lines of balance-of-power principles. In any event, collective security has been largely a failure. The League of Nations was reduced to impotence by Japanese and Italian aggression in the 1930s. The fact that the superpowers have depended on military doctrines of mutual deterrence, the construction of hostile military alliances, and the continuance of spheres of influence—all of which are identified with the traditional balance of power to which collective security is theoretically opposed—shows their lack of faith in the United Nations.

International Interactions

Policy Instruments and Forms of Interaction. Once an actor has decided on a strategy—an overall plan or method designed to achieve certain goals and objectives—it mobilizes its resources or its "instruments of policy." The kinds of policy instruments and techniques available to decision makers to pursue their objectives cover a wide gamut of options. Positive action is not necessarily a consequence of the decisional process, for a state may decide to do nothing. Beyond nonaction, instruments may be classified in such categories as diplomatic, political, psychological, cultural, economic, or military resources. Thus, interactions in the system are largely identical with policy instruments. For example, war and economic assistance are policy instruments as well as forms of interaction. When the instruments of state action, once selected through the foreign policy process, are implemented, they then constitute part of international political processes and result in patterns of interaction that give further structure to the system.

Capability analysis, a concept introduced earlier, is also essential to understanding international interactions. In fact, the most meaningful view of foreign policy capability theorizes a range of power relationships. Capability is relative with respect to other states; it cannot exist without having one party to assert claims and another to respond. Brazil is considerably more powerful than, say, Rumania; but the lack of significant interaction between them renders such an observation meaningless. A state may be weak in general terms vis-à-vis one state and powerful toward another. This principle would apply to the relations of Mexico to the United States and to Guatemala, respectively. A state may have power over another in one area of activity, but the roles may be reversed in another area. For example, in military terms, the United States is infinitely more powerful than Venezuela; but with regard to the energy needs of the United States, Venezuela, with its huge petroleum resources, often has great leverage in the relationship. Capability also depends on the problem or situation in which it is being exercised. In 1965 the United States was capable of invading the Dominican Republic, quelling domestic chaos there, and restoring public order; but afterward it was incapable of establishing the U.S. system of democracy for Dominicans.

Cooperation and Conflict. While we often classify the large number of diverse instruments and interactions in political, economic, military, and other categories, it is also useful to cut across these categories and think of them as either cooperative or conflictual in character.

"Cooperation" (or "collaboration," which is synonymous) means willingly working with others for a common purpose in harmonious relationships. It involves the conscious behavior of all of the actors, or differentiated units, designed to produce results of value to all of them. Cooperative measures include diplomatic representation, cultural activities, technical assistance, capital investment, economic aid, trade, military grants and aid, arms transfers, personnel exchanges, armed service missions, and other transactions. Thus, cooperation is perceived by the various actors as enhancing their own ability to achieve goals while also being compatible with the interests of others. Interests need not be mutual in the sense of sameness, but cooperation requires that they be complementary and noncontradictory, even if different. Cooperation implies a symmetry of relations acceptable to all parties, even if full satisfaction is lacking or some resentment is present.

Conflict is the opposite of cooperation. It refers to instruments of policy and patterns of politics involving coercion, contention, hostility, tension, struggle, divisiveness, and discord of action—in general, a variance of principles and interests and asymmetry of relations. Conflict is present in war, intervention, blockade, clandestine actions, subversion, hostile propaganda, covert intelligence activities; terrorism, guerrilla warfare, diplomatic nonrecognition of new governments, and rupture of relations; economic pressures such as embargoes, boycotts, frozen assets, blacklists, and denial of aid; and the nationalization and expropriation of foreign enterprise. International conflicts arise out of incompatible objectives between states, which often resort to threats and may lead to the use of force. The regulation of conflict and search for cooperation through direct negotiation, third-party activities (by states or IGOs), or creation of international regimes are among the most constant, persistent, and even poignant themes of international politics.

Diplomacy and Violence. The cooperation-conflict dichotomy is not exact nor is either category fixed or static. Even in the most cooperative relationships some level of conflict may arise; cooperative relations may become conflictual, and conflict may be transformed to cooperation. As a policy matter, cooperative and coercive instruments are rarely applied singly or in isolation; usually they come in some sort of tactical "mix" of tools. This being so, interaction processes are probably best understood in terms of diplomacy (bargaining) and violence (the threat or use of force).

The concept of diplomacy has more than one meaning. In a narrow sense, "diplomacy" refers to the conduct of negotiations and other relations between nation-states, the practices and procedures whereby states exchange official representatives and communicate with each other. In its broader meaning, "diplomacy" is synonymous with "bargaining." "Bargaining" is the general process, either formal or informal, whereby parties reach agreements. These agreements may relate to obligations undertaken in cooperative transactions or to the resolution of conflict. Bargaining entails the politics of influence, the process by which states and other actors seek to achieve their ends by influencing others to behave in a desired fashion through the mobilization of appropriate resources. Bargaining may include promises and rewards ("carrots") as well as threats and punishments ("sticks"). It may go on between friends, neutrals, opponents, or enemies.

The relationship between diplomacy and violence is a subject of debate. Some would define bargaining as the attempt to induce or persuade without resorting to direct physical coercion. In this view, diplomacy may require "the stick," but it falls short of the actual use of armed force or other forms of violence. That is, states resort to force only when diplomacy fails. Another school extends the meaning of diplomacy to include the selective use of force, or the "diplomacy of violence." Violence occurs often enough that many observers consider it to be not a breakdown or an aberration but rather a normal part of world politics. They consider war as an instrument of policy in the tradition of Clausewitz's dictum that "war is the continuation of policy by other means," a deliberate and rational part of bargaining.

A fine line separates the use of diplomacy and of force as bargaining vehicles, but it is a critical distinction because cost and risk tend to rise sharply once armed action is undertaken. Furthermore, the use of armed force may go far beyond the purposes of a bargaining tool. War may range from being a limited political instrument to a broad assertion of raw power; it may aim to influence, to compel, or to seize. It may be a rational bargaining exercise, or it may be irrational or accidental. Even if initially conducted rationally, war may get out of control, and its termination, under many circumstances, rational or otherwise, may be difficult.

International Regimes

A possible outcome of interaction processes is the adoption of international regimes—such as arms control and law of the sea—designed to control conflict and facilitate cooperation. Such regimes are attempts at international governance and regulation of international systems. Competition and conflict seem to be inherent in the nation-state system, based as it is on the concept of sovereignty and characterized by nationalism and a heavy emphasis on the role of power. States assume that they must use their own resources to achieve their objectives or to prevent successful challenges by other states. Consequently, the regulation of conflict—its limitation and adjustment—is a major concern for most states. At the same time, regulation also involves the search for cooperative measures designed to resolve problems relating to military force, economic interdependence, national development, and the physical environment itself. All of these problems have become more crucial and seemingly more difficult to resolve than at any period in the history of the nation-state system. International regimes focus on the congeries of forces at work in selected issue-areas and attempt to resolve historic tensions between order and disorder.

International regimes are mutually accepted rules and procedures ("governing arrangements") that allow international actors to deal with problems of mutual concern in the absence of higher authority. Regime building may occur on bilateral, regional, global, or other levels or on some combination of them (as in arms control). Formal treaties and international agreements, informal agreements, shared norms and values, and international organizational machinery may all form parts of regimes. Many different kinds of international problems have given rise to regimes, including the various forms of violence, arms races, economic development, scarcity of resources, borders and waterways, and other concerns.

Regimes are often but not always associated with IGOs. One of the principal roles of IGOs is to sponsor, facilitate, or serve as regimes, but they are not the exclusive source of international governance. Regimes may be organized outside of IGOs through special conferences, bilateral or multilateral treaties, or informal agreements. Because such regimes are designed to resolve conflict and promote cooperation, it is appropriate to devote special attention to international regimes in the study of IR.

INTERNATIONAL SUBSYSTEMS

Kinds of Subsystems

Regions may be considered component subsystems of the global international system at a level between nation-states and the worldwide system. Most of the elements of a system apply equally to subsystems. A subsystem is marked by differentiation and integration. The analysis of subsystems involves the concepts of distinct units (actors), foreign policy, interaction, regulation, and even further subsystems. Although some modifications must be made in these conceptual categories to accommodate the study of regional international relations, the same analytic questions and criteria already posed in the context of foreign policy analysis and the global international system are directly relevant.

Not all subsystems are geographic regions; in fact, several different kinds of international subsystems may be identified. Many examples of subsystems could be listed by examining the differentiation and integration of various actors—states, interstate organizations and associations, nonstate actors, and mixes of all kinds. The regularized interaction of two states could be considered a subsystem, such as that between the United States and Mexico or between Argentina and Brazil. International organizations of all kinds, irrespective of geography, may also be considered subsystems, such as the Organization of African Unity, the Association of Southeast Asian Nations, the Organization of American States, the Arab League, and the Economic Community of West African States, to name just a few. Ideological or common-interest groupings that form international subsystems include the industrialized states, the Communist world, the Third World, the Commonwealth of Nations, the Organization of Petroleum Exporting Countries, and others. Of particular importance, and of primary interest to this study, is the concept of the regional subsystem, such as Latin America, the Middle East, Europe, Asia, and so on.

International subsystems, although marked by differentiation and integration, are not considered independent systems. Today, one worldwide international system encompasses virtually all actors, subsystems, and their interactions. (The "boundary" of a system is defined as that limit within which all system components are contained and outside of which no system interaction takes place.) Regional groupings and other associations are considered to be subsystems even though they are marked by all of the elements of a system for several reasons: (1) Their units interact significantly with other units and subsystems beyond their boundaries; (2) outside actors are subsystem relevant; (3) regional actors may also form parts of other subsystems; and (4) subsystem groupings remain functionally inseparable from the global system.

Regional Subsystems

Although regions are relatively new foci for systems theory as such, the concept of the region has long been evident in both the study and practice of international relations. There is nothing new in the concept of regional politics, especially if one considers older concerns with regionalism, political and economic integration, and the voluminous literature on European international relations. International political processes have been interpreted to include regional spheres of influence in the balance of power, regional organization, regional integration (economic and political), regional security, and regional policies of the great powers, as well as the more recent notion of regional subsystems. An academic concern with regional topics appeared even before World War I, but such concerns were not widespread until after the failure of collective security under the League of Nations to prevent World War II and the sanction of "regional arrangements" by the United Nations Charter. Latin American studies were an exception, as inter-American organizations, beginning in 1889, were the object of historical and institutional-legal scholarship. If we consider inter-American relations in general, a significant literature had begun to develop even before 1889. By and large, however, strong scholarly interest in regional topics is a post–World War II enterprise.

The early postwar writings were caught up in the debate between regionalists and universalists about the best arrangements for creating world order. Regionalists were primarily concerned with security arrangements for keeping the peace in delineated geographic areas and with describing existing organizations in legal terms. The regionalism versus globalism debate centered on the regional commissions and activities of the United Nations and the activities of specialized regional organizations. In the mid-1950s, regionalist scholarly interest began to focus on economic and political integration; scholars searched for ways in which national political actors within defined geographic zones could shift at least part of their loyalties and decision making to supranational regional institutions for their mutual benefit. Finally, with the impact of systems theory on the study of politics in general and international relations in particular, regional concerns became part of systems theory.

All of these approaches to the study of regions are linked by the common idea that geographic proximity defines one of the limits of inquiry. Consequently, the problem of defining what constitutes a region is common to all. The fundamental difference is that the peacekeeping, functional, and integration approaches include prescriptive doctrines and normative statements of preference (although scientific studies have attempted to determine their effectiveness), whereas systems theory is designed to order the objective study of reality (it is flexible enough to allow prescriptions and judgments to be considered, but not accepted as norms). Furthermore, the view of a given region as a subsystem is topically more inclusive than in the other regional approaches because it deals with the totality of regional policies and relations among actors. It includes and integrates consideration of structures, processes, and issues in other approaches and goes beyond them with an array of systemic considerations.

BIBLIOGRAPHIC COMMENT

Important early sources drawing the analytic distinction between foreign policy and international politics are the two editions of *International Politics and Foreign Policy,* edited by Rosenau (1961, 1969), which are different enough to be considered separate volumes. A similar format, broadened to include a section on regional subsystems, is presented by Rosenau, Thompson, and Boyd (1976). Hermann, Kegley, and Rosenau (1987) edited a collection of sophisticated analyses on the comparative study of foreign policy. Some recent textbooks explicitly or implicitly analyzing IR from a systems perspective include Deutsch (1988), Farnsworth (1988), Holsti (1988), Papp (1987), and Pearson and Rochester (1988). Kegley and Wittkopf (1988) emphasize international political economy. Lafer (1982) is a sophisticated Brazilian view of international system transformation. World regions as foci for subsystem analysis is a relatively new enterprise, but the theoretical literature has flourished. Good books on the subject are by Boyd (1984), Cantori and Spiegel (1970), Falk and Mendlovitz (1973), Feld and Boyd (1980), Keohane and Nye (1977), Russett (1967), and Yalem (1970).

On the development and state of the study of Latin American international relations, see Cisneros-Lavaller (1982), Domínguez (1978), Gil (1985), Institute of International Studies (1965), Morse (1964), Muñoz (1987), Perina (1985), Tulchin (1983), and Alberto van Klaveren in Muñoz and Tulchin (1984). Also recommended are the introductory essays to the international relations sections of the Library of Congress, *Handbook of Latin American Studies.*

CHAPTER TWO

—————————— ■ ——————————

The Latin American
Regional Subsystem

THIS CHAPTER is divided essentially into two parts. The first defines the Latin American subsystem in terms of criteria applicable to any international regional subsystem with subregional components. In this regard, our understanding is enhanced by highlighting subsystems within Latin America where various conditions have obtained. The second part, which traces subsystem change, has a dual concern: Latin America's position in global politics, including external influences on Latin America and the various subregions; and relationships among the Latin American states themselves.

The primary (but not exclusive) factor in system structure and change is the international distribution of power and influence. In the previous chapter, concepts of power were related to policies pursued by states, patterns of international politics, and systemic conditions. This chapter emphasizes the last element—structure and change in the international system and in the Latin American subsystem as indicated by patterns of power distribution among the actors. The other uses of the concept of power are taken up in subsequent chapters.

IDENTIFYING REGIONAL SUBSYSTEMS

Relevant Criteria

Scholars have proposed differing definitions of regional subsystems, and their work on related issues is marked by conceptual disparity. A survey of the literature on regional subsystems by William Thompson (1973) stands as one of the most helpful in establishing what criteria should be applied in determining the validity of viewing geographic regions as international subsystems. He inventoried and evaluated twenty-one attributes that had been proposed by eighteen analysts to define a regional subsystem. Thompson concluded that three criteria were necessary and sufficient: (1) that the regional actors be in geographic proximity (this condition is implied by the term "region," and it includes the identification of the differentiated units); (2)

that there be both internal and external recognition of the region as a distinctive area; and (3) that the interaction among the actors and their patterns of relations exhibit a degree of regularity and intensity (this condition is implied by the concept of "subsystem" and is partly synonymous with the notion of integration). A regional subsystem, then, consists of a set of geographically proximate and regularly interacting states that share to some degree a sense of regional identity and are so perceived by external actors. These same criteria also identify further subsystems within the region.

Boundary and Actors

In studying a particular regional subsystem, one must first identify the boundary that delimits the region and sets it apart from other components of the larger international system. In an autonomous system, the boundary is defined as that limit containing all of the components and outside of which no system interaction takes place. Clearly, actors outside of a regional subsystem are significant because transboundary interaction takes place. The boundary must set off the components of one subsystem from those of others, although these distinctions may be less clearly defined than in an independent system.

The establishment of a typology of subsystem-relevant actors further helps to identify regional boundaries. In order to distinguish a subsystem from other system components, the differentiated units must be identified. These include the regional states within the boundary, the external states that have regularized interaction with the regional actors, and several kinds of regional and external non-nation-state entities.

Geographic proximity within a physical boundary is a necessary characteristic of a regional subsystem, but it alone does not define the subsystem. Students of regional studies must guard against geographic determinism and beware of unwarranted assumptions about the character of political relations within a given territory. The result may be a contrived region based merely on geographic convenience; if the proposed subsystem units have nothing more than their proximity in common, then the proposition is invalid. Therefore, after establishing the geographic limits of a region, the analyst must search for additional indications of subsystem qualities.

Perceptions

The second aspect of subsystem analysis is the extent of regional self-perception and the views of the external actors about the region. Shared attributes among subsystem actors may help to delineate the region if they contribute to a regional self-consciousness. In systemic terms, however, common sociocultural, economic, and political traits are not definitional requirements and there is no merit in putting such restrictions on regional designations. Proximate and interacting states may be rich or poor, culturally complex or simple, or politically and socially advanced or not (however defined) without violating the subsystem concept. The key consideration in subsystem analysis is the degree of mutual identity among the actors.

Interactions

The region, finally, is also defined by the regularity of relationships among the units, including the patterns and intensity of the various forms of interaction engaged in by the regional and external state and nonstate actors as well as the subsystem-related regulatory institutions and processes. What are the patterns and effects of such international contacts as diplomatic exchanges, communications, cultural relations, trade and investment, economic aid, and various kinds of military relations? Does an identifiable power configuration emerge among the regional actors or in regard to the region as part of the global structure? What is the role of regularized conflict, both within the region and with outside actors, in structuring the subsystem? What formal associations and organizations give further structure to regional politics?

Identifying the Latin American Subsystem

How valid is the view of Latin America as a regional subsystem? Do the thirty-three independent states in the region form a coherent entity for study? This question is the system theorist's version of the Latin Americanist's age-old query: To what extent can the area be regarded as a significant unit in the conduct of international affairs? In other words, do the independent states in the region form a coherent entity for study, or is Latin America only a convenient geographic description?

In the following discussion I argue that Latin America may indeed be regarded as a significant unit in the conduct of international affairs. I further assert, however, that the key to an accurate analysis of Latin America's international relations is to recognize several levels within the subsystem. That is, the structure and processes of Latin American international relations should be defined in a hierarchical series: (1) the entire region as a subsystem of the global international system; (2) subregions within the Latin American region; and (3) sets of bilateral relationships on the part of individual Latin American states. A variety of subregional subsystems are possible; in my view, the three most relevant ones are Mexico, the Circum-Caribbean, and South America beyond the Caribbean (the Southern Cone and Brazil). We will also discuss further subordinate levels within the Caribbean and South America, such as Central America, the Caribbean Commonwealth, the Amazon Basin, the Andean region, and others.

THE LATIN AMERICAN REGIONAL LEVEL

Geographic Demarcation and Actor Typology

The Regional Boundary. Identification of the regional line of demarcation begins with the notion of a geographic boundary delimiting the region and enclosing a set of physically proximate states. Latin America is thus defined as inclusive of that territory in the Western Hemisphere south of the United States. Measuring 7,000 miles from northern Mexico to Cape Horn at the

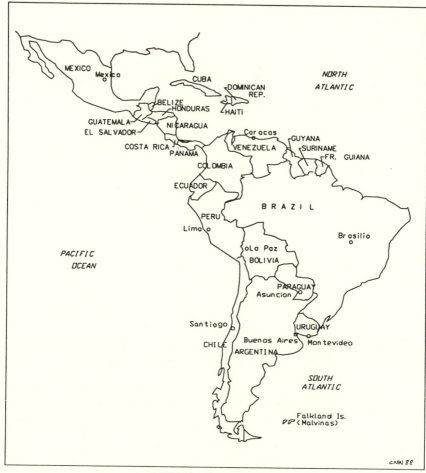

LATIN   AMERICA

far southern reaches of Chile and Argentina, this area is mostly occupied by thirty-three sovereign states (at the beginning of 1989), with the small remainder consisting of British, Dutch, French, and U.S. dependencies. The northern part of the region—Mexico and the Caribbean region—is mostly south of the United States. Almost all of South America, however, lies east as well as south of North America; the Natal region (the "Brazilian Bulge") is only 1,900 miles from the closest point on the African continent.

The Regional States. The regional states located within the subsystem boundary form the central focus of the subsystem's international politics. These states are usually subdivided into groupings that reflect their political culture and "age" as independent nation-states:

1. *Ibero-America* refers to the nineteen nations of Spanish and Portuguese origin, all of them the "old" or "traditional" states in the context of Latin American studies. Eighteen of them form *Spanish America*; they are, in alphabetical order, Argentina, Bolivia, Chile, Colombia, Costa Rica, Cuba, Dominican Republic, Ecuador, El Salvador, Guatemala, Honduras, Mexico, Nicaragua, Panama, Paraguay, Peru, Uruguay, and Venezuela. They occupy some 57 percent of the total Latin American land area. Most of them achieved their independence from Spain between 1810 and 1830; Cuba did so in 1898 but was not technically sovereign until the end of U.S. military occupation in 1902, and Panama was a province of Colombia until it became independent in 1903. *Portuguese America,* or *Luso America,* refers to Brazil, which was under the colonial rule of Portugal until becoming independent in 1822. This giant of Latin America, the largest regional state in both population and territory and larger than the continental United States, covers about 40 percent of the Latin American terrain.

2. The tiny island-nation of *Haiti* is the oldest regional state and at least peripherally a "traditional" one for Latin Americanists. Haiti broke away from France in 1804 in a successful black slaves' revolt and has maintained its West African culture to the present day.

3. The remainder of the regional actors are thirteen "new" states, twelve of which are former British colonies that gained their independence between 1962 and 1984 and are known collectively as the *Commonwealth Caribbean Countries*. They are Antigua-Barbuda, Bahamas, Barbados, Belize, Dominica, Grenada, Guyana, Jamaica, St. Kitts-Nevis, St. Lucia, St. Vincent, and Trinidad-Tobago. *Suriname,* a former Dutch colony, became independent in 1975 and represents what may be called "Netherlands America."

External States. The external sector is made up of those states outside the boundary that have significant relations with the regional actors. Political dependencies located within the regional boundary, numbering eleven administrative entities as of early 1989, represent continuing territorial intrusion by the controlling external states (the United Kingdom, France, the Netherlands, and the United States). Significant external states include not only those which possess regional territory but also those with any form of regularized interaction with the region in question, that participate in the regional distribution of power, have membership or participate in regional organizations, have alliances or alignments with regional actors, or participate with the region in other forms of international politics.

Historically the European states were among the most important components of the external sector, with Great Britain the single most important external actor in the nineteenth century. A number of them have recently reasserted their Latin American interests, especially since the early 1970s. The United States, important in the northern portion of Latin America in the nineteenth century, has been the most significant (but not unchallenged) external actor for much of Latin America during most of the twentieth century. The Soviet Union expanded its activities in about 1960 beginning with its alignment with Cuba, and Japan became a major economic force

28

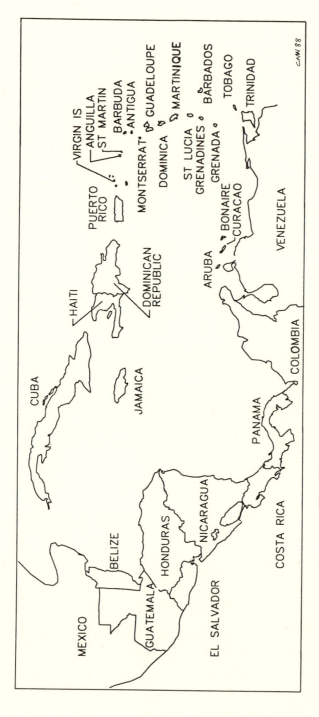

THE CARIBBEAN AREA

at about the same time. An array of other external states have special bilateral or other particular relationships in the Latin American region.

Nonstate Actors. Several kinds of nonstate entities also function as important actors in the Latin American subsystem. The oldest is the Holy See and the Roman Catholic Church organizational structure. Multinational corporations (MNCs) have also played important roles, as have, to a lesser degree, international labor movements. Subnational insurgency groups have long been active in Latin America, especially since the late 1950s and continuing to the present day. In addition, the importance of transnational political parties, most prominently those originating in Europe, has been increasing.

Perceptions

Regional Self-Consciousness. The evidence supporting the existence of a regional awareness is varied. Fundamental differences and even uniqueness are obvious in Latin America. Diversity and exceptionality should not be overemphasized, however; the Latin American states have much in common, and in certain important ways mutual identification is prevalent. Although few generalizations would apply to all of the Latin American states, a significant degree of commonality exists among them, and certain generally, if not universally, applicable patterns and shared experiences and traits emerge out of the diversity. (The next chapter discusses this complexity, noting elements of both commonality and multiformity.)

Regional consciousness is difficult to measure, but evidence suggests a "push-pull" force working in Latin American relations, an ambivalent situation of mutual repulsion and attraction. The most obvious expressions of ambivalence are found in the relations between Brazil and Spanish America. Great diversity exists among the eighteen Spanish American states, but they also exhibit the most cultural cohesion and mutual identity within the region. Within Spanish America, ambivalence is reflected especially in the competition for leadership between Mexico and Argentina and sometimes between Colombia, Chile, Peru, and Venezuela. Mutual identity is further revealed by the sensitivity of political groups in one state to developments in others. Military establishments seem to have regular communications with their Latin American counterparts, as, increasingly, do certain political parties and, to a lesser extent, labor unions. Although different developmental models have been posed by Mexican, Cuban, Brazilian, Peruvian, and other experiences, it seems significant that regional debates tend to center upon which *Latin American* solutions to the problems of change are most viable, with minimal reference to nonregional models.

External states have tended to increase subsystem cohesion in Latin America by their very presence. No Latin American state has been a great power in the mainstream of global politics; all have operated from a position of weakness relative to the world powers, with some recent special exceptions. Although some have come close to breaking this mold at certain times, most of them have tended to band together against threats, real and imagined, from the outside world. For example, Spanish American unity, from the time of the wars for independence from Spain until the mid-1860s, insofar as it existed, was based largely on fear of foreigners and a desire to ally against them. Plans for economic integration since World War II have been motivated not only by hopes for mutual economic benefit but also by the possibility of escaping from economic dependence on external industrialized states. Furthermore, Latin Americans have tended to side with each other when outsiders have exerted pressure in the region, even when individual state interests have not been involved. For example, U.S. intervention in the Caribbean during the first third of the twentieth century evoked strong protests even from the remote Rio de la Plata region, which was largely unaffected by U.S. actions. By the mid-1970s, the Panama Canal issue was no longer simply a confrontation between Panama and the United States but had become a matter of concern for virtually all of Latin America, which supported Panamanian interests against the United States. More recently, conflict in Central America led to organization of the Contadora Group by Mexico, Colombia, Venezuela, and Panama, which was subsequently endorsed by a "support group" of South American states not directly affected by the Central American crisis. Another example of regional unity was the majority decision among Latin American states to express support for Argentina in its 1982 war with the United Kingdom over the Falkland/Malvinas islands, despite their own unhappiness with Argentine aggression.

Regularity of Interaction

A considerable portion of this book is concerned with the interaction processes, and, where appropriate, the several criteria regarding subsystemic structures proposed in my definition of subsystem requirements are considered in the Latin American context. The general question to ask is whether a regularity of relations exists in these areas; if so, the concept of a Latin American subsystem would be strengthened. The following chapters discuss interaction processes that provide considerable evidence for the regional subsystem theory.

FURTHER SUBSYSTEMS

Mexico

A major state that borders a superpower, Mexico stands apart in Latin America because of its special structure of bilateral relations with the United States in addition to its inter-American and other international relations. Mexico is part of a North American subsystem separate from the rest of Latin America; it shares a continent with a great area outside of Latin America—Canada and the United States. Mexico has always been of significant interest to one or another of the world's great powers, but the United States has long been the principal foreign presence in Mexico (the foreign menace, in the eyes of many Mexicans). Consequently, the Mexican-U.S. relationship is largely divorced from the greater inter-American arena. Many of the issues are "North American" in content and closely associated with the domestic concerns in each country; the relationship has been determined primarily by territorial proximity and increasingly integrated economic and social structures.

The Circum-Caribbean

The boundary of the Caribbean subsystem in international politics has been perceived by both local and external states to include the islands of the Caribbean Sea and those nearby in the Atlantic Ocean, the entire Central American isthmus and Yucatan Peninsula, and the north coast of South America, which extends to the Atlantic Ocean and beyond the Caribbean Sea as such. Thus, Venezuela is considered a Caribbean nation; Colombia is increasingly considered a part of the Caribbean region, but it is also perceived as a Pacific nation. The two countries also become involved, from time to time, in the Andean South American subsystem. The idea of a "Caribbean Basin" that conforms to the above definition is often viewed by Europeans as a North American invention (the term is favored by U.S. policymakers); but in the nineteenth century Great Britain seemed to hold the same idea, as do Venezuela and Mexico today.

Caribbean states have been small, weak, and relatively noninstitutionalized, with the exceptions of Colombia and (more recently) Venezuela and Costa Rica. Consequently, the region has continuously been the object of rivalry, pressure, intervention, and domination by greater powers. There is nothing new about geopolitical conflict in the area. In this respect, international politics have not changed for centuries; only the actors have shifted. Throughout the twentieth century Caribbean states have generally been in the U.S. sphere of influence. The United States has been the international policeman in the area, more assertive and consequential there than in South America beyond the Caribbean; most of the area is part of a U.S. bilateral trading system.

The U.S. presence in the Circum-Caribbean has been one of the clearest cases of hegemony in the international political system. That hegemony, however, has not been total, constant, or simple and has suffered numerous challenges. The territorial holdings of the United Kingdom, France, and the Netherlands have constituted a constant diversion from U.S. primacy. More recently, the Soviet Union has aligned with Cuba and supported Nicaragua. Today a number of local Latin American and nonhemispheric states and organizations disagree with U.S. policies in Central America and are pressing for changes. Furthermore, U.S. actions in the Caribbean over the years have often engendered strong domestic opposition in the United States. On balance, however, U.S. power and influence have been and continue to be the primary factors in Caribbean international politics.

The Circum-Caribbean may be further subdivided. Central America, the isthmian area between Mexico and Colombia, displays systemic characteristics. Central American states have desired but failed to be politically united for more than a century and a half. They have banded together in political and economic unions but are sharply divided over a number of issues. The current Central American crisis of civil war and international conflict provides another structural element that helps define this area as a subsystem. The Commonwealth Caribbean states also make up a subsystem. They are located mostly in the eastern Caribbean zone except for Belize on the Central American isthmus. The Commonwealth states also exhibit an internal push-pull process; several of them failed to unite in the West Indies Federation and to become independent as a single state in 1962, but shortly thereafter they began their economic integration. They were further divided over the 1983 U.S. intervention of Grenada (a Commonwealth Caribbean Country), but they moved thereafter to repair the divisions.

The Southern Cone

The entire South American continent below Central America arguably forms an international subsystem. South America beyond the Caribbean, however, is a more coherent entity. In terms of international politics, this majority part of the continent is largely synonymous with what is often called the Southern Cone of South America. Actors in Southern Cone international relations are Argentina, Brazil, Chile, Uruguay, Paraguay, Bolivia, Peru, and sometimes Ecuador. Excluded are the northern tier states of Colombia, Venezuela, Guyana, and Suriname; the concerns of these states overlap those of the South American subsystem, especially on border questions, but the thrust of their international relations more often parallels the concerns of the Caribbean Basin.

The Southern Cone thus defined forms a regional subsystem distinguished by a number of characteristics. A principal one has been the region's relative isolation from the mainstream of international politics, largely a function of its strikingly unique geographic situation. In addition, the leading Southern Cone states are, in a relative sense, internally institutionalized, and they act independently in international politics, especially in comparison with most Caribbean countries. Their remote global location at great distances from Europe and the United States, combined with the relative strength of the key local states, has left the region free, for the most part, from inclusion in global balance-of-power rivalries and helped it resist outside influences in the handling of internal affairs. The region thus has not been part of a global balance-of-power system in which a great power has played the role of an international policeman enforcing the peace. This autonomy is dramatically different from the situation in northern Latin America.

Southern Cone states have a broad array of external relationships that add to their ability to balance outside influences. The subregion is a multilateralized trading area; unlike Mexico and most of the Caribbean, which are restricted to a bilateral economic network with the United States, the Southern Cone states and Brazil have long-standing cultural as well as economic ties with Europe. The region's trade with Europe, notably, includes arms transfers. Brazil, especially, has diversified its economy and developed a broad set of bilateral relationships. Argentina after 1979 made the Soviet Union its primary trading partner. The United States, by and large, has been one of several competitors in South America, never approaching a position of dominance as in the Circum-Caribbean or of primary importance as in Mexico. As a general matter, the United States, in its Latin American relationships, has had the least interest and influence in the Southern Cone, with the exception of Brazil, and its influence with Brazil has declined dramatically since the mid-1960s.

Relative isolation from global power politics has allowed the major Southern Cone states to establish independent patterns of interaction involving their own set of subregional issues. The issues have involved local rivalry for leadership as well as national searches for security, power, well-being, prestige, and resources, depending on the relative capabilities of the states involved. Subregional international politics have brought strategic-geopolitical components to the foreign policies of the major Southern Cone states. They have developed such calculations solely in regard to their own subregion, extended to include the South Atlantic and the Antarctic. Intraregional relations have been characterized by rather firm and persistent balances of power, in which the small states have served as "buffers" in rivalries among the larger states. The adoption of geopolitical perspectives further distinguishes the Southern Cone subsystem from the more northerly parts of Latin America. Particularly ominous, and in further contradistinction to the rest of Latin America, nuclear questions have been introduced into subregional international relations, with advanced capabilities on the part of Argentina and Brazil. Finally, as mentioned above, certain Southern Cone states have links to the South Atlantic region and interests in the Antarctic. These interests are peculiar to the South American subregional states within Latin America.

The Southern Cone subsystem, like that of the Caribbean Basin, may be further subdivided. Three subgroupings in particular have emerged, marked by formal organizations as well as other characteristics, such as border disputes. The Platine countries—Brazil, Argentina, Uruguay, Paraguay, and Bolivia—have a self-identification, reflected, among other ways, in their organization of the Cuenca del Plata accord in 1969 for regional infrastructure development. The Amazonic countries—Brazil, Suriname, Guyana, Venezuela, Colombia, Ecuador, Peru, and Bolivia—have a similar self-perception; they signed the Amazon Pact in 1978 for the controlled development of the Amazon Basin.

In an Andean subsystem that sometimes emerges, part of the Southern Cone overlaps with the Circum-Caribbean. The Andean countries—Venezuela, Colombia, Ecuador, Peru, Bolivia, and Chile—have considered themselves an international unit in several ways. For example, integration was fostered in 1966 by the formation of the Andean Group, and these states (except for Venezuela) are part of an emerging Pacific Basin trading system. For some of them, territorial interests also extend to the Pacific Ocean; the Easter Islands belong to Chile and the Galapagos Islands to Ecuador.

Brazil

Brazil, as indicated above, is geographically separate from the Southern Cone but is a key actor in the Southern Cone subsystem. It is the strongest state in that subsystem as well as in Latin America at large. In several respects its bilateral relationships should be viewed as a separate subsystem. Brazil has long stood apart from the rest of Latin America because of its Portuguese cultural heritage, large size (territory, population, and economy), and ambition and potential to be an influential state in global politics. Long the "sleeping giant" of Latin America, and once the junior partner in a cooperative alignment with the United States, Brazil has increased its self-confidence toward the United States and its overall ability to pursue an independent foreign policy. It has successfully expanded its bilateral relations and is not prepared to reemerge as subordinate in any future relationship. It now engages in relations with the United States without an assumption of mutual interests, prefers to approach other nations of the world in terms of bilateral relations rather than in concert with the rest of Latin America, and is open to a further broadening of its external relationships. It is significant, moreover, that Brazil has developed a multilateral network of international trade.

SUBSYSTEM CHANGE

Criteria

Systemic change or transformation is another important focus of inquiry for system theorists. How does a subsystem shift from one historical dividing line to another; that is, how does it move in time? How do we detect the transformation when a subsystem with certain characteristics becomes another kind of subsystem with different features? Analysts tend to measure transformations manifested by the form and nature of the balance or distribution of power. They search for shifts in the capability levels of the units, in the types of policy instruments they use, in the issues stimulating interaction, and in the patterns of politics and power configurations. Those few studies addressing subsystem change have mostly dealt with the European region, historically the center of the global system. But such studies are not necessarily of conceptual relevance for the analysis of other regions. Asian and African subsystems have not been so studied because they were largely colonial areas and therefore extensions of the European system. Latin America was not such a colonial extension after the early nineteenth century, but neither was it in the mainstream of European-dominated international politics. It has had a unique evolution during the twentieth century, even as it has become more globalized. Thus, Latin American subsystem change must be dealt with in its own terms.

After independence and through the mid-twentieth century, most of Latin America did not escape the pervasive influence of external states, first the nations of Europe and then the United States. Subsystem transformation depended not so much on intraregional changes as on changing external global systemic influences on the region as a whole and on the individual regional actors. After the mid-1960s, however, internal considerations became increasingly important. We may identify different eras in the development of Latin America in the global distribution of power. The Latin American subsystem and its subregional components have gone through distinct stages, with transitional periods signaling the end of one era and the initiation of another. However, the various subregions did not develop in exact parallel; thus, most dates assigned in the following discussion should be considered approximate.

From Colonies to Nations

The Latin American subsystem evolved out of the colonial period, from the late fifteenth to the early nineteenth centuries, when colonialism bound the entire region to European powers. During that three-century era preceding Latin American independence, most of the region was part of the Spanish and Portuguese crowns. Their control of the New World's territory and riches was an important factor in the European-centered global balance-of-power structure. Portugal led the European actors in their expansion of power around the globe through colonization and trade. In the early fifteenth century Portugal expanded southward along the African coast and eastward to the Orient. Spain followed, and after its discovery of the New World in 1492, the Americas became the object of contention for territorial control. Spain was the dominant world power throughout most of the sixteenth century, primarily because of its American empire, which eventually extended some 8,000 miles from San Francisco in North America to the Straits of Magellan. In 1530 Portugal finally began to settle Brazil and later pushed its frontier westward, but its American empire never rivaled that of Spain.

As Spain and Portugal became relatively weaker in international politics from the late sixteenth century onward, France, Britain, and the Netherlands challenged their Latin American primacy through pirate raids on shipping, some territorial acquisitions, and the establishment of trading relationships (legal and contraband). Nevertheless, Spain and Portugal were able to manipulate the European balance-of-power system sufficiently to maintain control over most of their American territory. By the end of the colonial period their empires were largely intact, with the relatively minor exceptions of the British, French, Dutch, and Danish West Indies.

Latin American independence, like that of the United States earlier, began largely as a sidelight of European international politics. That is, the European balance-of-power system, badly shaken by the Napoleonic Wars, facilitated the Latin American revolutions. By 1800 Spain was bankrupt and poorly governed, having continuously lost to France and England in eighteenth-century dynastic struggles. Portugal had declined into poverty and was closely allied with and dependent on Great Britain. When French armies invaded the Iberian peninsula in 1807–1808, the Portuguese royal family fled to Brazil aboard a British naval vessel while the Spanish king and his heir were imprisoned. By the time Ferdinand VII returned to the throne in Madrid in 1814, most of Spanish America was in revolt against him. Disorder within Spain itself further reduced his ability to deal with rebellious colonists. The last of the viceroys in Spanish America was vanquished in 1824, with some British assistance, and the once vast Spanish American empire was reduced to Cuba and Puerto Rico.

The Portuguese royal family returned to Portugal in 1821. The following year Brazilians declared their independence. In contrast to the long and bitter struggle between Spain and its colonies, Portugal relinquished control with little opposition. Brazilians called upon the Portuguese prince (the heir to the throne), who had remained in Brazil as regent, to make the declaration of independence and rule as monarch of the new state.

European Dominance

Subsystem Emergence. The nineteenth century after the mid-1820s roughly marks the first era of the independent Latin American subsystem. Before this transition, the regional states had largely been pawns in the rivalries among the great European powers. The severance of the colonial ties that had bound the region to overseas powers for more than three centuries, and had almost entirely isolated it from the rest of the world outside Spain and Portugal, submitted the new Latin American states to the power vagaries of the international political system. In addition, the independence of the vast Latin American territory affected the global system by changing the distribution of power among European states and stimulating rivalry among them to gain regional influence or control. From the beginning of national independence throughout the nineteenth century, the Latin American states played passive roles in global politics. Securing independence from Spain and Portugal had thrust the new states into the mainstream of international power politics, but they were still subordinate actors compared to the external great powers.

The major external powers were European and had a preponderance of economic, military, and technological capabilities as well as long experience in statecraft. The United States played an important role in areas contiguous to it, but it was otherwise weak in relation to the European states. Great Britain was the dominant (but not unchallenged) external actor and held the primary position in most of the region into the first years of the twentieth century. Britain's naval and merchant fleets dominated the Atlantic and discouraged other power excursions into the area until the turn of the century. It is true that Mexico lost half its territory to the United States between 1836 and 1848, that Mexico and the Dominican Republic were occupied by France and Spain, respectively, in the 1860s, and that other armed interventions were initiated in the area by France, Spain, the United States, Great Britain itself, and, later, Germany and Italy. Nevertheless, Britain shielded the Western Hemisphere from many other European designs, especially those of France and Spain, by largely controlling ocean communications between Europe and America. In the 1880s, a private French company began construction of the Panama Canal, but the project went bankrupt and was abandoned. Germany and Italy entered the scene with their respective national unifications in the 1870s; Germany became highly competitive, especially in commercial and military affairs.

Position of the United States. At the beginning of the nineteenth century, the United States was a relatively weak external actor. It steadily rose in power during that century, expanding its territory almost three times over from 1802 to 1852 and, after the end of its Civil War in 1865, developing its industrial and military capabilities and increasing its population at rapid rates. The United States finally emerged as a great power at the turn of the century. In general, it was not a major factor in the nineteenth-century balance of power beyond North America, although some European statesmen, particularly in Britain, recognized its power potential.

Despite the warning to Europe by President James Monroe in 1823 to keep "hands off" the Americas, the United States did not dominate affairs in the Western Hemisphere. This statement of the U.S. position was issued in the shadow of the British navy, for at that time the United States lacked the military power necessary to keep continental European forces out of the Americas while knowing that Great Britain could and would do so. As the Monroe Doctrine (as it was later called) was directed against Europe during a period of U.S. military impotence when the United States was preoccupied with its own nation-building and, later, with the Civil War, it remained virtually forgotten in the United States for many years. During the nineteenth century, the United States was the protégé of British sea power. The two states did not act in formal concert, but they shared coincidental interests in keeping continental powers out of the Americas. Thus, Great Britain realized Monroe's purposes in the sense that it assured to some degree the independence of Latin American nations from the imperial designs of continental Europeans.

Until the mid-1890s, the United States displayed little interest in Latin American affairs beyond its own continental expansion, the possibility of an interoceanic canal in Central America, and unrealized proposals to annex Cuba, the Dominican Republic, and the Danish West Indies. The major exceptions to U.S. weakness in Latin America were its relations with its immediate neighbor, Mexico, and with Great Britain in Central America. The United States acquired about half of Mexico's national territory as the result of the annexation of Texas and the later war settlement in 1848. Britain was the chief U.S. rival in Central America, where the construction of a transisthmian canal was of continuing concern to both states and brought them into serious conflict. The two states signed the Clayton-Bulwer Treaty in 1850 in order to soften their intense rivalry. It provided that neither would construct or exclusively control a canal or "exercise domain" over any part of Central America.

Subregional Development. Distinctive subregional structures and self-consciousness in Latin America were not as clear in the postindependence period as they would later become. For four decades after independence, from about the mid-1820s to the mid-1860s, Latin Americans (with the prominent exception of Brazil) were preoccupied with the often frustrating search for domestic stability as well as coherent foreign policies. This instability produced conditions that invited conflict with neighboring states and intervention by Europeans and sometimes the United States. Nevertheless, the various subregional subsystems had begun to emerge. Some of their elements were shaped during the colonial period. For example, Spanish control of the Caribbean, in contrast to its firm hold on other parts of the Spanish American empire, had been eroded by other European challengers who acquired territories there, and Brazil's separate identity was evident throughout the colonial period. Important South American conflicts—between Argentina and Brazil on the Atlantic side and, on the Pacific coast, between Chile and the alliance of Peru and Bolivia—that developed in the early independence period became continuing elements of the Southern Cone subsystem.

Intra–Latin American distinctions became clearer as the century progressed. The Mexican identity was shaped by the aggressive policies of outsiders—first the disastrous war with the United States in the 1840s and then the occupation by France in the 1860s. The Circum-Caribbean subsystem did not undergo major systemic change until the turn of the century, which saw the retirement of Great Britain and the emergence of the United States as the dominant power in the area. In contrast, during the 1860s the Southern Cone subsystem went through a transition period that solidified its identity and further set it off from northern Latin America. Southern Cone states developed more viable political systems; they strongly desired to modernize their nations in all respects and looked to foreigners for aid in doing so. Now secure from most threats of European intervention, they concentrated on internal problems and national development involving cooperative rather than conflictual relations with Europeans and the United States. The remoteness of these states played an important role in their development, as the external great powers concentrated on a new era of energetic imperialism in other parts of the world.

Southern Cone Balances. The Southern Cone balance-of-power system began with rivalry among the ABC states (Argentina, Brazil, and Chile), but it came to have implications for the entire subregion. (Burr, 1967a, is the primary source for this topic.) Major developments in Southern Cone international relations during the nineteenth century included Chile's Policy of the Pacific aimed at domination of the west coast; Argentina's determination to be preeminent in the Rio de la Plata area and to restore the old viceregal boundaries (which had included Uruguay, Paraguay, and part of Bolivia) under its control; and Brazil's preoccupation with expanding and securing its own borders. Thus, Argentina contended with Chile for influence in Bolivia and Peru, and with Brazil over Paraguay and Uruguay. In intraregional politics, the century witnessed a series of major South American wars or threats of war as well as other forms of power struggle.

The Southern Cone balance-of-power structure—in essence a microcosm, but not an imitation, of the European regional balance-of-power system—

began to change in the 1860s. Argentina developed rapidly after its unification as a nation in 1861. Brazil extended its territory greatly, actually beginning in 1851 and continuing into the 1900s, by gaining territory from all eight of its neighboring states except for Peru. Brazil, however, was unable to match Argentina's spectacular economic growth. The Argentine-Brazilian competition was inconclusive for the remainder of the century.

A period of "condominium hegemony" extended from 1883 until 1924 (Bailey, 1967:58). Chile began to think in broader terms; it sought to preserve its power position by continuing to curry favor with Ecuador and Colombia against Peru and with Brazil and Paraguay against Argentina— out of fear that Argentina might cooperate with Bolivia and Peru to challenge its Policy of the Pacific. Chile and Argentina, after narrowly averting war in the 1890s, reached an accord in the Pactos de Mayo (1902). They explicitly recognized each other's sphere of influence, agreed to naval parity, and formalized the balance of power system between them. This agreement temporarily left Chile secure in the west, but the Atlantic rivalry between Argentina and Brazil continued. Largely confined to the Rio de la Plata region in the nineteenth century, the rivalry expanded in the twentieth century when both parties adopted policies asserting leadership of South America. The ABC concept effectively ended in the mid-1920s as Chile clearly was left behind, in terms of power, by both Argentina and Brazil, although Chile continued to maintain its power position as best it could. The Argentine-Brazilian competition remained indecisive for about four more decades.

The Rise of the United States
and the Decline of Europe

The second era of subsystem development dates roughly from the 1890s until the middle of World War II. During that time, the United States and Britain were the most significant external actors, but the former expanded its power while the latter declined in influence. The United States emerged as a great power, signaled by its victory in war with Spain in 1898. Thereafter, the United States assumed a new role of international police power in the Caribbean region and converted most of it into a bilateral trade area. It engaged in various forms of coercive unilateral intervention that impinged on the sovereignty of many of the Caribbean states. Interventions were designed to preempt European meddling to enforce stability in the environs of the new Panama Canal, and to secure the Caribbean approaches to the isthmus, considered vital to U.S. strategic interests. That Britain largely retired from the Caribbean in the early 1900s, except for its territorial holdings, further relegated the region to the U.S. sphere of influence subject to a great deal of North American coercion. The principal exceptions to total U.S. hegemony were the territorial holdings of the United Kingdom, France, the Netherlands, and (until 1917) Denmark.

In the South American subsystem, however, the United States was only one of several competitors to the powerful British position; France and

Germany were also important contenders. U.S. influence outside of the Caribbean area did not begin to rival that of Europe until World War I. After the war, Great Britain, which had been the major source of capital for South America, continued to play a major role but yielded first place to the United States. The major Southern Cone states became active and more autonomous at the beginning of the twentieth century, even though their new roles coincided with the rise of U.S. power. With the opening of the Panama Canal under U.S. control, the U.S. domination of the Caribbean region, and the beginning of the Mexican Revolution in 1910, the Southern Cone subsystem was further set apart. Furthermore, there were far-reaching changes in Southern Cone social, economic, and political systems during the first three decades of the twentieth century, as well as in power relationships among the states of the area and with outside powers. Brazil emerged during these years from under the shadow of Great Britain and sought more autonomy in an "unwritten alliance" with the United States. Beginning with the Second Hague Peace Conference and continuing in the politics of World War I, the postwar League of Nations, and the evolving Inter-American System, South American states played an increasing role in global affairs—much greater than in the nineteenth century. In intraregional relations, however, many of the same conflicts continued.

U.S. Hemispheric Hegemony

The third phase of change in the Latin American regional subsystem began during World War II and continued throughout the postwar period until the mid-1960s. It was given impetus with the advent of the cold war but shifted direction after 1959 following the Castro revolution in Cuba and its alignment with the Soviet Union. This era corresponded in large measure to the cold war; the United States was the dominant actor in the region at large and gave form to the subsystem. The subsequent decline of global bipolarity was accompanied by a Soviet challenge to U.S. hegemony in Latin America.

Soon after World War II the international political system was characterized by a loose bipolarity. Most Caribbean states were U.S. clients; the Southern Cone subsystem was less strictly under U.S. domination, with Argentina most successfully resisting U.S. influence. The United States had replaced all foreign powers throughout the hemisphere, except for a few small but burdensome colonies; the long U.S. effort to convert the Caribbean into a sphere of influence and to "insulate" the rest of the region seemed complete. The United States was the region's largest trading partner and capital investor, and it monopolized military relations. Between 1945 and 1948 the Inter-American System was formalized by the Rio Treaty and the Charter of the Organization of American States (OAS), which organized the weaker Latin American states into a bloc under the leadership of the more powerful United States. The United States was able to convert the Inter-American System into an anti-Communist alliance. This move was accompanied by the largely successful U.S. effort to mold a mostly reliable Latin American voting bloc in the United Nations.

Outside powers offered little challenge to U.S. dominance because Latin America was not related to their primary concerns. West European states retreated from strong competition. They were first absorbed with their own recovery and reconstruction and then preoccupied with intra-European affairs, relations with the superpowers and their own security arrangements, and the dissolution of their empires in Asia and Africa. The Soviet Union indicated slight interest as well. It was fundamentally concerned with its own contiguous regions and the cold war with the United States and Western Europe; at the same time it regarded Latin America as inevitably a U.S. sphere of influence that precluded Communist advances. Infrequent perceived threats were dealt with individually by the United States; for example, the United States provided covert support for the overthrow of a leftist government in Guatemala in 1954. From the U.S. point of view, international communism posed little threat to Latin America, a calculation that, when coupled with the dominant U.S. power position, meant that the United States could devote minimal policy attention to the region.

Cuba aligned with the Soviet bloc after the Castro revolution in 1959. The Soviet Union accepted the opportunity to erode the U.S. power position in the Caribbean. This development posed the first significant challenge to U.S. predominance in Latin America since World War II. The United States consequently assigned a prominent position to Latin America in its global policies and temporarily devoted more resources to its overall Latin American policy. These policies included both cooperative instruments through aid programs and coercive means through various forms of intervention. The new policy emphasis had special implications for the Caribbean Basin.

Under these new policies, U.S. and Latin American interests converged in what came to be called the Alliance for Progress. From 1959 to the mid-1960s, the United States temporarily defined the concept of security to include national development, which coincided with the Latin American states' primary economic interests. The United States also pursued coercive strategies; these included an exile invasion of Cuba in 1961 and multilateral agreements in the Inter-American System to impose sanctions on Cuba in 1962 and 1964. Once Cuba left the fold, the United States said it would not allow a similar occurrence again and forcibly returned the Dominican Republic to its sphere of influence through military intervention in 1965 in order to prevent "another Cuba." That intervention effectively ended the Alliance for Progress and the convergence of U.S. and Latin American interests.

In the meantime, a major series of cold war events occurred with the U.S.-Soviet confrontation in the Cuban missile crisis of October 1962, which was viewed by both antagonists in terms of global balances of power. The confrontation over the presence of Soviet missiles in Cuba was a major episode in the cold war, the significance of which went far beyond the Caribbean area and the rest of Latin America. It was a great world crisis in which both sides seemed to perceive a potential shift in the global power balance. A debate over whether Soviet missiles in Cuba in fact could have altered the strategic military balance ensued at the time and has continued thereafter. At any rate, Fidel Castro was largely ignored in what was essentially a U.S.-Soviet confrontation; interaction took place between the superpowers with little reference to the Cuban leader. (The balance-of-power strategies engaged in by Soviet and U.S. leaders are analyzed in Chapters 4 and 5, respectively.) The outcome of the confrontation was that the Soviet Union agreed to remove its newly placed weapons in return for a U.S. pledge not to invade Cuba.

A lower-level U.S.-Soviet imbroglio in 1970 further clarified the latter's activities in the Caribbean area. The United States protested the building of a Soviet nuclear submarine facility at the Cienfuegos naval base in Cuba. President Richard Nixon warned the Soviet Union that the United States would view with alarm the establishment of a Soviet strategic base in the Caribbean. Apparently both sides viewed the base in terms of the strategic military balance. The Cienfuegos activity was consistent with similar Soviet efforts in other parts of the world to increase their capability to conduct continuous operations at great distances. Such bases reduced transit time between ports and allowed for more time on station in the high seas. The U.S. deputy assistant secretary of state for inter-American affairs, testifying before the Senate Foreign Relations Committee in 1973, referred in retrospect to "Cuba's cooperation in 1970 in Soviet efforts to establish a nuclear submarine facility at Cienfuegos which, had it succeeded, could have caused a disturbance" in the balance of military power. The Soviet Union, wishing to avoid another confrontation with the United States over Cuba, agreed in October 1970 to abide by its understanding with the United States on the same terms as those for ending the 1962 missile crisis. Apparently this reaffirmed understanding in 1970 did not cover Soviet navy operations or port calls in the Caribbean region, as the United States probably could have done little to prevent that Soviet presence.

Regional Pluralism

Changing Power Relationships. The Latin American subsystem entered its fourth and current era beginning in about the mid-1960s, when it became even more independent from outside powers, shaped more by the regional actors themselves than was traditionally the case. The hemispheric position of the United States was increasingly challenged, resulting in a relative decline in U.S. influence and an increased pluralism in the distribution of power. Developing international relationships involved changes in U.S. policy in response to shifting calculations of "the Communist threat," the revival of activities by extrahemispheric states in Europe and Asia, and rising Latin American assertiveness in international politics. It has been argued that, with the intense application of U.S. power in the Caribbean Basin after 1981, and the severe economic crisis and heavy debt burden throughout Latin America since about the same date, the subsystem has entered a new era of dependency relationships. The evidence suggests, however, that U.S. power and influence have been effectively applied in certain places and issue areas but remain highly limited in others.

For more than a decade beginning in the latter 1960s, the United States chose policies that again placed a low priority on Latin America, even in the Caribbean. South America recaptured its contours as an independent subsystem, eroded but still intact after the brief postwar period of U.S. predominance in the hemisphere. The Soviet-Cuban threat seemed to recede in the wake of the missile crisis. The United States abandoned developmentalist policies; thus, levels of funding for foreign assistance programs, both economic and military, declined sharply, and direct arms sales were severely limited. The United States sharply diminished its military presence beginning in the late 1960s. Certain bilateral relationships and specific issues were still important to the United States, such as negotiations with Panama over new canal treaties. Human rights policies pursued after 1976 further isolated the United States from those states subjected to U.S. sanctions.

The erosion of global bipolarity was evidenced by Latin American positions and actions toward the United States, as many of them consciously attempted to move out of the U.S. sphere—with some success. They clearly stated their lack of support for a united American front, which they viewed as a device to maintain their status in a U.S. sphere of influence. This attitude was a culmination of trends gathering force after the mid-1960s, which included expropriating foreign enterprises and assuming control of national resources, broadening contacts with other world power centers, challenging the United States in the Inter-American System, and devoting more attention to organizing among themselves and excluding the United States. In general, Latin American states were prompted to cooperate and unite in order to bargain with the United States; but their cooperative efforts were limited and their bargaining power undermined by their own continuing rivalries and disputes. Latin American states also increasingly identified themselves with the Third World, and they sought further foreign policy independence and concerted realization of their interests.

As U.S. influence waned in Latin America, external states initially showed little interest in taking advantage of those opportunities. Japan became an important economic force in the region; European governments and nonstate actors expanded their activities; and the Soviet Union increased its diplomatic, economic, and military presence. However, none of the external powers, with the possible limited exception of the Soviet Union in Cuba, made major efforts to increase their strategic power through Latin American operations.

Economic debilities bearing on the Latin American states in the 1980s, including a large external debt owed to U.S. banks, clearly reduced Latin American foreign policy capabilities. U.S. ability to influence events in Latin America increased because of the same problems faced by any debtor country, but this influence nevertheless remained limited, especially with the major nations. There was no question that the local states' ability to pursue independent foreign policies was eroded, but U.S. leverage as a creditor was far from absolute. The debt situations involved risks for all parties. This is not to argue that they placed equal constraints on creditors and debtors alike; indeed, Latin American governments were forced to adopt stabilization measures that caused domestic hardships and political tensions. Yet it is difficult to measure the extent to which debt rescheduling increases U.S. opportunities or how financial influence translates into political influence. All of the major Latin American states, and even some of the smaller ones, have maintained international orientations and policies in opposition to those of the United States.

Limitations on U.S. capabilities should not be overstated. The current subsystem era has seen the end of the U.S. "hegemonic presumption," but these changes exhibit different contours in the various parts of Latin America. Subregional distinctions have reflected different power realities.

Mexico. As mentioned above, many U.S.-Mexican issues are "North American" in content, a function of territorial proximity and increasingly integrated economic and social structures. They involve trade, investment, capital flows, energy resources and supplies, migration (legal and illegal), boundary settlements and sharing of water resources, border communities, tourism, fishing rights, and so on. "Latin American" issues—such as Central American conflicts, Cuba, intervention, human rights, arms transfers, trade and investment, and nuclear nonproliferation—are also highly important in the relationship; Mexico tends to differ with or oppose the United States on all of them.

The United States continues as the much stronger nation, but Mexico is far from being its client. Their relations have been increasingly characterized by mutual dependence. Mexican nationalism is strong, its foreign policy principles coherent, and its capability significant, so that the United States is in no position to bring about a reorientation of Mexican foreign policy in any fundamental way. Outside states have ample opportunity to align with Mexico on political issues but not to gain a significant share of Mexican trade. The United States is Mexico's largest trading partner, and Mexico occupies third place in total U.S. trade. Furthermore, Mexico is atypical in Latin America in that it generally opposes all types of direct foreign investment, an element inherited from its social revolutionary experience. Even with severe debt problems beginning in 1981, later accentuated by internal political and social problems, Mexico has not shifted its policies to accommodate the United States; if anything, it has stood by them even more self-consciously.

This view of the Mexican-U.S. relationship is sharply contested by some analysts who emphasize Mexico's vulnerability to U.S. power and relative weakness in most respects. To them the characterization of the relationship as mutually dependent is no more than rhetorical, since Mexico needs the United States and the latter can ignore or threaten the former when it wishes. I disagree; I see the relationship as a symbiotic and unavoidably linked one in which, in crude power terms, the United States cannot credibly coerce Mexico without damaging itself.

The Circum-Caribbean. After the Nicaraguan Revolution of 1979, U.S. strategic concern was revived in the Caribbean region. Relations with Cuba had already deteriorated because of its expanded African adventures in concert with the Soviet Union, and President Jimmy Carter had accused the Soviet Union and Cuba of increased activities in Central America. The Reagan administration, inaugurated in 1981, was determined to increase the U.S. presence in the Caribbean and recapture its influence, beginning in Central America. From the point of view of the United States, the principal challenge to Caribbean security arose from Soviet policies and their relationship to Cuban and Nicaraguan actions. If the United States expected an early or easy victory over international communism in Central America, however, it was disappointed. While the Soviet Union and its partners showed a certain caution in their Caribbean activities, they did not retire in the face of strongly assertive U.S. actions. Furthermore, U.S. activities engendered strong domestic political opposition in the United States itself. Important challenges came from other sources as well.

One of the most striking new conditions of Caribbean international politics was the concerted rise to power and assertiveness of Latin American states. Four of them—Mexico, Venezuela, Colombia, and Panama—organized the Contadora Group in 1983 to offer a formula for the negotiated settlement of Central American conflict. Four South American states later joined in a Contadora Support Group. Mexico was particularly independent in its opposition to the United States. Even more stunning was the multilateral peace plan agreed to by the five Central American governments in August 1987. The result of the initiative by President Oscar Arias of Costa Rica, for which he was awarded the Nobel Peace Prize, the Arias plan was opposed by the United States. Successful or not, the combined effects of the Contadora and Arias proposals represent a historic juncture regarding the U.S. position in the Circum-Caribbean. Latin American dissatisfaction with U.S. hegemony was also reflected in the Inter-American System, where U.S. leadership continued to be resisted; the Inter-American System was no longer available to legitimize U.S. actions. In sum, U.S. hegemony was challenged by the regional states themselves, including the weakest among them and those considered to be U.S. clients.

Numerous European actors also presented something of a challenge to U.S. domination of the Caribbean zone. Europeans do not view Latin America in terms of primary security interests because of geographic, cultural, and political distance and higher priority concerns elsewhere. None of them have attempted to increase their strategic power in the Caribbean zone, tending to defer to the United States on such matters. NATO members have only the contingency security concern that the Gulf of Mexico and Caribbean Sea be open for movements of military forces and supplies in the event of European war. After the Nicaraguan Revolution of 1979, Europeans took a political interest in the evolving Central American crisis and by and large dissented from the U.S. approach. Their concern had to do not so much with geopolitics, strategy, or balances of power as with the nature of commitments by the West to social change in the Third World in general. Europeans tended to agree that Soviet influence should be minimized and to be concerned about Nicaragua's authoritarian trends. They opposed unilateral coercion by the United States, however, and argued against military solutions. They applauded the Contadora initiative and the Arias plan.

But European opposition did not develop to the extent anticipated during the period immediately following the Nicaraguan Revolution when the situation was in flux. Europeans exercised little influence on Central American events or on restraining U.S. actions. Most of all, the 1983 U.S. military intervention in Grenada signaled a new and more serious phase. Without primary interests in the region, European governments drew back so as to avoid another alliance problem with the United States. At the same time, however, they warned the United States that the more coercive U.S. actions in Central America became, the more problems the United States would have with its European allies.

On balance, U.S. policy became increasingly isolated in the Circum-Caribbean during the 1980s. Yet U.S. power and influence continued to be the primary considerations in the subregion's international politics.

The Southern Cone. Certain continental and global trends converged to alter the traditional nature of international relationships and foreign policy issues in South America during this period. A more open international environment and diffused external influences allowed local actors greater latitude in the conduct of their foreign relations and permitted extraregional powers to institutionalize substantial involvement—some building on traditional relationships, others evolving into new ones. By the mid-1980s almost all of the subregional states had moved away from military regimes to constitutional democracies. Intra–Southern Cone relationships underwent dramatic evolution, particularly with more cooperative Argentine-Brazilian and Argentine-Chilean relationships. A Brazilian-Argentine rapprochement began in 1979, survived the Anglo-Argentine war of 1982 and dramatic changes of government in both countries, and was extended thereafter. Argentina and Chile settled their contentious Beagle Channel dispute. These were both historic changes, given the traditions of Southern Cone rivalries. The South Atlantic environment is also colored by the anticipation of an Antarctic Treaty review likely to begin in 1991.

On the extrahemispheric level, in addition to its long-standing ties to Europe, the Southern Cone established closer economic relations with Japan. Argentina after 1979 engaged the Soviet Union as its primary trading partner. Brazil established extensive trade relations in Africa and the Middle East. The way is open for a multiplicity of outside states and nonstate entities (especially European churches, labor movements, and transnational parties) to expand both economic and political relationships in the Southern Cone.

The U.S. presence in the Southern Cone and its relations with individual states—especially its economic relations—remain highly important, however, and should not be underestimated. Local states' freedom of action are diminished because of severe debt burdens. Any further U.S. collaboration with South American states will require some sort of mutually satisfactory resolution of the problem of debt structure and repayment. Their international debt problems are severe and tend to dominate economic processes; yet international banks and creditor nations have limited leverage because of the serious risks posed for them as well as for the debtors.

Brazil. U.S. influence with Brazil has declined dramatically since the mid-1960s. Brazil has developed a multilateral network of international trade, has become not only self-sufficient in military affairs but one of the world's major arms exporters, and has continued to reduce its dependence on imported oil. It has developed strong ties in Europe, the Middle East and Africa, and Japan, in addition to those with the United States. Brazil's freedom of action has been limited by its heavy debt burden, yet it still maintains a high degree of independence. Although Brazil suffers serious debilities as the world's largest portfolio-debtor nation, it also has a well-diversified economy, which is rated as the eighth largest in the world. Under military governments in the 1960s and 1970s, Brazil sought great power status; those ambitions have receded, but Brazil's determination and capability to pursue an independent foreign policy remain. For all external states, future cooperative relations with Brazil will likely stem from a convergence of mutual interests rather than from an assertion of superior power. Brazil will formulate most of its ends and means independently rather than follow the lead of the United States, or of any other country, as it interacts in international politics.

EXTRAREGIONAL SUBSYSTEMS

Latin America in the Third World

The membership of Latin American states in the Third World, transcending regional boundaries, perhaps constitutes another global subsystem. Latin Americans sought alternatives to traditional power politics and the redistribution of political and economic power by aligning with other like-minded states in other parts of the globe, thus creating subsystem changes. Conversely, it may be possible to learn more about Latin America's regional consciousness by determining the extent to which it behaves as a regional bloc within the Third World. Latin America is, at once, a regional unit with subregional distinctions and at least loosely part of the Third World, which in certain ways it leads.

The term "Third World" entered the popular vocabulary after World War II. It came to refer to the countries of Asia, Africa, and Latin America, thus containing the majority of the world's populations, as distinguished from the First World (the United States and its partners) and the Second World (the Soviet Union and its Communist-state allies). The Third World is viewed as mostly nonaligned in international politics and composed of poor developing countries economically dependent on the rich nations. Third World nations are said to have a sense of community based on their common conditions of poverty, colonial history, and economic dependency and consequently to share the foreign policy objectives of military and political nonalignment and economic independence and advancement.

There are some problems with this seemingly widely held view. When we attempt to make precise definitions and identify common characteristics among Third World members, we discover important exceptions that challenge the rules. Furthermore, Third World unity and sense of community is illusory. The Latin American region in particular defies easy or general categorization. Yet the concrete movements and organizations that have evolved reflect real concerns and aspirations. Thus, the complexities of this subsystem must be confronted. The Third World requires a more discriminating definition, and the associated structures and processes more precise analysis, than those given in the popular view.

The Third World evolved out of two separate but closely related associations, the Nonaligned Movement and the New International Economic Order. The Third World was first synonymous with the Nonaligned Movement, which began to emerge in the late 1940s and early 1950s. It initially referred to newly independent states in Asia and Africa (including the Middle East) that preferred policies of neutralism, nonalignment, and anticolonialism in the cold war between the United States and the Soviet Union and their respective alliances. Membership subsequently expanded dramatically to include an increasing number of Latin American states after 1961. As of the end of 1987, sixteen Latin American states were full members of the movement and an additional eight of them had attended Nonaligned conferences as observers; the remaining nine states had not participated.

A second Third World association came to be known as the New International Economic Order (NIEO). Almost all Latin American states have joined this association. The origins of the NIEO may be traced to the first United Nations Conference on Trade and Development (UNCTAD I), at which Third World states formed the Group of 77 coalition to unify their objections to global economic practices. The Group of 77 then expanded in number (but kept its original name). In the United Nations General Assembly in 1974, it adopted the Declaration on the Establishment of a New Economic Order. The NIEO created a north-south global confrontation between rich and poor nations on the idea that, by and large, the wealthy nations of the world were in the Northern Hemisphere and the poorer nations in the Southern Hemisphere; consequently, the meaning of Third World was extended to be synonymous with the "south" in economic and developmental terms. The NIEO has been pursued primarily through various United Nations organs.

Thus, two parallel Third World conceptions of the international system emerged, one in reaction to the cold war and its aftermath and the other in reaction to the gap between rich and poor nations. The distinctions have become blurred as each movement has extended its agenda and grown in size. Both have sought Third World unity through a series of international conferences focusing on a wide range of economic, political, and security issues. Concerted action has been difficult to achieve, however, given the large number of states involved, the diversity of their interests, and the divisiveness of regional and other issues. Nonalignment has been a multifaceted objective variously interpreted by Third World governments, including those in Latin America. These divergences and regional issues have generated tremendous strains in both movements.

The Latin American identification with the Third World, in the sense of both nonalignment and developmentalism, is a loose one. By and large, the Latin American states identify first with their own regional developmental problems; they perceive a unique development tradition and tend to coalesce among themselves when confronting the international aspects of development. In fact, a clear Latin American bloc has emerged within the Third World, in both the Nonaligned Movement and the NIEO, pressing regional positions on certain issues.

Other Levels of Analysis

It is possible that there are other international subsystems involving different combinations of Latin American states. A number of theoretical and ideological propositions seem to challenge the idea of the Latin American subsystem itself. In addition to the idea of Latin America as a part of the nonaligned and developing Third World as discussed above, both analysts and political leaders have proposed a Pan American subsystem involving Latin America's special relationship with the United States in the Western Hemisphere or Inter-American System. Some have also posited various Pan Latin connections between Latin America and Latin Europe (most prominently Pan Hispanism of Spanish America and Spain). Regional actors may also have overlapping memberships in nonregional subsystems, such as in the United Nations, where all of the Latin American states are members; Cuba in the Communist world; Venezuela and Ecuador in OPEC; and former British colonies in the Commonwealth. All of these alternatives to Latin American regionalism are discussed in subsequent chapters; some propositions are considered viable, others are not. The point for now is that such subsystem possibilities may complicate the structure of the Latin American subsystem (as well as the global system) but do not refute the regional concept. Actors may belong to more than one subsystem, which may overlap and need not be mutually exclusive. The analyst may choose from various levels of analysis; that of the Latin American region, including its regional subsystems, is both politically important and conceptually defensible. The Latin American region and its subordinate components conform to the definition discussed above sufficiently to be set apart within the larger international system.

BIBLIOGRAPHIC COMMENT

Thompson (1973) provides a definitive critique of regional subsystem concepts. Cantori and Spiegel (1970) include Latin America as one of five regions discussed and compared, and Rosenau, Thompson, and Boyd (1976) also have a chapter on Latin America. Yale H. Ferguson's chapter in Feld and Boyd (1980) is an excellent overview of Latin American IR from a subsystem perspective.

An increasing number of studies over the years have detailed general Latin American international relations. The most thorough early history is by Rippy (1938). Davis, Finan, and Peck (1977) provide a solid international history emphasizing Latin American points of view. Significant studies by Latin American scholars on regional diplomatic history include Quesada (1918–1920), Rodríguez Larretta (1938), Zea (1960), and Boersner (1982). Barclay (1971) covers the period 1917–1945. Bailey (1967) gives a brief, well-organized political science treatment of Latin American international politics. Valuable analyses of a broad range of Latin American international relations are Díaz Albonico (1977), Lagos Matús (1979), and Tomassini (1981). Contributions edited by Fontaine and Theberge (1976) emphasize the end of Latin American isolation in the international system; Jaguaribe (1985), a leading Brazilian analyst, evaluates the new international scene and Latin America's place in it.

A generalized treatment of balances of power with reference to Latin America does not exist. Burr (1967a) provides the most authoritative treatment of the South American balance of power. Caribbean international relations, inevitably including questions of power politics, are addressed by Erisman and Martz (1982), Heine and Manigat (1986), Ince (1979), Langley (1976, 1980, 1982), Millett and Will (1979), R. F. Smith (1981), and Tokatlian and Schubert (1982). See Parkinson (1974) on Latin America in the cold war. For analyses of the Cuban missile crisis, see the bibliographic comments following Chapters 4 and 5. Theberge (1973, 1974) analyzes aspects of Soviet power in Latin America. Kaufman (1976) compares U.S. and Soviet spheres of influence; Lowenthal (1976, 1983) articulates the U.S. "hegemonic presumption" and the decline of U.S. influence; Wesson (1982) edited a volume considering declining U.S. influence in Latin America in the 1980s; and Maira (1986) includes discussions by twelve Latin American experts about the reestablishment of U.S. hegemony by the Reagan administration.

PART TWO

■

The Actors

The next four chapters are concerned with the various actors in the Latin American subsystem. Chapters 3 through 5 explore the foreign policy processes of the regional and external states. They concentrate on the policymakers' perceptions of their interests and situations, the basic foreign policy orientations they have adopted, their ends-means and capability calculations, the role of strategic-geopolitical thinking (for those states whose policies have been based on such considerations), and the various policy doctrines that have been adopted. Commentary is also devoted to Latin American decision-making structures and processes. Such analysis is highly limited with respect to the external states, however, as the subject goes far beyond the scope of this book. Chapter 6 investigates the nature and interests of certain nonstate actors. More detailed discussions of specific policy decisions and the execution of policy through various instruments on the part of all actors are presented in Part Four.

CHAPTER THREE

—————— ■ ——————

The Latin American States

THE FOREIGN POLICIES of the Latin American states share certain basic elements. This chapter examines the motivations, strategies, and policy orientations of the regional decision makers from the perspective of the regional states themselves. The differences in their sizes and diversity in other respects makes comparative analysis difficult and any conclusions tentative. Nevertheless, such an analysis reveals a number of common traits as well as important distinctions.

Three broad questions are considered: (1) What important environmental factors shape Latin American foreign policies? (2) How is policy formulated? and (3) What orientations have been adopted toward the outside world? In general, the realities of Latin American capabilities and the nature of nationalism, combined with the primacy of domestic political processes, form the most important influences bearing on the choice of foreign policy orientations.

CAPABILITY

Geographic Factors

A capability analysis of the Latin American states must pay special attention to political geography. It is generally true that with the development of modern communications, weapons, and other technology, geographic setting and position are not as important to foreign policy calculations as in previous eras. In Latin America, however, political geographic factors continue to affect policies in a number of fundamental ways.

The geographic positions of different parts of Latin America, combined with other capability factors, have fundamentally shaped perceptions and orientations toward the outside world and affected relations with outside states. The northern part of the region—Mexico and the Circum-Caribbean—has always been subjected to intense foreign pressures. Mexico's position on the U.S. border has influenced Mexican foreign policy in important ways; for many years Mexico experienced the threat or actuality of military intervention as well as economic dominance. The Caribbean area was the scene of initial European rivalry, of U.S.-British rivalry in the nineteenth century, and then in the twentieth century was drawn into a sphere of pervasive U.S. influence, until that influence was challenged by the Soviet Union in Cuba and later Nicaragua. Thus, the intense interest of outside states in their affairs, based partly on geographic location, has been a primary policy-making factor for all states in this northern portion of Latin America.

The states in the Southern Cone subsystem have a strikingly unique geographic situation. The location of Brazil, Argentina, Uruguay, Paraguay, Bolivia, Chile, Peru, and Ecuador places them at great distances from both Europe and the United States, outside the mainstream of great power global politics and beyond the immediate sphere of U.S. influence. Their isolation has not been total, however; the area has been subject to external coercion (perhaps less so in the twentieth century than in the nineteenth) and relies on the outside world to provide its major export markets. Most of the time, however, distance has given those states located farthest from the world's great powers a measure of freedom in the international political system, allowing them to maintain relatively independent positions in world affairs and to pursue policies toward each other relatively free of outside considerations.

This fact of relative physical isolation has allowed the states in the Southern Cone subsystem to develop discrete perceptions, orientations, and actions within their subregion as well as toward the contiguous South Atlantic area and Antarctica. That is, in intraregional international politics, the local great powers (Brazil and Argentina) behave like great powers toward their neighbors; the middle powers (Chile and Peru) act accordingly; and the small powers (Uruguay, Paraguay, Bolivia, and Ecuador) are as concerned with the stronger local states as with outsiders. The weak states in the Southern Cone, although isolated from the mainstream of world power politics, have been intimately caught up in rivalries among Argentina, Brazil, Chile, and Peru. Uruguay, Paraguay, and Bolivia are located between larger and more powerful states that compete for leadership in their locale. This "buffer status" has greatly influenced their domestic and foreign policy. They have also had serious conflicts with each other.

Brazil, Argentina, and Chile are the only states in Latin America to have developed significant geopolitical strategic schools of thought, and these concepts have been fundamental motivators in their foreign policies. These states have regularly acted on the basis of the geopolitical nature of the Southern Cone–South Atlantic–Antarctic region as well as in response to their individual national interests; the others have done so to a lesser extent or not at all. This policy-making consideration shows up in stark contrast to the situation in the northern half of Latin America, where the geopolitical interests of outsiders and their activities as local international policemen have precluded the local states from developing such policies.

Geography has influenced intraregional politics in other ways as well. Brazil, the ambitious giant of Latin America, borders all states on the South American continent except for Chile and Ecuador, a fact not lost on the decision makers in the rest of South America. At the other end of the region, the proximity of five small Central American states to relatively huge Mexico has influenced their subregional policies since the 1970s, and the Central American crisis has, in turn, become of primary concern to Mexico. Venezuela's expansion of international influence in the 1970s, based on financial resources garnered from the sale of petroleum, extended to the rest of the Caribbean area; even with the decline of those resources in the 1980s, Venezuela joined Colombia, Mexico, and Panama in the Contadora Group in a sustained effort to deal with the threat posed to them in proximate geographic areas.

A number of physical features have also affected the intraregional policies of several states. Mountains form the dominant characteristic of much of Latin America. They are found in many of the Caribbean islands, beginning almost at the Mexican border with the United States and continuing south through Central America, along South America's Caribbean coast and western continental reaches, and in Brazil. The Andes mountain chain (*cordillera*) extends from the Patagonian region of southern Chile and Argentina along the west coast of the continent near the Pacific shores, to the Caribbean coast, traversing Colombia and Venezuela. In width they vary from less than 100 miles in the south to about 400 miles in a plateau in Peru and Bolivia. They have long provided a security barrier between Chile and Argentina, Chile and Bolivia, and Bolivia and Peru. The large Atacama desert between Chile and Peru serves the same function. The vast Amazon jungle basin, the heartland of South America and until recently undeveloped, has traditionally formed a barrier between Brazil and most of its neighbors. Few highways connect the Latin American nations, although South America contains several great river systems linking some nations. The Amazon River is the world's largest; it carries, by conservative estimate, 20 percent of the world's fresh water; 40 percent of the South American surface waters, found in the territories of eight nation-states, drains into it. Ocean ships are able to navigate some 900 miles upriver to Manaos, and smaller vessels can proceed 1,400 miles farther to Iquitos in Peru. Other important South American river systems are the Magdalena-Cauca in Colombia and the Orinoco in Venezuela, both of which rise in the interior and flow into the Caribbean Sea; both are navigable for considerable distances. The river complex of the Uruguay-Paraguay-Paraná-Pilcomayo, which empties into the Rio de la Plata estuary, is of great commercial and, in the minds of local leaders, military significance. Navigable for 2,000 miles by oceangoing vessels, the system connects southern Brazil, Uruguay, Paraguay, and Argentina.

In South America, physical barriers have offered military protection to all states. At the same time, they have impeded international trade and other peaceful forms of intercourse. In the early 1960s Brazil began constructing transnational highways and a transcontinental railroad network. Brazil had long been obsessed with the fear that some other power might take over the Amazon Basin. This development was met with mixed feelings by many South Americans. The opening of Brazil's interior simultaneously linked the entire continent, facilitating not only international trade but also the spread of Brazilian influence and, in the minds of the more fearful, aggression.

TABLE 3.1
Some Capability Indicators (estimates for end of calendar year 1987)

State (capital city)	Area (square miles)	Total Population (thousands)	Growth Rate (% annual)	Literacy (%)	GDP ($bn)	External Debt ($bn)	Regular Armed Forces (number of personnel)			
							Army	Navy	Air Force	Total
Antigua-Barbuda (St. Johns)	171	84	2.6	90	0.2	0.1				
Argentina (Buenos Aires)	1,072,068	31,328	1.6	92	68.3	48.4	40,000	18,000	15,000	73,000
Bahamas (Nassau)	5,389	265	1.8	89	1.6	0.3	(security forces)			992
Barbados (Bridgetown)	166	254	0.5	99	0.7	0.3				
Belize (Belmopan)	8,867	172	2.2	90	0.2	0.1	545	40	15	600
Bolivia (La Paz)	424,163	6,753	2.7	43	3.2	4.4	20,000	3,600	4,000	27,600
Brazil (Brasilia)	3,286,473	140,236	2.3	72	214.1	104.5	182,900	49,800	50,700	283,400
Chile (Santiago)	286,400	12,308	1.7	90	16.0	21.1	57,000	29,000	15,000	101,000
Colombia (Bogotá)	439,513	30,547	2.1	82	32.7	13.4	53,000	9,000	4,200	66,200
Costa Rica (San José)	19,653	2,785	2.6	93	3.6	4.5	(security forces)			6,500
Cuba (Havana)	44,218	10,333	1.1	96	17.2	3.9	130,000	13,500	18,500	162,000
Dominica (Roseau)	305	74	0.4	80	0.1					

Country (Capital)										
Dominican Republic (Santo Domingo)	18,703	6,955	2.5	68	4.7	4.7	13,000	4,000	4,300	21,300
Ecuador (Quito)	104,506	10,108	3.0	84	12.9	7.8	35,000	4,000	3,000	42,000
El Salvador (San Salvador)	8,083	5,906	2.5	65	5.6	2.1	38,650	1,290	2,700	42,640
Grenada (St. Georges)	133	86	0	85	0.1	0.1				
Guatemala (Guatemala)	42,040	8,858	3.0	50	9.4	2.5	30,300	1,000	700	32,000
Guyana (Georgetown)	82,978	773	0.3	85	0.5	1.3	5,000	270	180	5,450
Haiti (Port-au-Prince)	10,714	5,982	1.9	23	2.1	2.5	6,400	300	200	6,900
Honduras (Tegucigalpa)	43,277	4,801	3.3	56	3.4	2.5	17,000	700	1,500	19,200
Jamaica (Kingston)	4,470	2,349	1.0	76	2.1	3.2	1,780	150	170	2,100
Mexico (Mexico, D.F.)	759,530	81,162	2.7	77	175.4	98.0	105,000	28,000	6,500	139,500
Nicaragua (Managua)	53,668	3,452	3.3	66	3.3	4.4	69,000	1,000	2,000	72,000
Panama (Panama)	29,208	2,274	2.1	90	4.7	4.2	11,500	300	200	12,000

(Continued)

TABLE 3.1 (Continued)
Some Capability Indicators (estimates for end of calendar year 1987)

State (capital city)	Area (square miles)	Total Population (thousands)	Growth Rate (% annual)	Literacy (%)	GDP ($bn)	External Debt ($bn)	Regular Armed Forces (number of personnel) Army	Navy	Air Force	Total
Paraguay (Asunción)	157,047	3,739	2.4	75	5.8	1.9	12,500	2,500	970	15,970
Peru (Lima)	494,293	20,342	2.5	67	17.0	15.2	85,000	27,000	15,000	127,000
St. Kitts-Nevis (Basseterie)	150	40	0	80	0.1					
St. Lucia (Castries)	238	124	1.1	78	0.2					
St. Vincent-Grenadines (Kingston)	150	104	0.9	82	0.1					
Suriname (Paramaribo)	55,000	387	1.7	65	1.0	0.4	2,350	125	60	2,535
Trinidad-Tobago (Port of Spain)	1,864	1,221	1.5	89	5.8	1.6	1,500	580	50	2,130
Uruguay (Montevideo)	72,172	3,031	0.6	91	5.1	4.8	22,300	6,600	3,000	31,900
Venezuela (Caracas)	347,029	16,640	2.6	86	49.7	35.0	34,000	10,000	5,000	49,000
Total	7,872,639	413,473			666.9	393.2	973,725	210,755	152,945	1,344,917

Sources: Inter-American Development Bank, Economic and Social Progress in Latin America, 1986 Report; Central Intelligence Agency, The World Factbook, 1986; and International Institute of Strategic Studies, The Military Balance, 1985-1986. Projections and estimates by the author.

Territorial size is also a capability factor. With a total land area of about 8 million square miles, Latin America represents about one-sixth of the world's land area. The individual states, however, differ greatly in size. Brazil is the largest territorial state by a wide margin; its 3.3 million square miles represent more than 40 percent of the entire surface area of the region. The smallest continental state, El Salvador, covers only 8,083 square miles, and the smallest island nation, Grenada, only 133 square miles. Other large states are Argentina, Mexico, Peru, Colombia, Bolivia, and Venezuela. Mexico and Bolivia at one time encompassed twice the territory they have today, but as the result of military defeats, each lost half its national domain to neighboring states. Size alone, however, does not determine state power; other factors must be considered.

Population Factors

Quantitative and qualitative aspects of Latin American populations are important sources of foreign policy strengths and weaknesses. Underpopulation was a primary concern in the region after national independence. The entire Latin American population in 1810 was probably only 20 million, and in 1900 little more than 60 million. In 1975 the total population was in excess of 300 million, growing faster than that of any other major region of the world. By the mid-1980s it was approaching 400 million; if the 1986 annual rate of increase continues, Latin American population will reach about 600 million at the end of the twentieth century.

Population levels and density vary widely among the various states. Brazil's 140 million inhabitants make up about one-third of Latin America's total population. St. Kitts-Nevis is the least populous state, with 40,000 inhabitants. Some Latin American nations are among the world's most densely populated, such as Barbados and El Salvador. Others are very lightly inhabited, such as Bolivia. Most of Latin America is urbanized, and urbanization continues apace throughout. Argentina has the highest urban concentration: About two-thirds of its people live in cities and towns, almost half of them in greater Buenos Aires alone.

Latin America generally has much unoccupied territory, and several states could provide many more people with living space. Population variables, however, involve not only numbers of persons but qualitative considerations as well. For example, economic growth rates are not sufficient to dramatically decrease poverty levels, given the generally high population growth rates. Poverty, in turn, is correlated with socially undesirable traits, such as low literacy levels and lack of technical skills. Overall, poverty detracts from a nation's capability because productive human resources are undeveloped and because large numbers of discontented sectors increase divisive social tensions.

Some Latin American nations have much higher educational levels and standards of living than others. For example, estimated literacy in Argentina, Chile, Costa Rica, Cuba, Panama, and Uruguay ranges from 90 to 96 percent, and literacy rates in most of the Commonwealth Caribbean are very impressive. Literacy is lowest by a wide margin in Haiti, and low literacy rates are also found in Guatemala, Bolivia, Nicaragua, Honduras, and El Salvador. Higher literacy rates are not an unmixed blessing, however; they can result in increased expectations that, if frustrated, may have a socially destabilizing impact.

Social Factors

Social tensions and lack of homogeneity detract from the strength of some states more than others. Racial and cultural variety in Latin America and complex intermixing have had different social impacts in the various nations. Indigenous Indian peoples were the first Americans; by the time of European expansion into America after 1492, Indian civilizations ranged from primitive nomadic tribes to the advanced and complex cultures and empires of the Aztecs and Incas (superior to those of parts of Europe at the time). The Spanish and Portuguese, coming first as conquerors and then as settlers, ruled, reduced most Indians to servile status, and further populated most of what is today called Latin America. Africans were later introduced to certain less populated parts of the region in large numbers as slaves on sugar and cacao plantations or in gold, silver, and diamond mines. They were brought by the Spaniards and Portuguese as well as the British, French, and Dutch during the three-century colonial period. The British also brought East Indians (from South Asia) to their colonies as indentured immigrant labor from the 1830s until World War II. Chinese "coolies" were brought as "contract labor" to various parts of Latin America. Immigrants from virtually all parts of the globe migrated to the New World, mostly after Latin American states had achieved nationhood. As a result of racial and ethnic intermixing, the Latin American states are culturally complex and dissimilar in many respects, combining indigenous, colonial Iberian, and imported cultural heritages. Thus, racially and ethnically, there is no such thing as a "typical" Latin American individual or nation.

As a general rule skin color is correlated with class: The whitest persons are in the upper classes and, correspondingly, darker people are relegated to the lower social gradations. Strong class-consciousness has created social tensions, alienated large social sectors, and weakened national unity. Even in the largely homogeneous black-populated new nations and in Haiti, the class system is rigidly structured, and little effort has been exerted by the upper classes to involve the masses more fully in national life. The few states with relatively small noncaucasian populations have not been divided by the problems of integrating minority races into national life, but even in those states class-consciousness is strong, based on such factors as family and economic status. Generally speaking, more class mobility exists in the cities than in rural areas.

Political Factors

Political instability is both a source and an expression of weakness, whereas stable political processes add to national strength. The politically unstable states in Latin America are less united on international issues and less able to deal with their own national development; preoccupied with domestic problems, they tend to consider foreign policy as relatively less important. In contrast, the Latin American states with the most effective foreign policies are also the most politically stable. They are more able to devote resources to international questions, and they have gained a certain amount of respect from other states.

During the early national period, few Latin American states were able to maintain internally stable political systems. Conflict and factionalism, including civil war and rebellion, as well as corrupt administrative practices, were common. This weakness frequently invited foreign intervention. The international effectiveness of the major states has depended largely on their internal stability. Brazil experienced little turmoil in the nineteenth century and was the major exception in this regard. In the latter part of the century, Argentina and Chile began to move toward relatively stable systems, although a great deal of violence accompanied the process.

Mexico's political turmoil, beginning in 1910, for all practical purposes retired it from international politics for two decades. Mexico regained stability after the 1930s, however, and became an important actor in inter-American and, at times, world affairs, despite its geographic disadvantage in proximity to the United States. Brazil's stability since the mid-1960s, as in an earlier era, was fundamental to its uneven drive for world power. As Brazil's authoritarian government became fragmented in the late 1970s, however, its foreign policy followed suit. Brazil's main rival, Argentina, although loath to admit it, effectively dropped out of the Latin American leadership race, primarily because of problems directly related to political instability beginning in the late 1920s and accelerating after 1955. Argentina's return to popular civilian rule in 1983, replacing a military regime that terrorized its own populace, allowed a policy of "reinsertion" into the international system to be carried out. Chile's domestic political crisis beginning in 1970 caused severe foreign policy problems as well as weakness in dealing with them. A decade of civil war in Colombia beginning in 1948, and subsequent guerrilla insurgency and violence associated with narcotraffic, have kept Colombia from developing the international influence that should be possible, given its size and resources. In contrast, Venezuela's capability has been enhanced by a democratically legitimized political system and its vastly increased oil riches—especially in the 1970s—despite its small population and serious domestic social inequities. Even as Venezuela's national income dropped with the decline in oil revenues in the 1980s, its general domestic political consensus reduced the impact of economic crisis.

Political stability can be of importance to the foreign policies of small states as well. Uruguay, for example, influenced inter-American relations for many years because of its prestige stemming from stable democratic development. It suffered a great loss in prestige, however, when its political stability and democratic government deteriorated along with its economic life in the decade after 1966. Costa Rica is another example of a small state respected for its democratic stability, developed after World War II. But small states can also be seriously weakened by domestic political problems. For example, political instability in the Dominican Republic after 1961 led directly to the U.S. military intervention in 1965. Likewise, civil war and insurgency in Central America in the 1980s have led, variously, to U.S., Cuban, Soviet, and other external involvement in local politics, and internecine strife in Grenada was one reason for the U.S. military intervention there in 1983.

Military Factors

Although the military capability of Latin American states generally is not significant in world politics—the Cuban presence in Africa is the current exception—it has had substantial impact on inter-American relations. Throughout most of the nineteenth century and, in several instances, into the twentieth, Latin American armies were as a rule inadequately equipped, untrained militia led by officers lacking professional skills and knowledge. The armies tended to be bands of armed men loyal not to the nation or to any central government but to charismatic regional strongmen (*caudillos*). The Chilean army was the principal exception to this rule. The small navies were not much better, with the significant exception of Chile's and, to a degree, those of Argentina and Brazil. The major states of South America began important modernizing efforts in the late nineteenth century, and eventually all Latin American military establishments began the process of professionalization, all largely with foreign help.

Despite considerable modernization, the Latin American armed forces have remained vastly inferior to those of the world's great powers. Although some have reached relatively sophisticated levels, in worldwide terms they have remained unimportant. With some exceptions, the involvement of the nations in extraregional politics has not relied on military capability. Those exceptions include a Brazilian army battalion that fought in Italy in World War II, a Mexican aircraft squadron stationed in the Philippines at the same time, a Colombian ground unit that participated in the United Nations force in Korea, and the Cuban army presence in Africa in concert with the Soviet Union beginning in late 1975.

In regional terms, however, relative military capability has been of continuous significance since the wars for independence; military units were mobilized in inter-American wars beginning in the early national period and as late as 1967. Border disputes have erupted periodically, and relative military power has been a factor in their outcome. An Inter-American Peace Force settled the Dominican civil war of 1965–1966 (under de facto U.S. leadership), and a similar organization was instrumental in bringing warfare between El Salvador and Honduras to an end in 1967. The Central American crisis in the 1980s has actively involved the armed forces located in that subregion. In most Latin American states today, military capability is significant primarily in terms of internal problems—primarily as a domestic political arbiter and, variously according to place and time, as a defense against insurgency.

No nuclear weapons are possessed by Latin American states, but some have the potential to manufacture them. Existing civil nuclear power programs in Argentina, Brazil, and Mexico are oriented toward peaceful purposes, and no state seems to have embarked on nuclear weapons programs thus far. Nevertheless, their nuclear research centers and reactors have military potential, an inherent by-product of any nuclear power capability. Argentina is the most advanced in this regard, with Brazil close behind. Other Latin American states interested in developing nuclear power programs have either begun research or are planning to do so. In the 1980s, the prospects for nuclear weapons development in Argentina and Brazil have been reduced, at least temporarily, by a combination of a return to democratic rule and financial crisis. The latter consideration has also deterred nuclear development in other Latin American programs.

Economic Factors

Economic problems, another factor in judging a nation's capabilities, trouble most Latin American states, although examples of real economic strengths are also evident. Most of the regional states are characterized by economic monoculturism: National income depends heavily on the export of a few, perhaps only one or two, agricultural or mineral items, causing national economies to be strongly affected by the vagaries of world markets. Stagnation is averted as long as full export market demands exist, but economies tend to deteriorate when export products must compete in markets characterized by declining prices.

Weaknesses in the industrial sector are characteristics of economic monoculturism. Latin America traditionally has relied on external industrialized states for manufactured goods as well as investment capital, for which it has exchanged agricultural and mineral commodities. Industrialization has made some progress in most states and remarkable strides in a few, so that today industrial levels vary widely. Some economies are fairly well balanced industrially, including heavy industry; Brazil is especially notable, while Mexico, Argentina, and Chile have made certain advances in this regard. Others are in a "moderate" industrial development stage, such as Colombia, Cuba, Peru, Trinidad-Tobago, and Venezuela. The remainder have only the beginnings of industrialization or are virtually nonindustrial, such as Haiti and Grenada. Latin America in general has certain natural disadvantages that detract from its industrial potential. For example, coal resources are small and generally of low quality, and power sources are deficient; hydroelectric potential is great, but the best sites are remote from urban centers. Platine states in the Southern Cone subsystem, led by Brazil and Argentina, have cooperated to their mutual benefit in dam building projects to realize hydroelectric potential.

A continuing myth, dating from the discovery of the New World, pictures the Latin American region as possessing immense mineral resources that need only investment capital and managerial skills to be developed. The region is not generally rich in minerals, although a minority of states are especially well endowed in certain resources. Some of them rank high in world levels of reserves and production, such as Bolivia in tin; Chile in nitrates and copper; Mexico in silver, lead, and zinc; Peru in vanadium and bismuth; and Venezuela and Mexico in oil. Even though these minerals are crucial necessities for the external industrialized nations, the Latin American states have only seldom derived serious bargaining leverage, with the important exception of oil in the 1970s. Mining industries traditionally were dominated by foreign capital and decision makers. Nationalization of foreign-owned extractive industries in some nations eliminated many foreign economic elites, but if the heavy reliance on mineral resources continues, the problems of monoculturism will persist.

Special mention should be made of oil resources. Ten Latin American nations produce oil, but it is significant as an export in only four—Venezuela, Mexico, Ecuador, and Colombia. Venezuela's petroleum industry began to grow especially in the 1920s, and thereafter it has consistently been among the world's major oil producers and exporters. Mexican reserves and production have also achieved a very high volume in world terms. With the energy crisis of the 1970s and dramatic increases in world market oil prices, Venezuela and Mexico profited enormously. Conversely, the decline of the price of oil in the 1980s was an important factor in their economic crises.

The high levels of external debt in relation to the size of Latin American economies has been the most serious international economic problem throughout the 1980s. (The debt structure is discussed in detail in Chapter 10.) External debt is closely linked not only to trade balances but also to more general international relations and questions of internal stability. The analyst must ask how dependent Latin Americans are on the international economic system and whether they are able to respond to outside pressures and consider the effect of domestic austerity programs, negotiated with the International Monetary Fund in concert with external government and commercial bank creditors, on domestic developmental demands. Latin American leaders generally argue that too much austerity will bear too heavily on the poorest sectors of society, leading to social violence and ultimately to political chaos. Leaders of democratic polities, some of whom have only recently succeeded military regimes, further argue that their very democracies are at stake. Although the content and consequences of the debt issue have varied in different Latin American countries, it is safe to generalize that the question of external debt not only dominates economic issues but also has profound long-term implications for other areas of international politics.

NATIONALISM

The Analytic Problem

Nationalism is a fundamental force in Latin America's foreign policy. An analysis of this phenomenon is complicated, however, first by the lack of a precise and widely accepted definition and, second, because the Latin American variety of nationalism is highly complex. Despite definitional elusiveness and regional complexity, the importance of nationalism to Latin American foreign policy formulation cannot be denied. (The following discussion of nationalism follows the categories posited by Whitaker and Jordan, 1966.)

Classic definitions characterize nationalism as a "group consciousness" in which individuals identify themselves with and give supreme loyalty to the abstraction of the nation, which reinforces the state as the ultimate source of authority and legitimacy. This definition should be modified with the caveat that particular nationalists may use nationalism to attempt to capture control of the state and its authority, claiming to speak for "the nation" in order to gain advantage over political competitors. Nationalism is also a structural and institutional phenomenon; that is, it represents the lodging of social functions and their structural base in the nation-state.

Latin American nationalism involves several forms and different orientations. It assumes multiple ideologies and loyalties even within individual nations. Latin American nationalism, variously, stems from both internal and external sources, is based on indigenous social values, imitates the values of outsiders, or stands in opposition to external values or interference. The effects of nationalism have also been varied, ranging in style from militant, intolerant, xenophobic, aggressive, and divisive at the one extreme, to pacific, benign, internationally cooperative, and domestically unifying at the other extreme.

The diversity of nationalism has led to domestic political tensions and resulted in a variety of foreign policies. The following discussion will identify only those variants of nationalism that have relevance for Latin American foreign policy, ignoring those of essentially domestic consequence.

Early Nationalist Sentiments

The roots of Latin American nationalism are found in the colonial era, when some native elites developed a sense of separate identity from Spain and Portugal. Between 1810 and 1824, when most of Spanish America ended its colonial status and achieved national independence, the fighting intensified the anti-Spanish feeling that had been building for some time. This Spanish American aversion to foreigners has been called "creole nationalism," a term that grew initially out of the bitterness of *criollos* (Spaniards born in the New World) toward the privileged Spanish authorities in America (*peninsulares*). It survived throughout the nineteenth century, prodded on by continued Spanish hostility toward the lost colonies, and translated into a xenophobia among some Spanish Americans, to whom anything Spanish was anathema.

The nationalist outcome in Portuguese Brazil was very different. The royal Braganza family had fled from Portugal to Brazil during the Napoleonic invasion of the Iberian peninsula in 1807 and 1808 (the Spanish king and the heir to the throne had been arrested by the French). The Portuguese royal family returned to Lisbon in 1820, leaving Prince Pedro in America as regent to rule Brazil. He came under the influence of Brazilian nationalists and led that nation's successful independence movement in 1822 with little bloodshed. Anti-Portuguese feeling was to be found among many native Brazilians, but it was modified by the wide acceptance of a member of the old royal family as sovereign of the new nation until 1889.

A strong sense of "Americanism" and Spanish American solidarity existed among some leaders of the new Latin American states. Sometimes called "continental nationalists," such prominent patriots as Simón Bolívar and José de San Martín hoped for political unity in Spanish America and visualized some sort of league of states to be organized along the lines of the viceregal boundaries. Some Spanish Americans and Brazilians advocated the inclusion of Brazil. These plans were frustrated, however, as the Spanish American empire broke up into sixteen (later eighteen) separate nations. A number of boundary conflicts among the new states, inter-American wars, and foreign interventions helped to develop individual nationalist sentiments and to erode continental nationalism. Furthermore, loyalties were often local rather than national in scope, although international conflict promoted the perception of the need for national unity in the face of foreign threats.

A great deal of nineteenth-century Latin American nationalism, largely restricted to the small elite power groups, was often a superficial imitation of European and North American strains. Independence was won just as modern nationalism was taking shape in these other areas of the globe, stimulated by the American and French Revolutions (1776/1789). These elites, however, were divided among themselves.

In Spanish America, competing groups were organized into primitive political parties, actually cliques, labeled Conservative and Liberal (a European borrowing), each with a different nationalist perspective. Conservatives generally wished to perpetuate the colonial system, but with themselves rather than the Spaniards as leaders; they looked to the past for national identity and unity—a past that included authoritarian central governments, Roman Catholicism, rigid social stratification, and other elements of the Hispanic colonial tradition. Liberals rejected the colonial past; they were anti-Spanish to varying degrees and to some extent opposed the political, social, and educational roles of the Church, adopted anticlerical positions, and sought to replace the authoritarian political system with progressive forms and principles copied, especially, from France, Britain, and the United States.

Modernization and Nationalism

Current forms of Latin American nationalism are rooted in the values and tensions associated with the processes of political, social, and economic modernization. They date essentially from the late nineteenth century, when modernization, largely fostered by native elites in league with foreign interests, helped to develop national infrastructures and to create new, politically aware socioeconomic groups. The rise of new social classes stimulated nationalist sentiments among the mobilized groups as they attempted to establish a broad consensus that would better serve their interests as they challenged traditional elite power structures. In the mid-1980s, Latin American nationalism was further shaped by the continuing process of economic development and social conflict, which in turn were shaped by the earlier impact of two world wars, the repercussions of the interbellum worldwide depression, the cold war, and foreign military intervention, as well as investment and economic assistance. The main forms of nationalism stimulated by modernization are identified here as modernism, nativism, antiyankeeism, economic nationalism, military socialism, and revolutionary nationalism.

Modernism. Modernism refers to the pursuit of national unification and development by progressive elites, usually with foreign help. The drive to develop, beginning in the nineteenth century, was itself a nationalist urge, a nation-building process looking to Europe and the United States for inspiration and identified with political and economic liberalism and cultural cosmopolitanism. Modernist advocates asserted that the best way to strengthen the nation was to draw as fully as possible on foreign sources, including capital investments, managerial skills, and mass immigration. Modernism was especially vigorous in Brazil, Argentina, Chile, Uruguay, and Mexico, where foreign enterprise and European immigration (of less significance in Mexico than the others) assumed great importance in national development.

Nativism. Nativism, a Spanish-American concept, was a nationalist reaction to modernism. It was opposed the influx of foreign immigrants and other influences. It was based on both *criollo* national values and opposition to the values of others. Nativists such as the Argentines José Hernández, writing in the late nineteenth century, and Ricardo Rojas, in the early twentieth, urged that tradition be protected and that their nation be ridded of European cultural hegemony. Nativists often viewed their national pasts nostalgically and romantically and saw the nation's history as a struggle between native and immigrant forces.

Antiyankeeism. Antiyankeeism was related to nativism during the first third of the twentieth century. Traces of anti–North Americanism were found throughout the nineteenth century, but they were not sustained until many Latin Americans were outraged by U.S. military and economic intervention in the Caribbean area. The expansion of U.S. interests stimulated nationalism not only in politics and economics but in cultural matters as well. A number of literary expressions of *antiyanquismo* during that time declared disillusionment with the course the U.S. democratic experiment had taken and warned of the threat of North American materialism to Hispanic spiritualism. Such sentiments existed in Brazil, but they were less pronounced there than in Spanish America because Brazilian government leaders encouraged friendship with the United States. Brazilians, to the present day, do not hold the same suspicions and hostility toward foreigners, whatever their origins, as Spanish Americans.

The United States continues to be criticized for its interventions. Antiyankeeism increased gradually during the three decades after World War II, and sharply in the 1980s, not only because of such events as the military invasion of the Dominican Republic in 1965, subversion in Chile in the 1970s, and coercive policies in the Circum-Caribbean in the 1980s, but also because of resentment over U.S. economic and trade policies toward the area. U.S. policies have inspired anti-U.S. sentiments in their own right; at the same time, Latin American governments themselves have been under pressures stemming from economic dislocations and social change and the United States presents a tangible object for resentment.

Economic Nationalism. Economic nationalism was first embraced by the new upper middle class, primarily the industrial and entrepreneurial sectors, that emerged from the modernization process. It was later adopted by representatives of the other middle sectors, organized labor, and the student movement. (The appearance of the student movement paralleled modernization in the early twentieth century, and its presence has remained strong through the mid-1980s.) In contrast to the foreign orientation of the earlier modernists, economic nationalists have stood for a modified statism. Although economic nationalism allows for an important role for private enterprise, its basic tenets hold that the nation owns the subsoil and natural resources and that the national good prevails over private property rights.

Economic nationalism intensified after World War II and again in the late 1960s. In both periods the major stimulus was provided by U.S. economic policies. A major rallying point was a program of economic nationalism formulated by the United Nations Economic Commission for Latin America (ECLA) under the leadership of two Latin American economists, the Argentine Raúl Prebisch and the Mexican Víctor Urquidi. They argued that Latin America should develop its own industry by establishing protective tariffs, creating common markets, and obtaining massive external financial assistance. They also advocated commodity agreements and better terms of trade with other states in the United Nations Conference on Trade and Development (UNCTAD). They did not reject the use of foreign capital, but argued that foreign interests should not interfere with Latin American industrialization. Some radical schools of economic nationalism advocated the expropriation and nationalization of existing foreign enterprises and exclusion of further foreign investment; others would allow such investment, but only under closely supervised conditions.

Military Socialism. Military socialism is a variant of economic nationalism that is combined with calls for social justice and distinguished by the stress put on the dominant role of the armed forces. It involves reform-oriented military regimes that claim to have abandoned their traditional role as defenders of the status quo in alliance with the upper classes and are willing to nationalize foreign enterprise. This phenomenon has been called "Nasserism" after the example set by Egypt's nationalist leader, but a number of Latin American "Nasserists" preceded Nasser's appearance as a political figure. Some came to power by coup d'état, others by regular elections. In 1936 a notable revolutionary movement in Paraguay was led by military men advocating a socialist program. Military socialist governments in Bolivia were in power from 1936 to 1943.

The linking of military-led social reform with economic nationalism and anti–North Americanism was significant in the late 1960s and early 1970s, especially in the case of Peru. There, military men came to power in 1968 and embarked on a major social reform and economic development program counter to traditional upper-class interests; they also nationalized a subsidiary of Standard Oil Company and seized lands belonging to U.S. firms for a land reform program. The Peruvian military government clearly identified itself as a nationalist movement asserting national rights to the land and subsoil resources and stated that foreign companies would not be allowed to control the national wealth. A similar government took power briefly in Bolivia in 1969; it, too, moved against U.S. companies and succeeded in nationalizing a Gulf Oil Company subsidiary.

Revolutionary Nationalism. The radical left has attempted to use popular nationalism to further its cause. In the 1930s and 1940s Soviet-oriented Marxist movements tried to capture nationalism for the proletariat, often working with popular fronts composed of other leftist and sometimes centrist parties. While Communists supported populism, they never controlled it. Their greatest successes occurred in Chile. A Popular Front of Communists, Socialists, and Radicals governed under a Radical president from 1938 to 1952 (the Communists separated from this organization in 1947); and a coalition of leftist parties was again in power under President Salvador Allende, a Marxist, from 1970 to 1973.

Revolutionary nationalism as a recent phenomenon has been most vividly expressed by the Cuban Revolution of 1959. Fidel Castro's combination of Cuban nationalism (in the tradition of José Martí) and Marxism-Leninism during the 1960s forced Latin America as well as the United States to recognize the slowness of economic and social development in the region. The Castro revolution provided ideological inspiration for other groups that began to use violence aimed at overthrowing the existing order and to express virulent hatred for the United States. The new radical left was hostile to the orthodox Communist parties and scornful of their tactic of peaceful political coexistence; they abandoned traditional modernist social values, including peaceful constitutional political processes, claiming to have lost faith in the ability of "bourgeois democracy" (*democracia burguesa*) to achieve social justice. Revolutionary nationalism was not successful in gaining power outside of Cuba until the Sandinista movement captured control of the government in Nicaragua in the revolution of 1979.

The New States

Special mention should be made of the nationalist orientations of the "new states"—the twelve former British dependencies in the Caribbean Basin that gained their independence beginning in 1962, and Suriname (former Dutch Guiana), independent since 1975.

The former British colonies, never Latin and no longer British, searched for an American identity. They formed the West Indies Federation among themselves between 1958 and 1962, anticipating the emergence of a single independent state; it dissolved, however, and separate entities were created, with others remaining dependent on Great Britain. Only four years after the dissolution of the federation, however, the new states and dependencies began to establish Pan Caribbean ties, based on their common British colonial heritage, through economic integration organizations. The independent Commonwealth Caribbean States have also sought ties with other regional states. Most of them have joined the Organization of American States (OAS), thereby establishing organizational affiliations with the rest of the Americas. Guyana and Belize have not joined the inter-American organization because of ongoing unsettled territorial disputes with their neighbors, Venezuela and Guatemala, respectively, who are members. The independent states also continue their Old World ties and remain in the Commonwealth.

Cultural ties with the United Kingdom are elusive. An English cultural facade was superimposed, variously, on African, East Indian, Oriental, and other ethnicities. Barbados is the most "English" among these new nations, duplicating old-world ways to a remarkable degree. Trinidad-Tobago perceives itself as "American" more than the others but has not rejected the British tradition. All but Guyana are constitutional monarchies with a governor-general representing the British crown (but with no political power). Although criticism of British policies abound, especially regarding aid and trade, anti-British nationalism is minimal.

"Black power" movements in several of the new states emerged, for a time, as a specialized Commonwealth Caribbean form of revolutionary nationalism, anchored in a combination of economic nationalism and racial pride. Most of the nations share a predominantly African origin (with the exceptions of Guyana and Trinidad-Tobago). They also suffer massive unemployment, with the wealthy minority living apart from the poor majority. The main target of black power resentment was the small, wealthy, politically powerful upper class, composed of both blacks and whites and representing both local and foreign capital. "Wealthy" was not necessarily defined in racial terms, but the poor were almost exclusively black. They were resentful of what they considered to be the betrayal of the nation's interests by black governments and business to white, foreign financial interests. A certain solidarity existed in the movement in the Caribbean area. Although political leaders were sensitive to their resentment, the black power movement lacked leadership and declined in the 1970s. The basic elements for a coherent movement continued to exist but were never fully mobilized.

FOREIGN POLICY DECISION MAKING

The Primacy of Domestic Politics

Students of foreign policy emphasize the interplay between domestic politics and foreign policy, recognizing that the latter tends to be an extension of the former. In the case of Latin America, too, foreign policy tends to be a projection of domestic politics, even though foreign policy decision making by its nature differs somewhat from the domestic process (Harold E. Davis in Davis, Wilson, and others, 1975:11). In addition, foreign policy can be an important mode for furthering domestic political goals, especially in the hands of opportunistic politicians who lack popular support or wish to divert attention from domestic political crises by focusing on nationalist foreign policy causes. Political advantage has been sought, and often gained, by both government and opposition leaders by raising such issues as territorial disputes with neighboring states, intervention by external powers, imperialism by foreign entrepreneurs, and so on. Nationalization of foreign enterprises since the latter part of the 1930s, notably in Mexico, Bolivia, Argentina, Chile, Cuba, Nicaragua, Peru, and Venezuela, has been designed not only to further domestic economic development but also, in large measure, to gain popular political support.

The foreign policy formulation process differs from state to state in Latin America because of variations in capability factors, including proximity to greater powers, the degree and character of social complexity, political organization and style, specific experiences and issues, and so on. This diversity makes regional generalizations difficult. Nevertheless, assuming that commonalities do exist, and that the same social milieu gives rise to foreign policy decisions as to domestic ones, some tentative observations and conclusions may be set down.

A problem for the analysis of Latin American foreign policy formulation has been the erroneous assumption or impression, expressed especially by dependency theorists (see Chapter 13), that those processes are overwhelmingly dominated by foreign influences, especially from the United States. If, indeed, external inputs are dominant, we may easily dismiss questions of foreign policy formulation. Such has probably been the case, at least at times, for certain small states, as in the Caribbean area during the period of intense U.S. imperialism during the first third of this century and, to a lesser but still important extent, into the late 1980s. The same has been said for Cuba, which is often characterized as a Soviet "puppet," and for Nicaragua in its relationship with the Soviet Union under the Sandinista government. Even for the weakest and most externally dominated states, however, this generalization is not completely accurate even when foreign pressures are being applied. For example, in the 1980s El Salvador and Cuba, in their relations with the United States and the Soviet Union, respectively, exhibited some independence in their decision-making capacities. More important, this view of foreign dominance ignores the political complexity and relative foreign policy autonomy of the major regional states, as well as the isolated international environment of some of the smaller ones. This is not to deny that external factors play crucial roles in Latin American policy formulation, but it is to assert that those factors are not ubiquitous or omnipotent and are part of a more complex political process. Nor should we forget that many regional situations and issues require decisions largely divorced from U.S. or other external pressures.

Domestic Input Channels

Crucial among foreign policy factors are the views of politically powerful interest groups. Economic organizations, such as coffee growers in Colombia and meat and wheat producers in Argentina, especially attempt to influence foreign policy decisions. However, organized interest groups outside of the economic arena are rarely concerned primarily with influencing foreign policy, so that their impact on international relations tends to be a "spinoff" of domestic politics.

Foreign policy traditionally was monopolized by elite social sectors and represented their values and interests, with little reference to the larger public. Two sectors of the upper class, the landed aristocracy and wealthy commercial urbanites, have been internationally oriented, frequently with a special interest in foreign trade policy. Therefore, they have seen their interests served by friendly relations with foreign investors and the maintenance and expansion of foreign markets. Powerful agrarian, commercial, and sometimes industrial societies have been organized in almost every Latin American state to represent elite sectors and to promote their economic, including international, interests.

Economic development created new classes, which have challenged the upper class elite sector (who, ironically, had sponsored the development) for a share of social and economic benefits. As Latin America developed economically, the middle class expanded significantly. Today its size varies considerably from state to state, but it generally has challenged the modernist assumptions of traditional elites and has substituted economic nationalism as the dominant basis for foreign policy perspectives. Most of the middle class, however, has taken little interest in foreign policy and is more narrowly concerned with career and employment opportunities. However, as the middle class has expanded, become more secure, and acquired more political power, it has taken increased interest in foreign policy issues, usually urging more independent national roles in international politics but generally avoiding xenophobia.

Altogether new groupings have also appeared and expanded as a result of continuing modernization, most notably in urban and mining labor. The dominant foreign policy perspective seems to be anticapitalist and anti–United States. Labor unions have exercised varying impacts on policy throughout the region. They were particularly important in the mid-1980s in Argentina, Mexico, Bolivia, Venezuela, and Peru. Unions were highly influential in some countries in the past, as in Brazil and Chile before the advent of military regimes in 1964 and 1973, respectively, and are rising in importance in others, such as Ecuador and Colombia. Their influence is likely to increase in other countries as economies and societies become more institutionalized. In any event, the energies of labor unions are directed primarily at gaining more economic benefits for their members. However, when nationalization of important foreign corporations and government direction of internationally concerned local enterprises has occurred, labor has been drawn into the foreign policy arena, since the state becomes the manager toward whom labor must then direct its attention. Continued social change points toward a politically more powerful labor force whose demands, including foreign policy demands, will carry greater weight. This trend may foreshadow more conflictual relations with the industrialized external actors.

Peasants (*campesinos*), traditionally inert, are in some states demanding improvements in their socioeconomic conditions. Nowhere, however, are they organized to exert leverage in foreign policy, nor do they show any interest in doing so. They have been of foreign policy significance, however, in states where rural guerrilla activities have occurred or where drug trafficking has depended on their coca production—both often foreign-inspired and foreign-supported enterprises. Governments have been aware of the peasants' importance in the insurgents' strategies and the drug traffickers' operations and sometimes have been willing to exchange some agrarian reform for *campesino* support, which can translate into neutrality in guerrilla warfare or cooperation in attempts to stem the drug trade.

It is difficult to measure how much public opinion influences foreign policy. States with high literacy levels, good educational systems, and distinguished newspapers and other forms of communications that enjoy relative freedom of expression generally also exhibit a high level of public awareness of foreign policy issues. The list of states meeting these criteria in 1988 would include Argentina, Uruguay, Costa Rica, Mexico, Venezuela, Colombia, and even Chile. In these states, however, and certainly in the others, public debates over foreign policy are seldom carried on in a systematic way, and elections rarely hinge on foreign policy issues other than economic ones. Consequently, political parties tend not to pursue strong or consistent positions on international issues in their campaigns and other public statements. Although they have used nationalist themes as campaign issues, efforts have been directed more at winning elections than at forming a basis for policy. Exceptions have existed, however. In recent experience, for example, parties espoused nationalization programs during presidential elections in Chile in 1964 and 1970 and in Venezuela in 1974; these were important international issues to the electorate and indeed were carried out as policy once the parties came to power. The external debt question was a major issue in elections in 1980s but was closely linked to domestic economic and social concerns.

The Roman Catholic Church has also sometimes influenced foreign policy decision making. Church interests have traditionally been associated with the small oligarchies and their politics of the status quo. The church's political power has seriously eroded over the years to the point where it no longer has a strong influence on decision making. As its power declined, the church's policies, including those concerning international relations, changed from predictably supporting upper-class interests. Actually, deep divisions exist within the church—within individual national organizations, in Latin American regional meetings, and in relations with the Vatican (see Chapter 6).

Decision-Making Agents

The main feature of Latin American authoritative decision-making processes is the primary role of the chief executive and, conversely, the relative weakness of the legislative and judiciary branches in policy formulation. Executive power is derived not only from constitutional provisions—the president normally is charged with responsibility and authority in the conduct of external affairs—but even more from the traditional political culture, which places high confidence in the executive power, whether or not it is operating under republican constitutional procedures.

The idea of republicanism with the presidential system was adopted by almost all the Latin American states when they became independent in the early nineteenth century. However, the widespread existence of the *caudillo* in Spanish America, or the *coroneis* in Brazil (a local strongman, boss, or man on horseback), reflected a disposition for authoritarianism and *personalismo*, or an emphasis on individual personalities rather than public issues. *Caudillismo*, typical of the nineteenth century, declined as a governmental form in the twentieth century. Some caudillos were still found in the 1960s, but they had virtually disappeared by the end of the decade. The closest approximation in the late-1980s was the Pinochet dictatorship in Chile and that of Stroessner in Paraguay.

In the meantime, beginning in the late nineteenth and early twentieth centuries, constitutional democracies were established for various periods of time in several nations. Nevertheless, the executives, whether achieving office constitutionally through elections or arbitrarily through force, continued to be shaped by tradition. Personalism and even authoritarianism have been reflected in many democratic experiments; elected presidents in most instances have dominated their legislatures and exercised extraordinary powers. Even Fidel Castro of Cuba exhibits traditional Latin American attributes despite the Marxist-Leninist ideology of his movement; his followers rally not around the banner of communism but of Fidelismo. Another common form of government, especially in the 1960s and 1970s, was military rule, in which the armed forces became the government. In contrast to caudillos, who erected dictatorships over the military and consolidated personal power, military rule involved leaders who held power as agents for the entire military establishment and superimposed the military structure over governmental organization. Military regimes, though by definition not personalist, are clearly authoritarian.

While political culture provides the most important source of Latin American executive power in foreign (and other) affairs, constitutional provisions are also important sources of power as well as restrictions on executive freedom. Formal constitutional authority is divided between executive and legislative branches. Latin American constitutions, like most of those around the world that structure presidential systems, give the chief executive primary responsibility and authority in foreign affairs, including national defense. The president is charged with such matters as negotiating treaties, with congressional approval; making diplomatic appointments, also usually requiring congressional approval; and acting as commander in chief of the armed forces, although few presidents in recent years have taken the field at the head of their forces. Congressional constitutional roles in foreign policy stem from their required consent to treaties prior to ratification and their power to confirm diplomatic and military appointments, to interrogate ministers (in some countries), and, most important, to appropriate funds. Congresses must often grant permission to the executive to leave the country, and in numerous instances they have exercised their power to deny a president's travel request.

Presidential-congressional conflict in Latin America has often been tense, especially in multiparty systems. Congresses have often blocked international agreements negotiated by the executive; Argentina over the years is the prime example, but such conflict occurs in other states to some extent. Congresses have, from time to time, refused to approve appointments or appropriate monies to finance foreign policy projects or administration. These constitutional powers, however, are insufficient to allow congresses to compete effectively with executive position, prestige, organization, and other resources in foreign affairs.

The foreign minister usually makes day-to-day policy decisions and acts as a spokesperson for the chief executive. The foreign minister normally is a distinguished and notable public person. Latin America has produced, over the years, a number of skillful, internationally renowned *cancilleres* (foreign ministers). They are supported by permanent career foreign services, which have been increasingly professionalized, especially with the intensification of Latin American involvement in international politics since World War II. The diplomatic services traditionally were recruited from and dominated by the small upper-class elite. This situation continues in a large number of countries despite important changes in class mobility in the societies at large. Thus, Latin American diplomats traditionally have tended to have upper-class attributes—to be sophisticated, cosmopolitan, well-educated, and conservative—and to share upper-class interests and goals in foreign policy matters. They remain so in those countries where tradition continues. This description does not apply to nations with large middle classes or those that have undergone revolutionary or other rapid social change.

As pragmatic, professional diplomats, the foreign services tend to adjust and accommodate to changing administrations and policies. Foreign service academies have been established in the major Latin American countries, and the recruitment of diplomatic personnel according to merit is required by law in most states. Admission to the service in many states, however, is often the result of personal contacts or political influence. On occasion, ambassadors are well-known intellectuals or artists who carry a great deal of prestige with them to the nation where they are accredited. More often they are prominent political figures; sometimes they are appointed so as to remove them from competition for political power with the chief executive (a sort of genteel form of exile). Some career diplomats achieve ambassadorial rank, but they are usually not posted to major capitals.

Ironically, certain small countries seem to be the most effective in their foreign representation. The larger countries, such as Mexico, Brazil, and Argentina, have highly professional diplomatic corps that emphasize formal protocol in their dealings with governments to whom they are accredited. Others have been less reluctant to establish networks of personal contacts and to operate more as lobbyists than as traditional diplomats. Most examples come from the array of small states that have much to gain and lose in their foreign relations, especially in regard to the United States: the dictator Rafael Trujillo in the Dominican Republic from 1930 to 1961; the Somoza family dynasty in Nicaragua from 1936 to 1979; on occasion the revolutionary Nicaraguan government; the embattled governments in El Salvador after 1979; and Panamanian governments over the many years when aspects of the canal treaties were being negotiated. These and others became adept at operating within U.S. Government circles on an informal basis and appealing to U.S. public opinion.

Foreign ministries have been increasingly challenged by other bureaucracies in foreign policy administration. Ministries of the armed forces have had inherent interests in foreign policy. These concerns stem from their role in national defense, their regularized contacts with their counterparts throughout the Western Hemisphere, and their dependence on external states for arms and training. Consequently, military establishments play important roles in the negotiation and administration of international military matters. They have also been a force for industrialization, in order to build up their own countries' arms production, notably in Argentina, Chile, Mexico, and especially Brazil (which has become virtually self-sufficient in military arms and equipment and is now one of the world's principal arms exporters). The military often controls some or all intelligence services; for those services that are not formally part of the defense establishment, the armed forces supply active or retired personnel to direct and staff them. Finally, for two decades beginning in the early 1960s, many military establishments viewed themselves as having crucial nation-building roles, whether they exercised power as direct rulers or as a competing bureaucratic interest group, and consequently they were caught up in broad economic and social development issues and concerned with foreign policy decisions related to developmental strategies. With the decline of military governments in the 1980s, and with the loss of prestige that generally accompanied their exit from power, their foreign policy roles were reduced. They remained influential, however.

Other agencies have also been drawn into the foreign policy process. An interior ministry (usually called *gobernación*) generally controls the national policy forces and therefore often has paramilitary functions involving international concerns, especially as they have related to urban guerrilla warfare. The minister of interior often has a voice in general policy matters, because he is usually the ranking cabinet member according to law or practice. Other bureaucracies, such as the finance or economics ministry, the central bank, and many autonomous or semiautonomous economic and development agencies established in recent years are involved in matters relating to their provinces. For example, the extensive economic content of Latin American foreign policies often includes not only traditional concerns with foreign trade, investment, and immigration but also newer concerns involving international economic institutions, expropriation of foreign enterprises, regional integration, foreign economic aid, and "developmentalism" in general. The agencies concerned with economic matters operate with their own international staffs of technocrats, usually young, liberal, nationalist economists who are well trained in developmental economics.

FOREIGN POLICY ORIENTATIONS

Ends and Means

Objectives and Tactics. Latin American states pursue national interests that are common to all states as they attempt to ensure their survival, security, and well-being. In the Latin American context, these ultimate objectives translate into long-range goals that reflect the regional states' capability levels, national consciousnesses, and domestic politics. Their primary interests have been: (1) to maintain their sovereignty and independence from all outside powers; (2) to strengthen their economies; and (3) to achieve national prestige, or at least the respect of other nations (Burr, 1967b:80–81). In addition, some states seek to assert their leadership in inter-American affairs and, at times and on a more modest scale, in world affairs. In fact, in assessing policy, a basic distinction should be made between actions formulated for intraregional relations and those for relations with external actors.

The limitations of Latin American capability bear strongly on the choice of policy means as well as ends. In the global arena, the fact that Latin Americans have operated from a position of relative weakness has significantly affected their selection of policy instruments and strategies. Most Latin American states are small in a global sense, ranking low in the order of world power stratification. Some of them, however, have had the potential and ambition to change this status upward. Argentina, from the turn of the present century until the late 1920s, seemed to be headed for great power status but instead entered a long period of steady decline. Others, such as Chile, Mexico, Venezuela, and Colombia, have been significant in particular ways at certain times. Brazil in the 1980s perhaps rivals in power such important states as Spain, Italy, Indonesia, and India. In general, however, the range of techniques available to the Latin American states in global politics has been limited because they must rely on other than physical power, either military or economic.

The regional states tend to use the same means chosen by most small states in the world, exerting influence as best they can through such tactics as: (1) playing active roles in international organizations; (2) promoting international law and supporting such principles and procedures as nonintervention and peaceful settlement of disputes; (3) appealing to humanitarian sentiments and moral principles; (4) exploiting the rivalries of greater powers while remaining as noncommittal as possible themselves; and (5) bargaining with nations that provide markets for their natural resources.

Intraregional politics are more complex, in that Latin America is a microcosm of the global system with a wide range of relative power positions and, consequently, of ends and means adopted by the regional states toward each other. Latin American great powers have played the game of power politics within the regions—most notably in the Southern Cone—including the pursuit of imperialist goals and the use of military force as well as other techniques. The other states are thus reduced to using small-state tactics in their relations with the larger Latin American states as well as with the world powers. The smaller states attempt to restrain the larger ones through international organization and law and by capitalizing on regional rivalries— a combination of persuasion and manipulation.

Independence and Dependence. The desire for an independent or autonomous role in international politics is a reflection of Latin American national consciousness. The realization of independence in foreign policy, however, has been frustrated by capability deficiencies, and in important ways the regional states have been subordinate to or at times even subjugated by external states. Thus a corollary objective has been to reduce their political, military, and especially economic reliance on outside actors. Freedom of action is difficult for all relatively small states, and the notion of sovereign independence for them in a strict sense is fictional. Nevertheless, while many regional actors stand in a dependent relationship to external actors, others have achieved a modicum of autonomy, and independence is a serious aspiration with virtually all of them.

The pursuit of autonomy in foreign policy is not only difficult for many states but often paradoxical. Latin American states want to achieve or maintain independence in their international actions, but to do so they must be strong in relation to the outside world; to become strong they must obtain some sort of assistance from the outside world toward which they wish to be independent, thus increasing the chances for a dependent relationship. Much of Latin America's continuing dilemma, then, is this: How are nations to improve their capability and modernize their societies while preventing inordinate influence in their economies and political systems?

The greatest dependence on others has been economic and financial, areas in which the Latin American states are the most vulnerable to external influences. Their reliance on public and private investment and loans has circumscribed their independence to varying degrees. Furthermore, because export markets are crucial to their well-being, most Latin American states strive to maintain friendly relations with their best customers. They have long sought foreign investment capital and assumed it was necessary for economic growth. Increasingly, however, expropriation of foreign enterprise was demanded by certain nationalist groups and effected by some governments. Beginning in the 1930s and increasingly throughout the 1960s and 1970s, governments were forced to calculate the relative economic and political benefits and risks between maintaining their appeal to foreign investors and pursuing expropriation. The thrust for expropriation has declined in the 1980s.

Latin Americans have often attempted to remain independent from external actors by playing them against each other. The exploitation of great power rivalries has long been a favored technique. For example, Colombia played on the rivalries among Great Britain, the United States, and France throughout the nineteenth century and thereby maintained control of the isthmus of Panama; but when the rivalry faded after 1901 and the United States was left unchallenged, Colombia lost control of her valuable province. In addition, Latin American states frequently seek to "diversify" their dependence by accepting economic, military, and other aid from a variety of external states, hoping that no single one will have an overwhelming position of influence. On the inter-American scene, the small states have attempted to exploit local great power rivalries. For example, both Uruguay and Paraguay, with varying success, have tried to balance Argentina and Brazil. During part of the cold war, Latin Americans were well aware of U.S. concern about the growth of communism in Latin America and were able to exploit it to their benefit by persuading the United States to commit relatively large amounts of economic and military aid under the Alliance for Progress.

Leadership Aspirations. Latin American states' aspirations for playing important power roles have been modest. They have generally eschewed efforts to enhance their world power beyond ensuring their physical survival and garnering economic benefits. At times, however, several Latin American states have played key roles in inter-American affairs and on the world scene, so that there have been exceptions to this prevailing lack of international ambition. Brazil, and sometimes Argentina and Mexico, for example, have from time to time sought to play world power roles. They, and to a lesser extent Chile, Colombia, Peru, and Venezuela, have also tried to achieve regional leadership. None, so far, has been able to do so for a sustained period, although a few of them have the potential to do so. In the case of the Southern Cone, the aspirations of local states have led to long-standing intraregional rivalries; within the Circum-Caribbean it has generated new competition. In the restricted inter-American arena, some of the states have successfully challenged outside influences by playing key and independent roles in inter-American politics. As a bloc, the Latin American states have sometimes been important, as at the San Francisco Conference in 1945 that founded the United Nations. Even the aspiring local great powers, however, have not been taken seriously in power terms by the leaders of the international system, with the tentative exceptions of Argentina before World War I and Brazil after the mid-1970s.

Economic Policies. International economic policy represents the clearest nexus between Latin American domestic and foreign policy. In virtually every Latin American state since independence, foreign policy has to some degree been an extension of domestic economic interests and concerns. In most of them, some form of economic developmentalism or modernization, sometimes including social reform, has assumed the importance of an ultimate goal. Other objectives often are compromised for economic ones. For example, much of the increase in Latin American relations with Communist states since the late 1960s is probably best explained in terms of economic needs with minimal reference to ideological positions. Even the most conservative and anti-Communist (including military) governments adopted pragmatic stances toward the Soviet Union and Eastern Europe when trade relations were offered, especially with the Soviet willingness to accept a balance of trade skewed sharply in favor of Latin America.

The foreign trade of every regional state is crucial to its economic well-being. Exports are required to generate the foreign currency necessary to pay for essential imports and to help repay foreign debt. Export taxes and import duties provide a significant source of government revenue for various operations, including development programs. In general, trade is necessary to sustain economic growth and promote national prosperity. Therefore, Latin American foreign policies usually aim to maximize export opportunities, which includes both protecting and attempting to expand traditional markets as well as searching for new ones. Consequently, Latin American diplomats spend a great deal of their time aiding exporters to protect and develop foreign markets. They play the traditional diplomatic game of projecting a favorable national image—not only for prestige purposes but also to promote the confidence of outsiders in their economic worthiness.

Alignment

Isolationism and Neutralism. By and large, the Latin American states have come to accept their small power roles, with some important exceptions. Concomitantly, they have assumed noncommittal positions in great power conflicts as much as possible.

Upon becoming independent, most Spanish American states and Brazil were the first "new states" to understand and oppose imperialism by attempting isolationism and considering neutralism. Yet Latin Americans sought the support of European states to assist their national development and reconciled finally to the United States as chief guarantor of their sovereignty and security. During World War I, Latin America failed to respond to U.S. urging for hemispheric solidarity; the leading states of Argentina, Chile, Colombia, and Mexico were neutral. During World War II, however, only Argentina and Chile remained neutral until the latter months of the hostilities.

After World War II, Latin American states sought to remain aloof in the cold war, with varying degrees of success. Isolationist positions toward global rivalries were pursued in a political and military sense, but Latin Americans remained active in world economic relations. "Aloofness" and "isolationism" did not mean "neutralism" or "nonalignment," however, except in a few instances, and only a small minority of Latin American states adopted neutral positions in international politics. Then, in the late 1960s, a number of Latin American states began to adopt some form of the neutralist orientation.

One of the earliest and most important neutralist postures was *justicialismo* in Argentina, a "third position" claiming to reconcile capitalism and communism adopted under President Juan Perón (1946–1955). Even though Perón set a course divorced from both communism and capitalism, his strategy did not, in my view, represent the first link between Latin America and the Nonaligned Movement during the cold war. Perón did not identify with the Afro-Asian bloc; his concept seemed more akin to the independent "third way" advocated by President Charles de Gaulle of France. The third position was a Peronist version of Argentine traditions of neutralism, non-intervention, and policy independence, previously reflected in the rejection of alliances during the nineteenth century and neutrality in both world wars in the twentieth.

Neutralist orientations were articulated during the administration of Jacobo Arbenz Guzmán in Guatemala (1950–1954) and during the brief presidency of Jânio Quadros in Brazil (January–August 1961). Their neutralism paralleled the Nonaligned Movement's concept of "noncommitment," but neither of them became members of the movement (although Brazil sent observers to the Belgrade meeting in 1961).

Strong Latin American political forces worked against neutralism following World War II. The armed forces generally desired close relations with the United States, and the internationalist upper and middle classes recognized the importance of traditional trading relationships and the perils of radical change to their social and economic positions. In fact, all Latin American states joined in formal military alliance with the United States through the mutual security arrangements in the Rio Treaty of 1947. Beginning in the early 1960s, however, and accelerating thereafter, a large number of Latin American states indicated their desire to be independent of the United States by adopting nonaligned postures and joining the Nonaligned Movement.

Latin America in the Nonaligned Movement. Latin American nonalignment has been a multifaceted objective variously interpreted by Latin American governments. Interest in the Nonaligned Movement, especially since the 1970s, has revealed mixed motives, with domestic imperatives helping to explain the degree of commitment or level of activity. Although most Latin American states are still allied with the United States through the Rio Treaty, some have joined the Nonaligned Movement because they saw their interests as more congruent with those of Asia and Africa. Cuba withdrew from the treaty and aligned with the Soviet Union; Nicaragua has also sought political-military unity with the Soviet Union. For most of the other states the Rio Treaty is moribund. Only one of the new states (Trinidad-Tobago) has adhered to the treaty.

Nonalignment has also been part of the overall Latin American strategy aimed at reducing dependence on the United States through developing diversified external bilateral and organizational relationships as alternatives to the status quo balance of power. The Nonaligned Movement has had the practical advantage of placing participants in a position to bargain for assistance from both sides in the East-West competition. Other Latin American states have not participated in the Nonaligned Movement, some because their alignment with the United States is more beneficial to them and others because they found little value in taking a neutral posture.

At the beginning of 1988, sixteen Latin American states were full members of the Nonaligned Movement. They were Argentina, Belize, Bolivia, Chile, Colombia, Cuba, Ecuador, Grenada, Guyana, Jamaica, Nicaragua, Panama, Peru, St. Lucia, Suriname, and Trinidad-Tobago. Eight more had attended as observers: Barbados, Brazil, Costa Rica, Dominica, El Salvador, Mexico,

Uruguay, and Venezuela. The nine Latin American states not participating in the Nonaligned Movement are Antigua-Barbuda, Bahamas, Dominican Republic, Guatemala, Haiti, Honduras, Paraguay, St. Kitts-Nevis, and St. Vincent. In addition, three Latin American regional organizations—the United Nations Economic Commission for Latin America and the Caribbean (ECLAC), the Latin American Economic System (SELA), and the Latin American Energy Organization (OLADE)—have sent observers to nonaligned meetings over the years. (See Chapter 9 for further details.)

Strategy and Geopolitics

Geopolitical strategic visions have influenced the foreign policies of a number of Southern Cone states. Geopolitical schools of thought with roots in nineteenth-century writings are especially notable in Brazil, Argentina, and Chile, and particularly strong among military men and their civilian allies. They include general theories of IR, explanations of Southern Cone international politics, and specific prescriptions for state action (both domestic and foreign). These theories guided both domestic and foreign policies of Southern Cone military regimes for two decades from the early 1960s (and continue to do so in Chile as of the late 1980s). Geopolitical bases for policy have declined with the return to democratic civilian governments in most of the Southern Cone, but they have not disappeared. Many nationalists often refer to geopolitical themes. In my view Southern Cone geopoliticians do not espouse serious theories of IR; but their theories must be taken seriously as guides to understanding aspects of Southern Cone foreign policies.

Jack Child (1979b, 1985) defines geopolitics (certainly as used by Southern Cone proponents) as the relationship of geography to power politics. He warns against equating "geopolitics" with "political geography" or the wide-ranging relationship of politics to geography. (An earlier section in this chapter indicates how some geographical factors have influenced foreign policies—an exercise in political geography.) Political geography, he says, fails to capture the aggressiveness and theoretical content of Southern Cone geopolitics. Southern Cone thinking is based in the organic theory of the state, an approach in disrepute in Europe and the United States since its absorption by fascist theorists in the 1930s. It has nevertheless been carried on in Southern Cone writings and, from the 1960s into the early 1980s, formed the basis for military government practice. Those writings draw heavily on the German *geopolitik-realpolitik* traditions, extreme versions of power politics viewing international relations as a Darwinian process in which the strongest and most ruthless states survive and dominate the weaker ones. States are living organisms competing and struggling in a world where might makes right. They drive to expand to their full capacity, both geographically and in terms of power, through the extension of "living frontiers."

According to Child, Brazil has produced the most significant geopolitical schools, while Argentine thinking largely rests on perceptions of Brazilian expansionism and encroachment into Argentina's natural sphere of influence. Argentine schools adopt a more maritime orientation than the Brazilian ones. Chilean geopolitics is the least developed of the three; it is also largely maritime in content. One major theme in Southern Cone geopolitics is the "ABC" rivalry for influence, extended to include security and ambitions in the South Atlantic and Antarctica. Brazil's security concerns further extend to West Africa and Chile's extend to the South Pacific; Brazil also relates geopolitics to its thrust to be a world power (*grandeza*). Nuclear considerations have also entered Argentine and Brazilian calculations. During the periods of military regimes, the geopolitical theories have provided models for authoritarian national security states in their different forms.

BIBLIOGRAPHIC COMMENT

The study of Latin American foreign policies has until recently been a largely neglected scholarly pursuit, resulting in a limited literature explicitly analyzing policy decisions. Traditional studies of Latin American international relations were histories concerned almost exclusively with interactions rather than formulation. The first comprehensive work to apply foreign policy analysis is a textbook by Davis, Wilson, and others (1975), which contains chapters on the foreign policy processes of almost all of the regional states. A book by Burr (1967b, especially chapters 1, 4, 5, and 7) is a brief but insightful comparative Latin American foreign policy analysis. Since then a number of important foreign policy analyses (comparative and country case studies) have appeared. Among them are collections edited by Drekonja and Tokatlian (1983), Lincoln and Ferris (1984), and Puig (1984). A comparative foreign policy analysis of the English-speaking states is offered by Braveboy-Wagner (1986).

The most thorough general work on Latin American nationalism is by Whitaker and Jordan (1966), which should be read with Whitaker's later article (1973). See also readings collected and analyzed by Baily (1971). The leading works on Latin American geopolitical thinking are by Child (1979b, 1985), to which the reader should refer for citations of the significant Latin American writings. Pittman (1981) is an exceptionally thorough presentation of Latin American geopolitical writings. Hirschman (1963) is an early and important work on economic policy-making. Hirst and Russell (1987) is a good analysis of the relationship between democracy and foreign policy in Argentina and Brazil.

Some broad treatments of the foreign policies of individual Latin American states, both diplomatic histories and foreign policy analyses, are the following: *Argentina*: Bagú (1961), Conil Paz and Ferrari (1966), Ferrari (1981), González Hernández and Alvarez Conde (1984), Lanús (1984), Milenky (1978), and Ruíz Moreno (1961); *Bolivia:* Arze Q. (1984), Escobari Cusicanqui (1975); *Brazil:* Carvalho (1959), Lafer (1984), Meira Penna (1967), Rodrígues (1966), Schneider (1976), and Selcher (1978, 1981); *Chile:* Sánchez G. and Pereira L. (1977); *Colombia:* Cavelier (1960), and Lozano de Rey and Marulanda de Galofre (1982); *Cuba:* Blasier and Mesa Lago (1979), Domínguez (1982), Erisman (1985), and *Política Internacional de la Revolución*

Cubana; *Mexico*: Castañeda (1956), Díaz (1983), Gómez-Robledo Verduzco (1981), México (1985), Ojeda (1976), Pellicer (1983), and Seara Vázquez (1985); *Nicaragua:* Vanderlaan (1986); *Panama:* Castillero Pimentel (1961); *Venezuela:* Bond (1977). Latin American bilateral relations with individual external states and various specific policies are addressed in the bibliographic comments following subsequent chapters.

CHAPTER FOUR

Nonhemispheric States

THE LATIN AMERICAN INTERESTS of selected states outside the Western Hemisphere are examined in this chapter. Much of the study of Latin America's international relations has been preoccupied with the role of the United States. As the following discussion should indicate, however, other external states also have been intimately involved in the region. West European political, economic, and military involvement with and cultural impact on Latin America reached its greatest height prior to World War I; this involvement declined thereafter but was revived in the early 1970s and carried forward to the present day. The remaining American dependencies of the United Kingdom, France, and the Netherlands represent the residue of past influence. The involvement of the Soviet Union was notable after 1917 but not great until the connection with Cuba after 1959; it was given further impetus with the Nicaraguan Revolution of 1979 as well as increased connections elsewhere in Latin America. A broad array of other nonhemispheric states have also developed Latin American policies, with widely varying considerations underlying them. Three of them are treated in this chapter: Japan, a vigorous economic force with almost purely economic interests; Israel, with an essentially political approach toward Latin America and an important military supplier; and the People's Republic of China, a highly significant global actor with only hesitant and temporary Latin American policies. An analysis of the Latin American interests of these nonhemispheric states will help bring the wide range of outsiders involved in the Latin American subsystem into sharper focus.

EUROPEAN PERSPECTIVES
OF LATIN AMERICA

Origins of Policies

During the colonial period most of Latin America was ruled by Spain and Portugal, with the small Caribbean remainder belonging to other European masters. The region was of immense importance to the two primary imperial powers. For the challengers to the Iberian position in the Americas, actions in the region were a part of, and often a sidelight to, their competition with other European states on a broader, sometimes global, scale. Nevertheless, the foundations for Spanish, Portuguese, and other European views of Latin America as a weak and even inferior set of entities were established during the colonial era. Furthermore, certain Spanish, British, French, Dutch, and Danish colonies obtained during the active colonial presence, some as late as the first part of the nineteenth century, remained territorial intrusions in the Latin American subsystem throughout the nineteenth century; some them continue to the present day. In the meantime, after the successful movements for independence, the emergence of new Latin American states between 1804 and 1824 and their subsequent search for nationhood stimulated rivalry among the external powers to gain regional influence or control.

British Interests. The United Kingdom's interests in Latin America date from the colonial period (as England before 1707 and Great Britain after that date) when it gained territorial and commercial positions in the region. During an early stage of the Latin American movements for independence, while Spain was ruled by Napoleon, the British apparently intended to annex large portions of Spanish territory. However, after an unsuccessful military effort in the Plata River region in 1807 and 1808 and an aborted one in Mexico in 1808, Britain changed its approach. From 1808 to 1824 Britain covertly assisted the Spanish American patriots in order to prevent France from taking advantage of the situation, correctly assuming that Britain would be able to dominate the new states sufficiently to achieve its purposes without colonizing them. In 1825 Britain recognized the independent Latin American republics, even though it favored some kind of monarchy over the republican form chosen by most of them. Thereafter, Great Britain was the dominant external power and held a primary position in most of Latin America (with the important exception of Mexico).

British goals were first and foremost commercial in nature. Great Britain became the preeminent external actor in Latin America, interested primarily in extending its new industrial strength by consolidating and expanding its economic position in the region. Its merchant fleets and superior naval power dominated the Atlantic and served to support British commercial objectives while denying expansion by other external states. Great Britain became especially well-entrenched in southern South America, holding preeminent commercial positions in Argentina, Brazil, and Uruguay. British interests were not entirely economic, however, at least not in the Caribbean area. Ambitions to build and control a Central American canal and to protect existing colonies were exceptions to the primary British pursuit of direct economic advantage. Great Britain felt obliged to prevent or impede French intrusion and U.S. expansion into the area. Initially, however, it attempted to act in concert with the United States to deter other European expansion. In 1823, Britain proposed a bilateral declaration asserting that neither party had territorial designs on the Spanish Empire and opposing any attempt by the Holy Alliance and Spain to recapture the latter's colonies. U.S. President James Monroe refused to join in such a declaration and issued his own unilateral statement. Britain encountered strong U.S. opposition over the canal issue; in order to soften the intense rivalry, Britain agreed with the United States in the Clayton-Bulwer Treaty of 1850 that neither would unilaterally pursue a transisthmian canal project.

Acquisition of further territory was not an important aspect of British policy by this time. The only land annexed during the Latin American national period was the remote Falkland Islands in the South Atlantic Ocean, acquired by force from Argentina in 1833 but based on an earlier claim. Between 1844 and 1860, Britain exercised a protectorate over the Central American Mosquito coast, roughly the Caribbean coast of Nicaragua today. Already existing colonies have given rise to a number of boundary disputes with Latin American states, which continue in some manner in the mid-1980s. These disputes have included conflict with Argentina over the Falklands (called the Islas Malvinas in Argentina), with Venezuela over the British Guiana (now Guyana) boundary, and with Mexico and Guatemala over parts of British Honduras (now Belize).

Spanish Interests. Spain, the preeminent colonial power in Latin America, was reduced to marginal importance after Spanish American independence. Spain sought to recover its former colonies from time to time, but it was then a minor European power and did not figure prominently in regional affairs. After unsuccessfully opposing the independence of its American colonies, Spain was obsessed with the desire to regain the empire. When Ferdinand VII returned to the Spanish throne in 1815, he attempted to isolate his rebellious colonists from the rest of Europe and to gain support for Spanish reconquest of the region. Strong British opposition restrained France and other European powers sympathetic to Spain, and by 1824, reconquest was an unrealistic prospect. However, even after most of Spanish America was safely independent, Spain refused to recognize its ex-colonies and intermittently plotted to recover them.

For most of the nineteenth century, beginning in 1820, Spain was deeply divided by revolution and civil war; its American policies reflected the cleavages in most aspects of Spanish life. The Liberal government, which came to power after Ferdinand's death in 1833, temporarily abandoned plans for an American reconquest and pursued a conciliatory policy toward Latin America. Despite violent opposition from traditionalists, Spain began to recognize the sovereign independence of various Latin American states, beginning with Mexico in 1836. It also began to negotiate for indemnification for damages sustained by Spanish nationals during the preceding years of violence in Latin America and over the question of nationality status for Spaniards who had chosen to remain in America or who were then beginning to emigrate there. Questions of recognition, debt, and citizenship dominated relations until they were finally settled, with some exceptions, by the mid-1860s (Victor Alba in Davis, Wilson, and others, 1975:Ch. 4).

Portuguese Interests. In contrast to the bitterness that prevailed between Spain and Spanish America during the movements for independence and the early national period, Portugal relinquished control of Brazil in a relatively peaceful manner. Portugal had not exercised as strict control over Brazil as Spain had in its American empire, except during the Portuguese royal family residence in Brazil from 1808 to 1821 while the French occupied Portugal. When the Brazilians decided to declare their independence in 1822, they were led by the heir to the Portuguese throne, who was then regent in Brazil. Members of the Portuguese royal family ruled as emperors of Brazil until 1889. Portugal, unlike Spain, almost immediately reconciled itself to the loss of its American colony, recognizing the independent Brazilian state in 1825. This Portuguese policy was heavily influenced by Great Britain, which had maintained an alliance with Portugal since the early 1700s and continued to exercise influence throughout the nineteenth century and beyond. In 1810, Great Britain and Portugal, whose government was then in Brazil, signed trade agreements giving the British a preeminent position in Brazilian markets; the British had been responsible two years earlier for the royal family's escape to Brazil aboard a British ship during the Napoleonic invasions. Subsequently, Britain acted as the diplomatic intermediary between Portugal and Brazil during their negotiations for recognition. An independent Brazil was favorable to British interests, and Britain used its influence over the subservient Portuguese government. Portugal was also the weaker partner in the Portuguese-Brazilian relationship.

French Interests. By the time of Latin American independence, France had lost much of its American empire, but it persisted more than any other external state in its designs on Latin American territory during the nineteenth century. The French imperialist thrust eventually ended in total frustration. The vast Louisiana Territory, which France had acquired from Spain by treaty in 1800, was sold to the United States in 1803. France's prize possession, the western part of the island of Saint Dominique (today's Haiti), obtained in 1713, gained its independence in 1804 after a long slave revolt. France refused to recognize Haitian independence until 1837. France attempted to use the Holy Alliance, a continental European antirepublican league formed after Napoleon's final defeat in 1815, to assist Spain in regaining her American empire, after which France expected to have dominant influence. Britain, however, by then in control of the seas, made its opposition clear, and France abandoned the scheme in 1823. France later sent naval forces to blockade Vera Cruz and Buenos Aires in the 1830s, asserting the claims of its citizens in both cases, but to little avail. France joined Britain in another blockade of Buenos Aires from 1845 to 1849 in support of Argentines and Uruguayans opposing Argentine dictator Juan Manuel de Rosas, who was conducting his own seige of Montevideo, but again the intervention gained little.

The Latter Nineteenth Century
to World War I

General Considerations. European involvement with the new Latin American states reached its height during the latter half of the nineteenth century and in the twentieth century to World War I. Great Britain's commercial interests and France's frustrated imperial ambitions continued as before. Germany and Italy entered the Latin American scene in the 1870s as their respective national unifications were taking place. Germany became highly competitive; by the end of the century it occupied third place in total Latin American trade, behind Great Britain and the United States and well ahead of France. Italy sent large numbers of immigrants, especially to southern South America, and to Argentina in particular. Great Britain, France, the Netherlands, Spain (until 1898) and Denmark (until 1917) continued to maintain relatively small colonies, all in the Caribbean area except for the British Falkland Islands Colony. European armed interventions designed to protect various interests occurred from time to time, sometimes in concert. Increasingly, however, with the development of major South American states and the rise of U.S. power in the Circum-Caribbean, Europeans turned to more cooperative relationships. The last European military intervention was a combined British-German-Italian blockade of Venezuela in 1902–1903.

European objectives were mixed. Latin America was not an arena of European power politics and imperialism to the same extent as the rest of the world. It was, however, the object of rivalry for economic, political, cultural, and military influence. The rapid industrialization of European states led to an increase in their needs for food and raw materials and to a more intense search for markets for their manufactured goods, investment capital, technical and managerial skills, and surplus population. In addition, the international rules of the game dictated that if one great power aided in economic development, cultural exchange, or military modernization, the other great powers were obliged to follow suit. Various goals were interrelated. Thus, the exportation of military expertise and technology, or of cultural benefits, might bring increased exportation of economic goods and assist political expansion into a peripheral and neglected area at relatively low cost. For some statesmen and military men in Germany and France, Latin America may have assumed an importance in their strategic calculations for then present and future contingencies. From about 1885 until the outbreak of World War I, the European military missions in the Southern Cone, and the provisions for training Latin American officers in Europe, were aimed at strengthening military and political relations that might become important in the event of European war. They also served economic purposes and increased a nation's prestige. Of particular note were the activities of Germany in Chile, Argentina, and Bolivia, and of France in Peru, Brazil, Uruguay, and Paraguay—whereby they extended to the Americas their worldwide competition to establish useful military relations.

British Interests. British domination of the seas, aided by the possession of naval bases in Latin America, after the advent of steam shipping, was directed toward economic ends. Britain intervened at times to protect its citizens and investments and to collect debts, on occasion in concert with other European powers, but all in all it resorted to little military interference in Latin American affairs. Britain continued to be the major investor and trader. It was especially well entrenched in Argentina and had important investments in and trade with Brazil, Uruguay, Mexico, Venezuela, and Colombia. British emigration to Latin America was also important, but it did not approach the numbers of some other European countries. British settlers were largely, but not exclusively, connected with British capital enterprises.

Britain began to retire from the Caribbean at the turn of the century and to give the United States a largely free hand in the area. The Hay-Pauncefote Treaty of 1901 replaced the Clayton-Bulwer Treaty of 1850, allowing the United States to build and exclusively control an interoceanic canal. Britain maintained its Caribbean colonies and economic interests, but it became a secondary external state in the area. It retained major interests in South America, however, especially in commercial and financial affairs, although to its chagrin its preeminence eroded after the turn of the century through the efforts of the United States and Germany. Nevertheless, Britain's investments and trade levels in Latin America reached their peak on the eve of World War I; the investments constituted about one-fourth of Britain's overseas total, with special concentrations in Argentina and Brazil.

Spanish Interests. Throughout the remainder of the nineteenth century, Spanish foreign policy was fundamentally European oriented and Spanish America was of slight and mostly emotional concern. Spain again took up efforts to recover at least part of the old empire after the end of the Carlist civil wars. In 1861, taking advantage of political chaos in Santo Domingo, Spain persuaded its former colony to petition for reannexation; but Dominicans again rebelled in 1865 and regained their independence. Also in 1861, Spain joined Britain and France in a military intervention against Mexico for payment of debts, but Spain and England retired when French desires to occupy Mexico became clear; in this case there is no evidence of Spanish intention to extend control over Mexico. In 1864 Spain sent a small naval squadron to attack Peru and Bolivia; this squadron later bombarded Chile when the latter came to the aid of her neighbor. The adventure gained nothing for Spain.

Despite these events, a great deal of sympathy for Spain was found in Spanish America among conservative political groups. Liberals, on the other hand, tended toward hispanophobia and yankeephilia. Spain destroyed any remaining potential for Spanish American goodwill, however, by its harsh treatment of its remaining colony in Cuba (which included Puerto Rico). Latin American public opinion widely supported the Cuban patriot cause. After Spain relinquished its last American territory as a result of a brief war with the United States in 1898, however, sympathy with Spain was revived as hostility toward the United States increased.

In reaction to the war with the United States over Cuba, a number of well-known Spanish intellectuals promoted the idea of a common civilization or cultural community between Spain and Spanish America. The Spanish government expressed verbal sympathy for what was called *hispanismo* but devoted minimal resources to it beyond financing some cultural exchange. The Spanish government apparently saw cultural solidarity as a way to make

Spain more competitive economically and to promote Spanish influence and prestige in Latin America, but Spain's economy did not allow it to compete effectively in Latin American markets with the rest of Europe and the United States.

French Interests. French interest in Latin America by the time of World War I had became essentially economic, in contrast to the earlier nineteenth-century imperialist thrust. In addition, the height of French cultural influence and the beginnings of its military cooperation in South America occurred at the turn of the century and up to World War I. These changes in emphasis came, however, after France engaged in two more disastrous colonial adventures—its occupation of Mexico in the 1860s and its support for a private French company's Panama Canal enterprise.

Mexican civil war beginning in 1857 led to the repudiation of foreign debts and to a joint French-Spanish-British military intervention in 1861–1862 to force a debt agreement. After Great Britain and Spain withdrew, French troops took Mexico City; Prince Maximilian of Austria became emperor of Mexico in April 1864, supported by the French army. However, continued resistance of Mexican patriots under Benito Juárez, and U.S. opposition to the French occupation, coming at the end of the U.S. Civil War, ended French imperial ambitions in Latin America with a humiliating departure from Mexico.

France soon took up a new American scheme—the linking of the Atlantic and Pacific oceans with a transisthmian canal. With British and U.S. power neutralized in Central America by their 1850 treaty, a private French company began construction of the Panama Canal. Mismanagement, unsound engineering, yellow fever, and corruption led to the bankruptcy and abandonment of the project in 1888, with less than a quarter of the canal completed. The canal equity was eventually sold to the United States in 1902.

France had important economic interests in Latin America in the latter part of the century. During the 1890s and until the eve of World War I, it occupied fourth place among the great powers in commercial trade with the region, behind Britain, the United States, and Germany. France was not really competitive with the three leading powers, however, lagging far behind Germany. Moreover, France was already burdened at the time with heavy investments in Russia, Spain, North Africa, and the Middle East.

German Interests. Political, military, cultural, and economic relations were woven into a complex series of German policies toward Latin America after German unification in 1871, but economic objectives generally were dominant. A German interest in the region can be traced to the colonial period when Spain allowed individual German families to make economic investments in Venezuela. After Latin American independence, Germans were prominent in the great European migrations to America, and the city-states of Hamburg and Bremen established important trading relations in Latin America.

After German unification and the establishment of the empire in 1871, migrations of people and capital and trading relations increased. Germans settled in considerable numbers in Argentina and Brazil, and significant numbers went to Chile, Peru, Bolivia, Mexico, Guatemala, and Venezuela. Germany's economic performance was especially impressive from about the turn of the century to the eve of World War I. By 1913 Germany was third in both exports to and imports from Latin America. Argentina was Germany's most important trading partner, with Brazil, Chile, and Bolivia also of significance. The extent of German trade and investment in Latin America is all the more remarkable in view of the fact that Germany suffered from an inadequate supply of foreign investment capital during that period, and that the focus of its investment and trade was in Central Europe, even while it recorded impressive gains in the United States, Great Britain, and the Middle East. The spread of German enterprise around the world created an urge to establish colonies and naval strength to promote and protect German overseas markets. Germany did not seek Latin American colonies, however, presumably deterred by the possibility of British and U.S. economic retaliation.

The Interbellum Period

General Considerations. European interest in Latin America sharply declined as a result of World War I but was rekindled throughout the 1920s and 1930s. European policies, however, remained relatively constant in concept if not in intensity during the interbellum period. With the turn of the century, Latin American international relations had entered a four-decade period characterized by rising U.S. power and declining European influence. Great Britain retired from its preeminent position in the Caribbean, leaving the United States free to assert its hegemonic ambitions. In the remainder of South America, however, the United States continued as one of several competitors. All European states now pursued primarily commercial interests, with Great Britain retaining the largest share but strongly challenged by the United States, Germany, and France. In addition, Germany and France again played leading roles in the development of South American armies, with essentially the same partners as during the pre–World War I period. Because of a strong German presence in Latin America in the 1930s, supported by local political groups sympathetic to Nazi Germany and Fascist Italy, Europe temporarily and at least peripherally included the region in its strategic concerns.

British Policy. Great Britain had been the dominant external influence in Latin America during the nineteenth century, but its influence, which had begun to wane at the turn of the century, declined considerably after World War I. A mild boom occurred in the 1920s, when the Prince of Wales, later King Edward VIII, traveled in 1925 to Chile, Argentina, and Brazil attempting to bolster British trade with them. Argentina continued to be the most important state in British economic calculations. In almost every year until 1946, at least 10 percent of total British capital invested abroad, and 30 percent of the total in Latin America, was in Argentina. In 1947 the Perón government purchased the British-owned railway and tram lines, eliminating Britain's largest capital enterprise in Argentina.

Spanish Policy. Spain had little interest in Latin America between the wars. Its policy was restricted largely to an emotionalized form of cultural activity, although a modicum of economic, political, and even military action took place. Before (but not during) World War II, Spain received small numbers of Latin American officers at its training centers.

The Spanish Civil War from 1936 to 1939 sharply divided Latin American public opinion. After its conclusion in 1939, General Francisco Franco adopted a new form of Pan Hispanism called *hispanidad* and made it the basis for Spanish policy toward Latin America. Hispanidad was an amalgam of some of the cultural tenets of *hispanismo* with *falangismo*, the Spanish variant of fascism. The overblown rhetoric of hispanidad notwithstanding, the reestablishment of the American empire was an unrealistic goal. More likely, Franco aimed at most for the development of a sympathetic Spanish American bloc supportive of Spain in international politics; he was successful in only the most reactionary sectors.

German Policy. World War I seriously interrupted German relations with Latin America. During the Weimar period after World War I, Germany recovered its trading position somewhat, although it reached its prewar levels only in Argentina. German investments remained low. Germany was deeply affected by the world depression; its economic relations suffered drastically. Military relations with Latin America were revived in the 1920s along prewar lines—that is, with Chile, Argentina, and Bolivia, and with brief inroads in Peru—and continued to World War II.

German National Socialist (Nazi) policy in Latin America beginning in 1933 succeeded in increasing trade with Latin America, and by 1938 Germany had regained its prewar commercial position in the region. Germany's principal economic efforts in Latin American policy were consistent with past interests, but the policies took on new strategic overtones consistent with Germany's desire to stockpile war-related raw materials as well as to encourage German export of manufactured goods for the sake of balance of payments. Hitler reorganized the German Chamber of Commerce to assist in collecting information regarding military and political conditions abroad as well as financial and commercial intelligence information. His government also exerted pressure on German overseas firms to dismiss Jewish employees and to withhold advertising from newspapers unfriendly to the Third Reich (Heilman, 1973:83–94).

The Hitler regime introduced a new ideological factor in German foreign policy as it sought to mobilize German communities in Latin America in support of the Nazi Party in order to project a positive image of the New Germany and to further its economic goals there. Although the number of German communities existing in Latin America was small, the homeland considered them significant in cultural terms. Some cultural organizations had been established in years past, and Germany had always prevailed on German migrants to support the mother culture, but Hitler demanded political as well as cultural loyalty. The Nazi party had attempted to organize and control counterparts in Latin America as early as 1930, more than two years before coming to power in Germany, and it continued its efforts after 1933. The infusion of German overseas schools with Nazi ideology received special attention, along with other forms of propaganda and often clumsy fifth column efforts. All of these attempts caused friction within the German communities and between Germany and virtually every Latin American government where they were attempted, including Argentina and Brazil, where otherwise sympathetic regimes were in power. World War II again severed most German contacts with Latin America.

Post–World War II

Primary Considerations. Following World War II, war-exhausted European states retreated from strong competition in Latin America. Initial postwar European policies in Latin America were subordinate to their preoccupations with essentially European affairs. They were absorbed with reconstruction and then maintenance of recovered prosperity, relations with the superpowers, organizing the North Atlantic Treaty Organization (NATO), and developing formal European integration associations that culminated with the establishment of the European Community (EC). Several of them were also faced with making new arrangements with their old colonial empires. Latin America had only a peripheral place in these concerns.

Eventually, Europeans revived their interests in Latin America and again assumed important roles there. Especially after the mid-1960s, they expanded existing relations and initiated new ones in the way of diplomatic contacts, cultural exchanges, economic assistance, private investment, and, especially, trade relations, including arms sales. Trade and investment were of paramount importance, supported by increased diplomatic contacts and some economic assistance. Even with the expanded relationships, Latin America generally was not as important to the European states as other world regions.

Political Interests. None of the European states, in contrast to the United States, has viewed Latin America in terms of primary national security considerations. With few exceptions they have not made significant efforts to extend their national ideologies to the region. Europeans did not view Latin America in security terms in the post–World War II period because of geographic and political distance and higher priority concerns elsewhere, and they tended to defer to the United States on security issues. Their policies were not devoid of such content, however. NATO members had a contingency concern that the Gulf of Mexico and Caribbean Sea be open for movements of military forces and supplies in the event of European war. This concern has been latent, however, and not an essential factor in policy calculations.

From the early 1980s onward Europeans have emphasized three areas of concern regarding Latin America, largely in reaction to U.S. policies: (1) the question of debt (as a political as well as financial issue); (2) the problems of Latin American democracy (as most of the region moved away from military regimes); and (3) the phenomenon of Third World revolution (at least as manifested in Central America). European transnational parties as much as states—especially Social Democratic parties and the Socialist International, and Christian Democratic parties and the Christian Democratic World Union—began to pay more attention to their Latin American colleagues and emphasized these three sets of issues.

Some Individual State Interests. A number of political interests and activities in specific countries were particularly notable, sometimes including ideological elements, after World War II. Spain, under General Franco, courted Latin America through the medium of a mellowed, less aggressive version of hispanidad in an attempt to win its votes for Spanish entry into the United Nations. The first UN General Assembly refused membership to Spain because of its nondemocratic Fascist government, but finally, in 1956, Spain joined the world body, with the support of sixteen of nineteen Latin American votes. Thereafter, Spain attempted, with some success, to gain Latin American support in the UN for its otherwise quixotic quest to force Britain to return Gibraltar to Spain. Simultaneously, Spain turned more attention to Europe, as it had come to equate security and the economic future with European involvement, and paid scant attention to Latin America. The main remaining issues between Spain and Latin America involved continuing Mexican hostility toward Franco and the question of Cuban indemnification for Spanish property seized by the Castro government in 1959. After Franco's death in 1974, Spanish policymakers suggested a new era of Latin American relationships in the post-Franco era. After joining NATO and the EC, Spain made new overtures to Latin America and Europe, offering to serve as a cultural and political bridge between the two regions.

The postwar peace settlement restructured Germany, dividing it into east and west sectors, the latter constituting the Federal Republic of Germany (West Germany). This development ushered in a new foreign policy era for Germany. Ideological concerns motivated aspects of German policy. Germany wanted to break with its National Socialist past, but Nazi personalities who had migrated to Latin America caused embarrassment through occasional publicity. Of more importance were German attempts to prevent Latin American recognition of East Germany and to promote German reunification. The Hallstein Doctrine of 1955 stated that Germany considered the recognition of East Germany an unfriendly act. In general, Latin American governments strongly supported Germany regarding its problems toward Eastern Europe. But *Ostpolitik*, led by Willy Brandt beginning in 1969 and culminating in 1972 with a treaty between the two Germanys, defused the anti-Communist element of German policy to a considerable degree.

Meanwhile, the United Kingdom, France, and the Netherlands had Caribbean dependencies to accommodate. British policies also involved conflicts with Venezuela over Guyana, with Guatemala over Belize, and with Argentina over the Falklands (the Anglo-Argentine war of 1982 and its aftermath was the most dramatic of these). Other states also looked for Latin American support on individual matters in the United Nations; for example, Portugal sought and usually received Brazil's supporting vote in the UN, even on colonial issues. Other countries based certain policies on the fact that they had large national populations resident in Latin American countries, such as Italy's policies toward Argentina and Portugal's toward Brazil.

Economic Interests. In economic terms, Latin America has continued to be of importance to a number of European states. Economic relations, especially trade, superseded political activities for most of them. The postwar pattern of relations and degree of interest, however, varied greatly among the Europeans. British relations dropped sharply; the United Kingdom's first priority was to resupply its Commonwealth partners and to rebuild Britain itself, after which increasing attention was turned to relations with continental Europe. West Germany became heavily dependent on international trade after it was separated from its eastern agricultural resources.

In time, Latin America was the preferred region for private investment after Europe itself; Germany became the most aggressive European trader and investor, paying special attention to Brazil and Argentina. French trade levels in Latin America fluctuated widely and the pattern of trade also shifted. Prior to 1951 Argentina was France's largest regional buyer and seller; after that date, Brazil became its major trading partner in both imports and exports. Spain's economic relations with Latin America after World War II were limited but more than negligible. Spain increased its share of Latin American trade only slightly until the death of Franco in 1974, but renewed Spanish economic growth thereafter led to increased Latin American trade and investment. In contrast, Portuguese trade declined with Latin America; most of it remained with Brazil and on a lower level even there.

The European Community. The European Community (EC) is a new actor in Latin America. It plays an especially important role because European states tend to pursue their economic interests multilaterally through their regional integration organization more than bilaterally. In the early 1970s, the EC began to look beyond its own integration and to formulate policies toward the developing world. It established a Generalized System of Preference (GSP), which gave concessional terms of trade for certain Third World exports. The GSP, along with some direct development assistance, was aimed at helping developing economies (including those in Latin America) to be more competitive with industrial nations in gaining access to EC markets. In 1974 the EC signed the Lomé convention, which gave further special trade concessions, with a group of former European colonies, which in Latin America included only the small Caribbean new states.

The EC established permanent consultation mechanisms with Latin America on the ambassadorial level in Brussels. Beginning in 1971, a regular series of multilateral diplomatic meetings were held there semi-annually to discuss interregional relations. The EC worked directly with the several Latin American economic organizations and, in time, with the Latin American Economic System (SELA).

The fact that the EC created an entity specifically devoted to relationships between the two regions shows that its interest in the region had increased. The Institute for European-Latin American Relations/Instituto de Relaciones Europeo-Latinoamericanos (IRELA), located in Madrid and directed by the

German Latin Americanist Wolf Grabendorff, was founded in October 1984. It came into being through the initiative of the Commission of the European Communities. Among its several functions, IRELA organizes conferences and colloquia, collects and analyzes information on a range of specific subjects, and issues a number of publications.

EC concerns have gone well beyond economic relations with their role in Latin American subsystem conflict. Specifically, the EC took positions in the Anglo-Argentine war of 1982—a move that created discord among member states. After Argentina invaded the United Kingdom's Falkland Islands colony on April 2, 1982, the EC responded to a UK appeal for its support by deciding on April 16 to condemn Argentina for its aggression and to impose sanctions; it banned European arms sales to and embargoed imports from Argentina. Members made it clear, however, that the measures were designed to convince Argentina to abandon force and did not imply an endorsement of British counterforce. Support eroded especially after May 2, when a British submarine torpedoed and sank an Argentine cruiser, an act widely perceived to have violated Britain's own rules of engagement. The British engaged in intense diplomacy with their reluctant EC partners, and the majority decided to extend the sanctions indefinitely, although Ireland and Italy refused to vote in favor of this extension. Italy openly acknowledged its special relationship with Argentina based on the large proportion of the Argentine population of Italian descent. The EC lifted its sanctions on June 20, 1982, after British armed forces had prevailed in the South Atlantic.

THE SOVIET UNION

Latin America in Soviet Policy

In addition to those difficulties inherent in the foreign policy analysis of any state, the nature of Soviet politics gives rise to further analytic difficulties. The secretiveness of Soviet political processes make information difficult to obtain, and the apparent devotion of Soviet policy to Marxist-Leninist ideology complicates an assessment of the motives behind policy goals and the tactics selected for their pursuit. Nevertheless, Soviet policy is not a total mystery. A great deal is known about the details of Soviet actions and related ideological development; observation of past and present Soviet behavior forms bases for deducing policy goals.

After its establishment in 1917, the Soviet Union showed little interest in Latin America. Its policy was preoccupied with Europe, Asia, and the Middle East. The Soviet view of Latin America and commitment of minimal resources there conformed with the earlier Imperial Russian lack of interest. Tsarist Russia paid little attention to geographically remote Latin America and had only sporadic contacts with the region during the colonial period and throughout the nineteenth century. The first formal relations with a Latin American state did not occur until 1885, when diplomatic and commercial ties were established with Argentina. This development was soon followed by similar arrangements with Mexico in 1887 and Uruguay in 1890 (Theberge, 1974:2–3).

After the Russian Revolution of 1917, Soviet foreign policy espoused world revolution. Soviet leaders did not ignore Latin America—the Bolshevik government attempted to create and control Latin American Communist parties and sporadically established diplomatic relations with Latin American governments—but the region did not occupy a prominent place in their calculations. They publicly stated that other areas were more urgent for Soviet policy. The Soviet Union attached more importance to the Latin American area after World War II, but its interest was still limited. The rigidity of Stalinist policy and the intransigence of local Communist parties at the height of the cold war all but made it impossible for the Soviets to collaborate with the Latin American states. Only after Stalin's death in 1953 was the Soviet Union to establish diplomatic, commercial, and cultural ties.

The Soviet presence in Latin America became especially significant after the Soviet involvement in the Castro revolution in Cuba in 1960. Even then, the acceptance of Marxism-Leninism by the Cuban revolutionary leadership apparently took the Soviet Union by surprise, offering it unsought and unexpected opportunities in the Caribbean. Nevertheless, a close relationship with Cuba provided the Soviet Union with its first high-priority interest in the region. Soviet activities increased around the rest of Latin America after 1964, especially in the form of expanded trade and diplomatic relations. The new attention was reflected in the establishment in 1961 of the Institute of Latin American Studies in the Academy of Sciences of the USSR at Moscow; by 1975 the institute had grown from an initial group of four scholars to an assemblage of about 100. Even with this heightened awareness of Latin America, the area remained of relatively low priority in Soviet calculations compared to that of other world regions.

Evolving Policy Calculations

Since the Revolution of 1917, a difficult analytic question has been posed: To what degree is Soviet policy rooted in Marxist-Leninist ideology and to what extent does it simply reflect the pursuit of national interest by a state in the international political system? The ultimate Soviet objective may be to achieve political power in Latin America and to communize the area. The evidence suggests, however, that even in the long run this world revolutionary purpose is not a primary motivation for Soviet policy toward Latin America. Rather, Soviet goals seem to have been, and continue to be, aimed at weakening U.S. influence in the region and increasing Moscow's as much as possible. Soviet policymakers generally have perceived limited opportunities in Latin America and their actions have been cautious, the major exception being the attempt to install missiles in Cuba in 1962. Soviet tactics, by and large, have been prudent and opportunistic, taking advantage of existing conditions rather than attempting to create more favorable situations. The Soviet Union seems to concentrate modestly on building its own influence and detracting from that of the United States, whether or not situations seem to offer immediate prospects for Communist revolution. In sum, the Soviets assign Latin America a low priority, seek limited objectives there, and apply generally cautious policies.

It may be argued that Soviet policies on Latin America have resulted from the confluence of ideology and pragmatism. Pragmatic considerations have restrained Soviet policy and discouraged reckless "revolutionary" activities, and ideological justifications have fitted power calculations of cost and risk.

For a half-century prior to the Cuban Revolution, Soviet policymakers took into account several practical considerations, which were summed up in their concept of "geographic fatalism." They viewed Latin America as an area in which the Soviet Union was placed at a great disadvantage because of geography, which meant that few opportunities to influence regional affairs would arise. The area was physically remote from the Soviet Union and far from its primary concerns; vigorous Soviet activity would require resources it did not have or could not profitably invest. The concept of geographic fatalism would seem to differ little from traditional geopolitical views. More important, Latin America was seen to be dominated by the United States, which would tolerate no revolutionary government there nor allow Soviet influence to gain a strong foothold. The main constraint, however, was that the Soviet Union was deeply absorbed in its own domestic problems and involved in international affairs of higher priority than those with Latin America.

Events seemed to confirm the persistence of geographic fate. After the Bolshevik revolution through World War II, the Soviet Union worked primarily with Latin American Communist parties through the Latin American section of the Comintern. Direct diplomatic relations with other states were few and slow in coming, so that little opportunity was presented for interstate relations. From 1917 until 1933, most Latin American states followed the U.S. lead in refusing to recognize the Soviet Union. The Good Neighbor Policy after 1933 kept Latin America in line with U.S. desires even as the Soviet Union was recognized. After World War II during the cold war years, each Soviet probe into Latin America brought a strong response from the United States. For example, the United States successfully supported an intervention in 1954 against a leftist regime in Guatemala that had been mildly aided by the Soviet Union. Soviet activities in Latin America during the first fifteen postwar years were few, because the United States seemed to have a controlling influence in the area.

Related to the notion of geographic fatalism was the Soviet willingness to compromise its Latin American activities when good U.S. relations were desired. Prior to 1933 Soviet objectives in the region were shaped by its desire to attain formal U.S. recognition; after recognition was granted in that year, its objective was to maintain good relations with the United States. Partly for these reasons, Soviet activities in Latin America in competition with the United States were subdued. Later, the Soviet policy of peaceful coexistence with the United States during the 1960s and détente in the 1970s had the same effect.

The Cuban Revolution of 1959 and the unexpected survival of the Castro regime at least temporarily changed this Soviet view of geographic fatalism. The Soviet Union initially watched the course of the Cuban Revolution with skepticism and surprise, assuming first that it was not a radical revolution and then, when it proved to be one, that the United States would not allow it to survive. Under these circumstances, there seemed to be no advantage in supporting Castro's struggle in the 1950s; the Soviets made the first tentative contacts in 1960, when the new regime had been in power for more than a year. Within Cuba the Communist party did not ally with Castro until his victory had been virtually assured. Only then did the Soviet Union seem to believe that Castro represented a genuine Latin American social revolution that could resist the United States. The Soviets first gave Castro verbal support, then later gave economic and finally military support. After 1961 it seemed for a time that the United States might no longer be able to dominate affairs in the Caribbean, that Castro was a precursor of regional change toward leftist regimes and, consequently, that the Soviet Union could influence at least part of Latin America. But Soviet policy received a major blow when it was forced by the United States to remove its offensive missiles so boldly placed in Cuba in 1962.

The Missile Crisis of 1962

Soviet intentions and power calculations leading to the superpower confrontation in 1962 are difficult to assess because of the secretiveness of the Soviet decision making process. Nevertheless, strong opinions on the subject have been put forward. For example, former Secretary of State Dean Acheson (1966) argued that the Soviet Union had three objectives: (1) to increase the Soviet nuclear first-strike capability against the United States by about half again; (2) to discredit U.S. influence in Latin America; and (3) to force the United States to pay so high a price for the removal of the missiles as to bring further discredit to the United States in Europe and Southeast Asia.

The first strategic motivation mentioned by Acheson was held plausible by most of the participating U.S. decision makers at the time and has been accepted by a number of analysts. Graham Allison, for example, accepts as "the most satisfactory explanation" of Soviet action its attempt to close the "missile gap" with the United States, since the missiles in Cuba "amounted to a doubling of Soviet first strike capabilities." Acheson's second and third points have been widely disputed, however. Adam Ulam's authoritative analysis finds them highly questionable, concluding that such objectives were highly disproportionate to the means employed and the risks assumed.

Revised Policy Calculations

When the United States intervened in the Dominican Republic in 1965 to prevent a "second Cuba," it signaled the Soviet Union that it remained determined to dominate the Caribbean region. Nevertheless, the Castro revolution proved durable, and other governments hostile to the United

States emerged in several parts of the hemisphere. Most important, Marxist Salvador Allende was elected president of Chile. While these occurrences seemed to refute the notion of U.S. regional invincibility, other events were in the mold of past Soviet expectations. Cuban revolutionary hero Che Guevara died in 1967 while leading a guerrilla band against Bolivian military forces, and a reactionary military coup deposed Chilean President Allende in 1973. Both outcomes were linked to U.S. actions. The Soviet Union again tested the U.S. security position in 1970 by planning the construction of a submarine base in Cuba, but when the United States vigorously protested, it aborted the plan rather than risk another military crisis with the United States.

Other calculations seemed further to restrain Soviet policies in Latin America. Ironically, because of its "success" in Cuba, the Soviet Union became more aware of the financial and political costs and risks of policy and of its military limitations. The Cuban experience suggested three basic lessons for the Soviet Union. First, the financial costs of a Soviet commitment to an economically underdeveloped ally were high and tended to escalate. It was widely assumed that during the 1960s Cuba cost the Soviet Union the equivalent of between $350 and $400 million per year and that this cost rose to about $500 million annually in the 1970s and at least doubled to $1 billion in the 1980s. To support a comparable revolution in a larger Latin American nation presumably would cost proportionally more and would involve potentially staggering financial commitments.

Second, a close relationship with a Latin American state did not guarantee that the Soviet Union would have its way politically, nor that political gains would be worth the economic costs. Cuba at times asserted its independence from Soviet leadership and publicly attacked Soviet policies toward the rest of Latin America. The Soviet Union, by its very presence, stirred nationalist resistance to its overtures. As in other parts of the world, communism proved to be compatible with nationalism rather than monolithic and was subject neither to overriding intellectual orthodoxy nor necessarily to Soviet direction. Soviet military strength was not present in America to enforce compliance of Soviet desires as it was in Eastern Europe. Finally, political, economic, and military support to a movement like that in Cuba could not easily be reduced or terminated. The collapse of a regime closely allied with the Soviet Union because of insufficient assistance would mean a great loss of prestige. (The above line of analysis, further reflected in the following section, generally concurs with that of Draper, 1965; Dinerstein, 1967; Duncan, 1985; and Blasier, 1988.)

The Soviet Union and Central American Conflict

Soviet motivations for its Central American involvement since the late 1970s have been sharply debated. The Reagan administration, reinforced by the Kissinger Commission report of January 1984, offered one explanation of Soviet policies. It contended that the principal thrust was Soviet expansionism, in particular Soviet-backed and Cuban-managed support for violent revolution in Central America, aimed at establishing Cuban-style Marxist-Leninist dictatorships allied with the Soviet Union. The U.S. administration also advanced the "domino-theory"—that the Soviet Union, enjoying a permanent presence in the Caribbean through its Cuban surrogate, was acting to reinforce and expand this penetration into Nicaragua. Cuban assistance, the argument continued, sought to transform additional countries into Marxist states, beginning with El Salvador. From there communism would spread to the other small Central American countries and then threaten the major bordering states of Mexico to the north and Colombia and Venezuela to the south; Mexico was the "big domino." Certain implications evolved from this calculation of Soviet motives. In particular, Communist expansion, leading to a more extensive permanent presence, would offer the Soviet Union significant military advantages with the establishment of military bases in the region. Such bases, in addition to threatening the Panama Canal and lines of communication in the Caribbean, would allow the placement of hostile forces and weapons (conventional and nuclear) capable of striking deep within the United States and Latin American states. They would allow extended Soviet naval operations without the necessity of returning to the Soviet Union. Such a situation would force significant alterations in the current U.S. forward deployment strategy, as a previously secure area would either require resources to be diverted from other areas or the creation of new ones.

U.S. assumptions about the expansionist purposes of the Soviet Union and its aligned partners may be challenged by plausible alternative explanations. The Reagan administration–Kissinger Commission analysis about the sources of Soviet behavior, with its exclusionary emphasis on ideology and expansionism, is incomplete. Those who hold this view make assertions about Soviet motivations but do not ask the same questions about the Soviets that, we may assume, they ask of themselves. What goals are realistically attainable? What costs and risks are acceptable? If Soviet policy exhibits a certain ideological consistency, it also behaves as a state in the international system. We cannot ignore Soviet perceptions of historical inevitability and their impact on Soviet behavior, but, in the meantime, the Soviet Union must make more proximate strategic and tactical decisions. It seems plausible that maximum Soviet objectives in Central America conform to its traditional Latin American purposes—to weaken U.S. influence and increase its own as much as possible—but within the limits of modest political and financial cost and risk. That is, the Soviet Union probably sees Central America as a target of opportunity, not of deep strategic value, and as a vulnerable investment. Furthermore, viewing Cuba and Nicaragua simply as Soviet surrogates, proxies, or puppets erroneously assumes that Cuba and Nicaragua will simply follow the Soviet lead under any circumstances. Evidence suggests diverging as well as complementary interests among them.

Yet the Soviet Union has not responded to strong U.S. anti-Communist, antiexpansionist actions in Central America. This persistence defies the U.S. assumption that the Soviet Union would respond to strong counterpressures to its expansionist probing. The decline of U.S.-Soviet relations since 1979 under both President Carter and President Reagan helps explain the lack of Soviet response to forceful U.S. actions. That is, from the Soviet view, meddling in Central America was appropriate as long as "détente" and "peaceful coexistence" were already eroded. Conversely, better general relations with the United States, particularly regarding arms control, might lead the Soviets to reduce their Central American activities. In late 1988, it is not clear yet whether the recent summit meetings and the Intermediate Range Nuclear Forces (INF) Treaty between the superpowers will change the situation in the Caribbean.

The motivations behind Soviet behavior, however, are probably more complex than the above might imply. The world, including Central America, presents a highly complex picture; dialectically, it is dynamic and in constant flux. Soviet historicist ideology demands the promotion of Communist influence, but only under favorable circumstances. The Nicaraguan Revolution of 1979 gave heightened possibilities for Soviet influence in Central America and shifted its thinking about opportunities in the U.S. sphere of influence. But the latter part of the ideological equation ("under favorable circumstances") leads the Soviet Union to more pragmatic modes of ends-means and capability calculations. Although Soviet actions may respond to a "new détente," more important factors are probably at work. Among them are external problems involving Afghanistan, Poland, China, and the Middle East; internal economic and leadership concerns; and the recognition, after Cuba, of the high cost that goes with commitment to the survival of a revolutionary regime.

OTHER STATES

Japan

Japan historically had at most a modest interest in Latin America until after World War II. Its new and expanded role is impressive, restricted as it is to economic affairs and concern for overseas Japanese communities. After 1960 Japan greatly increased its activities to become a leading investor and trader, but there has been virtually no political dimension to its diplomacy. This approach has been consciously and carefully pursued by Japanese decision makers. (The following commentary is based on Peter Wehner and Eric Fredell in Perry and Wehner, 1985:Ch. 7.)

Japan's self-imposed isolation from the early seventeenth until the middle of the nineteenth centuries precluded ties with Latin America. Toward the end of the nineteenth century and thereafter, Japan gradually increased relations through trade treaties and emigration; even then, policies were fundamentally apolitical. Following World War II, Japan began markedly to expand its regional involvement, with policies again revolving around economic interactions and migration. Although Latin America does not rank high compared to most of Japan's other regional economic involvements, the development of relations with Latin America over the past three decades is particularly striking in view of Japan's past isolationism.

Japan undertook its postwar policies on Latin America in the context of its general foreign policy positions. Largely imposed after the war by the victorious United States, and reflected in Japan's new constitution, these positions also comported with the Japanese public's preferences. They focused energies almost exclusively on economic matters, allocating few resources toward defense and placing Japan under the protection of the U.S. security umbrella. In the mid-1970s Japan began to reappraise its defense doctrines, but this reappraisal had little impact on its Latin American outlook. Japan's alliance with the United States remained too important to be eroded by taking contrary positions on relatively peripheral political or security matters like the Central American crisis. Other benefits also derived from this apolitical diplomatic posture. Not only was it considered appropriate to Japan's purposes of economic expansion and protection of overseas Japanese, it allowed Japan to avoid involvement in local Latin American conflicts and to carry on its burgeoning trade with all regime types from right to left.

Latin America became Japan's principal postwar emigration outlet, with Brazil the most prominent recipient. About a million Japanese have migrated to South America since World War II. The vast majority settled in Brazil, with about 80,000 in Peru; 30,000 in Argentina; and 10,000 in Bolivia. Trade relations, virtually nonexistent in the 1950s, increased from only about $600,000 in 1960 to some $15 billion in the early 1980s; it was supported by a substantial amount of investment and financial and technical assistance. Japanese communities in South America, in turn, facilitated the trading relationships.

Japanese economic expansion in Latin America rests on a striking economic complementarity involving trade, investment, and technical and financial assistance. Japan must import raw materials and food, while certain Latin American economies need to export them; Japan must export large quantities of its manufactured goods, and Latin America provides promising markets. Japan aims its investment, as well as financial and technical assistance, at developing Latin American raw materials and agricultural products for export to Japan; the exchange earned is then devoted to purchasing Japanese goods. In this closed system process, Latin American partners receive capital and technology.

Israel

Israel, in sharp contrast to Japan, has approached Latin America in essentially political terms. Those political interests initially centered on gaining support for the creation of an independent Israeli state, later on combatting competing Arab influences, and always on protecting local Jewish communities. Policies have also focused on protecting Israel's domestic arms industry, with Israel earning foreign exchange through large arms sales to Latin American states, and supporting U.S. security interests in certain direct ways. Overall, Israel's objectives in Latin America may be described as active but of low priority. (The following commentary follows the analysis of Edy Kaufman, in Perry and Wehner, 1985:Ch. 8, and Kaufman, Shaipra, and Barromi, 1979.)

Prior to the establishment of the Israeli state in 1948, and even before World War II, the Zionist movement sought and gained Latin American support for the legitimation of an Israeli state. As Latin American membership in the UN initially constituted more than a third of the total, Latin American voting power was crucial to Israel for decisions made following the withdrawal of the British Mandate from Palestine. The Latin American bloc overwhelmingly supported the Israeli cause. Israeli policies toward Latin America developed very slowly thereafter, as Israel devoted its scarce resources to establishing a presence in Europe and the United States. Israeli aims in Latin America then and thereafter sought to protect the well-being of Jewish communities, found in all parts of the region, and to keep their support.

Israel began to place more importance on Latin America in the early 1960s. Some issues were temporary, such as the diplomatic crisis with Argentina over the kidnapping of the former Nazi Adolph Eichmann. More lasting were those issues related to the Israeli perception, during the chronic Middle East conflict, that Latin American support for its independence was eroding. As Arab states and, later, the PLO increased their activities in Latin America, Israel redoubled its diplomatic efforts. By 1968 Israel had diplomatic relations with seventeen Latin American states, only excluding certain small countries. Cuba severed ties in 1973 as part of Castro's drive for leadership of the Nonaligned Movement. Israel was shocked by the support of a number of Latin American delegations for the anti-Zionist resolution passed by the General Assembly in 1975. By that time, with the decline of Latin America's relative voting power and of Israel's position in the UN, Israel had shifted its instrumental emphasis in Latin America to bilateral diplomatic efforts.

Israel has attempted to garner what economic gains it could in Latin America, but economic aims have been of low priority and commercial transactions modest. Argentina, Chile, Brazil, Mexico, and Venezuela are its major trading partners in the area. Part of the activity is in banking, which is tied to local Jewish communities, particularly in Brazil. Oil imports from Mexico are a security matter for Israel, representing part of its effort to diversify its sources of the crucial commodity. Israel has become particularly active in the transference of armaments and related technical assistance as well as other forms of technology.

Arms transfers to Latin America are of commercial value to Israel, but they are also a function of the necessity to keep Israeli arms factories going during periods of relative peace. Military transfers are a post-1967 phenomenon; they began after the Six-Day War, when Israel decided to build its own heavy arms industry. When the domestic demand is low, exports keep the arms industry at a high level of readiness. In addition, with weaponry quickly becoming obsolete, the export sale of "older generation" products helps cover the high costs of defense. (See Chapter 10 for more details about the Israeli–Latin American arms trade.)

Arms export policies generally have bipartisan support in the Israeli Knesset, but some cleavages surface from time to time. Criticism has been voiced by prominent political leaders; yet both major parties when in power have made extensive arms sales to Latin America. Sales to Argentina when it was under military regime from 1977–1983 was a particularly sensitive issue because of the large number of Jews who were victims of repression there.

Israel sees Latin America as an arena where it can both further its own national interests and demonstrate its usefulness to its all-important ally, the United States. Consequently, Israeli diplomacy involved itself in Central American conflict after 1979 in Guatemala, El Salvador, and reportedly with the *contra* movement in Nicaragua, in order to supplement U.S. efforts in the region. Israel publicly expressed sympathy with the U.S. invasion of Grenada in 1983. Thus, part of Israel's Latin American policies stem from its perception of the region as a U.S. sphere of influence in which Israel might benefit its bilateral relations with the United States.

The People's Republic of China

From the establishment of the People's Republic of China (PRC) in 1949 following Mao Tse Tung's revolution, until the Cuban Revolution of 1959, the PRC evidenced slight interest in Latin America. Its lack of interest was based on a combination of factors, including China's preoccupation with consolidating its own revolution; its concerns with strengthening its relations with the Soviet Union and the United States; Latin America's geographic remoteness; and the Chinese assumption that it was in the U.S. sphere of influence. Chinese policy, to the extent that it existed, rhetorically opposed U.S. imperialism and advocated armed guerrilla struggle to overthrow Latin American regimes. Latin America generally followed the U.S. lead in isolating the PRC in world politics, including opposition to its admission to the United Nations.

The PRC attempted to establish a close relationship with Cuba after the Castro revolution. It stressed the parallel nature of their revolutions and the compatibility of Maoist and Fidelista theories of rural guerrilla warfare; by then China and the Soviet Union had fallen out over a number of fundamental issues. Thus, in Latin America only Cuba had diplomatic ties with the PRC and was the only one to support China's admission to the UN. The two states also commenced a modest barter trade of sugar for rice. The relationship turned conflictual, however, and Cuba refused to align with the PRC against the Soviet Union. Castro on several occasions accused the PRC of subversive activities in Cuba and complained of Chinese deceit in their trading relationship. The Soviet Union simultaneously outmaneuvered the PRC with economic and military assistance to Cuba.

The PRC developed only a modicum of other cooperative relations in Latin America. It began to trade with Mexico in 1963, then with Argentina and Brazil. The divisive Cultural Revolution (1966–1969) isolated the PRC in world politics and drastically reduced what contacts existed with Latin

America. Its relations increased after 1970 and changed in style, but the PRC did not become an important regional actor. With the end of the Cultural Revolution, PRC leadership shifted away from dogmatic revolutionary ideology, and U.S. overtures to the PRC in 1971 for friendlier relations enhanced China's acceptance among Latin Americans. A majority of Latin American governments voted for PRC entry into the UN in October 1971; China reciprocated by supporting Latin American governments in the law of the sea negotiations, in which they claimed 200-mile territorial sea limits.

PRC propaganda continued its antiimperialist rhetoric against both the United States and the Soviet Union and in support of armed struggle. In practice, however, the PRC expressed a desire for diplomatic and trade relations with Latin American governments, both civilian and military. Extensive diplomatic exchanges were established after 1970 with Chile, Peru, Argentina, Mexico, and Brazil, but international trade never developed beyond a small scale. Propaganda statements were softened in the 1980s.

BIBLIOGRAPHIC COMMENT

The first notable foreign policy analysis of the nonhemispheric states in Latin America is by Goldhamer (1972). Perry and Wehner (1985) edited a useful collection of essays on the subject, with chapters devoted to West German, British, French, Spanish, Dutch, Canadian, Japanese, and Israeli involvement in Latin America. The diplomatic histories cited at the end of the previous two chapters also refer to works on nonhemispheric interactions.

With reference to European interests, Grabendorff and Roett (1985) edited an important book; Duran (1985) is an excellent general treatment by a Mexican scholar. Mower (1982) is a good study of European Community policies. Wiarda (1986) is a thorough multiauthored investigation of Spanish and, to a lesser degree, Portuguese policies in Latin America; an interesting treatment of those policies is provided by Víctor Alba in Davis, Wilson, and others (1975).

Book-length studies devoted to describing and analyzing aspects of the Soviet Union's policies are Blasier (1988), Duncan (1985), Gouré and Rothenberg (1975), Jackson (1969), Theberge (1974), and Varas (1987); Dinerstein (1967) remains a valuable article. Clissold (1970) and Oswald (1970) bring together documentary collections of Soviet writings in translation. Soviet versions of the Cuban missile crisis are found in Gromyko (1972) and Khrushchev (1971); Horelick (1964) analyzes Soviet calculations. Vacs (1987) treats Soviet relations with Argentina.

On Japan's actions, see the article by Nakagawa (1983); Kaufman, Shapira, and Barromi (1979) is the best treatment of Israel. C. Johnson (1970) is an excellent book on the PRC and Latin America; it may be partially updated with Anguiano Roch (1980), a good study of China's "pragmatic" policies in the post-Mao era, and Ruilova (1978).

CHAPTER FIVE

———————— ■ ————————

The United States

THE UNITED STATES is the most important external actor in Latin America. The following discussion of U.S. interests and orientations begins with an analysis of Latin America's position in U.S. foreign policy calculations. The evolution of policy objectives, strategic calculations, and accompanying doctrines are then traced in some detail.

THE LATIN AMERICAN POSITION IN U.S. POLICY

Policy Ends and Means

U.S. relations with Latin America seem to be characterized by abrupt changes in U.S. policy, especially in the twentieth century after the rise of the United States to great power status. The intensity of U.S. interest in Latin America and the extent of its activities have varied considerably over time and according to the specific regions involved. At fundamental levels, however, U.S. policy has been consistent and continuous. That is, certain long-range goals have remained relatively constant since the beginning of U.S.–Latin American relations in the early nineteenth century.

U.S. purposes often have been couched in moral rhetoric but almost always calculated in terms of national security. Consequently, policymakers have been preoccupied with two major interrelated long-range objectives, which have been established as essential security goals. The United States has sought to minimize foreign intrusions and to promote Latin American stability as essential to its strategic, political, economic, military, and ideological interests (as specifically defined at different times). Thus, the degree of U.S. concern with Latin America and the level of its activities there have fluctuated with U.S. perceptions of foreign threats in the region and its views about Latin American political instability. A strain of paternalism has also run throughout U.S. policy—the United States has been reluctant to relinquish its thrust for predominance in Latin America, especially in the Caribbean area, and seems to have assumed that Latin Americans were incapable of handling their own affairs. Geographic distinctions and capability estimates have been factored into the security calculations shaping U.S. actions in the region. The United States has adopted differentiated views of the subregions within Latin America, and different capability considerations have been applied to these different policy arenas.

Shifting U.S. policy approaches—whether interventionist, noninterventionist, developmentalist, or benign neglect—spring initially from these two basic objectives—to exclude foreign threats and to encourage stability. First and foremost, the United States has attempted to prevent and exclude, as far as possible, foreign (nonhemispheric) influence and control in Latin America, including the penetration of hostile ideologies, and to assure the independence and self-determination of Latin America with regard to the other external states. This objective further serves the ultimate objectives of ensuring the United States' own military, political, and economic security. Since the early nineteenth century, the United States has feared some part of Latin America might serve as a military base of operations against it. The United States has also opposed hostile political-ideological threats, including European recolonization, monarchism, fascism, or communism. Further, the United States has competed vigorously against the economic influence of other external industrial states.

The U.S. objective to encourage or develop political stability in Latin America derives from the assumption by U.S. leaders that the overall interests of the United States, as a major, industrial, metropolitan, status quo state, are best served in a secure, peaceful, and stable world. This general goal, when applied to Latin America, has often been a corollary to the objective of excluding foreign influence. That is, the maintenance of Latin American stability has been presumed to be a prerequisite for reducing nonhemispheric threats in the region. Therefore, the United States has been vitally interested in the political stability of countries whose political systems it has often characterized as unstable.

Security against foreign threats has transcended all other considerations, evidenced by the fact that the intensity of U.S. interest and activities has paralleled its perceptions of outside threats. Historically, the United States has been most active in Latin America when nonhemispheric states seemed most threatening. Conversely, during periods when threats seemed to be low or nonexistent, the United States has become less concerned with Latin America and has pursued activities less connected with security goals, sometimes neglecting the region or parts of it. A lack of foreign threats has at times muted even the concern with stability, with the United States sometimes choosing the policy option of doing little if anything.

Once these preliminary concerns have been minimally satisfied—in other words, once Latin American independence from other external states has been established and some level of stability achieved—the United States has felt free to seek more proximate objectives. These include the consistent pursuit of commercial interests, the vacillating attempts at the "democratization" of Latin America, and other more specific policies. With Latin American security assured with respect to nonhemispheric actors, the United

States has generally pursued closer objectives. Although the United States has sometimes pursued these objectives on their own terms, it has usually justified them by linking them to long-term concerns with "foreigners" and instability. Consequently, proximate objectives have often served as "springboards" to realize superior objectives. For example, U.S. efforts to gain commercial advantage and to promote democracy have often been part of the quest for stability and have represented direct attempts to preempt foreign overtures by offering economic and political alternatives. Likewise, several of the myriad choices of policy instruments and techniques can be understood in terms of how they relate to the long-range goals.

In the 1980s, new or nontraditional security issues were recognized by U.S. policymakers. The "narcotraffic" and massive migration ceased to be viewed as mere "problems" and were elevated to priority status on the national security "agenda." Nevertheless, the conceptualization of policy tended to be rudimentary and policy actions ineffective (see Chapters 10 and 11). Some policy advisers, inside and especially outside of government, also argued for including the Latin American debt problem in the national security category. They argued that the potential for Latin American political and social destabilization directly threatened U.S. security as well as economic concerns. Overall U.S. policy toward the debt, however, continued to assume that it was essentially a financial matter, with only modest recognition of the political and social elements. In any event, nontraditional security concerns had now captured the attention of U.S. policymakers for the long term.

Policy Arenas and Strategic Perceptions

The United States has further formulated its Latin American policies on several subregional levels. Geographic and other environmental conditions have strongly affected U.S. perceptions and capabilities. Consequently, the United States has had overlapping but distinct policies toward the overall Latin American region, Mexico, the Caribbean Basin (and sometimes toward its subdivisions), and the Southern Cone of South America, with a special view of Brazil. It has simultaneously pursued the entire range of bilateral relations. In other words, distinct U.S. policy arenas follow along the lines of the various Latin American subregions identified in Chapter 2, and these distinct areas of policy and the structures of the subregions themselves have mutually influenced and reinforced one another.

U.S. policy toward Mexico has been determined primarily by territorial proximity and the increasingly integrated economic and social structures of the two nations. Many of the rules governing this relationship are largely divorced from those at work in the larger inter-American arena. Issues tend to be "North American" in content and closely associated with U.S. domestic concerns.

The United States has always considered the Circum-Caribbean—which it more often than not refers to as the Caribbean Basin—to be especially important to its security and well-being. Its actions there have been more assertive and consequential than in South America beyond the Caribbean.

During periods of intense interest based on perceived external threats, the United States has attempted to dominate the Caribbean, whereas it has usually been satisfied with a more restricted leadership role in the more southerly South American zones. The United States has intervened militarily only in Mexico and the Caribbean Basin; it has never landed its troops for such purposes in the Southern Cone. The most recent U.S. military intervention in Mexico was in 1914; the most recent in the Caribbean was in Grenada in 1983. Furthermore, only in the Caribbean Basin has the United States developed a continuing strategic view giving rise to an active policy. Elements of a strategic view of South America beyond the Caribbean have been expressed from time to time, usually in special circumstances such as World War II, but have not been long-term in nature.

Brazil has also occupied a special role in U.S. policy. The United States long cultivated amicable relations with the "sleeping giant" of Latin America, accelerating its efforts in the mid-1970s as Brazil seemed to be on the verge of realizing its world power ambitions. Once the junior partner in a cooperative alignment with the United States, Brazil has increased its ability to pursue an independent foreign policy. U.S. policies implied a regard for Brazil's increasing regional and even world importance.

The United States has relatively little interest in and influence with the other states in the Southern Cone. It has exerted influence in the region, especially economically, and has sometimes engaged in coercive measures. However, largely because of the Southern Cone's remote location at great distances from the United States, and the relative sophistication of most of the states located there, it has been relatively shielded from U.S. power. At the same time, the United States has only intermittently felt threatened by the activities of extrahemispheric interests in the Southern Cone and generally has not considered it to be part of its sphere of influence.

Democracy, Human Rights, and National Interests

One of the most perplexing and continuously troublesome aspects of U.S. policy on Latin America has been the question of the proper official attitude toward Latin American governmental forms and behavior and the extension of U.S values to other states. The fundamental issue is whether to pursue republican forms of government (representative democracy) and the protection of human rights as goals of policy. The U.S. government and its articulate populace have always sympathized with democratic elements in Latin America, and formal commitments to democratic processes have been made through several inter-American conventions. The actual promotion of democracy, however, has received shifting emphasis over the years.

U.S. attempts to extend the practices of representative democracy and protection of human rights have been ambiguous and vacillating. When resources have been committed to the goal of democratic development, it has usually been viewed as an instrumental objective aimed at achieving one or the other of the long-range goals. Determining the relationship between democratic development in Latin America and the maintenance of political

stability and prevention of foreign control is a long-standing problem in
U.S. politics. One position maintains that there is an inherent conflict between
democratic development and political stability, as the concern for stability
has caused the United States to tolerate and even support certain dictators
and military regimes. Because they cooperated with the United States, these
regimes were said to achieve stability. For the most part, the United States
accommodated itself to such dictatorships and military regimes and regarded
them as conducive at least to temporary stability.

Another policy view has maintained that ultimate stability can be achieved
not by dictators and armed forces but only through open democratic societies
and free elections in which all political groups share equal opportunity.
When dictators and military regimes have been perceived as detrimental to
achieving stability, U.S. policy has shifted against some of them. One reason
for supporting democratic development in Latin America, in addition to
fostering compatibility with U.S. values, has been the assumption that open
societies and popular participation are the soundest paths to progress and
therefore to political stability.

Especially since World War II, policy debates have focused on whether
instability is more the result of external subversion or of internal conditions.
Related arguments have concerned the relative merits of shoring up the
status quo or encouraging reform (but not radical solutions, which have
been assumed by both sides to risk foreign orientation). The assumption
that the departure of dictators creates chaos leading to opportunities for
local Communists linked to the Soviet Union had currency after the Cuban
Revolution of 1959 and again with the Nicaraguan Revolution of 1979.
The public debate revolving around the Reagan administration's Central
American policies in the 1980s is but a recent manifestation of these old
positions. In fact, policy actions have eventually tended to involve some
combination of both interventionist and cooperative means for dealing with
instability. As of the late 1980s, it appears that a consensus has been reached
within U.S. policy circles that democratic forms in Latin America best serve
U.S. interests and should be promoted; the debate continues, however, over
how to go about this enterprise.

EVOLUTION OF POLICY

The following interpretation of the historical development of U.S. actions
and related policy doctrines toward Latin America illustrates the interrelated
nature of the long-range security objectives. It also distinguishes between
the various views predominating in different policy arenas and the opposing
schools of thought regarding the exportation of U.S. democracy. Moreover,
it points out those times when U.S. interest in the region has waned and
nonstrategic activities, especially in the commercial field, rose to the fore.

The Nineteenth Century

Isolationism and the Western Hemisphere Idea. The U.S. foreign policy
orientation, beginning with its own independence in the late eighteenth

century and continuing throughout most of the nineteenth century, was characterized by isolationism. However, policy was never founded on a literally isolationist basis of absolute nonintercourse with the rest of the world. Isolationism was relevant primarily to Europe, and then in the special sense of political noninvolvement or "nonentanglement."

The principle of noninvolvement did not extend to U.S. relations with Latin America in the same sense that it was applied to European affairs. The initial U.S. orientation toward Latin America was contained in the Western Hemisphere Idea, also known as the Doctrine of the Two Spheres. This concept posited a special relationship between the United States and Latin America. It was based on the geographic separation of the Americas from Europe and on the notions of political, economic, and social separation of the morally superior New World from the evil, autocratic Old World. The essence of the idea was that the Western (American) Hemisphere was separate and distinct from Europe and had its own set of interests. In general, this notion served as the basis for both the isolation of the Americas from Europe and for binding ties among the Americas themselves. In accordance with this idea, the No-Transfer Resolution, passed by the U.S. Congress in 1811, stated that although the United States had no objection to Spain's retention of its American possessions, the transfer of lands bordering the United States to a third party (meaning Great Britain) would be viewed unfavorably. The Western Hemisphere Idea later provided a mystique for U.S. security and commercial policies.

Initial contacts were slow in developing. The United States began the recognition process in Latin America in 1822, not only out of sympathy with the Latin Americans, but also in the unfulfilled hope that they thereby would not be dependent on Great Britain. U.S. fear of nonhemispheric influences was further revealed in December 1823, in the midst of the recognition process, when President James Monroe issued a warning to Europe against trying to recolonize the area. Despite recognition and Monroe's pronouncement, the United States did not desire closer political relations. It turned down Latin American overtures to form an inter-American defense alliance against Europe. It was eager for expanded commercial contacts, but was preempted by British economic power.

The main U.S. policies were related to its ambition for continental expansion. Years of conflict with Mexico culminated in war between the two states (1846–1848), which resulted in huge territorial gains for the victorious United States. In addition, the United States felt that the destiny of the Caribbean region directly affected its security. Cuba was of special importance, with interest also shown in the possible acquisition of the Danish West Indies and in building a Central American isthmian canal. North Americans sympathized with Cuban insurgents revolting against Spanish authority between 1868 and 1878, but the United States remained neutral even though the Cubans requested its intervention in their favor. The United States also refused several schemes to purchase the Danish West Indies and to annex Santo Domingo as well as Cuba. Although the United States had special interests in Mexico and the Caribbean, it did not engage in extensive interaction with the rest of the hemisphere.

The Monroe Doctrine. The Western Hemisphere Idea and the isolationist orientation were reflected in what came to be known as the Monroe Doctrine. It defined the U.S. attitude toward Europe's relationship with the Americas, and that of the United States toward Latin America, for more than a century. It reflected more than anything else the U.S. desire to limit foreign influence in the Americas. The essence of the policy, first enunciated in 1823 and later considered the "cornerstone" of overall U.S. foreign policy, was a desire for Europe to keep its "hands off" the Western Hemisphere. The term "Doctrine" was not used until much later; the policy had its genesis in President Monroe's "declaration" or "principles." In a sense the Monroe Doctrine had already been partially stated by the U.S. Congress in the 1811 No-Transfer Resolution.

Monroe's statement, included in his annual message to Congress on December 2, 1823, was inspired by the perception of two separate threats. The first was the fear of Russian colonization of the North American Pacific coast, which led to the general declaration "that the American continents, by the free and independent condition which they have assumed and maintain, are henceforth not to be considered as subjects for future colonization by any European power." The second part addressed the challenge represented by Spain's desire to retrieve its New World empire with the help of the French-led Holy Alliance. After noting that "the political system of the allied powers is essentially different . . . from that of America," Monroe said:

> We owe it therefore to candor, and to the amicable relations existing between the United States and those powers, to declare that we should consider any attempt on their part to extend their system to any portions of this Hemisphere, as dangerous to our peace and safety. With the existing Colonies or dependencies of any European power, we have not interfered, and shall not interfere. But with the governments who have declared their independence, and have maintained it, and whose independence we have, on great consideration, and on just principles, acknowledged, we could not view any interposition for the purpose of oppressing them, or controlling them in any other manner, their destiny, by any European power, in any other light, than as the manifestation of an unfriendly disposition towards the United States.

Monroe also assured Europe of U.S. reciprocity: "Our policy in regard to Europe, which was adopted at an early state of the wars which have so long agitated that quarter of the globe, nevertheless remains the same, which is, not to interfere in the internal concerns of any of its powers."

Monroe's declaration was unilateral, fairly narrow in scope, and intended to be temporary. Its unilateral nature was made clear in two ways. First, the United States had turned down a British proposal that the two states issue a joint declaration. Second, immediately after making the pronouncement, the United States rebuffed Latin American suggestions for treaties of alliance. Monroe restricted his warning to future colonization and was tolerant toward existing colonies; he mentioned nothing of prohibiting other forms of European intervention or influence as later interpretations were to do. That the policy was intended to be temporary was indicated by the fact that, for most of the half-century following Monroe's pronouncement, it was largely ignored as a policy guide. Once the immediate danger had passed, and during the long period of U.S. military weakness and domestic preoccupations, Monroe's words were virtually forgotten in the United States. A number of European military interventions occurred in Latin America and the United States did nothing; Great Britain undertook responsibility for the protection of Latin America from the designs of other European powers.

Manifest Destiny. During the first half of the nineteenth century, the United States was preoccupied with continental expansion, expressed in the ideology of "manifest destiny." The idea that the United States was entitled to expand its control across the virgin continent from one ocean to the other was widespread. The process of continental expansion inevitably brought the United States into conflict with Mexico and eventually led to Caribbean imperialism.

In only fifty years, between 1803 and 1853, the territory of the United States expanded from the area occupied by the original thirteen colonies to essentially its present boundaries, with most of the added territory taken from what was originally Spanish America. The first and largest single acquisition was the purchase in 1803 of the Louisiana Territory from France, to whom Spain had ceded the area in 1800. Its addition more than doubled the U.S. territorial size. For fifteen years after the Louisiana Purchase, the United States negotiated with Spain for the "Floridas," actually seizing some territory in 1810 and 1813. In 1819, the two states signed the Adams-Onís Treaty (it went into effect in 1821), in which Spain ceded to the United States all of its Gulf Coast lands east of the Mississippi River.

The United States and Mexico clashed for decades over the Texas question. Texans won their independence in 1836 after a violent struggle, and finally, in 1845, Texas became a state in the union. Mexican objections to the annexation and continuing U.S. expansionist tendencies led to war (1846–1848). Under the Treaty of Guadalupe Hidalgo, signed in 1848, Mexico ceded half of its national territory to the United States, including what today constitutes much of the U.S. West and Southwest. In 1853, exactly fifty years after the Louisiana Purchase, the continental dimensions of the United States were completed, except for some later minor adjustments, with the Gadsden Purchase from Mexico. Although U.S. leaders from time to time considered pursuing territorial gains in the Caribbean region, no further Latin American territory was taken by the United States until after its war with Spain in 1898.

Democratic Policy and Pan Americanism. A U.S. policy tradition on the question of relations with nondemocratic regimes was established at the very start of inter-American relations. Throughout the nineteenth century and into the twentieth, Spanish American political processes were characterized by dictatorship (Brazil was successfully governed under a constitutional

monarch). The United States enunciated broad policy outlines in the spirit
of its recognition of the revolutionary French government in 1793. On that
occasion, Secretary of State Thomas Jefferson said: "We surely cannot deny
to any nation that right whereon our own government is founded that
everyone may govern itself under whatever form it pleases." Later, as president,
Jefferson established a policy tradition when he applied this principle specifically to Latin America. With few exceptions, such as Secretary of State
William H. Seward's opposition to monarchy in Mexico in 1865 (in fact,
in opposition to French occupation), this Jeffersonian tradition guided policy
until the presidency of Woodrow Wilson during World War I.

The United States inaugurated the Pan American movement in the 1880s,
primarily for the purposes of promoting hemispheric trade and developing
procedures for the peaceful settlement of disputes. It was not interested in
security questions, the primary Latin American concern, and consistently
strove to keep them off conference agendas. The First International Conference
of American States, held in Washington in 1889–1890, initiated the Pan
American policy of the United States. It reflected the interests of U.S.
businesspeople who had recently discovered trade and investment opportunities in Latin America. Policy was also motivated by the potential of the
Inter-American System as an instrument for promoting international stability
through peaceful settlement procedures and for gathering Latin America
together in a single organization under U.S. leadership, thus preempting
other foreign influences.

The Latin American policy of the United States from the last decade of
the nineteenth century through the first third of the twentieth was characterized by tension between the Monroe Doctrine and Pan Americanism;
the latter began in earnest in 1889 but the former dominated until the
1930s. Both of these policy approaches flowed from the Western Hemisphere
Idea positing a special relationship among the Americas. They were also
contradictory, however, in that the Monroe Doctrine was a unilateral policy
that came to justify U.S. intervention in the Caribbean area, while Pan
Americanism was based on the idea of international equality and cooperation.
Even though the inter-American conferences beginning in 1889 posited a
policy of U.S. cooperation with Latin America, especially in matters of
international trade, multilateral diplomacy was not a major aspect of U.S.
policy until the 1930s. Meanwhile, unilateral imperialism superseded multilateral cooperation.

The Twentieth Century to World War II

U.S. Imperialism. During the last few years of the nineteenth century,
the United States changed its policy orientation from traditional isolationism
to a rudimentary internationalism. The nation passed through a period of
policy transition that resulted in active participation in world affairs and
elevation to the status of a great power. The new orientation revived U.S.
interest in Latin America and ended its policy inaction; but it resulted in
the beginnings of imperialism and coercive policies in the Caribbean area

(as well as the far reaches of the Pacific Ocean). The United States demonstrated a new assertiveness in 1895, when it was willing to defy even Great Britain in the latter's dispute with Venezuela over the boundary with British Guiana. Richard Olney, secretary of state under President Grover Cleveland, asserted the Monroe Doctrine against Great Britain during the dispute. His note to the British foreign minister, which claimed U.S. hegemony in the Americas, was dubbed the Olney Corollary to the Monroe Doctrine.

A new wave of nationalism that swept the United States in the 1890s led to war with Spain and resulted in territorial acquisitions in the Caribbean area. A new interpretation of manifest destiny reaching beyond continental limits was typified by the "Expansionists of 1898" who molded U.S. public opinion; the Caribbean region loomed large in their strategic thinking. The most important of them was Captain (later Admiral) Alfred Thayer Mahan, who shaped official U.S. strategic thinking about the Caribbean area for many years to come. His converts and disciples included Senator Henry Cabot Lodge and President Theodore Roosevelt.

Mahan's thesis, developed from his study of naval history, revolved around his concern with the relationship of mercantilist imperialism and sea power to national security and progress ("destiny") (Mahan, 1918). In short, according to Mahan, national greatness depended on the three related factors of maritime strength, sea power, and imperialism; therefore, no great nation could be isolationist. U.S. policy action in the Caribbean area was crucial to Mahan and was one of the main subjects of his writing. He strongly advocated the construction of an isthmian canal because it would draw the Pacific, Atlantic, and Gulf Coasts of the North American continent closer together. Mahan also somberly warned of the "many latent and as yet unforeseen dangers to the peace of the western hemisphere, attendant upon the opening of the canal." He predicted that the then comparatively deserted Caribbean Sea would become, like the Red Sea, a great thoroughfare of shipping and would attract, "as never before in our day, the interest and ambition of maritime nations."

Mahan further warned that increased rivalry from Europe in the Caribbean as a result of "the piercing of the isthmus [would be] nothing but a disaster to the United States, in the present state of her military and naval preparation." With the enhanced commercial and military value of the Caribbean and the strategic importance of a future canal, the "indifference of foreign nations" would pass away. It would be dangerous for the United States to build a canal without also constructing its own continental defenses, building a strong naval force for offensive power, controlling the entire Caribbean area through the acquisition of bases, and fortifying and exclusively controlling any canal. The only protection for U.S. interests, Mahan said, was its own power to enforce them.

Mexico as an object of policy occupied a position distinct from the Caribbean area and the rest of Latin America. According to Mahan, although Mexico's location on the southern boundary of the United States made it of considerably more interest than the Southern Cone, Mexico was of less strategic importance than most of the Caribbean. In 1897 Mahan surveyed the strategic features of the entire Gulf of Mexico–Caribbean Sea region and concluded that "from the mouth of the Mississippi to the tip of the Yucatan peninsula there is no harbor satisfactory for ships of war of the larger classes." Partly because of the lack of potential Mexican naval facilities, Mahan considered it important for the United States to acquire bases in the Caribbean islands circling the eastern approaches to the isthmus.

The war with Spain in 1898 lasted only ten weeks, after which a peace treaty was concluded under terms dictated by the United States. As a result, the United States annexed Puerto Rico, established a protectorate over Cuba, and occupied some smaller Caribbean islands. Furthermore, U.S. leaders became unequivocally determined to build and exclusively control a trans-isthmian canal, and concrete arrangements were so made. In 1917 the United States purchased the Danish West Indies (the U.S. Virgin Islands). With Spain now completely ejected from the hemisphere and Great Britain willing to retire from the Caribbean area, the new U.S. strategic position was supported by public opinion. The United States had overcome external challenges in those parts of Latin America where it had asserted its power.

The broadest extension of Monroe's principles by far was enunciated in 1904 by President Theodore Roosevelt. Known as the Roosevelt Corollary, the principle asserted that U.S. interventions in the Caribbean were justified. Two years before, Germany, Great Britain, and Italy had blockaded Venezuela to enforce their financial claims, but at the behest of the United States they agreed to submit the dispute to the Hague Court of Arbitration. The court's ruling, which upheld the argument of the European powers that they should receive preferential treatment in the payment of their claims, set a precedent for the use of force in the collection of public debts. In 1904 European creditor nations threatened force against the Dominican Republic to collect defaulted debts as they had in Venezuela. In response to the Dominican situation, Roosevelt included a statement in his annual message to Congress in 1904; this statement became his Corollary to the Monroe Doctrine and was also known as the "big stick policy." Roosevelt said this:

> Chronic wrongdoing, or an impotence which results in a general loosening of the ties of civilized society, may in America . . . ultimately require intervention by some civilized nation, and in the Western Hemisphere the adherence of the United States to the Monroe Doctrine may force the United States . . . in flagrant cases of wrongdoing or impotence, to the exercise of an international police power.

The United States invoked the Roosevelt Corollary for the next quarter-century to justify its many interventions in a number of Caribbean states. Interventionist policies begun under President Roosevelt continued under Presidents William Howard Taft, Woodrow Wilson, and Calvin Coolidge. Several coercive instruments were employed, including the use or threat of armed invasion and military occupation, the imposition of treaties giving the United States the right to intervene, the establishment of customs receiverships and financial control, the recognition and nonrecognition of new governments used to influence their policies, and the supervision of elections.

Both long-range U.S. goals in Latin America—the exclusion of foreign influence and promotion of Latin American stability—were objectives of the active military, fiscal, and political interventions in the Caribbean. More specifically, interventions were used to secure and later protect the Panama Canal, to maintain law and order and protect the lives and property of citizens, to support North American investments and loans, and later, to encourage representative democracy. It is reasonable to assume that U.S. imperialism was aimed primarily at preventing other outside influences from dominating the area and at preempting European intervention; but after the U.S. position against outside threats was secured and stability enforced, it vigorously pressed for further advantages.

Not all of these proximate goals were sought at once by all U.S. administrations, but all of them were considered to be concomitant with national security interests. For example, "dollar diplomacy," encouraged by the Taft administration, involved the manipulation of loans and investments by U.S. consortia in the Caribbean region (especially Nicaragua and Honduras). This practice was followed by military landings ("pecuniary intervention") to protect private U.S. commercial interests. Dollar diplomacy appeared at the time to simply further the interests of the investors, but historians have since concluded that, from the point of view of the U.S. government if not that of the investors themselves, dollar diplomacy was also aimed at serving broader goals. U.S. investments, it was hoped, would keep out other foreign interests (especially British) as well as support stability in small Caribbean states. Military intervention would protect and encourage U.S. investors at the same time that it would enforce a degree of political stability in the Caribbean. In short, U.S. investors benefited from coercive U.S. diplomacy, but they did so as a part of U.S. security policy.

When President Woodrow Wilson came to office in 1913, he altered the traditional U.S. view of Latin American regimes and revised U.S. democratic policies. The Wilson credo reconciled the president's liberal political principles with his policy of frequent intervention in the Caribbean by considering the following: Political instability in Latin American (Caribbean) countries was a threat to North American interests; instability was caused by political immaturity; maturity was measurable by the extent of progress toward constitutional democracy. As a policy matter Wilson assumed that democracy could be imposed by external pressure or force and that the United States, as the most politically mature (democratic) and powerful nation in the Western Hemisphere, was responsible for taking an active role in the political development of Latin America.

The Good Neighbor Policy. U.S. policies from 1929 to 1945 contrasted sharply with those of 1895 to 1928. Basic U.S. goals, however, remained constant. The direct interventionary techniques were largely abandoned by the United States under the Good Neighbor Policy, but the long-range goals of foreign exclusion and Latin American stability remained, to be sought through cooperation rather than coercion. The reasons for the policy change lie in U.S. calculations of a changing strategic situation. After World War I European threats to hemispheric security were virtually nonexistent, and Latin American instability posed little direct threat to the United States. In addition, Latin American governments had made it clear that significant inter-American cooperation depended on the U.S. abandonment of interventionist practices. As no serious European threat existed and intervention aroused bitter resentment in Latin America and opposition in the United States, U.S. coercion was greatly reduced.

The features of what became known as the Good Neighbor Policy were tentatively established during the administration of Herbert Hoover (1929–1933); Franklin D. Roosevelt, inaugurated in 1933, explicitly enunciated the policy and expanded it. President Hoover repudiated the Roosevelt Corollary to the Monroe Doctrine and significantly reduced Caribbean intervention. A memorandum written by Under Secretary of State J. Reuben Clark in 1928 and circulated to the Latin American governments in 1930 dissociated the Roosevelt Corollary from the doctrine, although it did not renounce the use of intervention as a policy instrument. Some U.S. troops were removed from the Caribbean area, and certain U.S. investors were told that they must seek local Latin American remedies for their problems.

President Roosevelt made the Good Neighbor Policy explicit; he gave up intervention as a policy instrument, in both law and practice, and reinvigorated Pan American cooperation. In his inaugural address on March 4, 1933, he vowed that "in the field of foreign policy I would dedicate this nation to the policy of the good neighbor." The following month, Roosevelt specifically applied the Good Neighbor Policy to Latin America in a Pan American Day speech, with these words: "The essential qualities of a true Pan Americanism must be the same as those which constitute a good neighbor, namely, mutual understanding, a sympathetic appreciation of the other's point of view. It is only in this manner that we can hope to build up a system of which confidence, friendship, and good will are the cornerstones."

A salient aspect of the Good Neighbor Policy, as directed by Secretary of State Cordell Hull and by Sumner Welles in his various official positions, was the Pan Americanization of the Monroe Doctrine. That is, direct intervention was renounced by the United States and regional organization was embraced as a major (but far from exclusive) policy instrument. In 1933 the United States accepted, with reservations, an inter-American treaty stipulating nonintervention by one American state in the affairs of another. Three years later it accepted another treaty without reservation agreeing to the principle of absolute nonintervention (see Chapter 8 for details). Nonintervention was implemented with the U.S. abandonment of its five Caribbean protectorates—in Cuba, Haiti, the Dominican Republic, Nicaragua, and Panama—including the abrogation or revision of the treaties on which they were based. Situations that before probably would have occasioned intervention were dealt with through direct bilateral diplomatic negotiations, notably the expropriation of U.S. oil company properties by Mexico.

Policies of nonintervention required a return to tradition with regard to U.S. efforts at democratization. Abandoning the nonrecognition of unconstitutional governments and adopting a policy of noninterference in the internal affairs of others meant dealing with dictatorships often on a partnership basis. As a result, nonintervention came under attack because it permitted the continued existence of dictators and allowed others to seize power. The United States rejected the criticism, restated its commitment to nonintervention, and complained that those who deplored the effect of nonintervention were the very ones who had opposed prior intervention.

With the rise of the Fascist governments in Europe and their increased activities in Latin America, and especially with the threat of European war in the late 1930s, the United States was again concerned with foreign influences and Latin American stability. With intervention discredited, a cooperative hemispheric security system was constructed beginning in the late 1930s and strengthened throughout World War II. Extensive political, economic, and military collaboration took place during the war, on both bilateral and multilateral bases, including U.S. military and economic assistance programs. Most Latin American states, with some important exceptions, cooperated with the United States during the war, and the domestic status quo was generally maintained.

The Truman and Eisenhower Administrations

The United States emerged from World War II as the most powerful nation in the world with involvements on a global scale. Beginning in 1947, criteria related to the cold war were fundamental to U.S. policy formulation. The connected themes of worldwide interests and concerns about the cold war shaped U.S. policy on Latin America in the postwar period. As a result, the degree to which Latin America received attention in U.S. policy priorities depended essentially on the extent of the Communist threat in the other Americas and the degree of U.S. involvement in other parts of the world. As an arena of cold war conflict, Latin America was only a minor theater until the advent of Castro's Cuba in 1959; by the mid-1960s the Cuban Revolution seemed an atypical case and Latin America again received little attention. The United States resumed direct interventionist techniques from time to time, especially in the Caribbean area.

The Western Hemisphere Idea of a "special relationship" among the Americas lost most of its meaning after World War II. With its acceptance of broad international roles and pursuit of intimate relations with Europe, the United States all but abandoned the idea of two separate and distinct world spheres. The idea lingered on, at least in U.S. rhetoric concerning its Latin American policy, but in reality no special inter-American relations existed in the sense of either exclusivity or high priority. The Alliance for Progress period in the early 1960s and Caribbean policies in the 1980s both placed high priority on Latin America, and each policy in its own way was pursued in the context of East-West conflict.

The United States showed declining interest in Latin America during the latter part of World War II as Secretary Hull's ideas about globalism became dominant. "Good Neighbor" rhetoric was continued after the war, but U.S. interest in Latin America was superseded by the problems of war—the devastation of Europe, the "containment" of the Soviet Union, and later, by communism in Asia. The apparent lack of a serious foreign (i.e., Communist) threat in Latin America did not allow the region to be easily fitted into global cold war policies. Soviet expansion in Latin America seemed as remote as the prospect of internal Communist subversion. President Harry S Truman and his secretaries of state, George C. Marshall and Dean Acheson, made clear to Latin America that U.S. leaders felt that world problems were more crucial elsewhere. They candidly stressed the remoteness of Latin America from cold war problems.

The Republican party roundly criticized the Truman administration during the 1952 presidential campaign for its "neglect" of Latin America. After President Dwight D. Eisenhower was inaugurated in 1953, he and Secretary of State John Foster Dulles indicated that bold Latin American policy departures were imminent. President Eisenhower appointed his brother, Dr. Milton Eisenhower, a scholar with Latin American interests, to visit and report on the region with a view to U.S. policy reform. Dr. Eisenhower's subsequent report, submitted on November 18, 1953, stressed the need for additional U.S. economic assistance to the area and for a general upgrading of Latin America in U.S. policy priorities. As it turned out, the Eisenhower policy contained little that was new for Latin America; the emphasis in U.S. policy continued to focus on the cold war outside the hemisphere.

The only significant cold war events in Latin America prior to the Castro revolution in Cuba had to do with Communists in Guatemala gaining important positions in the leftist government of Jacobo Arbenz Guzmán (1951–1954). The United States obtained the adoption of a formal declaration against communism in the Americas at the Tenth Inter-American Conference at Caracas in 1954. Shortly thereafter the United States covertly sponsored a military coup that overthrew Arbenz. Except for the Guatemala case, the United States did not perceive a Communist threat in Latin America. Secretary Dulles, never complacent about communism, said at a press conference on November 5, 1957, that "we see no likelihood at the present time of communism getting into control of the political institutions of any of the American republics." In its Pan American policies, the United States aimed primarily to convert the Inter-American System into an anti-Communist alliance.

U.S. policy changed during the last two years of the Eisenhower presidency. The first catalyst for change was the treatment of Vice President and Mrs. Richard M. Nixon while conducting a "goodwill" tour in 1958. Violent riots in Peru and Venezuela, at times threatening the Nixons' physical safety, dramatized Latin American dissatisfaction with U.S. policy. The second and more important impetus for change was the Castro revolution in Cuba, coming to power on January 1, 1959. Castro's highly nationalist movement was strongly anti–United States in its ideological content; *antiyanquismo* eventually led to the embrace of Marxism-Leninism and alliance with the Soviet Union and its East European bloc. An important foreign intrusion was present in the Caribbean region, shaking the United States from its complacent assumption of Latin American immunity from the cold war. The president proposed his "Eisenhower Plan" in 1960 for increased economic aid to Latin America, and corresponding funds were appropriated by Congress. Further plans were laid for forceful intervention against Castro. Both policy approaches—increased aid and intervention—were carried out by the succeeding Kennedy administration.

Policies toward the different types of Latin American regimes and democratization again vacillated in the postwar period. Toward the end of World War II, during the Truman presidency, the United States briefly returned to the idea of intervention on behalf of democracy and in opposition to dictatorship. In addition, political interventionist policies were pursued in Argentina in 1945 and 1946 as the United States actively opposed the presidential candidacy of then Fascist-inclined Colonel Juan Perón. He subsequently won the presidency with ease; shortly thereafter, the United States ceased advocating intervention in the name of democracy.

After World War II, foreign aid programs, especially military, became caught up in policies and debates concerning Latin American dictators and democrats. Both the Truman and Eisenhower administrations signed mutual defense assistance pacts with several Latin American governments, including dictatorial and military regimes. The United States insisted that in each case the granting of aid was determined by its value in promoting mutual security rather than by the political form of its recipient. Dr. Milton Eisenhower recommended continuance of this policy in his 1958 Latin American policy report. He said that although the United States should maintain strictly formal relations with dictators and reaffirm its belief in democracy, it should not withdraw economic and military programs from countries governed by dictators. Further, he said, "reasoning which caused one to feel that we should do so would lead logically to the conclusion that throughout the world we should cease cooperating with any nation in which democracy is not complete. Patently, such a policy would paralyze the conduct of all foreign relations."

The Kennedy and Johnson Administrations

During the abbreviated presidency of John F. Kennedy and the first part of Lyndon B. Johnson's administration, Latin America assumed a major position in U.S. policy under the Alliance for Progress. In his inaugural address on January 20, 1961, Kennedy offered a "special pledge" to Latin America, promising to convert U.S. "good words into good deeds, in a new alliance for progress, to assist free men and free governments in casting off the chains of poverty." At a White House reception for Latin American diplomats on March 13, 1961, the president proposed a ten-year Alliance for Progress plan of U.S.–Latin American cooperation for economic, social, and political development in Latin America. In August, the Alliance for Progress was formally multilateralized at an inter-American conference, which enacted the "Charter of Punta del Este" detailing the goals and means of the broad development effort.

President Kennedy stressed that economic development and social reform should take place within an emerging democratic framework with political freedom. He had been highly critical of the Eisenhower administration's policies toward Latin American dictators and military regimes. The multilateral charter stated twelve goals for the Alliance, the first of which was "to improve and strengthen democratic institutions through application of the principle of self-determination by the people."

Thus, U.S. policy on Latin America assumed a position of high priority under the Kennedy administration. Nevertheless, policy continued to be formulated in a cold war context and in pursuit of traditional long-range goals. The United States feared that Communists would capture the revolutionary aspirations of a dynamically changing Latin America; that is, that Fidelismo would spread from Cuba to other parts of the region. Policy was directed at preventing foreign influence and maintaining political stability against communism through "developmentalism." It was hoped that social reform and economic growth would create political stability and deter Communist success. The purpose of economic assistance always had been to create the necessary economic conditions conducive to political stability; now social conditions were also included in the stability formula. The efforts toward democratic development were also based on the premise that a counterideology to communism was needed. The purpose of military assistance was clearly stated to be a support for political stability, aimed especially at counterinsurgency and the maintenance of internal order considered necessary for economic and political development, with only modest attention paid to defense against offshore incursions. In addition, the United States attempted further to consolidate the Inter-American System into an anti-Communist alliance; it succeeded in gaining multilateral agreements to exclude Cuba from participation in the OAS in 1962 and in 1964 to impose diplomatic and economic sanctions on the Castro regime.

The anti-Communist, antimilitary, prodemocracy, and developmentalist goals of the Alliance for Progress suggested a belief that Latin America sorely needed to pursue material and social progress; if it did not come about within a democratic framework, Latin Americans would be tempted to embrace radical solutions of the Castro-Communist type. Much was made of the fact that Castro had succeeded dictator Fulgencio Batista, with whom the United States had enjoyed cordial relations. It was implied that the United States would not only promote democracy, but would also oppose military coups and governments. This return to Wilsonian principles was motivated by the idea that dictators bequeathed a political vacuum to their successors that facilitated the Communist alternative. Therefore, the best way to oppose communism was to oppose repressive regimes, which make their nations vulnerable to political chaos and communism.

In addition to developmentalist strategies, the United States practiced military intervention. In April 1961 a U.S.-organized and financed band of Cuban exiles invaded Cuba at the Bay of Pigs hoping to stimulate a popular uprising that would overthrow Castro. The intervention, planned under Eisenhower and carried out by Kennedy, was a total failure. The invaders were subdued and Cuba became a base for subversion of other Latin American states.

The Alliance for Progress immediately faced serious problems. From 1961 to 1963 military coups overthrew constitutionally elected governments in seven Latin American countries. The success of these coups challenged the ideological (democratic) commitment and assumptions of the Alliance. The United States generally refused to recognize the new governments, suspended diplomatic relations, and terminated economic and military assistance. Then, in 1963, the U.S. position regarding military aid and democracy shifted; the new position remained unchanged until the mid-1970s. With some doubt about the effectiveness of antimilitary measures, the Kennedy policies took a pragmatic turn and accommodated to military regimes. Latin American military establishments came to be viewed as important parts of the political-social structure that played valuable and necessary roles in the process of modernization and nation building.

In the meantime, Soviet influence in Cuba had increased to the point where Soviet ballistic missiles, bombers, and combat troops were stationed on Cuba's soil. The dramatic "missile crisis" of October 1962—a confrontation between the United States and the Soviet Union over the weapons in Cuba—ended with Soviet withdrawal of the missiles. Intense U.S. decision making and action ensued during the thirteen days following the discovery of the missiles on October 14, 1962. President Kennedy organized his advisers as the Executive Committee of the National Security Council (Excom), although all of them were not permanent members of the NSC.

His objectives were to compel the Soviet Union to remove its offensive nuclear weapons from Cuba while avoiding nuclear war. According to Robert Kennedy (1969), all of the president's deliberations were guided by "an effort not to disgrace Khrushchev, not to humiliate the Soviet Union, not to have them feel they would have to escalate their response because their national security or national interests so compelled them." The costs and risks of several options were assessed by Excom and congressional and military leaders. The president finally decided to impose a blockade of Cuba, which was euphemistically referred to as a "quarantine." He had apparently decided that the presence of operational Soviet weapons in Cuba would constitute an adverse fundamental shift in the balance of world power and that therefore they must be removed, but he favored pressing for their removal rather than destroying them through direct military action. Those favoring air strikes or invasion contended that, as the missiles had already arrived in Cuba, a blockade would be futile. In addition, when the president announced the quarantine, he warned that any missile launched from Cuba on the United States would invite a U.S. retaliatory blow not on Cuba but on the Soviet Union.

The Cuban missile crisis came to an end in November 1962. The Soviet Union agreed to stop building bases in Cuba and to withdraw its nuclear weapons, bomber aircraft, and ground combat troops. In return, the United States lifted the blockade and pledged nonintervention in Cuba, subject to verification that Soviet weapons had been withdrawn. Thus, the United States was successful on the issue of ballistic missiles in Cuba; the Soviet Union did not, however, withdraw its combat unit as promised.

The Alliance for Progress was carried on by President Johnson after his inauguration in November 1963 following the assassination of President Kennedy. In April 1965, Johnson initiated a massive U.S. intervention in the Dominican Republic in order to prevent "another Cuba." But as the United States became more involved in the Vietnam conflict, its concern with Latin America receded. Furthermore, the Cuban case eventually proved to be atypical of Latin American politics; Cuba failed to export its revolution and after 1967 it abandoned serious attempts to do so for more than a decade. The lack of a Communist threat to the hemisphere coincided with U.S. congressional disillusionment with foreign aid as a policy technique in the world at large and a general decline in available U.S. economic and military assistance funds. Latin Americans again complained that the United States was neglectful of their problems, despite U.S. protestations to the contrary.

The Johnson administration's approach to military governments continued to reflect a disagreement with the former policy and a belief in the need for "realism" as well as an optimistic attitude toward the military role in economic development and social reform. The United States also argued that it must work with existing military establishments even if they were corrupt or unprofessional in order to transform them through training over a period of time. The United States did not raise the issue of democracy in its relations with military governments coming to power from 1963 to 1968 in the Dominican Republic, Brazil, Peru, and Panama.

The Nixon and Ford Administrations

During the Nixon and Ford administrations (1969–1977), Latin America continued to be viewed as a low-priority area. President Nixon's regional policy was decidedly slow in appearing after his inauguration in January 1969, despite his insistence that Latin American problems would have the "highest priority." Then, in his first major address on Latin American relations before the OAS on April 14, 1969, the president indicated an abandonment of "developmentalism." He referred to the Alliance for Progress as a "great concept" but expressed disillusionment with the results of its programs. President Nixon then sent Governor Nelson Rockefeller of New York on a series of "study missions" to twenty Latin American states in May and June of 1969. The governor met with violence in many places; visits to three states were cancelled because of rioting, and fourteen others experienced serious disorders upon his arrival. The Rockefeller Report was submitted on September 3, 1969, but few of its recommendations were implemented as policy.

President Nixon further outlined his policy in an address on October 31, 1969, adopting what came to be known as a "low-profile" approach. He called for a "new partnership" in inter-American affairs in which the United States "lectures less and listens more." He again rejected the social and economic developmental content of the Alliance for Progress, but he promised increases in economic aid and certain trade concessions. President Nixon (and President Ford after him) showed no inclination to alter the pragmatic policies toward military governments already established.

U.S. policy under Nixon was said to be based on the principles of respect for diversity, mutual cooperation, and peaceful resolution of differences. Latin Americans were expected to take a larger leadership role in hemisphere affairs. In practice, the region was largely ignored, except for Castro in Cuba and the Marxist government of Salvador Allende, which came to power in Chile in October 1970, and such specific issues as border questions with Mexico, nationalization of U.S. properties in Peru, and revision of the Panama Canal treaty. The U.S. Congress was unwilling to approve increased economic aid for Latin America, and the executive vacillated on trade concessions.

In October 1973, soon after becoming secretary of state, Henry Kissinger announced that Latin American policy was in the process of reformulation aimed at starting a New Dialogue with the other American states. The gist of Kissinger's policy statements, reinforced by remarks made by President Nixon and other U.S. officials, was to urge a new spirit of inter-American collaboration within the context of an interdependent world. The United States, the secretary said, recognized Latin American complaints that Washington had put aside its special commitments to the hemisphere, but he asserted that it sought not dominance but community and a sharing of responsibilities with Latin America. He promised that the United States would not impose its political preferences on Latin American states and would seek a close and free association with them. The United States was prepared to consult with those nations and to adjust its positions on trade and monetary matters, rules regarding private investment and the roles of multinational corporations in underdeveloped nations, law of the sea, food and population programs, the transfer of technology, energy problems, development assistance, and restructuring of the OAS. Kissinger pointed out that the United States and Mexico had solved their long-standing Colorado River salinity dispute, that the United States and Panama had made significant progress toward a new canal treaty, and that the United States and Peru had settled their dispute concerning compensation for nationalized property.

Prospects for the New Dialogue declined beginning in mid-1974. President Nixon's attention was primarily directed toward defending himself against possible impeachment by the U.S. Congress, and Secretary Kissinger's energies were concentrated on problems in the Middle East. After Nixon's resignation in August 1974 and the succession of Gerald Ford to the presidency, U.S.–Latin American relations further deteriorated. President Ford contradicted the principles of the New Dialogue at a press conference in September 1974 by defending CIA activities in Chile preceding the fall of Allende, which he claimed were in the best interests of the Chilean people. The 1974 Trade Act excluded Venezuela and Ecuador from a generalized system of trade preferences because of their OPEC membership, even though they had not participated in the earlier OPEC-sponsored oil embargo. Consequently, Latin Americans insisted on postponing the meeting of foreign ministers that had been scheduled for March 1975 in Buenos Aires as the next step in the New Dialogue.

The United States then attempted to reconcile its difficulties with Latin America. President Ford asked Congress in April 1975 to grant him the authority to waive restrictions in the 1974 Trade Act, which he said had an unintended impact on Latin American relations. Secretary Kissinger offered, in a speech in Houston on March 1, 1975, "to continue the dialogue in a spirit of friendship and conciliation" despite some "temporary interruptions." The United States ceased opposing the Latin American majority that wished to end the isolation of Cuba, and in August 1975 the OAS essentially dropped the sanctions that had been imposed in 1964. The United States also expressed its own complaints about Latin America. A State Department publication entitled *United States Foreign Policy: An Overview* (May 1975: 19–20) chided Latin America for succumbing to "the temptation to blame disappointment on the intrigues and excesses of foreigners," complaining that "Latin America is perennially tempted to define its independence and unity through opposition to the United States," thus delaying the New Dialogue when it was most needed.

Balance-of-power thinking during the Nixon-Ford administrations, with foreign policy directed throughout by Henry Kissinger, helps to account for Latin America's continuing low priority in U.S. policy calculations. Détente between the superpowers indicated that the United States and the Soviet Union shared a mutual interest in maintaining the existing distribution of rewards and power in the international system. In this arrangement the United States assumed key responsibility for system maintenance in Latin America, sometimes as "policeman" and at least as power broker. Thus, with no strategic threat to the United States posed by either the regional states themselves or by an external state operating in the region, the United States was free to concentrate its efforts in other areas of the world.

The Carter Administration

President Jimmy Carter (1977–1981) stated at Notre Dame University in May 1977 that "we are now free of that inordinate fear of communism which once led us to embrace any dictator who joined us in that fear." After discounting the Soviet threat, Carter rested his global policies on three commitments: (1) to consider human rights as a fundamental tenet of U.S. foreign policy; (2) to reduce the danger of nuclear proliferation and the spread of conventional weapons; and (3) to rely on all forms of military cooperation as exceptional rather than normal instruments of policy. President

Carter's policies on Latin America, based on these commitments, further isolated the United States from much of Latin America. U.S. relations with numerous states were strained over human rights, nonproliferation, and other issues. Furthermore, the Carter administration did not respond to Latin America's primary interests—namely, its economic demands, especially better access to U.S. capital and technology and more concessions for their commodity exports.

U.S. relations with Southern Cone states were reduced to low levels of activity. The United States banned Argentina, Chile, Paraguay, and Uruguay from receiving further arms transfers and certain forms of economic aid. Brazil, offended by the State Department's 1977 report on its human rights situation, refused to accept any more U.S. military assistance. President Carter further annoyed Brazil by opposing its acquisition of a nuclear reactor from West Germany, citing his commitment to nuclear nonproliferation; Brazil insisted that it was related to development of energy sources and had nothing to do with weapons.

In 1977 President Carter discussed placing a new emphasis on the long-neglected Caribbean region. High-level official visits were made around the area. At the same time, the president proposed restoration of U.S.-Cuban relations and tolerance for various ideologies in the region. However, his Caribbean policies met with several difficulties. U.S.-Cuban relations deteriorated after the Soviet Union and Cuba expanded their military activities in Africa. U.S. sanctions related to human rights abuses were applied to El Salvador, Guatemala, and Nicaragua. New canal treaties were signed with Panama and ratifications exchanged, but debate in the U.S. Senate and throughout the nation was vociferous, even though the treaties had been negotiated by four presidents from both political parties. Their conclusion reflected an official U.S. view, held since the mid-1960s, that the strategic and economic importance of the canal and the Caribbean had greatly decreased.

U.S.-Mexican relations were awkward despite the Carter administration's intent to improve them. The two governments strongly disagreed over several issues, especially those of Mexican migration to the United States and the price of Mexican natural gas exports.

The Carter administration's Latin American policy underwent important adjustments after 1979. His global policies were compromised as he confronted the harsh realities of international politics. By the end of 1979, the disillusioned president publicly admitted that the Soviet Union was more threatening and less accommodating than he had anticipated. In the meantime, he revised his policies toward certain parts of the Caribbean because of increased Soviet-Cuban activity; his policies toward the rest of Latin America, however, remained essentially unchanged. After the overthrow of Somoza in Nicaragua, U.S. policy in time was antagonistic toward the Sandinista-dominated government on the grounds that it was providing Soviet arms to guerrillas in El Salvador. Fearing that events in El Salvador would parallel those in Nicaragua, the Carter administration in January 1981 (only five days before the end of Carter's term of office) lifted its ban on military assistance and resumed shipments to the military government despite the absence of any substantive reforms. In the meantime, the United States also responded with hostility to a 1979 coup in Grenada led by the leftist New Jewel Movement, to which the Soviet Union and its East European had bloc extended various forms of aid (as had numerous non-Communist countries).

The Reagan Administration

When Ronald Reagan became president in 1981 he resolved to regain a dominant hemispheric role for the United States. He had been highly critical of President Carter's Latin American policies and set out to reverse them. President Reagan's world view was based on the proposition that international disorder and terrorism resulted from the activities of the Soviet Union and its surrogates, of which Cuba was the most important. Opposition to Communist expansionism formed the basis for his global and regional policies. This approach necessitated reducing human rights concerns to a secondary position—not abandoning them but greatly reducing their emphasis. His anti-Communist policies also included a resuscitation of arms transfers and other military programs, which had been considerably diminished in prior years. While the administration viewed all of Latin America in terms of East-West conflict, its most intense concern was with the Caribbean Basin, particularly Central America. Consequently, with the exception of Mexico, U.S. efforts concentrated on small countries and paid relatively little attention to the major nations in South America until events forced an extended range of concern.

The Reagan Doctrine (critics called it a rationale for simplistic anticommunism) was articulated early in the Reagan presidency. It emphasized the need to reverse what was perceived as the continuing expansion of Soviet influence in strategically important Third World regions of Central America, Africa, and Asia throughout the previous decade. The creation of Soviet clients (referred to as surrogates and proxies)—Angola, Ethiopia, Mozambique, South Yemen, Libya, Afghanistan, Vietnam, Nicaragua, and Cuba—provided bases for subversive Communist operations against neighboring states, created the beginnings of an infrastructure for a global terrorist network, and made military bases available for Soviet use. Soviet activities in these surrogate nations enhanced the chances for Marxist revolutions while minimizing the risk of direct confrontation with the United States. The Vietnam experience had paralyzed U.S. resistance to Soviet expansionism. The Soviets, however, also had vulnerabilities, the most basic of which was the failure of Marxist revolutions to meet popular expectations. Reagan said that the United States should exploit these vulnerabilities. That is, the key assumptions of the Reagan Doctrine were that a "democratic revolution" was under way in the Third World and that various forms of direct U.S. support for anti-Marxist forces would stop Soviet expansionism and further the democratic revolution. The administration, however, did not further define an explicit doctrine and preferred to take a case-by-case approach (Bode, 1986).

Central America immediately became a front line in the new global cold war. The Reagan administration evolved a geopolitical strategic view of the Caribbean Basin with an emphasis on Central America. In July 1983 President Reagan appointed members to the National Bipartisan Commission on Central America, headed by former Secretary of State Henry Kissinger, and charged them with the task of formulating and recommending long-term U.S. strategy and tactics. The Kissinger Commission report, issued in January 1984, reinforced the administration's assumptions and policies but with important qualifications and extensions. The report served as the basis for subsequent administration proposals to Congress and provided authority for its strategic rationale.

The principal assumption was that the global balance of power could be shifted by the advance of Soviet power in Central America. The security of the Caribbean Basin was vital to the United States, whose interests were threatened by activities aimed at establishing Cuban-style Marxist-Leninist dictatorships allied with the Soviet Union. The "domino theory" was advanced. The Soviet Union, already enjoying a permanent presence in the Caribbean through its Cuban surrogate, was seen as acting to reinforce and expand this penetration into Nicaragua. At the same time, Cuban assistance to El Salvador threatened to convert that state to Marxism. From there, the argument continued, communism would spread to the other small Central American countries and then threaten the major bordering states—Colombia and Venezuela to the south and, most ominously, Mexico to the north.

This calculation of U.S. interests and Soviet-Cuban motives led to a number of further assumptions: (1) Vital Caribbean sea lanes and unimpeded passage through the Panama Canal, already threatened by Cuba's geographic position, would be more vulnerable with additional Soviet surrogates; (2) a more extensive permanent Soviet presence would offer the Soviet Union other significant military advantages by allowing the placement of hostile forces and weapons (conventional and nuclear) capable of striking deep within the United States and in Latin American states, as well as extended Soviet naval operations; (3) all of these factors would force significant alterations in the current U.S. forward deployment strategy, since a previously secure area would either require new resources to be created or existing ones to be diverted from other areas; (4) Communist takeovers would inevitably cause a vast increase in illegal immigration to the United States; and (5) U.S. worldwide credibility was at stake—in the words of the Kissinger report, "The triumph of hostile forces in what the Soviet Union calls the 'strategic rear' of the United States would be read as a sign of U.S. impotence." The final conclusion was obvious: The United States must act to prevent the transformation of its southern border into a region of hostile states.

The United States instituted a program of assistance to the anti-Sandinista Nicaraguan guerrillas known as the *contras*, to the armed forces in El Salvador engaged in counterinsurgency efforts, and to Honduras for related services. U.S. actions were also directly interventionist; the most notable of these were the military invasion of Grenada in October 1983 and the mining of

Nicaraguan harbors in March 1984. They were also developmental. The administration proposed the Caribbean Basin Initiative (CBI), which, at least in its initial form, insisted on the necessity for continued aggressive opposition to Soviet expansionism but also recognized poverty as a source of instability and outlined a program for trade preferences and economic aid to friendly Caribbean governments. The administration placed increasingly strong pressure on the Salvadoran government to follow a centrist course, effectively institute an agrarian reform program, hold free and fair elections, and curtail right-wing death squads; a similar course was urged on other Central American states.

The Reagan Doctrine faced serious obstacles. The problems addressed were intractable to begin with. Moreover, the doctrine met with little support, and much criticism, among U.S. allies, and domestic consensus was clearly lacking. Leading members of Congress, and the public opinion to which they were sensitive, expressed skepticism about the administration's view of the Communist threat and were reluctant to support strong measures. They talked of "another Vietnam," a fear shared by certain key military leaders, in which the United States would become mired in an unwinnable Central American war unsupported by the American people. Despite considerable effort, the Reagan administration did not resolve the Central American problems it set out to rectify.

In the meantime, other subregional and transregional problems intruded. Because U.S. policies in the Southern Cone had revolved around questions of human rights and military assistance during the Carter administration, President Reagan had to observe legislative controls and prohibition of arms transfers because of human rights violations in Argentina, Chile, Paraguay, and Uruguay. Among several actions taken to reverse human rights policies toward the Southern Cone, the Reagan administration introduced legislation to repeal the ban on U.S. arms sales to Argentina and Chile. Congress agreed but required a presidential certification that both countries had made significant progress on human rights problems. These efforts came to an abrupt end, however, with the outbreak of the Anglo-Argentine military conflict in 1982 (see Chapter 11). After the return to democracy in Argentina in December 1983, the administration certified to Congress that Argentina had improved its human rights record and was eligible for military transfers that had been prohibited since 1977. With the return to democracy in other Southern Cone states (Uruguay, Brazil, and Bolivia joined Argentina; Peru had followed constitutional procedures since 1978), General Augusto Pinochet in Chile and Alfredo Stroessner in Paraguay stood alone as military heads of government. Prior U.S. prohibitions on arms transfers remained in effect for Chile and Paraguay; they were lifted elsewhere. Bolivia and Peru were central to U.S. efforts to control the international narcotics traffic, but bilateral programs designed to cut off the drug flow at its sources enjoyed little success. The debt question was a particularly difficult problem in U.S. policy toward all Southern Cone states.

The Reagan administration made some effort to smooth relations with Brazil. Brazilian-U.S. relations were dominated by the related questions of

Brazil's enormous foreign debt, owed mostly to U.S. commercial banks, and certain trade practices by both partners. President Reagan visited Brazil in December 1982 and was cordially received. Basic differences remained, however, with the related questions of debt, trade, and energy paramount among them. The United States ended a trade agreement in 1984 and imposed a monetary penalty in 1987, charging Brazil with violating treaty pledges by subsidizing its exports and engaging in unfair trade practices. The United States was also displeased with Brazil's arms exports to Libya, which transshipped a portion to Iran.

Transregional problems of debt, narcotraffic, and migration became increasingly important during the Reagan administration. By 1988, even as the administration continued to expend a great deal of effort on Central America, some officials acknowledged that these issues transcended the problem of Soviet expansionism. In particular, there was a sense that the flow of illicit narcotics from Latin America into the United States in response to the North American demand for drugs presented the principal security threat to the United States.

BIBLIOGRAPHIC COMMENT

The first general survey of U.S. relations with Latin America was a diplomatic history by Latané (1900), later revised and retitled (1920). This pioneering work was followed by Stuart, who produced six editions beginning in 1922, the latest coauthored with Tigner (1975). Another early history was by Robertson (1923), followed by Bemis (1943), Mecham (1965), Connell-Smith (1974), and Molineu (1986). Good political science surveys came later; the recent ones include Blasier (1985), Hayes (1984), Kryzanek (1985), Lowenthal (1987), and Schoultz (1987). Martz and Schoultz (1980) is an excellent collection of essays on a variety of themes. U.S. Senate Foreign Relations Committee (1960) is a compilation of studies still of interest. Leading U.S., Latin American, and European scholars debate major issues in U.S. policy in Middlebrook and Rico (1986). Wesson and Muñoz (1986) is a collection of Latin American views.

Child (1979a, 1980) provides a good overview of U.S. strategic concepts of Latin America and related military doctrines. Mahan (1918) is one of the admiral's numerous influential works. Schoultz (1981) is one of the best treatments of U.S. human rights policies; Kirkpatrick (1979, 1981) formed the basis for Reagan's initial approach to human rights in Latin America, which he later abandoned; Farer (1981) is a sharp critique of the Kirkpatrick thesis. Keogh (1985) edited a balanced set of essays on U.S. human rights policies in Central America.

Caribbean imperial policies are analyzed by Munro (1964, 1974), Perkins (1966), and R. F. Smith (1981). Findling (1987) is a good history of the United States in Central America from 1800 to the mid-1980s. Langley (1980, 1982) thoroughly analyzes U.S. actions in the Caribbean in the twentieth century. On recent U.S. policy formulation in Central America, see *The Report of the President's National Bipartisan Commission on Central America* (1983), U.S. Senate Select Committee on Secret Military Assistance to Iran and the Nicaraguan Opposition and U.S. House of Representatives Select Committee to Investigate Covert Arms Transactions with Iran (November 1987), and Etheredge (1985). For further works on the conflict, including criticisms of U.S. policy, see the Bibliographic Comment after Chapter 11. Baily (1976) focuses on the United States and South America, and Pike (1977) on the United States and the Andean region.

The major works on the Monroe Doctrine are by Alvarez (1924), a classic Latin American interpretation by the eminent Chilean jurist; May (1975); and, especially, Perkins (1927, 1933, 1937, 1963); see also J. R. Clark (1930). J. A. Logan (1961) analyzes the "no transfer" principle. Whitaker (1954) is the major work on the Western Hemisphere Idea; his interpretation is challenged by Rippy (1958). See also Callcott (1968) on the subject. Weinberg (1935) provides the leading study of Manifest Destiny. Wood (1961) is the best source on the Good Neighbor Policy; Wood (1985) also interprets the later dismantling of that policy. Analyses of U.S. actions during the Cuban missile crisis, selected from a voluminous body of writing, include Allison (1971)—the premier treatment—Chayes (1974), and Dinerstein (1976). Treatments by U.S. officials include those by Acheson (1969), Kennedy (1969), Schlesinger (1965), and Sorenson (1965). Sigmund (1982) and Lowenthal (1983) review the Reagan administration's early approach. Bode (1986) gives an official explanation of the Reagan Doctrine; and Sanchez (1983), who was then deputy assistant secretary of defense for inter-American affairs, argues the strategic rationale for Central American–Caribbean policies.

A sampling of the sources concerned with the problem of Puerto Rican economic development and political status are by Bhana (1975), Clark (1975), Heine and García-Passalacqua (1983), and Wells (1969). On the Virgin Islands, see Lewis (1972), and O'Neill (1972).

The following few selections are taken from the voluminous literature on bilateral U.S. relations with individual Latin American states: *Argentina:* Peterson (1964); *Brazil:* Wesson (1981); *Chile:* Pike (1963); *Cuba:* Bonsal (1971), Langley (1968), and Smith (1960); *Dominican Republic:* Atkins and Wilson (1972); *Mexico:* Cline (1963), Gómez-Robledo V. (1981), Grayson (1984), S. K. Purcell (1981), Schmitt (1974), and Vázquez and Meyer (1985); and *Peru:* Carey (1964), and Sharp (1972). See also the Bibliographic Comment following Chapter 3.

CHAPTER SIX

—————————— ■ ——————————

Nonstate Actors

INTERNATIONAL POLITICAL ANALYSIS focusing exclusively on the policies of nation-states ignores the important impact of other kinds of international actors. The nation-state has never been the sole actor in the modern international political system, nor politics the result of state interaction alone. Sovereign states remain the prime actors, but the nonstate actors have shown a high degree of autonomy and have played central roles in politics. This chapter deals with five categories of nonstate entities that have been significant actors in the Latin American subsystem: the Roman Catholic Church, multinational business enterprise, international labor organizations, guerrilla insurgency groups, and transnational political parties. These entities are not the only nonstate actors operating in the Latin American subsystem, but they are considered to be the most important ones.

THE ROMAN CATHOLIC CHURCH

The Church as Global Political Actor

Church policy and influence in Latin America, emanating from the papacy in Rome, is a complex subject for several reasons. First, the Roman Catholic Church is a special kind of international actor; the Holy See is not only a state presided over by the pope but is also the headquarters for a worldwide religious organization. Second, the church is not a transnational unit as monolithic as its internal and global structures might imply; nationalism, in Latin America and in other parts of the world, plays an important role in matters of religion and church politics as in other social arenas. Finally, deep divisions within the church over many issues, which have been evident since even before the Latin American national beginnings, have complicated the policies of Rome and its relations with Latin American churches and states, as well as inter–Latin American church relations.

The Holy See and the Vatican State. The nature of the Roman Catholic Church as an actor in the modern international political system is unique. References to the papacy as a nonstate actor are technically inaccurate since the Holy See and the Vatican in fact constitute a sovereign state; but the church predates the emergence of the modern nation-state by more than a millennium and has special characteristics. It is the oldest important actor in the current international political system and formally recognized by most of the nation-states. The church's independent attributes and sovereign status date from the Peace of Westphalia of 1648; the Lateran Pacts signed with Italy in 1929 (revised in 1984) further confirmed its status.

The Holy See constitutes the central government of the Roman Catholic Church. Its ancient sovereignty is vested in a sacerdotal monarchy (the papacy) with governmental jurisdiction and temporal and spiritual authority as the capital of the global Roman Catholic Church. The Holy See has legal personality in international law, which allows it to enter into treaties as a juridically equal state and to engage in formal diplomatic relations. The Holy See has exchanged diplomatic missions since the fourth century and today engages in a broad scope of diplomatic activity. It is formally recognized by about 120 nation-states and carries on diplomatic relations with them, including most of the Latin American states. Participation in international organizations includes membership in a number of IGOs and NGOs and permanent observer status in the United Nations System, the Organization of American States, and the Council of Europe. The Holy See is signatory to many treaties, including the nuclear Non-Proliferation Treaty of 1971. The State of the Vatican City is the territorial base of the Holy See, superseding the former Papal States; the pope is head of state. Created in 1929 to administer the properties belonging to the Holy See, the Vatican also possesses personality under international law and enters into international agreements; it does not, however, exchange diplomatic representatives. (This definition draws on U.S. Department of State, 1987.)

Until the latter part of the nineteenth century, the pope not only led the universal church but also headed a relatively large European state. The Italian peninsula was divided into a number of separate entities, among them the Papal States with Rome as the capital city. During the revolutions and wars attendant to the unification of Italy under a monarch, the papacy lost control over much of its territory. By 1861 the Papal States had been conquered by military force and annexed to the Kingdom of Italy; in 1870 Italian troops occupied Rome and the pope withdrew to the Vatican. Finally, the papacy and Italy signed the three Lateran treaties of 1929. Italy recognized the sovereignty of the Holy See and the creation of the State of the Vatican City, the pope dropped all claims to the former Papal States, and they both agreed on certain arrangements between church and state in Italy. Two additional pacts (concordats), signed by the Vatican and Italy in 1984 and put into effect the following year, revised parts of the Lateran treaties. These revisions changed certain aspects of the relationship between the Vatican and Italy but had no real consequence for the international activities of the Holy See.

Decision Making. Church divisiveness over current social issues is instructive with regard to its policy-making procedures and revealing of the decentralized nature of the church as a transnational actor. Thomas Sanders (1970) pointed out the gap between the ideal church decision-making model and the way in which policy is really formulated. According to the ideal model, broad policies are made by the pope at the top of the church structure and then move downward through the hierarchy for implementation by bishops around the world, finally being applied by priests and lay people. The emphasis throughout is on initiative and authority from above and obedience below. In fact, according to Sanders, official church teachings have tended to lag far behind social change, and the upper echelons of the hierarchy have been slow to absorb new social thought. The pope and most bishops have not been policy innovators; revision of papal policy usually has been in response to public pressures and to initiatives taken by church officials at lower levels of the hierarchy who eventually have been able to influence Vatican authorities. Church decisions and actions with regard to issues in Latin American international relations through the latter 1980s provide continuing evidence to support Sanders' thesis.

Latin American Perceptions. A perception of Latin America as a distinct region has been revealed in church organizational structures. In 1858 the papacy established the Latin American Holy College (Colegio Pío Latinoamericano) in Rome, and in 1899 it sponsored the Latin American Plenary Council at the Vatican (Víctor Alba in Davis, Wilson, and others, 1975:106, 108). Much later, in 1953, Latin American bishops established a regional organization, the Conferencia Episcopal Latinoamericana (the Conference of Latin American Bishops, or CELAM). CELAM became an important inter–Latin American Catholic Church forum for debate and communication; the papacy has attempted to influence it in matters of Vatican policy. CELAM searches for common positions among the bishops, takes into account papal teaching, issues policy statements, and offers guidance to national church officials. It has served the important function of regionally integrating the church in Latin America and eroding the old system of largely isolated national churches.

The traditional Catholic political parties in Latin America tended to be narrowly based nationalist groups advocating religious intolerance, and sometimes anti-Semitism, and opposing secularization; they were of little political consequence and have virtually disappeared. Much more important have been the Christian Democratic parties, which began to appear in the mid-1930s (the first was in Chile) and were modeled after their European counterparts. They were initially influenced by the writings of the French theologian Jacques Maritain, a leader in the revival of thomism (scholasticism), who advocated church support for representative democracy and civil rights and liberties. Christian Democrats viewed capitalism as humanly degrading but rejected Marxism as anti-Christian. They sought to implement principles of social justice contained in certain papal encyclicals through political action.

One Roman Catholic order that maintains extensive formal diplomatic relations with Latin America is the Sovereign Military Hospitaller Order of St. John of Jerusalem, of Rhodes, and of Malta (also known as the Knights of Malta, or the Knights of St. John, or the Knights Hospitallers). Founded in eleventh-century Jerusalem, this religious order later fought in the Crusades and eventually acquired great wealth and military power, including fortresses and fleets. Over the years it moved to Cyprus, to Rhodes, and to Malta, in the process becoming a powerful territorial state. French armed forces dislodged the order from Malta in 1798, after which its headquarters were located in Rome and dependent on the Holy See. Thus, by the time of Latin American independence, the Knights of Malta were no longer a military power and had lost their territorial base. Nevertheless, the order maintained its state status and supported diplomatic relations with the Holy See and with numerous nation-states around the world, today including nineteen states in Latin America. The order is, therefore, an actor in the Latin American subsystem. It still calls itself an order of chivalry of laymen and priests with mixed religious and military purposes, although in fact its activities in Latin America and elsewhere are concerned almost exclusively with various kinds of welfare work.

Mention should also be made of the important role played by foreign priests in the Latin American churches. After the nineteenth-century Latin American movements for independence, the church was subject to political attacks, often involving violence, by anticlerical liberal governments. As a result, the church was in a continuing state of crisis, unable to recruit sufficient clergy from local populations. Thus began the flow of clergy from Europe and subsequently from the United States. That movement has continued since World War II, and today the percentage of foreign clergy is as high as 80 percent in some countries and is significant in almost all others. Most of them come from France, Spain, and the United States.

Papal Relations with Latin America

The papal role in Latin America has never been as great as might be expected, given the hierarchical church structure that stresses obedience to higher authority and the fact that some 90 percent of all Latin Americans profess faith in Roman Catholicism. Rome's presence was minimal during the Latin American colonial period, despite Catholic Spain's aim to conquer and rule its part of America in the name of God and the Gospel as well as for Gold and Glory. The Spanish Crown jealously controlled religious as well as other affairs in the colonies, successfully resisting papal intrusion through the system of "royal patronage" (*patronato reál*), in which the crown made ecclesiastical appointments, controlled finances, and made basic policy decisions. Portuguese officials followed the Spanish lead and also insisted on independence regarding church governance in Brazil. The Holy See generally accepted Spanish and Portuguese sovereign power over the church in America, taking little action to assert itself there.

During the Spanish American wars for independence, the pope supported the Spanish king. In 1816 the pope issued an encyclical calling for Spanish American Catholics to be faithful to the king (Alba in Davis, Wilson, and others, 1975:104). The church in Spanish America was divided, however. Many of the lower clergy participated as patriots in the independence movements; the Mexican struggle, for example, was begun by two priests. The high clergy tended to be royalist until revolutionary success was evident, whereupon they generally supported the new nations against Spain.

During the Latin American national period, three forms of international relations involving the papacy have stood out: (1) the transition from conflict to diplomatic linkages in the nineteenth century; (2) papal third-party conflict resolution in the twentieth century; and (3) a series of papal visits to the region beginning in 1969.

In the first stage, the early national period, papal relations with the Latin American states were largely conflictual. Papal influence was mixed but, by and large, not great. The Holy See continued its close ties with Spain and the Holy Roman Empire, which, in turn, were often hostile toward Latin America. The Vatican's relations with Brazil were much better than those with other Latin American states. Rome was closely tied to Portugal, but the Brazilian independence movement had been nearly bloodless, and independent Brazil was governed as a monarchy by the heirs to the Portuguese throne until 1889, so that Luso-Brazilian relations were relatively friendly. The Holy See and Brazil exchanged diplomatic representatives in 1830 and continuously maintained relations afterwards.

During this period, the Latin American churches were deeply divided over political issues and in sharp conflict with the temporal state. Church-state conflict existed virtually everywhere in the region to some degree; it was especially intense in Mexico and Colombia. The churches were caught up in the political struggles of their nations, largely fought out between opposing upper-class cliques organized into primitive political parties. Conservatives advocated traditionalism and authoritarianism, while liberals sought constitutional republicanism. One major issue stemmed from the nature of church-state relations inherited from the colonial period. During that time the church had enjoyed the legal status of an autonomous "estate," which included a number of special privileges such as maintaining its own judicial system. Liberals wanted to end the church's special status as part of their overall attempt to create societies in which all individuals were subject to common constitutional provisions and legal systems. Liberal anticlericalism was also directed against church wealth in several states.

The church hierarchy in Latin America responded to the liberal challenge by allying with conservatives and some of the most reactionary elements of society, thus gaining a reputation for opposing social change and perpetuating economic injustice. The Vatican further alienated its detractors by systematic attacks on such liberal tenets as rationalism, public education, economic progress and materialism, and separation of church and state (as in the encyclical *Quanta Cura* in 1864), and by the doctrine of papal infallibility proclaimed in 1870, which made the pope's word final in matters of faith and doctrine.

The Latin American church-state conflict declined in the late nineteenth century, soon after the pope had suffered the loss of the Papal States in Italy and had become isolated in the Vatican. In this environment, the papacy pressed for expanded diplomatic relations, and by the beginning of the twentieth century it had established them with all Latin American states. These diplomatic channels were used to defend the church's property interests against liberal opposition. Anticlericalism remained strong among liberals, but an accommodation with the church was beginning to take place.

Two notable cases of successful papal mediation in serious Latin American conflicts, one involving Haiti and the Dominican Republic in the 1930s and the other Chile and Argentina in the 1970s and 1980s, illustrate papal activity in different parts of the region over time.

In October 1937, Dominican military forces attacked and killed large numbers of Haitian peasants near the border between the two countries. It was a bloody and tragic chapter in the long history of border disputes. A complex series of diplomatic maneuvering followed, and in time the dispute was taken up under two general inter-American treaties to which both countries were signatory. The agreement reached was widely acclaimed as a successful utilization of the Inter-American System's structure for peaceful settlement. In fact, as the U.S. minister in the Dominican Republic observed at the time, the actual instrument of the settlement was the diplomacy of the papal nuncio who was accredited to both countries. The church offered a common meeting ground in an otherwise distrustful and hostile situation. The convention finally signed in the context of inter-American treaties was in fact the protocol originally drafted and urged on the two states by the papal nuncio (Atkins and Wilson, 1972:56).

Argentina and Chile over the years contested the entire length of their mutual border. One issue involved a contentious and dangerous dispute over three islands in the Beagle Channel near Cape Horn. In 1971 they agreed to allow the British Crown to arbitrate the dispute, and six years later an award was handed down that largely favored the Chilean claims. The Argentine military government rejected the decision, and in late 1978 the two countries were on the verge of war. The Holy See's observer to the Organization of American States (OAS) urgently proposed papal mediation, which was readily accepted by both countries in January 1979. Almost two years later, in December 1980, the pope presented his peace proposal. Chile seemed ready to accept it, but Argentina stalled on responding. The effort was interrupted by the Anglo-Argentine war of 1982, but the papal role as third-party mediator was successfully revived. In January 1984, a month after the inauguration of civilian Argentine President Raúl Alfonsín, the two countries signed a declaration at public ceremonies in the Vatican pledging to solve the "southern question" in the framework of papal mediation. In November 1984 the two countries signed a treaty, again at the Vatican.

The possibility of a papal role in the Central American crisis was sometimes raised during the 1980s. During the papal visit to the region in 1985, the Venezuelan president alluded to the Contadora negotiations and said that the pope's presence brought hope for dialogue and peace in Central America. Speculation grew after the pope said during a mass that he extended a special "embrace of peace" to the embattled churches of El Salvador and Nicaragua.

He later made it clear, however, that the situation was not propitious; the requirements for a successful effort on his part did not exist. The pope seemed to defer to other peace efforts being pursued.

Over the years, papal nuncios have attempted to mediate in internal as well as other international conflicts. They did so when dictators fell in the 1940s and 1950s in Colombia, Costa Rica, and Venezuela, for example, and they attempted to avoid civil war in the Dominican Republic in 1965.

When Pope Paul VI arrived in Bogotá on August 22, 1968, he became the first pontiff to visit Latin America. He attended the World Eucharistic Congress and, afterward, addressed the meeting of CELAM at Medellin. Pope John Paul II made an extensive series of visits to all parts of Latin America after becoming pope in October 1978. In February 1979 he visited the Dominican Republic, Mexico, and the Bahamas; in July 1980 he traveled to Brazil; and in 1983, to Central America. In January and February 1985 he visited fifteen cities in twelve days in Venezuela, Ecuador, and Peru, with a stopover in (Anglican) Trinidad-Tobago. In July 1986 he spent a week in Colombia; in April 1987 he spent two weeks visiting ten cities in Chile and Argentina; and in May 1988 he visited Southern Cone nations.

This extensive papal attention to Latin America is due to the fact that, before the end of the twentieth century, the region will contain a majority of the entire world's Roman Catholics. Moreover, the Latin American church is severely divided over an array of fundamental issues. In fact, it is the region that has most given rise to new and controversial movements within Roman Catholicism. Those movements are intimately related to the issues of Latin American social change.

The Church and Social Change

After World War I, new issues began to transcend those previously associated with church-state conflict. New social and economic concerns increasingly divided the church and complicated papal–Latin American relations. Important religious changes entered in the Latin American political experience in the 1930s with the formation of Christian Democratic parties, Catholic Action groups, and Catholic labor unions. The upper clergy still tended to be conservative, but many local priests and laypeople became concerned with questions of the church's role in achieving social justice and economic development.

Beginning in the 1960s, social and economic change in Latin America accelerated dramatically. In response, church people included the entire spectrum: obedient conservatives, intransigent reactionaries, progressive reformers, and radical challengers seeking revolutionary transformations. In the 1960s the papacy finally addressed these issues directly, most notably in Pope John XXIII's encyclical *Mater et Magistra* (1961) and *Pacem in Terris* (1963) and Pope Paul VI's encyclical *Populorum Progreso* (1967). The worldwide ecclesiastical convention called Vatican II (1962-1965) dealt extensively with social and economic issues. Papal positions were also articulated during the numerous visits to Latin America. In general, papal policy moved away from supporting the political and social status quo, opting for some measure of reform and opposing both reaction and revolution. Despite papal statements for moderate change, however, the church was far from united; if anything, divisions intensified over social issues.

The lack of consensus within the church was clearly demonstrated during the visit of Pope Paul VI to Colombia in 1968 and those of Pope John Paul II between 1978 and 1988. The debate from the beginning solidified opposing positions that have been maintained into the late 1980s. Both popes reiterated their support for social progress but also maintained their theological conservatism and thus failed to appeal broadly to any faction. They chastised both conservatives and radicals, arguing that the church must lead in the fight against poverty and injustice and oppose the concentration of wealth and power in the hands of the few as well as abuses of political authority. They rejected as un-Christian and impractical the idea that violence was necessary to counter these injustices; but they also alienated many progressives who would otherwise agree with notions of orderly peaceful reform by reemphasizing the ban on artificial contraception contained in the encyclical *Humanae Vitae*. Church progressives and, increasingly, Latin American governments argued that without birth control and family planning programs, economic development would be impossible and, consequently, social injustice would persist.

Papal relations with the more radical movements within the Latin American church became increasingly important, and by the late 1980s related issues seemed to dominate the debate about the role of the church in social change. Some priests and laypeople argued the relevance of Marxism to Christian social change. Some expressed admiration for revolutionary hero Che Guevara, and certain "Third World" priests joined guerrilla bands and engaged in violent acts. The young Colombian priest Camilo Torres Restrepo, for example, was killed by a Colombian army unit in 1966 while fighting as a member of a guerrilla group. In fact, few church people joined guerrilla movements; the much more important radical phenomenon was what came to be known as liberation theology and the movements associated with it.

Liberation theology is, in sum, a theology of the poor. It argues that the church should play a central political role in the struggles for human rights and social and economic justice for the popular masses. A Peruvian priest, Gustavo Gutiérrez, is considered the first theologian to write about the various tenets that had been developing since the late 1950s in Latin America in terms of theology as such; in time he was joined by perhaps two dozen more liberation theologians around the region, such as the Brazilian priest Leonardo Boff. Some of their writings utilize Marxist concepts for analyzing society and some raised the question of whether violence had theological significance. For the most part, however, they emphasized the importance of the church's political role on behalf of the poor, on the grounds that since the causes of poverty were part of social and economic structures, political action was necessary if those structures were to be changed. In particular, liberation theologians helped spawn "base communities" (*comu-*

nidades eclesiales de base—CEBs). In practice, most CEBs were composed of groups of poor people who emphasized lay leadership and stressed experience and biblical traditions as sources of valid religious values.

Critics and opponents charged that liberation theology was Marxism in Christian disguise, that the gospel and atheistic materialism were inherently contradictory, and that it represented an inappropriate challenge to church authority and politicization of religion. Liberationists and their supporters replied that they sought to recover the two-millennium Judeo-Christian tradition of biblical radicalism and that Marxist analysis was merely an analytic tool for understanding modern class conflict and poverty. Peter Hebblethwaite (1985) argued that Pope John XXIII's encyclical *Pacem en Terris* justified such thinking in holding that "good and commendable elements" could be found in systems of thought that also contained "falsity." Supporters also pointed out that the charge of "politicization" implied that Latin American religion in past ages was not political, clearly an unsupportable proposition; what was new were the issues being addressed, not a political role for the church.

Pope John Paul II remained unconvinced, however. He directly confronted liberation theology on each of his trips to Latin America; in September 1984 the Holy See published a paper pointing out its errors. The papacy issued warnings to the Peruvian hierarchy about the dangers of liberation theology, silenced Leonardo Boff, and censured the two priests—Miguel D'Escoto and Ernesto Cardenal—who served in the Nicaraguan revolutionary government. The pope's opposition to liberation theology was based partly on opposition to political action on the part of the clergy—they should stress traditional pastoral concerns—and partly on the principle of obedience and defense of papal authority. Furthermore, Pope John Paul II objected to "those who distort the evangelical message and put it at the service of ideological and political strategies in search of illusory earthly liberation"; the gap between wealth and poverty was evil, he said, but the church's spiritual mission must never be relegated to a secondary place behind social concerns.

BUSINESS ENTERPRISE

Corporations as System Actors

Evolution of Corporate Actors. A multinational corporation (MNC) is a group entity with a legal personality; while corporate control remains centered within some sovereign state, the corporation exhibits a great deal of independence as an actor in the international political system. The prefix "multi" indicates that MNCs have business activities in a number of nations and have extensive resources. Most major global corporations today are MNCs; these corporations dominate the world industrial order but remain national entities domiciled in the industrial states.

Although private business enterprise has long been a part of the international scene, the MNC is a relatively new actor in world politics. International companies originally were creations and subjects of the state. For example, in colonial America the Dutch West Indies Company was chartered by the sovereign monarch and, while funded by private capital, it was subject to royal control and entitled to state protection. Over the years, however, the nature of overseas business enterprises underwent dramatic changes and, consequently, their roles as international actors changed accordingly. In the nineteenth century, business corporations began to develop in the capitalist economies in Great Britain, Western Europe, and the United States. They were not multinational in character, however; their activities and power were restricted by the states granting corporate charters. International firms were generally limited to a specific economic activity, such as banking, mining, agriculture, or manufacturing, and their life spans and total assets were limited by law. By the time of World War I, however, according to Raymond Vernon (1971a:1–2), "corporations could be formed by practically anyone for practically any purpose without limit of time or size." Even more important, he said, "corporations by this time had acquired the extraordinary right to own other corporations." Consequently, separate companies could be created to perform different aspects of a total business activity, but all of the activities would be subject to centralized control, coordination, and support. Modern corporations acquired a distinct multinational character as they began to branch out into several different sovereign jurisdictions with various enterprises linked together by a single corporate structure.

The growth of MNCs was especially significant after World War II. The size of their overseas assets dwarfed those of the past. North American, European, and Japanese companies increased their foreign assets at rapid rates in virtually all parts of the world. Later, MNCs evolved in newly industrializing parts of the world, including Latin America. Some 4,000 MNCs now exist, accounting for about 15 percent of the gross world product, but a great proportion of the activity is controlled by a small number of large corporations in a few industrial sectors. In the petroleum industry, the "Seven Sisters" dominate—Exxon (Standard Oil of New Jersey), Standard Oil of California, The Royal Dutch Shell Group, Texaco, Gulf, Mobil, and British Petroleum. Together they account for almost two-thirds of the world's oil production outside of the Communist states, control more than half of the oil tanker tonnage, and retail about half of the petroleum products on world markets. Eight automotive producers—General Motors, Ford, Chrysler, Volkswagen, Fiat, British Motors, Nissan, and Toyota—dominate global automotive markets. The electronics industry, the third largest industrial sector, is composed primarily of International Business Machines (IBM), International Telephone and Telegraph (ITT), Westinghouse, Philips, Siemens, and Hitachi. A half-dozen mining companies account for three-fourths of the international trade in metals and other ores, and only a few companies control world chemical markets.

Corporate Actors in Latin America. The growth of business enterprise in Latin America has been an important aspect of the region's international relations. Latin America has been a major recipient of foreign investment and the scene of organized business activity throughout its national history.

British capital accounted for most of the foreign investment in Latin America from the early national period until the world depression of 1930. Toward the end of the nineteenth century, French, German, and U.S. capital became significant; by then, Latin America was receiving investments from virtually every nation in Europe and some from Japan. Most of the investment was portfolio in nature, financing projects through the purchase of Latin American government bonds and leaving operational administration to local management. However, important operations were also begun by foreign entrepreneurs through direct investment and management.

Toward the end of the nineteenth century, international business actors who were to enjoy many years of large-scale activity in Latin America began to appear. The most important sectors for foreign direct investments included extractive operations (petroleum production and tin, copper, and nitrate mining); forestry and agriculture (coffee, sugar, meats, and tropical fruits, including bananas); banking; and some specialized manufacturing areas. U.S. investors, unlike investors from other nations, were as interested in direct as in portfolio investments, and Latin American markets were seen to offer U.S. companies important opportunities. After 1930 portfolio investments greatly declined for a variety of reasons (see Chapter 10) and direct investments increased. U.S. capital came to assume a dominant position; in the 1930s and 1940s no more than 300 U.S. companies dominated foreign business operations in Latin America, and by 1950 U.S. investments were twice as large as all others combined. European and Japanese investments were sharply reduced, especially by the impact of two world wars.

A few examples suffice to illustrate the growth of business actors in the Latin American region. Richard Van Alstyne (1955) offered the following case of George Drabble of Manchester as an illustration of British nineteenth-century enterprise:

> Toward the end of the 1840s Drabble left England for Buenos Aires to look after the interests of the family firm, Drabble & Bros., exporters of cotton goods. Becoming a permanent resident of Argentina, Drabble played a part in the formation of every important enterprise in that country during the next two decades. His name was connected with the Buenos Aires & Great Southern Railway (the first line to be built in Argentina), the Bank of London and the River Plate, the Buenos Aires Tramway Company, the Buenos Aires & Rosario Railway, and the River Plate Fresh Meat Company.

Beginning in the late nineteenth century in Argentina, Armour and Company and Swift and Company competed with British concerns in meat processing and exporting. Both companies expanded to Uruguay and Paraguay, and through the 1960s those three nations were important suppliers for both companies' overall operations. In Chile and Peru, U.S. mining companies dominated copper and other mineral extraction from the late nineteenth century until the 1960s; the most important of these companies were Kennecott, Anaconda, and Cerro de Pasco. By 1906 they had a combined investment in Chile of about $0.5 billion. The Singer Company was founded in Boston in 1850; from the early days of its sewing machine business it established foreign subsidiaries. By World War I, Singer was well established in all of Latin America. It remained so in the mid-1980s, with the Brazilian subsidiary one of its largest branches.

In Peru in the 1870s a Yankee adventurer and railroad builder, Henry Meiggs, built lines across the Andes and created a financial empire. In Peru at about the same time, a young Irish immigrant, William Russell Grace, began a small business of servicing ships that transported guano fertilizer. He parlayed this modest beginning into the large and highly diversified W. R. Grace and Company headquartered in New York, a trading firm operating in all of Latin America. Known as Casa Grace in Latin America, its regional operations by the 1970s had dwindled to only a minority of its global business. During the latter part of the nineteenth century, Henry Meiggs's nephew, Minor Cooper Keith, established railways in Central America and then developed some banana plantations and shipping lines to U.S. ports. In 1899, after thirty years of intense rivalry with his competitors, Keith took over most of the other small banana companies and organized the United Fruit Company, thereafter a major political actor in Central America, with headquarters in New York. In 1970 the company acquired John Morrell and Company, adding meat packing to its Chiquita banana enterprise and changing its corporate name to United Brands.

The activities of oil companies have also been important in Latin America. The Standard Oil Company of New Jersey (created in 1873 by John D. Rockefeller as the Standard Oil Trust) and the binational Royal Dutch Shell Group (a merger in 1897 of the Royal Dutch Petroleum Company and the British-owned Shell Transport and Trading Company) established major operations in Mexico and Venezuela after the discovery of oil in both nations in the 1890s. The largest single petroleum operation in Latin America for many years was run in Venezuela by the Creole Oil Company, a subsidiary of Standard Oil. Both Standard and Shell had difficulties with Mexico beginning with the revolution in 1910 and were expropriated in 1938. In the 1930s Venezuela became the principal supplier for both companies, remaining so until their Middle East operations surpassed Venezuelan production in the 1960s. Venezuela nationalized the Standard and Shell operations in 1975. Gulf, Texaco, and other oil companies have also been active in a number of Latin American nations. They continue to operate in several countries, although they, along with Standard and Shell, have been important targets of Latin American nationalists and have suffered expropriations, such as in Peru and Bolivia in the late 1960s.

European banks became well established in the region during the nineteenth century and have remained so to the present day. Among the most important was the Bank of London and South America (BOLSA), a joint Canadian-British chartered enterprise. It was acquired by Lloyds Bank of London in 1971. The U.S. Federal Reserve Act became effective in June 1914, allowing U.S. banks to establish overseas branches. They were led by the National City Bank of New York (later First National City Bank, and then Citibank), which in 1914 opened its first overseas branch in Buenos Aires; considerable and continuous activity throughout the region ensued. Other U.S. banks followed suit, with the Chase Manhattan Bank, the Bank of Boston, and the Bank of America prominent among them.

After World War II, U.S. and European companies placed a new emphasis on manufacturing, retailing, communications, and service industries in addition to the traditional concentration on extractive, agricultural, and trading concerns. International Telephone and Telegraph (ITT) became a major and controversial actor in Latin America. Founded in 1920 by Virgin Islander Sosthenes Behn as a small telephone company in Puerto Rico, ITT became a worldwide telephone and cable communications firm operating extensively in Latin America. The Ford, Chrysler, General Motors, Volkswagen, Fiat, and Renault automotive companies placed assembly plants in Argentina, Brazil, and Mexico. Sears, Roebuck and Company founded a chain of stores in several parts of the region, selling goods produced mostly by local industries. The hotel industry expanded far beyond the long-popular tourist areas in Mexico and the Caribbean. Much of the business initially belonged to the Intercontinental Hotel Corporation, a subsidiary of Pan American World Airways. In the 1960s the Sheraton and Hilton chains expanded significantly into Latin America; Sheraton was acquired by ITT. Japanese corporations did not engage in overseas production facilities to the same extent as U.S. and European companies; rather, they sold products through large trading companies serving the industrial firms through overseas offices.

Important investment companies have also appeared on the Latin American scene. Atlantic Community Development Group for Latin America (ADELA) was established in 1956 as a private multinational consortium sponsoring private foreign investment in Latin America. It is capitalized by contributions from U.S. and European firms to provide financial backing for new enterprises by Latin American businesspeople in a variety of fields. International Basic Economy Corporation (IBEC) was started by Nelson Rockefeller in 1947 to introduce new ventures to underdeveloped areas for both profit and local development. Significant Latin American ventures included the hybrid corn business in Brazil and the introduction of "supermarkets" to Venezuela, Peru, and Argentina.

Several multibusiness associations having a primary concern with Latin America have been organized. A nonprofit organization supported by member corporations, the United States Inter-American Council, was founded in New York in 1958. Its name was changed to Council for Latin America in 1965 and, in 1970, to Council of the Americas; it also opened a Washington office. The Council's stated purpose is "to further understanding and acceptance of the role of private enterprise as a positive force for the development of the Americas." The Inter-American Council for Commerce and Production (known by its Spanish acronym CICYP) was established in 1960 by U.S. and Latin American companies, individual businesspersons and economists, and developmental organizations. At its meetings in U.S. and Latin American cities, CICYP has stressed the role of private enterprise in Latin American economic integration, active business participation in the making of public economic policy, and the need to stimulate foreign private investments through such vehicles as ADELA.

Business Foreign Policy

The main operational goal of both foreign and domestic corporate policy is assumed to be the maximization of profits. Business enterprises, like states, act in their own interests, which, ultimately, are survival, security, and well-being. Once the fundamental concerns of assuring survival and securing resources are provided for, policy success is measured in terms of monetary profit and corporate growth. Thus, foreign operations are rationalized in economic terms, principally the beneficial employment of capital resources. Modern technology has increasingly stimulated the growth of large companies requiring access to global markets, and the world economy encourages direct overseas investment. But international and multinational business relations, involving as they do corporate relations with both foreign and home governments, are inseparable from politics. Companies have used many of the same strategies in external relations as states have, including cooperative ones such as negotiation and persuasion as well as coercion and subversion. Consequently, MNCs have foreign departments or overseas divisions devoted to "foreign policy-making" and execution—these operations are complete with a foreign service and interact with sovereign states.

The image of MNCs in Latin America continue to suffer from past and present excesses. They have negotiated with sovereign states, but they have also engaged in espionage; they have pursued unsavory activities designed to influence foreign officials, such as bribery; and they have been involved in the subversion of governments. Spectacular examples of past business intervention include United Fruit Company activities in Central America from the early part of the twentieth century through the 1930s. Coercion through threats of violence to force small farmers to sell exclusively to United Fruit at company prices, bribery of public officials, and even the sponsoring of coups earned United Fruit the popular name of *el pulpo* (the octopus). Oil company ventures in Mexico and Peru also often involved corrupt practices. In a more recent example, oil companies whose interests had been expropriated in Cuba by the Castro regime exerted pressure on the U.S. government in favor of the Bay of Pigs intervention. In addition, ITT took measures in Chile to disrupt the Marxist government of Salvador Allende in 1970–1973. Bribery of Latin American officials by U.S. companies, including United Brands in Honduras and Gulf Oil in Bolivia, was revealed in 1975. Questions remain about whether coercive and corrupt tactics are the exception or the rule, and whether the dramatic cases mentioned above are atypical or fairly representative of activities by business actors in Latin America.

Evidence also exists to support the view that U.S. companies cooperate with their Latin American hosts as good corporate citizens. For example, Stephen Rosenfield, writing in the *Washington Post* on January 28, 1972, reported on a series of discussions about relations between U.S. business firms and Latin American government officials, sponsored by the Council on Foreign Relations in 1971. He concluded that the proceedings revealed "not a calculated or malevolent or exploitation-minded conspiracy of the bureaucratic-investment complex"; rather, "there was evident an inclination to consider new forms of American economic participation on terms politically acceptable in the hemisphere, and a parallel inclination to avoid the kinds of political confrontation that would spoil the chances for future profit."

The issue of excessive foreign business profits from Latin American operations is difficult to analyze. Ascertaining the profits of foreign enterprises has never been easy, especially since the arrival of holding companies and large corporations with networks of branches and affiliates in several nations, which often issue "no-par" common stock (Rippy, 1958:47). As Hunter and Foley (1975:208–209) noted, no definition exists of what constitutes a "fair" or "excessive" rate of return; furthermore, the meaningfulness of available data is questionable. These authors, defining an annual rate of return as the ratio of total earnings to the total outstanding investment before the payment of corporate income taxes, pointed out that caution should be exercised in analyzing published figures, primarily because of the nature of accounting procedures. Rates of return depend on the value placed on assets, which is difficult to determine precisely; capital is often invested in kind as well as money, and inflation makes further valuations problematical. In addition, in order to show a lower rate of return, foreign companies may purposely overvalue their assets or sell their locally produced products to their external parent at low prices.

Having entered the above caveats, some tentative conclusions may be made about foreign business profits in Latin America. With regard to British investments, Van Alstyne (1955:153) concluded "that few British investors enjoyed anything better than a small return for their money, that the risks in many cases (particularly mining) were great and the losses considerable, and that salaried employees, manufacturers in Great Britain, exporters and shipping companies benefitted more than did the direct investor." Research by J. Fred Rippy focusing on U.S. investments during the first half of the twentieth century disclosed high yields for a few business organizations. Dividends paid by some small mining companies in Mexico were fantastic— one paid an annual average dividend of 945.8 percent from 1903 to 1927, and another an annual average of 124.5 percent from 1908 to 1926. Rippy calculated that the large mining and petroleum companies probably made large profits on their Latin American investments. He noted that Creole Petroleum Company in Venezuela paid an annual average dividend of 31.8 percent on its common stock from 1936 to 1951, and that International Petroleum Company in Peru and Colombia returned an average annual dividend of more than 40 percent from 1921 to 1950. However, Rippy said, many foreign business organizations in Latin America yielded only moderate profits or suffered heavy losses. Most agricultural enterprises had only a few profitable years, with the exceptions of the Cuban American

Sugar company and the United Fruit Company; those attempting to grow plantation rubber in Mexico and Central America from 1890 to 1910 lost heavily. Finally, railways and public utilities were not among the business organizations enjoying high yields.

For the first ten years following World War II, the highest returns for U.S. investors in Latin America came from petroleum (24.4 percent) and agriculture (16.8 percent—mainly sugar). Returns came to 11.5 percent from mining, 14.4 percent from manufacturing, and 17.3 percent from trading companies. The lowest returns were from public utilities. The average return for the decade was 14.6 percent per year. During the period from 1960 to 1967, average rates of return for U.S. investments in manufacturing were generally lower in Latin America (10.3 percent) than in all other world regions except Canada (Rippy, 1958:47–52; Hunter and Foley, 1975:208).

Latin American Multinational Corporations

MNCs based in developing states, a relatively new phenomenon, are emerging as an important force in international relations. Since the early 1970s, a significant number of them have established or acquired foreign subsidiaries and joint ventures. In Latin America, the most important firms have come from Argentina and Brazil, joining those from Hong Kong, India, the Philippines, Singapore, South Korea, and Taiwan in taking the lead among newly industrialized and other developing states. Argentine firms started overseas investment as early as the 1950s; their annual foreign investments reached an average of about $4 million during most of the 1970s and increased after 1977. About half of those investments were in manufacturing, including machine tools, food, and automobiles. Brazilian investments, mostly in the nine neighboring South American countries, reached $60 million by 1978. Brazilian firms have also started manufacturing operations in several African countries, with foreign expansion led by state-controlled enterprises.

LABOR ORGANIZATIONS

Labor Unions as International Actors

A number of regionally organized labor organizations, comprising national Latin American members and usually affiliated with some larger world movement, have been significant twentieth-century actors in the Latin American subsystem. International and multinational labor development has been slow and sporadic, however, and conflicts have often arisen between the different organizations. Latin American labor movements—stimulated by industrialization and the growth of the urban proletariat beginning in the late nineteenth century, but also including mine workers as an important labor sector—have tended to be organized along national rather than international lines. Labor eventually became politically strong in some states, especially Mexico, Chile, Argentina, Bolivia, Venezuela, Colombia, and Peru, and gained importance in Brazil, Uruguay, and Costa Rica. It has enjoyed less success in the rest of Latin America. The first regional organizations were founded soon after World War I, but their development was slowed by disputes among national members about goals, and they were characterized by clashes between contending workers with opposing ideologies.

The Pan American Federation of Labor (PAFL), was organized in 1918 largely on the combined initiative of the American Federation of Labor (AFL) and the Regional Confederation of Mexican Labor (CROM), which was founded in the same year. PAFL was effective only until the late 1920s, although it was not formally disbanded until after World War II. Its most active members, in addition to U.S. and Mexican unions, were largely those from Central America and the Caribbean islands. PAFL engaged primarily in extending financial assistance to its poorer members and in public protests about U.S. imperialism in Mexico and the Caribbean.

About the time that PAFL ceased to be effective in the late 1920s, two new and more radical regional labor confederations appeared. Both were established in 1929 and reflected the split within Latin American labor movements between anarcho-syndicalists and Communists. Those unions associated with the former ideology founded the Continental Association of American Workers (Asociación Continental Americana de Trabajadores— ACAT). By 1929 anarcho-syndicalists had lost control of much of the Latin American labor movement to Communists, and ACAT never had much political impact even though it continued to maintain a formal organization. Of more importance was its Communist-dominated rival, the Latin American Syndicalist Confederation (Confederación Sindical Latino Americana—CSLA), a product of the period of Communist history during which the Communist International instructed local Communist parties to establish separate labor union organizations under their control. Consequently, national affiliates of CSLA were established in those Latin American states where Communist parties existed. Some important national trade union organizations, insisting on autonomy of action, refused to join CSLA because it was directed from the Soviet Union. The most important example was the refusal of CROM of Mexico to join, even though it had declared itself both socialist and syndicalist. CSLA was dissolved in 1938 and superseded by a more broadly based labor organization.

The Confederation of Latin American Workers (Confederación de Trabajadores de América Latina—CTAL) represented the most ambitious and important effort to establish an all-inclusive regional trade union to date when its founding congress met in Mexico City in 1938. CTAL involved collaboration among most Communist, socialist, and liberal labor unions and paralleled popular front political party coalitions being formed at the same time. The guiding personality and long-term leader of CTAL was Vicente Lombardo Toledano, the radical Mexican intellectual, politician, and labor leader. Lombardo organized CTAL with the help of other Latin American trade union leaders, most prominently those from Cuba, Chile, and Colombia. Within a few years after its founding, CTAL's leadership became Communist-dominated and pro-Soviet. Lombardo's personal power declined after 1946 when his own union in Mexico, which he had founded in 1936, repudiated his leadership. Furthermore, with the onset of the Cold War in 1947, collaboration ended between Communists and non-Communists in political parties and labor movements, and Communist labor influence declined drastically. CTAL lost the affiliation of several national unions that left in 1948 to found the Inter-American Federation of Labor. Until then CTAL had been the only labor confederation existing in Latin America. In 1950 it became the regional affiliate of the World Federation of Trade Unions (WFTU). Most national trade unions belonged to WFTU, a worldwide labor confederation, with headquarters in Paris, founded in 1945. But in 1949 most of its non-Communist affiliates withdrew; in 1956 WFTU headquarters were moved to Prague. Generally a Communist-dominated association with policy largely determined by the Soviet government, CTAL eventually was disbanded and replaced by the Single Central Association of Latin American Workers (Central Unica de Trabajadores de América Latina—CUTAL), but it lost a number of national member unions during the process of reorganization.

The Inter-American Federation of Labor (Confederación Interamericana de Trabajadores—CIT) was organized in 1948 by non-Communist exmembers of CTAL and other trade unions with the specific purpose of countering Communist influence in the Latin American labor movement. The efforts of the AFL of the United States and the Aprista party of Peru constituted the driving force behind the founding of CIT. CIT membership was inter-American in character, comprising twelve Latin American national labor confederations and the AFL of the United States and of Canada. CIT was superseded in 1951 with the founding in Mexico City of the Inter-American Regional Organization of Workers (Organización Regional Interamericana de Trabajadores—ORIT), which absorbed additional affiliates of CTAL at the time of its founding. ORIT was the American affiliate of the International Confederation of Free Trade Unions (ICFTU), founded in London in 1949 under U.S. and British labor leadership by those unions that withdrew from the Communist-controlled WFTU; its headquarters later moved to Brussels. ICFTU has worked closely with labor-oriented agencies in the United Nations system; it is especially interested in worker training and education. The AFL-CIO of the United States has ties with ORIT and has given it financial and technical aid.

A potentially powerful rival to both CTAL and ORIT appeared in 1952 with the formation of the Unionized Latin American Workers' Group (Agrupación de Trabajadores Latino Americanos Sindicalizados—ATLAS) by Argentine president Juan Perón. ATLAS, under the direction of the General Confederation of Labor of Argentina, was intended as an instrument of Peronista foreign policy to help extend Argentine influence in Spanish America. As an international labor organization, it organized and affiliated as members a number of national labor confederations outside of Argentina. ATLAS was only of temporary importance, however; it disbanded after Perón fell from power in 1955. CTAL had offered an alliance to ATLAS in 1953, but it had been refused; after 1955 former ATLAS unions either joined ORIT or steered an independent course.

In 1954 an additional regional labor organization was founded, the Latin American Confederation of Christian Trade Unionists (Confederación Latino Americana de Sindicalistas Cristianos—CLASC). This organization is the Latin American regional affiliate of the International Federation of Christian Trade Unions founded in The Hague in 1920; its headquarters was later moved to Brussels. The parent world organization's program originally was based on the papal encyclical *Rerum Novarum* (1891), and later on the *Quadragerimo Anno* (1931), although its affiliates include Protestant as well as Roman Catholic federations. CLASC also has links to international associations of Christian Democratic political parties and trade unions. Its own national affiliates in Latin America include Christian trade unions and federations and a Catholic workers' association. CLASC, clearly leftist, is critical of the larger ORIT, which it considers to be dominated by the conservative U.S. labor movement. CLASC is also anti-Communist, however, and thus opposes the moribund CUTAL.

U.S. Labor and Latin America

The U.S. labor movement has exhibited alternating periods of concern with and indifference to Latin American regional organizations. After its involvement with PAFL from 1918 until the late 1920s, the AFL had few contacts with the Latin American labor movement until after World War II, when it was instrumental in organizing CIT and the successor ORIT. In 1946 the AFL sent Serafino Romualdi as its "labor ambassador" to Latin America. Romualdi negotiated with non-Communist trade unions and federations both in and out of the Communist-led CTAL, and within two years the rival CIT had been established. Romualdi had served briefly with the Latin American department of the International Ladies Garment Workers Union before going to Latin America. Upon his return in 1948 he became head of the inter-American affairs section of the AFL and held a similar position with the AFL-CIO after the U.S. labor merger in 1955. Romualdi also served as assistant secretary of ORIT and labor adviser to the Alliance for Progress; he retired in 1964. Romualdi died three years later in Mexico while on a lecture trip to the Cuernavaca Labor College run by ORIT.

In 1961 the AFL-CIO and a group of U.S. business corporations active in Latin America founded a U.S. government–financed union-industry group called the American Institute for Free Labor Development (AIFLD). Romualdi was appointed its first director. The purpose of AIFLD was to encourage the development of non-Communist trade unions in Latin America. A staff study by the U.S. Senate Foreign Relations Committee in 1968 criticized the AIFLD for being preoccupied with anticommunism in its Latin American operations. After noting that "the problem of Communist subversion of the Latin American labor movement has been central" to AIFLD activities, the study concluded:

This overriding preoccupation has led to three results: (1) It has tended to give AIFLD the appearance of being little more than an instrument of the cold war; (2) It has led to a polarized view of the political spectrum in Latin American labor; and (3) It has involved the AFL-CIO in some awkward contradictions of its principle that trade unions should not be tied to political parties.

Changes in the foreign policies of U.S. labor in the late 1960s, extending into the 1980s, have had important implications for its Latin American relations—namely, a long period of reduced contacts. The AFL-CIO supported free trade as long as the balance of trade was favorable to the United States. The only qualifications were that agreements should be negotiated with states whose exports were harming specific U.S. industries and that the government should pay adjustment allowances for workers who were displaced because of foreign competition. But in the late 1960s, when the United States began to suffer large trade deficits, labor policy changed. The AFL-CIO began to champion protectionism in U.S. trade, favored a decrease rather than an increase in world economic interdependency, and drew back from its own commitments to international labor organizations.

In the early 1970s, U.S. labor leaders began to argue that protectionism was the only way for U.S. labor to guard against the effects of international competition. That position has continued into the late 1980s. As trade balances turned against the United States, U.S. labor turned against free trade. Labor leaders complained that the tariff code and tax laws encouraged U.S.-based MNCs to manufacture in foreign settings at a lower cost and return finished products back to the United States. Consequently, they charged, U.S.-based MNCs were destroying jobs at home in their search for cheap labor abroad; in other words, by exporting jobs to their foreign subsidiaries and affiliates where lower labor costs prevailed, in order to produce goods that underpriced U.S.-made products, MNCs were quickly eliminating U.S. jobs. Arguing that labor was helpless in the changed international situation, U.S. labor leaders changed their trade policies away from supporting free-trade legislation.

TRANSNATIONAL POLITICAL PARTIES

Political Parties as Independent Actors

Political parties are groups that seek to obtain public office and political power by presenting candidates to the electorate. Transnational political parties transcend national boundaries and seek international acceptance in an organized way. The affiliates to a transnational party share a philosophy and common goals to some degree, coordinate their interests and ideas, and offer mutual support. The national identities of transnational parties may be primary, but their connections across national boundaries are discernible.

A number of transnational parties have been active in Latin America. The most important ones originated outside the region and later established Latin American counterparts, including the Communist parties organized in the

Communist International, the Social Democratic parties in the Socialist International, and the Christian Democratic parties in the Christian Democratic World Union. Political parties in the United States are only peripherally relevant to Latin America. The Democratic and Republican parties are essentially national parties and not internationalized. They have interests and sympathies abroad, but have not established systematic transnational ties with kindred parties. Their Puerto Rican counterparts are active only in the context of U.S. national elections, in which Puerto Ricans vote.

The Comintern and the Socialist International both emerged from the nineteenth-century European socialist movement. The First International, originally called the Workers' International Association, was formed by Karl Marx in 1864 and dissolved in 1876. The Second International (the Labor International) held its first meeting in 1889 and continued until its collapse in 1914 with the outbreak of World War I. Neither the First nor Second International involved Latin America; except for small sections in the United States, both were European organizations.

Members of the internationals shared the goal of uniting the workers of the world and taking power from their class enemies, but tensions increased over the years between totalitarian and democratic strains of Marxism. They achieved separate identities after World War I and thereafter went their separate ideological and organizational ways as bitter rivals. The Third International, also called the Communist International and known as the Comintern, was founded by Lenin in 1919 following the successful Bolshevik Revolution of 1917 and the establishment of the Soviet Union. With the purpose of organizing revolutions through Communist parties in every country throughout the world, the Comintern developed extensive Latin American connections. It was dissolved in 1943.

Social Democrats opposing Bolshevist totalitarianism claimed to reconvene the Second International in 1920; in 1923 they called themselves the Socialist and Labor International and explicitly disassociated from the Comintern as a rival organization. The Socialist International remained an essentially European movement, with only a few small American elements. It was interrupted by World War II, but in 1945 it reorganized as the International Socialist Conference with headquarters in London. It took the name Socialist International in 1951 at the pivotal Frankfurt Conference, which adopted the "Principles and Tasks of Democratic Socialism." In time the Socialist International expanded to include Social Democratic and Labor parties in many countries, including those in Latin America.

In the meantime, another competing party emerged with yet another distinct orientation. Christian Democratic parties appeared around Europe in the 1890s espousing a sort of clerical Fabian socialism. More interest groups than political parties, they defended Roman Catholic interests on the grass-roots level. The European organizations broadened their bases and became real political parties in the 1920s. They were still Roman Catholic in outlook, but they sought to appeal to the interests of broader segments of the electorate. They also shifted from socialism to traditional liberalism.

This fundamental change was in opposition to events within the socialist movement—both the adoption of bolshevism in the Communist International and the rise of trade union socialism in the Socialist International. The transnational Christian Democratic World Union was not formed until the late 1940s. By then its traditional liberal tenets (such as individualism, limited government roles, and laissez faire economics) were identified with postwar conservatism. The transnational organization included Latin American counterparts.

Both the Social Democratic and Christian Democratic parties in Europe went through evolutionary stages of development that are relevant to understanding their Latin American connections. They gained governmental power in the 1920s and 1930s in Europe, but their general ineffectiveness convinced them of the need for broader electoral appeal. The religious base of the Christian Democrats precluded their appealing to anticlerical elements, while the trade unionist Social Democrats could make few inroads with propertied classes or industrial interests. After World War II they reduced their ideological insistence in a successful concerted effort to broaden their political bases and consequently became the two major European parties. At the Frankfurt Conference in 1951, the Social Democrats acknowledged the utility of mixed private and public economic sectors, depending on individual national conditions, and in 1959 they formally disavowed Marxism and social revolution. Soon thereafter the Christian Democrats came to accept a degree of state intervention into economic and social affairs. Fundamental differences remained, however. In general, Christian Democrats may be characterized as moderate conservatives with a strong right wing, and the Social Democrats as moderate socialists with a strong left wing. Latin American counterparts did not necessarily follow the same process.

The Communist International and Latin America

In an earlier era international communism could have been called a major global transnational political party. After its founding in March 1919, the Comintern headquarters was in Moscow throughout its twenty-four-year existence. The Comintern included members in almost all countries, and they sent delegates to Moscow to plan the promotion of Communist revolutions outside of the Soviet Union. The Soviet government denied that the Comintern was an instrument of the Soviet state, although in fact it viewed the transnational organization as a tool of Soviet policy.

The founding of local Communist parties and the Latin American section of the Comintern created opportunities for extending Marxist-Leninist revolutionary activities in the region. Under Comintern guidance, the Mexican Communist party was more successful in fostering communism in Central America than in Mexico itself, as Mexicans preferred to make their own revolution without outside assistance. In South America the Argentine Communist party was the first to join the Comintern. A South American Comintern secretariat was set up in Buenos Aires in 1930 and assigned the

task of strengthening Communist influence and supervising the flow of
agents in the Southern Cone.

Between the two world wars, Soviet policy was aimed at creating loyal
and disciplined local Communist parties. Some success was achieved. In
Chile, the organization of a strong Communist party contributed to formation
of a popular front coalition that brought the Radical party to power in
1938. Thus, Chile became the third country, after France and Spain, to be
ruled by popular fronts. Otherwise, the Soviet strategy was a failure.

Communism faced the continuing dilemma of reconciling Soviet foreign
policy interests, the narrow Comintern sectarian approach, and the needs of
local Communist parties. In Latin America in the late 1920s and throughout
the 1930s, Comintern tactics made little progress toward revolution, but
they did provoke a rupture of Soviet diplomatic relations with Mexico and
Argentina in 1930, Chile in 1932, and Brazil and Uruguay in 1936. Dogmatic
Comintern directives to local Communist parties and the Soviet preoccupation
with domestic and proximate international problems did not enhance revolutionary chances. Furthermore, radical Latin American nationalists initially
were more inclined to opt for Italian fascism than for Soviet communism.

In 1943 Moscow announced that the Comintern had been dissolved.
Throughout the 1920s and 1930s, the Soviet Union had remained the world's
only Communist country; obviously, the Comintern purpose of sparking
revolution elsewhere had not succeeded. Thereafter, Communist parties
continued to work for the overthrow of established governments without
the Comintern; in Latin America they have succeeded nowhere. For a brief
period during and immediately after World War II, from about 1941 to
1947, the Soviet Union and Latin American Communist parties did enjoy
influence in the region. The wartime alliance between the Soviet Union and
the Western powers facilitated the expansion of Soviet diplomatic contacts
in the region, and Latin American Communist parties achieved a certain
level of prestige. Those parties were directed by Moscow to support the
Allied war effort and to use their influence to prevent strikes and the
disruption of war production. The onset of the cold war in 1947, however,
reversed the trend. Soviet relations with Latin America became increasingly
strained as Stalin bitterly criticized Latin American governments for their
close ties with the United States and demanded that the local parties publicly
declare their loyalty to the Soviet Union. Wartime goodwill toward the
Soviet Union dissipated and the newly intransigent Communist parties were
outlawed. Better relations were not possible until after Stalin's death in
1953; but the internecine strife among various revolutionary groups after
the Castro revolution of 1959 severely detracted from the Communist parties'
positions.

The Socialist International and Latin America

Social democracy has a long history in Latin America. Some local parties,
borrowing their social-democratic inspiration from Europe, date from the
first decade of the twentieth century. The importance to Latin America of

the Socialist International (SI), however, is a much more recent phenomenon. In fact, its real impact as an actor in Latin American international relations dates from about 1976 when it began taking more interest in the Third World. Since then, the SI has been more active in Latin America than in any other region outside of Europe.

Despite the expressed desire at the Frankfurt Conference in 1951 to open to the Third World and develop closer links with Latin American, Asian, and African parties, the SI kept its essentially European character. In the 1970s some European leaders, notably Willy Brandt, Bruno Kreisky, and Olaf Palme, strongly advocated expanding membership into Third World regions. They argued that social democratic solidarity and mutual support would have a positive influence in furthering the struggle for social and economic equality on the part of popular movements. Willy Brandt accepted the presidency of the SI at its general Geneva Conference in November 1976, partly on the condition that the SI would actively seek institutional cooperation with like-minded Third World parties and movements. Political parties and organizations from forty-two countries were represented at the Geneva Conference. By the mid-1980s, the SI global membership comprised sixty-four parties and affiliated groups from fifty countries, fifty-two observer parties and liberation fronts from thirty seven countries, and ten international organizations as observers. Those from Europe were in a distinct minority.

Latin American membership in the SI grew rapidly. Two of the three heads of state present at the Geneva Conference in 1976 were from Latin America: President Carlos Andrés Pérez of Venezuela representing the Democratic Action party, and President Daniel Oduber of Costa Rica for the National Liberation party. The SI organized an ongoing Regional Conference on Latin America and the Caribbean, which held periodic meetings in different Latin American capitals. By 1983 Latin American parties and organizations who were members of the SI included the Dominican Revolutionary party, the National Liberation party of Costa Rica, the Radical party of Chile, the Democratic Action party of Venezuela, the Febrerista Revolutionary party of Paraguay, the Ecuadorian Democratic Left, the Popular Socialist party of Argentina, the Jamaican People's National party, the New Jewel Movement of Grenada, the Progressive Labour party of St. Lucia, the Working People's Alliance of Guyana, the Independence party of Puerto Rico, APRA of Peru, the Democratic Labor party of Brazil, the Nicaraguan Sandinist Front, the Panamanian Democratic Revolutionary party, the Bolivian National Revolutionary Movement of the Left, and certain groups in El Salvador, Haiti, and Honduras.

The SI has addressed a large number of issues concerning Latin America, both directly and indirectly. Among the first and continuing issues have been the New International Economic Order (NIEO) and disarmament and arms control. At Geneva in 1976 the first great issue discussed was the new economic world order resolution asking for the reduction of inequalities, a commitment to economic solidarity, and satisfaction of the vital needs of all nations. The NIEO continued as a major topic at subsequent meetings, reflecting Brandt's views on the NIEO and the SI's new openness to the Third World. Calls were made for a new international financial and monetary system that would diminish the debts of the developing countries. Other resolutions emphasized disarmament, partly on the grounds that it would release resources for development. The Latin American nuclear-free zone treaty was viewed with great favor. The SI also backed the 1983 reports of the Brandt Commission and the Paline Commission on development and disarmament, respectively.

A second set of major issues with particular relevance for Latin America dealt with democracy, dictatorship, and human rights. Over the years a number of resolutions were passed on general subjects as well as on issues involving specifically named countries. Resolutions were passed, for example, expressing regret over the proliferation of military dictatorships institutionalizing the use of terror and torture; supporting the peoples' struggles for a democratic system that respects human rights and social development; and calling for an end to arbitrary detention, tortures, and killings and demanding the restoration of political freedom and the right of political parties and trade unions to work freely and openly. Other resolutions denounced disappearances, arbitrary detention, and persecution in Chile, Argentina, Uruguay, El Salvador, and Guatemala; expressed solidarity with democratic elements in Guyana, Suriname, Haiti, El Salvador, Bolivia, and Paraguay against dictatorial regimes; welcomed democratic elections in the Dominican Republic, Ecuador, Peru, Bolivia, Brazil, Argentina, and Uruguay; and hoped that the end of the Somoza dynasty would lead to the democratization of Nicaragua as well as of all of Central America. Other statements expressed support for the Sandinistas and denounced U.S. policy toward Nicaragua; supported the New Jewel Movement in Grenada; supported the Panamanian-U.S. treaties for the decolonization of the Panama Canal; declared solidarity with the Puerto Rican Independence party; and asked for humane treatment of illegal immigrants. An attempt by the Portuguese Socialist party to denounce the Cuban dictatorship was not carried, although the presence of Soviet, Cuban, and East German forces in Ethiopia was condemned. In August 1977 the SI organized a meeting with the Chilean Popular Union to elaborate an action program for the democratization of Chile. The Central American crisis beginning in the late 1970s occupied a great deal of SI attention, continuing into the late 1980s. While the SI was able to make collective statements unfavorable to U.S. policy, deep divisions existed over attitudes toward the Sandinista government in Nicaragua.

GUERRILLA GROUPS

Guerrilla Insurgents as International Actors

Guerrilla groups have been a part of the Latin American scene since the early nineteenth century wars for independence and of international significance since that time. They have been most prominent, however, since the latter half of the 1950s. The importance of guerrilla groups in Latin America declined in the 1970s as counterinsurgency operations by governments (including especially repressive military regimes) proved effective. In certain states, however, they remained or reappeared as important actors.

The nature and scope of the meaning of guerrilla insurgency should be made clear. John D. Martz (1970:143) defined guerrilla warfare as "armed protest against nationally constituted authority by an organized force other than the regular military establishment pursuing a set of broadly explicit objectives which extend beyond a mere change of governmental personnel and denial of legitimacy to the existing regime." In the same vein, Samuel P. Huntington (1974:3) said that insurgency, which challenges political systems at a fundamental level and employs violence to bring about the collapse of an incumbent regime, should be distinguished from other forms of violence aimed at reaping rewards from the political system (such as power, money, or recognition).

A further definitional problem is the indiscriminate way in which the terms "terrorist" and "terrorism" have come to be used. These terms have emotional content that may reveal political preferences rather than analytic precision. It has become a cliché to note that one person's terrorist is another's freedom fighter. The result has been a certain conceptual confusion surrounding the subject of subnational entities that engage in violence against the existing order. (The following discussion on this point is suggested by Radu, 1984.)

Terrorism is the intentional use of violence against the general public (noncombatants) or against government officials for political purposes. For terrorists, terrorism is the principal component of ideology and the use of terror an exclusive instrument. This concept of "terrorist" is too narrow to define the organized insurgent guerrilla groups, which are the important actors in the Latin American context. Guerrillas do not necessarily employ the use of terror, and when they do, it is part of a larger set of instruments. Thus, guerrillas may avoid indiscriminate use of violence and still be defined as guerrillas, whereas terrorists, by definition, engage essentially in terrorism. While all guerrilla groups in Latin America have eventually used terror on some level (some have refrained more than others), few purely terrorist groups have existed. In the late 1960s, however, with the rise of urban guerrilla warfare, this distinction between insurgency and terrorism was blurred. The revival of guerrilla warfare in the late 1970s seemed to once again emphasize the distinction. Many terrorists have come from the radical right, such as the death squads that have operated in Argentina, Brazil, Guatemala, and El Salvador. They usually have had government connections and have been devoted to preserving the status quo, not destroying it.

Guerrillas and terrorists have other distinguishing characteristics. Terrorists tend to aim at the general public and individual government officials but recognize that they are not equipped to confront security forces effectively and try to avoid them. Guerrillas engage the security forces as primary targets. Terrorist groups tend to be small, organized around isolated cells in order to escape detection. Guerrillas have more complex organizations and utilize a hierarchical military command structure.

Latin American Guerrilla Movements

The model for guerrilla groups in contemporary Latin America was provided by the successful Castro movement in Cuba. In December 1956 Fidel Castro and his band of eighty-two guerrillas landed on the northeastern coast of Cuba in the old yacht *Granma*, initiating a two-year insurgency against dictator Fulgencio Batista. The small group, known as the 26th of July Movement, suffered initial heavy losses in encounters with the regular army, and only a dozen survivors made their way into the mountainous eastern portion of the island called the Sierra Maestra. From there guerrilla activities increased and the Batista regime was overthrown; on January 1, 1959, Castro marched into Havana and assumed power as the leader of the Cuban state.

Fidelista movements became widespread around Latin America, seeking to emulate the Cuban success and looking to Havana for leadership. Not until twenty years later in Nicaragua, however, did a second movement succeed in destroying an existing political system and gaining control of the state. While most Latin America guerrilla groups looked to Cuba for leadership and Castro exercised some influence over them, only a modicum of effort was made to organize these groups internationally. In December 1965 the Organization of Latin American Solidarity (OLAS) was organized under Cuban auspices as an agency to coordinate regional guerrilla activity. OLAS, a confederation of twenty-seven Latin American revolutionary movements, held its first conference in Havana in 1967. Later, four South American groups (from Argentina, Chile, Uruguay, and Bolivia) established the Revolutionary Coordinating Committee (JCR), which operated at times across national borders in mutual support.

Significant guerrilla groups outside of Cuba first appeared in Peru. In October 1959 a group of young radicals committed to Fidelismo broke away from the reformist Aprista party. They called themselves APRA Rebelde for a brief time, until they reorganized as the Movement of the Revolutionary Left (MIR). MIR was led by Luis F. de la Puente Uceda and Guillermo Lobaton until both were killed in 1965 fighting the Peruvian army. MIR was relatively inactive thereafter, although it continued to exist in the 1970s. In 1962 a group of Peruvian Communist party members, led by Héctor Bejar, broke away and formed the National Liberation Army (ELN); it, too, declined after 1965 but did not disappear. A peasant movement led by Trotskyite Hugo Blanco, the Revolutionary Leftist Front (FIR), was very active from 1962 to 1964; but Blanco and other leaders were imprisoned, and FIR dissolved.

In the meantime, another Peruvian insurgency developed and in the 1980s posed a serious threat to Peruvian governments. Following the Sino-Soviet split in 1964, the Peruvian Communist party split into pro-Soviet and pro-Chinese groups. The Maoist factions in turn divided and realigned, out of which emerged in 1970 the Sendero Luminoso (SL), meaning "Shining Path." The SL's principal leader from the beginning has been Abimael Guzmán Reynoso (Comrade Gonzalo), a professor at the San Cristobal de Huamanga University in Ayacucho. Guzmán left the university sometime in the 1970s to build an armed organization in the countryside, and in May 1980 the SL first made its paramilitary presence known with hundreds of acts of sabotage and terrorism. Although the SL's ideology combines Maoism (the theory of revolution beginning with rural peasant warfare eventually encircling the cities) with the Peruvian Indian historical tradition of resistance to Spanish colonial rule and then to white and mestizo domination, the SL appears to have had an urban structure from the beginning. The first guerrilla operations included urban warfare in Lima, although action was concentrated in the mountainous Ayacucho Department. The SL thereafter proved to be a disciplined, effective, and particularly ruthless guerrilla movement. In 1986 it expanded its activities to other parts of the country, both rural and urban. As the SL considers itself an indigenous nonaligned group and is openly contemptuous of other movements and their ideologies, it has not sought or received outside assistance. It uses modern weapons captured from the police and army and dynamite stolen from mining operations, which it hurls with slingshots of ancient Indian design called *huaracas*. The SL counts on support from *campesino* communities. Among other early groups were those organized in Venezuela, a major target of Castro's own international activities. In 1960 a group split from the ruling reformist Democratic Action party and formed the Movement of the Revolutionary Left (MIR), led by Domingo Alberto Rangel. MIR engaged in joint operations with the guerrilla element of the Venezuelan Communist party, organized in 1962 under the leadership of Douglas Bravo and called the Armed Forces of National Liberation (FALN). By 1966 the two organizations had withdrawn from armed revolutionary tactics and largely entered the regular political process, although some active guerrilla remnants remained. In early 1973 several small insurgency groups merged to form the Revolutionary Integration Organization (OIR), but it had little success.

One of the most effective groups operated in Uruguay. The National Liberation Front (FLN), popularly called the Tupamaros, was organized in 1963. Its operations increased in 1966 and it enjoyed considerable success for the next six years. In 1972, however, the Uruguayan army was given extraconstitutional powers and finally brought the Tupamaros under control.

Guerrilla activities in Colombia have been among the most persistent and long lasting. The National Liberation Army (ELN) was formed in 1964 as a Fidelista group under the leadership of Fabio Vásquez Caastaño. It was this group with whom the former Jesuit priest Camilo Torres, discussed earlier, was associated. A number of its leaders were killed in late 1972, and Vásquez defected in 1976. The ELN then adopted an essentially defensive posture, led by Nicolás Bautista. The Armed Forces of Colombia (FARC) was organized in 1966, led by peasant-born Pedro Antonio Marín (pseudonym: Manuel Marulanda Vélez). A principal leader, Ciro Trujillo, was killed in

1968. FARC became the most important guerrilla group in Colombia; in 1984 it accepted a truce proposed by Colombian President Belisario Betancur. The small Peking-oriented Popular Liberation Army (EPL) was formed in 1967, led by Rafael Vergara Navarro. The group suffered severe losses in the late 1960s and early 1970s and became a minor factor. Vergara departed Colombia in 1979. Unusual in its origins was the 19th of April Movement (M-19). Organized in 1974, it took its name from the election of April 19, 1970, when former dictator Rojas Pinilla was defeated. Its founder and leader, Jaime Bateman Cayón, had originally belonged to FARC; he died in an airplane accident in 1983 while en route to a unification meeting with EPL guerrillas. In 1984, M-19 joined FARC in accepting the amnesty law aimed at national reconciliation.

Insurgency in Brazil was fragmented. Competing groups were organized along local rather than national lines. Two groups stood out among the many organizations that proliferated under frequently changing leadership. They were the National Liberation Action (ALN) and the Popular Revolutionary Vanguard (VPR). The two organizations cooperated in the spectacular kidnapping of the U.S. ambassador in 1969. The ALN persisted most strongly, but its original leader, Carlos Marighella, was killed by police in 1969. Both the ALN and the VPR were virtually eliminated by Brazilian forces in 1973, a date by which all Brazilian guerrilla forces had lost their effectiveness.

In Chile the most important of several guerrilla organizations was the Movement of the Revolutionary Left (MIR), formed in 1965 as a Fidelista group advocating armed struggle. It did not join Marxist President Allende's coalition government of 1970–1973 and, in fact, was highly critical of it. Most MIR leaders were arrested after the military coup in 1973. Its principal leader, Miguel Enriquez, was killed by Chilean police in 1974. MIR continued to exist into the late 1980s, led by the late President Allende's nephew, Andres Pascal Allende.

Insurgency organizations in Argentina were among the most active. Some were organized in the early 1960s, but they did not become prominent until late in the decade. The three most important groups were the Montoneros (MPM), the Peronist Armed Forces (FAP), and Revolutionary Armed Forces (FAR). The three closely linked groups claimed to be both Fidelista and Peronista, although they were as much as ejected from the Peronist party in 1973 and 1974. Large numbers of terrorist political murders in the 1970s inspired like retaliation by extremist right-wing groups. An intensive and bloody antiguerrilla campaign was begun by the Peronist government in 1976; this campaign intensified after the military coup in 1977 in what was called the "dirty war." The guerrilla organizations were eliminated, but military actions went far beyond antiterrorism to deal brutally with many other people as well. The Montoneros were led by Mario Firmenich, who left Argentina in 1977 to participate in the Nicaraguan Revolution. He was arrested in Brazil in 1984.

Bolivian guerrilla groups are of special interest because of their direct connection with Cuban revolutionary leaders. Ernesto "Che" Guevara, who had been with Castro aboard the *Granma* and was a major figure in the subsequent insurgency movement and then in the revolutionary government, disappeared from Cuba in April 1965. He went to the Congo for about nine months and then returned to Cuba to lay plans for guerrilla action in Bolivia, hoping to stimulate a South American continent-wide insurgency movement. He arrived in Bolivia in November 1966 and organized the National Liberation Army (ELN). It was initially composed of twenty Cubans (four of whom had been members of the Cuban Central Committee), twenty-nine Bolivians, and three Peruvians. After some initial successes in the Bolivian mountains, the ELN suffered increasing losses at the hands of the Bolivian army. The celebrated East German Tamara ("Tania") Bunke served as the ELN's urban liaison until she joined the guerrillas in the mountains. In October 1967, Che, Tania, and all but five guerrillas were killed by Bolivian military forces—an event that dealt a major blow to insurgency groups throughout Latin America. The ELN continued after Guevara's death, but in 1969 the new leadership was captured by government forces and the ELN was disarmed. The Bolivian Movement of the Revolutionary Left (MIR), formed in 1971, suffered heavy losses the following year. The MIR had been led by Jaime Paz Zamora, who became Bolivia's vice president under President Siles Zuazo in 1982.

The first important guerrilla groups in Central America operated in Guatemala beginning in 1961. Three major ones were organized: the Revolutionary Armed Forces (FAR), the 13th of November Revolutionary Movement (MR-13), and the Organization of the Armed People. Guatemalan violence was extreme in the 1960s as right-wing groups responded in kind to guerrilla terrorism. The Guatemalan army conducted a brutal counter-insurgency campaign in the early 1960s, along with large-scale Indian population resettlements. The guerrillas were weakened but managed to keep operating in remote areas. In 1982 the three guerrilla groups formed the Guatemalan National Revolutionary Union. The principal guerrilla leader was then Rodrigo Asturias (pseudonym: Gaspar Ilmo), son of the Guatemalan Nobel Prize–winning writer Miguel Angel Asturias. On October 2, 1987, the Guatemalan government and the guerrilla alliance announced a cease-fire and then began talks in Madrid seeking to end the twenty-six-year insurgency. The peace talks complied with the Central American peace agreement that had been signed by all Central American presidents on August 7, 1987.

In Nicaragua, a small Castroite organization was founded in 1961 called the Sandinist National Liberation Front (FSLN). It became inactive in 1970 when its founding leader, Carlos Fonseca Amador, went to Cuba. Two years later the FSLN was again activated, as popular discontent with the ruling Somoza dictatorship increased, but Fonseca was killed in a skirmish with the Nicaraguan National Guard. The Sandinistas and their allies finally overthrew General Somoza in 1979.

As soon as the Nicaraguan guerrillas became governors, they were in turn opposed by counterrevolutionary guerrilla groups. Numerous organizations coalesced into three alliances. In time they were collectively known as the *contras*, but they were loosely connected and had continuous internal disputes. The Reagan administration supported the contras as the key to its anti-Sandinista policies.

The National Democratic Front (FDN) coalition was formed in 1981 by Colonel Enrique V. Bermudez, former member of Somoza's National Guard and his last military attaché to the United States. Many FDN members also were former National Guard officers; they recruited widely within Nicaragua and in time their ranks included many teenagers. The key civilian leader of the FDN was Adolfo Calero, a conservative businessman who had strongly opposed Somoza but had also resisted the Sandinista regime. He left Managua in 1983 and allied with Bermudez. The FDN was based in Honduras and operated in northern Nicaragua; it sought to overthrow the Nicaraguan Revolution.

A coalition of Indian groups—the Sandinista Unity of Miskito, Sumas, and Ramas (MISURASATA)—was transformed into an armed resistance. This organization was founded under another name in 1979 to oppose Somoza and was reorganized by the Sandinistas in 1979; but the group defected in 1981. The government's resettlement of Indians as part of counterinsurgency operations led MISURASATA to join loosely with the FDN. In 1985 the Indian coalition was reorganized, drew in some other smaller groups, and reconciled certain differences.

In stark contrast to the FDN, ARDE consisted of moderate political forces operating out of Costa Rica, which sought to return the Sandinista revolution to its original political pluralism. The two dominant forces were Eden Pastora's Sandinista Revolutionary Front and Alfonso Robelo's Democratic Movement. Pastora was a folk hero as Commander Zero in the revolution against Somoza; his departure in August 1981 was a bitter blow to the Sandinistas. Robelo had been a leading businessman opponent of Somoza and a non-Sandinista member of the Junta of Government after 1979; he departed in 1982. Robelo, Pastora, and others (such as Alfredo Cesar, a Social Democrat and leader of the Southern Opposition Bloc) put together their revolutionary front in early 1982 and made clear their distance from the FDN because of its *somocista* background and different political objectives. They were joined by Arturo Cruz, a prestigious banker, early Sandinista supporter, and a member of the Junta of Government, until his resignation in 1982. Cruz subsequently stood as a candidate for president of Nicaragua in 1984, but he withdrew before the election.

In July 1985 the United States persuaded the feuding contras to form the United Nicaraguan Opposition (UNO) to serve as an "umbrella" organization for the various rebel groups. Underlying the UNO effort was an attempt to enhance contra acceptability with the reluctant U.S. Congress. Calero, Cruz, and Robelo formed the three-man UNO Directorate; but Calero and his military ally, Bermudez, also acted independently. Cesar refused to join but worked with Robelo. Pastora, badly injured in an assassination attempt in May 1984, had left the struggle.

The FDN had begun its operations with assistance from Argentine military intelligence officers and U.S. CIA agents. Most U.S. support went directly to the FDN, considered to be the best fighting force. CIA relations with Eden Pastora were always tense; Pastora received some CIA subsidies, but they were suspended in April 1984. In late 1984 legislation prohibited direct CIA help; in 1986 Congress authorized an overt assistance program, but with restrictions. The Iran-contra affair in 1987, revealed in detail in congressional hearings, ended a covert operation directed out of the National Security Council (NSC) and relying on private funding and logistical support designed to overcome the post-1984 congressional prohibitions.

The contra leadership remained badly split. Arturo Cruz, central to contra reform efforts and always a reluctant insurgent, resigned from the movement in March 1987 in disillusionment. His departure led to a reorganization of contra leadership—the Nicaraguan Resistance was created as the new "umbrella" unit, with a five-member directorate. The power struggle continued, however, given impetus by two factors: On February 3, 1988, the U.S. Congress rejected any further public aid to the contras; and on March 23 the contra leadership and the Sandinista government signed a temporary cease fire and began negotiations to make it permanent. Calero, who supported the peace process, was pitted against his former ally Bermudez, who was skeptical. In May 1988 dissident FDN officers refused to take orders from Bermudez and demanded his removal; they had long-standing grievances concerning his conduct of field operations. The contra alliance, which had been held together by a common enemy and U.S. support, was badly fractured.

In El Salvador, the Nicaraguan Revolution of July 1979 reinvigorated insurgent movements. The Farabundo Martí National Liberation Front (FMLN) was formed in October 1980 to integrate five armed organizations. The Farabundo Martí Popular Forces of Liberation (FPL) was the largest; it had been founded by Salvador Cayetano Carpio in 1974. The FPL suffered from violent internal disputes, leading to the murder of Chief Deputy Mélida Anaya in 1982 and the subsequent suicide of Cayetano. A second FMLN guerrilla group was the Revolutionary Army of the People (ERP), led by Joaquín Villalobos. The Armed Forces of National Resistance (FARN) also joined. Its original commander, Ernesto Jovel, mysteriously died in 1980; he was succeeded by Eduardo Sancho Castañeda (pseudonym: Ferman Cienfuegos). The Salvadoran Communist party, led by Secretary General Shafick Jorge Handel, decided to join the armed conflict in 1979 in alliance with the FMLN. The small Central American Workers' Revolutionary party (PRTC), founded by Roberto Roca, adhered in late 1980.

The Democratic Revolutionary Front (FDR) was also established in 1980. It was a separate political wing attached to the FMLN that operated as a government-in-exile in Mexico, but with no control over military decisions. The FDR was made up of democratic left organizations. Most important was the National Revolutionary Movement, a Social Democratic organization and member of the Socialist International. It was headed by Guillermo

Manuel Ungo, a former member of the post-1979 military-civilian junta that sought to reform the political system. Ungo became president of the FDR in December 1980. The Popular Socialist Christian Movement (MPSC) was also part of the FDR; it was composed of former Christian Democrats who left the party in early 1980. Rubén Zamorra was a central figure.

Much of the FDR membership had concluded that peaceful progress in El Salvador was no longer possible. The FMLN initially followed a "total victory" strategy, which ended with the failure of the "final offensive" in January 1981 (just prior to the U.S. presidential inauguration). The insurgents then turned to sabotage of the country's infrastructure (the destruction of roads and bridges, communications facilities, electrical and water sources, and industrial plants). They refused government offers to participate in elections; they occasionally negotiated directly with the government, but the civil war continued unabated and stalemated. In October 1987 intense negotiations occurred in compliance with the general Central American peace accord; however, following the government's defeat in legislative elections in March 1988, and the subsequent announcement of President Duarte's terminal illness, the FMLN decided to press for a full-scale insurrection.

What Kind of Revolution?

Considerable differences in ideology and tactical preferences were found among Fidelista revolutionaries and between them and Soviet-supported Latin American Communist parties advocating orthodox Marxist-Leninist thought. Matters were even more complicated by China's positions on various issues and by its support for revolutionary activity in Latin America; by the survival of Maoism in Latin America after it had declined in the PRC itself; and by the influence of other ideologies, such as those of Trotsky, Bakunin, and certain Spanish theorists. In addition, an array of Latin American writers added their contributions to revolutionary literature. The most important Latin American theories, however, were the *foco* (rural cadre) concept of Fidelismo and ideas related to urban warfare.

The Castro experience served as the original principal source for guerrilla warfare doctrine. Che Guevara's statements provide a starting point for an analysis of insurgency doctrine. Long before his death in Bolivia, Guevara was a hero to revolutionaries and had great influence on their activities through his writings on guerrilla strategy. Guevara reflected to a degree the theories of Mao Tse-tung and Ho Chi Minh, in that he sought to establish a rural peasant base for revolution. He differed from Soviet theory by insisting that it was unnecessary to wait until all of the objective conditions for revolution were present, as he believed that an insurrectional cadre or core (*foco*) could create the conditions. He wrote in 1969 that "a nucleus of thirty to fifty men" would be "sufficient to initiate the armed struggle in any country of the Americas." He also departed from Soviet doctrine by insisting that the guerrillas need not be tied to a political party; they were in "the vanguard," and after they gained power a true revolutionary party could arise. This course was said to have been followed by the Cuban

Revolution. The fundamental concept was that the guerrilla *foco* would operate in the countryside (as in the Sierra Maestra) and create a peasant revolution. Unlike the theories of Mao and Ho, the *foco* would lead the revolution, not blend with the peasantry.

Regis Debray (1967) wrote a long pamphlet that also was viewed as a handbook on guerrilla warfare. Debray was the radical intellectual scion of a wealthy, conservative, aristocratic French family. He taught at the University of Havana after Castro came to power and later was with Guevara in Bolivia. He used the Castro experience as the model for further Latin American revolution, dismissing all other strategies, and drew heavily on Guevara's and Castro's writings and speeches. Debray argued, in sum: (1) that guerrilla struggle was the only effective means of achieving political and social change in Latin America; (2) that revolutionary power resided not with political parties but in guerrilla cadres and their military leadership; (3) that, since Castro was correct in his dictum that "cities are the graveyards of revolutionaries," war must be fought in the countryside; and (4) that mobile guerrilla *focos* would make the revolution, eventually gaining mass support. Debray claimed that Castro's unique contribution to Marxism-Leninism was his insistence that the guerrilla must assume both political and military leadership of the revolution and defer the creation of a party.

Some writers have argued convincingly that Fidelismo was more a matter of tactics than of consistent ideology. They point out that Castro's guerrilla warfare was not in fact set in the theoretical mold that he and others later claimed. He pragmatically used ideology as it suited his needs, coming to power through the confluence of several factors that did not conform to subsequent theoretical explanations. Castro won not with peasant militia (or the proletariat) but with middle-class revolutionaries, the argument continues, and his *foco* did not create a revolutionary situation where none had existed but, rather, victory was due to nonguerrilla factors. Guerrilla determination was important, but so were the mistakes and incompetence of the enemy. The turning point in the Cuban Revolution was when Batista responded to Castro by trying to control the major cities through repression, turning the urban middle class against him and losing his ability to rule. The regular armed forces were corrupt, undisciplined, and easily demoralized; the Sierra Maestra provided a guerrilla sanctuary only because the army was unwilling to enter. Many significant revolutionary events occurred in the cities, initiated by urban guerrillas. (The above assessment conforms with that of Draper, 1965; Suárez, 1967; and Karol, 1970.)

When Bolivian troops seized Guevara on October 8, 1967, they found a 30,000-word personal handwritten diary, which was subsequently published in several editions. It detailed his activities from his arrival in Bolivia to the day before capture, a chronicle of the eleven-month guerrilla campaign. Guevara repeated much of his earlier guerrilla doctrine in the diary, and yet it is a major source of evidence to argue the nonuniversality of the Cuban Revolution and its inapplicability to certain other situations. Guevara stressed in numerous diary entries the "continental magnitude of the task," writing that he wanted to create a series of "Vietnams" beginning in Bolivia and moving to neighboring nations. Despite Guevara's transnational perspective, his largely foreign band found it difficult to understand Bolivian politics and culture; none of them spoke Quechua, the primary language of the Indians in their area of operations. Furthermore, the Bolivian government was able to capitalize on the fact that "foreigners" were attempting to capture the Bolivian nation, a situation that guerrillas had not faced in Cuba. Guevara complained about the "disloyal and stupid" Bolivian Communist party, which refused to support him, thus substantiating the antiparty aspect of Guevara's theory.

From the outset Guevara was hampered by dissension in his own ranks and harassed by government forces. The regular Bolivian army (especially its Ranger units), unlike Batista's army in Cuba, was well trained, received U.S. aid, and was willing to encounter and able to defeat guerrillas in a mountainous environment. Most important, the diary bitterly described the Indian peasants' lack of support for the guerrillas and even their betrayal of the movement. (There were no Indians in Cuba, whereas they constituted a majority in Bolivia.) Bolivian Indians tended to be apolitical and suspicious of outsiders, and they resisted change even though they lived at a subsistence level. They did not hesitate to inform the Bolivian army about guerrilla activities. The guerrillas were unable to replenish their personnel losses with a single peasant recruit.

Urban warfare theory rose to prominence following Guevara's defeat in Bolivia. A widely read booklet that advocated the initiation and development of guerrilla forces in urban areas was the forty-one-page *Minimanual of the Urban Guerrilla*, written in 1970 by Carlos Marighella, a Brazilian. It received Cuban support with its publication in the official organ *Tricontinental* and was circulated abroad. Marighella, a dissident former member of the Brazilian Communist party and founder of the urban terrorist group ALN in Brazil, was killed in a police ambush in São Paulo at the end of 1969. He had long opposed the rural guerrilla warfare thesis. Cuban support of his alternative strategy signified a fundamental change in Latin American insurgency thinking. Marighella summed up his strategy, in fact the fundamental statement about terrorism, in this manner: "It is necessary to turn political crisis into armed conflict by performing violent actions that will force those in power to transform the political situation of the country into a military situation. That will alienate the masses who, from then on, will revolt against the army and the police and thus blame them for this state of things."

This scenario for civil war—the strategy of militarization through urban terror that will invite repression and pave the way for popular revolt—proved to be utopian. Urban guerrillas discovered that the frequent popular response to indiscriminate terrorism was revulsion, and that if a government was sufficiently ruthless, effective repression was more likely to occur than popular uprising.

BIBLIOGRAPHIC COMMENT

The general concept of nonstate international system actors is discussed by Mansbach, Ferguson, and Lampert (1975) in a book that includes two chapters on Latin America. Papal diplomacy in Latin America is analyzed by Víctor Alba in Davis, Wilson, and others (1975) and Manhattan (1946). Works on the Latin American church, including some transnational aspects, include Considine (1964), Levine (1986), *Los Obispos Latinoamericanos* . . . (n.d.), Mecham (1966), Mutchler (1971), Sanders (1970), and Schmitt (1972). Guimarães (1979) analyzes the 1979 papal visit to Mexico and Puebla, and Ferllini, Díaz, and Castillo (1983) include pronouncements and speeches by Pope John Paul II during his 1983 visit to Central America and Haiti. The classic work on liberation theology is Gutiérrez (1973); Boff (1985) and Cardenal (1976–1982) are of interest. On the debate over liberation theology, see Berryman (1987), an informative and sympathetic treatment by a U.S. priest; and Novak (1987), a negative critique by a leading U.S. conservative intellectual; see also Hebblethwaite (1985).

General treatments of business enterprise, with substantial reference to Latin America, are provided by Barnet and Muller (1975), Eells (1976), Sampson (1973, 1975), Vernon (1971a, 1971b), and Wilkins (1970, 1974). Studies of international enterprise in Latin America include Behrman (1972), Sigmund (1982), and Irish (1978). Stewart (1946) is an interesting biography of Henry Meiggs; the same author (1964) is also the biographer of Minor Cooper Keith. On international banks, see Baster (1935). On the new phenomenon of Latin American multinationals, see Díaz-Alejandro (1977) and White (1981). On international labor organizations and activities in Latin America, see Alba (1968), Alexander (1965), Levenstein (1971), Poblete Troncoso and Burnett (1960), Rens (1959), and Romualdi (1967).

Analyses of transnational political parties and Latin America are sparse. On communism (and its variants) and Communist parties in Latin America, with reference to the Soviet role, see Aguilar (1968), Alexander (1963, 1973), Herman (1973), Poppino (1964), and Ravines (1951). Braunthal (1967–1980) provides a comprehensive three-volume history of the Socialist International. Williams (1984) gives a sympathetic treatment of the Socialist International; Mujal-Leon (1983) is an excellent article on the Socialist International and Central American conflict.

The relevant literature regarding Latin American guerrilla groups is extensive. General works include Bambirra et al. (1971), Duff and McCamant (1976), Gott (1970), Martz (1970), Mercier Vega (1969), Moss (1972), Radu (1984), Radu and Tismanlanu (1986), and Schump (1971). On the Cuban Revolution and Castro, see R. L. Bonachea and San Martín (1974), R. E. Bonachea and Valdes (1972), Draper (1965), Karol (1970), Matthews (1961), and Suárez (1967). See also writings and speeches by Guevara (1961, 1973–1974), and those edited by Gerassi (1968). The editors of Guevara (1985) comment on Che's writings and add information on current insurgencies. Of the many editions of Guevara's Bolivian diary in several languages, the most useful in English are those edited by Scheer (1968), which contains an introduction by Fidel Castro, and James (1968), which includes "other captured documents" and an introduction by the editor that is highly critical of Guevara. Also of interest is an analytical document issued by the Pan American Union (1968) regarding the diary. See also the writings of Debray (1967, 1970, 1976). Works by and about other Latin American guerrillas are by Bejar (1970), Blanco (1972), Soto (1986), Gilio (1972), Hodges (1973), Marighella (1970, 1971), McClintock (1984), Mercado (1982), Movimiento de Liberación Nacional (1971), Palmer (1986), and Porzecanski (1973).

PART THREE

■

International Institutions

The next three chapters deal with the large number of international governmental organizations (IGOs) relevant to Latin American international relations. IGOs sometimes behave as subsystem actors, and IGOs themselves often constitute subsystems where regularized interaction takes place. They also serve as policy instruments by other actors and provide regulatory elements at various levels of international politics. Latin American states, since their national beginnings, have used international organizations as favored policy instruments. Thus, a large number of Latin American–relevant IGOs need to be analyzed as a category unto themselves.

This part of the book proceeds through a hierarchy of IGOs. Chapter 7 deals with the Latin American level, both regional and subregional, analyzing attempts to form organizations aimed at political and economic integration and other interstate associations. Chapter 8 addresses the Inter-American System of organization and law, which reflects the Western Hemispheric search for security, peace, and national well-being. Chapter 9 is concerned with global institutions and specialized extrahemispheric organizations in which Latin American states have participated. They range from the Hague Peace Conferences, the League of Nations, and the United Nations System to commodities agreements and the Nonaligned Movement.

———————— ■ ————————

CHAPTER SEVEN

Latin American Integration
and Association

LATIN AMERICAN state participation in international organizations at the regional and subregional levels is the subject of this chapter. Initiatives toward some sort of integration or association among some combination of Latin American states date from the movements for independence to the present day. The nineteenth-century Spanish American congresses for political union are discussed as well as Central American efforts continuing through the twentieth century. Post–World War II projects aimed primarily at economic union are then taken up, along with other South American associations looking to facilitate cooperation for development. The chapter ends with a discussion of Latin America–wide organizations designed to promote both political and economic cooperation among the member states and to increase the region's bargaining power with the rest of the world.

THE MOVEMENT FOR
SPANISH AMERICAN UNION

Americanismo

Subregional integration was first attempted in Latin America during the nineteenth century when some Spanish American states attempted to form larger political entities and to join in mutual security alliances on a confederation basis. The first efforts began during the movements for independence and continued for about a half-century thereafter; they were largely abandoned after 1865. An ambivalent intra–Spanish American "love-hate" relationship was then revealed that has survived to the present day. The early integration efforts were often referred to by Latin Americans as Americanismo or, sometimes, "continental nationalism." Some advocates of union were also found in Brazil. Usually, however, Americanismo was the idea of a kindred Spanish American spirit growing out of a common colonial heritage, revolutionary experience, and culture; a common perception of Spanish American community that might form the basis of political unity. Americanismo also

175

referred to patterns of unity among Spanish American states against outside powers. Its advocates, who thought of themselves as Americans in the sense of not being European, had a strong sense of solidarity among Spanish American peoples based on historical and cultural sameness and a desire to band together against external threats.

Americanists variously wanted to form anywhere from one to four sovereign states out of the Spanish empire in America, but geographic realities, localism and regionalism, and interstate disputes led instead to the establishment of separate states that were often in conflict with one another. The chief advocate of Americanismo and the most active exponent of Spanish American solidarity was Simón Bolívar, the prestigious leader of independence in northern South America. Other important leaders similarly were inspired to advocate permanent cooperation among the newly independent American states, but Bolívar more than they attempted to translate theory into practice. He first articulated the idea of the union of American states in his famous "Jamaica letter" of 1815. He envisaged three Spanish American federations, roughly composed of Mexico and Central America; the Spanish portions of northern South America, including Peru and Bolivia; and southern South America. In 1826 he proposed the total unification of Spanish America.

The four viceroyalties of the Spanish American empire soon divided into sixteen (later eighteen) separate states. Mexico and Central America formed a single empire in 1821, but Central America broke away and formed a separate federation in 1823 and then split into five more states in 1838. In 1830 Gran Colombia divided into the three nations of Colombia, Venezuela, and Ecuador. The leaders of Buenos Aires attempted to mold a single independent state out of the Viceroyalty of La Plata, which they misnamed the United Provinces of La Plata; but it disintegrated into modern day Argentina, Uruguay, Paraguay, and part of Bolivia. Chilean and Argentine leaders worked to frustrate attempts at union between Bolivia and Peru; after Peru gained independence in 1824, its province of Upper Peru separated to form the state of Bolivia. Other Spanish American states later emerged without regard for considerations of Americanismo.

Spanish American Alliance

Another effort at political union was aimed at forming some sort of federation or alliance among Spanish American states geared toward mutual security against external threats. As the separate nation-states were developing a self-conscious sense of their unique national identities and traditions, they also attempted to associate on an international level. Four unsuccessful international Spanish American congresses were held between 1826 and 1865. Other conferences were suggested during the nineteenth century to consider the possibilities of union, but none were held. Thus, not only did some of the state entities that initially emerged from the independence movements fragment, but attempts at alliance among the sovereign states were also frustrated. The latter efforts were hampered by a general Latin American lack of interest and ended in disillusionment.

Certain Spanish American states desired to gain strength relative to external powers by pooling their resources through mutual security agreements. The four general political conferences held between 1826 and 1865 adhered to the Bolivarian concept of Americanism in the sense of close cooperation among former Spanish colonies for their mutual development and protection. Participation at these conferences was primarily limited to the Spanish American states, with only a small minority of them attending. Participants signed agreements occasioned by fear of external threats, but once those threats subsided the proposals for union or alliance disintegrated into nationalism and particularism. Only one of the treaties, signed in 1848 (discussed below), actually went into effect. (Bailey, 1967:161–165 and Mecham, 1965:85–92 provide numerous details for the following discussion of the four conferences.)

On December 7, 1824, the Colombian government, led by Bolívar, sent invitations to several states to attend a congress in Panama (a Colombian province), with the primary objective of establishing a Spanish American union. The possibility that Spain, with help from the Holy Alliance led by France, would attempt to reclaim its American empire by force was a special concern. Great Britain and the Netherlands, both enemies of Spain, sent unofficial observers to the conference at the invitation of conference organizers. Only four American states were represented—Colombia, Peru, Mexico, and the Central American Federation. Mexico was a reluctant participant, itself ambitious to be the leader of Spanish America and jealous of the Colombian initiative. Argentina declined to attend, stating that it intended to follow an independent course. Apparently, Argentina too was unwilling to accept Colombia's regional leadership.

Brazil and the United States received invitations, although Bolívar originally had opposed their attendance. He felt that Brazil had no common aversion to Spain and that the U.S. presence might offend Great Britain. The United States was invited because some Spanish American leaders believed that the recently enunciated Monroe Doctrine might be used as the basis for an inter-American alliance. Brazil declined, little interested in helping to strengthen Spanish America. The United States hesitantly agreed to participate, apparently because of the possibility of increasing its trade with Latin America, but it made clear its lack of interest in making any mutual political or security commitments with the other American states. As it turned out, neither of the two U.S. delegates sent to Panama attended the congress. One died en route and the other arrived after the meeting had adjourned.

The Congress of Panama met from June 22 to July 15, 1826. The major theme was Spanish America's unity and defense of its new sovereignty and territorial integrity. Four agreements were signed: (1) to establish principles for preserving peace among the American states; (2) to create a mutual defense organization; (3) to promote nonintervention as an international legal concept; and (4) to provide for future meetings to be held on a regular basis. The Treaty of Perpetual Union, League, and Confederation stated, in part: "The object of the perpetual compact will be to uphold in common, defensively and offensively, if necessary, the sovereignty and independence of all and every one of the confederated powers of America against all foreign domination." The treaties provided for members of the league to aid each other with armed forces if attacked by foreign nations, for all disputes to be settled by arbitration, for rights of citizenship to be extended mutually among them, for renunciation of the traffic in slaves, and for the guarantee of the territorial integrity of each state.

Even as the Panama Conference was in session the threat from Spain and the Holy Alliance was subsiding and nationalism increasing among the Spanish American states. Only Bolívar's Colombia ratified the agreements, and his plan for a Spanish American political system ended in failure.

A second meeting was not held until almost two decades later. After the Panama gathering, Mexico took the initiative for Spanish American unity as part of its drive for regional leadership. Mexican attempts to organize conferences in the 1830s and 1840s, however, never came to fruition, and Mexico abandoned its leadership efforts after its defeat in the war with the United States. The movement for Spanish American union thereafter shifted to South America, but still without Argentine cooperation.

A conference in Lima, called the American Congress, was held from December 11, 1847, to March 1, 1848. Five South American states were represented—Bolivia, Chile, Ecuador, Colombia, and Peru. Mexico, preoccupied with its war with the United States, did not attend; Venezuela, Argentina, and Brazil declined their invitations. The United States received an unauthorized invitation from Colombia and an informal one from Peru, but they were refused. Indeed, the conference was partly motivated by fear of the United States because of its war with Mexico, and the organizers retracted the earlier invitations. The primary threat, however, was perceived to be Spain's brief attempt to reconquer the west coast of South America.

The American Congress drew up several treaties, the most important of which was a Treaty of Confederation. Its stated purpose was to "sustain the sovereignty and independence of all and each one, to maintain the integrity of their respective territories, to assure in them their dominance and sovereignty, to refuse to consent that they should be permitted to suffer outrage or offense." The treaty loosely provided that the contracting parties should aid one another with land and naval forces in the event of attack by a foreign power, that regular meetings should be held, and that disputes be peacefully settled according to a specified set of procedures. The delegates also signed a treaty of commerce and navigation, a consular convention, and a postal convention. The other American governments, including the United States, were invited to subscribe to the several conventions, but the response was unanimously negative. Furthermore, the consular convention was the only one eventually ratified by the states represented at Lima, and the only one drafted by the several Spanish American congresses to be entered into force.

The third general conference, a one-day meeting, took place in Santiago, Chile, on September 15, 1856. Only three states—Chile, Ecuador, and Peru—attended what was called the Continental Congress. Again, cooperation was inspired in part by fear of foreign aggression. This time the filibustering expeditions of William Walker and other North Americans in Central America and Mexico heightened existing apprehensions over U.S. territorial ambitions. The conference adopted yet another convention for alliance and confederation called the Continental Treaty. It established a permanent league of Latin American states with a permanent congress and included mutual aid provisions and the pledge to prevent the organizing of hostile expeditions by political emigrés within any of the allied states. The other Spanish American states and Brazil were invited to join the union; this time the United States was not approached. None of the parties ratified the Continental Treaty.

The Second Lima Conference, the fourth and last Spanish American conference, was held from November 14, 1864, to March 13, 1865. It was attended by Bolivia, Chile, Colombia, Ecuador, El Salvador, Guatemala, Peru, and Venezuela. Argentina and Brazil still refused to consider plans of confederation. Peru proposed inviting the United States, but after some discussion, the suggestion was turned down. The threat of U.S. aggression had been halted by the Civil War, but several European interventions urgently renewed the question of political union. The French occupation of Mexico, the Spanish reoccupation of Santo Domingo, and the Spanish war with Peru and Chile all led to the Second Lima Conference. The resulting Treaty of Union and Defensive Alliance again agreed to confederation and pledged mutual defense against aggression. Additional conventions called for the compulsory arbitration of disputes and for cooperation in commercial navigation and postal exchange. None of the treaties was ratified.

The Failure of Americanismo

Although the vision of Americanismo emphasized Spanish American cultural homogeneity, agreements reached at the four congresses held between 1826 and 1865 were based more on fear of the outside world. The kindred Spanish American spirit was probably sincerely felt by many leaders, and surely it was a factor in calling the congresses, but what unity was developed was based instead on perceived threats emanating from the outside world. When external dangers seemed to pass, unity declined. The Spanish American states showed uniformity and even solidarity in their views of the world outside their region, but in their relations with each other the newly independent states were more often plagued by mutual suspicion or indifference. Moves toward union were hampered by interstate territorial disputes and other controversies and exacerbated by separatist movements within states. Integration ultimately failed because outside threats were not consistently sustained and because of disruptive forces both in the relations among the regional states and within those polities.

After the Second Lima Congress in 1865, the Latin American states abandoned initiatives directed toward union and began to place their reliance on international law. International legal conferences included the Congress of Jurists at Lima from 1877 to 1879, the Bolivarian Congress at Caracas in 1883, and the first South American Congress at Montevideo in 1888–

1889 (attended by delegates from Peru, Chile, Paraguay, and Uruguay). Shortly thereafter, in 1889, Latin Americans combined their emphasis on international law with regional organization by founding the Inter-American System in cooperation with the United States. Later, it participated in global international organizations, beginning with the Hague System at the turn of the century and then in the League of Nations and the United Nations System. However, in the late 1940s and early 1950s, new initiatives toward Latin American unity emphasized economic integration without abandoning regional or global approaches to organization and law.

INTEGRATION MOVEMENTS
AFTER WORLD WAR II

The Impetus to Economic Integration

Post–World War II economic integration efforts continued to illustrate an inter–Latin American "love-hate" relationship. The 1960s especially were years of great expectations for economic integration. Subsequent efforts, however, tended to be gradual and formalistic, even though the Latin American states' economic and social problems continued to grow and their desire for more independence from external powers remained unabated. Yet the fact of continued subregional integration efforts (as well as the organization of the Latin American Economic System, discussed below) represents at least a partial commitment to cooperation for economic purposes. Within such an ambivalent situation, this question remains unanswered: Is Latin American economic and political integration an idle effort, or might integration succeed in stimulating increased international economic independence, domestic social progress, and regional political cohesion?

Initial Concepts

Latin American integration efforts after World War II differed fundamentally from the earlier nineteenth-century attempts. The thrust for direct political union was replaced by an emphasis on economic unity, reflecting the shift in Latin American priorities from security and defense to economic development. The idea that political union might ultimately grow out of economic integration was expressed, perhaps reflecting a continuing Latin American desire for political unity, but the basic drive in modern Latin American integration was clearly economic. Another linkage with the past was a continuing ambivalence in the constant clash between the desire for unity and national rivalries.

Latin American economic integration organizations initially grew out of immediate post–World War II United Nations proposals, specifically those of the Economic Commission for Latin America (ECLA). A suborganization of the UN Economic and Social Council, ECLA was founded in 1948 and headquartered in Santiago, Chile. (It was later retitled the Economic Commission for Latin America and the Caribbean—ECLAC—after eastern Caribbean entities began to become independent.) Its general purpose as a regional economic commission was to coordinate policies designed to promote Latin American economic development; economic integration was considered an important aspect of this enterprise. ECLA commissioned studies and sponsored conferences and negotiations; as a result, the Central American Common Market (CACM) and the Latin American Free Trade Association (LAFTA) were formed under its auspices.

The initial integration efforts included both economic and political considerations. From a purely economic standpoint, free-trade theory was embraced and applied to regional integration theory. Free trade was assumed to mean more trade, redounding to everyone's benefit. Therefore, the best organization, in terms of this assumption, was universal free trade with no barriers such as tariffs, taxes, or quotas. Given the unlikely prospect of a worldwide free trading system, the second best solution was some form of regional economic integration. Proponents further assumed that successful integration required complementary economies among the member states, meaning that the national economies must produce different goods. With complementarity, "economies of scale" would develop, a modern version of the classic economic concept of "comparative advantage." In economies of scale, there is economic specialization in each national economy, with each member state exporting those products that it produces most efficiently and importing those that others produce most efficiently. Thus, the theory goes, various products originate at their most efficient and therefore least expensive source, which leads to lower prices. With costs and prices lowered to everyone's benefit, markets expand, giving incentive to increased investment and, consequently, to the expansion of existing industries and the creation of new ones. In sum, the theory of economies of scale within a regional integration context predicted that increased, sustained, and mutually beneficial economic growth would occur among member states.

The dangers of regional economic integration were also recognized. If economies of scale did not exist—that is, if "substitute" rather than complementary economies were the rule—the result of integration would be trade stagnation or trade diversion. Stagnation would occur because similar economies had little to trade. Trade diversion was the opposite of trade creation—instead of creating low-cost sources, trade is diverted from foreign sources to higher-cost regional sources; in this scenario, integration could worsen rather than better the economic situation. For example, before integration, a South American state imported automobiles from Europe, where particular models were produced most efficiently. Economic integration revised the common tariff structure, making the European source more expensive, and the state then imported similar automobiles from a regional state. However, the automobiles were produced less efficiently and more expensively than at the prior (preintegration) European source, and the integration thus resulted in higher costs.

Early Planning Efforts

ECLA proposed at its first meeting in 1948 that the Latin American states consider arranging themselves into a series of subregional customs unions. The rationale for subregional groupings was that their markets would be more cohesive and viable than a single larger regional one and that, after subregional markets became operational, they could be melded into a larger entity. ECLA later urged that the subregional approach be abandoned in favor of integrating the entire Latin American region. The shift in emphasis, occurring in about 1958, apparently was based as much on political as on economic concerns; that is, ECLA theorists envisioned Latin American integration as a counterpoise to U.S. regional hegemony. They theorized that the integration of all the Latin American states, and increased regional economic power, would result in more collective economic leverage. In fact, ECLA influence on economic integration in Latin America should not be overstated. Most political economists today acknowledge that ECLA gave impetus to the initial stages of integration and especially to the CACM but that it had little guiding influence on LAFTA's subsequent development and decreasingly on CACM's policies. They recognize that, as of the early 1970s, ECLA's theories (such as import substitution) were widely discredited in Latin America and of little political influence.

The Inter-American System also gave impetus to and supported economic integration in Latin America. Official multilateral statements favored region-wide integration over subregional markets. Economic integration was officially adopted by the Inter-American System as part of the multilateralization of the Alliance for Progress in the 1960s. A major statement issued from a meeting of American presidents at Punta del Este in 1967; on that occasion U.S. President Johnson formally endorsed integration as a means of promoting Latin American economic growth. The American presidents agreed to the establishment of an organization linking the CACM and LAFTA and making it fully operative by 1985. The Inter-American Development Bank (IDB), created in 1959, actively supported economic integration. It lent funds to the CACM for integration projects and underwrote multinational programs in South America aimed at physical infrastructure development tying the nations together. The IDB founded the Institute for the Integration of Latin America (INTAL) in Buenos Aires in 1966. INTAL served as an economic integration research institute, training center, and technical assistance source, issuing policy studies and training (as well as attempting to persuade) Latin American government, business, and labor officials. The IDB, like ECLA, made its contribution to the integration movement but declined in influence in the 1970s.

Latin American integration involved both regional and subregional approaches, with actual practice favoring the latter. Planning for the integration of five Central American states was well under way by the time ECLA shifted its position away from subregional integration, and those states were unwilling to give up their own common market (established in 1959) and join a larger enterprise. LAFTA, composed of eleven members, was founded in 1960. It did not truly form a Latin American regional economy because all of the regional states were not members; nevertheless, it included all of the large states and most of the region's population and resources. Efforts continued to create an all-inclusive market, but without success.

Further subregional integration did take place. The Andean Group was organized in 1966 within LAFTA, at about the same time that the Caribbean Free Trade Association (CARIFTA) was being organized. (CARIFTA incrementally integrated more intensely to become the Caribbean Community.) In 1980 LAFTA was abolished and superseded by a new organization, the Latin American Integration Association (ALADI). Leaders of the various markets debated the merits of widening their membership or linking with other markets, but no important movement in this direction occurred. In fact, the formation of the Andean Group and ALADI signaled a move away from institutional convergence; this trend indicated a variety of problems besetting the LAFTA community and led to new ways of thinking about economic integration in Latin America. Central American and Caribbean integration shared these problems but also had unique concerns impinging on their organizations.

Problems of Economic Integration

Despite ECLA and Inter-American System initiatives and support and official commitments by Latin American states and the United States, economic integration proceeded unevenly and, to its advocates, disappointingly. By the end of the 1960s, economic integration had slowed considerably. Among the problems were deeply ambivalent attitudes toward integration in both Latin America and the United States (Grunwald, Wionczek, and Carnoy, 1972).

At first the integration concept conflicted with U.S. policy traditions of bilateral relations and support of private economic enterprise and free trade. Under the Alliance for Progress, the United States generally endorsed and subsidized integration efforts because they promised to aid in Latin American economic development and, presumably, political stability. From the late 1960s onward, however, U.S. material assistance and policy commitments in fact did not support integration. U.S. preoccupation first with the Vietnam War and then with domestic problems, and decreasing foreign aid expenditures, precluded Latin American policy commitments in general, including support of economic integration.

Economic integration had wide appeal in Latin America, both as an "independence movement" against external (especially U.S.) economic domination and as a means to Latin American development. Important political and economic groups whose cooperation was necessary for successful integration, however, did not accept or were ambivalent toward integration policies. Military and business establishments were divided over integration issues. Certain industrialists and exporters formed important interest groups that urged continuation of trade barriers; they were never won over by economists promoting integration. Furthermore, a general Latin American opinion developed that integrated markets would be especially vulnerable to U.S. economic penetration; the change in U.S. policy after about 1967 further fueled these misgivings.

A number of problems also worked against the development of a Latin American regional market and reduced the effectiveness of existing subregional organizations. The chief problems included the sheer size of Latin America and the difficulties created by distances among states; the wide disparities in size, diversity, level of development, and rate of growth of the different national economies; and nationalism, national rivalries, and competing ideologies. Central American international conflict was particularly disruptive of the CACM. At the same time, certain successes also were evident, and significant efforts toward economic integration continued among most Latin American states outside of the Central American region.

Changing Concepts

The Andean Group approach conformed to positions worked out by theorists who challenged the free-trade model of regional integration on the grounds that the economically more advanced members of an integrated market tended to benefit more than the less developed members. For example, with reference to the poor lands of the world, Gunnar Myrdal (1957) had asserted that, in general, the free play of market forces would "work more powerfully to create regional inequalities and to widen those which already exist." Furthermore, according to Philippe Schmitter (1972), the economic integration of developing states based on free-market forces actually increases the chances for foreign penetration, especially by multinational corporations, rather than strengthening the member states relative to the rest of the world and allowing them increased independence in their collective policy-making. These and other critics of free trade recommended controlled markets to some degree, in order to include various forms of preferences or compensation for weaker states and conditions for external capital investment. The Andean Group was organized in consonance with this school of thought. The free-trade model for economic integration, the original basis for CACM and LAFTA operations, had been discredited in the view of Andean Group leaders. They favored cooperative regional development aimed at freedom from external actors through central planning and "directed economies" (*dirigisme*) rather than through laissez-faire free markets and private enterprise. "Developmental nationalism" and *dirigisme* generally prevailed over laissez faire, although member support for the former was not unanimous.

Traditional concepts were further changed with the formation of ALADI to replace LAFTA. Whereas LAFTA exclusively called for multilateral integration agreements, ALADI called for extensive bilateral arrangements among member states to parallel multilateral agreements.

CENTRAL AMERICAN INTEGRATION

Early Central American Organizations

Attempts to integrate Central America into a single nation-state date from the earliest days of independence. As noted above, the colonial Spanish captaincy general of Guatemala (i.e., Central America) declared independence from Spain in 1821. It briefly joined the Mexican empire, but two years later opted for separate nationhood as the Federation of Central America, composed of five provinces. Foreign incursions from Mexico, Colombia, and Great Britain resulted in territorial losses in various parts of the region. Integration based on fear of foreigners, however, was superseded by the disintegrative impetus of internal conflict. The violence of party politics (liberals against conservatives), coupled with localism and emerging nationalism, resulted in popular uprisings and civil wars, leading in 1838 to the dissolution of the Federation. Five separate states were established (Guatemala, El Salvador, Honduras, Nicaragua, and Costa Rica).

The idea of Central American union continued after the Federation was dissolved. Several further agreements to unify the five states were negotiated during the nineteenth century, but none involved all of the states and none endured. The most important early twentieth-century expression of unity was the establishment of the Central American Court of Justice. Created by all of the Central American states at the Washington Conference in 1907, the Court was designed as a supranational instrument for the peaceful settlement of international disputes in Central America. The Court successfully averted some armed conflicts, but certain justices exhibited considerable national partisanship. In 1917 the Court ruled that the Bryan-Chamorro canal treaty between Nicaragua and the United States injured Costa Rica and El Salvador. Nicaragua then withdrew from the court, and it ceased to exist in 1918.

The Organization of Central American States

The Organization of Central American States (ODECA) was founded in 1951 to promote Central American political and economic integration. ODECA had its headquarters in San Salvador and was composed of the traditional five Central American states. The ODECA Charter of San Salvador was signed on October 14, 1951, but did not go into effect until 1955. A revised charter of the same name signed on December 12, 1962, in Panama City became effective in 1965; it describes ODECA as the highest organization of the Central American states. Article 1 states that the five member states "are an economic-political community, which aspires to the integration of Central America," for which purpose ODECA was established. More specifically, in the preamble the members agreed that "it is necessary to provide the five States with a more effective instrument by establishing organs which assure their economic and social progress, eliminate the barriers which divide them, improve constantly the living conditions of their peoples, guarantee the stability and expansion of industry, and strengthen Central American solidarity."

A complex structure of eight principal organs involving high-level national officials was established to achieve ODECA's multiple purposes. They were the Meeting of Heads of State, the Conference of Ministers of Foreign Affairs, the permanent Executive Council, the Legislative Council, the Central American Court of Justice (reviving the early twentieth-century regional court idea), the Central American Economic Council, the Cultural and Educational Council, and the Central American Defense Council. In addition, the General Secretariat, known as the Central American Bureau (not mentioned in the 1962 Charter) was eventually created to coordinate the work of the various ODECA organs. Their combined purposes were broad ranging, involving high-level communications within ODECA and between ODECA and member states, and included promoting uniform Central American legislation; deciding legal conflicts; planning and coordinating Central American economic integration; promoting educational, scientific, and cultural interchange; achieving uniformity in the region's educational systems; and advising on regional defense and mutual security.

ODECA never proved effective in realizing its purposes. It was of some importance in assisting economic unity, but its companion organization, the Central American Common Market, took the lead once founded. ODECA was confronted with a variety of disputes after its inception and had little success in settling them. For example, in December 1967 the foreign ministers met in Managua and sought, without success, to settle a border dispute between Honduras and El Salvador; the associated conflict was in fact resolved by the Inter-American System. The accelerating Central American international crisis and sharp intraregional conflicts after 1979 effectively ended ODECA's functioning.

The Central American Common Market

The idea for Central American economic integration developed during the June 1951 meetings of ECLA in Mexico City, the year that ODECA was founded. In 1952 ECLA established the Central American Economic Cooperation Committee (CCE), composed of the five Central American ministers of economy; the committee's studies led to the creation in 1954 of the Central American Advanced School of Public Administration (ESAPAC), located in San José, Costa Rica, and in 1956 to the establishment of the Central American Institute of Industrial Research (ICAITI) in Guatemala City.

A series of treaties signed from 1958 through 1960 finally led to the creation of the Central American Common Market. The process culminated in 1960 with the signing of two agreements: the General Treaty of Central American Economic Integration and the Convention Chartering the Central American Bank for Economic Integration. Together they consolidated, extended, and superseded the prior integration agreements. The General Treaty provided for the gradual realization of a Central American customs union, envisioning the eventual elimination of all trade barriers among its members and the establishment of a common external tariff for the rest of the world. It also projected a common customs administration, a unified fiscal policy, a regional industrial policy, and coordinated policies in public health, labor, education, transportation, and agriculture. It became effective for Guatemala, El Salvador, and Nicaragua on June 4, 1961; for Honduras on May 6, 1962; and for Costa Rica on September 9, 1963.

The CACM institutional structure consisted of the Economic Council, the Executive Council, and the Permanent Secretariat (located in Guatemala City). The Central American Bank for Economic Integration (located in Tegucigalpa) and the Central American Clearing House, both established in 1961, were recognized by the General Treaty. The two training schools (ESAPAC and ICAITI) came under CACM sponsorship. Mexico participated in the CACM by joining the clearing house, providing funds to the banks, and lending technical advisers to various bodies. Panama became a member of CCE in 1958; both Panama and the Dominican Republic expressed interest in joining CACM, but this eventuality was postponed because of increasing intraregional conflict in Central America after 1979.

CACM was highly successful in many ways during its early years. Elimination of most tariff barriers between member countries during the first nine years (1961–1970) brought about a 700 percent increase in interregional trade and a 10 percent increase in trade with countries outside the market. The spectacular increase in trade stimulated the utilization of previously idle industries and promoted technical efficiency, particularly in textiles. It also created a favorable investment climate; as a result, many small industries were established, such as tire factories and food-processing plants. CACM was almost wholly responsible for increased foreign investment in the area and was an important factor in the GNP increases in the Central American region. Economic benefit went mostly to the industrial sector, which accounted for only about 16 percent of the region's GNP. Agriculture, the greatest contributor to the GNPs of individual countries, involved few economies of scale, was not emphasized in CACM policy, and was little affected by the common market.

The CACM faced economic disagreements from the beginning that created serious conflict among its members. Economic gains, in terms of increased trade and industrial growth, were not shared equally by member states, and the CACM was unable to equalize the benefits of the increased trade. Honduras and Nicaragua, the two least developed members, benefited only slightly, while Guatemala and El Salvador, the most developed states of Central America, improved their trade considerably. Costa Rica held a middle position in both development and benefits. Nicaragua and Honduras imported more from their colleagues than they exported to them. They also suffered from trade substitution; that is, they said that products they imported from other CACM members were not only more expensive than similar products they had formerly imported from the United States and Europe, but also inferior to them.

The problem of industrial growth was a particularly thorny issue. The market agreements had envisioned the planned distribution of industries among member states through an integrated industries scheme that assigned plants and production rights. Guatemala and El Salvador benefited the most from trade in their manufactured products, while Honduras and Nicaragua received the least new industry. The CACM unsuccessfully encouraged industries to locate in the less developed countries of Honduras and Nicaragua, and it was unable to implement reforms benefiting the least developed countries. El Salvador and Honduras went to war in 1969, further complicating the economic tensions and seriously disrupting the CACM. Honduras had become heavily indebted in its payments position to Guatemala, Costa Rica, and Nicaragua, and in late 1970 it imposed tariffs on its interregional trade. The other members retaliated with tariffs on Honduran goods, effectively removing Honduras from the CACM. In the meantime, surpluses were created in the semimanufactured goods produced by Guatemala and El Salvador for the Honduran market; Costa Rica imposed trade controls to check their flow into its market; and El Salvador, Guatemala, and Nicaragua closed their borders to Costa Rican goods. Eventually all members except El Salvador lifted their various trade restrictions and reestablished full participation; but the economic difficulties were superseded by political and military conflicts after 1979 and continuing through the 1980s. Intraregional conflict as much as ended common market activities and virtually dissolved the organization in all but name.

CARIBBEAN INTEGRATION

Early Caribbean Integration

The United States and Great Britain cooperated in 1942 to establish the Anglo-American Caribbean Commission (AACC). (This section relies on Corkran, 1972.) The bipartite commission was designed to deal with certain wartime emergencies in the U.S. and British Caribbean dependencies; it developed measures to relieve the lack of ocean shipping and disruption of world markets and devised plans to defend them from attack. In 1940 the United States had leased British West Indian areas for use as military and naval bases, giving it a direct interest in the conditions in those areas governed by Great Britain (at the time threatened by German invasion) as well as its own Puerto Rico and Virgin Islands. The AACC largely succeeded in dealing with immediate economic and military emergencies; in addition, it began long-term economic projects and stimulated inter-Caribbean cooperation.

In 1946 the AACC was reconstituted as the Caribbean Commission and broadened to include the participation of France and the Netherlands acting on behalf of their Caribbean dependencies, as well as the participation of delegates from the nonsovereign Caribbean entities themselves. More formal than the AACC, the four-power Caribbean Commission held the regularly scheduled West Indian Conference. Its Caribbean Research Council and the General Secretariat were located in Trinidad and headed by a secretary general. During its fifteen year life, the Caribbean Commission undertook projects in agriculture, trade, fisheries, education, health, and other "functional" areas.

The four metropolitan powers agreed in 1959 to end the Caribbean Commission in two years. It was succeeded by the Caribbean Council in 1961; the members of the new council included the Caribbean entities themselves, except for France participating as a member "on behalf of" its American overseas departments. The Caribbean Council survived for three years. Among the problems leading to its dissolution (on June 30, 1965) were the breakup of the West Indies Federation in 1962, one of its largest members; the awkward position of France; and the impatience of Puerto Rico over what it perceived as the council's ineffectiveness in dealing with Caribbean problems.

Another organization promoting cooperation among nonsovereign Caribbean entities was created under Puerto Rican leadership but was an agency of the Puerto Rican government rather than an international organization. The Caribbean Economic Development Corporation (CODECA), a public corporation chartered in Puerto Rico with the "approval" of other West Indian entities, was established on July 1, 1965. CODECA's purpose was to enter into agreements with counterpart agencies in other territories for regional projects in an effort to bridge the differing levels of self-government in each. But a new Puerto Rican government elected in 1968 was unenthusiastic about the idea and brought an end to CODECA.

The West Indies Federation

After World War II, British arrangements for its American colonies became its prime concern in the region. The British dependencies generally began to travel the road to self-government in the immediate postwar period as Britain attempted to divest its empire in an orderly manner. After the political eclipse of Winston Churchill, both major British political parties agreed that the colonial territories around the world should be guided toward independence within the Commonwealth through economic, social, and political development. It was admitted that some were deficient in population or resources to the point that self-government should not go beyond internal affairs. By 1955 the British territories in Latin America were grouped together in ten Crown Colonies. The British Caribbean Territories, also known as the British West Indies, included nine Crown Colonies; the Falkland Islands, far removed from the Caribbean area, were a separate Crown Colony within a grouping called the Atlantic Ocean Dependencies (which also included the Crown Colonies of St. Helena and Ascension). A closer association of the British Caribbean Territories, including the idea of an independent federal state composed of some of them, had been discussed for many years. Planning to this end had been undertaken in 1945 by the British Colonial Office in cooperation with the local governments involved. After considerable debate they agreed to establish a federation of Caribbean territories, a goal that was finally accomplished in 1958 when the West Indies Federation was established.

The West Indies Federation was composed of ten entities—Antigua, Dominica, Montserrat, St. Christopher-Nevis-Anguilla, St. Lucia, St. Vincent, Barbados, Grenada, Jamaica, and Trinidad-Tobago. It was to be internally self-governing for a four-year transition period, with Great Britain responsible for foreign affairs and defense. After this transitional period the federation was to be given complete independence as a single, sovereign federal state. In 1962 the most important entities, Jamaica and Trinidad-Tobago, decided to secede in favor of separate independence, and the federation was dissolved.

After the collapse of the West Indies Federation, Britain was forced to develop new constitutional arrangements. The possibility of a new federation was discussed, but no agreement could be reached. In 1966 the British and dependency governments agreed to end the latters' colonial status and to make them "States in Association with Great Britain." An associated state was "semi-independent" on an individual basis, as the federation collectively had been during its brief existence. Each was internally self-governing, but the United Kingdom was responsible for defense and foreign affairs. Most of them subsequently opted for sovereign independence, despite suspicions that they lacked the resources for viable independence. Barbados opted for complete independence in 1966; by 1983, all of the remaining members of the defunct federation had also become independent, except for Montserrat and Anguilla (which refused to be appended to St. Christopher).

The Caribbean Free Trade Association

The agreement establishing the Caribbean Free Trade Association (CARIFTA) was signed in Antigua on December 15, 1965, by Antigua, Barbados, and British Guiana. Two years later, when additional entities agreed to join the association, the agreement was revised at a conference in Barbados. CARIFTA came into being on May 1, 1968, and eventually its membership included four independent states, seven semi-independent States in Association with Great Britain, and one British colony; they all were located in the Circum-Caribbean and were members of the British Commonwealth. Prime Minister L.F.S. Burnham of Guyana was the principal leader in the formation of CARIFTA and its subsequent development.

The CARIFTA charter established a free-trade area. CARIFTA members opted for the free-market approach and pledged to eliminate tariffs and quota systems on each other's products on May 1, 1968. The inclusion of lists of "reserved commodities," on which trade barriers were to be gradually reduced until eliminated, allowed for exceptions based on the assumption that varying levels of economic development among the members required additional time for adjustments in certain areas. Member states were divided into two categories—the More Developed Countries (MDCs), made up of the independent states, and the Less Developed Countries (LDCs), composed of the nonsovereign entities. LDCs were given preferred treatment in the lifting of trade barriers.

CARIFTA's governing body was the Council of Ministers, made up of representatives from each member entity and responsible for broad policies aimed at furthering the process of regional economic integration. Administration was lodged with the Commonwealth Caribbean Regional Secretariat, located in Georgetown, Guyana. In 1969 CARIFTA established the Caribbean Bank (CARIBANK) as its financial institution, with headquarters in Bridgetown, Barbados. The members contributed to the general fund, as did Canada and Great Britain. The bank also established a Special Development Fund and an Agricultural Development Fund for soft-currency loans, to which various members and the United States contributed funds. CARIBANK directed much of its efforts toward the LDCs, assisting in the formation of development plans, providing financial and technical aid, fostering public and private investment, and other activities.

The Caribbean Community

CARIFTA's founders had envisioned the association as a first step in Caribbean Commonwealth economic integration. In April 1972 the heads of government of CARIFTA member states met in Guyana and drew up the Georgetown Treaty establishing the Caribbean Common Market (CARICOM). Four states (Barbados, Guyana, Jamaica, and Trinidad-Tobago) adhered on July 4, 1973; most of the remaining CARIFTA members ratified the treaty on May 1, 1974. The thirteen members, at the end of 1988, were Antigua-Barbuda, the Bahamas, Barbados, Belize, Dominica, Grenada, Guyana, Jamaica, Montserrat, St. Christopher-Nevis, St. Lucia, St. Vincent, and Trinidad-Tobago. Three local non-Commonwealth Caribbean states were given permanent observer status: the Dominican Republic, Haiti, and Suriname.

CARICOM's objective, as set forth in its charter, was the economic integration of the member states through the establishment of a common market. CARICOM hoped to bring about accelerated and balanced development, greater economic independence from the outside world, and increased effectiveness "in dealing with states, groups of states and entities of whatever description." In addition to the removal of tariffs among the members, CARICOM also established a common external tariff; some articles were excepted, but these exceptions were to be "progressively eliminated." In addition, a Common Protective Policy was adopted to "operate by way of imposing quantitative restrictions for promoting industrial and agricultural development." The LDCs, apprehensive about the distribution of benefits, were again given special opportunities and preferred status.

CARICOM's governing board was the Conference of Heads of Government. It was assisted by the Common Market Council, composed of a minister from each participating member state. On August 1, 1973, the Commonwealth Caribbean Secretariat became known as the Caribbean Community Secretariat, to serve as the administrative organ for both CARIFTA and CARICOM. Seven additional institutions were mentioned in the charter, including four standing committees of ministers in the fields of agriculture, finance, labor, and mines, and three "associate institutions"—CARIBANK, the Caribbean Investment Corporation (created on June 1, 1973, to support investment programs in LDCs), and the Regional Shipping Council. CARIBANK resources were also expanded. In addition to its eligibility to borrow from the World Bank and continued contributions from the United Kingdom, Canada, and the United States, it received contributions from Colombia, the Federal Republic of Germany, France, Italy, Mexico, the Netherlands, Sweden, and Venezuela.

CARICOM leaders considered their political objectives to be important. The charter established a Standing Committee of Ministers of Foreign Affairs, "to the end that Member States aim at the fullest possible coordination of their foreign policies within their respective competencies and seek to adopt as far as possible common positions in major international issues." This standing committee, made up only of representatives from the sovereign state members, was advisory in nature and made recommendations to CARICOM. Noneconomic functional relations were also provided for in CARICOM activities. The charter created a Conference of Ministers of Health and a number of other associate institutions in such areas as education and meteorology, with provision for others to be established as needs arise.

The Organization of Eastern Caribbean States

In July 1981, seven of the smaller Commonwealth Caribbean island-states formed the Organization of Eastern Caribbean States (OECS) within CAR-ICOM. The members are Antigua-Barbuda, Dominica, Grenada, Montserrat, St. Christopher-Nevis, St. Lucia, and St. Vincent. Their primary purpose originally was to pool economic resources; a peripheral goal, and a voluntary one at that, was to coordinate foreign affairs and defense arrangements. As it turned out, however, the OECS was most noteworthy for its role in the U.S. invasion of OECS-member Grenada in October 1983, only two years after its formation. Ignoring provisions of the Rio Treaty and the OAS Charter, the United States chose a minor provision of the OECS Charter (of which it was not a signatory) as legal justification for the intervention. The United States persuaded the OECS to request its military assistance. The subsequent U.S. invasion of Grenada involved participation by certain OECS members. Not all members supported the action, and the Grenada intervention deeply divided the OECS as well as CARICOM. (This and other aspects of the Grenada intervention are discussed in Chapter 11.)

TRANSREGIONAL INTEGRATION

The Latin American Free Trade Association

After ECLA discarded its policy of urging subregional economic groupings in Latin America, negotiations began for a free-trade area covering most of the region. However, the Central American states stood aside because they felt they needed to press forward with their own integration before they would be strong enough to face the larger states. Finally, in February 1960 seven Latin American states signed the Treaty of Montevideo establishing the Latin American Free Trade Association (LAFTA; or Asociación Latino-americana de Libre Comercio—ALALC). The seven charter members when the treaty went into effect on June 1, 1961, were Argentina, Brazil, Chile, Peru, Paraguay, Mexico, and Uruguay. Four more states subsequently joined— Colombia and Ecuador later in 1961, Venezuela in 1966, and Bolivia in

1967—bringing the total number of members to eleven. Thus, the market area included most of South America plus Mexico.

LAFTA, with headquarters in Montevideo, was administered by an annual conference where members negotiated trade liberalization and established various programs. The Permanent Executive Committee, composed of ambassadorial representatives, assisted by a secretariat, implemented the conference decisions. In 1965 the LAFTA states created a series of high-level ministerial councils (foreign ministers, heads of central banks, transportation and communications ministers, and agriculture ministers) in an attempt to stimulate integration beyond the level of the free-trade area.

LAFTA's goals, expressed in the Treaty of Montevideo, were "to establish, gradually and progressively, a Latin American common market," and for the members "to pool their efforts to achieve the progressive complementarity and integration of their economy on the basis of an effective reciprocity of benefits." LAFTA did not undertake to unify tariffs toward the outside world; rather, it sought to establish only a free-trade area in which the members eliminated tariffs and other restrictions on "substantially all" of their trade with one another. The elimination of internal trade barriers was to be achieved incrementally over a twelve-year period and completed by 1973.

After the treaty went into effect, certain tariff reductions were resisted by some members. Difficulties stemmed from the diversity in the levels of economic development among the eleven member states. The less developed ones were unwilling to drop their import trade barriers irrevocably without parallel controlled allocation of industrial growth from which they would benefit. They felt that the "Big Three" economies—Mexico, Brazil, and Argentina—were benefiting disproportionately from intramarket trade and should make concessions to the weaker states. The Treaty of Montevideo had recognized Ecuador and Paraguay as "least developed" members that required certain special treatment, but the other members (at the time, Chile, Colombia, Peru, and Uruguay) insisted that, relative to the Big Three, they, too, were disadvantaged. Consequently, in 1963 the idea of allowing free-market forces to determine economic growth was essentially discarded and the middle-level economies were classified as "insufficient markets." Complementation agreements allowed the members to negotiate restricted accords to participate in some aspect of a particular industrial enterprise. The Big Three were unwilling to agree, however, to the demand that they not manufacture products assigned to other states under the complementarity program. Other inducements included some preferential tariff treatment, escape clauses in certain trade concessions, and limited financial and technical assistance.

The 1963 compromises, however, were insufficient to realize a regional mutuality of interest, and LAFTA's progress during the 1960s was unimpressive. By 1968 intramarket trade amounted to an average of 10 percent of each member's total trade as compared to about 7 percent in 1960; however, that average had ranged from 8 to 9 percent from 1950 to 1952

(Grunwald, Wionczek, and Carnoy, 1972:51). Trade barriers were not lowered on schedule, and industry was not stimulated to the extent hoped for. By 1968 LAFTA had virtually ceased to function, deadlocked over the free-trade versus regional-planning issue. In 1969 LAFTA members signed the Protocol of Caracas, which extended the deadline for establishing a free-trade area from 1973 to 1980. Colombia and Uruguay refused to ratify; few complementation agreements were signed. The failure to agree upon a program of joint development was the principal factor slowing the tariff-cutting process among LAFTA members; this situation led to its moribund state and then to the creation of the Andean Group.

The Andean Group

The Andean Common Market, usually referred to as the Andean Group, was formed by LAFTA members who were dissatisfied with the course of integration but unwilling to resign from LAFTA or to abrogate the Treaty of Montevideo. The governments of Chile, Colombia, Venezuela, Ecuador, and Peru joined in the Declaration of Bogotá on August 17, 1966, announcing their intention to form a common market aimed at accommodating the differing levels of development of their national economies. The declaration stated the signatories' dissatisfaction with LAFTA but emphasized their desire to integrate on a subregional basis within the LAFTA structure. They hoped to revitalize LAFTA and move toward a common market through planned industrialization rather than relying on free-market forces. Two treaties were subsequently drafted, one creating the Andean Development Corporation to help finance development projects and the other establishing the Andean subregional common market itself. The charter of the Andean Development Corporation was signed on February 7, 1968, and the Andean Pact (the Agreement of Cartagena) was signed on May 26, 1969, and entered into force on October 16, 1969. The charter Members of the Andean Group were Bolivia (which had joined the negotiations in 1967), Chile, Colombia, Ecuador, and Peru. Venezuela delayed joining because of domestic pressure from industrialists who opposed ending protection of their high-cost industries but eventually dropped its demand for special status and became a member on February 13, 1973.

The Andean Pact contained four objectives: (1) to create a common market with virtually no trade barriers among its members and a common policy toward the outside world; (2) to establish an internal market for industrial production, with new industries assigned exclusively to different members; (3) to limit the power of multinational corporations in their dealings with the common market; and (4) to accommodate the less developed members (Bolivia and Ecuador) with special concessions. The pact established organizational machinery, with headquarters in Lima, Peru, that included the following bodies: (1) the Mixed Commission of ambassadorial representatives as supreme organ; (2) a council charged with presenting technical proposals to the commission; (3) an advisory consulting committee of integration experts; and (4) an economic and social council representing the interests of business and labor groups. A separate convention later established the Andean Development Corporation to serve as a regional development bank.

The Andean Pact called for a free-trade area to be created by eliminating tariffs among members in progressive, automatic, irrevocable steps over a ten-year period until 1982; tariffs were eliminated on schedule. In addition, a common external tariff was instituted by 1976 to encourage the manufacture of certain goods within the market. Industrial development was to be stimulated further by an investment program and complementation agreements.

The Andean Group gave special attention to the role of private foreign investment in the integrated market, a reflection of growing Latin American economic nationalism and recognition of the economic power of MNCs. Andean Group leaders said that MNCs had been the major beneficiaries of other integrated economy arrangements, claiming that MNCs used their large resources and mobility to establish industries within the region and to produce for protected and expanded markets. Those leaders, however, also acknowledged their need for foreign capital and proposed to control rather than exclude it.

The Andean Pact Statute on Foreign Capital ("Decision 24"), adopted on January 1, 1971, and later modified, represented the only multilateral Latin American attempt to control investment in the region. The statute was a comprehensive industrialization policy and foreign investment code. It provided for step-by-step reductions of foreign-controlled investment, regulation of the international transfer of technology, planned distribution of industries throughout the Andean zone, conversion of foreign manufacturing firms to at least 51 percent local ownership, and restrictions on existing foreign banks.

The Andean Group was faced with a number of economic and political difficulties, especially from 1972 to 1976. A major problem emerged with regard to Decision 24. Waivers and exceptions were granted extensively by Bolivia, Chile, and Peru; Chile was particularly adamant that the regulations be severely modified. After the 1973 coup in Chile, the military regime adopted free-market economic policies directly opposed to the Andean Group strategy; in 1976 Chile withdrew from the agreement. A more general problem was the fact that most members had insufficient markets to support the development of industries that would be large and efficient enough to compete effectively with external industries in terms of cost and price. Long-standing intraregional boundary and territorial disputes, and changing governments with opposing political philosophies, further complicated economic cooperation.

After 1976 the Andean Group members substantially modified the Cartagena agreement with a series of protocols and formal decisions. Decision 24 was so severely modified that it was rendered virtually ineffective. Deadlines for internal free trade and common external tariffs were extended. Industrial programs were delayed and state roles in them reduced. The organizational structure was also extended, with the creation in 1979 of the Andean Tribunal of Justice, the Andean Parliament, and the Council of Ministers of Foreign Affairs. With the formation of the foreign ministers council, the Andean Group, for the first time, became overtly political and active. For example, a resolution was passed by the Andean foreign ministers on June 16, 1979, recognizing the popular forces in Nicaragua (the Sandinistas) as a belligerent in their fight with the Somoza dictatorship, thus legitimizing them with legal personality and opposing the U.S. view of the matter.

The Andean Group went through another crisis in 1980 and 1981 owing to a coup in Bolivia and border fighting between Ecuador and Peru. The members formally declared a "relaunching" of the integration movement in September 1981. Since then progress has been slow and the original *dirigisme* all but forgotten.

The Latin American Integration Association

In the late 1970s LAFTA members decided to reform extensively their integration arrangement. A new Treaty of Montevideo was signed on August 12, 1980, and adhered to by all LAFTA members. It instituted the Latin American Integration Association (Asociación Latinoamericana de Integración—ALADI) establishing a new juridical order for economic integration. The treaty entered into effect with full ratification in March 1981; it superseded the 1960 treaty and replaced the LAFTA structure. Further development of ALADI took place during a transition period in which a number of measures were applied and further negotiations took place.

In certain ways ALADI is a continuation of LAFTA. (The following description is based on ALADI, 1980.) The members of ALADI consider integration to be the appropriate means for promoting regional development and cooperation. They posit the long-range goal to be the establishment of a region-wide Latin American common market. Moreover, specific aspects of the old scheme have been incorporated into the new one.

Notwithstanding these continuities, the 1980 treaty introduced fundamental changes in both the concept and operation of economic integration. First, ALADI provides for multiple levels of negotiation and cooperation. In fact, Argentina and Brazil had been the prime movers behind ALADI so that they could make bilateral agreements between themselves and Mexico. ALADI also allows for multilateral agreements not involving the full membership. LAFTA had sanctioned only multilateral agreements of a full-market scope. Second, ALADI expanded LAFTA's basic commercial character by specifying three additional basic functions: the promotion and regulation of reciprocal trade, the creation of economic complementation, and the development of enlarged markets. Third, while LAFTA had recognized a special status for the relatively less developed economies, the new scheme incorporates more extensive provisions in their favor; it also defines the category of intermediate economic development to include countries that also receive special treatment. Finally, ALADI provides for limited participation by certain nonmember countries and private entities.

In sum, ALADI was designed to have greater negotiation and operational flexibility than LAFTA, to recognize the different levels of economic development among member countries, and to provide for a wider range of agreements. In fact, the following three types of agreements were fashioned that reflected the overall new design.

1. *Regional Tariff Preference.* The preference would vary with different economic sectors, and member countries would be allowed to exclude a certain number of products. The most developed countries (Argentina, Brazil, and Mexico) would be allowed the fewest number of exceptions; intermediate countries (Chile, Colombia, Peru, and Uruguay) would be allowed more exceptions; and the least developed (Bolivia, Ecuador, and Paraguay) would enjoy the most exceptions. The regional tariff preference is a mechanism of a full multilateral character that applies preferences to the prevailing economic level of the various members and with reference to particular products.

2. *Agreements of Regional Scope.* These are agreements in which all member countries participate. They cover extensive activities, including economic complementation, agriculture, promotion of commerce, financial accords (such as for payments and credits), scientific and technological cooperation, promotion of tourism, and more. The first agreements were those "inherited" (*patrimônio histórico*) from LAFTA. Thereafter, a large number of new ones were instituted under ALADI itself.

3. *Agreements of Partial Scope.* Such agreements constitute a clearly distinctive element in the new treaty and immediately became the most dynamic factor. These measures specify a limited restriction to the principle of multilaterality. All agreements between pairs or among groups of countries must be open to eventual multilateralization through negotiation and, at the same time, be automatically open to the least developed members on a most-favored-nation basis. While only member countries may initiate them, the adhesion of nonmembers is possible. This category is intended to overcome the disparity of economic development that plagued these states in the past because all agreements were not appropriate for all members.

With regard to both regional and partial agreements, all old LAFTA accords were renegotiated after 1980. The process was not completed until early 1988. New treaties under both categories were completed at about the same time, mostly as sets of bilateral treaties. Particularly notable were a voluminous series of treaties between Argentina and Brazil.

SOUTH AMERICAN ARRANGEMENTS

The Cuenca del Plata Accord

On April 23, 1969, five South American states (Argentina, Bolivia, Brazil, Paraguay, and Uruguay), all part of the complex Rio de la Plata system, signed a treaty for the development of the river basin (*cuenca*). An example of the integration of physical infrastructure resources, the Cuenca del Plata accord called for the multilateral development of international communications and water resources, especially hydroelectric power potential. The accord provided for a standing intergovernmental committee and annual meetings on the ministerial level. A consortium of international financial institutions, led by the Inter-American Development Bank, agreed to cooperate, and a foreign ministers' meeting of members in June 1974 established a development fund.

The Cuenca del Plata group achieved successes but revealed serious debilities as well. Some highway and hydroelectric projects were completed, but no development funds were expended. The most serious problem was essentially political, involving rivalry between Argentina and Brazil over strategic concerns and competition for influence with the buffer states in the Southern Cone. Mutual suspicions resulted in several uncoordinated bilateral river project agreements.

The Cuenca del Plata's fortunes improved in the 1980s. The solidification of an Argentine-Brazilian rapprochement after 1979 facilitated cooperation in basin projects. Construction of the Itaipu dam on the Paraná River—a project that created the world's largest source of hydroelectric power—was finally completed after years of delay due to Argentine-Brazilian bickering.

Amazon Pact

Representatives of eight Amazon region states signed the Amazon Cooperation Treaty in Brasilia on July 3, 1978. They were the foreign ministers of Bolivia, Brazil, Colombia, Ecuador, Guyana, Peru, and Venezuela, and the prime minister of Suriname. The treaty committed the signatories to coordinated development of the Amazon Basin's communications and transport systems and natural resources and protection of the region's fragile ecology. It also gave Latin American enterprises the first opportunity to develop the region. In sum, the treaty called for Amazonic regional cooperation that would enable member nations to benefit from the basin's resources and spelled out the projects to be accomplished. The organizational structure was simple: Meetings of ministers were to convene annually in a different member country each year.

REGION-WIDE ASSOCIATIONS

The Special Latin American Coordinating Committee

In 1964 the Latin American states joined informally in the Special Latin American Coordinating Committee (Comité Especial para la Coordinación Latinoamericana—CECLA). It was a caucusing group designed to increase regional unity for economic bargaining power with external states and international organizations. Foreign ministers from all Latin American states except for Cuba attended CECLA's first meeting in February 1964. They gathered at Alta Grácia (near Córdoba), Argentina, to establish regional policy positions for the imminent UNCTAD I (United Nations Conference on Trade and Development). Although no formal agreement was signed and no organizational apparatus was established, CECLA became a continuing conference that could be reconvened as its participants desired. The ministers held a series of meetings after 1964 to plan regional bloc positions for UNCTAD II (1967) and III (1971) and worked together within other international fora such as the General Agreement on Tariffs and Trade (GATT), the International Monetary Fund (IMF), and the World Bank (IBRD). CECLA operated as a caucusing group within the Organization of American States, especially in the work of the Inter-American Economic and Social Council. CECLA also provided a medium for joint Latin American negotiations with the United States and the European Economic Community (EEC).

CECLA enjoyed some success but also confronted difficulties in achieving Latin American unity. One of the most significant CECLA statements was the Consensus of Viña del Mar, formulated at a meeting in June 1969 at the Chilean resort town of the same name. This set of common Latin American positions on trade and economic development issues was sent directly to President Nixon. The following year CECLA used the same tactics toward Europe; meeting in Buenos Aires in July 1970, Latin American foreign ministers issued a joint statement, called the Declaration of Buenos Aires, calling for more favorable terms of trade with and increased economic assistance from the EEC. CECLA reacted again in 1971 in response to the Nixon administration's general 10 percent trade surcharge: It issued the Manifesto of Latin America, pointing out that Latin America had a net deficit trade relationship with the United States and therefore was not responsible for the unfavorable trade balance in the United States. It asked that the United States exempt Latin America from the surcharge and, further, that it develop a system of general trade preferences for the region.

CECLA achievements were limited. Latin Americans generally were disappointed with the outcomes of the UNCTAD meetings. President Nixon responded favorably to the Consensus of Viña del Mar, dropping some U.S. trade and aid restrictions, but the U.S. Congress was unwilling to give in to many of Latin America's demands. In 1970 the EEC agreed to explore ways to improve its trade relationships with Latin America, but on a nonpreferential basis. The United States exempted Latin America from the 1971 trade surcharge. CECLA meetings resulted in a high degree of Latin American unity and coordinated positions on a number of economic issues, but intraregional disagreements similar to those within the economic integration organizations also arose. The economically more advanced nations, especially Mexico, Brazil, and Argentina, tended to differ from the rest over economic policy positions. In addition, rivalry among the larger states for leadership of CECLA, a reflection of their general regional rivalry, reduced CECLA's unity.

Latin American Economic System

The establishment of the Latin American Economic System (Sistema Económico Latinoamericano—SELA) was almost entirely the result of initiatives taken by Mexican President Luis Echevarría. At a meeting in Caracas in November 1974, Echevarría persuaded President Pérez of Venezuela to establish a joint permanent consultation arrangement in order to arrive at common economic and social policies, especially those regarding Latin American natural resources. The bilateral agreement was opened up to the adherence of all other Latin American states, without exception.

Meeting in Panama on October 12, 1975, twenty-three Latin American states signed a formal constituent act, virtually identical to the earlier Mexican-Venezuelan declaration, establishing SELA. Additional new Caribbean states later signed the charter, bringing SELA's membership to all thirty-three states making up the Latin American regional subsystem.

According to the SELA charter, it is "an organization for consultation, coordination, and joint economic and social promotion." The agreement proposed to pool the resources of member states in order to form agencies for the production and sale of Latin American raw materials, thus opening the possibility of forming multilateral state-owned transnational companies to develop and sell those commodities (such as bauxite, nickel, chrome, sugar, and cotton). In addition, SELA serves as an international bargaining tool based on the assumption that regional unity increases the strength of individual members toward the rest of the world, and in this sense it is a political arrangement. Because SELA proposed to formulate common regional positions prior to attending other international meetings, and was juridically organized, it replaced the informal CECLA as the Latin American regional caucus. SELA is not an economic integration scheme and did not propose to replace or unify the existing integration arrangements. However, it has the declared purpose of supporting regional integration.

SELA's principal organ is the Latin American Council, composed of ministers meeting at least once yearly. The initial council meeting was held in Caracas in January 1976 in order to agree on unified regional positions prior to the meeting of the developing nations' Group of 77 in Manila (March 1976) and a session of the UN Conference on Trade and Development (UNCTAD IV) in Nairobi (May 1976). Council decisions, usually adopted by a two-thirds majority, are nonbinding; members are committed only to multilateral consultation. The Latin American Council is authorized to appoint a series of ad hoc Action Committees to supervise approved projects. A Permanent Secretariat, located in Caracas, provides operational support; it is headed by a secretary general serving a four-year term. The first secretary general was Jaime Moncayo García of Ecuador. Budget contributions are assigned to members in amounts decided by their relative ability to pay.

BIBLIOGRAPHIC COMMENT

Nineteenth-century attempts at Spanish American union are the subject of studies by Cuevas Cancino (1955) and Lockey (1920). The general subject of post–World War II integration efforts is analyzed by Gauhar (1985), Grunwald (1978), Grunwald, Wionczek, and Carnoy (1972), Herrera (1986),

Hilton (1969), Krause and Mathis (1970), Maritano (1970), Nuñez del Arco, Margain, and Cherol (1984), Urquidi (1962), and the U.N. Economic Commission for Latin America (1956, 1959). The Inter-American Institute for International Legal Studies (1968) has provided a useful documentary collection.

The following works deal with Central American union and integration: Cochrane (1969), Cohen Orantes (1972), Holbrik and Swan (1972), Karnes (1961), McClelland (1972), Schmitter (1972), and Shaw (1979). The only complete treatment of the Anglo-American Caribbean Commission and its successor agencies is by Corkran (1972). On the West Indies Federation, see D. Lowenthal (1961), Mordecai (1968), and Springer (1962). On the economic integration of the Commonwealth Caribbean, see Axline (1979) and Segal (1968). LAFTA is the subject of works by Cale (1969) and Milenky (1973b); on ALADI, see ALADI (1980). On the Andean Group, see Avery and Cochrane (1973), Council of the Americas (1973), Kearns (1972), Milenky (1973a), and Switzer (1973). Studies of the Cuenca del Plata projects include Greño Velasco (1972) and Levin (1972); on the Amazon Basin Treaty, see Franco Filho (1979) and Ware (1980). The United Nations (1972) has provided a collection of CECLA documents, and M.J.R. Martz (1979) wrote an excellent assessment of SELA.

CHAPTER EIGHT

———————— ∎ ————————

The Inter-American System

WESTERN HEMISPHERIC ORGANIZATIONS for law, peace, security, and national development collectively form the Inter-American System of institutionalized multilateral cooperation among the American states. Largely institutionalized since 1948 in the Organization of American States (OAS), the Inter-American System traces its genesis to 1889 through a direct lineage of international American conferences and other institutional paraphernalia. With membership by the United States as well as the Latin American states, these regional international institutions transcend the territorial scope of the Latin American regional subsystem as such. The institutions of the Inter-American System have helped to regulate international politics, both between Latin America and the United States and within Latin America itself, by simultaneously offering opportunities for and imposing limitations on the foreign policies of the member states. The systems' level of effectiveness has had a checkered and complex history, and it has suffered a general and severe decline over the past two decades.

REGIONAL ORGANIZATION AND LAW

The Pan American Idea

The Inter-American System is the political expression of Pan Americanism, a movement whose principles predate formal inter-American organization. According to Joseph B. Lockey (1920), the term "Pan American" came into use in the 1880s in connection with proposals that, at the time, resulted in arrangements for the first inter-American conference. The underlying concept, however, was an earlier outgrowth of the Western Hemisphere Idea (see Chapter 5). The notion of a "special relationship" among the Americas because of their separation from Europe had provided the point of departure for the Monroe Doctrine as a unilateral policy of the United States toward Europe and the rest of the Americas; it also represented the ideological underpinnings for inter-American cooperation and organization. Some North American leaders supported the idea of an inter-American regional system early in the nineteenth century, but they were in a distinct minority. Likewise, some Latin American leaders were interested in some sort of an alliance based on Monroe's principles, but the United States rebuffed them. The Monroe Doctrine and Pan Americanism were incompatible despite the fact that they both stemmed from the Western Hemisphere Idea, for one was strictly unilateral in scope and the other was inherently multilateral.

Eventually the United States and Latin America concurred that the Americas had common interests that should be promoted by institutionalized multilateral cooperation, although the tensions between unilateralism and multilateralism have persisted throughout the history of Pan Americanism to the present day. Furthermore, agreeing on mutual interests has often been difficult.

An early advocate of juridical Pan Americanism was Alejandro Alvarez (1868–1960), an eminent Chilean jurist. Alvarez developed important concepts of public international law, including the separation of inter-American from general international law. He considered inter-American law the legal extension of the Western Hemisphere Idea and Pan Americanism. Beginning in 1905 Alvarez advanced the idea that "because of geographical, ethnological, historical, social, political, economic, moral, and spiritual reasons the states of the New World were developing an American international law which supplemented existing international law and would eventually lead the way in molding the future of nations" (Bemis, 1943:238–239).

At the inter-American conference in 1910 the Chilean delegation, led by Alvarez, proposed a separate codification of American international law to be presented to the Third Hague Conference (which was never held). As head of the Rio Commission of Jurists, established in 1912, Alvarez supervised the project of drafting a separate code of inter-American law; he submitted a report on this project at the fifth Pan American conference in 1923. Alvarez continued his work on the Rio Commission after it was reestablished in 1923; he also served for many years as a judge on the World Court. James Brown Scott of the United States, also a longtime member of the Rio Commission, strongly supported Alvarez's views in his own work and writings. The U.S. government, however, did not; it had taken exception to the idea of the separation of international law proposed at the inter-American conference in 1910, negated the recommendation for the Third Hague Conference, opposed Alvarez's designs for many years, and thereafter continued to prefer global applications of international law.

Regional Organization as a Policy Instrument

Because of the romanticism and sentimentality that have sometimes been attached to Pan Americanism and the Inter-American System, the point should be emphasized that international organizations are created and sustained because member states perceive that in some manner they serve their national interests. The Inter-American System seems to have worked best, in the sense of maximum cooperation for complementary objectives and minimal conflict among the member states, when mutuality of interests has been present. Convergence of interests has by no means always occurred, however.

Latin American and U.S. foreign policy instruments have always reflected diverging long-range fundamental goals. For its part, the United States has generally sought to exclude other foreign influences in Latin America and to support political stability in the region. To these ends the United States has attempted to unify Latin America in a formal organization characterized by friendly relations but under primary U.S. leadership (Larman C. Wilson in Davis, Wilson, and others, 1975:Ch. 3). In fact, the United States has pursued most of its region-wide Latin American policies through the formal multilateral institutions of the Inter-American System, seeing the system as a formal way of organizing all of Latin America under its leadership and preempting nonhemispheric influences.

Most Latin American states have sought to achieve as much autonomy as possible in world affairs, but their capability deficiencies have made them dependent to some degree on outsiders for protection and assistance. Given this state of affairs, they have attempted to limit the coercive actions of external states while gaining assistance from them through international organization. Through the Inter-American System, the Latin Americans have worked for international economic cooperation, for development funds, and for trade preferences and rules more compatible with their interests. International organization also provides machinery for the peaceful settlement of disputes and for mutual security—concepts compatible with the interests of militarily weak states. In addition, the rule of law, under which might does not necessarily make right, may be sought through international organization. Inter-American law, developed largely through the efforts of Latin American statesmen, stresses the corollary of nonintervention and urges all states to pledge noninterference in the affairs of others.

Latin American attitudes toward regional organization tactics vary from state to state. For example, Argentina traditionally has had an aversion to American regionalism, which it felt was dominated by the United States, in favor of universalism. This attitude has been shared by Cuba since 1962, when it was denied participation in the OAS under U.S. pressure, and by Panama in pursuing its conflict with the United States over the canal in the United Nations. Brazil, after the late 1960s, reduced its use of international organization as a primary instrument of foreign policy; with its newly realized capabilities as a relatively strong nation, it placed more emphasis on widening its bilateral relationships. In general, however, most Latin American states most of the time have viewed the Inter-American System as serving their interests, even if they disagree among themselves on specific tactics to be followed.

Systemic Considerations

The systemic patterns at work in the Inter-American System reflect the structure of the Latin American regional subsystem. The behavior and alignments of state members within the Inter-American System are based on the Latin American regional consciousness of those members. Inter-American politics tend to divide member states into distinguishable camps with ambivalent views toward one another. The basic division places the United States on one side and all of Latin America on the other, in constant dialogue, and simultaneously attracted, repulsed, and mutually dependent. Within Latin America the eighteen Spanish American states tend to identify with each other, at the same time quarreling among themselves, with Brazil deeply involved but standing apart. Haiti and the newer nations tend to operate on the periphery. The United States has created unity among some of the disunited states of Latin America, both intentionally and unintentionally. Latin American unity was fostered partly by the attraction-repulsion syndrome between Latin America and the United States and partly by overt U.S. attempts to unify the region under its leadership, U.S. coercion leading to Latin American opposition for its mutual protection, and U.S. economic power stimulating regional bargaining for developmental resources.

ORGANIZATIONAL STRUCTURES

Institutional Development

The institutional history of the Inter-American System began with the First International Conference of American States, held in Washington in 1889–1890. The conference did not adopt a U.S. proposal for a Pan American customs union, but it established a rudimentary regional structure by creating the International Union of American States and a permanent organ called the Commercial Bureau of the American Republics. The Inter-American System developed in an ad hoc manner over the next fifty-five years. Seven more regular International Conferences of American States and three special conferences were held between 1901 and 1945 in different Latin American capital cities; various organs and procedures were established at these meetings. The official name of the overall system was changed at the Buenos Aires conference in 1910 to the Union of American Republics and in 1928 at the Havana conference to the Union of American States. (See Table 8.1 for full titles of inter-American meetings, referred to in the text in a "shorthand" manner.)

The Commercial Bureau, established in 1890, was located in Washington within the Department of State and charged with collecting and disseminating commercial information. It was reorganized at the Mexico meeting (1901–1902) as the International Bureau of the American Republics. A resolution at the Buenos Aires conference in 1910 created the Pan American Union as the organization's secretariat, replacing the International Bureau as the agency overseeing day-to-day operations. At first, it was administered by a director general with control vested in a Governing Board. It functioned essentially as an economic organization with no political activities with its functions dominated by the United States. Members agreed on certain reforms of the Pan American Union at the meetings held in 1923 and 1928; these reforms

TABLE 8.1
Principal Inter-American Conferences, 1889-1988

International Conferences of American States

First (Washington, 1889-1890)
Second (Mexico, 1901-1902)
Third (Rio de Janeiro, 1906)
Fourth (Buenos Aires, 1910)
Fifth (Santiago, 1923)
Sixth (Havana, 1928)

Seventh (Montevideo, 1933)
Eighth (Lima, 1938)
Ninth (Bogotá, 1948)
Tenth (Caracas, 1954)--name
   changed to Inter-American
   Conference

Special Conferences

International Conference of American States on Conciliation and Arbitration
   (Washington, 1928-1929)
Inter-American Conference for the Maintenance of Peace (Buenos Aires, 1936)
Inter-American Conference on Problems of War and Peace (Mexico, 1945)
Inter-American Conference for Maintenance of Continental Peace and Security
   (Rio de Janeiro, 1947)
First Meeting of American Presidents (Panama, 1956)
First Special Inter-American Conference (Washington, 1964)
Second Special Inter-American Conference (Rio de Janeiro, 1965)
Third Special Inter-American Conference (Buenos Aires, 1967)
Second Meeting of American Presidents (Punta del Este, 1967)

Meetings of Consultation of Ministers of Foreign Affairs

First (Panama, 1939)
Second (Havana, 1940)
Third (Rio de Janeiro, 1945)
Fourth (Washington, 1951)
Fifth (Santiago, 1959)
Sixth (San José, 1960)
Seventh (San José, 1960)
Eighth (Punta del Este, 1962)
Ninth (Washington, 1964)
Tenth (Washington,1965-1966)

Eleventh (Washington, Buenos
   Aires, Punta del Este, 1967)
Twelfth (Washington, 1967)
Thirteenth (Washington, 1969)
Fourteenth (Washington, 1971)
Fifteenth (Quito, 1974)
Sixteenth (San José, 1975)
Seventeenth (Washington, 1978)
Eighteenth (Washington, 1979)
Nineteenth (Washington, 1981)
Twentieth (Washington, 1982)

Regular General Assembly Sessions

First (Washington, 1971)
Second (Washington, 1972)
Third (Washington, 1973)
Fourth (Atlanta, 1974)
Fifth (Washington, 1975)
Sixth (Santiago, 1976)
Seventh (St. Georges, 1977)
Eighth (Washington, 1978)
Ninth (La Paz, 1979)

Tenth (Washington, 1980)
Eleventh (Castries, 1981)
Twelfth (Washington, 1982)
Thirteenth (Washington, 1983)
Fourteenth (Brasilia, 1984)
Fifteenth (Bogotá, 1985)
Sixteenth (Guatemala, 1986)
Seventeenth (Washington, 1987)

essentially gave member states freedom to choose their own representatives to the Governing Board. Latin Americans attempted without success to replace the U.S. secretary of state as chairman and to rotate the director general's office, and U.S. dominance of the Pan American Union prevailed. Latin Americans often pointed out that the location of the Pan American Union building in Washington (constructed with funds donated by Andrew Carnegie and completed in 1910) between the State Department and the White House symbolized U.S. control of the Inter-American System.

A number of specialized agencies were created between 1902 and the end of World War II. The Pan American Health Organization was established in 1902, the Inter-American Children's Institute in 1927, the Inter-American Commission of Women and the Pan American Institute of Geography and History in 1928, the Inter-American Indian Institute in 1940, the Inter-American Institute of Agricultural Sciences and the Inter-American Defense Board in 1942, and the Inter-American Statistical Institute in 1945. In addition, important institutional developments beginning in 1938 provided the first political-security organs. The Lima conference in that year created the Meeting of Consultation of Ministers of Foreign Affairs to consider emergency security matters, at that time in the context of impending European war. The conference considered giving the consultative function to the Pan American Union, but decided against allowing the Governing Board any such political role.

Integrated Constitutional Bases

From 1945 to 1948 the institutions of the Inter-American System were formally codified and expanded. Most important, the Inter-American Treaty of Reciprocal Assistance (Rio Treaty) was agreed upon and the Organization of American States (OAS) was established. In 1967 the Inter-American System underwent some restructuring, and in 1975 further amendments were proposed that are still before member states for consideration.

Five conferences produced documents that, if taken together, form the consitutional bases for the present Inter-American System. At the first of these meetings, a special conference held in Mexico City in 1945 (the Chapultepec Conference), the codification and consolidation of the regional arrangements that had developed over the previous five and a half decades was envisioned. Latin Americans were fearful that the Inter-American System was in danger of being downgraded or even dissolved because of U.S. enthusiasm for the global United Nations then being organized; they wanted to give the regional organization a permanent juridical basis. To this end, the Chapultepec Conference authorized the drafting of three basic integrated documents: (1) a treaty of reciprocal assistance to enable the American states to meet in concert acts of aggression from either within or outside the hemisphere; (2) an act to serve as the basic constitution for regional organization; and (3) a treaty to coordinate and consolidate the many agreements on the pacific settlements of disputes.

The triad of inter-American documents was soon forthcoming. The Special Rio de Janeiro Conference in 1947 resulted in the Inter-American Treaty of Reciprocal Assistance, commonly referred to as the Rio Treaty or Rio Pact. It went into effect on December 3, 1948, after ratification by the required two-thirds of the member states. In the meantime, the Bogotá Conference in 1948 issued several major documents. One was the Charter of the Organization of American States (Charter of Bogotá), to serve as the basic constitution for the American regional organization. The charter went into effect on December 13, 1951, although in practice its provisions were adhered to soon after the Bogotá meeting. The conference also issued the Inter-American Treaty on Pacific Settlement (Pact of Bogotá) outlining procedures for the peaceful resolution of inter-American disputes. Unlike the Rio Treaty and the charter, the Pact of Bogotá entered into force only with respect to those states ratifying it. It has been ratified and is still in force among thirteen states; for other states, previous treaties that they have ratified are still in effect. The conference also approved a third document, the American Declaration on the Rights and Duties of Man, apparently considered less important than the others. Later, the Fifth Foreign Minister Meeting (1959) created the Inter-American Commission on Human Rights as an OAS advisory group headquartered in Washington, D.C.; it began to function in 1960 with limited powers.

The special Buenos Aires conference in 1967 approved the Protocol of Amendment to the Charter of the OAS. This Protocol of Buenos Aires, which amended the original OAS organization and functions, entered into force in February 1970. The amendments strengthened economic and social functions relative to political ones, reflecting a shift in organizational emphasis away from the political-security interests of the United States toward the economic-social interests of the Latin American members.

The Inter-American Specialized Conference on Human Rights, held in Costa Rica in 1969, produced the American Convention on Human Rights (Pact of San José). The convention finally went into effect in 1978; eleven states have ratified it. The United States signed in 1977 but the Senate Foreign Relations Committee has not held hearings or voted on whether or not to recommend ratification. The convention incorporated and extended the 1948 American Declaration on the Rights and Duties of Man and related subsequent acts. It "recreated" the Inter-American Commission on Human Rights, composed of seven jurists selected by the Permanent Council to four-year terms, and further defined its procedures. It also created the Inter-American Court of Human Rights, located in Costa Rica, with jurisdiction limited to cases voluntarily brought by state adherents to the convention.

Only three years after the Protocol of Buenos Aires charter amendments went into effect and brought about important institutional changes, another movement to restructure the OAS charter as well as the Rio Treaty was under way. In 1973 the General Assembly of the OAS created the Special Committee to Study the Inter-American System and to Propose Measures for Restructuring It (CEESI, an acronym after the Spanish title). CEESI's deliberations, from June 1973 through February 1975, resulted in four proposals. The Protocol of Amendment to the Inter-American Treaty of Reciprocal Assistance (Rio Treaty) was submitted to and approved by a Conference of Plenipotentiaries in July 1975 and sent to member states for ratification; it has failed to receive enough ratifications to become effective. The Draft Amendments to the Charter of the OAS were taken over by the Permanent Council of the OAS in April 1976 for further consideration and languished thereafter; further amending of the charter became a dead issue. The Draft Convention on Cooperation for Development, with wording similar to that of the draft charter amendments calling for a comprehensive approach to economic development, also became a dead issue. Consideration of the Draft Convention on Collective Economic Security for Development, which expressed concepts already included in the proposed amendments to both the Rio Treaty and the charter, was postponed indefinitely.

OAS Structure

The 1948 Charter. The 1948 charter, called the Charter of Bogotá, provided for four principal organs to govern the OAS. The Inter-American Conference (the new name for the International Conference of American States), a general decisional body to establish and reassess broad policy guidelines, was established as the supreme OAS organ. It was to meet every five years at least, but the last time delegates assembled was at Caracas in 1954. The next conference, scheduled for Quito in 1959, was indefinitely postponed because of a generally unfriendly atmosphere generated first by conflict between Peru and Ecuador and then between the United States and Cuba. An ad hoc conference was held in its place, and major OAS business then came to be conducted by the foreign ministers' meeting.

The Meeting of Ministers of Foreign Affairs was also made one of the principal organs. The charter provided for the foreign ministers of each of the member states to meet in order to consult on such matters as dealing with threats to hemispheric peace, settling inter-American disputes, and resisting external attacks on the Americas. The ministers were advised by the Advisory Defense Committee, composed of high-ranking military officers from the states represented at foreign ministers' meetings.

The third major organ was the Council of the Organization of American States (COAS), composed of one permanent ambassadorial representative from each member state. The COAS handled any matters referred to it by the Foreign Ministers' meeting and the Inter-American Conference; it also supervised the Pan American Union and coordinated the activities of the Specialized Conferences. The Rio Treaty authorized the COAS to act provisionally as the Organ of Consultation when hemispheric security or peace was threatened. The charter created three organs subordinate to the COAS. The most important, as it turned out, was the Inter-American Economic and Social Council (IAECOSOC), which in 1962 established subordinate entities with special responsibilities in the administration of Alliance for Progress programs. A second COAS subsidiary was the Inter-American Council of Jurists, served by the Inter-American Juridical Committee; the third was the Inter-American Cultural Council, with a subagency called the Committee for Cultural Action.

The Specialized Conferences (not to be confused with the Special Conferences mentioned above) consisted of twelve organizations, institutes, agencies, committees, boards, and commissions created to deal with technical matters or specialized inter-American activities covering a wide range of endeavors. They operated either autonomously within the OAS or under "working agreements" with other OAS bodies. Eight of these organizations had been created prior to the adoption of the Charter of Bogotá in 1948. Three additional ones were established after the charter went into effect: the Inter-American Committee on Human Rights in 1959, the Special Consultative Committee on Security in 1962, and the Inter-American Nuclear Energy Commission in 1964. The Inter-American Peace Committee had been established by resolution in 1940, but it did not hold its first meeting until 1948. In addition, the Inter-American Defense College, a dependency of the Inter-American Defense Board, opened in Washington on October 9, 1962.

After the Mexico City conference in 1945, the Pan American Union was headed by a secretary general, serving for a ten-year elected term. The first secretary general under the new system was Alberto Lleras Camargo, who served for eight years from 1946 to 1954, when he resigned in frustration. Lleras returned to his native Colombia to help end civil strife there and to serve as president of the nation, thereafter becoming publisher of the news magazine *Visión*. The second secretary general was Carlos Dávila, a Chilean political leader, journalist, and diplomat. Dávila served for a brief period from 1954 until his death on October 19, 1955. In January 1956 the COAS elected the former Uruguayan Foreign Minister José A. Mora as interim secretary general for two years and then to a full ten-year term, which expired in May 1968.

The 1967 Amendments. The 1967 Protocol of Buenos Aires amended the 1948 Charter of Bogotá and made some basic organizational changes. It abolished the moribund Inter-American Conference and created the General Assembly as the new supreme organ of the OAS. The 1967 protocol directed the General Assembly to meet at least annually to decide on general policy guidelines. It may discuss any matter of interest to the members and may coordinate the work of other organs. The General Assembly also assumed some functions of the old COAS, such as approving the OAS program budget, electing the secretary general and assistant secretary general, approving the admission of new members, and establishing working standards for the General Secretariat (formerly the Pan American Union, and still known informally by its traditional name).

The General Assembly has two subordinate bodies. The Inter-American Juridical Committee is a merging of the old Inter-American Council of Jurists and its subordinate Inter-American Juridical Committee. The new committee, composed of eleven jurists, is elected by the General Assembly from separate states for four-year terms on a staggered replacement basis. It advises the OAS on juridical matters and promotes the further development and codification of international law, including that related to regional economic integration. In addition, the charter amendments raised the status of the Inter-American Commission on Human Rights from that of a Specialized Conference to an organ supervised by the General Assembly, charged with promoting the observance and protection of human rights in the Americas and investigating complaints of their violation.

The amendments did not change the composition or functions of the Meeting of Consultation of Ministers of Foreign Affairs. However, its relative importance in the OAS was reduced with the elevation of two other organs to equal status. The Inter-American Economic and Social Council was raised from a subordinate position to full council level and charged with increased responsibilities. It coordinates economic and social development programs sponsored by the OAS in member states, evaluates the progress of those states receiving development assistance, and promotes Latin American economic integration. The other major organ, the Inter-American Council for Education, Science, and Culture, is an expanded and updated form of the old Inter-American Cultural Council. Its primary purpose is to promote educational, scientific, and cultural cooperation and exchange among the American states. Both councils meet at least annually.

The Permanent Council (PCOAS) succeeded the COAS but does not hold the central position formerly occupied by the latter. The level of authority is on a par with the foreign ministers' meetings and the two new councils; its basic role is that of a peacekeeping mediator handling matters referred to it by the General Assembly or the Meeting of Ministers of Foreign Affairs. The PCOAS also serves as the preparatory committee for the General Assembly; it prepares draft agendas, reviews the various matters to be considered by the latter, and recommends measures to the General Assembly regarding standards and functions of the General Secretariat. The PCOAS may act as the Provisional Organ of Consultation when emergency situations arise until a meeting of foreign ministers may be convened. The Inter-American Committee on Peaceful Settlement was established as a subsidiary body assisting the PCOAS with its peacekeeping responsibilities, replacing the Inter-American Peace Committee, which had been one of the Specialized Conferences.

The Specialized Conferences were reorganized into ten entities, including six Specialized Organizations and four Other Entities. All of the current Specialized Conferences had been organized prior to the 1967 amendments, which made no important changes in their functions.

The General Secretariat occupies a key position in the revised organization. It serves the entire organization and its member governments in some capacity. The amendments increased the duties and services of the Secretariat and established a more flexible relationship between it and the other OAS organs. The secretary general is responsible to the General Assembly and is a nonvoting participant in all OAS meetings. The assistant secretary general, among other duties, serves as secretary to the PCOAS. Both officials are elected by the General Assembly for a five-year term; they may be reelected once and their successors may not be of the same nationality.

In practice, the secretary general is always a Latin American (that is, not a U.S. citizen). When José A. Mora completed his twelve years in the post in May 1968, he was succeeded by Galo Plaza Lasso, a former president of Ecuador and United Nations official, in a hotly contested election. Plaza was succeeded in July 1975 by Alejandro Orfila, who had been serving as the Argentine ambassador to the United States. Orfila resigned his post in 1984, a year before his second five-year term ended, and was succeeded by João Clemente Baena Soares, a professional Brazilian diplomat who had spent most of his career in international organization posts.

Membership

Pan Americanism, based on the idea of a special relationship among the peoples of the Western Hemisphere, implies the desirability of universal membership of sovereign American states in the Inter-American System. A large majority of them have always belonged, but membership has never reached universality.

In 1889, at the first inter-American conference, all eighteen of the existing Latin American states plus the United States were present. Cuba and Panama joined subsequent conferences after they became legally sovereign in 1902. Membership remained at twenty-one states until the 1960s, when British Caribbean dependencies began to gain independence and join the OAS. Membership for the new states in the Inter-American System involved adherence to the OAS charter but did not require adherence to the Rio Treaty. Barbados and Trinidad-Tobago were added in 1967 within a year after gaining their independence. Jamaica achieved independence in 1962 but delayed joining the OAS until 1969, when it received assurance that its membership did not require adherence to prior OAS sanctions imposed on Cuba. Other new states subsequently joined the OAS, bringing the total number of member states to thirty-two as of 1988. Belize and Guyana have not become members because of unsettled boundary disputes with member-nations Guatemala and Venezuela, respectively. Guyana, however, has been granted permanent observer status. The Rio Treaty currently has twenty-one signatories participating in its procedures; Trinidad-Tobago is the only participant from the group of new nations.

An apparently common misunderstanding about the multilateral sanctions imposed on Cuba in 1962 (discussed below) should be clarified. Cuban membership was not revoked; the charter makes no provision for expulsion of a member. Rather, the Castro government was denied participation in the OAS and other agencies and conferences of the Inter-American System. Thus, although Cuba's activity was temporarily suspended, it technically remains a member of the Inter-American System. Cuba is not, however, a member of the IDB, and it unilaterally abrogated the Rio Treaty.

The OAS allows representatives from nonhemispheric states to attend its meetings as permanent observers. As of 1988, twenty entities enjoy observer status. They include Austria, Belgium, Egypt, Federal Republic of Germany, France, Greece, Israel, Italy, Japan, Morocco, the Netherlands, Portugal, Saudi Arabia, South Korea, Spain, and Switzerland. The United Nations and the Holy See are also permanent observers, as are the American states of Guyana and Canada. The United Kingdom has declined such participation because of its continuing disputes with Argentina and Guatemala.

The question of Canadian membership has recurred throughout the history of the Inter-American System. Until about 1948 Canada declined periodic invitations to join the organization. With the establishment of the OAS, Canadian governments evidenced increasing interest in their role in hemispheric affairs but still refused OAS membership and continued to deal with the other American states on bilateral bases. Canada cited its British Commonwealth ties as its formal reason for declining membership in the Inter-American System, arguing that any adherence to Pan Americanism would weaken its influence in the Commonwealth system and perhaps endanger the trade benefits it had accrued. But membership in the OAS on the part of the new Caribbean nations, which were also members of the Commonwealth, along with the British entry into the European Community and the decline of Commonwealth trade privileges, eroded this Canadian argument. In the 1960s Canada stated that it preferred freedom to maintain diplomatic and trade relations with Cuba over OAS membership if the latter meant having to adhere to OAS sanctions against Cuba. With the de facto dropping of most sanctions in 1975 Canada was free to join the OAS without jeopardizing its Cuban relationship but did not do so.

Apparently Canada's real reason for remaining aloof from Pan Americanism, based on its perception of U.S. primacy in the Inter-American System, was its aversion to submitting to a further form of U.S. dominance in addition to existing U.S. economic and cultural influence. Many Canadian nationalists feel that Canada already has too many ties with the United States. Nevertheless, Canada joined the Inter-American Development Bank (IDB) in 1972; its membership reflects the primacy of its economic interests, particularly in the Caribbean region, over political concerns.

The 1959 charter of the IDB lists its member states. As of 1988, forty-four states were IDB members, including twenty-four Latin American members of the OAS plus the United States, Guyana, Canada, and seventeen non-hemispheric states. The seven OAS members not belonging to the bank are Antigua-Barbuda, Cuba, Dominica, Grenada, St. Christopher-Nevis, St. Lucia, and St. Vincent. Canada joined on May 3, 1972, having already contributed funds for a number of years. A special amendment to the bank's charter named Canada specifically as a member and opened the way for nonhemispheric states to join. On July 9, 1976, nine nonregional states joined the IDB—Belgium, Denmark, Federal Republic of Germany, Israel, Japan, Spain, Switzerland, United Kingdom, and Yugoslavia. Eight more later joined—Austria, Finland, France, Italy, the Netherlands, Portugal, Sweden, and the Holy See.

INTER-AMERICAN POLICIES

Conflicting Purposes in the Inter-American System

The various constitutional bases for the Inter-American System created the machinery described above in order to implement a number of Pan American principles that are reiterated in the constitutional instruments. The many principles developed since 1889 guiding inter-American policies and activities may be grouped under five main categories: (1) nonintervention and sovereign equality; (2) mutual security; (3) representative democracy and human rights; (4) peaceful settlement of disputes; and (5) economic cooperation and development. None of the policies appeared full-blown at the start; they were introduced at different times and evolved thereafter. Furthermore, they have been assigned different priorities and levels of commitment by the various member states—a tendency that reveals the often conflicting purposes at work in the Inter-American System.

The Pan American movement has gone through several historical phases of shifting hostilities among the member states, with the cleavage usually between Latin America and the United States. The first phase of the Inter-American System spanned the years from 1889, when the First International Conference of American States was held, to 1928, when the Sixth Conference revealed such bitter Latin American hostility toward the United States that the survival of the movement was in jeopardy. During that time the United States was primarily interested in expanding commercial relations with Latin America; secondarily, it sought to establish procedures for the peaceful settlement of Latin American disputes, which would promote regional political stability, facilitate international trade, and preempt nonhemispheric influences. The United States was not interested in a regional mutual security arrangement, preferring to pursue security unilaterally. The Latin American states shared U.S. interests in trade expansion and pacific settlement but viewed Pan Americanism first and foremost as a way to achieve security against outside intervention, primarily from Europe and then from the United States itself. After the U.S. enunciation of the Roosevelt Corollary in 1904 and subsequent extensive intervention in the Caribbean region, Latin American dismay with the regional organization increased. Restrained hostility toward the United States in the early 1900s developed into bitter public denunciations by the late 1920s. Latin Americans were unwilling to risk abandonment of the Inter-American System despite their disappointment in its course.

The second era of Pan Americanism, beginning in the late 1920s and continuing through World War II, was marked by a general harmony of interests. The principal developments involved the progressive acceptance of nonintervention by the United States, followed by the building of regional security arrangements. Most members saw mutual advantages and concurring interests in regional organization, and the period represented the most harmonious in the history of the movement.

The third phase, from the end of World War II to the late 1950s, was again marked by diverging goals and conflicting relations. During this time the United States and Latin America completely reversed their respective views of inter-American organization from those initially held between 1889 and 1928. The United States pursued primarily mutual security goals in the context of a global cold war, while Latin America urged regional organization essentially to promote its economic interests. A brief period of converging interests, during what came to be known as the Alliance for Progress, extended roughly from 1959 to 1965. During this period, the United States broadened its notion of security to include economic and social concerns. As a result, a temporary convergence of U.S. and Latin American interests occurred even though they rested on different motivations.

The current phase began in the mid-1960s. In the years from 1965 to 1979, the United States did not perceive a serious threat in Latin America, so its interest in the region's economic development declined. Latin American states were unified by their general consensus that U.S. trade and aid restrictions were a major source of their economic problems, and they sought through the Inter-American System to gain more favorable arrangements. Since 1979, when the Nicaraguan Revolution gave renewed strength to the U.S. perception of security threats in the Caribbean Basin, the importance of the Inter-American System has declined for most parties. On the one hand, the Latin American states refused to respond to hesitant U.S. steps to reinvigorate the mutual security procedures of the system; with no encouragement from Latin America, the United States pursued its regional security policies without the Inter-American System. At the same time, the United States was unwilling to commit significant resources to the system's developmental programs.

In the following sections, each of the five categories of principles, policies, and activities identified above will be analyzed on its own terms.

Nonintervention

The principle of state sovereignty and its corollary of nonintervention has come to be the cornerstone on which the Inter-American System is built. The Latin American determination to press for nonintervention as a doctrine of international law predated the First Inter-American Conference in 1889. Afterward the Latin American states were vitally interested in the idea as a fundamental organizational principle. They finally succeeded in the 1930s in having nonintervention adopted as a concept of American international law and the primary principle of Pan Americanism.

Early Doctrines. A doctrine enunciated by the famous Argentine jurist Carlos Calvo, in his book published in 1868, became the rallying point for early Latin American desires to establish nonintervention as a rule of international conduct. The Calvo Doctrine challenged the European legal position that foreign residents had rights to "just" treatment by their host states, especially with regard to pecuniary claims based upon injuries during civil war, acts of violence, and breaches of contract, whether or not the same standards were accorded national citizens. Calvo asserted that intervention by foreign governments to enforce the claims of their own citizens residing abroad was illegal, no matter what sort of treatment had been given them, because it violated the host state's sovereign independence. In sum, Calvo stressed the absolute equality of states and the inviolability of sovereignty, concluding that intervention to enforce pecuniary claims under any circumstances was invalid.

A resolution incorporating the essence of the Calvo Doctrine was proposed at the Washington Conference in 1889. It declared that states were under no obligation to favor foreigners with more protection than was afforded to native citizens and that the former had only the same legal rights as the latter. The United States opposed the resolution and was the only conferee voting against it.

The Calvo Doctrine was modified in 1902, when three European states threatened Venezuela with intervention in order to collect public debts. The Argentine Foreign Minister Luis M. Drago proclaimed the illegality of armed intervention to force payment of foreign governmental debts, but with reference to public rather than private debt. The Drago Doctrine, like that of Calvo, stressed absolute sovereignty and territorial inviolability as superior to pecuniary claims. This position received wide support in Latin America and became the new point of departure for their demands within the Inter-American System.

The Drago Doctrine was initially advanced in response to European intervention, but it was soon directed toward the United States when the interventionist features of the Monroe Doctrine became clear. The Roosevelt Corollary, enunciated in 1904, and the subsequent U.S. interventions in the Caribbean area based on it, definitively shifted Latin American fears from Europe to the United States.

Evolution of the Current Doctrine. For some three decades, Pan Americanism revolved around Latin American resistance to U.S. interventions in the Caribbean area. The first two inter-American conferences (1889/1890 and 1902) had been held prior to sustained U.S. intervention in the Caribbean, but at the next four conferences, convened between 1906 and 1928, the United States attempted to keep the conference agendas devoid of the intervention issue. The Latin American states, however, succeeded in using the meetings to attack U.S. intervention as both unjust and illegal. They protested U.S. interference in their domestic affairs as violations of their sovereignty and attempted to persuade the United States to accept the principle of nonintervention as the legal corollary of sovereignty. The ensuing debate reflected conflicting views as to what kinds of acts constituted intervention. Whereas the Latin American definition of intervention was a broad one including diplomatic, economic, and military actions, the United States had a narrow view limiting intervention to military activities justified as necessary for the security of all the Americas.

By the time of the Havana Conference of 1928, an impasse had been reached over the intervention issue. Latin Americans made it clear that future cooperation was contingent on the United States dropping its resistance to nonintervention. This open hostility threatened to destroy the Inter-American

System. Because of the urgency of the problem, and because of the lack of European threats to the hemisphere, the United States abandoned the Roosevelt Corollary and accepted nonintervention as a part of American international law. The United States had indicated a changed attitude as early as 1928 (see Chapter 5); by 1933 it was willing to proceed along multilateral lines.

At the Montevideo Conference in 1933, the United States accepted a nonintervention treaty, although with reservations. The conference adopted the Convention on the Rights and Duties of States, embodying the Calvo and Drago doctrines as well as broader nonintervention principles long championed by Latin Americans. The key clause in Article VIII flatly stated that "no state has the right to intervene in the internal or external affairs of another." The United States signed and ratified the convention, but with the ambiguous reservation of its rights "by the law of nations as generally recognized." This unclear reservation cast doubt on the degree of U.S. commitment. Three years later, however, the United States accepted nonintervention as an unqualified legal principle. All of the American states adhered to a convention signed at the Buenos Aires Conference in 1936 entitled Additional Protocol Relative to Non-Intervention. This document, reaffirming the principles adopted in 1933, emphatically declared as inadmissible any intervention "directly or indirectly, and for whatever reason, in the internal or external affairs of the parties."

Nonintervention Provisions. After 1936 nonintervention was reaffirmed at various conferences and incorporated into other treaties, most notably in the OAS Charter. The most relevant articles in the original (1948) charter were numbered 15 through 20; in the amended charter (1967) they are numbered 18 through 22:

Article 18. No state or group of States has the right to intervene, directly or indirectly, for any reason whatsoever in the internal or external affairs of any other State. The foregoing principle prohibits not only armed force but also any other form of interference or attempted threat against the personality of the State or against its political, economic, and cultural elements.

Article 19. No State may use or encourage the use of coercive measures of an economic or political character in order to force the sovereign will of another State and obtain from it advantages of any kind.

Article 20. The territory of the State is inviolable; it may not be the object, even temporarily, of military occupation or of other measures of force taken by another State, directly or indirectly, on any grounds whatever. No territorial acquisitions or special advantages obtained either by force or by other means of coercion shall be recognized.

Article 21. The American States bind themselves in their international relations not to have recourse to the use of force, except in the case of self-defense in accordance with existing treaties or in fulfillment thereof.

Article 22. Measures adopted for the maintenance of peace and security in accordance with existing treaties do not constitute a violation of the principles set forth in Articles 18 and 20.

Interpretations and Applications. One reason why it is so difficult to distinguish between legally permissible and impermissible acts of intervention is that there is little agreement on the exact meaning of the concept. The members of the Inter-American System, after many years of debating the subject and using the concept in a variety of treaty provisions, have not devised a listing of the specific acts constituting intervention or agreed on a satisfactory general working definition of the phenomenon. General agreement prevails that the use or threat of military force is interventionist, but intervention has been further conceived to indicate a wide range of actions in economic, diplomatic, legal, moral, and political contexts. That is, it may refer to almost every form of international influence. To be useful as an analytic or operational concept, intervention needs to be defined more precisely than merely as a synonym for influence or, in effect, equated with almost all international politics.

The inter-American law of nonintervention has not deterred the United States from intervening in Latin America—nor has it deterred Latin Americans from interfering in each other's affairs. The United States has departed from the nonintervention principle on seven important occasions, all of which qualify as interventionist even according to a minimal definition: in Argentina in 1945–1946; Guatemala in 1954; Cuba in 1961; the Dominican Republic in 1965; Chile in 1970–1973; Grenada in 1983; and Nicaragua in 1984. Latin Americans also have been guilty of intervention, especially in a series of acts in the Caribbean region beginning in the late 1940s and continuing, off and on, into the late 1980s. In my judgment, however, the Latin American consensus did succeed in deterring the United States from committing more extensive acts of intervention, and OAS actions generally were effective in enforcing the rule of inter-American law, at least prior to the decline of the Inter-American System beginning in the mid-1960s.

Mutual Security

Development of Hemispheric Security Principles. Mutual security—the idea of "one for all and all for one" in combatting aggression—eventually developed into one of the main purposes of the Inter-American System. The prohibition of unilateral intervention required the fashioning of multilateral security arrangements. Such arrangements were first incorporated into the American regional system in 1938; they were refined during World War II and then stated in the OAS Charter and, most prominently, in the Rio Treaty. Some inter-American security concepts were aimed at preparing for defense against aggression from outside the hemisphere, but most of it involved disputes and interventions among the American states themselves.

The initial development of mutual security principles closely paralleled the resolution of the nonintervention issue—specifically, the changing nature of the Monroe Doctrine. From the time of Monroe's enunciation of these principles in 1823 until the threat of world war in the late 1930s, the United States considered the Monroe Doctrine to be a unilateral security concept. During World War I the United States desired a united American front against the Central Powers, but Latin America failed to comply. Of the eight Latin American states declaring war, Brazil was the only major one, and the only one from South America. The other leading states—Argentina, Chile, Colombia, and Mexico—remained neutral. U.S. intervention in the Caribbean was prevalent, and hemispheric solidarity clearly was lacking.

From time to time a Latin American state would suggest that the Monroe Doctrine be multilaterally defined and enforced. One of the most important of those proposals was made in April 1920 by President Baltasar Brum of Uruguay. The Brum Doctrine, as it came to be known, called for the multilateralization of the Monroe Doctrine and the establishment of an American League of Nations. This proposal was submitted to the Santiago Conference in 1923, but neither the other Latin American states nor the United States offered encouragement. The former were intent on attacking the latter for its intervention in the name of the Monroe Doctrine, while the United States insisted on pursuing unilateral security policies.

In the 1930s the Monroe Doctrine was finally transformed from a prime principle of U.S. unilateral policy to a basis for multilateral Pan American mutual security agreement. This transformation has been referred to as the multilateralization, Pan Americanization, or continentalization of the Monroe Doctrine. It occurred in two stages, the first of which was the abandonment of the Roosevelt Corollary. The second phase, more directly related to the principle of mutual security, involved the acceptance of the idea of multilateral hemispheric defense. Inter-American machinery was then created to implement the newly accepted principles.

The first tentative step toward the defense of the entire hemisphere, which simultaneously applied the Monroe Doctrine to the principle of a multilateral defense, was taken at the Buenos Aires Conference in 1936. There, the United States urged some sort of hemispheric defense plan, thus revealing a willingness to change its unilateral security policies. The conference adopted only a rudimentary form of the "one for all and all for one" principle in the Convention for the Maintenance, Preservation, and Re-establishment of Peace. It provided that, "in the event that the peace of the American Republics is menaced," the members of the Inter-American System should "consult together for the purpose of finding and adopting methods of peaceful cooperation."

More important measures were adopted at the Lima Conference in 1938. After considerable debate, the conferees adopted a statement of hemispheric solidarity known as the Declaration of Lima. It stated, in part, that all American states "affirmed the intention of the American Republics to help one another in case of a foreign attack, either direct or indirect, on any one of them." This declaration represented a significant step toward multilateralizing the Monroe Doctrine. Moreover, the Declaration of Lima formed the basis for subsequent wartime inter-American security collaboration.

Three foreign ministers' meetings were held during the World War II period—in 1939, 1940, and 1942. Soon after the German invasion of Poland on September 1, 1939, the First Meeting of Consultation of Ministers of

Foreign Affairs was held in Panama. The ministers agreed on the General Declaration of Neutrality, which affirmed and defined inter-American neutrality in the European war and established a neutrality zone around the Americas. The American states agreed to consult further as necessary and created the Inter-American Neutrality Committee, composed of seven international lawyers and located in Rio de Janeiro.

The second foreign ministers' meeting convened in Havana in July 1940, shortly after the fall of France. It adopted, among other things, the Declaration of Reciprocal Assistance and Cooperation for the Defense of the Americas, which further multilateralized the Monroe Doctrine in precise terms. It clearly stated that an attack by a non-American state would be considered an attack on all the Americas, and that cooperative defense measures would be taken after consultation.

After the Japanese attack on Pearl Harbor (December 7, 1941), the third foreign ministers' consultation was held in Rio de Janeiro in January 1942 in pursuance of the Havana declaration. The United States desired a resolution requiring the severance of diplomatic relations by all the American states with Japan, Germany, and Italy, and most Latin American states were willing to accept such a measure. Opposition by Argentina and Chile, however, resulted in a resolution that recommended only the rupture of relations. Another resolution created the Inter-American Defense Board, composed of military and naval advisers from all member states charged with studying the problems of hemispheric defense and recommending solutions. In addition, the Foreign Ministers agreed to establish the Emergency Advisory Committee for Political Defense, a seven-member body located in Montevideo, to investigate and coordinate measures to counter Axis subversive activities. The Inter-American Neutrality Committee was renamed the Inter-American Juridical Committee and its focus shifted to the legal problems of war.

Prior to the Rio meeting, twelve Latin American states had severed diplomatic relations with the Axis and nine of those had declared war. After the meeting, all other regional states except Argentina and Chile broke relations, and four more of them declared war. Chile and Argentina eventually ruptured relations and declared war in 1944 and 1945, respectively. Most of Latin America's armed forces did not have a major position in hemispheric defense and generally were assigned to supporting roles. There were important exceptions, however. Brazil sent an expeditionary force into combat in Italy, and the Brazilian navy assisted that of the United States in antisubmarine patrols off the Atlantic coast of South America; Mexico dispatched an aircraft squadron to the Philippine Islands. Most Latin American states cooperated in breaking Axis espionage networks and granted U.S. requests for base rights.

One of the results of the Mexico City Conference in 1945 was the Act of Chapultepec, which broadened the scope of aggression covered under mutual security arrangements to include attack by any state, meaning other American ones as well as non-American ones. Inter-American security principles and consultation procedures had been fully defined by 1945 but had lapsed at the conclusion of the war. Therefore, at the Mexico City Conference, the drafting of a permanent treaty of reciprocal assistance was authorized to be one of the first postwar actions taken by the Inter-American System. The Rio de Janeiro Conference of 1947 produced the Inter-American Treaty of Reciprocal Assistance, or Rio Treaty, reaffirming the various wartime principles on a continuing basis. It is noteworthy that the Rio Treaty of 1947 was the first permanent collective defense treaty entered into by the United States and served as an initial guide for other arrangements during the cold war.

Mutual Security Provisions. The Rio Treaty is the primary source of mutual security principles and procedures; these principles are repeated in summary form in the OAS Charter. The Rio Treaty distinguishes between armed attack and other forms of aggression and between aggression occurring within and outside of a designated geographic zone and specifies the collective responses called for under the various circumstances.

The first two paragraphs of Article 3 are worded as follows:

> The High Contracting Parties agree that an armed attack by any State against an American State shall be considered as an attack against all the American States and, consequently, each one of the said Contracting parties undertakes to assist in meeting the attack in the exercise of the inherent right of individual or collective self-defense recognized by Article 51 of the Charter of the United Nations.
>
> On the request of the State or States directly attacked and until the decision of the Organ of Consultation of the Inter-American System, each one of the Contracting Parties may determine the immediate measures which it may individually take in fulfillment of the obligation contained in the preceding paragraph and in accordance with the principle of continental solidarity. The Organ of Consultation shall meet without delay for the purpose of examining those measures and agreeing upon the measures of a collective character that should be taken.

The above provisions applied in case of an armed attack within a precisely designated geographic region, which ranged from pole to pole and included all of the continental territory of the American states (including Alaska) and the adjacent islands but not the Hawaiian Islands. Canada and Greenland were covered by the treaty even though they were not signatories.

When an armed attack took place outside the zone, presumably against the overseas possessions or other national territory or against the military forces of an American state, or when other forms of aggression occurred inside or outside the zone (the treaty does not define specific acts), Article 6 applied. It reads in part:

> The Organ of Consultation shall meet immediately in order to agree on the measures which must be taken in a case of aggression to assist the victim of the aggression or, in any case, the measures which should be taken for the common defense and for the maintenance of the peace and security of the Continent.

Article 8 listed the measures that could be applied to aggressors, singly or in combination. They were "recall of chiefs of diplomatic missions;

breaking of diplomatic relations; breaking of consular relations; partial or complete interruption of economic relations or of rail, sea, air, postal, telegraphic, telephonic, and radiotelephonic or radiotelegraphic communications; and use of armed force." Articles 17 and 18 provided that decisions by the Organ of Consultation be taken by a two-thirds majority vote, but in the case of inter-American disputes the directly interested parties were excluded from voting. Article 20 stipulated that decisions would be binding on all member states "with the sole exception that no State shall be required to use armed force without its consent."

Applications of Security Procedures. Regional security procedures under the Rio Treaty have been applied in actual cases, and the OAS Charter has been brought to bear on certain occasions. Between 1948 and 1983 the Rio Treaty was applied in twenty instances to deal with perceived threats to hemispheric peace. Most of the cases involved inter-American disputes, and all but one of them dealt with the Caribbean area. Sanctions were applied three times: against the Dominican Republic in 1960 and against Cuba in 1962 and 1964.

A series of eleven cases considered by foreign ministers' meetings—all but one convened under the Rio Treaty—involved long-standing and evolving Caribbean tensions and rivalries. They were: (1) conflict between Costa Rica and Nicaragua, 1948–1949; (2) conflict between the Dominican Republic and Haiti, 1949–1950; (3) conflict involving the Dominican Republic against Haiti, Cuba, and Guatemala, 1950; (4) conflict between Costa Rica and Nicaragua, 1955–1956; (5) conflict between Honduras and Nicaragua, 1957; (6) conflict between Panama and Cuba, 1959; (7) conflict among Nicaragua, Costa Rica, and Honduras, 1959; (8) conflict between Venezuela and the Dominican Republic, 1960–1962 (sanctions imposed on the Dominican Republic were the first levied under the Rio Treaty); (9) conflict between the Dominican Republic and Haiti, 1963–1965; (10) civil war in the Dominican Republic, 1965 (the foreign ministers met under the OAS Charter); and (11) war between El Salvador and Honduras, 1969. The Inter-American System generally was able to halt hostilities among the disputants, if not to resolve the underlying causes of the conflict.

The situation between Panama and the United States in 1964 was a special case and represented the first involvement of a non–Latin American party in an application of the Rio Treaty. Panama accused the United States of acts of aggression against its sovereignty during clashes between Panamanians and U.S. residents of the Canal Zone. The OAS Council met under the Rio Treaty, and at its urging the disputants agreed to reestablish diplomatic relations and begin friendly high-level negotiations to resolve their differences.

Seven further applications of mutual security procedures in the Caribbean were closely linked to U.S. efforts to make the Inter-American System an "anti-Communist alliance" and its subsequent decline. One case involved Guatemala in 1954. The Cuban missile crisis in 1962, and four cases related to the Cuban situation from 1962 to 1975, also involved applications of these procedures. Finally, consultation took place in 1979 in the midst of the Nicaraguan Revolution. In only two instances were cases outside the Circum-Caribbean undertaken. The Nineteenth Meeting of Ministers of Foreign Affairs was called under the OAS Charter at the request of Ecuador in January 1981 to consider armed conflict between Ecuador and Peru; the disputants consequently agreed to a cease-fire. The last case involved three meetings, one under the OAS Charter and two under the Rio Treaty, to consider the Anglo-Argentine South Atlantic war in 1982.

The *"Anti-Communist Alliance."* The evolution of an anti-Communist ideological orthodoxy began with the Tenth Inter-American Conference in Caracas (1954). The conference reflected the tension between the U.S. concern over Communist subversion and the Latin American desire for economic assistance. The United States prevailed in obtaining a declaration of inter-American commitment to collective intervention against international communism. This declaration was tacitly directed against Guatemala, which the United States presumed to be the victim of international communism, and foreshadowed the intervention in Guatemala later that year. After vigorous debate, a U.S.-sponsored resolution was adopted that said, in part:

> The domination or control of the political institution of any American State by the international communist movement extending to this Hemisphere the political system of an extracontinental power, would constitute a threat to the sovereignty and political independence of the American states, endangering the peace of America, and would call for a Meeting of Consultation to consider the adoption of appropriate action in accordance with existing treaties.

In June 1954 ten member states, at the behest of the United States, asked for the convocation of the Organ of Consultation of the Rio Treaty. They cited their concern with "the demonstrated intervention of the international communist movement in the republic of Guatemala and the danger which this involves for the peace and security of the Continent." The OAS Council met provisionally as the Organ of Consultation and called for a foreign ministers' meeting, but after the leftist Guatemalan government was replaced by a rightist military regime the meeting was canceled. The Guatemalan situation had been resolved not by the Inter-American System but by the United States, which unilaterally and covertly supported a local military intervention.

Sanctions were applied against Cuba at the Eighth Meeting of Consultation of Ministers of Foreign Affairs in Punta del Este (January 1962). The convocation was requested by Colombia and strongly supported by the United States. A resolution entitled "Exclusion of the Present Government of Cuba from Participation in the Inter-American System" was adopted. It declared "that as a consequence of repeated acts, the present government of Cuba had voluntarily placed itself outside the Inter-American System" and resolved, among other things, the following:

> That adherence by any member of the Organization of American States to Marxism-Leninism is incompatible with the Inter-American System and the align-

ment of such a government with the communist bloc breaks the unity and solidarity of the hemisphere.

That the present Government of Cuba, which has officially identified itself as a Marxist-Leninist government, is incompatible with the principles and objectives of the Inter-American System.

That this incompatibility excludes the present Government of Cuba from participation in the Inter-American System.

The resolution instructed the OAS Council "and the other organs and organizations of the Inter-American System [to] adopt without delay the measures necessary to comply with the resolution." Further limited economic sanctions were imposed by another resolution. Specifically, the foreign ministers decided "to suspend immediately trade with Cuba in arms and implements of war of every kind."

A few months later, during the Cuban missile crisis in October 1962, the OAS followed President Kennedy's "quarantine of Cuba" with a meeting of the OAS Council. A resolution insisted on "the immediate dismantling and withdrawal from Cuba of all missiles and other weapons with any offensive capability" and urged members to "take all measures, individually and collectively, including the use of armed force."

Multilateral sanctions against Cuba were expanded at the ninth foreign ministers' meeting in July 1964. This time Cuba was found guilty of aggression against Venezuela. A resolution increased the limited sanctions of 1962: all members were called upon to end their diplomatic and consular relations with Cuba; to suspend all trade except for food, medicine, and medical equipment; to suspend all sea transportation with Cuba except for that related to humanitarian purposes; and to warn Cuba that any continued acts of aggression could invite armed force against it. In 1967, Venezuela, strongly backed by the United States, charged Cuba with further aggression. The twelfth meeting of foreign ministers in that year condemned Cuba anew, but not as strongly as Venezuela and the United States had desired, and the resolutions in reality lacked force.

Eventually a clear sentiment in favor of reconsidering the Cuban case developed and spread, leading in 1975 to a major modification in the sanctions. Despite the changing Latin American views, the United States resisted any relaxation of Cuban isolation and for a time persuaded Latin American states not to ease any of the sanctions. At the fifteenth meeting of foreign ministers in November 1974, twelve Latin American states voted to end the sanctions—a majority of those who had imposed them earlier but two votes short of the necessary two-thirds majority. However, at the sixteenth meeting in July 1975, the foreign ministers enacted a "Freedom of Action Resolution." It released member states from their obligation to enforce the 1964 sanctions. Sixteen states voted in favor of the resolution, including the United States and Venezuela; Chile, Uruguay, and Paraguay opposed it; and Brazil and Nicaragua abstained. The 1962 sanctions denying Cuba participation in the Inter-American System were not addressed and continued to stand.

Proposed Rio Treaty amendments dating from 1975 indicated general Latin American dissent from the anti-Communist alliance. In fact, the Latin American view of U.S. coercion and intransigence over the Cuban issue led to most of the amendment proposals. The preamble to the treaty incorporated the principle of "ideological pluralism," stating as one of the purposes "to reaffirm and strengthen the principle of non-intervention as well as the right of all states to choose freely their political, economic, and social organization." The notion of such a plurality of systems ran counter to the U.S.-sponsored proposition that Marxism-Leninism was incompatible with inter-American principles. Another provision of the protocol, apparently motivated by past U.S. acts against Cuba, said that only a "vote of absolute majority" would be required to "rescind the measures" taken by a two-thirds vote. Finally, the treaty broadened the definition of aggression to include acts such as blockades; allowing territory to be used by another state for perpetuating acts of aggression against a third state; and sending armed bands, groups, irregulars, or mercenaries to carry out acts of armed force against another state (i.e., those instruments used by the United States against Cuba).

The Anglo-Argentine War. Continuing Latin American dissatisfaction with the state of mutual security processes was further revealed during the Anglo-Argentine War. On April 2, 1982, Argentina invaded the United Kingdom's Falkland Islands colony in the South Atlantic Ocean, asserting that it was enforcing its rightful sovereignty over the territory. The United Kingdom dispatched a naval force to the South Atlantic and appealed to the United Nations and the European Community for support. The Argentine invasion and British counterforce created a bizarre situation for the Inter-American System. Argentina had, in the view of most American states, committed aggression against a non-American state, but British counterforce required them to take up the conflict at the behest of Argentina. The United States was in a particularly uncomfortable position, not wanting a situation that, in effect, pitted its own alliances in Europe and the Americas against each other. The United States remained neutral in the conflict until April 30, 1982, attempting through its direct third-party efforts to reconcile the disputants. Perhaps inevitably, it finally sided with its European interests at the cost of further damaging its Latin American ones.

At Argentina's request, a meeting of the PCOAS under provisions of the OAS Charter was held in Washington, D.C., from April 5 to 13, 1982. Argentina was seeking inter-American support as a counter to UN condemnation and anticipated EC backing of the United Kingdom, but it was disappointed with the restrained Latin American response. With all twenty-nine participating members of the OAS present, debating, and voting, the council passed a "resolution of concern." Less than a week later, Argentina called for another inter-American meeting, this time invoking the Rio Treaty. The Twentieth Meeting of Consultation of Ministers of Foreign Affairs was called as the Organ of Consultation under the Rio Treaty procedures. Only the twenty-one signatories of the Rio Treaty were eligible to participate, thus excluding eight of the nine English-speaking Caribbean states, seven of whom were strongly pro-British. By now British forces had penetrated the hemi-spheric security zone as defined by the Rio Treaty; Argentina proposed that the British threat to hemispheric peace be met with collection sanctions as provided for in Article 8. The foreign ministers adopted a compromise resolution supporting Argentine claims to sovereignty over the Malvinas, but they refused to invoke sanctions against the United Kingdom.

The twentieth meeting was reconvened May 27–29. In the meantime, the United States had abandoned neutrality; it sided with the United Kingdom and strongly opposed Argentina. British forces had landed on the islands and were advancing. The final resolution condemned "most vigorously" the United Kingdom's "unjustified and disproportionate attack" against Argentina and called on the United States to stop assisting the UK and end its sanctions against Argentina. But the foreign ministers again refused Argentina's request for sanctions against the UK. Resolutions were passed by the same votes at both sessions of the twentieth meeting: seventeen in favor, none opposed, and four abstentions (Chile, Colombia, Trinidad-Tobago, and the United States). The majority felt compelled to demonstrate solidarity on the issue of sovereignty but had clear reservations about Argentina's use of force to assert its claims. The military campaign came to an end on June 14 with the surrender of Argentine forces, and inter-American mutual security procedures were no longer appealed to in this issue.

Peaceful Settlement

Evolution of Principles. Concern for the peaceful settlement of disputes dates from the very beginning of the Inter-American System. An important proposal for compulsory arbitration of inter-American disputes was on the agenda at the Washington Conference in 1889. Because of Chilean objec-tions—it was unwilling to jeopardize its recent territorial gains in the War of the Pacific—a compromise was adopted. Arbitration was accepted as a principle of American international law, obligatory except for those cases in which a state determined that its independence would be compromised. Eleven states signed the treaty; but fifteen ratifications were required to place it in force, and none were forthcoming. Despite the initial impasse, important inter-American provisions for the peaceful settlement of disputes were sub-sequently established. Consequently, pacific settlement principles and pro-cedures, some of them contradictory, are contained in several treaties, and the current regime presents an uncoordinated system.

A compulsory arbitration treaty was signed at the Mexico City Conference in 1902. However, so many reservations were entered that the original compulsory intent was severely eroded. Of the nine states signing the treaty, six subsequently ratified it; for them the instruments dating from 1902 remain in force. The Santiago Conference of 1923 established further peacekeeping procedures with the adoption of the Treaty to Avoid or Prevent Conflicts Between the American States. Sponsored by Dr. Manuel Gondra, the foreign minister of Paraguay, it is known as the Gondra Treaty. It is in force for twenty member states; that is, for all except Argentina and the new Caribbean Commonwealth members. It provides that all disputes that threaten to lead to armed conflict and cannot be settled through direct diplomatic negotiation be submitted to one of two commissions of inquiry, one in Montevideo and the other in Washington, D.C. The signatories agree to make no preparations for war from the time the commission is convened until six months after its report is issued, up to a total time span of eighteen months. The Gondra Treaty is designed primarily to establish a "cooling off" period for inter-American disputes.

The special Washington Conference (1928–1929) added two more conventions to the corpus of pacific settlement treaties. The General Convention of Inter-American Conciliation remains in force among eighteen member states, and the General Treaty of Inter-American Arbitration continues to be adhered to by sixteen members. The General Convention, intended as a supplement to the Gondra Treaty, adds conciliatory functions to the duties of the commissions of inquiry and provides for states to resort to the commissions on a voluntary basis. The General Treaty binds the contracting parties to submit to arbitration any international dispute arising from a claim of right that could be decided by an application of legal principles. Four years later, in 1933 at Montevideo, six states agreed to the Anti-War Treaty of Non-Aggression and Conciliation sponsored by Argentine Foreign Minister Carlos Saavedra Lamas (for which he received the Nobel Peace Prize). At the special Buenos Aires Conference in 1935, the signing of the Inter-American Treaty of Good Offices and Mediation, later ratified by fifteen states, completed the pre–World War II pacific settlement regime. In addition, a number of bilateral treaties of arbitration, inquiry, and conciliation were signed by several American states in the 1920s and 1930s.

Attempted Coordination. Those attending the Mexico City Conference (1945) perceived a need for a single treaty to coordinate the various measures providing for the peaceful settlement of disputes in the Inter-American System. It ordered a draft treaty, which was presented at the Bogotá Conference (1948). The resultant Inter-American Treaty of Pacific Settlement (Pact of Bogotá) called for obligatory settlement by the signatories. It sanctioned all the standard peaceful techniques as satisfactory alternatives, including good offices, mediation, investigation, conciliation, and arbitration, both by regional bodies and before the World Court. The debate over the treaty's adoption reflected a long-standing division, with some states contending that all states should be obligated to submit all their disputes for some sort of third-party settlement, and others favoring the availability of voluntary standing settlement procedures.

The treaty entered into effect only for those states ratifying it and superseded all prior agreements to which they were party. Thirteen states have ratified the pact: Brazil, Colombia, Costa Rica, Dominican Republic, El Salvador, Haiti, Honduras, Mexico, Nicaragua, Panama, Paraguay, Peru, and Uruguay. Earlier instruments remain in force for the remaining states as well as for disputes between ratifying and nonratifying parties.

The OAS Charter refers to the desirability of peaceful settlement of inter-American disputes. The Rio Treaty, while primarily concerned with mutual security, also has provisions relevant to pacific settlement.

Democracy and Human Rights

Early Latin American Propositions. Several early Latin American doctrines attempting to resolve the tension in Pan Americanism caused by the conflicting demands of democracy and nonintervention preceded the formalization of the two principles in treaties. There have been three major Latin American exponents of democracy and human rights: the Chilean Pedro Felix Vicuña, the Argentine Juan Bautista Alberdi, and the Ecuadorian Carlos R. Tobar. (This section relies on Wilson, 1964:85–88, and Bemis, 1943:412, n.40).

Vicuña was perhaps the earliest American advocate of collective action to promote democracy. His plan, set forth in a pamphlet published in 1837, called for a "Great American Congress" to support democratic governments and popular revolutions and to oppose tyrannies. The regional organization would intervene on the side of constitutional governments, thus combining physical power with moral force. In 1844, Alberdi, the principal architect of the Argentine Constitution of 1853, supported Vicuña's idea of an American Congress. He further proposed an American Court with the right to intervene against any state violating its decisions. This court would be supported by the Latin American states and certain European states, but not the United States. Alberdi believed in national sovereignty and nonintervention, but he argued that ultimate sovereignty and rights of collective intervention resided with the international community to protect humanity and oppose tyranny. In 1907, Tobar, a retired Ecuadoran diplomat, proposed a policy of collective nonrecognition of governments coming to power by other than democratic means. The Tobar Doctrine argued that the American republics "should intervene, at least mediately and indirectly, in the internal dissensions of the republics of the continent. This intervention might be, at least, by denying recognition to governments *de facto* born of revolutions against the constitutional order."

Other Latin American propositions were interventionist and thus challenged the above doctrines. Principal among them was the Estrada Doctrine, advanced by Mexican Foreign Minister Genaro Estrada in 1930, which challenged the Tobar Doctrine. Estrada asserted the principle of continuous diplomacy and said that new governments should be automatically recognized—an act that did not indicate approval of a regime but rather acknowledged its existence and its political control of a state.

Inter-American Principles in Conflict. A dilemma between democracy and nonintervention has long existed for the Inter-American System. The American states have committed themselves to the promotion of representative democracy and the protection of human rights (that is, to democracy in both its procedural aspects and its substantive or ethical content) at the same time that they have posited nonintervention as a basic principle. Consequently, they have been faced with this question: How can representative democracy be promoted and human rights enforced, including opposition to nondemocratic regimes, without violating the principle of nonintervention? Most Latin American states have adopted a preferential position toward nonintervention. From time to time, others have taken a more complex view and have been willing to allow some sort of collective intervention in certain instances.

In late 1945 and early 1946 the American states considered a proposal by Uruguayan Foreign Minister Eduardo Rodríguez Larreta appealing for collective intervention to oppose dictators and promote democracy and human rights. Rodríguez's plan (often erroneously referred to in English as the "Larreta" doctrine) was implicitly directed against Argentina, small Uruguay's then Fascist-inclined and more powerful neighbor. However, it had broad implications for general inter-American relations. Rodríguez argued that peace was safe only where democratic principles of government prevailed and that the inter-American obligation to promote democracy and human rights should transcend the principle of nonintervention. He proposed that in the case of the violation of the basic rights of man in any American state, "the community of nations should take collective multilateral action to restore full democracy there" (U.S. Department of State, *Bulletin*, November 25, 1945:864–866).

The United States fully endorsed the plan, and it was supported with some reservations by six Latin American governments. The remainder of the Latin American states, however, rejected the proposal outright or made such serious qualifications as to be tantamount to rejection. The Latin American view prevailed that no modification of the nonintervention principle was permissible, despite the awareness that absolute nonintervention tended to insulate oppressive governments from community action.

Principles of democracy and human rights were strongly reaffirmed in both the Rio Treaty and the OAS Charter. The Rio Treaty preamble stated that "peace is founded . . . on the effectiveness of democracy for the international realization of justice and security." The preamble of the OAS Charter declared: "The true significance of American solidarity and good neighborliness can only mean the consolidation on this continent, within the framework of democratic institutions of a system of individual liberty and social justice based on respect for the essential rights of man." Article 5 of the charter, devoted to "Principles," included the statements that "the solidarity of the American States and the high aims which are sought through it require the political organization of those states on the basis of the effective exercise of representative democracy," and that "social justice and social security are bases of lasting peace." The same document, however, also posited nonintervention as a fundamental principle. Furthermore, at the Bogotá Conference in 1948, the United States led a move for a return to the principle of continuous diplomacy advocated in the Estrada Doctrine. Consequently, a resolution was adopted declaring that "continuity of diplomatic relations among the American States is desirable," and that "the establishment or maintenance of diplomatic relations with a government does not imply any judgment upon the domestic policy of that government."

Article 22 of the amended charter (Article 19 in the original) provides for collective intervention under certain circumstances, offering a possible solution to the dilemma. Most of the Latin American states, however, have been unwilling to invoke it or to compromise the rule of nonintervention in any manner. For them, nonintervention transcends even democratic development. The majority view nonintervention as an absolute legal obligation and the commitment to democracy as a relative moral obligation. This Latin American consensus has been made clear in several debates and decisions.

Shortly after the Rodríguez Larreta plan was rejected, inter-American judicial procedures began to be applied to Caribbean conflicts. These conflicts largely resulted from ideological differences between closely proximate dictatorial and (more or less) democratic states. The problem for the Inter-American System was that two fundamental Pan American principles—the doctrines of nonintervention and democratic development—had been pitted against one another. The principle of nonintervention received higher priority. The OAS Council, at its meeting on April 8, 1950, resolved the following:

> [Considering] that both the principle of representative democracy and that of nonintervention are established in many inter-American pronouncements, and that both are basic principles of harmonious relations among the countries of America; and that there exists some confusion of ideas as to the means of harmonizing the effective execution and application of the basic principle of nonintervention and that of the exercise of democracy; [be it resolved] to reaffirm the principles of representative democracy [but] to declare that the aforementioned principles do not in any way and under any concept authorize any governments to violate inter-American commitments relative to the principles of nonintervention.

The Inter-American System appeared in one case to serve as an "antidictatorial alliance," but this case, too, exhibited its commitment to the nonintervention principle (Slater, 1967:Ch. VI). The sixth foreign ministers' meeting in August 1960 condemned the harshly dictatorial Trujillo government in the Dominican Republic for its assassination attempt against Romulo Betancourt, the democratically elected president of Venezuela. The foreign ministers voted to impose sanctions on the Trujillo regime, including the breaking of diplomatic relations and imposing an arms embargo. The debate did not revolve around a preoccupation with nonintervention, and the Trujillo dictatorship was almost universally detested. However, the Dominican government itself had violated the nonintervention principle and was guilty of aggression as well as the violation of human rights. The reason for the sanctions was not primarily to promote democracy and human rights but rather to punish that state for intervening in Venezuelan affairs. Since the end of the Trujillo regime in 1961, no indications of "antidictatorial alliances" were found until the Nicaraguan case in 1978/1979.

The Nicaraguan Situation. The OAS became involved in the Nicaraguan civil war, but the United States had only limited influence in the process. The Seventeenth Meeting of Consultation of Ministers of Foreign Affairs convened in Washington on September 21, 1978, in response to the request by Venezuela to consider the worsening conflict in Nicaragua. The Somoza government in Nicaragua favored the convocation so that it could "demonstrate to the world how foreign interventions are trying to implant Marxist-Leninist ideals" in Nicaragua. The deliberations led to a visit by the Human Rights Commission to Nicaragua; its subsequent report in October 1978 was highly critical of human rights violations by the Somoza government. The OAS attempted to mediate the situation, but the Somoza government rejected as "interventionist" the ultimate plan that called for an OAS-supervised referendum and Somoza's resignation.

Thereafter, the revolutionary National Liberation Sandinist Front (FSLN) gained strength against the Somoza regime, and border disputes between Costa Rica and Nicaragua increased in number. In mid-October, at their seventeenth meeting, the foreign ministers censured Nicaragua for its air attacks near the Costa Rican border in which bombs and machine guns were used against Costa Rican civilians.

In June 1979 the seventeenth meeting again reconvened, at U.S. request, to consider the "critical situation" in Nicaragua. After referring to mounting evidence of involvement by Cuba in the internal affairs of Nicaragua, U.S. Secretary of State Cyrus Vance submitted a resolution calling for the establishment of a government of national reconciliation and providing for the presence of an inter-American force for the maintenance of peace in Nicaragua. The proposal was rejected; the idea of a peace force again raised fears of intervention. The final resolution, adopted on June 23, referred to the inhumane conduct of the Somoza regime and called for its immediate replacement by a pluralist representative government, for the guarantee of respect for human rights for all Nicaraguans, and for the holding of free elections as soon as possible. It also resolved that OAS member states scrupulously respect the principle of nonintervention. The resolution was unprecedented; for the first time the Inter-American System had called for the replacement of a head of state. Somoza and other dissenting military governments argued that the resolution was interventionist, but to no avail.

Human Rights Cases. Included in the provisions of the American Convention of Human Rights are the right to life, liberty, personal security, habeas corpus, due process, equality before the law, fair trials, freedom from arbitrary arrest, and freedom of speech, assembly, association, political participation, and religion. The Inter-American Commission on Human Rights was established in 1960 as an OAS advisory group; its power is limited to moral suasion and it is required to work in concert with an accused government. Cuba refused to allow the commission to investigate its situation in the early 1960s, and later Guatemala was unwilling to receive it in an investigatory role. The commission then played an active role in the Dominican crisis of 1965–1966 under an expanded mandate from the inter-American conference at Rio de Janeiro in 1965. It followed with investigations in Honduras, El Salvador, and Haiti; its factual findings were accepted, but no further actions were taken. In 1970 the commission was made an official body of the OAS, empowered to "keep vigilance over the observance of human rights." Its membership is composed of seven jurists elected by the council to four-year terms.

The reluctance of OAS members in the 1970s and 1980s to apply multilateral sanctions in cases of human rights violations has been reflected in a series of cases. In 1970, in response to complaints filed against Brazil, the Human Rights Commission was refused permission from the Brazilian government to conduct an on-the-scene investigation. It continued to investigate from outside the country for four years, however, and presented its report to the OAS General Assembly at its 1974 meeting in Atlanta. The detailed account, containing considerable evidence gathered despite Brazil's opposition, concluded with a presumption of grave human rights violations, including torture and murder of political prisoners. The General Assembly voted unanimously to take note of the report with thanks to the commission for its work, but not to discuss it, and to table the study and its unprecedented charges.

The Human Rights Commission received complaints against the military government in Chile after the Allende government was overthrown in September 1973. The commission made a two-week visit to Chile in July–August 1974. Its investigations resulted in a 175-page report that found "extremely serious violations," citing summary executions, torture, mass detention, and various deprivations of legal and political rights. Chile strongly objected to the charges. Two years later, in March 1976, three of the seven commission members—jurists from Uruguay, Argentina, and the United States—announced that they would not seek reelection, and in April the executive secretary from Bolivia, who had served for sixteen years, resigned the post. All of them cited the lack of OAS action on their report on Chile as a major reason for their resignation. They questioned whether OAS members sincerely desired to further the cause of human rights.

The OAS General Assembly meeting in Santiago in June 1976 further revealed serious divisions over these basic questions. Three agenda items concerned human rights: the Human Rights Commission's annual report; its special report on Chile and the latter's reply; and a proposal by Chile to limit the commission's mandate. The Human Rights Commission's annual report found flagrant human rights violations by sixteen member states, including the United States, and documented large numbers of abuses. The chief target was Chile, the subject of a special report charging that most human rights abuses continued. Chile issued a denial. The General Assembly again voted to "take note" of the commission's findings and to continue monitoring human rights in the hemisphere with special attention to Chile. Chile and Brazil abstained in the voting; the United States strongly supported the commission and its charges against Chile.

At the General Assembly meeting in 1977, U.S. Secretary of State Cyrus Vance introduced a resolution stating, in part, that "there are no circumstances which justify torture, summary executions or prolonged detention without trial contrary to law." The resolution passed by a vote of 14–0, with 8 abstentions (Argentina, Brazil, Chile, Colombia, El Salvador, Guatemala,

Paraguay, and Uruguay) and 3 absences (Bolivia, Honduras, and Nicaragua). At the General Assembly meeting in 1981, however, Secretary of State Alexander Haig emphasized the Communist threat in Central America and dismissed the human rights issues. The Human Rights Commission had submitted reports on violations in Argentina, Bolivia, El Salvador, Guatemala, and Nicaragua. The assembly simply acknowledged their receipt.

Economic Cooperation

During the initial stages of the Inter-American System in the late nineteenth century, the United States was primarily interested in expanding its commercial relations, while Latin Americans were attracted for political and legal reasons, especially the need for security from outside incursions and promotion of the nonintervention principle. The U.S. proposal at the Washington Conference in 1889–1890 for an American customs union received almost no Latin American support. During the period of U.S. interventionism during the first third of the twentieth century, Latin Americans were suspicious of U.S. economic overtures while remaining more interested in political and security rather than economic matters.

Important developments in inter-American economic cooperation occurred during the period surrounding World War II. The First Meeting of Consultation of Ministers of Foreign Affairs (1939) created the Inter-American Financial and Advisory Committee (FEAC), consisting of an economic expert from each member state, to anticipate economic problems consequent to war. The Second Meeting of Consultation in 1940 expanded FEAC's functions and endorsed a number of its projects. These included programs for marketing surplus products, concluding commodity agreements, and establishing the Inter-American Development Commission (in June 1940) to aid in Latin American economic diversification. The Third Meeting of Consultation, held in 1942 soon after the Japanese attack on Pearl Harbor, gave FEAC the additional tasks of developing programs for the production of strategic materials, obtaining capital investments, improving transportation facilities, and breaking economic relations with Axis states. FEAC was one of the most active wartime inter-American agencies (Mecham, 1965:133–135, 142–145, 150).

During the initial post–World War II years, the United States was primarily interested in persuading the Inter-American System to organize itself against communism in the Americas, while the Latin Americans emphasized multilateral technical assistance and economic development programs. Concomitant to the establishment of U.S. technical assistance programs on a worldwide scale after 1949, the OAS conducted relatively small but effective programs. The United States clearly was unwilling to establish large multilateral economic development programs.

When Latin American pressure mounted in the late 1950s, U.S. positions began to change. In September 1958 President Juscelino Kubitschek of Brazil proposed an "Operation Pan America" to an informal meeting of American foreign ministers in Washington. This economic development program was designed primarily to raise Latin American social and economic living standards. The foreign ministers recommended two important measures: (1) the establishment of an inter-American financial institution for economic development (something Latin Americans had been suggesting for decades); and (2) the creation of a committee to recommend additional measures for economic cooperation.

Action soon followed. The Inter-American Development Bank (IDB) was established on December 31, 1959. In 1960 the United States formally proposed an economic development program to be administered by the IDB; this Eisenhower Plan received inter-American support in the Act of Bogotá of 1960. The Alliance for Progress, articulated by President Kennedy in 1961, was multilateralized by the Charter of Punta del Este, enacted on August 17, 1961. The charter listed twelve goals toward which the American states agreed to work during the decade of the 1960s. In sum, they committed themselves to policies that would achieve substantial and sustained growth, more equitable distribution of income, economic diversification and industrialization, increased agricultural productivity, agrarian reform, educational advances, increased and improved public health, increased availability of low-cost housing and public services, stable price levels, strengthened international economic integration, and stabilized earnings from primary product exports.

The IDB was the world's first regional multilateral bank, a lending agency designed to promote the economic and social development of its Latin American members. The first president was the eminent Chilean economist Felipe Herrera. He served two five-year terms, from the bank's inception until October 1970. Herrera was succeeded by Antonio Ortiz Mena in November 1970. Ortiz Mena, a former Mexican finance minister, was IDB president for seventeen years; he resigned in February 1988 during his fourth term. Uruguayan Foreign Minister Enrique Iglesias assumed the IDB presidency in April 1988. A prestigious economist and diplomat, he had been executive secretary of the UN Economic Commission on Latin America (ECLA) for thirteen years (1972–1985) prior to being named foreign minister.

IDB operations have been financed largely by member contributions as well as by special funds donated by individual states and the sale of bank bonds. When the bank was first organized an ordinary capital account was established for "hard loans" of an orthodox nature, and the Social Progress Trust Fund was created to finance social development projects with longer terms and lower interest rates than the ordinary loans. By 1965 the trust fund had been almost entirely disbursed; its remaining resources were transferred to the new and further capitalized Fund for Special Operations (FSO) to continue "soft loans." Total IDB capital resources had risen from $1.4 billion in 1960, to $11.5 billion in 1975, to $44 billion in early 1988; negotiations for the terms of a $20–25 billion increase had begun in 1985.

The United States has been the largest subscriber to the IDB from the beginning. It reduced its support in the early 1970s, leading the bank to search for additional capital resources from other states. Canada, new Caribbean states, and then nonhemispheric state members pledged additional capital shares. Expanded membership broadened the IDB's financial base, with Latin Americans hoping that it would erode U.S. domination.

The issue of U.S. predominance in IDB lending decisions has been debated throughout the life of the bank, with the debates focused on the fact that voting power is weighted according to the size of a member's contribution in proportion to the total. The Board of Directors approves loans from the ordinary capital account by simple majority. FSO loans, however, require a two-thirds majority. Until 1976 the United States had about 40 percent of the FSO weighted voting; with new member contributions after that date, the U.S. voting proportion dropped, standing at 34.5 percent in early 1988. Latin American members then collectively controlled 54 percent, and the remaining nineteen members, 11.5 percent.

From its inception, both advocates and critics of the bank's operations have viewed the institution as a "borrowers' bank," as voting power has been as much in the hands of loan recipients as in those of the principal contributors. The United States has argued that it should have an even greater share of the weighted voting. The U.S. Treasury, which has the primary voice in U.S. international financial matters, has since the late 1960s resisted the vision of development elaborated by Felipe Herrera. For example, the IDB pioneered in agrarian reform lending, a practice the United States considered outside the realm of sound development standards. The United States also expressed displeasure from time to time (especially during the Reagan administration) at the lack of a free-enterprise approach in Latin America and at the notion of the state as the primary force for economic development. Since 1985 the United States has clashed with the bank over expansion of its capital resources. The Reagan administration made its offer of an additional $9 billion contribution over four years contingent on an increased share of the weighted voting. When the Board of Directors rejected a formal U.S. proposal to that end, the United States delayed any increase in its capital contributions.

Latin Americans fear that ceding more control to the United States would allow it to impose its preferred development model on the entire region. U.S. standards, they said, did not apply to their developmental needs. While Latin Americans were willing to accept the U.S. approach to the debt crisis after 1982, they resisted its ideas about economic development in the private sector. Latin Americans further claimed that at times the United States had, in effect, a veto power. They pointed out that the United States had blocked new developmental assistance to Peru in the late 1960s, Chile in the early 1970s, and Nicaragua in the 1980s when it was having bilateral political conflicts with those states. Moreover, they argued that development loan decisions must be restricted to economic criteria and must not be based on political and ideological debates.

BIBLIOGRAPHIC COMMENT

Comprehensive studies of the Inter-American System and the OAS with historical or political frames of reference tend to be dated but are still useful.

They include Connell-Smith (1966), Fenwick (1963), Fernández-Shaw (1963), Mecham (1961), Sepúlveda (1973), and Thomas and Thomas (1963). Martz and Schoultz (1980) edited an excellent set of analytical essays. Documentary collections and legal studies include Carnegie Endowment for International Peace (1931, 1940, 1943) and Inter-American Institute for Legal Studies (1966). Pan American Union (1981) reproduces the OAS Charter, Rio Treaty, and Convention on Human Rights. For views of the proposed charter amendments, Rio Treaty reforms, and the draft convention on collective economic security, see Pan American Union (1973–1975).

The distinguished jurist Sepúlveda (1975) wrote on the old question of American international law; Latin American views of international and inter-American law, and analyses of the latter's development, are presented by Alvarez (1922), Caicedo Castilla (1970), Jacobini (1954), Rodley and Ronning (1974), and Taylor (1963). Bryan (1986) discusses Commonwealth Caribbean perspectives of the OAS.

Various Pan American principles and practices have received considerable scholarly attention. Díaz Albonico (1977) analyzes a wide range of activities. Wilson (1986) dissects contemporary Central American conflict in terms of international law and nonintervention. Child (1980) wrote the leading work on the inter-American military system; Gómez Robledo (1959) provides an earlier general treatment of security arrangements. On post–World War II Caribbean conflict, see Corominas (1954), Jameson (1950), and U.S. Department of State (1962); for applications of the Rio Treaty through 1972, see Pan American Union (1973). On inter-American security as it related to Castro's Cuba, see Oliver (1964) and the reexamination by Jamison (1980). Buergenthal, Norris, and Shelton (1983) is an authoritative, detailed textbook on the Inter-American System's regional approach to human rights. Still of interest on matters of democracy and human rights are Sandifer and Scheman (1966) and Wilson (1964). Inter-American Development Bank works (1966, 1974, 1984, 1985) relate to multilateral economic relations. On the Inter-American Development Bank, see Dell (1972) and Inter-American Development Bank (1974); see also Herrera (1970). Scheman (1987) is a current assessment of the Inter-American System.

CHAPTER NINE

■

Global and Extraregional Arrangements

THE ROLE OF THE LATIN AMERICAN STATES in a number of international institutions beyond the Western Hemisphere is the subject of this chapter. Most of these institutions are twentieth-century creations. The chapter deals with Latin American participation in the Hague Peace Conferences, the League of Nations, the United Nations System, and in an assortment of commodities agreements and the Nonaligned Movement. In general, Latin American states have made the same uses of extraregional organizations as they have of regional and subregional ones. That is, to the extent that they can, they seek to restrict the actions of more powerful states and to gain substantive economic and other benefits for themselves. The global and extraregional arrangements themselves not only regulate certain aspects of the international system in which Latin American states participate but also reflect certain policies of the external states toward Latin America.

GLOBAL ORGANIZATION TO WORLD WAR II

The Hague System

Two great currents of international politics, arbitration and disarmament, played conspicuous roles in the international system at the beginning of the twentieth century. The first attempts to devise universal multilateral approaches to the problems of war and peace took place at two peace conferences at The Hague in 1899 and 1907. The Permanent Court of Arbitration (the Hague Court) was established in 1899 and revised in 1907, and declarations in both years placed limited prohibitions on certain instruments of war. Plans for holding a third conference were dropped because of the increasing conflicts among nations immediately preceding World War I.

Planners of the First Peace Conference at The Hague (1899) largely ignored the Latin American states. Only Brazil and Mexico were invited, and only the latter attended. However, all twenty Latin American states were invited to the Second Peace Conference (1907) at the behest of the United

States. Eighteen of them participated; only Costa Rica and Honduras passed up the forty-four–nation gathering. The Prestigious Latin American representatives played active roles at the conference, especially Ruy Barbosa of Brazil, Luis M. Drago of Argentina, and Santiago Pérez Triana of Colombia. U.S. Professor Leo S. Rowe, later director general of the Pan American Union, said at the 1907 meeting of the American Political Science Association that Latin American participation "was but the formal recognition of an accomplished fact—the establishment of a group of sovereign and independent states in the southern hemisphere, whose political importance can no longer be ignored." In fact, their participation brought the Latin American region into international prominence for the first time.

Once they were offered the Hague Conference as a forum, the Latin American states mounted a concerted effort to have nonintervention accepted as a principle of international law. This effort paralleled their attempts to do the same in inter-American law. A resolution had been approved at the International Conference of American States at Rio de Janeiro in 1906 recommending that the forthcoming Hague Peace Conference discuss the Drago Doctrine regarding the legal prohibition of force for the collection of public pecuniary claims. With U.S. support, the Latin American delegates succeeded in having a version of the Drago Doctrine adopted as a principle of general international law, but they were greatly disappointed over the extent to which it was modified. The conference adopted the Porter Doctrine (submitted by U.S. delegate Horace Porter), which prohibited the use of force in the collection of public debts unless the debtor state refused to submit the claim to arbitration or, having gone to arbitration, failed to comply with the decision. The Drago Doctrine itself tolerated no intervention whatsoever. No South American government ratified the convention, and the four Latin American states that did ratify it made reservations restoring the treaty to absolute nonintervention (Wilson, 1964:36–38, and Mecham, 1965:99). Despite their failure to have their version of the law adopted, Latin Americans had made it clear that another community existed championing international legal rules differing profoundly from those generally accepted in Europe and the United States.

Because of the insignificance of Latin American armed forces in 1907, they received little consideration in disarmament questions. Yet one South American arrangement was of some importance. During discussions on the limitation of armed forces, the arms control agreements between Argentina and Chile (the "Pacts of May" of 1902) were given serious consideration by the European representatives, who viewed the Argentine-Chilean agreements, providing for the arbitration of all differences between the two states and the limitation of their naval forces, as among the most modern of arms control arrangements.

The League of Nations

The Latin American states that had declared war on or severed relations with Germany during World War I participated in the subsequent Versailles

Peace Conference. They strongly supported President Woodrow Wilson's project for a League of Nations. Ten of them signed the Versailles Treaty, which included the Covenant of the League of Nations, and thereby became charter members of the organization. Eventually, all twenty Latin American states joined the League for at least a limited time. Latin American participation in the League was intermittent, however; never were all of them members at the same time. Fifteen Latin American states were members when the first League Assembly met in 1920. By 1923 all of them except the Dominican Republic, Ecuador, and Mexico were members; in 1934 only Brazil and Costa Rica, both of which had withdrawn in 1926, did not belong.

A regional consciousness was reflected both in Latin American behavior in the League and in the attitudes of the other members toward Latin America. An informal Latin American bloc was formed, primarily in order to assure the election of Latin American representatives to the Assembly and the Council and to obtain positions for their nationals in the Secretariat. The League itself, anxious to keep Latin Americans as members in pursuit of the ideal of universality, established a special Liaison Bureau for the region and dispatched the Secretariat on a regional visit to Latin America (Bailey, 1967:146, and Rippy, 1958:519).

Latin American delegates in Geneva used every opportunity to lecture about their contributions to world peace. They also expressed basic principles that anticipated their later actions under the UN System. For example, in 1927 Chile proposed a system of regional Latin American agreements designed to prevent any competitive armaments; security requirements in the region, the delegates said, were unique and European standards therefore should not apply. Furthermore, security should be achieved by means of a system of arbitration and conciliation. Indeed, most Latin American states opposed arms control through global arrangements, emphasizing that the region was appreciably different from the rest of the world. In 1928 Argentina declared arbitration to be "an essentially American principle" and a sufficient guarantee of security.

The Latin American states were attracted to the League for several reasons, including the prestige that membership might bring, the League's adherence to such principles as arbitration and judicial settlement, and its potential as a counterpoise to U.S. interventionism. The League offered little opportunity for Latin America to press for economic advantages in the way of aid or trade preferences, as such activities were of peripheral importance to the organization. The Latin American states succeeded in accumulating a certain amount of prestige from their League activities and participation; they gained nonpermanent seats on the League Council and representation on the World Court and elected presidents of the Assembly. On the other hand, the League paid little attention to Latin American disputes and played almost no role in limiting U.S. power in Latin America.

The first major disappointment for Latin Americans occurred at the Versailles Conference when the League Covenant was adopted. Article X of the Covenant seemed to fulfill the Latin American desire for an international law of nonintervention. It read: "The Members of the League undertake to respect and preserve as against external aggression the territorial integrity and existing political independence of all Members of the League." However, Article XXI, included despite Latin American protests that it contradicted Article X, stated: "Nothing in this Covenant shall be deemed to affect the validity of international engagements, such as treaties of arbitration or regional understandings like the Monroe Doctrine, for securing the maintenance of peace." Article XXI was designed to make the Covenant more acceptable to the U.S. Senate; it prompted two Latin American delegations to withdraw from the Versailles Conference. The Covenant made no other mention of regional arrangements.

Later events further eroded the League's utility as a counterweight to U.S. power in Latin America. The United States refused to join the League, freeing it from the limitations that could have been imposed by membership. Furthermore, the League largely refrained from dealing with inter-American problems. It ignored the Tacna-Arica dispute involving Chile versus Peru and Bolivia, as well as a dispute between Panama and Costa Rica, largely because of U.S. protests in both instances. In two cases the League attempted to settle inter-American disputes—the Chaco War between Bolivia and Paraguay, and the Leticia conflict between Peru and Colombia—but both times it deferred to U.S. actions.

Intermittent clashes in the Chaco area between Bolivia and Paraguay beginning in 1927 led to full-scale war between them from 1932 to 1936. In September 1932, two months after the war broke out, the League Council established a commission to offer alternative plans to settle the war, but none was accepted. An inter-American committee, established at about the same time for the same purpose, deferred to the League Commission in 1933, but the effort still failed. In 1935 the League labeled Paraguay as the aggressor, making it the first state to be the object of League sanctions; Paraguay promptly withdrew from the League. When the disputants in 1936 became exhausted by the tragic and bloody conflict and were prepared to accept third-party assistance in its settlement, another inter-American commission was organized, in which the United States played an important role. The Inter-American System, not the League of Nations, finally arranged a settlement that Paraguay and Bolivia both accepted in 1938.

On the surface the League action in the Leticia affair might appear to have been successful, but in fact the United States played the leading role in its settlement. In 1933 Colombia appealed to the League Council to settle its decade-old argument with Peru over the ownership of the small Amazon River town of Leticia and the surrounding area. The international body established a special Administrative Commission for the Territory of Leticia, consisting of representatives from Spain, Brazil, and the United States. The commission administered the Leticia area for about a year in 1933–1934—the first police action in the history of general international organization—while mediation between the disputants was carried on. In 1934 sovereignty was awarded to Colombia. Neither the United States nor

Brazil was a member of the League at the time; Brazil was closely aligned with the United States, and Spain was unassertive in the matter. Consequently, the United States controlled the commission of an international body to which it did not belong. Furthermore, the League was ignored in the protocol terminating the conflict, in which Colombia and Peru referred to their "historical, social, and sentimental ties" as members of the "American community" (Bailey, 1967:147–148).

THE UNITED NATIONS SYSTEM

Latin American Participation and Regional Consciousness

Regional participation in the United Nations has been universal and continuous, in contrast to the intermittent nature of Latin American membership in the League of Nations. Consequently, the Latin American states have always formed a significant proportion of the UN membership, although their relative voting strength has declined as UN membership has increased. The number of Latin American members remained constant at twenty from 1945, when the first General Assembly convened, until 1962. At that time, the first new states within the Latin American region began to join the world body and total regional membership eventually grew in number to thirty-three. At the same time, total UN membership increased from fifty-one original members in 1945 to 162 as of 1987, reducing the Latin American proportion from about 39 percent to about 20 percent. Prior to 1955, reaching a decision in the General Assembly over united Latin American opposition was a difficult proposition. The reduction in relative Latin American strength since the mid-1950s has been offset somewhat by a degree of voting solidarity among the regional states. Their influence is greatest on "substantive" questions in the General Assembly requiring a two-thirds majority for adoption.

The relatively high degree of consistency with which the Latin American states have voted together in the world body indicates a measure of regional cohesion, although they have not always voted en bloc in the way that the iron curtain countries once did. Prior to 1960 the regional states generally supported the United States on cold war issues, but their twenty votes were never automatically assured. On "anticolonial" (dependent area) questions, they tended to favor increased colonial self-government and independence, including UN supervision of the independence process. Latin American states joined the other developing nation members in calling for maximum funding of technical assistance and economic development projects. They also urged the creation of an Economic Commission for Latin America within the Economic and Social Council.

Latin Americans were less amenable to U.S. leadership in the 1960s and began to divide on cold war issues. Cuba joined the Soviet bloc after 1960; others increasingly adopted independent stances. They also began to divide on colonial issues, although they were virtually unanimous in condemning racism in South Africa. Most Latin American members continued to vote consistently to extend economic and technical programs and voted with considerable unity on humanitarian and social cooperation and administrative matters. They also tended to vote as a bloc in UN elections.

Latin America's regional self-perception has been enhanced by their membership in the UN System. They formed a bloc at the San Francisco Conference in 1945. Thereafter, they met as a caucusing group during annual General Assembly meetings so as to ensure that Latin American interests were represented and maximum voting strength assured. The caucuses were informal in nature until the Ninth General Assembly convened in 1953 when the procedures were formalized. Thereafter, the self-named Latin American Caucusing Group held regular biweekly meetings chaired by the Latin American delegate who had been elected a vice-president of the General Assembly. When the OAS in 1964 imposed sanctions on Cuba isolating it diplomatically, the Latin American Caucusing Group reverted to informal meetings to which Cuba was not invited (with one exception in March 1973). Cuba was finally readmitted on January 29, 1975, when the caucus chairman convened a formal meeting with Cuba attending and no other Latin American state objected. The formal Latin American Caucusing Group was reinstituted with all regional states participating.

The Latin American caucus is the longest-standing regional grouping in the UN. Although its decisions are not binding on members, it has succeeded in defining regional positions on issues before the UN, gained general agreement on tactics to be pursued, and negotiated the election of Latin Americans to fill offices in various UN bodies.

The UN's Relationship to the Inter-American System

Some early proponents and founders of the global UN organization argued that the global institution was incompatible with regional organizations. More of them, including U.S. Secretary of State Cordell Hull, accepted the existence of regional organizations but insisted that they be superseded by the UN in authority. Enough pressure was brought to bear at the organizing conference at San Francisco in 1945, particularly by the Latin American states acting as a bloc, to have the UN Charter sanction regional organization. The effort was led by Alberto Lleras Camargo of Colombia (who became secretary general of the Pan American Union in 1946). The charter subjects regional arrangements to considerable direction by the UN, but in practice, the Inter-American System enjoyed considerable autonomy until it began to erode in the early 1970s.

Article 51 of the UN Charter recognized regional arrangements as being compatible with global organization and especially appropriate to the settlement of regional disputes. The provision gave the Security Council the right to intervene in those settlements and allowed individual states the right to appeal directly to the global body. In practice, however, the UN has deferred to the Inter-American System. Although some regional disputes have been taken directly to the UN, and some OAS decisions have been appealed there, the Inter-American System for the most part has been the only forum for issues relating to American peace and security, with little UN action forthcoming.

A few examples suffice to illustrate the UN relationship with the Inter-American System. In June 1954 Guatemala appealed to the Security Council in accusing Honduras and Nicaragua of aggression. (Guatemala was not then a party to the Rio Treaty or the OAS Charter.) The Latin American members of the Security Council, supported by the United States, wanted to refer the matter to the OAS, but a resolution to that effect was vetoed by the Soviet Union. A French resolution calling for a cease-fire was then adopted. The Security Council considered a subsequent Guatemalan request for another review of the issue but then declined to place the issue on its agenda.

The OAS decision to apply sanctions against the Trujillo regime in the Dominican Republic for its assassination attempt against the president of Venezuela was appealed to the UN in 1960. The Soviet Union initiated a move in the Security Council to authorize the sanctions under Article 53 of the UN Charter, appearing to support U.S. policy. In fact, adoption of the resolution would have established the Security Council's authority over regional enforcement actions, providing a future opportunity for the Soviet Union to cast a veto in the eventuality of regional sanctions against Cuba. The Soviet proposal was voted down.

After the Bay of Pigs invasion in 1961, Cuba charged the United States and certain other Caribbean states with aggression and appealed to the Security Council for support. The council took no action. In settling the Cuban missile crisis in 1962, the United States and the Soviet Union agreed to have UN observers in Cuba monitor the removal of Soviet missiles, but Castro refused to receive a UN team and it was never sent. In 1967, at the Twelfth Meeting of Consultation of Ministers of Foreign Affairs of the OAS, the ministers expanded OAS sanctions against Cuba and reemphasized the practice of only reporting regional actions to the UN rather than gaining UN approval. They recommended that acts by Cuba that violated UN resolutions condemning armed intervention and subversion be brought to the attention of the UN by each OAS state. Also in 1967 the OAS established a permanent observer at the UN to act as liaison between the two organizations. In 1973 the attention of the Security Council was directed to disputes between the United States and Panama and between Britain and Guatemala over Belize. No actions were taken.

The most recent and direct UN activities in hemispheric conflict were during the Anglo-Argentine War of 1982 and in the Central American conflict. The Security Council, secretary general, and General Assembly were all involved in the South Atlantic conflict. On April 1, with an Argentine naval task force moving toward the British Falkland Islands Colony, the Security Council adopted a statement urging both states to refrain from the use of force and to seek a diplomatic solution. On April 3, the day after Argentina in fact invaded and took control of the islands, the council approved Resolution 502, which demanded an immediate cessation of hostilities and withdrawal of Argentine forces and called on both governments to seek a diplomatic solution. The resolution became the foundation for British diplomacy throughout most of the crisis and the point of departure for other efforts to avert warfare.

The resolution assigned no role to UN Secretary General Javier Pérez de Cuellar, a Peruvian diplomat who had assumed his position less than four months before the Argentine invasion. For his part, Pérez de Cuellar supported and deferred to a third-party effort undertaken by the United States. With the failure of the U.S. effort and the end of U.S. neutrality on April 30, however, the mediation efforts shifted to the secretary general. On May 7, Pérez de Cuellar commenced a two-week mediation process at UN headquarters in New York. Both disputants agreed "in principle" to the secretary general's proposal for a cease-fire and mutual withdrawal of forces, temporary UN administration of the islands, and subsequent negotiations under UN sponsorship. They could not agree, however, on the critical issue of sovereignty, and the mediation effort collapsed.

On May 22, as fighting spread in the South Atlantic, the UN Security Council again debated the dispute. On May 26 the Council adopted Resolution 505 asking the secretary general to negotiate "mutually acceptable terms for a cease-fire" while "bearing in mind" his earlier proposals. He reported a week later, on June 2, that "the positions of the two parties do not offer the possibility of developing at this time the terms for a cease-fire which would be mutually acceptable."

The military campaign came to an end on June 14 when Argentine units in the islands surrendered to British forces. In the aftermath of the crisis, a reshuffled Argentine military government repeated its intention to seek UN support on the sovereignty issue. Nineteen other Latin American nations joined Argentina in introducing a resolution in the General Assembly calling for British-Argentine negotiations. Unlike the Security Council no member had a veto power in the General Assembly. The resolution was overwhelmingly passed on November 4 by a vote of 90–12, with 52 abstentions. Ironically, the resolution was based on Security Council Resolution 502 of April 3, which had chastised Argentina and served British diplomacy. The United States voted for the resolution in a conciliatory gesture toward both Argentina and the rest of Latin America, despite British Prime Minister Margaret Thatcher's personal appeal to President Reagan to abstain. Referring to the nonbinding nature of the resolution, Thatcher said that the United Kingdom was confident of its title to sovereignty and had no intention of negotiating with Argentina.

In another case before the UN, Nicaragua appealed in 1984 concerning its conflict with the United States. In March the United States had mined Nicaraguan ports as part of a series of actions against the revolutionary government in Managua. The most prominent of these actions had been the U.S. support of the anti-Sandinista Nicaraguan guerrilla groups (the contras). On March 29 Nicaragua asked the UN Security Council to consider this "escalation of acts of aggression." In the subsequent debate, all fourteen members of the Security Council other than the United States condemned the mining. Nineteen additional UN members were also allowed to participate in the debate: Fifteen of them, including Mexico, sustained the Nicaraguan position; four Central American representatives supported the United States. On April 4 a resolution was proposed condemning the mining as a violation of international law, affirming the right of free navigation, and supporting the work of the Contadora Group. Thirteen votes were in favor (including those of two NATO members), the United Kingdom abstained, and the United States cast a veto.

The issue then went to the International Court of Justice (ICJ). Nicaragua instituted proceedings on April 9, 1984, charging the United States with using military force in violation of international law. The application noted that both the United States and Nicaragua had accepted the court's compulsory jurisdiction. Three days before, on April 6, the United States had informed the UN secretary general that it was temporarily modifying its acceptance of compulsory jurisdiction by ruling out cases involving Central America for the next two years. This modification was clearly an attempt to preempt Nicaraguan plans to bring the case before the court. After the Nicaraguan application, the United States argued that the ICJ did not have jurisdiction in the case. A month later, on May 10, the court asserted its competence in the case, rejected the U.S. request that it not be heard, issued an injunction against further U.S. action against Nicaraguan ports, and called on the United States not to violate Nicaraguan sovereignty with other illegal military or paramilitary activities. The vote was 14–1, with only the U.S. judge dissenting.

The case then went to trial in November 1984. The first question addressed was the matter of ICJ jurisdiction. The court ruled 15–1, with the U.S. judge again dissenting, that it had authority to hear the case. The majority argued that Article 36 of the court's statute would be meaningless if compulsory jurisdiction could simply be rejected when disputes actually arose. The United States continued to maintain that the court had no jurisdiction and announced that it would participate no further. Nicaragua insisted that the case proceed, and the court agreed to continue.

As a result of the Nicaraguan case, the United States, on October 7, 1985, terminated its general acceptance of the ICJ's compulsory jurisdiction. It argued that while the United States had agreed to limited jurisdiction over particular cases, Nicaragua had never validly accepted the court's compulsory jurisdiction and therefore had no right to sue. In addition, Nicaragua's claims concerned collective security and self-defense matters that the UN Charter assigned to political bodies for resolution. The United States also argued that Nicaragua's evidence in the case was faulty. Nicaragua alleged that U.S. support for the Nicaraguan resistance was illegal because Nicaragua had not intervened against its neighbors. The United States argued, however, that Nicaragua's deep involvement in support of the Salvadoran insurgency gave the United States the right to act against Nicaragua as a matter of collective self-defense. On January 18, 1985, the United States withdrew from further participation in the case, which proceeded nevertheless. The ICJ decided that it had jurisdiction and that the Nicaraguan claims could be appropriately settled in the court.

The ICJ handed down its decision on June 27, 1986, ruling on sixteen separate counts. The court rejected U.S. justifications of collective self-security for its interventions, held that the United States had violated international law in mining Nicaraguan harbors, and ruled that it should make reparations. The key issues were decided by votes of 12–3; the dissenting judges were from the United States, Japan, and the United Kingdom. However, the court unexpectedly rejected Nicaragua's argument that actions taken by the U.S.-supported contra guerrillas could be imputed to the United States. The majority acknowledged U.S. collaboration but saw insufficient evidence that the United States exercised such control that the contras were operating on its behalf. On July 31 the Security Council took up a Nicaraguan resolution calling for full compliance with the ICJ decision and cessation of support for the contras. The United States vetoed the resolution. Neither the court nor the council, however, had the capacity to enforce U.S. compliance.

Economic and Financial Institutions

ECOSOC and ECLAC. With the establishment of the United Nations System, Latin American states immediately turned to various UN agencies as alternatives both to bilateral U.S. assistance and, increasingly, to OAS agencies, which they viewed as dominated by the United States. Their first major accomplishment was the creation in 1948 of the Economic Commission for Latin America (ECLA) as a subagency of the UN Economic and Social Council (ECOSOC). (In 1984 it was retitled the Economic Commission for Latin America and the Caribbean—ECLAC—after eastern Caribbean entities began to become independent.) Within its framework, they formulated Latin American economic theory, policy positions, and ideology concerning development, trade, and regional integration. ECLAC is headquartered in Santiago, Chile.

ECLA membership was opened to UN members in the Americas and to states that had dependencies in the area. In 1988 ECLAC had forty members: the thirty-three Latin American states, the United States, Canada, France, the Netherlands, Portugal, Spain, and the United Kingdom. In addition, four entities were admitted as "associate members": Monserrat, British Virgin Islands, U.S. Virgin Islands, and Netherlands Antilles. ECLAC usually meets every two years.

ECLAC's executive secretaries, all well-known Latin American economists, have combined theory with diplomatic activism. The post was first filled by the Argentine Raúl Prebisch (1948–1963); he was succeeded by the Mexican Víctor Urquidi (1963–1972), who was in turn replaced by the Uruguayan Enrique Iglesias (1972–1985). Their personal influence on institutional activities was significant. Norberto González of Argentina has been executive secretary since 1985.

ECLA initially served as a major advocate of unorthodox development theory and policy. Acting as a promoter and political pressure group, ECLA influenced Latin American economists and government officials to a considerable but then declining degree. Prebisch was once the director of the Central Bank of Argentina; he was Latin America's best-known economist and, in time, a leading spokesman for the world's economically underdeveloped nations. ECLA became a proving ground and proponent for his structuralist theory (see Chapter 13), which basically said that underdevelopment is caused by a combination of domestic and international economic structural realities. His thesis originally provided an explanation only for persistent Latin American inflation; he later elaborated it into a comprehensive Latin American economic development theory and then extended it to the entire underdeveloped world. Prebisch left ECLA in 1963, but his influence continued as he became head of the United Nations Conference on Trade and Development (UNCTAD); he remained in that post until 1968.

Yale Ferguson (in Lincoln and Ferris, 1984:37) has noted that under Prebisch's leadership ECLA provided most of the ideological inspiration for postwar regional and subregional cooperation and that its prescriptions profoundly shaped Latin American thinking about development as well as U.S. policies in the Alliance for Progress. However, Ferguson went on to say that with the end of the Alliance, ECLA ceased to be a leading regional actor. Nevertheless, ECLAC retained an important if not leading position.

Víctor Urquidi followed the basic structuralist lead as successor to Prebisch at ECLA, but he also placed his own philosophical stamp on ECLA activities. An economist of international repute, his writings and speeches revealed an optimistic view of Latin American development and a perception of Latin America as a unique, regional whole. He appealed to the people and governments of Latin America to perceive themselves as part of "*a* Latin America and *a* Latin American economy" where he found more positive than negative factors.

Enrique Iglesias was also one of Latin America's leading economists and diplomats. He headed ECLAC for thirteen years and incrementally shifted his own thinking and the organization's approach. He moved the institutional position from one that vigorously promoted state intervention for economic development and import-substitution industrialization to a reliance on developing a combination of internal and external markets and recognizing an important role for private enterprise in Latin American development. In the 1980s ECLAC made recommendations regarding the external debt and helped organize conferences on the problem in Caracas (1983), Quito (1984), and (under Iglesias' successor) Mexico (1987). Iglesias resigned in 1985 to become Uruguayan foreign minister as that country returned to elected civilian government; in 1987 he was appointed president of the Inter-American Development Bank.

UNCTAD. The United Nations Conference on Trade and Development (UNCTAD) was originally organized as an institution attuned to the interests of underdeveloped nations. Latin Americans had important influences in

UNCTAD through their own concerted bloc action and by virtue of the fact that it was headed by Prebisch from 1963–1968. A sequence of global meetings were held, attended by representatives of both the underdeveloped and the developed nations of the world. UNCTAD has been convened in plenary session about once every four years: UNCTAD I (Geneva, 1964); UNCTAD II (New Delhi, 1968); UNCTAD III (Santiago, 1972); UNCTAD IV (Nairobi, 1976); UNCTAD V (Manila, 1979), UNCTAD VI (Belgrade, 1983), and UNCTAD VII (Geneva, 1987).

Latin American states have caucused as a regional bloc prior to each UNCTAD session, first in the Special Latin American Coordinating Committee (CECLA) before UNCTAD I, II, and III, and then in the Latin American Economic System (SELA) (see Chapter 8). They adopted common regional strategies of developmental nationalism that became dominant themes during the global meetings. The largely unproductive effort to improve terms of trade for underdeveloped nations was a great disappointment to them; it was apparently a source of frustration for Prebisch as well and perhaps led to his resignation as secretary general of UNCTAD after the 1968 conference. He was succeeded by the Venezuelan Manuel Pérez-Guerrero.

UNCTAD from the beginning was the centerpiece of the Third World effort to create a New International Economic Order (NIEO). This international regime, centered in UNCTAD but involving numerous other organizations and activities, is discussed in more detail in Chapter 12.

The World Bank and IMF. The International Bank for Reconstruction and Development had some operations in Latin America after it started business in 1946. The UN Development Program (UNDP) instituted programs in Latin America from its beginning in 1953. Two IBRD affiliates, the International Finance Corporation (IFC) and the International Development Agency (IDA), were established (in 1956 and 1960, respectively) in response to the demands of underdeveloped nations for increased loans on more flexible terms than those originally offered by the IBRD.

The World Bank became caught up in the Latin American debt crisis in the 1980s. Former U.S. congressman Barber B. Conable became bank president in March 1986, stating that he wanted to draw it more deeply into the various efforts dealing with the debt problems. One of the Democratic party's leading authorities on economic policy, Conable strongly endorsed the role of the bank envisaged by U.S. Treasury Secretary James A. Baker in his "initiative" regarding the debt (see Chapter 10). As a congressman Conable had criticized the Reagan administration's initial suspicion of and hostility toward the World Bank.

The International Monetary Fund (IMF), also established in 1946, was designed to encourage trade by contributing to the maintenance of stable currencies and rates of exchange. It lent from funds contributed by member nations to ease inflationary pressures and to cover trade deficits. Interest rates were nominal, but when negotiating "standby arrangements" for "drawing rights" with a potential recipient, the IMF often insisted that credits be accompanied by conditions for internal economic reforms. Those reforms were based on orthodox monetarist policies in direct opposition to the ECLA structuralist approach. The IMF called for various austerity programs that it expected to bring economic stability, but ECLA claimed that these programs would retard economic growth. In general, Latin American governments allied with ECLA while the United States supported the IMF. Latin Americans tended to view the IMF as an instrument of creditor nations, especially the United States, and it became a frequent target of nationalist enmity.

After becoming IMF director in 1962, Pierre-Paul Schweitzer of France was able to improve the IMF reputation somewhat in Latin America. In 1972 U.S. efforts to have him replaced were strongly opposed by most Latin American states. Schweitzer was more willing than his predecessors had been to recognize that some IMF conditions were politically unacceptable to Latin American governments, and he was more sympathetic to their needs. For example, he assisted them in negotiations with creditors when they fell behind in payments—in the instances of Chile, Argentina, and Brazil in the early 1970s, for example. The next two IMF managing directors were also from France: Jacques de Larosiere, who served from 1978 to January 1987 (resigning about a year and a half before his second five-year term expired); and his successor, Michael Camdessus, formerly governor of the French central bank.

Tensions between the IMF and Latin American governments returned, however, with the onset of the Latin American debt crisis in 1981. Faced with the mounting inability to make payments due in late 1982, Latin American governments sought agreements with the IMF and the principal creditors. The IMF, as the key multinational institution, was at the very center of Latin American debt negotiations. It remained committed to orthodox economics stressing debtor austerity in order to reduce inflation, lower imports, and increase exports—all measures aimed at enhancing the ability to service debt and invest internally for sustained development. Creditor banks and governments generally required debtors to come to an agreement with the IMF as a prerequisite to renegotiating lending arrangements. When agreed-upon austerity and credit targets were not met, the IMF did not hesitate to withhold portions of loans and private creditors to interrupt loan disbursements.

Debtor countries were reluctant to adopt the austerity measures because of internal political opposition and fear of social disruption. Governments complained that the IMF-mandated austerity measures threatened their popularity and limited their developmental options. However, the IMF had clearly increased its power in the national affairs of those states seeking to reschedule debts and acquire new loans. Management of the foreign debt became the predominant issue of most Latin American foreign policies and its impact was felt in other issue areas. Consequently, the IMF and its adjustment programs were an obvious source of government and public dissatisfaction and became a target for the political opposition. IMF policies toward the Latin American debt crisis are discussed in more detail in Chapter 10.

COMMODITY AGREEMENTS

Latin American states joined, and sometimes led, "commodity agreements," a process often referred to as "resources diplomacy." Both expressions are euphemisms for "cartel." Nations that produce primary materials, often having monocultural economies, were attracted to commodity agreements as a way to control markets for their export products. They sought to raise and then stabilize prices in world markets and assure export earnings over a long period of time. In general, commodity agreements represented further efforts on the part of Latin American (and other) states to gain economic strength in relation to the more industrialized and richer states.

Organization of Petroleum Exporting Countries

One of the earliest and clearly the most successful commodity agreements was the Organization of Petroleum Exporting Countries (OPEC). Five relatively obscure underdeveloped states banded together in 1960 to form OPEC. It eventually comprised thirteen members, with its headquarters located in Vienna. Venezuela was a charter member and Ecuador joined in 1973. A Venezuelan oil expert and government official, Juan Pablo Pérez Alfonso, played a prominent role in establishing OPEC. The stimulus occurred in 1959 when the major global oil companies, the "Seven Sisters," acted in concert to reduce the price they paid for oil to the producing nations. The original five OPEC members met in Baghdad the following year in order, according to their charter, "to create an organization for regular consultation and for the coordination of oil policies." OPEC came into prominence with the "energy crisis" in the 1970s. By mid-1973, thirteen years after its modest beginnings, OPEC was powerful enough to quadruple the price of petroleum on world markets and bring about a major redistribution of international income in favor of its member states.

The Coffee Agreement

A commodity agreement predating OPEC also enjoyed some success. An International Coffee Agreement signed in 1962 was the culmination of earlier efforts. Brazil had attempted from 1940 to 1945 to regulate production and achieve price stability in the global coffee market. The 1962 agreement, renewed for five years in 1968, was subscribed to by Brazil and Colombia (the world's largest coffee producers at the time), Ecuador, the Central American states, and a number of African producers. Consuming nations also joined in agreeing to stabilize coffee prices. In 1962, when U.S. policy toward Latin America was cast in the context of the Alliance for Progress, any price increases resulting from the coffee agreement were viewed as a form of foreign aid for development. Despite a great deal of internal dispute, especially between the Latin American and African groups, world coffee prices were brought under a modicum of control.

The coffee-producing nations allowed the agreement to expire in 1973. They apparently felt that they no longer needed a formal agreement with the consuming nations. Nevertheless, they were faced with the financial inability to limit coffee sales in order to keep prices at a desirable level. To this end, Venezuela in November 1974 announced that it would lend some of its profits from petroleum sales to Central America so that Central America could withhold part of their coffee production from international markets. Brazil and Colombia said they would finance their own stockpiling.

Other Efforts

OPEC's success catalyzed efforts to regulate other commodities through associations of producer nations. Other cartels with Latin American participants were created. An organization of copper producers, the Intergovernmental Council of Copper Exporting Countries (CIPIC), was established in 1967 and made up of Chile, Peru, Zambia, Zaire, and, later, Indonesia. The Organization of Iron Ore Exporting Countries (IOEC) was composed of Venezuela (a major leader), Chile, Peru, Brazil, Algeria, India, Australia, Canada, Sweden, Liberia, and Mauritania. Bolivia belongs to the International Tin Agreement. Jamaica is the chief producer and leader of the International Bauxite Association. Latin American banana producers organized the International Organization of Banana Exporters (IPEB).

Problems

Serious doubts exist about the long-term viability of the cartels, including OPEC. A successful cartel requires that producers be willing and able to withhold enough of their products to affect prices and that consumer demand remain relatively constant despite increased prices. These conditions are hard to satisfy, because producers often are unable to finance stockpiling or reduced production and consumers often turn to substitutes or are willing to do without. Petroleum seemed to be the exception, because producers had the financial ability to control the volume of supply and consumers had little choice other than to buy the crucial commodity at current world market prices. However, even OPEC ran into serious problems of supply, demand, and organizational cohesion. Furthermore, high prices stimulated the major consumers to increase oil conservation efforts, seek alternative energy sources, and, for those able to do so, increase their own oil production.

THE NONALIGNED MOVEMENT

Latin American Membership

The Nonaligned Movement traces its beginnings to the onset of the post–World War II cold war between East and West. Certain independent nations of Asia and Africa, most of them former European colonies that had recently gained their independence, were the first participants. They sought to avoid political and military entanglements in the cold war by forming a Third World in the bipolar structure between the First and Second Worlds dominated by the United States and the Soviet Union, respectively. Membership in the

Nonaligned Movement was first indicated by attendance at a series of informal conferences beginning in 1947; the first major meeting was at Bandung, Indonesia, in April 1955. Leaders of twenty-nine Asian and African states, including the People's Republic of China, attended the landmark event and proclaimed themselves to be a third force in world affairs. They called for nonalignment in the cold war and condemned colonialism as an evil that should be immediately ended. No Latin American state attended any of these meetings.

The Belgrade Conference of 1961 was a significant gathering. It was the first nonaligned summit meeting (the twenty-five delegates were heads of state) and it expanded Third World membership beyond Africa and Asia with the attendance of Yugoslavia and Cuba. Third World leaders had considered inviting several Latin American states to attend, but the Latin American states approached were not interested in attending because they had not been consulted about Cuba's presence at the conference. However, Bolivia, Brazil, and Ecuador sent observers to Belgrade.

By agreement reached in Belgrade in 1961, summit Conferences of Nonaligned Nations (to be attended by heads of state) would be held approximately every three years. Seven additional nonaligned summits have convened: Cairo (1964), Lusaka (1970), Algiers (1973), Colombo (1976), Havana (1979), New Delhi (1983), and Harare (1986). The ninth summit meeting is scheduled for Lima in 1990. Numerous ministerial level and other meetings have also been called over the years. Latin American membership increased steadily and, by the beginning of 1988, sixteen of the thirty-three Latin American states were full members and another eight had attended nonaligned meetings as observers. Three Latin American regional organizations had also sent observers: UN Economic Commission for Latin America and the Caribbean (ECLAC), Latin American Economic System (SELA), and Latin American Energy Organization (OLADE).

Latin American states have played varied roles in the Nonaligned Movement. Cuba, under the revolutionary leadership of Fidel Castro, became the region's most active and prominent member. Castro was a leading figure at the Algiers summit in 1973; he became president of the movement in 1979 for a four-year term. Bolivia continued to attend as an observer, finally becoming a full member at the Havana summit in 1979; Ecuador, in time, also became a member. Brazil has continued as an observer but has never undertaken membership, consonant with its determination to pursue an independent foreign policy with a minimum of "entangling alignments."

Argentina has attended nonaligned meetings as an observer beginning in 1964. Juan Perón returned to power in 1973 and resuscitated the "Third Position," continuing to view both communism and capitalism as exploitative. Argentina became a full member at the Algiers meeting in 1973. Military governments in Argentina after 1977 continued membership, as they had poor relations with the United States and also sought Third World support of their claims against the United Kingdom over the Falkland/Malvinas Islands. President Alfonsín since 1983 has ambiguously indicated "selective participation" in the movement.

Chile became an observer at the Cairo conference in 1964 at the start of Eduardo Frei's Christian Democratic government, which advocated non-capitalist and non-Communist policies. Chile's Marxist President Salvador Allende (1970–1973) attempted to establish himself as a Third World spokesman, and Chile joined the Nonaligned Movement as a full member in 1971. Allende's ultimately unsuccessful attempt to socialize Chile through constitutional means while remaining independent of the major world powers was closely watched by other nonaligned states. Chile has not attended the nonaligned meetings since the rightist military coup of 1973, but it has not formally withdrawn its membership.

Peru was an observer at a lower-level nonaligned meeting in 1970 and became a full member in 1973. Peru's nationalist and socialist military government from 1968 to 1975 under General Velasco Alvarado was essentially neutral in orientation and achieved prominence in the Nonaligned Movement. More conservative governments after 1975, both military and civilian, played no more than formal roles; but President Alan García, whose APRA party has long advocated Latin American neutrality, resumed active participation after his inauguration in 1986.

The revolutionary government of Nicaragua joined as a member of the movement after coming to power in 1979. It has sought to play an active role, but, like Cuba, has been viewed with some suspicion because of its relationship with the Soviet Union.

Colombia and Venezuela, who began participating as observers in the 1970s, applied for membership in 1983 after the Seventh Nonaligned Summit Meeting at New Delhi. Colombia was admitted, but Venezuela's application was tabled because of its border dispute with Guyana. (Venezuela has blocked Guyana's membership in the Inter-American System on the same grounds.) Mexico has not gone beyond observer status, despite the Nonaligned Movement's desire for it to be a full member and Mexican President Luis Echevarría's attempts to be a Third World leader from 1970 to 1976.

Finally, most of the new Caribbean Commonwealth Countries and Suriname have joined the Nonaligned Movement. Guyana, Jamaica, Trinidad-Tobago, Belize, Grenada, and St. Lucia became members soon after gaining independence, as did Suriname. Belize was granted observer status in 1976, even before achieving independence. Barbados and Dominica have attended as observers. These new states share the colonial legacies of Africa and Asia and have joined them on questions of racialism and colonialism. They have also maintained ties with the United Kingdom in the Commonwealth and have sought closer economic relations with the United States. Only Trinidad-Tobago, however, has signed the Rio Treaty.

The Havana Meeting and After

The sixth summit meeting in Havana in 1979, with Fidel Castro presiding, and its aftermath were of particular significance. (Information in this section is based on Willetts, 1984:54–57.) The members threatened to split over Castro's proposal that the Soviet Union was the "natural ally" of the

Nonaligned Movement in the struggle against imperialism and that the policies of nonaligned states should reflect the Soviet position. President Tito of Yugoslavia and other delegates to the conference strongly opposed Castro, maintaining that imperialism and colonialism in whatever form should be condemned. Little support for the Cuban view was forthcoming, and the opposition led by Tito won an overwhelming victory in expunging references to the natural allies thesis from the documents finally adopted. In addition, the annual Ministerial Meeting of the Coordinating Bureau (the executive committee of the movement) was abolished, depriving Castro of an important medium to express his views.

The Cuban chairmanship ran into further trouble in the immediate aftermath of the summit meeting. The annual meeting of nonaligned foreign ministers and delegation leaders in New York at the opening of the UN General Assembly session failed for the first time ever to produce any substantive statement or serious discussion of priorities for handling the UN debates. At the same session of the General Assembly, Cuba stood for election as a nonpermanent member of the Security Council. It should have been assured an easy victory, with a potential of eighty-eight votes from the nonaligned UN members, plus twelve from the Soviet bloc. However, Colombia was put up as a candidate against Cuba and a total of 154 ballots produced a deadlock with neither side obtaining the necessary two-thirds majority. The Soviet Union's invasion of Afghanistan further eliminated Cuba's chances. Both candidates stood down in favor of Mexico, which was not a member of the Nonaligned Movement.

The Reagan presidency after January 1981 led to a number of U.S. foreign policy changes on development issues, law of the sea, the Middle East, southern Africa, Central America, and military expenditures. Much of the Third World saw these changes as an unwelcome return to the cold war. The result within the Nonaligned Movement was a substantial shift in Cuba's favor against U.S. policy. In March 1983, after almost four years as president of the Nonaligned Movement, President Fidel Castro was succeeded at the New Delhi summit by Indira Gandhi, prime minister of India.

BIBLIOGRAPHIC COMMENT

Scott (1909) provides a general work on the Hague Conferences with references to Latin American participation; Alvarez (1907) discusses the role of Chile, and Cunha (1977) that of Ruy Barbosa of Brazil. Latin America in the League of Nations is analyzed by Edwards (1937) and Kelchner (1929). On Latin America in the United Nations, including the idea of a Latin American bloc and the participation of certain individual states, see Houston (1956), Hovet (1960, Ch. 3), Kelly (1971), and Wood and Morales (1965). The relationship of the OAS to the UN is studied by Canyes Santacana (1963) and Trindade (1985). On the activities of the specialized agencies of the UN System in Latin America, see United Nations (1961) and World Bank Group (1972). Fisher (1972) is a good study of the International Coffee Agreement. Shaplen (1983) addresses the development of the Nonaligned Movement, including, especially, the Cuban role.

PART FOUR

■

Instruments and Interaction

The policy instruments selected by the various actors in Latin America and the resulting patterns and processes of interaction are addressed in this part of the book. Chapter 10 deals with bargaining and Chapter 11 with violent conflict and accommodation. Both chapters identify policy considerations behind the choice of political, economic, military, and other instruments; the patterns of relationships resulting from their interaction; and the functions of the distribution of power and of international organizations. Chapter 12 takes up the specific international regimes that have been created to deal with certain Latin American conflicts through mutually accepted rules of governance.

Cooperation, bargaining, conflict, accommodation, and regime building are not discrete categories but overlapping dynamic processes. The categories are intended to indicate an analytic continuum: (1) bargaining, which may involve both cooperation and a range of coercive measures short of the use of violence; (2) conflict, involving hostility and compulsion, and its possible resolution, which may lead to cooperation; and (3) governance, through the making of international regimes designed to resolve conflict and promote cooperation. These processes and outcomes are not inevitable but provide a logical starting point for discussion of foreign policy instruments and international interactions.

CHAPTER TEN

■

Bargaining

THE BARGAINING USES of economic, military, diplomatic, and cultural foreign policy instruments chosen by Latin American subsystem actors, and the international patterns they create, are examined in this chapter. Although these instruments and interactions are essentially cooperative in nature (as defined in Chapter 1), they also have a coercive element as actors attempt to sway one another. External actors have attempted to accrue influence in the region through their involvement with Latin American economies and military establishments. Latin American actors have also been the purveyors of influence, not only in intraregional relations, but increasingly toward the outside world as well.

ECONOMIC RELATIONS

Patterns of Commercial Relations

Once Latin American barriers to investment and trade were dropped along with their dependence on Spain and Portugal in the early nineteenth century, Britain immediately dominated Latin American commerce and maintained an advantage over other industrial powers. In the late nineteenth century British preeminence eroded, especially through the efforts of the United States and Germany. The Latin American states mainly had colonial plantation economies. The economically more powerful external states sought export markets for their manufactured goods, investment capital, technical skills, and surplus populations and cultivated Latin American sources of food and raw materials. The most efficient Latin American industries were often foreign owned and managed and produced for foreign rather than domestic markets.

Foreign capital was more attracted to portfolio than to direct investments. Beginning with Argentina in 1824, most Latin American government bonds were sold in the London money market, with the remainder primarily in France and the United States. By 1827 every bond sale had been defaulted, a situation postponing further flotations for three or four decades (except for Brazil). British capital again financed large bond issues by fifteen Latin

American governments in the 1860s and 1870s; by 1877 more than two-thirds of the total value was in default. In the 1880s Latin American debt servicing improved. But French investors who purchased bonds in the 1860s and 1870s in Haiti, Mexico, Honduras, Peru, and Argentina suffered heavy losses when they were defaulted (Rippy, 1958:331–333).

Direct foreign investment was also important. Britain was especially well entrenched in Argentina, with holdings there representing between 40 and 50 percent of Britain's total Latin American investment. Britain also had substantial levels of investment in Brazil, Mexico, Venezuela, and Colombia. Some private U.S. capital migrated to Latin America before 1830; by 1870 virtually every Latin American state had received some North American investments, with the preponderance in Mexico, Cuba, and Chile. U.S. capital flows increased dramatically after the Civil War; at the turn of the century about two-thirds of the U.S. investment in Latin America was concentrated in Mexico (Bernstein, 1966). The main recipients of French capital were Brazil, Chile, and Mexico.

J. Fred Rippy (1958:334) made the following summary:

> By the turn of the century, foreigners owned all the oceanic shipping lines communicating with Latin America; nearly all of Latin America's railways and most of the river shipping companies; all the submarine cables; the majority of the gas plants and tramways; many of its port facilities; most of the enterprises exploiting the nitrate deposits and many large companies engaged in the mining of metals; numerous ranches, plantations, and farms; several firms taking out forest products; a multitude of mercantile firms and many commercial banks; and the most efficient manufacturing and processing plants.

As Latin American populations grew rapidly after 1900, demands for consumer goods increased. But these goods were not available from domestic industries, and the region's international trade expanded dramatically. Total Latin American trade increased from less than the equivalent of $1 billion in 1885 to about $3 billion in 1913 on the eve of World War I (Rippy, 1958:390). Britain remained the principal trader and investor in Latin America, but the United States registered the greatest increases in trade and investment and ranked second in both areas. German and French trade and investment also remained significant.

World War I cut off much of Europe's trade with Latin America, but it recovered soon after the war. The region's total trade increased to more than $6 billion in 1920. This figure contracted somewhat in the 1920s but reached a level well above $5 billion in 1929. U.S. investments more than tripled during the postwar period until 1930, with almost every Latin American state receiving some U.S. capital. British investments remained relatively stable until they began to decline after 1928, never to recover to their pre-1928 levels. German and French holdings declined in the 1920s.

Regional trade shrank drastically during the world depression beginning in 1930, sinking to only $1.6 billion in 1932 and recovering to only $3.2 billion by 1939. Foreign investment also declined severely. The lack of capital and the shrinkage of purchasing power in markets around the globe were exacerbated by protectionist policies adopted by most trading partners. In addition to adopting economic controls, some Latin American states expropriated foreign enterprises, notably oil company subsidiaries in Mexico and Bolivia in 1938.

World War II stimulated Latin American international trade, especially with the Allies, who purchased the region's raw materials in large amounts for their war effort. However, new investment capital did not flow into the region until after the conflict was settled in 1945. During the postwar period, foreign corporations in Latin America still produced food and raw materials for export to industrial states, and the Latin American states continued to import capital machinery and manufactured goods; a number of them also imported significant amounts of agricultural products. Foreign exchange reserves accumulated during the war were partly used to retire bonds at a rapid pace in order to reduce levels of portfolio investments. Some states repatriated a number of foreign enterprises. Argentina took over British railways and other transportation facilities, and several governments purchased public utilities from their foreign owners. However, total direct investments increased, with the United States the main source of capital; the levels of portfolio investment increased only slightly.

Trade and investment figures illustrate U.S. economic dominance during the postwar era. For most Latin American states, at least one-third (often more) of their total trade was with the United States. Through the 1960s U.S. investments accounted for about 40 percent of the total invested in Brazil, about half of that in Colombia and Peru, and almost 75 percent in Chile; the largest single U.S. investment in Latin America was in Venezuelan petroleum. Other nations were also active. Germany and Japan were the strongest competitors to the dominant U.S. position. British investments and trade fell off sharply after World War II; France also had a low level of trade, except with Brazil. The United States and other investors suffered severe losses with the nationalization and expropriation of foreign enterprise in Cuba after 1959; in Chile and Peru in the late 1960s and early 1970s; and especially in Venezuela in the mid-1970s. The Soviet Union and China mounted drives in the 1960s and 1970s to increase their trade with Latin America, but they held a minor share of the total, except for the Soviet relationship with Cuba.

The 1980s Debt Situation

Latin American international economic relations have been dominated since the early 1980s by problems of external debt. While they are part of a global phenomenon, debt problems have special relevance for Latin America. The current regional situation is distinguished from previous ones by its sheer magnitude. All Latin American countries have accumulated high levels of debt in relation to the size of their economies and have encountered serious problems with servicing them. Almost two-thirds of all bank loans to developing countries beginning in the early 1970s went to Latin America.

Activities related to the resolution of debt issues continued to dominate U.S., European, and Japanese relations with the individual Latin American nations. Those problems further affected political and military relations, and until questions of debt are resolved by mutually acceptable arrangements, collaboration in other areas will be inhibited.

The problem began in the late 1960s when Latin American governments and private enterprises decided to accelerate domestic development by borrowing abroad from international lending institutions and private commercial banks. The arrangements included two types of creditors: private suppliers, such as commercial banks, which provided direct loans and markets for the flotation of bonds; and public sources, including bilateral government agencies and the multilateral (general and regional) financial institutions. Borrowers included Latin American governments, government agencies, and private sector entities. The doubling of oil prices in 1973 spurred further borrowing to pay for higher-priced oil imports; a reduction in interest rates after 1976 accelerated borrowing even further.

Debt-service capacity remained satisfactory, except for occasional problems, until the end of the 1970s. Commercial banks competed vigorously to place loans in the profitable market. They operated on the theory that governments, by definition, were not vulnerable to bankruptcy as private corporations were, and on the assumption that the IMF would rescue governments that encountered liquidity problems. Latin American governments, for their part, saw no need to adjust monetary or fiscal policies or engage in domestic austerity programs, and fiscal deficits increased. Moreover, in a number of important cases, a significant portion of borrowed funds was diverted from developmental purposes to budgetary support, military expenditures, and capital flight. High-level corruption was sometimes a serious problem as well.

Not only did the size of public debt increase dramatically, but its structure also changed significantly. The greatest change was the increase in medium-term loans granted by private banks. Latin Americans gained unprecedented access to international bank syndicates and the Euromarket, and by 1980 the level of private-lender participation had grown from an insignificant proportion to more than two-thirds of the total.

A set of factors converged at the end of the 1970s to create the Latin American debt crisis. Another round of oil price increases worsened terms of trade. Moreover, a renewed global recession sharply depressed prices for commodity exports, and interest rates increased. All of these problems added to debt-service burdens. They were initially perceived as temporary phenomena that could be bridged through short-term borrowing. But the situation discouraged domestic savings and investment and encouraged massive capital flight, and Latin American economic growth rates declined for the first time in four decades. Furthermore, borrowers had increasingly undertaken risky, short-term, variable-rate loans, further adding to the debt-servicing burden. Banks then began to refuse new loans, denying access to capital markets when debt servicing was the most difficult.

The debt problem became a crisis when Mexico, the world's second largest debtor, announced on August 12, 1982, that it could no longer meet its external debt-service obligations. Thereafter other governments indicated illiquidity and inability to meet their foreign debts.

With the advent of the debt crisis in 1982 and the accompanying decrease in borrowers' creditworthiness, Latin Americans increasingly requested debt rescheduling. Complex negotiations subsequently developed between the borrowing entities and private banks, multilateral financial institutions, and creditor governments. (The following discussion of actors and negotiations draws on Parkinson, 1987.)

At the time of the Mexican announcement in 1982, Latin American external debt totaled about $315 billion. The three largest economies (Brazil, Mexico, and Argentina) accounted for about two-thirds of the total. Brazil was the world's largest debtor, having reached a level of about $100 billion in 1982. Chile, Colombia, Peru, and Venezuela together held much of the remainder. All Latin American countries, however, had borrowed heavily in relation to the size of their economies. U.S. bank claims in Latin America totaled some $82.5 billion, about a quarter of their overseas lending. Two-thirds of that total was held by the nine largest U.S. banks. The exposure of European and Japanese banks was sizable but far smaller as a percentage of their total international claims. Many smaller banks participated in external credits through syndicates.

Two "clubs" represented creditor governments and private banks, respectively. The Paris Club was composed of sovereign representatives engaged in government-to-government loans. Originally established in 1956 to deal with the serious financial situation in Argentina, it operated again in the general financial crisis after 1982. The London Club of commercial banks was organized in the mid-1970s to systematize the proliferation of banking syndicates (themselves formed to raise the vast sums involved in the 1970s lending). It operated informally, meeting only when negotiations with a particular borrower were in progress. Neither club had a fixed membership or an institutional structure. The Paris Club was concerned with the interests of commercial banks but did not allow them to participate in its proceedings.

The Cartagena Group emerged to represent most of the Latin American debtor governments. When the presidents of Mexico and Brazil met soon after the onset of the crisis, they considered but rejected the repudiation of debts in favor of rescheduling them. The United Nations Commission for Latin America and the Caribbean (ECLAC) and the Latin American Economic System (SELA) subsequently issued a joint report and sponsored several meetings to discuss collective action. The most important of these meetings took place in Quito in January 1984, attended by representatives (including presidents and prime ministers) from twenty-six Latin American governments. The final report postulated a program of reduced debt payments and interest rates, a lengthening of maturities, and elimination of trade barriers by developed countries. The indifferent response by creditors inspired eleven Latin American governments (Argentina, Bolivia, Brazil, Chile, Colombia,

Dominican Republic, Ecuador, Mexico, Peru, Uruguay, and Venezuela) to meet at Cartagena, Colombia, in June 1984 to further consider a multilateral position. They issued a document establishing a formal consultative mechanism known as the Cartagena Group and agreed to meet on a regular basis.

Two dissenting Latin American leaders offered their own widely publicized propositions. Peru's new President, Alan García (succeeding the Peruvian government that had been present at the formation of the Cartagena Group), stated at his inauguration in July 1985 that he intended to set aside no more than 10 percent of Peruvian export earnings for debt servicing. In April 1986 García further announced his intention of setting his own interest rate for servicing the debt. Cuban Premier Fidel Castro in July 1985 recommended direct creditor-debtor negotiations but said that if creditors were recalcitrant, then unilateral collective repudiation of debts should follow. Cuba was not a member of the Cartagena Group.

Almost all Latin American governments were involved in continuing negotiations with the International Monetary Fund (IMF), in which the United States played a major role, and with a consortium of private international banks led by Citibank of New York. The IMF insisted that the governments adopt austerity programs aimed primarily at controlling inflation, reducing imports, and stimulating exports so as to generate foreign exchange for debt servicing and lessen the need to borrow from abroad in future years. The banks made refinancing of existing loans and negotiation of new ones contingent on such agreements; the IMF, in turn, made "bridging loans" to ease the shocks of austerity. The United States and the Bank for International Settlements (BIS) also provided some short-term bridging loans to help countries meet external liquidity requirements. When austerity and credit targets were not met, the IMF did not hesitate to withhold portions of loans and private creditors to interrupt loan disbursements. Debtor countries were reluctant to adopt the austerity measures because of internal political opposition and fear of social disruption. This consideration was particularly important for delicately balanced democratic governments with open political processes and those in the midst of moving toward democracy.

The U.S. government concurred in the positions taken by the IMF and commercial banks. In 1985, however, a modest change in emphasis evolved with what came to be called the "Baker Initiative." U.S. Treasury Secretary James Baker unveiled his initiative at a combined meeting of the IMF and the World Bank Group in Seoul, Korea, in October 1985. He proposed to build on the current approach and seek sustained growth in the debtor countries that would restore their creditworthiness. Baker called for a three-year term package of new commercial bank loans netting $20 billion to fifteen principal debtor countries, ten of whom were from Latin America. Those countries would be required to undertake long-term comprehensive structural reform policies. This tactic would be combined with a continued central role for the IMF, the opening of the economies to foreign trade and investment, and an expanded role for multilateral banking institutions. The initiative amended only marginally, not fundamentally, the original strategy.

Negotiations, as of late 1988, have resulted in a partial restoration of the confidence of private lenders, a gradual renewal of credit to the stronger Latin American borrowers, and fiscal and economic austerity in the borrowing states. Some have experienced positive growth, most importantly Brazil; the Venezuelan situation has not required an IMF standby agreement. In general, however, the public and private external debt levels are still projected to grow at rates exceeding economic growth. Most Latin American governments are committed to servicing their debts, but are paying more in interest on existing loans than are received in new ones. Furthermore, they must also respond to the demands of their own citizens for increased prosperity and equity. Renewed global recession or a sharp increase in interest rates could revive the crisis, threaten the international financial system, and lead to Latin American social and political turmoil. The prediction is commonplace that the debt cannot and will not be repaid. A panoply of proposals has come forward—radical and conservative, imaginative and orthodox—for various kinds of debt restructuring and ways to deal with the situation.

U.S. Economic Policies and Aid Programs

An early source of U.S. assistance to Latin America was the Export-Import Bank of Washington (EXIM), established in 1934 to help promote the recovery of U.S. foreign trade after its sharp decline during the world depression. According to the EXIM report of December 31, 1941, a total of $48.5 million in loans had been disbursed to the twenty Latin American states as of that date. The most significant single project consisted of assisting in the export of U.S. equipment and services for the construction of a steel plant at Volta Redonda, Brazil. After the fall of France in 1940 and throughout World War II, EXIM loans to Latin America were aimed at developing sources of strategic raw materials and combatting Axis economic penetration of the area, as well as building the Pan American highway and other projects. The EXIM report of July 1, 1945, listed more than $4 billion in authorizations to Latin America from 1940 to 1945.

The first publicly funded U.S. technical assistance programs in Latin America were instituted in 1939; they survived at low levels in the 1980s. The programs were not designed for major capital investments or to promote large scale economic development. Rather, they were intended to give limited assistance to specific projects jointly financed by the United States and the host government. In 1939 President Roosevelt established the Interdepartmental Committee on Scientific and Cultural Cooperation, which spent a total of $678,000 in Latin America through 1945. Most of the projects were in agriculture (notably a rubber development program), geology, civil aviation, child welfare, and statistical services. Another agency created in 1940, eventually called the Office of Inter-American Affairs, was devoted to U.S. technical assistance programs in Latin America; it was originally headed by Nelson A. Rockefeller. Viewed as a wartime agency only, it supervised a large number of cultural and commercial relations between the United States and Latin America. Technical assistance programs costing the United

TABLE 10.1

U.S. Export-Import Bank Loans (U.S. fiscal years; millions of dollars)

Recipient	Postwar Period, 1946- 1952	Mutual Security Act, 1953- 1961	Foreign Assistance Act 1962- 1982	1983	1984	1985	1986	Total, 1946- 1986
Argentina	101.7	304.2	1,193.1	----	----	----	----	1,478.8
Bahamas	----	----	63.8	----	----	----	----	55.9
Barbados	----	----	6.1	----	4.3	----	----	10.0
Belize	----	----	*	----	----	----	----	----
Bolivia	19.3	7.1	44.6	----	----	----	----	74.2
Brazil	158.5	996.8	2,051.3	29.3	28.5	37.4	124.4	3,686.8
Chile	104.2	169.1	381.5	----	----	1.3	----	1,024.4
Colombia	23.5	144.3	828.1	3.8	4.0	130.0	----	1,201.3
Costa Rica	----	19.4	42.7	----	----	----	----	70.5
Cuba	12.0	25.5	----	----	----	----	----	93.8
Dominican Rep.	----	----	111.3	----	----	----	----	107.1
Ecuador	11.6	10.4	64.6	----	----	----	----	82.5
El Salvador	----	3.2	18.7	----	----	----	----	23.4
Grenada	----	----	----	----	----	----	----	----
Guatemala	----	13.4	100.3	----	----	----	----	46.2
Guyana	----	----	9.6	----	----	----	----	9.1
Haiti	14.0	11.0	3.1	----	----	----	----	38.8
Honduras	----	2.7	34.0	----	----	----	----	30.5
Jamaica	----	----	95.8	----	----	----	----	90.4
Mexico	180.1	301.9	3,123.6	37.2	66.5	10.1	----	3,096.7
Nicaragua	0.6	12.5	28.3	----	----	----	----	40.9
Panama	4.0	13.0	139.1	----	----	----	----	139.1
Paraguay	----	10.3	66.9	----	----	----	----	19.6
Peru	19.9	161.3	226.8	26.3	----	----	----	438.4
Suriname	----	----	5.8	----	----	----	----	5.9
Trinidad-Tobago	----	----	336.3	----	39.0	16.3	----	333.9
Uruguay	2.6	----	22.3	----	----	----	----	38.6
Venezuela	12.2	51.2	589.2	12.0	----	----	----	572.0
Other[+]	3.0	28.1	110.8	4.5	----	----	----	87.6
Total	667.4	2,285.4	9,697.6	113.0	142.3	195.1	124.4	12,936.3

* Less than $50,000.

[+] Includes Latin American regional, Central American regional, and other West Indies-Eastern Caribbean programs.

Note: Row totals include any "capitalized interest" and "net deobligations" and may not add to sum of annual loans; column details may not add to totals due to rounding.

Source: Agency for International Development, U.S. Overseas Loans and Grants and Assistance from International Organizations: Obligations and Loan Authorizations, July 1, 1945-September 30, 1986 (1987).

TABLE 10.2
U.S. Economic Assistance: Loans and Grants (U.S. fiscal years; millions of dollars)

Recipient	Postwar Period, 1946- 1952	Mutual Security Act, 1953- 1961	Foreign Assistance Act					Total, 1946- 1986
			1962- 1982	1983	1984	1985	1986	
Argentina	*	51.3	186.5	*	0.1	----	*	199.4
Bahamas	----	0.3	*	----	*	----	*	0.3
Barbados	----	----	3.7	*	0.1	*	----	3.8
Belize	----	1.4	11.2	17.8	5.4	25.2	12.1	72.6
Bolivia	4.1	192.5	717.0	63.0	78.0	50.6	74.6	1,047.9
Brazil	20.3	314.2	2,230.3	0.4	*	0.8	0.7	2,447.0
Chile	6.2	170.7	1,060.4	2.8	1.7	1.3	1.1	1,198.3
Colombia	3.3	106.5	1,384.1	3.9	8.2	11.3	11.5	1,405.8
Costa Rica	6.0	52.2	281.8	214.1	169.9	220.0	162.8	1,099.3
Cuba	0.5	3.8	----	----	----	----	----	4.0
Dominican Rep.	0.8	2.1	795.4	63.1	98.2	170.6	101.8	1,215.8
Ecuador	5.1	49.3	333.6	26.6	28.9	51.9	60.4	603.9
El Salvador	2.4	11.1	539.8	245.6	215.9	433.9	322.6	1,777.8
Grenada	----	----	----	----	48.4	11.3	*	59.7
Guatemala	9.9	121.3	341.6	29.7	20.3	106.9	116.7	751.4
Guyana	*	2.3	133.8	0.1	*	0.1	3.2	115.5
Haiti	2.7	61.0	297.8	46.2	46.5	55.6	77.7	539.9
Honduras	2.5	35.1	418.9	106.0	95.0	229.0	136.6	995.3
Jamaica	----	6.7	404.3	103.5	110.0	158.1	126.6	903.1
Mexico	93.9	40.2	227.8	8.2	8.4	11.1	11.9	385.3
Nicaragua	6.2	33.6	374.8	*	0.1	----	----	387.6
Panama	3.0	54.9	407.1	7.4	12.0	74.5	33.4	570.5
Paraguay	4.4	35.5	157.6	3.2	2.7	3.5	3.3	203.5
Peru	12.4	101.4	722.7	93.5	164.6	79.1	58.4	1,195.0
Suriname	----	2.9	3.6	0.1	----	----	----	6.4
Trinidad-Tobago	----	7.9	35.9	----	----	----	----	40.9
Uruguay	2.8	34.0	138.5	1.0	0.6	*	14.4	176.3
Venezuela	1.6	16.3	185.2	0.1	0.4	0.8	0.1	202.8
Other[+]	1.8	43.7	1,294.7	124.9	101.2	197.1	160.4	1,905.2
Total	195.9	1,552.2	12,687.2	1,160.7	1,216.6	1,892.6	1,490.2	19,514.3

*Less than $50,000.
[+]Includes Latin American regional, Central American regional, and other West Indies-Eastern Caribbean programs.
Note: Row totals include any "capitalized interest" and "net deobligations" and may not add to sum of annual loans and grants; column details may not add to totals due to rounding.
Source: Agency for International Development, U.S. Overseas Loans and Grants and Assistance from International Organizations: Obligations and Loan Authorizations, July 1, 1945-September 30, 1986 (1987).

266

TABLE 10.3
Assistance from International Organizations, 1946-1986 (millions of dollars)

Recipient	IBRD	IFC	IDA	IDB	UNDP	Other UN	Total
Argentina	2592.1	446.0	----	3232.8	58.2	3.6	6332.7
Bahamas	22.8	----	----	2.8	4.6	*	30.2
Barbados	70.2	0.3	----	29.7	5.6	0.2	106.0
Belize	5.3	----	----	----	2.8	1.1	9.2
Bolivia	296.0	9.3	174.8	951.2	44.1	11.8	1487.2
Brazil	13044.4	1228.9	----	5306.2	87.9	21.7	19689.0
Chile	1343.8	142.7	19.0	2389.6	65.1	7.9	3968.1
Colombia	5524.3	162.0	19.5	1451.4	62.7	28.0	7247.9
Costa Rica	489.9	6.7	4.6	301.6	12.2	3.5	818.5
Cuba	----	----	----	----	39.0	4.2	43.2
Dominican Rep.	337.9	33.7	22.0	300.3	26.4	7.1	727.4
Ecuador	964.1	48.2	36.5	1670.7	46.5	12.2	2778.2
El Salvador	215.1	1.0	25.6	634.2	23.8	7.2	906.9
Grenada	----	6.0	5.0	----	0.1	----	11.1
Guatemala	471.6	18.2	----	925.1	25.3	11.3	1451.5
Guyana	79.4	3.7	47.3	112.6	20.3	2.1	265.4
Haiti	2.6	3.2	256.4	284.8	40.0	13.7	600.7
Honduras	547.6	11.0	82.6	713.6	29.7	6.3	1390.8
Jamaica	693.4	32.3	----	301.0	24.9	1.8	1053.4
Mexico	8700.4	815.6	----	2669.5	53.8	21.2	12260.5
Nicaragua	231.1	9.5	60.0	405.4	23.8	6.8	736.6
Panama	595.8	69.0	----	572.2	26.8	4.5	1268.3
Paraguay	457.6	18.0	45.5	533.8	28.0	7.5	1090.4
Peru	1690.9	100.1	----	1466.7	54.5	15.7	3327.9
Suriname	----	----	----	14.0	11.1	0.7	25.8
Trinidad-Tobago	119.9	268.0	----	25.0	20.0	0.8	433.7
Uruguay	551.4	35.5	----	238.4	25.7	0.9	851.9
Venezuela	348.0	25.4	----	866.2	36.2	2.1	1277.9
Other[+]	43.0	10.0	24.0	752.7	170.9	50.5	1015.1
Total	39438.6	3504.1	822.8	26115.4	1070.0	254.4	71205.3

*Less than $50,000.
[+]Includes Latin American regional programs, and other West Indies-Eastern Caribbean programs, and Bermuda.
Abbreviations: IBRD=World Bank; IFC=International Finance Corp.; IDA=International Development Assoc.; IDB=Inter-American Development Bank; UNDP=United Nations Development Program.
Source: Agency for International Development, U.S. Overseas Loans and Grants and Assistance from International Organizations: Obligations and Loan Authorizations, July 1, 1945-September 30, 1986 (1987).

States $110 million through 1945 concentrated on the fields of health, agriculture, and education.

The Truman administration through 1952 attempted to explain to Latin America that problems in other parts of the world, first in Europe and then in Asia, were more pressing than those in Latin America and that Latin Americans should thus depend primarily for funds on the newly created international lending agencies (the World Bank and the International Monetary Fund), and private investment capital, rather than on direct U.S. economic assistance. Technical assistance programs, however, were continued. Economic policy was geared closely to the cold war, and Soviet expansion into Latin America seemed as remote as the prospect of internal Communist revolution.

Beginning in 1945 EXIM was authorized to finance some foreign development projects on the assumption that they would increase markets for U.S. exports. EXIM was the main source of U.S. postwar economic assistance to Latin America, but it gave Europe priority, and the sums authorized for Latin America were relatively small. EXIM projects in 1951, in response to the military needs of the Korean conflict, were aimed at facilitating Latin American strategic raw material production. The Interdepartmental Committee on Scientific and Cultural Cooperation and the Institute of Inter-American Affairs (IIAA), a subagency of the Office of Inter-American Affairs that was transferred to the State Department when its parent was abolished, continued their technical assistance projects in the fields of agriculture, public health, elementary education, and vocational training. From 1946 through 1949 the Interdepartmental Committee expended $10.4 million in Latin America, and the IIAA, $21.6 million.

The United States inaugurated a worldwide technical assistance program in 1950 under the Act for International Development. The program was popularly called "Point Four" because it was the fourth point of President Truman's economic policy announced in his inaugural address of 1949. U.S. experience with technical assistance in Latin America largely provided the basis for global Point Four programs. Yet the region itself received less assistance than did Europe and Asia. Public administration and the improvement of industrial productivity were added as new fields of endeavor in 1951.

The Mutual Security Act (MSA) of 1951 emphasized the relevance of economic and technical aid to security concerns in the context of the cold war. The Communist threat in Latin America was not considered great, however, and the area was of low priority in MSA programs. Truman, and then the Eisenhower administration, continued to stress the "trade not aid" concept in Latin America and opposed large-scale development spending. Nevertheless, Latin America benefited from several MSA programs, even if not to the extent it desired. In addition, the Agricultural Trade Development and Assistance Act of 1954 (PL480), an effort to reduce U.S. farm product surpluses in a constructive manner, provided for several programs, among them the overseas sale of surplus agricultural products followed by loans of "counterpart" funds that subsequently accumulated.

After Vice President Nixon's ill-fated Latin American trip in 1958, U.S. officials indicated a need to reexamine U.S. economic policy toward Latin America and showed a willingness to make changes. The Castro revolution in Cuba in 1959, and its association with the Soviet Union, further inspired U.S. attention to economic programs in the region. New developmentalist policies emerged toward the end of the Eisenhower administration. The Inter-American Development Bank was established in late 1959 with U.S. backing. In July 1960 the United States announced the $500 million Eisenhower Plan for Latin American economic development aimed at halting "the further spread of communism in the Western Hemisphere." Finally, at U.S. urging, the "Act of Bogotá" was adopted in September 1960 at an inter-American meeting to give multilateral support to the Eisenhower Plan.

The new program represented some fundamental changes in U.S. economic policies toward Latin America. The provision of long-term loans for social purpose projects such as low-cost housing, improved education, and land reform, repayable in soft currency, revised the former policy of extending hard-currency loans to be spent primarily on U.S. products. The United States continued to urge Latin Americans to provide an attractive climate for foreign investors in the economic development process, but it no longer insisted on private capital as the primary economic source.

The Alliance for Progress and After

Soon after his inauguration in 1961, President Kennedy proposed a ten-year Latin American economic and social development program to be known as the Alliance for Progress. Recipients of U.S. assistance were to agree to undertake measures seeking to assure maximum social progress. The Alliance for Progress built on programs initiated by the Eisenhower administration. It was further inspired by Brazilian President Kubitschek's proposal in 1958 for an "Operation Pan America" to raise dramatically Latin American living standards. A few months after Kennedy's proposal, an inter-American agreement known as the Charter of Punta del Este was signed. This agreement made the Alliance a multilateral program. In general, the United States promised to give long-term development assistance to Latin America in a "decade of progress." The program, to be administered by the Inter-American Development Bank, promised significant financial contributions as well as assistance in development planning and social reform. The new economic and social aid was closely linked with the U.S. fear that the Castro revolution would spread to other parts of the region.

The developmentalist policy of the Alliance for Progress continued through the Kennedy and Johnson administrations, but the Nixon administration quickly shifted to a "low profile" in economic as well as other affairs concerning Latin America. In his first presidential address on hemispheric policy on April 14, 1969, President Nixon referred to the Alliance as a "great concept" that had "done much good" in some countries. Although Nixon did not propose a formal end to the Alliance, he seemed to indicate that it would be downgraded on the grounds that it had not stimulated sufficient economic growth; he made no mention of its social purposes. Latin American economic aid expenditures declined after 1969, and policy rhetoric moved away from ideas and projects aimed at social change and economic development. The importance of trade over aid and of foreign investment capital for economic development was reemphasized. The Ford administration after 1974 made no basic changes in Nixon's economic policy toward Latin America. The Carter administration emphasized the human rights factor in its aid polices, but this policy mainly affected military assistance programs, and economic assistance in general was not emphasized.

The Caribbean Basin Initiative

President Reagan announced the Caribbean Basin Initiative (CBI) at a meeting of the OAS in February 1982. Congress subsequently passed the Caribbean Basin Economic Recovery Act, which went into effect on January 1, 1984. Twenty countries and territories were designated as beneficiaries: Antigua-Barbuda, Barbados, Belize, British Virgin Islands, Costa Rica, Dominica, Dominican Republic, El Salvador, Grenada, Guatemala, Haiti, Honduras, Jamaica, Montserrat, the Netherlands Antilles, Panama, St. Christopher-Nevis, St. Lucia, St. Vincent and the Grenadines, and Trinidad-Tobago. In addition, the Bahamas was designated in March 1985, and Aruba (formerly a part of the Netherlands Antilles) in April 1986. Cuba and Nicaragua were excluded from the program; Grenada initially was proscribed, but it was declared eligible after the U.S. military intervention in 1983 and the end of the New Jewel Movement government there.

The CBI as initially conceived closely fitted the Reagan administration's geopolitical views of the Caribbean Basin sketched in terms of East-West conflict and reflected changing views of the causes of Central American conflict. It blended opposition to Soviet expansionism with regional developmentalism and the president's free-enterprise philosophy. President Reagan's speech before the OAS and subsequent administration declarations all revealed this combination of concerns. Reagan emphasized the Caribbean Basin's strategic importance to the United States. He also highlighted economic interests of trade and investment as well as regional economic problems. He suggested that the economic crisis in Latin America threatened political and social stability and created conditions that could be exploited by the Soviet Union and Cuba. In addition, economic problems increased illegal immigration and facilitated the production and export of narcotics to the United States. In sum, the view predominating in the Reagan administration was that a major border of the United States threatened to consist of hostile states. The United States, therefore, had a vital interest in preventing economic collapse or the creation of Marxist-Leninist regimes in these poor neighboring countries.

The economic aspects of CBI programs were aimed at Caribbean export expansion and diversification and increased outside investment. The CBI "centerpiece," to use the administration's language, was the provision for twelve years of duty-free access for most exports from designated Caribbean countries into U.S. markets. The exceptions included textiles and apparel, petroleum, and footwear. Sugar imports would receive limited duty-free treatment in order to protect the already-existing U.S. domestic sugar price support program. Ethanol imports would have to conform to special rules in the 1986 tax law. A "textile initiative" added in 1986 allowed special access to the United States for apparel assembled in the Caribbean region from materials manufactured in the United States, and a "safeguard mechanism" was provided for U.S. industries injured by increased CBI imports. The CBI also offered a convention tax benefit allowing U.S. companies to deduct expenses for business meetings in CBI countries.

U.S. economic assistance to the region was increased, focusing on balance-of-payments support and development and commodity assistance. The levels of aid were not high, however, and were reduced in 1987. Puerto Rico and the U.S. Virgin Islands received special consideration. The measure provided for excise taxes on their exported rum to be rebated, allowed their industries to have access to the same safeguards as mainland industries, and gave them duty-free access to mainland markets.

The United States stressed the multilateral nature of the CBI. Consultation with other governments did take place—in particular, with Mexico, Venezuela, Colombia, and Canada, and their efforts did supplement the U.S. programs. But it was agreed that each state would develop its own approach, with only a modicum of coordination among Latin American states in order to avoid duplication. Much of the effort on the part of these and other actors (Europe, Japan, and international financial institutions) in fact predated the CBI itself and, presumably, would have continued without it.

Aid Policies of Other Actors

The United Kingdom, France, and the Netherlands tended to concentrate their "Latin American" aid in their American dependencies or former colonies. This practice left few resources for assistance to the vast majority of the region. Europeans generally tied aid closely to their exports, looking to improve their own balance of trade more than to promote Latin American economic development. Assistance was designed to improve commercial positions, and credits and loans usually were granted only to finance Latin American purchases of European products. Germany was the exception. Like the United States, Germany perceived that its interests were best served by a stable and prosperous world and linked its aid to anti-Communist ideology and the East-West conflict. Consequently, German economic aid to Latin America fit into its overall concern with the underdeveloped nations of the world and centered on economic development programs initiated in the mid-1950s. Commercial goals were not lacking, however; development aid credits were used as a means of developing new export markets. In 1974 the German government reduced its development aid programs, stating, in effect, that easing its domestic tax burden took precedent over foreign assistance. That calculation had not changed as of mid-1988.

By the mid-1970s, most members of the European Economic Community (later integrated into the European Community—EC) had decided to direct their trade and aid policies toward Latin America through regional institutions. More than 80 percent of the trade between the EC and Latin America has been with the seven largest Latin American economies (Argentina, Brazil, Chile, Colombia, Mexico, Peru, and Venezuela). The EC is Latin America's largest trading partner after the United States, although the level of trade has tended to decline in the 1970s and 1980s. The relationship with Latin America is of much less significance to Europe than it is to the United States. As of 1985, Latin American countries accounted for 2.9 percent of EC exports and 3.4 percent of its imports. Nevertheless, Latin America receives a proportionally higher level of exports from the EC than do other Less Developed Countries (LDCs), probably because it is the most economically advanced LDC region. Furthermore, although Latin America represents a minor part of the EC's total trade, the area is a principal source of food and raw materials and an important market for manufactured surpluses.

The EC has established a Generalized Preference Scheme (GPS) as its principal concessionary policy toward LDCs. The main preference has to do with exemptions from customs duties, according to a sliding scale, on which industrialized nations must pay the common external tariff. The purpose is to adjust competitive relations between LDCs and industrialized countries by allowing certain agricultural products to enter duty-free or at reduced tariff rates. The GPS was introduced in 1971; items have occasionally been added to the preferred list. The EC has also opened its markets to some Latin American and Asian manufactures and semifinished goods.

Latin Americans have been highly critical of EC practices. EC officials have acknowledged the Latin American complaint that the system is too restrictive and that preferences are given on very few of the products in the first rank of Latin American exports. Problems of a more specific nature have also arisen. In July 1974 the EC imposed a ban on beef and veal imports in order to protect its internal markets from the world surpluses that had developed at the time. Although this ban was later relaxed, certain Latin American countries suffered severe declines in product trade, especially Argentina, Brazil, Paraguay, and Uruguay. The EC agreed to a new beef-import system beginning in April 1977, but after this experience, Latin American producers concluded that they had to cultivate new markets in Japan and elsewhere.

The EC established special trade preferences for the former colonies of its member states in February 1975, when, after lengthy negotiations, the Lomé Convention was signed between the EC and forty-six states in Africa, the Caribbean, and the Pacific (the ACP countries). The convention took effect on April 1, 1976. The number of eligible ACP countries and the benefits offered have increased with subsequent treaty renegotiations and extensions. Eligible parties within the Latin American region, as they became independent, include only the Caribbean Commonwealth Countries and Suriname as former colonies of the United Kingdom and the Netherlands, respectively. The Lomé system provides for preferential markets in many products, a commodity export price stabilization agreement, cooperation in industrial and technical matters, increased aid disbursements through the European Development Fund, assistance in regional integration, and new joint institutions.

The majority of Latin American states are not party to the convention and have expressed displeasure with the Lomé arrangements. Their major complaint is that the preferential markets include products that make up more than 20 percent of Latin American exports—beef, bananas, coffee, sugar, iron ore, cotton, and cocoa—threatening them with the loss of export markets. They have reiterated pleas that the EC adopt a global policy toward LDCs and not favor the ACP partners to the detriment of others. The EC, in turn, has acknowledged the CBI and the Central American economic crisis in at least modest ways. In November 1985 the EC agreed to double its financial assistance to Central America over the next five years.

Japan adopted an increasingly global foreign policy as it became the world's second largest market economy. Most of Japan's aid to Latin America has been in the form of export credits rather than economic development grants, similar to the U.S. practice through EXIM. Japanese relations with Caribbean Basin countries developed slowly, commensurate with its relatively limited interests in the region, but its engagement in the region is expanding. Japan has actively traded with Cuba, and it lent $10 million to Jamaica in 1981 for developmental purposes. Moreover, in early 1986 Japan increased its trade credits and developmental assistance to the Circum-Caribbean countries.

Latin America was not an important part of Canada's foreign assistance program until 1964. Thereafter, bilateral aid and some Canadian contributions to the Inter-American Development Bank were restricted to purchases of Canadian goods. Canadian assistance to Circum-Caribbean countries increased after the onset of Central American conflict in the late 1970s and the debt crisis of the early 1980s. Specifically, in early 1982 Canada announced an increase in developmental assistance to Central American countries, committing $105 million over the next five years. Four years later Canada announced a program to double its bilateral aid to the Commonwealth Caribbean for the ensuing year (into 1987) and simultaneously to implement a preferential free-trade arrangement for those countries along the lines of the CBI.

The Soviet Union's economic aid program in Latin America outside of Cuba is small, but its trade concessions are generous in nature if not in amount. Soviet economic aid to Cuba includes balance-of-payments credits, technical assistance costs, project credits, and sugar subsidies. The Soviet Union normally does not provide aid in the form of either grants or outright loans. However, it gives trade transactions the character of economic assistance by allowing repayments in the form of commodities rather than currency (Goldhamer, 1972:184). This barter arrangement, however, is automatically tied to Soviet products; Latin Americans have complained about the inferior quality of Soviet goods and their overvaluation in account settlements. Except for Cuba, Latin American states enjoy a trade surplus with the Soviet Union. Offers of economic aid and trade, however, often are linked to the reestablishment of diplomatic relations between the Soviet Union and its Latin American trading partners.

The Holy See sponsors a development assistance program in support of papal pronouncements concerning social and economic justice for the poor. Pope Paul VI in 1969 established a Vatican Development Fund for Latin America to be funneled through the Inter-American Development Bank. Interest-free long-term loan projects would be selected by the bank in consultation with the Vatican. According to a church communiqué, the fund would be used in "the fields of agrarian reform, over-all human well-being, workers' organizations and other areas of social and economic reform and general improvement in the developing countries which are members of the bank."

Assistance programs have also been sponsored by the stronger Latin American states themselves. Brazil, Mexico, Argentina, and Venezuela for a time provided economic aid and technical assistance to the poorer Latin American states. The most important programs were pursued by Venezuela, which used its new oil wealth in the mid-1970s to enhance its emerging influence in Latin America as well as to avoid the inflationary consequences of investing more money in the domestic economy than it could absorb. In 1974 Venezuela contributed more than $500 million for loans to be made through the Inter-American Development Bank and the World Bank. In December of that year Venezuela compensated the six Central American nations for holding back part of their coffee harvests in order to raise prices. It also provided subsidies to those particularly hurt by rising oil prices and gave direct aid to the most underdeveloped of them (such as Honduras). In addition, Venezuela promised to deposit $3 billion of its 1974 oil profits and 50 percent of future revenues into the Venezuelan Investment Fund.

Latin American assistance activities were reduced with the debt crisis in the 1980s, but certain efforts nevertheless continued. In 1980 Mexico and Venezuela established a joint oil facility for the energy-deficient countries in the Circum-Caribbean. The program finances almost a third of the petroleum requirements of nine countries (El Salvador, Guatemala, Honduras, Costa Rica, Nicaragua, Panama, Barbados, Jamaica, and the Dominican Republic), valued at a total of about $300 million annually. The facility continued despite the debt problems in both countries. In addition, Mexico grants trade preferences to El Salvador, Guatemala, Costa Rica, Panama, and members of CARICOM and finances technical assistance programs around the Caribbean area. Venezuela has further assisted some of those economies in the 1980s by contributing direct Central Bank deposits (in Nicaragua, the Dominican Republic, Costa Rica, and Jamaica) and granting developmental project loans to Central American countries. Finally, Colombia has offered substantial trade credits and modest technical assistance programs to several countries in the Caribbean subregion.

The Narcotics Traffic

In the early 1980s, inter-American relations entered an era of "drug diplomacy." While the narcotics traffic in the hemisphere had existed for many years, its expansion after the late 1970s made it an enormous business enterprise and created a major policy dilemma for all governments involved. The "narcotraffic" became one of the most compelling and acrimonious issues in U.S.–Latin American relations.

Market demand stemmed primarily from drug consumption in the United States, which provided the world's largest market for illicit drugs. In the latter 1980s, U.S. consumers spent about $110 billion annually on illegal drugs, a figure corresponding to almost 3 percent of GNP. Those consumers numbered some 25 to 30 million marijuana smokers, 5 to 6 million cocaine users (including the cocaine derivative "crack"), and more than a half-million heroin addicts. With the growth of drug-related urban crime and violence, narcotics financing of organized crime, and the devastating social consequences of increasing numbers of youth involved with drugs, the narcotraffic became a major public issue in the United States.

Suppliers in other countries, especially in Latin America, responded to the U.S. demand. Latin America was the source of all the cocaine, four-fifths of the marijuana, and two-fifths of the heroin consumed in the United States. Nine countries accounted for most of the illegal marijuana, cocaine, and heroin entering the United States each year in terms of growing crops, refining and transshipping products, and laundering proceeds. Mexico produced about 40 percent of the marijuana and heroin and transshipped about one-third of the cocaine imported into the United States. Mexico was Latin America's only heroin-producing country—the remainder came from non–Latin American sources such as Pakistan and Burma. Colombia provided about 25 percent of the marijuana destined for the United States and cultivated up to 10 percent of the cocaine. The Colombian Medellin Cartel was the largest cocaine cartel in the world. It came to control as much as 75 to 80 percent of the cocaine exported from the Andean region. Its wealth was so vast that it publicly and credibly offered in 1988 to pay off Colombia's $10 billion external debt in return for the cancellation of Colombia's extradition treaty with the United States. Peru, the world's largest cultivator of coca leaf (cocaine's raw material), produced 50 percent of the cocaine destined for the United States. Bolivia was the second largest producer, accounting for 40–45 percent. Jamaica produced up to 15 percent of the marijuana that entered the United States and was a major transshipment country for cocaine. Belize accounted for up to 10 percent of the marijuana and became an alternate trafficking route. The Bahamas was a favored site for laundering money and a major transshipment point for the cocaine and marijuana traffic. Panama was a transit point for cocaine and a major center for money laundering.

Anti-drug programs aimed at the countries mentioned above led, after the mid-1980s, to trafficking activities elsewhere. Some coca production was begun in Argentina, Brazil, Ecuador, Paraguay, and Venezuela. The Dominican

Republic, islands in the Eastern Caribbean, Guyana, and Suriname became alternate trafficking routes.

The narcotraffic had fundamental consequences for Latin American societies. The immense wealth of drug traffickers enabled them to corrupt civil, police, and armed forces officials; they were willing to assassinate those who refused to cooperate. Corruption undermined the legitimacy of governments, and violence intimidated them. Drugs became a major source of income for many Latin American farmers; they financed a large underground economy outside of state authority. In time the traffickers arranged with insurgency groups to exchange money for protection.

The supply of cocaine grew at an estimated annual rate of 10 percent throughout the 1980s. As the U.S. market became saturated, traffickers looked for new markets to absorb the increasing supply. By the end of 1986, Europe had begun to import significant amounts of illicit drugs, and by mid-1987 it was evident that even Latin American societies were subject to increasing cocaine abuse.

Cooperative international drug eradication and interdiction programs, led by the United States, were undertaken throughout the 1980s. President Reagan declared a "war on drugs." U.S. policy makers determined that they could not quickly modify domestic consumer behavior and decided to attack the source and flow of drugs. Certain multilateral efforts were undertaken. In April 1986 in Rio de Janeiro the OAS adopted a program for regional antinarcotics cooperation, and the following November an Inter-American Drug Abuse Control Commission was created. In October 1986 ministers of justice and attorneys general from thirteen Latin American countries and the United States met in Mexico to discuss narcotics problems, and in March 1987 a Caribbean Regional Conference on Drug Abuse was held in Belize (U.S. Department of State, 1987b).

The most important efforts, however, were U.S.-led bilateral actions. Interagency field efforts were undertaken with Mexico. (In 1985, a U.S. drug enforcement agent, Enrique Camarena Salazer, was kidnapped, tortured, and killed in Mexico by drug dealers.) Colombia agreed to extradite its citizens to the United States for trial on drug charges. As a result, in October 1987, Carlos Lehder, a founder of the Medellin Cartel and one of the world's leading cocaine dealers, went on trial in Jacksonville, Florida; he was convicted after a seven month trial. The United States entered into agreements with Peru in 1982 and Bolivia in 1983 designed to eradicate the supply of drugs and to induce and assist small farmers to switch to other crops. In 1986 the United States and Bolivia cooperated in an exercise called Operation Blast Furnace. The United States provided army helicopters to airlift Bolivian National Police on a series of raids aimed at destroying the laboratories that processed the coca leaf into cocaine or the fields in which the leaf was grown. In 1988 Operation Snowcap, headed by the U.S. Drug Enforcement Agency assisted by U.S. Special Forces, the U.S. Border Patrol, and police in several Latin American countries, conducted anti-cocaine activities.

The U.S. Anti-Drug Abuse Act of 1986 was designed to strengthen the U.S. antinarcotics efforts at home and abroad. It sought to lower domestic demand with tougher law enforcement, educational programs, drug testing, treatment and rehabilitation programs, and increased penalties for traffickers. It increased resources for the interdiction of the drug traffic and for eradication, crop substitution, and enforcement programs abroad. The law mandated the annual International Narcotics Control Strategy Report to assess the situation in the drug producing and trafficking nations around the world, nineteen of which were in Latin America. The president was required to certify whether those countries were cooperating fully with the United States in narcotics control before they could receive foreign aid; trade and economic sanctions were also provided for. Sanctions were imposed on Bolivia in 1986 and 1987 for not acting seriously to eradicate its coca crop. In 1988 the Reagan administration "decertified" Panama because of the activities of General Manuel Noriega. (Noriega, while cooperating with the CIA and DEA, had created a large narcotics trafficking and money laundering center; he was convicted in absentia of drug-related charges by a federal court but his extradition was highly unlikely.)

Eventually progress was made in the efforts to eradicate the source of narcotics and to interdict its flow. Increased government resources were devoted to antinarcotics programs; the volume of seizures of all categories of illicit drugs went up dramatically, and arrests on drug charges increased sharply. Nevertheless, production and drug supply remained many times the amount consumed by drug abusers, and government action interdicted only 3 percent of the marijuana and 10 percent of the cocaine entering the United States. Antinarcotics programs faced immense problems, and international cooperation was hampered by a variety of factors. Markets in the United States were not diminished and they grew in Europe; the reduction of demand was ultimately the sine qua non for resolving the drug problems. In the United States, policies were undermined by inadequate resources, lack of bureaucratic coordination, and their subordination to "national security" concerns—such as the toleration of Noriega for years because he was a useful anti-Communist "asset" despite evidence he was involved in the drug trade (Bagley, 1986). In Bolivia the introduction of U.S. military forces was widely condemned and such an instrument was rejected by other governments in the region. The Medellin Cartel recovered from the loss of Lehder; through violence and its threat, the cartel succeeded in forcing the Colombian government to suspend extraditing traffickers to the United States. In Latin America official corruption, mismanagement, and rivalry made strong action difficult if not impossible. Peasants resisted change; coca had been their mainstay for centuries and was considerably more profitable than other crops.

MILITARY RELATIONS

Latin American Military Modernization

Toward the end of the nineteenth century, Latin American states consciously began to develop their military establishments—most of which had been born during the earlier wars for independence—as a concomitant to the general thrust for national modernization. Since then, Latin American governments generally have conceded that their continuous attempts to modernize and professionalize their military establishments have required substantial foreign assistance. The Latin American armed forces have undergone extensive development with active assistance from Europe and the United States, both in terms of professional training and in the acquisition of arms and equipment. As a result, levels of military modernization and foreign military influences in the region vary widely and complex patterns of international military competition are at work.

The motives of the extraregional states in giving military assistance have been several; in general terms it has been used as a way to gain political and economic as well as military influence in Latin America. Cooperative military instruments have included sending military missions and instructors to other states, providing training and educational facilities for foreign personnel, pursuing diplomatic activities (such as exchanging armed service attachés, making visits, and awarding honors), and engaging in the arms trade.

Patterns of Relations to World War I

From the late nineteenth century until World War I, Latin American plans for military and naval reorganization and development led to sharp competition among the external states who vied to be entrusted with the task. Some foreign influence existed in the regional armies and navies dating from the wars for independence, but it was not until the Latin American states decided to develop their military establishments systematically that foreign training became an important part of Latin American international politics. (This and the following section are based on Epstein, 1941, and my own research in collaboration with Larry V. Thompson.)

In the pre–World War I period, Germany and France were the most important military competitors, and Great Britain and the United States, both renowned commercial shipbuilders, retained the most influence in naval affairs. The German and French armies enjoyed high prestige and the support of their home governments in overseas activities; their competition for military influence in Latin America and elsewhere was an extension of Franco-German antagonism in Europe. Germany was predominant in Chile's and Argentina's military affairs, while France prevailed in Peru, Uruguay, and Brazil. The two states competed with rough equality in Bolivia, Paraguay, and Guatemala. The United States exerted direct military influence on armies in those states in the Caribbean where it practiced post-1898 intervention. Influence was mixed in Ecuador, Venezuela, and Colombia; it was insignificant in the remaining regional states.

External military assistance usually came in the form of armed forces missions and instructors sent to Latin America and offering the use of military facilities in the external state. German and French missions and instructors were invited to perform a variety of tasks in the major South

American states. Chile, the first state to begin military modernization, received its first German adviser in 1885; thereafter the number of German officers increased, and they achieved positions far in excess of foreign officers elsewhere in Latin America. They reorganized the Chilean army, organized a general staff, established general conscription, reformed military education, and assumed direct command and training of troops. The German role became important in Argentina in 1899, when a military mission was engaged to organize and staff the new Army War College; it later was involved in other training schools and in writing Argentina's obligatory conscription law. Peru was the first Latin American state to establish close military collaboration with France and became a center of French military influence in Latin America. A French military mission arrived in 1896 and reorganized the Peruvian army along French lines. France also held a leading military position in Brazil. A French mission was engaged by the state of São Paulo in 1906 to train public forces and to establish a cadet school. Latin American military personnel were assigned overseas for professional training and education, regimental service, and observation at maneuvers. A few were sent to the United States, but most went to Europe, primarily to those states that sent missions to Latin America.

Latin American states also entered into armaments contracts with European munitions firms and U.S. and European shipbuilders, committing most regional armies and navies almost completely to foreign manufactures. Armaments orders were largely by-products of foreign service mission employment. The Latin American states, as a rule, were not weapons manufacturers and imported almost all of their armaments and equipment. The competition in military affairs affected the general competition in the export trade, as military orders could increase a country's volume of export trade considerably. In the industrial sphere, bitter rivalry developed among Krupp of Germany, Schneider-Creusot of France, and other arms manufacturers. Leading European armament firms made advances to Latin American governments—Schneider-Creusot seems to have led this practice—until improved Latin American financial situations enabled them to make immediate payment. In addition, the French government, in granting general-purpose loans to Latin American governments, insisted on linking them to purchases from Schneider-Creusot. In spite of the French efforts, the German firms of Krupp and Mauser held the largest share of the Latin American military market prior to World War I. In the commemoration volume celebrating the Krupp factory's centenary in 1912, the firm boasted that it had sold weapons to fifty-two states outside of the Reich and other German states, eighteen of which were in Latin America.

The Interbellum Period

After World War I Latin American military leaders complained that their lack of actual war experience seriously handicapped service training. By then the last wars in which they had participated were more than a generation removed, and only a few Latin American officers had observed the recent war in Europe firsthand. They had been left behind by the revolutionary developments in military technology and tactics. Latin American military men, lacking recent experience and knowledge in modern war, felt that it was essential for them to learn from those who had.

Outside of those small Caribbean nations where the United States was directly intervening, at first it seemed that France would be free of military competition in Latin America. Not only was France's military reputation at its zenith as the leading European power, but the Versailles Treaty prohibited Germany from sending military missions and instructors abroad and abolished all German military educational institutions that might receive foreign officers. The treaty bound thirteen Latin American states and prohibited Germany from aiding the military forces of any other state in any way. French military circles confidently expected to inherit the prewar German position in South America in a period marked by severe legal restrictions on Germany. As it turned out, however, the Versailles Treaty proved to be ineffective and Germany soon returned to a position of influence.

The first years after the war witnessed a surge in French influence in Latin American armies, but the region soon received training missions not only from France, and eventually Germany, but also from Italy, Great Britain, the United States, and even Switzerland and Spain. The number of missions contracted by Latin American governments increased substantially in the 1920s and 1930s. Air and police missions were added to the traditional army and naval missions. Especially notable was the accelerated employment of air force training missions consequent to the rapid development of military aviation during the war. Italy entered the South American military scene in the 1920s and eventually gained extraordinary influence in Latin American military aviation. Britain and the United States initially followed their tradition of viewing military relations in essentially commercial terms, but in the 1930s they began to aim at counterinfluencing the presence of Germany and other Axis states for political reasons. Japan attempted to compete in the arms market but was relatively unimportant. A small number of Russian officers of the old Tsarist army, several of high rank and reputation, came to Latin America for military employment after the Bolshevik Revolution of 1917; some of them participated in the Chaco War between Bolivia and Paraguay in the 1930s. An interesting phenomenon was the surrogate role played by Chile and Peru, for Germany and France, respectively, when they sent their own training missions and instructors to other Latin American states or received other Latin American military personnel in their own military institutions, thus transmitting their mentors' systems to a broader audience.

As in the prewar period, the South American states were the most important arenas of competition during the years between the world wars. Chile reengaged German military instructors in 1924 over vigorous French protests based on the Versailles Treaty. Chilean officers themselves taught methods learned from their German mentors to other Latin Americans. Chilean missions were sent to Colombia, Ecuador, El Salvador, Nicaragua, and

Paraguay. German officers returned to Argentina in the 1920s and remained until 1940. Moreover, Germany had a military monopoly in Bolivia between the wars until 1935 (the end of the Chaco War), after which an Italian military mission was engaged. Military relations remained intimate between France and Peru, with French officers assuming important army positions. France also sent air and naval missions to Peru, although the United States later sent a naval mission and replaced the French position in the Peruvian navy. France also resumed its work in Brazil in the 1920s in the state of São Paulo; it added missions to the Brazilian federal army and air force, including direction of the general staff school. However, a large and influential U.S. naval mission went to Brazil in 1922. Paraguay, Ecuador, Colombia, Venezuela, and Guatemala continued their eclectic ways, turning to more than one external military source.

The external states continued to perceive the economic advantages inherent in dominant military influence, since the Latin American states required foreign armaments to continue their military modernization. They hoped that the partisan efforts of their officers would lead to extensive arms contracts. Furthermore, Latin American military establishments were expected to urge the adoption and imitation of foreign production practices and techniques within their own newly established armaments industries, which would lead to foreign industrial involvement in the region. The persuasive counsel of foreign military advisers gave the initial impetus for this development. Thus, the arms trade continued to be closely linked to military diplomatic activities. Foreign military officers were instrumental in establishing and promoting the new armaments industries because they were interested in seeing the Latin American units armed with implements with which the instructors were familiar. Strong evidence indicates that military and diplomatic personnel cooperated closely with the representatives of their home commercial arms firms. Often the commercial representatives in Latin America were either retired officers or reserve officers. Thus, the employment of instructors and missions was a stimulus to the international traffic in arms.

Post–World War II

During the period surrounding World War II, the United States sought to displace European military influence in all of Latin America beyond the Caribbean area, where it was already predominant. As a result, military cooperation was established between the United States and almost all of Latin America, and the phase of European military influence in Latin America ended. With the rise of fascism and threat of war in Europe, and the consequent dangers perceived for the Americas, the United States urged the establishment of multilateral inter-American arrangements for hemispheric defense. During the war, an additional set of bilateral military relationships were established, which set precedents for postwar interaction. By the time war broke out in Europe in September 1939, the United States and other American governments had issued neutrality proclamations. However, most Latin American states were unable to patrol their own coastal waters effectively, so the United States felt it necessary to secure permission for military bases and certain other rights and facilities from them. After the fall of France in 1940, U.S. negotiations with most Latin American states led to further base rights agreements, whereby U.S. requests were granted for airfields to be used as aircraft ferry relay points. The United States constructed or refurbished some Latin American naval bases, and agreements were signed permitting the United States to use Latin American airports, to fly over their territories, and to station maintenance personnel in the area.

In the late 1930s the United States began to substitute its military missions and instructors for those of the European states, continuing its efforts during the war and immediately after. By 1946 the United States was the only external power maintaining missions in Latin America, with seventeen of them in thirteen states. The United States extended bilateral military assistance to certain Latin American states through the Lend-Lease program. The Lend-Lease Act of March 11, 1941, ended legal restrictions on the supplying of arms to Latin America. It was the enabling act for worldwide U.S. military aid, designed to assist U.S. allies most directly involved in the European war; the president was empowered to transfer military articles to any state whose defense was deemed vital to the security of the United States. All Latin American states were declared eligible for aid except Argentina and Panama; Argentina had refused to cooperate with hemispheric defense plans, whereas Panama had other special military arrangements with the United States. Brazil received by far the largest portion of Lend-Lease arms furnished to Latin America; most of them were used to equip its expeditionary infantry force that saw action in Italy. Mexico (which sent an aircraft squadron to the Philippines), Chile, and Peru received most of the remainder.

After World War II the United States became Latin America's main source of military assistance, providing both standardized military equipment and training. In the first part of the postwar period the United States continued to rationalize military assistance in terms of the need for cooperative efforts toward a common hemispheric defense. The wartime principles of hemispheric defense were reaffirmed on a continuing basis in the Inter-American Treaty of Reciprocal Assistance (Rio Treaty) of 1947. Thereafter, the Rio Treaty became the "cornerstone" of U.S. military commitments to Latin America and provided the framework for regional and bilateral military programs.

From the end of World War II until 1952 the United States had no well-organized program of military assistance in Latin America. President Truman asked the U.S. Congress on two occasions, in 1946 and 1947, for authority to institute a program of inter-American military cooperation, but Congress refused the requests. The United States continued to supply some military equipment under the Lend-Lease Act, but only that which had previously been committed for delivery as of the end of the war. Under the Surplus Property Act of 1944, which authorized direct sales of U.S. military surpluses at reduced prices, Latin Americans purchased small arms, light naval vessels, and artillery pieces. The Mutual Defense Act of 1949 enabled Latin Americans, as signatories of the Rio Treaty, to purchase arms from the United States.

TABLE 10.4

U.S. Military Assistance: Loans and Grants (U.S. fiscal years; millions of dollars)

Recipient	Postwar Period, 1946-1952	Mutual Security Act, 1953-1961	Foreign Assistance Act					Total, 1946-1986
			1962-1982	1983	1984	1985	1986	
Argentina	----	4.2	261.5	----	----	----	----	236.6
Bahamas	----	----	----	----	----	*	*	0.1
Barbados	----	----	0.2	----	0.1	0.1	----	0.3
Belize	----	----	*	0.1	0.5	0.6	0.6	1.8
Bolivia	----	2.5	79.9	----	0.1	3.4	1.5	86.0
Brazil	26.9	206.7	413.9	----	----	----	----	640.0
Chile	6.7	64.3	146.0	----	----	----	----	217.0
Colombia	3.5	50.2	199.0	0.7	25.3	0.8	4.3	283.1
Costa Rica	----	0.1	9.0	4.6	9.1	11.2	2.6	36.7
Cuba	0.6	15.4	----	----	----	----	----	16.1
Dominican Rep.	----	8.1	47.4	6.6	6.4	8.7	4.5	81.5
Ecuador	2.3	30.7	87.0	4.6	6.7	6.7	4.5	142.6
El Salvador	----	0.3	140.1	81.3	196.6	136.3	121.8	676.1
Grenada	----	----	----	----	0.1	0.1	----	0.1
Guatemala	----	1.7	40.2	----	----	0.5	5.4	47.3
Guyana	----	----	0.1	*	----	----	----	0.1
Haiti	----	3.9	3.2	0.7	1.0	0.7	1.9	11.4
Honduras	----	1.3	71.5	48.3	77.4	67.4	61.1	327.1
Jamaica	----	----	4.8	3.5	4.2	7.7	8.0	28.0
Mexico	----	3.9	11.3	0.1	0.2	0.2	0.2	15.8
Nicaragua	----	2.2	30.6	----	----	----	----	32.4
Panama	----	0.1	20.7	5.5	13.5	10.6	8.2	58.4
Paraguay	----	0.8	30.0	0.1	0.1	0.1	0.1	30.6
Peru	3.7	73.6	175.5	4.6	10.7	8.7	0.6	276.9
Suriname	----	----	0.1	----	----	*	*	0.2
Trinidad-Tobago	----	----	----	----	----	*	0.1	0.1
Uruguay	2.8	29.3	57.6	0.1	0.1	0.1	0.1	89.6
Venezuela	----	31.5	121.5	0.1	*	0.1	0.1	152.6
Other[+]	----	----	1.1	3.3	7.2	5.2	12.8	29.4
Total	46.5	530.8	1,952.1	163.9	359.2	269.1	238.4	3,544.8

*Less than $50,000.

[+]Includes Latin American regional, Central American regional, and other West Indies-Eastern Caribbean programs.

Note: Row totals include any "capitalized interest" and "net deobligations" and may not add to sum of annual loans and grants; column details may not add to totals due to rounding.

Source: Agency for International Development, U.S. Overseas Loans and Grants and Assistance from International Organizations: Obligations and Loan Authorizations, July 1, 1945-September 30, 1986 (1987).

However, no grant aid was available and requests for material far exceeded the amount available.

The most important basis for U.S.–Latin American military relations during most of the 1950s and until 1961 was the Mutual Security Act of 1951, passed in response to the Korean War. Portions of the legislation dealing with Latin America made military assistance contingent on the recipients' participation in "missions important to the defense of the Western Hemisphere." The act made it clear that it would be desirable to standardize the equipment, organization, and methods of the Latin American armed forces, and to orient them toward the United States and mutual security, in order to prevent Latin American arms purchases elsewhere, which might invite nonhemispheric military missions and advisers to the region. The United States also wanted to ensure the accessibility of strategic raw materials. Most of all, U.S. policy pronouncements claimed that the United States was not anxious to assume major responsibilities in Latin America in case of war. It desired to help the Latin American countries achieve a capability to protect their own territory, thus sparing the United States the necessity of assigning large numbers of troops to the region.

But the assertion that the primary purpose of military aid was to strengthen Latin America's own capability to contribute to hemispheric defense cannot be accepted as the basis for U.S. policy. An all-out Soviet attack on Latin America was a remote possibility and seemed to be recognized as such by U.S. military planners. Even if such an attack had occurred, the United States obviously would have assumed the burden of defense and retaliation. The military resources of Latin America in relation to the Soviet Union were so limited that massive aid would have been required to enable them to withstand a major attack; even with such aid, the contribution they could make to self-defense against military aggression would inevitably be small. The United States at the time considered Latin America to be far behind the front lines of the cold war. The fact is that military equipment assigned to Latin America was small in quantity and obsolete in quality. Clearly, U.S. armed forces would have been necessary to resist certain kinds of external attack. The conclusion to be made, therefore, is that military aid was extended to preempt Latin American relations with other external actors and to promote internal stability in the Latin American nations.

Under the provisions of the Mutual Security Act, Latin American states were able to make cash purchases of weapons and equipment. In addition, the act authorized direct grants of military equipment for selected states under bilateral agreements called Mutual Defense Assistance pacts; a total of sixteen such agreements were signed in the 1950s. Two kinds of U.S. military missions were authorized under the Mutual Security Act: (1) Military Assistance Advisory Groups (MAAG) to administer military transfers under the Mutual Defense Assistance agreements; and (2) Service Training Missions to help train Latin American armed forces in an advisory capacity. Every Latin American state received at least one kind of mission and sometimes both. In addition, Latin American personnel were trained at U.S. military centers in the United States and Panama.

With the Alliance for Progress and an emphasis on economic and social development in Latin America, U.S. policy shifted from an emphasis on hemispheric defense to combatting internal subversion. The shift began near the end of the Eisenhower administration, was consummated in 1961 at the beginning of the Kennedy presidency, and continued as official policy thereafter. General economic and social development were assumed to occur best in a stable political environment; military aid aimed at countering internal Communist subversion and insurgency was said to help promote that stability. A modicum of resources, such as small amounts for antisubmarine warfare, continued to be put into hemispheric defense, but this concept was considered outmoded and internal stability clearly was the overriding goal.

Military assistance programs continued to consist of furnishing technical advisers, supplying grant material, and sponsoring formal training, as well as selling equipment for cash. The content of these programs, however, was changed to support Latin American counterinsurgency capabilities. Throughout the 1960s, U.S. officials, stressing the low probability of attack on Latin America from outside the hemisphere, attempted to discourage Latin American states from building up large conventional military forces and particularly discouraged arms purchases involving sophisticated aircraft and expensive naval vessels. Such expenditures were considered unwarranted diversions of resources from economic and social development projects; military replacement items should be of a kind and cost that would increase internal capabilities and enhance national development. In 1963 the International Police Academy was established in Washington, D.C., operated by the Office of Public Safety in the Agency for International Development. It was charged with assisting Latin American police forces to maintain civil security—specifically, to combat urban guerrilla activities.

Under the Alliance for Progress, Latin American armed forces placed a new emphasis on civic action, substantively supported by U.S. funds, equipment, and advisers. A number of enterprises fell under this rubric. Byproducts of military training transferred to civilian life ranged from literacy training of recruits to teaching technical skills enhancing civilian occupations. Other functions were directly aimed at assisting economic and social development, such as exploration of remote areas and opening new land, building schools and highways, improving sanitation and health facilities, and other projects useful to civilians, especially in rural areas.

A wide variety of objectives were pursued and variously stressed as functions of civic action. Emphasis was placed on economic and social development through nation building and on strengthening the economy by modernizing basic facilities and improving the infrastructure. A related idea was that the armed forces should justify their expensive public maintenance by helping to develop their nations. Improving the image of the military and the central government in the eyes of a skeptical public was yet another goal. Special stress was placed on the relationship of civic action to counterinsurgency (the two doctrines were developed simultaneously in the 1960s). Here the goal was to rectify those conditions believed to inspire insurgency, such as poverty and unfulfilled expectations for a better life.

The United States sharply diminished its military presence in Latin America beginning in the late 1960s. Officials declared that not only was the hemispheric defense concept outdated, but that internal insurgency threats also were at a low level and only sporadic activity existed. Furthermore, they said, Latin American counterinsurgency capabilities had improved. Consequently, personnel assigned to military groups were reduced and grant assistance funds were cut. A reduced training program and grant assistance fund were maintained.

An important debate in the U.S. Congress in 1967 revolved around the concern that scarce Latin American resources were being unduly devoted to military expenditures to the detriment of social and economic development. The Foreign Military Sales Act of that year imposed a limit of $75 million on direct arms sales to Latin America. Latin American states simply turned to other suppliers, especially West European ones. In 1971 President Nixon exercised his discretionary authority and raised the ceiling to $150 million, a figure then agreed to by Congress in the legislation for fiscal year 1972. The rationale for the increased limit was that Latin Americans had a legitimate need to update their military equipment and that experience had shown that, if the United States was unresponsive to their requests, they would simply acquire what they wanted elsewhere at an increased cost. They would also view the U.S. position as indifferent and paternalistic. U.S. balance-of-payments problems gave further impetus to increased arms exports, and the sales ceiling was eliminated altogether in 1974.

Competitors in the Arms Trade

The United States was Latin America's chief, but not exclusive, source of military assistance for the first two decades after World War II. After the war, France, Britain, Italy, Spain, West Germany, and Belgium again received small numbers of Latin American officers in their educational and training institutions. However, other states had a primary concern with trade and lacked security interests in the region. With the exception of Soviet relations with Cuba under Castro, with Peru after 1968, and with Chile from 1970 to 1973, sales of military equipment by external states other than the United States were essentially only of economic significance, related to the balance of payments rather than to the balance of power. Great Britain and France pursued a policy of virtually unrestricted arms sales in the profitable Latin American market; Germany, beginning in the late 1960s, adopted a similar policy after lifting prior restrictions on arms transfers to developing nations.

When the United States deemphasized its counterinsurgency military programs and restricted arms sales to Latin America, the regional states turned to Europeans as their chief suppliers. At the same time, the larger South American states competed vigorously to modernize their armed forces. Consequently, the volume and sophistication of arms transfers to Latin America in fact increased dramatically. According to a study by the U.S. Department of State (1973) surveying arms sales to Latin America (excluding Cuba) from 1966 to 1973, Latin American states placed a total of $1.7

billion in orders during that period, 75 percent of them in Western Europe (mainly Britain, France, and West Germany). The United States received 13 percent of those orders, Canada 10 percent, and Australia 2 percent. Six South American states (Argentina, Brazil, Chile, Colombia, Peru, and Venezuela) placed 97 percent of the orders. Naval and air forces accounted for about 90 percent of arms expenditures by the six states, and ground forces the remaining 10 percent.

The Soviet-Peruvian military relationship that began in 1973 continued through the latter 1980s. Peru was the only South American nation receiving military transfers from the Soviet Union, primarily sales of helicopters and tanks. Soviet military advisers and technicians were resident in Peru, and Peruvian military personnel were trained in the Soviet Union. In addition, the Soviet fishing fleet that operated off the South American Pacific coast was granted access to Peruvian ports for support and maintenance.

The Human Rights Factor

Further dramatic reductions in U.S. military assistance to Latin America began in 1976 with congressional action and were extended by President Carter after 1977. The International Security Assistance and Arms Export Control Act of 1976 virtually eliminated several key elements of the traditional aid program. It directed the elimination of U.S. military advisory groups around the world unless specifically authorized by Congress. Those in Latin America were reduced to three military personnel, with some exceptions specifically authorized by law.

President Carter introduced far-ranging executive restrictions on U.S. arms transfers. He stated that henceforth U.S. arms transfers would be viewed as exceptional rather than normal foreign policy instruments, that the United States as the world's largest arms exporter would take the initiative in reducing arms sales, and that human rights considerations in recipient countries would be an important factor in military assistance decisions. Congress approved the new presidential orientation. In 1976 Congress had required that reports be issued on those countries for which security was proposed and mandated an associated review process; the extent of the "report cards" and the review process were expanded during the Carter administration. As a result, the United States ended its military assistance and prohibited arms transfers to Argentina, Chile (beginning in 1976), El Salvador, Guatemala, Nicaragua, Paraguay, and Uruguay. Brazil was not so prohibited but refused to accept further military aid in reaction to the publication of negative reports on the status of human rights there. All claimed unwarranted interference in their internal affairs.

Arms Transfers Revived

The Reagan administration resuscitated military options in Latin America, emphasizing transfers of weapons and equipment. This revival of arms transfers logically formed part of Reagan's policies based on opposition to Soviet-Cuban expansionism. Reagan's approach differed from Carter's in three main ways: (1) Arms transfers would again have a central role in U.S. diplomacy for hemispheric security; (2) human rights concerns would be subordinate to security instruments in decisions about military relations; and (3) commercial sales would be encouraged and would include making the most sophisticated weapons available to Third World armed forces.

President Reagan signed a directive on July 8, 1981, laying out certain guidelines and his rationale for arms transfer policy. The directive and subsequent administration testimony before Congress emphasized a policy designed to counter "massive" Soviet arms transfers that "destabilize regions of strategic importance" to the United States. Furthermore, the United States would be viewed as a reliable supplier, thereby strengthening ties with allies. The policy was described as steering a middle course between unrestricted sales without reference to the military needs of recipients, on the one hand, and Carter's policy of restraint on the assumption that such sales inherently had a negative impact, on the other hand. The Carter policy, it was said, had been proven ineffective because the Soviet Union and other major arms suppliers had not slackened their activities. Officials denied charges that commercial considerations were the main driving force behind the new policy, which in practice amounted to a license for U.S. industry to sell anything anywhere.

While the Reagan administration sought to reelevate military assistance as an instrument of policy, legislative prohibitions and congressional controls in terms of human rights continued. Earlier decisions prohibiting arms transfers to Argentina, Chile, Paraguay, Uruguay, and Guatemala remained in effect, and questions were raised about human rights conditions in El Salvador. The administration itself chose to chastise Nicaragua, with whom it had hostile relations, about its human rights record. Reagan's effort to create an inter-American front against Communist penetration in the Southern Cone involved improving relations with military regimes in Argentina, Chile, Uruguay, and Paraguay. Cultivating their friendship and cooperation required, as a first step, reversing extant sanctions.

In April 1981, the administration introduced legislation to repeal the ban on arms sales to Argentina. Later, a similar request was made with respect to Chile. After considerable resistance, Congress agreed to lift sanctions on both countries, but only after the president had given Congress a report certifying that they had made significant progress on human rights problems. The State Department decided to consider the Argentine and Chilean cases simultaneously because of their dispute over islands in the Beagle Channel, not wanting to appear to take sides. Certification of Chile was difficult because Chile would not cooperate in resolving the murder case of Orlando Letelier, former Chilean ambassador to the United States, and an associate, both killed in a bomb blast in Washington. The Anglo-Argentine war of 1982 suspended certification considerations for a year and a half.

On December 10, 1983, inauguration day of the newly elected Argentine civilian President Raúl Alfonsín, President Reagan certified to Congress that Argentina had improved its human rights record and was eligible for the resumption of military transfers. A similar move was taken toward Uruguay in 1984 with the end of the military regime and return to democracy there. By then, General Augusto Pinochet of Chile and Alfredo Stroessner in Paraguay stood alone as authoritarian military heads of state. U.S. prohibitions on arms transfers remained in effect for both governments. The U.S. Congress continued to require better human rights conditions in both countries before allowing the end of prohibitions, an unlikely prospect as long as Pinochet and Stroessner remained in power.

Human rights concerns in Central America posed special considerations. In Guatemala, General Roméo Lucas García presided over probably the most violently repressive regime in Latin America. The Reagan administration indicated its willingness to resume military aid to help combat Guatemala's insurgency problem, but the scale of state terrorism was so high that the administration could not convince Congress to resume military ties. Congress relented in the case of El Salvador, but by law required the executive to certify that El Salvador was making a "concerted and significant effort to comply with internationally recognized human rights," was "achieving substantial control over all elements of its armed forces," and was "committed to the holding of free elections at an early date." Certification was made in February 1981. With the subsequent holding of free elections in El Salvador, the end of the Lucas García dictatorship in Guatemala and the holding of elections there, and resumption of the electoral process in Honduras, and the improved but still problematical human rights situations in all three countries, U.S. military transfers were unfettered. Arms transfers were again conducted, this time in the larger context of Central American conflict (see Chapter 11).

The administration was free to act independently when arms transfers did not involve questions of human rights. As a candidate, Reagan had pledged to promote weapons sales abroad, and once in office he did so. The State Department instructed U.S. diplomats, including armed services attachés, to assist U.S. manufacturers in marketing arms abroad. It canceled President Carter's order prohibiting such cooperation. Reagan approved sales of highly advanced F-16 aircraft to Third World nations. Venezuela was a principal recipient, as the Reagan administration acceded to its request to purchase eighteen F-16s on a cash basis. The sale amounted to about $615 million. Concerns were expressed that the sale presaged unrestrained transfers of highly advanced weaponry in Latin America. As it turned out, however, other countries did not have the economic resources to buy extensive military arms.

DIPLOMATIC AND CULTURAL RELATIONS

Diplomatic Relations

Latin Americans were eager to have their sovereign existence recognized during their movements for independence, but such action by the external states was slow in coming. The United States was the first to recognize the new Latin American states, but it did not do so until 1821. U.S. leaders viewed the revolutions against Spain with sympathy, but they were engaged in difficult negotiations with Spain to secure the Floridas and felt that recognition would jeopardize those efforts. With the ratification of the Adams-Onís Treaty of 1821 providing for the cession of the Floridas, the United States began to recognize Latin American sovereignties in defiance of European governments. Great Britain soon followed the U.S. lead. It was interested primarily in unrestricted trade with the Americas and in keeping Europe, especially France, from interfering in the revolutions. Britain granted full recognition to the new states in 1825, giving them at least moral support to resist Spain's attempts to reconquer its empire for the next half-century.

Spain, in its bitterness, sought to isolate Spanish America by refusing recognition. Only after the death of Ferdinand VII in 1833, which brought the liberals to power, did Spain temporarily abandon reconquest. Mexico was the first of the new states to be recognized by Spain, in 1836; delays in recognizing the others occurred because of intermittent hostility and pending negotiations over indemnification for Spanish losses in the revolutions and over the citizenship status of Spanish emigrés. Most of Spanish America had been recognized by 1864, but the process was not completed until the early 1890s (Víctor Alba in Davis, Wilson, and others, 1975:88–89).

The position of the Soviet Union has been a major factor in Latin American diplomacy in the twentieth century. Since the Bolshevik Revolution of November 1917, Soviet diplomatic relations with Latin America have been linked to Latin American Communist parties. Soviet policy focused first on developing Communist parties within the Comintern framework and secondarily on formal state-to-state diplomatic relations. The first Latin American Communist parties were founded in Argentina (1918), Mexico (1919), and Uruguay (1920); the first diplomatic relations were not established until 1924 with Mexico, and then with Uruguay in 1926. Several other states recognized the Soviet Union and made diplomatic exchanges, but by 1939 all diplomatic relations had been severed because of subversive activities by local Communist parties.

During World War II, the Soviet Union, as a member of the Allies, resumed diplomatic ties with Latin American governments, beginning with Colombia in 1941; a total of fourteen countries were included by the end of the war. With the onset of the Cold War in 1947, however, those ties again were restricted. By 1953 diplomatic relations were maintained only with Mexico, Argentina, and Uruguay, and further relations were not established until the 1960s. The special relationship with Cuba developed after the Castro revolution in 1960. To achieve its aims of strengthening Soviet influence wherever possible in Latin America, the Soviet Union was willing to cooperate with virtually any type of Latin American government, even militantly anti-Communist ones. The Soviet diplomatic offensive in Latin America resulted in numerous diplomatic ties established after the mid-1960s.

Throughout the Spanish Civil War (1936–1939) the incumbent Republican government maintained diplomatic relations with all but two Latin American states; in 1939 all of them except Mexico recognized the victorious Franco government and maintained relations throughout World War II. Mexico continued refusing to recognize the Franco government despite Mexican adherence to the Estrada principle advocating universal recognition and continuity of diplomatic relations.

Culture and Propaganda

States commonly seem to assume that cultural exchange facilitates the realization of political goals. Although cultural exchange may be unnecessary when interests are complementary and cannot overcome wide divergences of interest, cultural relations may assist cooperation or mitigate conflict. Some states have emphasized the economic value of cultural exchange. French officials, for example, have said that foreign students trained in French culture were the best promoters of French products, commercial methods, and technology (Goldhamer, 1972:131–132). Cultural relations have also been pursued in essentially ideological terms, such as the French "civilizing mission," the U.S. "democratizing mission," and the Spanish pursuit of "racial solidarity."

While cultural relations in a broad sense have existed throughout Latin American history, systematic governmental activity is a fairly recent phenomenon. For example, educated Latin Americans (especially South Americans), throughout the nineteenth century and well into the twentieth, were attracted to French culture; they read French books, adopted French philosophies, traveled to France, and sent their children to be educated there. Most of that interchange, however, was by way of private rather than official means. The French government seemed unwilling to enter into official cultural exchange with Latin America even during the height of its cultural influence at the turn of the century and up to World War I.

Spanish cultural policies toward Latin America have been of special interest. A small precursor cultural movement began in the mid-nineteenth century, but the idea received little attention until the 1890s. This Pan Hispanic movement, known as *hispanismo* or, sometimes, *hispanoamericanismo*, was advocated by a group of Spanish luminaries that included Rafael Altamira, José Ortega y Gassett, José F. Gómez, Adolfo Gonzáles Posada, Miguel de Unamuno, and others. They were highly active in their own transatlantic correspondence, travel, and lecturing, and in attempting to persuade the Spanish government to establish official programs based on their ideas. The movement was later fostered by institutes for Spanish-American studies in Spanish universities, several journals on the subject, student and professorial exchanges, and Pan Hispanic political and commercial organizations.

Early advocates of *hispanismo* championed not only a cultural community among Spanish-speaking peoples, stressing kindred race and cultural solidarity, but also political rapprochement and increased economic interaction for the mutual benefit of Spain and America. Some writers called for some sort of confederation or league among Hispanic peoples, but this idea remained vague. Hostility toward the Pan American movement sponsored by the United States was a constant theme; *hispanoamericanistas* viewed yankee imperialism and materialism as a major threat to hispanic values in Latin America. Antiyankeeism was stimulated by the war of 1898 and given further impetus by the long period of U.S. intervention in the Caribbean that followed. A Hispano-American cultural and economic congress was held in Madrid in 1900 with Spanish American attendance, signaling the official beginning of *hispanismo*; further congresses assembled in different Spanish cities in 1908, 1910, 1912, and 1914. The Spanish government modestly supported the movement, sending representatives to Spanish American centenary celebrations (beginning with Argentina in 1910) and subsidizing several Pan Hispanic political and commercial organizations. It also sponsored scholarships and fellowships for student and professor exchange (Rippy, 1958:205–209, 512–515). Latin American hostility toward Spain lessened somewhat and trade slightly increased.

Most students of the movement have viewed *hispanismo* basically as a cultural, partially economic, nonaggressive liberal movement stressing race, culture, and commerce, designed to promote Hispanic civilization and solidarity and to defend the culture against U.S. incursions. An important work by Frederick Pike (1971) confirms these features but also emphasizes that the Spanish adherents of the movement held antirevolutionary sentiments and represented the status quo. Pike believes that Spanish liberal and conservative supporters of *hispanismo* alike wished to prevent social revolution on both sides of the Atlantic. This sharing of social conservatism, in effect, left as the main difference between them the conservatives' rigid Roman Catholicism and the liberals' strong anticlericalism.

In the late 1930s, after falangist dictator General Francisco Franco came to power, *hispanismo* was converted to *hispanidad*, a concept fundamentally different from its predecessor. *Hispanidad* was widely popularized by Ramiro de Maeztu, an ex-anarchist turned falangist, in his book *Defensa de la Hispanidad* published in 1934. He described the concept in mystical and reactionary terms, seeking revindication of Spanish world power. For inspiration, he turned to the sixteenth century, when Spanish imperial power had reached its zenith. According to the falangists, the bases for Spanish greatness had been devotion to the church, military and naval strength, and a hierarchical social order. That greatness had declined, and Spain had suffered three centuries of humiliation, the theory continued, because of the pagan Renaissance, the Protestant Reformation, and the consequent eroding effects of relativism in religion, egalitarian political ideals, and economic materialism. Falangists admired and felt a spiritual kinship with Italian fascism and German nazism. But they insisted that falangism was distinctly Spanish, rooted in the values of the Middle Ages when, it was claimed, Spain was already Fascist. To promote Spanish regeneration in the 1930s, falangists called for reinstitution of religious intolerance and the Inquisition, the recovery of military strength and military values, and the resumption of empire in America (including large portions of the United States). England continued to be the eternal enemy, and France was vilified, but the United States and Pan Americanism received the most vociferous hostility. Falangism was also antimasonic, anti-Semitic, antidemocratic, antisocialist, and anti-Communist. The reestablishment of the American empire was absurd as a practical policy goal. Franco probably sought at most some degree of Spanish American sympathy for his regime.

Immediately after the Civil War and during World War II, organizations associated with the falangists engaged in a propaganda campaign in Latin America, sometimes in concert with German Nazi and Italian Fascist groups, even though Spain remained neutral throughout the war. Brazilian dictator Getulio Vargas initially sympathized with falangism and allowed Rio de Janeiro to serve as the Latin American center for Spanish propaganda activities, but Brazil nevertheless eventually sided with the Allies in World War II. (Actually, Vargas first sympathized with the Salazar brand of fascism in Portugal, which was older than the Franco regime.) Spain also cultivated relations with authoritarian governments in Argentina and Peru; it was active in Chile but eventually broke relations with that government. Spain financed the travel of sympathetic Latin American politicians, intellectuals, and students to Spain and established an Institute of Hispanic Studies in Madrid to give a scholarly veneer to *hispanidad*. Pan Hispanism was enthusiastically received in Latin America by right-wing elements; its appeal was essentially restricted to those elements by the end of World War II and the defeat of the Axis powers.

During World War I and the following interbellum period, the leading external competitors disseminated propaganda in Latin America. During the war the regional states were courted by both sides of the conflict: by France, Great Britain, and then Italy and the United States on the one hand; and by Germany, supported by neutral Spain, on the other. Notable at the time was the work of the American Committee on Public Information (the Creel Committee), the first U.S. experiment in government-supported cultural exchange in Latin America. Created by President Wilson in 1917 and headed by journalist George Creel, the agency established a network of contacts around Latin America. These contacts—usually resident U.S. newspaper correspondents but sometimes government officials and Latin American nationals—received and distributed various kinds of communications media and advised on the information content best received in their areas (Mock, 1942).

During the 1920s and especially the 1930s, as international frictions increased, external propagandizing in Latin America continued apace. Italy, Germany, and Spain actively sought to take advantage of their national communities in the region, but with mixed success. Those communities often were deeply divided among themselves over loyalty to European governments, even though they generally had affection for the former national homeland. After the United States announced its Good Neighbor Policy in 1933, European propaganda lost much of its appeal because it had a high antiyankee content. The United States signed multilateral cultural exchange conventions with Latin American states in 1936 at the Buenos Aires Conference, and in 1938 the Department of State organized its Division of Cultural Relations to administer official activities and to assist private agencies in their cultural programs (Mecham, 1965:128–130).

Regularized cultural exchange programs have been prevalent since World War II. The most important ones have been maintained by France, the United States, West Germany, Great Britain, Spain, and the Soviet Union, although the People's Republic of China, East Germany, Italy, Iran, Korea, and the United Arab Republic (UAR) also undertook some modest activities in the region. In addition, Argentina, Brazil, Mexico, Chile, and Cuba developed intraregional communications and educational exchange programs (Agor and Suárez, 1972).

Several external states have maintained publicly funded cultural centers around the region. Most of them are private organizations receiving financial support from their home governments, including France's Alliance Francaise, West Germany's Goethe Institute (which contracted with the government in 1969), the United Kingdom's British Council (founded in 1934), Spain's Instituto de Cultura Hispanica, and the United States Information Agency (USIA, a public agency supervised by the Department of State). All of them have engaged in a wide range of activities. They have given high priority to language classes (except for the Spanish-run centers), the operation of libraries, and various cultural programs. They have provided scholarships for Latin Americans to study abroad; offered travel programs for the exchange of artists, intellectuals, and athletes; and distributed films, books, magazines, and newspapers. Most of the major external states have also sent government-supported teachers to staff schools originally intended to serve the children of their own nationals, but enrollments in these schools include large numbers of Latin American children as well. Government broadcast services are aired to Latin America by Radio Moscow, Radio Peking, Voice of America, the UAR broadcast service, British Broadcasting Corporation, the French broadcast service, and the East German broadcast service (Goldhamer, 1972: Ch. 9).

BIBLIOGRAPHIC COMMENT

General texts on Latin American economics, political economy, and international economic relations are provided by Fishlow and Díaz-Alejandro (1984), Glade (1969), Grunwald (1978), Hartlyn and Morley (1986), Hirschman (1972), and Hunter and Foley (1975). Analyses of trade and investment include books by Baerresen, Carnoy, and Grunwald (1965), Bernstein (1966), Platt (1973), and Rippy (1959). See McBride (1981) and Purcell (1981, 1982) on U.S.-Mexican economic relations. Broad treatments of the debt problem and its adjustment include Bianchi, Devlin, and Ramos (1985), Economic Commission for Latin American and the Caribbean (1985, 1986), Inter-American Development Bank (1984, 1985), Pastor (1987),

Thorp and Whitehead (1987), and Wiarda (1986b); Roett (1984) addresses the relationship of debt to democracy, and Parkinson (1987) the legal-institutional aspects. On U.S. economic programs and policies, see U.S. Department of Commerce (1951) and the annual hearings by the U.S. Senate and House regarding mutual security appropriations (1951–1960) and foreign assistance appropriations (since 1961). See U.S. House Committee on Foreign Affairs (1981) on the Caribbean Basin Initiative. Latin American economic relations with the Soviet Union are treated by Evanson (1985) and Goldman (1966). CEPAL (1982) is a primary source on Latin American relations with the CMEA. Ferrer (1973) and Mower (1982) discuss Latin American economic relations with the European Community.

On drug trafficking, see Bagley (1986), Craig (1981a, 1981b, 1983, 1985), and Lupsha (1981). Migrations of peoples related to Latin America in a wide variety of contexts are studied by Audera (1955), Bastos de Avila (1964), Bates (1957), Ferris (1987), Murillo-Castaño (1984), Pastor (1984), Saunders (1986), and Teitelbaum (1984).

On pre–World War II external (especially European) military activities in Latin America, see Epstein (1941)—an unpublished rough draft but still a highly valuable source. On U.S. military policy and programs, see Kemp (1970), U.S. House Committee on Foreign Affairs (1946, 1947, 1950), and U.S. Department of State (1973); see also the annual congressional hearings on foreign assistance cited above. Barber and Ronning (1966) is still the best work on counterinsurgency, civic action, and related U.S. assistance. Latin American military expenditures are detailed by Heare (1971) and the annual U.S. Arms Control and Disarmament Agency, *World Military Expenditures*. Brigagão (1986) analyzes the Brazilian arms industry.

Works on cultural relations include Bernstein (1961), Maeztu (1941), Mock (1942), Pike (1977), Shapiro (1968), and Wood (1972). Schoultz (1981) is excellent on questions of human rights. Brown (1985) presents findings on human rights experiences in nine Latin American countries. Relatively broad treatments of U.S. recognition policy toward Latin America include Cochran (1968), Cochrane (1972), Dozer (1966), Goebel (1915), and the U.S. Department of State (1975). On expropriation and national-ization, see Gordon (1941), Ingram (1974), and Lowenfeld (1971).

CHAPTER ELEVEN

■

Violence and Accommodation

CERTAIN REALITIES AND NORMS of Latin American international politics have been violent in nature. This chapter deals with conflict involving the threat or use of force in the regional subsystem and efforts to resolve such conflicts. The analysis identifies the sources of contention, the principal actors and their calculations, conflict-resolution measures undertaken, and the outcomes or current status. Conflict analysis is facilitated by first identifying a number of general considerations about the phenomenon of violence in the Latin American subsystem. These considerations are then applied to a series of case studies in specific regional and subregional contexts.

SOME GENERAL CONSIDERATIONS

The Sources of Conflict

Violence in the Latin American subsystem has arisen essentially from five sets of sources or causes: (1) boundary and territorial disputes, (2) competition for resources, (3) imperial and power disputes, (4) ideological competition, and (5) migration of people and goods. Considerable overlap occurs among these sources, and specific cases may involve some combination of them. (The following commentary has been influenced by Child, 1985:Ch. 1, and Grabendorff, 1982.)

Border conflicts flow from disagreements over frontiers between contiguous sovereignties. They are related to territorial disputes in that they may lead to or be part of larger conflicts involving sovereign claims. Nationalist sentiments invariably accompany border and territorial conflict. Territorial conflicts usually stem from disputes over the possession of land terrain but may extend to oceanic rights. Strategic assertions entail important terrain and islands, transisthmian canal locations, or sea lanes. Resource conflicts have become increasingly important in furthering national development and economic well-being. While the disputes themselves involve land or ocean territory, it is often the vital energy, strategic, or food resources that are at stake (petroleum, natural gas, minerals, hydroelectricity, fish, and so on).

"Influence conflict" refers both to historic imperialism and to more recent competition to project national power; both are closely associated with balance-of-power systems. This type of conflict usually includes questions of prestige or some other version of "national honor" and is often intertwined with ideological conflict. The ideological category goes beyond simple power considerations, however. Ideological conflicts deal with the struggle to impose, or resist the imposition of, political, economic, and social values. The principal rivalries have been between dictatorships and democracy, civilian and military regimes, and democratic capitalism versus various forms of Marxism. They have been pursued not only by the great powers but by regional states on all levels and by a range of nonstate actors.

Conflicts arising from the migration of people and goods are also multifaceted. A majority of the nineteenth century European interventions were responses to problems arising from commerce, investments, and immigrants; foreign investors and resident aliens appealed to their governments for redress when Latin Americans defaulted on their debts or mistreated foreign persons and property. Those governments demanded indemnity from Latin American states and at times threatened or used military force to gain compliance. Other migration conflicts deal with strains caused by the movement of people and goods across frontiers. Strife has often been caused by people migrating for essentially economic or political reasons from one polity to another. The flow of illicit drugs (the "narcotraffic") has become increasingly important; it has led to considerable violence on the part of traffickers and to contentious interstate relations.

Regional and Subregional Patterns

Latin American regional and subregional patterns, especially those involving the distribution of power, are directly linked to conflict analysis. Latin American history includes a significant amount of region-wide or transregional conflicts. Boundary disputes have been prevalent within the region: Every Latin American state with a common land frontier with another has engaged in such conflict; that is, only the Caribbean island states with no contiguous neighbors have avoided such quarrels. Furthermore, a series of European military interventions and other forms of power politics occurred in all parts of Latin America throughout the nineteenth century. Soviet attempts at subversion were widespread during the twentieth century interbellum period, as were U.S. covert paramilitary activities during the cold war. Guerrilla warfare, beginning in the late 1950s, has been a common regional phenomenon. Migration conflicts have caused long-standing regional problems, and the narcotraffic has recently given rise to considerable transregional conflict.

Certain geographic and political factors have been especially significant in helping to determine subregional politics and the choice of policy instruments. Because of Mexico's position as an important state bordering the powerful and vitally interested United States, and the role of relatively weak Circum-Caribbean states in the great power competitions of the nineteenth century and as a sphere of U.S. influence in the twentieth, Mexico and the

Circum-Caribbean have long been the most susceptible of the Latin American regions to external force, although the last intervention in Mexico took place in 1914. If one excludes the very special case of the Anglo-Argentine war of 1982, no military interventions have occurred in the Southern Cone in the twentieth century, partly because of the region's remoteness from the mainstream of international politics. In the Circum-Caribbean, however, the United States applied military force extensively during the first third of the century; the latest case in the long history of such actions was the U.S. invasion of Grenada in 1983.

Furthermore, in the Southern Cone, intraregional conflicts with little involvement from external powers have been especially important; the impetus for such conflict has been provided by the power calculations of the principal local states. Such calculations are not as relevant to the policy-making of other Latin American states. The legacy of conflict in the Southern Cone includes a long list of discrete territorial and boundary disputes, national power struggles that have led to warfare and threats of war, claims of sovereignty, and competition for resources. Southern Cone rivalry has been extended to the sea and seabed and to Antarctica, and nuclear questions have been introduced.

NINETEENTH-CENTURY PATTERNS AND CASES

Mexico and International Conflict

In the nineteenth century, Mexico was often of interest to one or another of the external powers. Spain sent an expedition to Mexico in 1829 in response to a Mexican law expelling Spanish citizens, but it was repelled by disease and the Mexican army. In 1838 France bombarded Vera Cruz and forced payment of claims to its nationals. The most important conflict, however, occurred in relations with the United States and France. The former took half of Mexico's territory as the result of war, and the latter occupied Mexico and temporarily made it a part of its empire.

Mexico's relations with the United States were dominated by boundary and territorial questions in the nineteenth century. The territorial limits between the United States and Mexico had not been fixed when the latter won its independence. An 1819 treaty, reaffirmed in 1828, agreed to the Sabine River as the frontier. The United States, however, was expanding westward across the continent to realize "manifest destiny," and U.S. leaders wanted to designate the Rio Grande as the new boundary. They unsuccessfully employed diplomatic means to purchase the additional territory from Mexico, as well as more devious measures, such as bribing Mexican officials.

The area that now forms Texas was originally part of Mexico, but the Mexican government largely ignored it and allowed "Anglo" settlers to migrate there. U.S. citizens who began to settle in the sparsely inhabited territory in the 1820s eventually clashed with the central Mexican government.

In 1836 Texas declared its independence and defeated a Mexican army sent to put it down. Texans wanted to be annexed as a U.S. state, but statehood was denied, largely because of the slavery issue. They thereupon established an independent republic, which was recognized by the United States in 1837. Despite the opposition of Britain and France, who wanted Texas to serve as a buffer state between Mexico and the aggressive United States, Texas was annexed by the United States in 1845.

Continued disputes over the extent of the Texas territory after annexation resulted in the U.S.-Mexican war (1846–1848). Mexico said that Texas ended at the Nueces River; the United States claimed the Rio Grande. U.S. troops were sent to Texas, where they clashed with Mexican units in the disputed territory. Full-scale warfare followed, resulting in U.S. military invasion and occupation. The war was terminated by the Treaty of Guadalupe Hidalgo, signed on February 2, 1848. Under its terms, Mexico quit its claims to Texas, allowed the United States to fix the Texas boundary at the Rio Grande, and ceded the rest of its northern territory from Texas to the Pacific Ocean. The settlement cost Mexico almost half its national territory. The vastness of the new acquisition did not satisfy some expansionists in the United States, however; an "all-Mexico" movement demanded total annexation, but their ambitions were frustrated by the slavery issue. The United States paid Mexico $15 million, and U.S. troops withdrew in August 1848. Five years later, in 1853, the U.S. Minister to Mexico, James Gadsden, negotiated the purchase from Mexico of the Gila River valley in southern Arizona and New Mexico for $10 million.

Mexico was rocked by civil war beginning in 1857, and the liberal government of Benito Juárez in July 1861 declared bankruptcy and repudiated all foreign debts. France, Britain, and Spain collaborated to coerce Mexico to honor their nationals' heavy claims, some of which were fraudulent. Their combined fleet appeared at Vera Cruz in 1861. The following year Britain and Spain reached agreements with Mexico and withdrew their troops. Napoleon III had more than pecuniary claims collection in mind, however; he wanted to establish a French empire in Mexico. His motives seem to have been to enhance French commerce, to "contain" U.S. continental expansion, and to curry favor with the church in France by punishing Juárez and other anticlerical Mexican liberals.

After French troops occupied the capital, France formed the Empire of Mexico and named prince Archduke Maximilian of Austria, a Catholic, as chief of state. He and his wife, Princess Carlota, arrived at Mexico City in June 1864. The following year, at the end of its own civil war, the United States demanded that French forces be withdrawn. The United States had continued to recognize the Juárez government throughout the French occupation, and Mexican forces had continued their resistance outside the capital city. Napoleon III removed French troops from Mexico, not only because of the U.S. position, but also because of opposition in France and a tenuous political position in Europe. With French military support gone, Juárez's army deposed Maximilian; he was convicted by court martial and shot.

The 1848 peace treaty between Mexico and the United States did not end border friction. Numerous incidents continued to occur in the last half of the nineteenth century and into the twentieth. The U.S. Marines landed in Mexico in 1913 as the Mexican Revolution took an exceptionally violent turn. The United States captured Vera Cruz in 1914 and held it for almost seven months; General John J. Pershing led a U.S. military expedition into northern Mexico in an unsuccessful attempt to capture General Francisco (Pancho) Villa. This expedition was the last U.S. military intervention in Mexico.

Southern Cone Conflicts

The nineteenth century witnessed a series of major South American wars or threats of war and power struggles. Involving in one way or another all of the subregional states, the wars were part of a larger expression of Southern Cone power politics and geopolitical thinking. The most intense traditional leadership rivalry was among Argentina, Brazil, and Chile, the "ABC" states.

The rivalry between Argentina and Brazil for control of the Rio de la Plata region centered on Uruguay in the early national period. Portugal and Spain had contested the region for two centuries in the colonial era, it being the major point of contact between the two great Iberian empires. Argentina unsuccessfully tried to maintain the viceroyalty of La Plata under its control during the wars for independence, and afterward it actively meddled in the other La Plata states. Brazil, after gaining independence in 1822, pursued an aggressive policy of "manifest destiny," clashing with Argentine ambitions. Uruguayan patriots claimed independence from both Spain and Portugal and seceded from Buenos Aires, but Argentina still considered Uruguay one of its own provinces. In 1822, however, Uruguay was annexed as the Cisplatine province of the independent Brazilian empire. In 1825 Uruguay declared its independence from Brazil, and Argentina entered the dispute on the side of the rebels; Argentine troops and Uruguayan patriots fought an indecisive three-year war against Brazil. Britain, its commercial interests in the area disrupted, intervened to force a settlement. It pressured Argentina and Brazil into signing the Treaty of Montevideo (1828), in which they both agreed to recognize Uruguayan independence, thus creating a buffer state between the two South American rivals.

Despite the 1828 treaty, attempts to control Uruguay continued throughout the nineteenth century. Intermittent civil war in Uruguay invited Argentine and Brazilian intervention and claims for territory. One of the most important developments was what Uruguayans called the Great War, beginning in 1836. An alliance between Argentine dictator Juan Manuel de Rosas and an Uruguayan political faction, the Blancos, conducted a siege of Montevideo from 1841 to 1851 against another faction, the Colorados, allied with anti-Rosas Argentines. From 1845 to 1850 French and British naval units blockaded Buenos Aires and simultaneously supported the Montevideans; after their withdrawal, Brazil joined the anti-Rosas alignment (partly because it was assured of a favorable settlement of its Uruguayan boundary) and was soon victorious. In 1851 Brazil forced a treaty upon Uruguay in which the latter renounced an earlier claim to almost half its national territory along the northern frontier. Brazil thereafter expanded into the territories of each of the remaining seven contiguous states except Peru, but it did so through peaceful diplomatic negotiations.

From 1865 to 1870 the Uruguayan Colorados united with Argentina and Brazil to resist the expansionist moves of Paraguayan dictator Francisco Solano López. This union produced the Paraguayan War, known in Paraguay as the War of the Triple Alliance. A Blanco government, having poor relations with both Argentina and Brazil, had responded to Paraguayan overtures for a common policy in 1862. López had in mind a Paraguayan-led empire of central South American states, including Uruguay and Bolivia. Paraguay invaded Argentina and Brazil near their Uruguayan borders, and in May 1865 the triple alliance of those two states plus Uruguay was formed. The resulting war went on for five years until March 1870, ending with Paraguay's complete defeat. The majority of its male population was killed, and Argentina and Brazil took portions of its territory. Paraguay, no longer a power contender, was left as a buffer state between its neighbors.

The entire boundary between Argentina and Chile from north to south was disputed following the movements for independence. In 1881 a vague settlement provided for the frontier to run along the "highest peaks" of the Andes dividing the watershed. This provision was interpreted differently by each state. War was narrowly averted over a portion of the northern frontier known as the Puna de Atacama. After failing to reach agreement through direct diplomacy, Chile and Argentina agreed to arbitration by the United States, and in 1899 the U.S. arbiter divided the disputed territory. Objections were voiced in Chile, but the decision was accepted by both sides. Parts of the southern boundary remained in dispute, however. The 1881 treaty had divided Tierra del Fuego between the two states; it had given sovereignty over Patagonia to Argentina and that over the Strait of Magellan to Chile, which agreed to neutralize the area. Disagreements arose over the precise demarcation, however. They turned to the British Crown for arbitration in 1896, and King Edward handed down his award in 1902.

Important conflicts on the west coast of South America that developed in the early independence period continue in some respects to the present day. Chile, intent on dominating the Pacific coast, pursued aggressive policies toward Bolivia and Peru. In 1836 Bolivian President Andres Santa Cruz took advantage of political divisions in Peru to form a Peru-Bolivian Confederation. Chile immediately opposed it, perceiving a threat to its economic interests and strategic position, and went to war against the Confederation in 1836. Argentina did the same the following year, but, feeling less threatened than Chile, it played a minor military role. Chile invaded Peru in 1838 and defeated the combined Peru-Bolivian army the following year, bringing an end to the Confederation. Chile built up its military and naval forces thereafter and in 1879 again went to war against the combined forces of Peru and Bolivia.

The War of the Pacific (1879–1883), along with the Paraguayan War, was the most serious nineteenth-century Latin American international conflict. The 800-mile Bolivian Pacific coastline was composed mostly of the barren Atacama Desert; few Bolivians settled there. In 1866 Chileans discovered vast nitrate deposits near the site where the town of Antofagasta was built, and in 1874 Bolivia ceded a portion of its Atacama territory to Chile. The Chileans mined and exported the nitrates under an agreement with Bolivia until 1878, when a dispute over taxes led to military confrontation. Chile attacked the Bolivian desert regions in 1879, and Peru entered the war on the side of Bolivia, allied by a second treaty in 1873. Some major actions were fought at sea; Peru was initially victorious, but Chile eventually achieved supremacy in the naval war. Peru also bore the brunt of the Chilean land offensive, which involved another invasion of Peru by Chile and the sacking and occupation of Lima. U.S. and European governments, beginning in 1880, unsuccessfully attempted to terminate the war through mediation. Chile finally defeated the Peru-Bolivian alliance and made substantial gains through the peace settlements.

In the Ancón Treaty of October 20, 1883, Peru permanently ceded its province of Tarapacá to Chile. Chile was to occupy the Peruvian provinces of Tacna and Arica for a ten-year period, after which a plebiscite was to be held to determine their future status. Chile and Peru could not agree on the terms of the plebiscite, however, and its continuous postponement after 1893 embittered relations between the two states for the next thirty-five years. A compromise was finally reached through U.S. good offices in the Washington Protocol of 1929. Chile annexed Arica and returned Tacna to Peru.

A truce signed between Chile and Bolivia on April 4, 1884, provided for an indefinite armistice and for Chilean occupation of Atacama. In 1888 Chile unilaterally relabeled the territory of Atacama as the province of Antofagasta. A treaty formally ending the war was not signed until October 20, 1904. Under its provisions Bolivia gave up the territory, thereby losing its coastline and access to the sea. In return, Chile indemnified Bolivia and agreed to build a railroad from La Paz to Arica for Bolivian use. Chile later allowed Bolivia to use Arica as a free port, but it failed to satisfy Bolivian needs or its nationalist goals and Bolivia never abandoned the idea of regaining its own Pacific port. In 1920 it appealed to the League of Nations for a seaport on the grounds that the 1904 treaty was null and void, but the League refused to intervene. Neither did Bolivia participate or receive concessions in the 1929 settlement between Chile and Peru. After losing its Pacific littoral, Bolivia turned to the east for an outlet to the Atlantic—a concern that provided one of the bases for the Chaco War (discussed below).

Origins of the Falklands/Malvinas Dispute

The Falkland Islands, known in Argentina as the Islas Malvinas and located some 300 miles east of southern Argentina, had an ambiguous early history that complicated later claims to its ownership. The dispute dates from the discovery of the islands in 1592 and the subsequent contending colonial claims. France, Spain, and Britain at one time or another occupied and abandoned the islands between 1764 and 1811. In 1820, Argentina (then the United Provinces of La Plata) took possession based on rights of succession to Spanish territory. Britain later claimed ownership; at the same time, private U.S. sealing vessels were trespassing on the islands. The Argentine governor seized three of the vessels; this move opened up a diplomatic controversy between Argentina and the United States, during which the *U.S.S. Lexington* destroyed the Argentine colony on the Malvinas. Britain took advantage of the situation by occupying the islands with military force in 1833. A British naval unit drove off an Argentine settlement and established effective British control for the next century and a half. Argentina never accepted British rule, and it regularly protested and asserted its own sovereign claims.

TWENTIETH-CENTURY PATTERNS AND CASES TO WORLD WAR II

U.S. Imperialism in the Caribbean

During the first third of the twentieth century, the United States behaved as a great imperialist power. That behavior was especially based on geopolitical-strategic calculations about the Caribbean region combined with economic motives and, sometimes, democratic purposes. The operational beginnings of U.S. imperialism in the Caribbean region date from the U.S. victory in its ten-week war with Spain.

The United States intervened often in Caribbean affairs during the first third of the twentieth century. It established protectorates in Cuba and Panama, colonized Puerto Rico, and gained treaty rights to intervene in Haiti. It intervened on numerous occasions and in various ways during this period in seven states—Cuba, Panama, Haiti, Dominican Republic, Nicaragua, Honduras, and Guatemala. Intervention assumed the forms of troop landings and military occupations (U.S. troops entered all seven states between 1898 and 1934), the establishment of customs receiverships, and electoral supervision. Most of the interventions were carried out with concern for the security of the Panama Canal. In the initial stages of imperialism after 1898, the United States asserted its new world power with little hesitation in order to attain canal rights and to secure the Caribbean approaches to the Central American isthmus. Later, a secondary motive of intervening developed—intervention in the name of democracy and antidictatorship. Some interventions occurred to protect the lives and property of U.S. citizens, and for a time, the primary focus was on the protection of capital investments ("dollar diplomacy").

U.S. imperialism increased after the conclusion of the last European military intervention in a sovereign Latin America state—Venezuela in 1902/1903. Europeans residing in Venezuela had been heavily damaged in a civil war, but Venezuelan dictator Cipriano Castro excluded foreign claims against

Venezuela. External states issued ultimatums and, when they were not met, Germany, Great Britain, and Italy blockaded Venezuela in concert. The United States had previously stressed that the Monroe Doctrine forbade territorial aggrandizement, but it did not protect any state against punishment for fiscal misconduct. After the blockade began, the United States successfully pressured the European states to accept arbitration of their grievances. Consequently, in 1905, President Roosevelt issued his corollary to the Monroe Doctrine, and the United States thereafter engaged in its own Caribbean intervention in order to preempt that of the Europeans.

U.S. troops were continuously based in Panama from 1902 to 1914 during the construction of the canal. They intervened there during local disturbances from 1918 to 1920 and in 1925. The United States exercised its rights of intervention in Cuba by establishing a provisional military government from 1906 to 1909; it also briefly sent in troops in 1912 and again in 1916 (with some troops remaining until 1922) and threatened to do so again on numerous other occasions. U.S. forces intervened in the Dominican Republic in 1905 to restore order; another troop intervention in 1916 was followed by the establishment of a U.S. military government that lasted until 1924. U.S. Marines occupied Nicaragua from 1912 to 1925 and from 1926 until 1933. Marines were sent to Haiti in 1914; after a brief withdrawal they returned in 1915 and remained until 1934. U.S. troops were in and out of Honduras between 1903 and 1925. A brief military intervention occurred in Guatemala in 1920 to protect U.S. diplomats and private interests during political disturbances in that country.

It was during the Taft administration (1909–1913) that the United States began to practice "dollar diplomacy." Secretary of State Philander C. Knox manipulated U.S. investments and loans in the Caribbean region by encouraging North American financial groups and consortia to extend them in Santo Domingo, Haiti, and Nicaragua. This private capital involvement led to the landing of U.S. Marines to protect U.S. lives and property. The United States pursued arms control in Cuba, Nicaragua, and Mexico through supervision of sales and embargoes. U.S. "fiscal intervention" took place under U.S.-administered customs receiverships in the Dominican Republic beginning in 1905, in Nicaragua from 1911, and in Haiti starting in 1916. The receiverships involved U.S. fiscal control of the economies and were designed to bring about responsible management and to arrange for a restructuring of international debts.

U.S. armed forces carried out "civic action" projects during their occupations of Cuba, Panama, Nicaragua, Haiti, and the Dominican Republic. Under their aegis, internal order was restored, legal systems reformed, highways constructed, public education improved, and sanitation and public health programs instituted; public schools were constructed, teachers were trained, and public administration programs were developed. Little political development took place, however, beyond "pacification" of the populaces.

Intervention in the name of democracy and antidictatorship began with the administration of Woodrow Wilson in 1913. A sharp distinction should be drawn between the landing of troops and the nonrecognition of governments as two very different modes of intervention. Troop interventions were not used to bring down dictatorships, nor were they immediately occasioned by constitutional-democratic motives, whereas nonrecognition or its threat was employed in such cases. Once military occupation was begun, however, some local military and police forces (in Nicaragua, Haiti, and the Dominican Republic) were trained, organized, and led by U.S. Marines in the hope that they would be apolitical forces protecting future constitutional governments upon the withdrawal of U.S. forces (a hope totally unrealized). The United States also pursued "electoral intervention," with military supervision of elections prior to ending its occupations. U.S.-supervised elections were held in Cuba, Panama, the Dominican Republic, Haiti, and Nicaragua. These practices developed by Wilson were continued by his successors, Presidents Harding, Coolidge, and for a time, Hoover.

U.S. conflict with Latin America was reduced considerably beginning in 1930 with the adoption of noninterventionist policies. President Hoover reduced the number of troops in the Caribbean, and President Roosevelt largely based his Good Neighbor Policy on nonintervention. The last troop contingents left Nicaragua in 1933 and Haiti in 1934, leaving no U.S. troops in Latin America for the first time since 1919; no further direct military interventions occurred until 1965, when forces were sent to the Dominican Republic. President Roosevelt resisted State Department pressures for armed intervention in Cuba in 1933 against the repressive Machado dictatorship; furthermore, the 1903 treaty with Cuba giving the United States interventionist rights was abrogated in 1934 (the United States retained the Guantanamo naval station). Likewise, the United States concluded a treaty with Panama in 1936 giving up rights to intervene in Panamanian affairs. The last customs receiverships, in Haiti and the Dominican Republic, were closed in 1941.

Soviet Subversion

After the Bolshevik Revolution of 1917, the Soviet Union attempted to create loyal Communist parties in Latin America and establish traditional diplomatic relations at the same time. These lines of policy proved to be contradictory. After Uruguay recognized the Soviet Union in 1926, the Soviet embassy in Montevideo served as Latin American headquarters for the Comintern and the dissemination point for its revolutionary propaganda. Soviet efforts to stimulate armed insurrections through local Communist parties were attempted in Mexico (1929), Argentina (1930), Chile (1931), El Salvador (1932), Chile (1932), Cuba (1933), and Brazil (1935); Uruguay severed relations with the Soviet Union in 1935 because Soviet diplomats in Montevideo had helped organize the subversive activities in Brazil. All of the insurrections were suppressed, and they led to widespread outlawing of Communist parties and ruptures of relations with the Soviet Union (by 1939 all diplomatic relations between Latin American states and the Soviet Union had been severed). Soviet policy was much more cautious after 1935, with Moscow instructing local Communist parties to participate in popular front coalitions.

Inter–Latin American Conflict

Haiti and the Dominican Republic, both located on the island of Hispaniola, view each other with suspicion and enmity. After the Dominican Republic broke away from Haiti in 1844 and formed a separate state, border conflicts were frequent. According to Larman Wilson (in Davis, Wilson, and others, 1975:202), "the history of border disputes between the two countries of Hispaniola has had a racial dimension, the border having always been viewed as a barrier against a Haitian black invasion or a Dominican mulatto invasion." In 1874 the two states agreed to a vague boundary, which was to be delineated by subsequent negotiations, but it remained undefined for the next six decades and frequent border clashes occurred. In 1934 and 1935 the presidents of the two states exchanged visits; they announced that all border difficulties had been resolved and that a treaty would go into effect in 1936. As it turned out, the difficulties were more excruciating than ever. In October 1937 Dominican military forces attacked and killed at least 12,000 and perhaps as many as 25,000 Haitian peasants near the border. Why the massacre took place has never been fully explained, although little doubt exists that the Dominican dictator, Rafael Trujillo, was responsible. A settlement was worked out using the peacekeeping machinery of the Inter-American System. The disputants signed an agreement on January 31, 1938, in which the Dominican Republic agreed to pay the sum of $750,000 as indemnity to Haiti and to fix responsibility for the "incident"; both parties agreed to prevent recurrences of such violence.

The most recent South American war was between Bolivia and Paraguay from 1932 to 1935. The Chaco War originated in disputes over undetermined national frontiers. The area of the Chaco Boreal, a triangle of territory bound by the Pilcomayo, Paraguay, and Parapeti rivers, was a void area until both Paraguay and Bolivia took increased interest in it. Paraguay desired to recover some of its lost national prestige after the War of the Triple Alliance, and after the War of the Pacific, Bolivia wanted ports on the Paraguay River to give it access to the Atlantic through the Rio de la Plata system. Several frontier treaties were signed, but none went into effect. In 1906 Bolivia began building small forts (*fortines*) in the disputed region, and Paraguay soon followed suit. The controversy was intensified by rumors of the discovery of oil in the Chaco. Armed clashes occurred beginning in 1927, and full-scale war began in 1932. Attempts at mediation by the League of Nations and the Inter-American System failed. By 1935 Paraguay was in control of most of the Chaco and, with both sides exhausted, a truce was agreed to. Most of its provisions were included in a 1938 peace treaty signed through U.S. good offices. Paraguay, as the military victor, annexed about 20,000 square miles, or most of the disputed Chaco area. The financial and human costs were huge for both sides. Some 50,000 Bolivians and 35,000 Paraguayans died in the war.

Peru and Ecuador had serious boundary disputes that dated from their earliest relations. Upon independence they both claimed the sparsely inhabited Amazon provinces of Jaen and Maynas lying to the north of the Marañón River (which eventually flows into the Amazon River). After 1910 Peru was in control of the most valuable portion of the disputed region. In that year the two states agreed to settle the question by direct negotiations or, if that method failed, to submit it for an arbitral award by the U.S. president. Nothing came of the agreement, however, and it was terminated in 1938.

Relatively large-scale military movements by both sides occurred in the area between July 1941 and January 1942, but no major fighting took place. The United States, which had entered World War II in December 1941, was unwilling to allow the destabilizing influences of fighting in South America and forced a settlement of the dispute. The relatively weaker Ecuador was prevailed upon to accept Peruvian sovereignty over the disputed territory, guaranteed by the United States, Argentina, Chile, and Brazil. An agreement was signed in Rio de Janeiro on January 29, 1942, after which a mixed Ecuadorian-Peruvian Boundary Commission was appointed to fix the agreed-upon boundary. After about 95 percent of the frontier had been marked, however, Ecuador protested that it did not conform to the Rio de Janeiro agreement. The commission's work was halted. In 1959 Ecuador declared the 1942 protocol void and renewed its claim to the disputed provinces. Lima rejected the claims and the dispute remained unresolved thereafter.

Colombia and Peru signed a treaty in Lima in 1922 fixing the boundary between them in the Amazon River Basin. In 1930 the demarcation was fixed by a bilateral commission. Under this plan, Colombia occupied a strip of territory called the "Leticia Trapezium," which included the Amazon River port town of Leticia. In September 1932, an armed irregular band of Peruvians seized the town and ejected the Colombian officials. The Peruvian government at first repudiated the act, but later it supported the seizure, sent regular troops into the area, and declared the 1922 treaty invalid. Colombia responded by sending military forces to the Leticia territory via the Panama Canal and the Amazon River, and in February 1933 the disputants severed diplomatic relations. Attempts at settlement by the Inter-American System and by Brazil failed because of Peru's uncompromising position. Finally, after a change of government in Peru, the disputants allowed the League of Nations' Special Commission for Leticia to arrange a settlement. Colombia and Peru evacuated their troops from the area, and the commission took over its administration in June 1933, remaining for almost a year. Peru and Colombia continued their negotiations in Rio de Janeiro, with Brazilian mediation, from October 1933 until May 1934, when an agreement was reached. A protocol was signed in which Peru expressed regret for the incidents causing the dispute, reestablished diplomatic relations, and confirmed the Lima Treaty of 1922. Colombia then reoccupied Leticia.

POST–WORLD WAR II
PATTERNS AND CASES

U.S. Cold War Interventions

A new factor entered the Latin American subsystem after World War II with the creation of the U.S. Central Intelligence Agency (CIA). During the cold war period, CIA officials deliberately participated in the assassination of foreign leaders; trained private armies; bribed chiefs of state, labor union leaders, and other official and political figures; and engaged in other activities designed to discredit or remove what were considered to be leftist Latin American governments. Among the most serious revelations in the mid-1970s was that the U.S. government, through the CIA, was involved in several assassination attempts on the lives of Latin American chiefs of state, most notably Fidel Castro of Cuba.

The CIA's covert interventions in Latin American politics became the subject of considerable controversy as a general picture of CIA activities in Latin America emerged from a variety of sources. In the 1970s a great deal came to be known about them, especially through U.S. congressional committee hearings and books written by former CIA agents.

A book by former CIA operations officer Philip Agee (1975) requires special mention as an early account of clandestine activities in Latin America. Agee spent much of his twelve-year CIA career from 1957 to 1969 in Ecuador, Uruguay, and Mexico. He portrayed himself as a "true believer" in the cold war against communism who, having become disillusioned with the deceit, hypocrisy, incompetence, and corruption of The Company (the CIA), determined not only to expose the agency but to urge its dismantlement. Agee, bitterly referred to by CIA officials as "our first defector," does not explain his conversion from zealous cold war devotion to anticapitalist Marxism; but he offers a convincing account of covert CIA operations in Latin America. Those operations included the manipulation of foreign agents, news media, political parties, public officials, political leaders, and trade unions and the use of bribery, blackmail, propaganda, wire-tapping, and other means of espionage. Agee discussed CIA interventions in elections and its role in assassination attempts and coups d'état, all aimed at weakening leftist forces. The foreign CIA agents and collaborators he listed by name included prominent figures from all walks of Latin American life.

In 1974 and 1975 the U.S. intelligence community was investigated by a presidential commission and select committees in the House and Senate. Recent directors of the CIA testified before Congress and stated their opposition to further assassinations as an instrument of U.S. foreign policy, a position reiterated by President Ford. Since then, as John Prados observed, demands for intelligence reform have given way to equally strident ones for an "unleashed" CIA. The reform movement proved abortive. Congress made do with the half-measure of "oversight," while CIA agencies interpreted their reporting requirements as narrowly as possible. The Reagan administration gave free rein to the CIA. One result of that policy was the 1983–1984 mining of Nicaraguan harbors, which flouted the oversight prerogatives of the Senate Select Committee on Intelligence. As it turned out, questions about appropriate activities for an intelligence organization in a democratic nation and the legal basis for those activities still have not been resolved.

A new controversy in the 1980s, under the Reagan administration, involved the National Security Council's covert operations in Latin America in concert with private individuals and organizations. Congressional hearings in 1987 revealed that these operations were designed to circumvent congressional prohibitions on the covert use of the CIA as well as more direct U.S. armed force. Perhaps more startling were the circumvention of U.S. Defense Department and CIA supervision and the privatization of covert actions. While the effort had long-term and global ambitions, it focused on Central American conflict.

The first important case of cold war conflict and U.S. covert intervention in Latin America occurred in Guatemala in 1954. The situation had its roots in 1944, when Dictator-General Jorge Ubico was overthrown after thirteen years in power. The following year an elected civilian president, Juan Arévalo, was inaugurated, who subsequently promoted fundamental social reform. He was succeeded in 1951 by President Jacobo Arbenz Guzmán, who initiated a number of radical economic and social changes. His efforts eventually brought opposition from the United States, which accused him of bringing Communists into his government and allowing them too much influence in Guatemalan politics. Arbenz attempted to integrate the Indian majority into the mainstream of Guatemalan national life through labor organization and agrarian reform, bringing strenuous opposition from the powerful landowning class. He also alienated influential foreign business interests, especially the United Fruit Company. Arbenz expropriated their properties, further straining Guatemalan-U.S. relations. In addition, he employed Guatemalan and foreign leftists in his government (including the Argentine Ernesto "Che" Guevara) and broadened Guatemala's diplomatic contacts with Communist states.

By early 1953 Guatemalan exiles were being trained in the neighboring states of Honduras and Nicaragua with assistance and support from the CIA. U.S. Secretary of State John Foster Dulles pushed an anti-Communist resolution through the Tenth Inter-American Conference at Caracas in 1954 that aimed at weakening Guatemala's position in the Inter-American System. The U.S.-sponsored exile force, led by Colonel Carlos Castillo Armas, invaded Guatemala from Honduras on June 18, 1954. The Arbenz government appealed to the UN Security Council, which deferred the matter to the OAS over Soviet opposition. Before an OAS fact-finding team could arrive in Guatemala, Castillo had taken over the government and sent Arbenz into exile.

U.S. conflict with the Castro government in Cuba was the dominant focus of covert U.S. actions after 1959. Castro's 26th of July Movement, which seized power on January 1, 1959, originally seemed dedicated to liberal democracy, and the United States recognized the Castro government on January 7, 1959. By the end of 1961, however, it was clear that Castro was running a dictatorship. On May 1, 1961, Castro formally announced that Cuba was "a socialist state," and the following December he stated that he would be a "Marxist-Leninist until the last day of my life." These developments were accompanied by an increasing orientation toward the Soviet Union. Castro defied the United States early in his regime. He confiscated U.S. and

British oil refineries when they refused to process Soviet oil and confiscated other U.S. investments and property; he abrogated the Cuban mutual assistance pact with the United States and expelled U.S. military missions; and he mounted an intensely hostile propaganda campaign against the United States.

The Eisenhower administration canceled all imports of Cuban sugar on July 6, 1960. Three days later Soviet Premier Nikita Khrushchev proclaimed Cuba a protectorate and threatened to defend it with missiles against the United States. Cuban-U.S. diplomatic relations were ruptured on January 3, 1961. The United States attempted both to lead multilateral action and to take unilateral measures against Cuba (for OAS actions, see Chapter 9). The principal early unilateral effort by the United States consisted of its support of a Cuban exile invasion to overthrow Castro in April 1961. The 1,500-man force, which included a large number of disillusioned former Castro revolutionaries, landed at the Bay of Pigs on Cuba's southern coast in hopes of catalyzing a popular uprising. The United States organized and financed the operation; planned under President Eisenhower and carried out under President Kennedy, it was an utter failure. The Cuban armed forces easily subdued and imprisoned the invaders. Although the United States pledged to desist from any further invasions of Castro's realm as part of the settlement of the missile crisis with the Soviet Union in October 1962, it apparently continued attempts to assassinate the Cuban premier. In 1975, Senate hearings on CIA assassination attempts revealed that eight efforts were made on Castro's life through various intermediaries from 1960 to 1965.

The United States sent troops to the Dominican Republic in 1965 in the first overt military intervention in Latin America since 1933. It took place in the aftermath of the thirty-one–year Trujillo dictatorship, ending with his assassination on May 30, 1961, and in the context of U.S. experience with Castro's Cuba. Dominican individuals and groups with conflicting purposes had struggled with each other since Trujillo's death; none had been satisfied with the results, and an unstable political situation existed. On April 24, 1965, a rebel army faction known as the "Constitutionalists," led by Colonel Francisco Caamaño, attempted a coup in support of civilian reformist politician Juan Bosch (who had been elected president and inaugurated in February 1963 but overthrown by a coup seven months later). The opposing military "Loyalist" faction, led by General Antonio Imbert (who had participated in the assassination of Trujillo), was supported by most military units and the national police. The rebels were supported by a large number of civilians who had acquired arms by raiding a police arsenal. Military advantage fluctuated between the two sides during a civil war lasting more than four months and culminating with U.S. military intervention. The United States landed 405 Marines in the capital city on April 28; the complement was increased thereafter, reaching a high of 23,000 troops (mostly from the U.S. Army) in the restricted vicinity of Santo Domingo, with 10,000 more standing by offshore.

The United States justified the initial troop landing on April 28 as protection for its nationals residing in the Dominican Republic. In an address to the nation on May 2, however, President Johnson asserted that Communists had joined the rebels and threatened to take control. After saying that "what began as a popular democratic revolution" had been "seized and placed into the hands of a band of Communist conspirators," he said that the U.S. goal had changed "to help prevent another Communist state in this hemisphere." The United States then received OAS endorsement of its intervention; after an exceptionally bitter debate, the OAS multilateralized and thereby legitimized (in the U.S. view) the action. The U.S. command was transformed into an international peacekeeping force. In fact, except for the Brazilian contribution, the Latin American presence was a token one. The external military peacekeeping units supported the Loyalist military faction in the Dominican civil war. Finally, in late August, a settlement was signed by both sides at U.S. urging. A year later, in September 1966, the peace force, reduced to less than 5,000 troops, was withdrawn.

A broad set of clandestine operations was centered in Chile as the United States employed several tactics to disrupt the elected Marxist government of President Salvador Allende from 1970 to 1973. The Chilean election of 1970 was thrown into the congress when no candidate received a majority. ITT, the U.S. corporation, then offered a million dollars to the Nixon administration for a bribery scheme to seek Allende's defeat in the Chilean congressional runoff; the offer was made through John A. McCone, former director of the CIA and then an ITT board member. The U.S. government, which had financed Allende's opposition in the campaign, declined the offer on the grounds that it would be unworkable, but thereafter it made several efforts to "destabilize" the Allende government and discredit his experiment of "socialism in democracy."

U.S. officials (including military personnel) encouraged Chilean military dissidents to make a coup prior to Allende's inauguration. As a prelude, certain Chilean officers attempted to kidnap General René Schneider, the commander in chief of the armed forces, who had refused to cooperate in a coup; but Schneider was accidentally killed in the clumsy kidnapping event on October 22, 1970. After Allende's inauguration, the United States encouraged and financed a wide spectrum of opposition groups, including other parties, certain trade and labor organizations, middle-class housewives, and right-wing terrorist groups; strikes and demonstrations were funded and coordinated through the CIA station in Santiago. In addition, the United States used its influence and voting power in the international lending agencies to put a "credit squeeze" on Chile; it did not stop grants and loans that had already been approved, but it blocked the approval of new ones. Finally, by mid-1973, Chile was in a desperate economic and social situation. The Chilean military overthrew Allende on September 11, 1973, in a brief but bloody coup in which Allende died.

The later disclosure that the CIA had financed the strikes that preceded the Chilean coup was confirmed by President Ford in a news conference in September 1974. Ford said that U.S. actions had been carried out in an attempt to help preserve opposition newspapers and parties in Chile; in fact, the opposition press continued to print during the Allende years, and opposition parties, including the most hostile, continued to function; only after the coup was the press suppressed and political parties banned. Ford justified U.S. subversion in Chile as being "in the best interests of the Chilean people."

Guerrilla Warfare

Contemporary guerrilla warfare was introduced with Fidel Castro's successful exile invasion of Cuba and subsequent defeat of dictator Fulgencio Batista. Similar conflicts emanated from the Caribbean but extended into South America and, to an extent, Mexico. After about a year of consolidating his power after January 1, 1959, Castro openly encouraged violent revolution in the rest of the hemisphere through active assistance to guerrilla movements, especially in Venezuela, Peru, and Guatemala. Guerrilla activities in Latin America intensified in 1963 and 1964, and Cuban support continued until about 1968. During that time, Cuba added Colombia to its list of targets and initiated the insurgency in Bolivia led by Che Guevara.

While Cuba urged and actively supported violent revolution in the rest of the region, the Soviet Union favored peaceful relations through traditional diplomatic and economic channels. Soviet policy had continued to be generally unprovocative during World War II and through the 1950s. The Soviet Union's approach was ambiguous; it vacillated in its covert activities and support for revolutionary groups in Latin America after the war. The Soviet Union urged caution in the early 1960s following Castro's success in Cuba and throughout the extended period of guerrilla warfare. Most orthodox (Moscow-oriented) Communist parties followed the Soviet lead and rejected armed insurgency in favor of more cautious tactics. China supported the militant Cuban posture emphasizing the need for violent overthrow of existing regimes through armed struggle, although it simultaneously attempted to increase its own diplomatic and trade contacts with Latin American states.

By late 1968 growing evidence indicated that Castro had come to terms with the Soviet Union and had tacitly accepted the Soviet doctrines of peaceful coexistence and evolutionary transition to socialism. Major guerrilla efforts had been liquidated in Peru and Bolivia and effectively controlled in Colombia, Venezuela, and Guatemala. Furthermore, economic problems forced Cuba to rely more on the Soviet Union; as the Cuban economy faltered, Soviet influence increased, and Cuban ideological conformity may have been the price for continued Soviet assistance. Castro largely withdrew his support of insurgency movements; he seemed to resign himself (at least temporarily) to the futility of exporting his revolution. By 1970, after a year and a half of Cuban silence toward Latin American revolution, insurgent leaders began to criticize Castro sharply for his withdrawal of support. The Soviet Union generally preferred cooperative state-to-state interaction after the mid-1960s, but it occasionally supported simultaneous subversive activities. Such activities led to conflict with several Latin American states (in

Colombia in 1967, Uruguay in 1968, Mexico and Ecuador in 1971, Bolivia in 1972, and Chile in 1973).

Soviet-Cuban support of guerrilla warfare revived with the successful Sandinista-led Nicaraguan Revolution of 1979 and increased insurgent activities in other Central American countries. In the new insurgent era, as before, the Soviet Union and Cuba disagreed about the appropriate approach; their positions had reversed, however, with Cuba urging caution and the Soviets seemingly accepting higher risks. Their actions are discussed further below in the context of current Central American conflict.

Continuing British Boundary and Territorial Disputes

Great Britain and Venezuela had disputed a large portion of British Guiana from the beginnings of Venezuelan independence. The problem continued after the British territory was granted independence in 1966 as Guyana. The dispute, dating from the early nineteenth century, seemed settled in 1899 when the decision of an international court of arbitration was accepted by both parties. However, in 1962 Venezuela reasserted its claims, declaring the 1899 agreement void because of illegal proceedings. Venezuela had hired U.S. attorneys to represent its case in 1899; in 1962 it used the will of one of those attorneys as new evidence. The will stated that a "deal" had been made between the British representatives and a Russian arbiter.

Venezuela wanted the boundary to be moved some 150 miles to the east to the Essequibo River; this change would give Venezuela about 53,000 square miles of territory constituting approximately three-fifths of Guyana. Venezuela protested Guyanese independence, asserting that the boundary question should have been settled prior to its grant. In 1966, Great Britain, Guyana, and Venezuela signed an agreement establishing a mixed border commission and providing that, if the commission failed to solve the problem by May 1970, the dispute was to be referred to the World Court or the UN secretary general. The mixed commission failed in its mission, and after direct negotiations the three states signed another agreement on June 18, 1970. The new agreement suspended the 1966 protocol and provided for a twelve-year "cooling-off" period, to be extended automatically unless either Venezuela or Guyana decided against the extension. The agreement was so extended in 1982. In the meantime, Guyana was free to develop the disputed area and Venezuela was to press no further claims.

There has been a history of conflict over the ownership of Belize, formerly the colony of British Honduras. That conflict for many years complicated the process of its becoming an independent state. Spain claimed the area in the sixteenth century but did not occupy it. A small number of English settlers arrived by way of a shipwreck in 1683, but Britain did not refer to British Honduras as a colony until about 1840. Guatemala and Great Britain signed a treaty in 1850 in which Guatemala recognized British sovereignty over Belize in return for certain concessions, one of which was the construction of a road connecting Guatemala City with the Atlantic coast. Since Britain never built the road, Guatemala declared the treaty void in 1939 and reasserted its claims to Belize on the grounds of inherited territory from Spain. Britain replied that Spain never effectively controlled the area, that it was not a part of the colonial Guatemalan jurisdiction, and that, anyway, Spain had ceded the area to Britain in 1670. Britain maintained control.

Guatemala reasserted its claims in the 1950s, when Britain was beginning to consider granting independence to Belize. Belize did not join the short-lived West Indies Federation formed in 1958 and refused a Guatemalan proposal in 1960 that it become an internally self-governing "free associated state" under Guatemalan sovereignty. Guatemala broke diplomatic relations with Britain in 1963 when the latter allowed Belize internal self-government. Guatemala and Belize both rejected a proposal set forth in 1971 by the United States, acting as mediator, that British Honduras be granted immediate independence after which it would "consult" with Guatemala on foreign and defense affairs. Britain and Guatemala continued their talks sporadically. Belize desired independence but feared a Guatemalan military invasion once British protection was gone; Britain was willing to grant independence but not to provide a defense guarantee to the new state. Discussions between the United Kingdom and Guatemala broke down in the summer of 1981; Belize received its independence on September 1 of that year. Guatemala has not recognized the new Belize state. Britain reluctantly relented on the security issues, and a British force remained in Belize to guarantee its territorial integrity.

Mexico also had claims to part of Belize based on succession rights to Spanish sovereignty, but it did not press them as vigorously as Guatemala. Mexico asserted a right to participate in any discussions on the status of the area, but it stated that it would not reactivate its dormant claims if a solution was based on the wishes of the Belizen people.

The Falklands/Malvinas Dispute

In 1965 the United Nations General Assembly, at Argentina's behest, approved a resolution urging Britain and Argentina to negotiate a peaceful resolution of the sovereignty question concerning the Falklands/Malvinas islands. The United Kingdom acquiesced, and in 1971 agreements were reached on matters of commerce, communications (including air service), educational and medical facilities, and cultural exchanges. The dispute was quiescent until 1975, when a British government study reported the possibility of oil in the surrounding continental shelf. This possibility reawakened interest in the islands on both sides. (This section is taken from Atkins, 1984:22–33.)

The United Kingdom subsequently proposed a "lease-back" scheme whereby Argentina would be granted formal sovereignty but Britain would continue administrative control in order to allow the Falklands inhabitants sufficient time to adjust to eventual Argentine governance. Settlers had eventually migrated to the Falklands after the assertion of British control in 1833;

they numbered about 1,800 in 1980 and were engaged primarily in sheep-raising. Most of the Falklanders were of British stock and strongly desired the status quo, wanting neither annexation to Argentina nor independence. The lease-back formula was defeated in the British Parliament in the face of vigorous opposition by the Falkland lobby in London.

On March 2, 1982, the Argentine government warned that if a solution was not soon forthcoming, it would pursue "a procedure that better suits its interests." A month later, Argentina sought to recover the Malvinas by force. On April 2, 1982, Argentina invaded and took military control of the inhabited portions of the United Kingdom's Falkland Islands colony, asserting that it was enforcing its rightful sovereignty over the Islas Malvinas. Costly naval, air, and land warfare ensued. The war effectively ended on June 14 with Argentina's defeat at the hands of British armed forces. The conflict seemed to begin as a series of events in a remote corner of the globe, but it ended with important consequences for international politics on several levels.

A number of factors may explain why Argentina resorted to military force. Argentine President General Leopoldo Galtieri said that Argentina had "recovered" the Malvinas, "which by legitimate right are part of the national patrimony." He justified the use of force by accusing the United Kingdom of perpetuating colonial rule "through interminable successions of delays and evasions" during diplomatic negotiations. The Argentine government also adhered to a South Atlantic geopolitical strategic view that placed considerable significance on the Malvinas. Argentine geopoliticians in 1982 and 1983 advocated military action to recover the Malvinas in order to protect and expand these long-standing interests. The invasion came at a time of increasing domestic political opposition and violence; it was, until the defeat, an immensely popular undertaking. Finally, the timing seems to have been based on a set of miscalculations about external responses. Argentine leaders apparently decided that the United Kingdom would not respond militarily to problems in a hostile and remote region. Perhaps they counted on their new friendship with the Reagan administration in the hope that the United States would restrain the British from pursuing a military response. They probably expected that support would be forthcoming from the Inter-American System, the Third World, and the Soviet Union. Argentina badly failed to anticipate British resolve, primary U.S. North Atlantic interests, and the reluctance of other actors (including most Latin American states) to validate its use of force.

The British government, led by conservative Prime Minister Margaret Thatcher, dispatched a naval force to the South Atlantic, 7,000 miles from southern English ports, and appealed for support from the United Nations and the European Community. The UN Security Council responded with Resolution 502, which condemned the Argentine action, demanded an immediate withdrawal of Argentine forces, and called on both governments to seek a diplomatic solution to their differences. The Soviet Union did not veto the resolution, apparently satisfied with the dilemma facing the United

States. The European Community (EC) also responded favorably to the British appeal, agreeing to condemn Argentina for the invasion and impose sanctions. In a resolution adopted on April 16, the Commission of the EC condemned the illegal Argentine aggression against a territory linked to the Community and urgently appealed to Argentina to implement UN Security Council Resolution 502. The EC banned arms sales to and embargoed imports from Argentina.

Soon after the Security Council action, the United States engaged in an intense mediation effort as a neutral third party. Hoping to commence negotiations and avoid open warfare, U.S. Secretary of State Alexander Haig pursued a mission of "shuttle diplomacy" from April 7–19 with visits to London and Buenos Aires and interim returns to Washington. The Thatcher government argued that democracies should not appease dictators and must resist aggression, and she insisted that Britain would not consider negotiations until Argentina unconditionally withdrew its troops in accordance with the Security Council resolution. A "paramount consideration" for the British was that the resident Falklanders (who adamantly opposed Argentine control) be consulted and their wishes and rights respected in any future negotiations. The Argentine government, in turn, said it would not remove its troops nor begin negotiations until the United Kingdom recognized Argentine sovereignty over the islands and recalled its naval task force. The U.S. effort effectively ended in impasse on April 19.

Argentina turned to the Inter-American System for support as a counter to UN Resolution 502 and EC sanctions. The initial response from other Latin American states was restrained, however; a meeting of the OAS Permanent Council from April 5–13 resulted in a "resolution of concern" that offered its "friendly cooperation in the search for a peaceful settlement." Argentina invoked the Rio Treaty just as the U.S. mediation effort ended; the Twentieth Meeting of Consultation of Ministers of Foreign Affairs was convened April 26–28. By this time British forces had penetrated the hemispheric security zone as defined in the Rio Treaty. Argentina asked for collective sanctions against "the British threat to hemispheric peace." The foreign ministers adopted a resolution supporting Argentine claims to sovereignty but refused to invoke any sanctions against the United Kingdom.

The United States ended its neutrality on April 30, in favor of the United Kingdom and in strong opposition to Argentina. In announcing the change in policy, Secretary Haig said that "in light of Argentina's failure to accept a compromise, we must take concrete steps to underscore that the United States cannot and will not condone the use of unlawful force to resolve disputes." Consequently, among other measures, the United States suspended all military exports and Export-Import Bank credits to Argentina. It promised to respond positively to requests for material support for British forces short of direct U.S. military involvement. The United States then supported a short-lived Peruvian peace plan, presented on May 2, that strongly resembled earlier U.S. proposals; Argentina immediately rejected it.

The EC, UN, and Inter-American System continued their efforts as military action escalated. EC support for the British position had faltered, especially with the sinking of an Argentine cruiser on May 2 with heavy loss of life; it was widely perceived that the British had violated their own rules of engagement and that its moral advantage as the victim of aggression had eroded. Following relentless British bargaining, however, the majority overcame their objections and decided to extend the sanctions against Argentina indefinitely. In the UN Security Council, Secretary General Javier Pérez de Cuellar reported that his efforts had brought no agreement. He was instructed to try again, and he again reported failure on June 2. The third inter-American meeting was held May 27–29 with the reconvening of the foreign ministers meeting. The final resolution—adopted after a particularly acrimonious debate expressing widespread hostility toward both Britain and the United States—condemned British counterforce but again refused to undertake sanctions.

The military campaign came to an end on June 14, seventy-four days after the invasion, when Argentine units on the Falklands surrendered. The European Community lifted its sanctions against Argentina on June 20, warning that they would be reimposed if Argentina resumed warfare. On July 12 President Reagan announced that U.S. economic sanctions against Argentina were no longer necessary (the ban on military transfers, predating the conflict and requiring a human-rights certification to Congress, was not lifted until December 1983 when a new civilian government was inaugurated in Buenos Aires). The United Kingdom kept in place its unilateral sanctions against Argentina as well as the 200–nautical mile exclusion zone around the islands.

The United Kingdom remained in full control of the Falklands. It reintroduced British military power to the area ("Fortress Falklands") for an indefinite time, despite the expense to the British treasury and the depletion of its NATO forces. The disputants remained without diplomatic relations and technically were still at war, as Argentina had not formally declared an end to hostilities. Some communication did occur, with Argentina and the United Kingdom speaking through their intermediaries—Brazil and Switzerland, respectively. Secret talks were held for some weeks beginning in December 1983, but each side blamed the other for their failure and the talks broke down. Prime Minister Thatcher firmly reiterated that under no circumstances would Britain negotiate the question of sovereignty. President Alfonsín made the matter of sovereignty Argentina's highest priority.

The conflict seems impervious to resolution by international organizations. The Inter-American System faces an obvious problem of jurisdiction, since the United Kingdom is not a party to the controlling treaties or subject to its procedures. The United Nations is the more appropriate international forum, but it cannot play a decisive role without the voluntary consensus of both parties to negotiate. Without such consensus, it is unlikely to overcome such obstacles as the Security Council veto and the nonbinding nature of General Assembly resolutions. Argentina has, nevertheless, continued to press its case in the UN General Assembly, where it has gained overwhelming support. It introduced a resolution there in November 1982, less than five months after the end of the war, and followed with further ones. The issue has remained alive but unresolved through the late 1980s as Argentina has continued to press its case in the United Nations.

Inter–Latin American Disputes

The Beagle Channel. The dispute between Argentina and Chile over ownership of three islands in the Beagle Channel involved competing geo-political and strategic calculations, access to possible petroleum and other resources, and the status of conflicting claims in the Antarctic. In 1971, Argentina and Chile agreed to submit their century-old dispute to binding arbitration as prescribed in existing bilateral treaties. Accordingly, the British Crown appointed a five-judge international court of arbitration (all of the judges were members of the International Court of Justice). After six years of hearings and studies, the court rendered a decision in 1977 finding that the three islands (Picton, Lennox, and Nueva) were "unquestionably Chilean," thus giving Chile control of the resource-rich sea area. From Argentina's point of view, Chilean possession of the islands negated the virtually absolute Argentine bioceanic principle that Chile was by nature a Pacific coast power and that Argentina must have hegemony in the Atlantic zone. Argentina also feared that Chilean rights in the Atlantic Ocean would threaten its Antarctic claims. The geopolitically minded Argentine military government rejected the ruling in January 1978.

The disputants were on the verge of war in late 1978 when the Holy See's observer to the OAS urgently proposed papal mediation. Both governments readily accepted this offer. The entire southern boundary zone, including the Beagle Channel and the contiguous oceanic triangle, was submitted for papal consideration. Two years later, on December 12, 1980, the pope presented his peace proposal. Chile was given sovereignty over the three islands plus a narrow fringe of territorial waters. Contiguous Atlantic waters were designated a condominium "sea of peace" reserved for common or concerted activities. Chile seemed ready to accept the papal decision, although it had resisted the sea-of-peace idea because the ocean resources were more important than the islands as such. Argentina again displayed intransigence; it did not reject the proposal outright, but it stalled on responding, reluctant to accept a Chilean presence in the Atlantic.

The process was interrupted by the Anglo-Argentine war of 1982. In the aftermath of that conflict, the negotiating climate for Argentina and Chile seemed unpropitious. Chile was convinced that Argentina had not negotiated in good faith since 1971 and had been too willing to consider the use of military force. Argentina strongly resented Chile's neutrality in the 1982 Anglo-Argentine war, which it saw as actually aiding the United Kingdom. The British Crown had been removed from its traditional role as intermediary between Argentina and Chile, and the United States was in no position to take initiatives. The United Nations lacked precedents in regional American disputes, and the disputants were not inclined to submit to the Inter-American System. Vatican mediation remained open, but Argentina's stalling tactics seemed to devalue that option. Yet the new civilian government in Argentina was determined to do something about the dispute and overcame the difficulties.

The papal role as third-party mediator was successfully revived. On January 23, 1984, the foreign ministers of Argentina and Chile signed a declaration in the Vatican pledging to solve the "southern question" in the framework of papal mediation. On October 10, they returned to the Vatican to sign a protocol confirming their intent to accept the treaty; they signed the treaty itself on November 29, 1984. It was ratified by both governments and went into effect in 1985.

In the treaty, Chilean possession of the three islands was recognized, with sovereignty extending south to Cape Horn. Chile also gained maritime jurisdiction over a surrounding twelve-mile–wide zone, in which Argentina would be able to exercise free navigation. However, specific limitations on Chilean rights removed the possibility of maritime projection or claims of sovereignty that would normally accompany territorial possession. That is, Chile had physical access to the Atlantic Ocean but did not hold rights to juridical claims. Argentina was given maritime jurisdiction over the area outside the twelve-mile zone. The sea-of-peace idea from the 1980 proposal had been eliminated. The treaty specified that Argentine jurisdiction was not limited by requirements related either to sovereignty or joint economic exploitation. The bioceanic principle was recognized, and Cape Horn was established as the base for maritime boundaries. Argentina and Chile agreed to create a binational commission to facilitate the economic integration of the region and agreed to abstain from warfare in the area. Finally, the treaty provided for a five-year suspension of all disputes that might arise along the entire length of the common national boundary.

The agreement was a clear compromise aimed at satisfying the fundamental concerns of each side. Chile received the islands and access to surrounding resources. Argentina retained control of the Atlantic area near the islands, as well as jurisdiction over the eastern mouth of the Strait of Magellan to the north.

Caribbean Turmoil. After World War II a number of ideological, boundary, and territorial clashes occurred in the Caribbean states. External actors joined in urging, opposing, or resolving the conflicts in various patterns. The conflicts initially entailed disaffected exiles invading their own national homelands, and then extended to guerrilla warfare both in the Caribbean area and throughout much of the rest of Latin America.

Shortly after World War II, exiles from a number of Caribbean states gathered in other nearby states to plan revolutionary attempts. Charges and countercharges of intervention among several nations ensued, along with a great deal of Caribbean conflict. An organization known as the Caribbean Legion, sponsored by "reform" governments in the Caribbean area (in Cuba, Guatemala, and Costa Rica), was composed of political exiles and adventurers representing a broad spectrum of political and other motivations. It was dedicated to the overthrow of dictatorships in the Caribbean. Charles Ameringer (1974: Chap. 2) concludes that the Caribbean Legion in fact never existed as a military organization with a permanent central command; rather, he says, "the term was applied indiscriminately to a series of exile military operations and plots" with different leadership, sponsors, and objectives. The dictators (especially Rafael Trujillo of the Dominican Republic and Anastazio Somoza of Nicaragua) in turn encouraged activities against their at least nominally democratic neighbors. The government of Haiti, which was not so easily classifiable, was also involved in the dispute. To identify the Caribbean conflict solely in terms of a confrontation between "democracies" and "dictatorships" would distort reality; personal grudges and adventurism also motivated certain participants.

In 1950 an OAS investigating committee reported that exiles fighting against the government of their homelands tended to join with other nationalities who had similar purposes. The report said that many of those exiles were idealistic individuals who had been deprived of democratic guarantees in their own states and were seeking a return to political life; but others were "adventurers, professional revolutionaries, and mercenaries whose primary objective was the promotion of illegal traffic in arms and expeditions against countries with which they have no ties whatsoever." A U.S. Department of State official wrote in 1950 that the dissident Caribbean Legion groups sought to bring about political changes by intimidation or armed invasion; he noted that revolutionary groups had been inspired by political exiles who aimed to return to active political life in their homelands, by force if necessary. Whatever their motives, their activities involved the use of territory by states in violation of international obligations.

The most recent "conventional war" in Latin America involving state forces occurred in 1967 between El Salvador and Honduras over boundary and migration issues. For most of the twentieth century, Salvadorans had left their densely populated homeland and migrated, legally and illegally, to lightly populated Honduras across an ill-defined border. Their search for work and land provoked Honduran resentment, and skirmishes frequently occurred between troops of the two states. The worst fighting in sixty years occurred in a week-long undeclared war in July 1969. Honduras instituted a land-reform program affecting the Salvadoran land squatters just as an emotionally charged soccer championship series was being played by the two national teams. Following the rioting at the *futbol* match, Honduran mobs attacked Salvadoran aliens. Diplomatic relations were suspended and troops were placed on alert. The conflict was dubbed the "soccer war" or "football war." Finally, the armed forces launched full-scale attacks. The OAS arranged a truce, which went into effect on July 18, and maintained a peacekeeping team on the frontier. An estimated 3,000 persons were killed during the conflict and 7,000 injured; extensive property damage also accompanied the conflict. The dispute was set aside with the onset of the Central American international crisis after 1979.

CENTRAL AMERICAN CRISIS

Complexities of the Crisis

The Nicaraguan Revolution of 1979 triggered an exceptionally complex and long-lasting crisis in Central America. The conflict exacerbated old problems in the subregion's international relations and created new ones and tapped into deep mutual suspicions among Central American neighbors. Regional developments, however, were overshadowed by the involvement of external actors. For the United States, Central America became a primary area of foreign policy concern and a significant source of domestic and international debate. The United States continued to play the leading role in the area, but other nations and groups were also prominent. Far from being an exclusive U.S. preserve, Central America became an internationalized arena. One of the most striking new conditions of Circum-Caribbean international politics was the concerted rise of assertiveness by local Latin American states in opposition to U.S. policy actions. The principal initiatives for conflict resolution, greeted with a distinct lack of enthusiasm by the United States, were undertaken by local states in concert. IGOs, both the OAS and the UN, played minor roles.

The topical context of Central American conflict has been discussed in prior chapters. The following narrative outlines the major events and then concentrates on proposals for conflict resolution.

After coming to office in 1977, President Carter imposed sanctions related to human rights abuses against the Somoza regime in Nicaragua, the military junta in El Salvador, and the Lucas García dictatorship in Guatemala. After the Sandinista-led revolution overthrew Somoza in 1979, President Carter accused the Soviet Union and Cuba of increased subversive activities in Central America. He was antagonistic toward the new Nicaraguan regime on the grounds that it was shipping Soviet-provided arms to leftist guerrillas in the emerging civil war in El Salvador. U.S. military transfers were resumed to the Salvadoran government despite the lack of substantive reforms, and the distribution of aid to Nicaragua was suspended.

The Reagan administration, inaugurated in 1981, was determined to recapture U.S. control of Central American events. President Reagan stated that the United States had to act decisively to deter the Soviet-Cuban threat on the U.S. "southern flank." The administration charged Nicaragua with transshipping Soviet-bloc arms to Salvadoran insurgents and accused Cuba of providing arms and advisers to Central American guerrilla groups. The United States pursued a number of coercive and interventionist measures; it also broadened its policies to include persuasive and developmental strategies in response to domestic and international criticism and the growing recognition, on the part of at least some members of the administration, of the complexities involved. Nevertheless, the thrust of policy and rhetoric remained the same: The United States was unwilling to accept a Marxist government in Nicaragua and sought a military victory over leftist forces in El Salvador.

In July 1983 President Reagan appointed the National Bipartisan Commission on Central America, headed by former Secretary of State Henry Kissinger, to recommend policies. The report, issued in January 1984, made a strategic case for the importance of Central America and the rest of the Caribbean Basin to U.S. interests, called for substantial economic aid and some more military assistance, and paid attention to issues of democracy and human rights with special reference to Nicaragua and El Salvador. Overall, the preferred approach favored, in the short term, a military victory over the insurgents and, in the long term, a rectification of the sources of instability that were taken advantage of by hostile ambitious outsiders. Any form of U.S. withdrawal was rejected; strong U.S. commitments to negotiated regional settlements or internal power-sharing arrangements with leftist governments or movements were not encouraged. The report, in substance, reinforced and justified as well as influenced government policy.

From 1981 to 1988, key U.S. policies included putting coercive pressures on Nicaragua and combining aid with various overtures to other Central American states, with El Salvador being the central concern. The United States armed, financed, and advised anti-Sandinista guerrillas (the contras), conducted military maneuvers in and with Honduras and naval exercises near Nicaragua, applied an economic boycott against Nicaragua, and even mined its harbors. In the meantime, the U.S. invasion of Grenada in October 1983 led to speculation that it would be followed by military intervention in Nicaragua (in retrospect probably not a likely event after the end of 1981, although U.S. officials never ruled it out). In sum, the Reagan administration's actions toward Nicaragua were unprecedented: It justified its largely unilateral coercive measures (including support of insurgent forces, the mining of harbors, and economic boycott) in terms of collective defense and, in effect, carried out an undeclared war while continuing formal diplomatic relations.

Military arms and advisers and economic aid to El Salvador increased dramatically. Honduras received increasing emphasis for similar assistance; a significant portion of the contra force operated out of Honduras, and at U.S. behest, Honduras allowed training of Salvadoran forces on its territory. Guatemala, ruled by a corrupt and repressive regime, received only marginal U.S. aid. The United States also prevailed upon the military government in Argentina, a country with no traditional interests in Central America, to give direct assistance. Argentine military advisers were sent to Guatemala and El Salvador and, more controversially, advised Honduras on intelligence matters and trained the contra anti-Sandinista guerrillas along the Nicaraguan border. Argentina's South Atlantic war with the United Kingdom in 1982, and the accompanying hostility toward the United States, brought the withdrawal of the Argentine military presence in Central America.

The United States also bargained with friendly governments. The Caribbean Basin Initiative (CBI), proposed in 1981 and implemented in 1984, provided for trade preferences and economic aid to friendly governments. It was framed in terms of the Soviet-Cuban threat, but it also recognized poverty as a source of instability. Increasingly strong pressure was asserted on the

Salvadoran government to follow a centrist course, institute an effective agrarian reform program, curtail right-wing death squads, and hold free and fair elections. The United States also sought to legitimize governments in Honduras and Guatemala with elections and to improve their human rights records. U.S. policy enjoyed a certain success in these regards, as elections were conducted in all three countries and human rights behavior improved (although serious violations continued to occur).

Cuba made no secret of its strong support for the Nicaraguan government. Large numbers of Cuban teachers, medical and technical personnel, and military advisers were sent to Nicaragua, and Nicaraguans were trained in Cuba. There seemed little doubt that guerrilla forces in El Salvador received training and equipment from Cuba. On the whole, the Soviets limited their direct involvement in the region, leaving much of the socialist bloc's activities in Nicaragua to East Germans, Czechs, and Bulgarians. Soviet military equipment was supplied, most notably tanks and helicopters, but sophisticated aircraft were denied.

Nicaragua's reputation abroad was damaged by its substantially increased military power, by its domination by Marxist Sandinista leaders, by the departure of disillusioned members of the government (both Sandinistas and non-Sandinistas), and by its silencing of the opposition and forced resettlement of the Miskito Indian population. Nevertheless, U.S. policy was never fully supported at home and was sharply criticized in Europe.

Europeans exercised little influence on Central American events or on restraining U.S. actions. They drew back from supporting Nicaragua as it increasingly mistreated the opposition and moved away from pluralism and nonalignment. Most of all, the Grenada invasion signaled that the Central American crisis had entered a new and more serious phase; European governments wanted to avoid another alliance problem with the United States. Nevertheless, they made it clear that they opposed U.S. military solutions in Central America and supported Latin American peace initiatives.

Latin American states proposed important measures for conflict resolution, directly challenging the United States with formulas for negotiated settlements of Central American conflict.

Conflict Resolution

The Central American conflict differed from previous situations mainly by virtue of the resistance of Central American states to simple U.S. great-power settlement. Despite the strong and sustained assertion of U.S. power, it did not prevail. The United States appointed a special representative early in the conflict, and later appointed another, to explore the possibilities of negotiated settlements in the region. Mexico offered to mediate in February 1982; the Reagan administration acknowledged the proposals and suggested direct talks with the Nicaraguans. The Mexican effort came to nothing, but high U.S. officials from time to time negotiated directly with Nicaraguans. Central American issues were placed on the agenda of U.S.-Soviet negotiations. The several parties charged their opponents with intransigence and insincerity;

little was accomplished toward ending the conflict. The Inter-American System was involved in various aspects of the Central American conflict, but its effectiveness had declined by then and mutual security provisions were not invoked. Indeed, the irrelevance of the Inter-American System to the Central American crisis largely explains why certain Latin American states rallied around the Contadora Group as a substitute multilateral forum.

Latin American states comprising the Contadora Group (Colombia, Mexico, Panama, and Venezuela) organized themselves at a summit meeting held on the Panamanian island of Contadora in January 1983. The group proposed to serve as a mediator in seeking peaceful negotiated outcomes in Central America. It drew up a set of twenty-one principles designed to facilitate discussions between the United States and Nicaragua and, in El Salvador, between the government and insurgents. The principles included, among other things, limiting arms flows, prohibiting all foreign bases, withdrawing external advisers (including Cuban, East European, and U.S.), and ending support for insurgents (both Salvadoran guerrillas and Nicaraguan contras).

Members of the Contadora Group had special interests in the Central American conflict and were anxious for a peaceful settlement for both external and internal reasons. They felt threatened by nearby isthmian conflict, although they did not consider themselves the ultimate "dominos" and saw the situation and solution differently than did the United States. They considered insurgency to be rooted in the internal conditions of Central American societies, not Soviet-Cuban inspired, and saw Cuba as being flexible enough to deal with through peaceful means. Furthermore, Contadora members also had their own domestic political concerns. Venezuela and Colombia were democratic polities, and Mexico was subject to intense internal demands to broaden political participation; they all feared that a clear victory in Central America for either the extreme left or the repressive right would adversely polarize their own delicate internal consensuses.

In time all five Central American states agreed to the list of Contadora principles. Four South American states joined in a Contadora Support Group. In addition, European governments and political groups generally applauded the Contadora initiative, and their own policy preferences tended to follow the Contadora line. Europeans, despite their second thoughts and increasing ambivalence, remained concerned with Central America. An extraordinary meeting, held in September 1984 in Costa Rica, was attended by all European Community foreign ministers, representatives of the four Contadora countries and five other Central American countries, and observers from Spain and Portugal. Europeans did not commit large sums of money, but the conference issued a formal endorsement of the Contadora proposals.

The United States indicated verbal support but in fact gave no substantive encouragement to the Contadora Group. The Kissinger report proposed a "comprehensive regional settlement" but refused to accept any regime (i.e., Nicaragua) that might serve as a "crucial stepping stone for Cuban and Soviet efforts to promote armed insurgency in Latin America." With direct reference to the Latin American initiative, the report said: "The United

States cannot use the Contadora process as a substitute for its own policy." The Contadora initiative declined with time and events—and, its supporters argued, with U.S. intransigence.

In the wake of the impasse in the Contadora process, President Oscar Arias of Costa Rica proposed a peace plan (for which he won the Nobel Peace Prize) that became the basis for an important conflict resolution effort. On August 17, 1987, the five Central American presidents of Costa Rica, Guatemala, El Salvador, Honduras, and Nicaragua met in Guatemala City to consider the Arias proposal. They signed a document entitled "Procedure for the Establishment of a Firm and Lasting Peace in Central America." It was known informally as the "Esquipulus II Accords," named after the town of Esquipulus in Guatemala where an earlier meeting (in June 1986) of the five presidents had taken place to discuss regional problems.

The plan had three interrelated purposes. It sought political reconciliation within each of the Central American nations, the democratization of their domestic political processes, and the cessation of civil and international hostilities. It mandated a number of measures. In order to achieve national reconciliation, it called for the combination of a cease-fire in those countries where irregular or insurgent groups were active, amnesty policies to facilitate the cease-fire, and the beginning of dialogue between governments and all unarmed opposition groups as well as those who had accepted amnesty. In addition, governments committed themselves to promoting pluralist and participatory democracy, including restoration of individual freedoms and free and honest elections at an early date. Each state would create a broadly representative National Commission of Reconciliation to verify compliance and to monitor the democratization process. Urgent measures would be taken to attend to the problems of refugees and displaced persons.

The cessation of hostilities further and critically depended on certain international processes. Governments in and outside of the region were asked to cease aid of any kind, open or covert, to any irregular forces or insurgent movements and to prevent the use of their territory and the extension of logistical aid in support of aggression against other nations. To ensure compliance, the plan provided for the creation of an International Commission for Verification and International Follow-up (*seguimiento*), to be composed of the secretaries general of the OAS and UN or their representatives and the foreign ministers of Central America, the Contadora Group, and the Support Group. This commission would undertake to verify and confirm compliance with the various commitments.

A timetable was established with a series of preferred deadlines. The cease-fire was to be accomplished within ninety days from the signing of the accord (that is, by November 7, 1987), and all assistance to insurgents halted within 120 days. Elections would take place simultaneously in all Central American countries during the first six months of 1988 on a date to be agreed upon by the presidents. Within ninety days, the presidents would sign the commitments relating to amnesty, cease-fire, democratization, cessation of aid to irregular forces or insurgent movements, and nonuse of territory to attack other nations. Within 120 days the international commission would analyze the progress of these actions. Within 150 days the five presidents would meet and receive a report from the international commission and make pertinent decisions.

Luís G. Solís-Rivera, chief of staff of the Costa Rican Ministry of Foreign Affairs and a principal adviser to President Arias, articulated Costa Rican thinking and explained the assessments behind the Arias plan. Solís (1987) said that Central American agreement to the plan represented the region's determination to forge its own destiny. Until then all peace initiatives had come from outsiders. Even the Contadora process, led by Latin American countries, was an external effort from the point of view of Central Americans. The Esquipulus document acknowledged the Contadora efforts and the encouragement of the Support Group, the European Community, and Pope John Paul II with appreciation. It also noted, however, that Central Americans must take the lead in solving their problems and that these external groups must work with Central Americans as partners rather than as tutors. It emphasized the equally important idea that Central American peace would not be lasting unless founded on effective democracy. Furthermore, it said that democracy could not be achieved with the prevailing social injustice and impoverishment of the masses. Peace could not be seen as a return to the pre-1979 status quo, which had caused many reformers to adopt radical attitudes.

Solís went on to say that the Arias proposal was meant to overcome the impasse in the Contadora process. One of the weaknesses of the Contadora plan was that negotiations were left open with no timetable for the enactment of specific measures, allowing the initiative to linger in diplomatic limbo. The Esquipulus procedure attempted to resolve this deficiency but to mandate only the most crucial dates so as not to overburden the agreement. Symmetry was also an important principle. That is, the prior Costa Rican view of Nicaragua as the central problem in Central America was an impediment to a realistic regional arrangement; all Central American governments had to be measured by the same standards if the agreement was to be credible. Finally, simultaneity of measures was crucial to success. A vicious circle had plagued discussions about the conflict, with those arguing that democracy had to come before suspension of armed force on one side and those persuaded that no political concessions could be made until military actions had ceased on the other. The plan sought to break this circle by calling for the simultaneous application of security and political measures, thus giving guarantees to all. Simultaneity, Solis said, had allowed the signing of the Esquipulus plan.

With regard to the United States, Solís made this sharp realistic assessment:

> Hard as it may be for some people to admit, there will be no peace and no development in Central America without the United States' direct and active involvement in the region's future. This is more than an accident of geopolitics, and has to do with economic reasons and mutual security considerations as well. By the same token, Central America cannot continue to be regarded by the U.S.

as its "backyard," for the years of uncontested hegemony are gone. The international context calls for new rules under which mutual respect and cooperation could be ensured.

Finally, from the Costa Rican point of view, the times were propitious for a settlement. The Sandinista government had grown into a repressive and undemocratic regime and had drawn closer to the Soviet bloc, so that Europeans, the Socialist International, and others formerly enthused with the Sandinista experiment had become weary with it. No longer was the threat of the U.S.-supported contras credible as a justification of Sandinista behavior. On the other hand, the Iran-Contra scandal in Washington had badly eroded the Reagan administration's credibility. Furthermore, the Soviets were caught up in foreign policy difficulties in their own proximate regions and the exigencies of economic reform and were concerned with developing strategic rapprochement with the United States. The Nicaraguan Revolution was perhaps interesting to them but not of high priority; this reality was understood in Managua. The way was thus opened to the Costa Rican initiative.

BIBLIOGRAPHIC COMMENT

Grabendorff (1982) constructs a good model of Latin American interstate conflict, and Child (1985) authoritatively focuses on South American conflict and its geopolitical origins. The subject of boundary and territorial disputes in Latin America has received considerable attention. Ireland (1938, 1941) wrote early general treatments. The Cisplatine War is analyzed by Carneiro (1946); the Paraguayan War by Beverina (1921–1933), Box (1929), Cárcano (1939–1942), and Kolinski (1965); the War of the Pacific and the Tacna-Arica dispute by Bulnes (1955), Bywater (1925), and Dennis (1931); and the Chaco War by Estigarribia (1950), C. J. Fernández (1955–1967), Rout (1970), and Zook (1960). Wood (1966) addresses Latin American wars in the decade 1932–1942. Anderson (1981) and M. J. R. Martz (1978) provide excellent analyses of the "soccer war" between El Salvador and Honduras. On the U.S.-Mexican War, see Price (1967) and Singletary (1960).

A voluminous literature, much of it nationalist, exists on specific territorial and boundary conflicts; the following list is highly selective. On Ecuador's various problems, see Pérez Concha (1961–1964); Zook (1964) analyzes the Ecuador-Peru dispute, and Barrera Valverde (1982) gives an extensive account of the 1982 Ecuador-Peru border dispute from an Ecuadorian perspective. Area (1984) and Venezuela (1983) published valuable collections of documents and chronologies regarding Venezuelan-Colombian territorial controversies; Valois Arce (1970) and Vázquez Carrizosa (1983) articulate the Colombian point of view. Venezuela (1984) documents the Venezuelan dispute with the United Kingdom over Guyana territory, also treated by Braveboy-Wagner (1984). Sabaté Lichtschein (1985) provides a legal analysis of the entire range of Argentine territorial and boundary problems; Amuchástegui Astrada (1980), Goñi Garrido (1984), and Melo (1979) analyze the Beagle Channel controversy from Argentine perspectives. United Kingdom (1982) gives its case for sovereignty over the Falklands, and The Sunday Times of London Insight Team (1982) supplies a good account of the Anglo-Argentine war.

Studies of various aspects of European interventions in the region include Arnáiz y Freg and Balaillon (1965) on France in Mexico, Cady (1929) on foreign intervention in the Río de la Plata, and W. C. Davis (1950).

A few general works and "country studies" on U.S. interventions prior to the Good Neighbor Policy are by Calder (1984), Cummins (1958), Feis (1950), Foner (1972), Kane (1972), Munro (1964), W. T. Perkins (1981), Ronning (1970), and Schmidt (1971). Among the writings on post–World War II interventions are these: *Guatemala*—Immerman (1982); *Cuba*—Bender (1974), H. B. Johnson et al. (1964), Wyden (1979); *Dominican Republic*—Draper (1968, 1971), Gleijeses (1978), A. F. Lowenthal (1972), and Slater (1970); *Chile*—Petras and Morley (1975). Dinges and Landau (1980) and Branch and Popper (1982) give accounts of aspects of the 1976 Letelier assassination.

On CIA activities in Latin America, see Agee (1975), Prados (1986), U.S. Senate Select Committee to Study Governmental Operation with Respect to Intelligence Activities (1975a, 1975b, 1976), and U.S. House Committee on Foreign Affairs (1975). On covert activities under Reagan, see Marshall et al. (1987) and U.S. Senate Select Committee on Secret Military Assistance to Iran and the Nicaraguan Opposition and U.S. House Select Committee to Investigate Cover Arms Transactions with Iran (1987).

Post–World War II Caribbean turmoil is handled by Ameringer (1974) and U.S. Department of State (1962). For works on guerrilla activities see the Bibliographic Comment following Chapter 6, and for those on Soviet subversion, that following Chapter 4.

A large number of works have appeared on Central American conflict from the late 1970s through the 1980s. Among the most useful are Blakemore (1984), Blachman, Leogrande, and Sharpe (1986), Burns (1987), Erisman (1982), Erisman and Martz (1982), Falcoff and Royal (1987), Feinberg (1982), Leiken (1984), Leiken and Barry (1987), Newfarmer (1984), Pastor (1987), Ropp and Morris (1986), Valenta and Duran (1987), and Walker (1987); see also The Report of the President's Bipartisan Commission on Latin America (1983). On the Grenada intervention of 1983, see Lewis and Mathews (1984), a collection of key documents relating to several actors; and Seabury and McDougall (1984), an analysis of those captured documents relating primarily to Grenada's international relations. On the Contadora initiative, see Cepeda and Pardo (1985), Ortega (1985), and Bagley (1987). Solís-Rivera (1988) explains the Arias peace proposal. Mesa-Lago and Belkin (1981) present essays on the Cuban presence in Africa, and Fernández (1988) analyzes Cuban policy in the Middle East.

CHAPTER TWELVE

— ■ —

International Regimes

THE AGENDA OF ISSUES involving Latin America has often required international attention and has led to several efforts at regime building. This chapter analyzes selected regimes, involving different institutional forms of governance, that are of particular relevance to Latin American international relations. They include bilateral, multilateral, and near-global arrangements. Specifically, the chapter addresses regimes related to the Panama Canal, Mexican–United States riverine problems, the body of arms control treaties, the Antarctic Treaty, the law of the sea, and the North–South–oriented New International Economic Order. This is not a complete list of issues and efforts related to Latin America and international governance, but it includes some of the major problems and endeavors involving the regional actors.

THE PANAMA CANAL

Early Interests

The idea of a canal across the Central America isthmus dates from the Spanish conquest in America. Columbus had made his voyages in search of a shorter sea route from Europe to Asia, and Cortés proposed that a canal be constructed along one of the routes that even today are considered to be the most practicable. Although Spanish kings were interested in such a project, they never actually began construction (Stuart and Tigner, 1975:184). After Latin American independence and through the remainder of the nineteenth century, the idea was taken up by the external states, particularly Great Britain, the United States, and France. The issue created a great deal of conflict between them as well as between Europe and certain local states.

The United States took the first important step to secure control of a Central American route. On December 12, 1846, the United States and New Grenada (now Colombia) signed a treaty that, among other things, guaranteed the right of passage across the Colombian province of Panama to the United States. In the meantime, Great Britain had secured an important position in Central America; it had established sovereignty over British Honduras (now Belize) and the Bay Islands and, in 1844, proclaimed a protectorate over the "Mosquito Kingdom," which consisted roughly of today's Caribbean coast of Nicaragua. In 1849 the United States signed treaties with Nicaragua to obtain a concession for a canal, contravening British claims in the area, and a treaty with Honduras granting U.S. control of Tigre Island in the Gulf of Fonseca. Britain promptly sent a naval force that took possession of the island. A compromise was achieved in the Clayton-Bulwer Treaty of 1850, in which both the United States and Great Britain, in essence, promised not to claim exclusive control over any canal in Central America and to guard the safety and neutrality of any canal that should be built.

With U.S. and British canal interests mutually neutralized, the French position became dominant. A private French company, organized by Ferdinand de Lesseps, the Suez Canal engineer, purchased a Colombian concession in 1879 to construct a canal across Panama. Construction began in February 1881, but eight years later the enterprise ended in bankruptcy and scandal with only about one-third of the canal completed.

The United States Gains Control

With the emergence of the United States as a great power after the war with Spain in 1898, its desire to build and control a canal increased. By then Great Britain was more amenable to compromise (see Chapter 4). The U.S. secretary of state, John Hay, and the British ambassador to Washington, Lord Pauncefote, negotiated treaties intended to settle their Central American differences. After one treaty was rejected by the U.S. Senate, a second was ratified by both parties. The Hay-Pauncefote Treaty of 1901 expressly abrogated the Clayton-Bulwer Treaty, giving the United States the legal freedom to build and exclusively control a canal. It provided that the canal should be equally open to commercial and war vessels of all nations with no discriminatory charges. Since the treaty contained no prohibition to the contrary, the United States also had the right to fortify and defend the canal. With U.S.-British conflict over a transisthmian canal settled, the canal issues shifted to disagreements between the United States and Colombia and, later, between the United States and Panama.

With British interests in retreat, the United States was free to choose a canal route. The Walker Commission had been charged by Congress in 1899 to study all possible routes, and it issued a voluminous report on November 1, 1901. The commission had narrowed the possibilities down to a choice between two routes, one through Panama and the other through Nicaragua. When the French project failed in 1889, a new Panama Canal Company had taken over the property and attempted to sell its interest to the U.S. Congress. The Walker Commission calculated the total value of the Panama Canal Company's rights and property to be $40 million, as opposed to the company's demand for more than $109 million. The commission favored the Panama route from an engineering standpoint, but it recommended the Nicaraguan site because of the high Panamanian price. The U.S. House of Representatives, in accordance with the Walker Commission's recommendations, passed the Hepburn Bill in January 1902 authorizing the construction of a canal across Nicaragua. The French company responded, apparently in panic, by offering to sell its interest to the United States for $40 million. Consequently, the Spooner Amendment to the Hepburn Bill authorized the Panama route as an alternative to the one across Nicaragua.

The United States negotiated an agreement with Colombia, which then ruled Panama. The Hay-Herrán Treaty of 1903 granted the United States exclusive rights to construct and operate the Panama Canal and authorized the French Panama Canal Company to transfer its concession. The U.S. Senate promptly consented to ratification, but the Colombian Senate decided to press for more advantages and unanimously rejected the treaty. French creditors were dismayed by the jeopardy in which their interests were placed, as the United States still had the Nicaraguan option. Consequently, agents of the French company organized a rebellion in Panama against Colombia, taking advantage of deep provincial resentment against the central government. Panamanians long had felt neglected, and now, considering the canal as a great potential benefit to them, they saw their local interests threatened.

The Panamanian revolt began on November 2, 1902. A U.S. warship prevented Colombian troops from interfering by blockading their only route over water to Panama. Four days later, on November 6, the United States recognized Panama's sovereign independence. A Panamanian employee of the French canal company became the first president of the Republic of Panama; the former chief engineer, Philippe Bunau-Varilla, who also had engineered the revolution, was appointed Panama's minister to the United States. He negotiated a canal treaty with the United States that was signed on November 18, 1903.

The Hay-Bunau-Varilla Treaty provided for U.S. use, occupation, and control, "in perpetuity," of a ten-mile strip of territory extending across Panama (the Canal Zone). In addition, the United States gained the use and occupation of other "lands and waters" outside the zone necessary to the canal's "construction, operation, or protection." Panama also agreed to U.S. legal (treaty) rights to intervene in Panamanian domestic affairs if necessary to maintain order and ensure Panamanian "independence" so as to protect the future canal. (The Panamanian Constitution of 1904 included Article VII of the 1903 treaty, which permitted U.S. military intervention "in case the Republic of Panama should not be, in the judgment of the United States, able to maintain . . . order.") In return, the United States agreed to pay Panama $10 million plus an annual subsidy of $250,000 beginning nine years after ratification of the treaty.

With the Panamanian route secured, the United States purchased the French company's assets. Construction began in 1906 and the Panama Canal opened to traffic in 1914.

Treaty Amendments

The U.S. Good Neighbor Policy coincided with the rise of Panamanian nationalism, which centered on protests about the canal. The agitation culminated in the Hull-Alfaro Treaty in 1936 to amend the original 1903 treaty. The United States renounced its right to intervene in Panamanian affairs; in case of aggression endangering Panama or the canal, the two governments were to consult about mutual defense. The annual U.S. rental subsidy was raised to $430,000, and the United States accepted stricter limitations on the conduct of business and rights of residence in the Canal Zone. During World War II, after a series of difficult negotiations Panama gave the United States temporary permission to use certain existing military facilities and to construct new ones in Panama outside of the Canal Zone. In 1947 the two states signed a treaty providing for U.S. retention of fourteen military bases, but a strong negative public reaction in Panama forced nonratification by the Panamanian National Assembly. The United States evacuated the bases.

Continuing Panamanian dissatisfaction over the treaty arrangements led to further changes. Negotiations begun in late 1953 resulted in a 1955 treaty further amending the original one. The Eisenhower-Remón Treaty increased the U.S. annuity to $1.93 million and transferred certain U.S. rights and properties to Panama.

The 1936 and 1955 amendments represented concessions on the part of the United States, but Panamanians considered the changes inadequate and felt that they did not address their most fundamental interests. They continued to agitate against the arrangement, sometimes in a violent manner. Riots and clashes between Zonians and Panamanians occurred on several occasions. Especially serious was a confrontation in 1964 in which four U.S. citizens and twenty-two Panamanians were killed. As a result, treaty revision talks were resumed, introducing a new era in the long, complex, and conflictual U.S.-Panamanian relationship.

Beginning in 1964, Panama specifically asserted a number of its long-standing resentments. It complained that during the 1903 negotiations its dependence on the United States for national survival forced it to accede to U.S. demands, and that Bunau-Varilla, the principal negotiator for Panama, primarily represented the interests of the French canal company rather than those of the Panamanian nation. Panama also charged that all along it had been inadequately compensated for its concessions to the United States and expressed resentment over the affluence of people who lived in the Canal Zone. Most objectionable of all, in the Panamanian view, were treaty provisions giving a foreign power virtual sovereignty over a portion of Panama that physically divided the nation.

Following discussions of the canal issue in the Organization of American States and the United Nations, Panama and the United States agreed in 1964 to pursue bilateral negotiations for a new treaty. Basic U.S. objectives were that the canal should continue to be available to all commercial vessels on a nondiscriminatory basis at relatively low toll costs, that it should be operated and defended by the United States for an extended but specific time period, and that the United States should have the right to expand the canal capacity. Agreements were reached in 1967 in three draft treaties that provided for canal operation by a joint U.S.-Panamanian authority and for U.S. defense of the existing canal and any new facilities for the duration of the treaties. In 1968 a nationalist military government came to power in Panama and formally rejected the treaties. In the meantime, considerable opposition was voiced in the U.S. Congress.

Negotiations, resumed in 1971, were intense but inconclusive. Panama, to the chagrin of the United States, brought up the issue before the UN Security Council during the meeting in Panama City in March 1973. Panama criticized the U.S. posture on the canal question and introduced a resolution calling for a treaty giving Panama "effective sovereignty" over the Canal Zone. The United States blocked the resolution by casting a veto, but it agreed to adjust its differences with Panama. U.S. Ambassador at Large Ellsworth Bunker, a highly experienced and prestigious diplomat, visited Panama in late 1973 and early 1974 to discuss the bases for a new treaty. The result was a Statement of Principles signed on February 7, 1974, by U.S. Secretary of State Kissinger and Panamanian Foreign Minister Juan Tack. Designed to serve as guidelines for further treaty negotiations, the principles emphasized general areas of agreement but left some major specific issues open for later discussion.

Considerable opposition in the U.S. Senate, which had to advise and consent by a two-thirds majority prior to ratification, delayed the treaty-making process. The opposition's basic argument was simply that the Canal Zone was U.S. territory, legally agreed to by Panama, and that under the principles decided upon in 1974 the United States unnecessarily gave away an important possession. Their battle cry was "we bought it, we paid for it, it is ours." In 1976, then California Governor Ronald Reagan made the canal an issue during the presidential primary campaigns.

The final negotiation and signing of new treaties was left to President Jimmy Carter. On September 7, 1977, President Carter and the President of Panama, General Omar Torrijos, signed two Panama Canal Treaties. At the same time, a protocol to the neutrality treaty was signed by most other Latin American nations, thereby showing their strong approval. The bilateral treaties were sent to the U.S. Senate, where a particularly bitter and acrimonious advising and consenting process took place. The mobilization of the opposition was impressive. Supporters of the treaty, who finally but narrowly prevailed, led a public defense of the new arrangements. They argued that the new treaties would remove a major source of friction not only in U.S.-Panamanian relations but in inter-American affairs in general and would signal an era of hemispheric cooperation. They pointed out that Panama had gained widespread support in Latin America. They argued that both the economic and military security importance of the canal, while still significant, had declined considerably. Treaty proponents said further that under the proposed new relationship the United States would have operational and defense rights for a time sufficient to work out future contingencies. They also raised the possibility of sabotage if agreement was not reached, noting that the canal was particularly vulnerable.

The new treaties and certain supporting documents finally went into effect. They were approved by national plebiscite in Panama, and by advice and consent of the Senate in the United States. The Senate approved the neutrality treaty on March 17, 1978, and the canal treaty on April 18 by votes of 68–32 (one more than necessary). Prior to Senate approval, the two governments had negotiated and signed a clarifying Statement of Understanding in response to certain demands of a number of U.S. Senators, an exercise that was necessary to secure sufficient senatorial votes. The two treaties were then ratified by both heads of state and, on October 1, 1979, entered into force. Detailed instructions for implementing the treaties were spelled out in subsequent U.S. congressional enabling legislation, the Panama Canal Act of 1979 (Public Law 96-70).

The Revised Canal Regime

The two treaties ratified in 1979 provide for the new Panama Canal regime. The basic Panama Canal Treaty governs the canal until the year 2000, arranging for its operation, maintenance, and defense through December 31, 1999. Its salient articles provide for: (1) assigning to Panama the normal local government functions in the former Canal Zone; (2) joint United States–Panamanian management and defense of the canal until the end of the century; (3) increasing Panamanian participation at every level of operations leading to its eventual unilateral management; (4) continuing control by the United States of all land and water areas necessary for the operation and defense of the canal; and (5) increasing the annuity paid to Panama with money derived from tolls and other canal revenues. The United States will continue to operate the canal, with Panamanian participation, until the year 2000, when Panama will assume control. Until that time, a nine-person board of directors will operate the canal, with five members from the United States and four from Panama. The canal was expected to be self-supporting, with income shared by the two countries.

The other treaty document, the Treaty Concerning the Permanent Neutrality and Operation of the Panama Canal, has no termination date and makes provisions for the canal after the year 1999 when Panama will be in charge of its operation. It guarantees that the canal will be kept permanently neutral in times of both peace and war, and that nondiscriminatory access and tolls will be provided for the vessels of all countries. Furthermore, the United States is permitted to act militarily to defend the neutrality regime and to keep the canal open.

The additional Statement of Understanding clarifies U.S. rights under the neutrality treaty. It confirms that the United States has a permanent right to protect and defend the canal against any armed attack or threat to its security or to the free passage of ships of all nations. Furthermore, U.S. warships have the permanent right to transit the canal expeditiously and without conditions and, in case of need or emergency, to go to the head of the line of vessels (when the United States deems it necessary). The same obligations apply with regard to any other canal constructed in Panama.

Although the former U.S.-administered Canal Zone ceased to exist when the treaties went into force, the United States retains the right to use areas and facilities necessary to the operation and defense of the canal. The United States may take the military action necessary to make sure the canal remains open and safe; but it does not have the right to intervene against Panamanian territorial integrity or political independence.

To comply with the basic bilateral framework established by the new treaties, the U.S. Congress passed the Panama Canal Act of 1979. (The treaties and U.S. obligations under them would have gone into effect whether or not the implementing legislation had been adopted.) The salient provisions of the act accomplished the following: (1) established a new U.S. government agency, the Panama Canal Commission, to manage and operate the canal until the end of the century; (2) specified the basis for setting tolls; (3) provided for U.S. participation in various binational bodies established by the treaties, including a Joint Commission on the Environment; (4) authorized an employment system covering Panama Canal Commission employees, including special retirement conditions and other provisions; (5) phased out the previous Canal Zone court system and established arrangements to cover the initial 30-month transition period; (6) provided for the immigration to the United States of long-term local employees of the canal; and (7) directed the president to report annually to Congress on the implementation of the treaties.

Three parallel transition processes were provided for, all dating from October 1, 1979. The first was a thirty-month transition, which ended March 31, 1982, as envisioned. On that date Panama assumed total responsibility for local government and the U.S. community became subject to Panamanian authority. The U.S. judicial and police functions were phased out and, when the period ended, transferred to Panama. The United States continued to play a dominant role in the administration, operation, and defense of the canal itself. The transfer of full canal control to Panama entailed two more transitional phases. One is scheduled to end on December 31, 1989, when the U.S. administrator of the Panama Canal Commission will be replaced by a Panamanian. The final phase will close at midnight on December 31, 1999, when Panama will assume full responsibility.

U.S. military forces of the Southern Command continued to operate from bases in Panama, as provided for in the treaties. On October 1, 1984, the Reagan administration complied with the provisions of the treaties and turned over Fort Gulick, the home of the U.S. Army School of the Americas on the Atlantic side of the former Canal Zone, to Panama.

Certain modernization and capital improvement projects have been undertaken and revenues and tonnage of transiting ships have increased. In 1982 the United States, Panama, and Japan (the second largest canal user) began to study long-term alternatives to the present canal but no concrete plans evolved.

MEXICAN-U.S. RIVERINE AGREEMENTS

The Chamizal Dispute

A U.S.-Mexican treaty in 1884 created the mixed International Boundary Commission to decide frontier questions. Some problems were settled by the commission, but not the important Chamizal dispute. The Rio Grande had continuously shifted its course southward, especially rapidly in the 1860s, transferring about 630 acres known as the Chamizal to the Texas side of the river. The Boundary Commission was unable to resolve conflicting claims and referred the problem to an international arbitral commission, which in 1911 gave the Chamizal to Mexico. The United States refused to accept the award and the dispute dragged on for another half century. Finally, in 1962, the United States agreed to abide by the 1911 decision. In the Chamizal convention of 1963 the United States acknowledged Mexican sovereignty over the region and Mexico ceded the northern half of Córdova Island, lying in the Rio Grande, to the United States. The agreement also provided for the construction of a channel to divert the river so as to place the Chamizal on the Mexican side and for the building of three highways and two railway bridges across the river. Costs of these projects were to be shared equally by the two states.

The Colorado River Problem

The dispute concerning the Colorado River, flowing from Nevada into Mexico south of California, arose from the fact that, in an apparent treaty violation, the United States was not delivering water of adequate quantity or quality to Mexico. In 1944 the United States agreed to deliver a minimum amount of water to Mexico from the Colorado River, received from the Morelos International Dam on the Mexico-Arizona border. In 1961 the U.S. Wellton-Mohawk Reclamation District began rinsing soil with methods involving the pumping of highly saline waters into the Gila River near its confluence with the Colorado; contaminated water began to kill the cotton crops in the Mexicali Valley of Mexico. After a decade of dispute, an agreement was put into effect in 1973. Under it the United States agreed to cleanse the water to a certain degree before sending it to Mexico; the Mexican government did not ask for indemnification for the damaged land.

ARMS CONTROL

Various Latin American states have adhered to a wide range of arms control agreements since the late 1950s. The regime governing arms control in Latin America is diffuse, including several treaties negotiated in different forums. The Antarctic Treaty of 1959 was the earliest of the post–World War II arms control treaties involving Latin American states; because it goes beyond arms control as such and involves an array of other issues it is discussed separately below. (Much of the information in this section is based on U.S. Arms Control and Disarmament Agency, 1975.)

UN-Sponsored Treaties

The Charter of the United Nations, unlike the Covenant of the League of Nations, gave disarmament and arms control no particular priority. Eventually, however, the UN Disarmament Commission was established in 1952. At first the preserve of the major world powers, the commission was broadened to allow membership of smaller states and reconstituted in 1961 as the Eighteen Nation Disarmament Committee (ENDC). In 1969 membership was increased from eighteen to twenty-six and the body was reorganized as the Committee on Disarmament (CCD). The ENDC included Brazil and Mexico; Argentina was added when the CCD was organized. Several multinational agreements to which Latin American states are a party emerged from the work of these two committees.

A series of international arms control agreements were negotiated in the 1960s and 1970s under the auspices of the United Nations. The Limited (or Partial) Test Ban Treaty (Treaty Banning Nuclear Weapon Tests in the Atmosphere, in Outer Space, and Under Water, signed August 5, 1963, and entered into force October 10, 1963) prohibits nuclear weapons tests as indicated in its formal title. While it is of primary relevance to the nuclear powers, the treaty was open to all states. Eventually 103 states signed it. The Outer Space Treaty (Treaty on Principles Governing the Activities of States in the Exploration and Use of Outer Space, Including the Moon and Other Celestial Bodies, signed January 26, 1967, and entered into force October 10, 1967) is based on the concept of some of the provisions of the Antarctic Treaty. It seeks to prohibit military competition in outer space before it begins. Two agreements of special importance to Latin America, the treaty for a Latin American nuclear-free zone and the nuclear nonproliferation treaty, were signed in 1967 and 1968, respectively; they are discussed below in some detail. The Seabed Arms Control Treaty (Treaty on the Prohibition of the Emplacement of Nuclear Weapons and Other Weapons of Mass Destruction on the Seabed and the Ocean Floor and in the Subsoil Thereof, signed February 11, 1971, and entered into force May 18, 1972) also sought to prevent the introduction of international conflict and nuclear weapons into locations that had been free of them. Finally, the Biological Weapons Convention (Convention on the Prohibition of the Development, Production, and Stockpiling of Bacteriological and Toxin Weapons and on Their Destruction, signed April 10, 1972, and entered into force in 1975) prohibits the development, production, stockpiling, or acquisition of biological agents or toxins "of types and in quantities that have no justification for the prophylactic, protective, or other peaceful use," as well as weapons and means of delivery.

Another antibiological warfare treaty, originally negotiated in 1925, was revived by the United Nations in 1969. The Geneva Protocol (Protocol for the Prohibition of the Use in War of Asphyxiating, Poisonous, or Other

Gases, and of Bacteriological Methods of Warfare, signed June 17, 1925, and entered into force February 28, 1928) had been adhered to only by Chile, Mexico, and Venezuela among the Latin American states. A product of the 1925 Geneva Conference for the Supervision of the International Traffic in Arms, the protocol restated certain provisions of the earlier peace treaties concluding World War I. In sum, it prohibited the use of gases and bacteriological weapons of war. Problems of treaty interpretation prevented the adherence of many states until 1969, when the CCD supported UN Secretary General U Thant's plea that the 1925 protocol be widely adopted with the simple acknowledgment that it prohibited the use of all chemical and biological weapons of war. Thereafter, a number of states, including nine in Latin America, adopted the 1925 protocol.

The Latin American Nuclear-Free Zone

In the early 1960s Brazil took the lead in proposing that Latin America be made a nuclear-free zone. It noted that there were no nuclear weapons present in the region and argued that their introduction would have a destabilizing effect on Latin America's international politics. Brazil feared that any regional nuclear weapons acquisitions would stimulate an extremely expensive and dangerous arms race. In 1961 Brazil formally proposed that the Latin American region be made a nuclear-free zone in a draft resolution to the UN General Assembly. Cuba supported the idea but insisted that Puerto Rico and the Panama Canal Zone be included and that foreign military bases (such as the U.S. naval station at Guantánamo Bay) be removed. The General Assembly did not vote on the resolution.

The Cuban missile crisis of 1962 supported fears that nuclear weapons would serve as a destabilizing element in Latin American international politics and gave great impetus to the establishment of a Latin American nuclear-free zone. Following the initiative of President João Goulart of Brazil, the presidents of Bolivia, Brazil, Chile, Ecuador, and Mexico signed a Five Presidents Declaration expressing readiness to sign an enabling treaty. The UN General Assembly formally supported the declaration on November 27, 1963. Mexico then assumed the initiative, led by Ambassador Alfonso García Robles, Mexican deputy foreign minister (and later recipient of the Nobel Peace Prize). A Latin American conference held in Mexico City in November 1965 created a commission to prepare a draft treaty, and in due course a draft was presented to the Latin American states for their adherence. The Treaty for the Prohibition of Nuclear Weapons in Latin America was signed on February 14, 1967, in Tlatelolco, the section of Mexico City where the Foreign Ministry is located, and is therefore known as the Treaty of Tlatelolco. The UN General Assembly endorsed the Treaty on December 5, 1967; it entered into force April 22, 1968.

The Tlatelolco treaty is the first seeking to establish a nuclear-free zone in a populated world region. In fact, the fundamental concept of the treaty is to prevent the introduction of nuclear weapons into a geographic region already free of them. Article 1 unambiguously states the obligations of the

Latin American signatories: They "undertake to use exclusively for peaceful purposes the nuclear material and facilities which are under their jurisdiction," and they agree to prohibit "the testing, use, manufacture, production, or acquisition" of any nuclear weapons, as well as their "receipt, storage, installation, deployment, and any form of possession of any nuclear weapons, directly or indirectly." Article 13 places all peaceful nuclear activities in the Latin American zone under the safeguards system of the International Atomic Energy Agency (IAEA), a UN-sponsored organization with headquarters in Vienna. In 1969 the Organization for the Prohibition of Nuclear Weapons in Latin America (OPANAL) was established as a further control mechanism.

The idea of a nuclear-free zone has been accepted by an overwhelming majority of Latin American states. By 1985, twenty-six regional states had signed the treaty, leaving only five Latin American states that have not signed. Cuba justifies its nonadherence by the strained status of U.S.-Cuban relations and the U.S. presence at Guantánamo. The new states of Dominica, St. Christopher-Nevis, St. Lucia, and St. Vincent and the Grenadines are still considering the measure. Two others—Belize and Guyana—have not been invited to subscribe to the treaty. They have been prevented from doing so by Guatemala and Venezuela, respectively, asserting Article 25 excluding states with territories subject to litigation or claims by other Latin American states. Argentina has signed but not ratified the treaty; Brazil and Chile have ratified but with the reservation that the treaty would not enter into force for them until all other eligible states had ratified it (i.e., Argentina). Both Argentina and Brazil have refused to accede to IAEA safeguards or to renounce nuclear explosions.

The basic treaty is restricted to the Latin American states themselves, but it was supplemented by two protocols designed to further ensure the region's nuclear-free condition. Protocol I commits external states with dependent territories inside the zone to place those territories under the same restrictions. Among the states responsible for territories within the geographical treaty limits, the Netherlands, the United Kingdom, and the United States have signed and ratified the protocol. The United States, whose territories include Puerto Rico, the Virgin Islands, and the naval base at Guantánamo, delayed ratification until 1981. France signed but did not ratify the protocol; thus French Guiana, Martinique, and Guadeloupe are not militarily denuclearized. France argues that those Caribbean entities are integral parts of the metropole and that it has the prerogative to move or establish nuclear devices on French territory if and when it so wishes.

Under Protocol II, nonregional nuclear weapons states agree to respect the nonnuclear status of Latin America, not to contribute to violations of the treaty by states in the zone, and not to use or threaten to use nuclear weapons against them. Five nuclear powers—the United States, United Kingdom, France, the People's Republic of China, and the Soviet Union—have ratified Protocol II. The United States ratified it in 1971. French and Chinese adherence to Protocol II represents their first participation in any post–World War II arms control agreements.

The Treaty of Tlatelolco is the only example of a regional pact in which an arms control regime applies to an entire inhabited continent. However, the denuclearized status of the region is threatened as long as Argentina and Brazil—the regional states with the most significant nuclear programs—do not subscribe to it. They have repeatedly stated that their programs are dedicated exclusively to peaceful ends, but their refusal to undertake full safeguards has raised suspicions that they have been developing nuclear weapons capabilities. It is difficult to envisage contingencies, however, in which either country would find it necessary or advantageous to use nuclear weapons or find any concrete applications for "peaceful" nuclear explosions. Furthermore, since 1979 there has been a trend toward rapprochement between neighboring Argentina and Brazil, including nuclear collaboration. While both have decidedly kept their nuclear weaponry option open, neither has rejected the treaty approach and neither has made a concerted drive to build weapons. Neither government presently desires to reactivate the historical bilateral rivalry, which would surely occur should either one "go nuclear." Nonetheless, outside nuclear states have willingly supplied both with nuclear technology that has potential military applications. The Carter nonproliferation restraints proved impotent in the face of other willing suppliers, especially Germany and the Soviet Union selling to Brazil and Argentina, respectively, and the Reagan guidelines for nuclear technology transfers are permissive.

The Nonproliferation Treaty

The United States had a monopoly on nuclear weapons until 1949, when the Soviet Union achieved a nuclear capability. By 1964 the United Kingdom, France, and the People's Republic of China had joined the "nuclear club." The Partial Test Ban Treaty of 1963, written by the United States, the Soviet Union, and the United Kingdom, reflected a general concern about the spread of nuclear weapons and was intended to inhibit their proliferation. Virtually all states except France and China expressed approval of the nonproliferation concept contained in the 1963 treaty. In 1967 a draft nonproliferation treaty was developed through the initiative of both nuclear and nonnuclear states. The following year, the Conference of Non-Nuclear Nations opened for signature the Treaty on the Non-Proliferation of Nuclear Weapons, usually referred to as the Non-Proliferation Treaty (NPT); it was signed July 1, 1968, and entered into force March 5, 1970.

The major thrust of the NPT is to prohibit those states possessing nuclear weapons from transferring them to nonnuclear states and to prohibit the latter from building or acquiring such weapons. Negotiations over the 1967 draft treaty revealed deep suspicions on the part of many nonnuclear states; as a result, important modifications, representing concessions by the nuclear powers, were included in the NPT that was finally adopted. The nonnuclear states argued that, since they were giving up the choice of "going nuclear," the nuclear states should accept safeguards ensuring they were not violating treaty agreements. The NPT provides for a system of safeguards to be administered by the IAEA, and for a Review Conference to be held every five years after the treaty entered into force. In addition, the nuclear states committed themselves to negotiations aimed at ending the strategic stalemate and seeking general and complete disarmament, and they agreed to make peaceful nuclear technology available to the nonnuclear states on a nondiscriminatory basis.

The NPT was opened for signature in 1968, and in July 1988—on the twentieth anniversary of the treaty—it was in force for 128 states (including the Holy See), four-fifths of the UN membership, and a record number of adherents for an arms control agreement. However, two nuclear powers—China and France—have not joined NPT, and at least six countries with significant nuclear activities remain outside the treaty. Moreover, the nuclear powers were slow after the conclusion of SALT I to meet their obligations to attempt to halt the arms race and achieve disarmament "in good faith."

As of mid-1988, twenty-seven Latin American states were party to the NPT: Antigua-Barbuda, Bahamas, Barbados, Belize, Bolivia, Colombia, Costa Rica, Dominica, Dominican Republic, Ecuador, El Salvador, Grenada, Guatemala, Haiti, Honduras, Jamaica, Mexico, Nicaragua, Panama, Paraguay, Peru, St. Lucia, St. Vincent-Grenadines, Suriname, Trinidad-Tobago, Uruguay, and Venezuela. The six nonadherents were Argentina, Brazil, Chile, Cuba, Guyana, and St. Kitts-Nevis.

Brazil was one of the original nonnuclear member states of the ENDC in 1961, and Argentina was included on the CCD in 1969. Brazil earlier had been a leader of the disarmament movement; in the late 1950s President Kubitschek had attached great importance to world disarmament and argued that nonnuclear states should spend resources on development rather than arms. By 1968, however, Brazil had been ruled for four years by an ambitious military government and was a potential nuclear power reluctant to adhere to the NPT. Argentina, also governed by a military regime, apparently felt it must have the same options as Brazil, its long-time rival. The NPT's unequal treatment of the five nuclear powers compared to the rest of the world is one of the main points of criticism made by such nonsignatories as Argentina and Brazil. With rapprochement between the two states dating from 1979, and the return to constitutional civilian governments in both countries in the early 1980s, the possibility for their adherence was reopened but they have not yet done so.

THE ANTARCTIC TREATY

Most Southern Cone states extend their geopolitical concerns to Antarctica, and other issues, such as the Falklands/Malvinas dispute, the Beagle Channel settlement, and Argentine-Brazilian rivalry, are often linked to territorial claims and competition for resources in Antarctica. The Antarctic is also of global interest. By the 1950s seven states had claimed sovereignty over some part of the Antarctic continent. Eight more states had explored the region but made no territorial claims and rejected those of other states. While relations in the Antarctic among the interested parties had been relatively peaceful, potential conflict was present.

The Antarctic Treaty of 1959 established a multinational collaborative regime for the region. It was signed in Washington on December 1, 1959, and entered into force on June 23, 1961, after ratification by the twelve signatory nations. Among them were the seven states who had claimed sovereignty over some part of the Antarctic continent (Argentina, Australia, Chile, France, New Zealand, Norway, and the United Kingdom; the claims made by Argentina, Chile, and the United Kingdom had overlapped considerably). The other five signatories—Belgium, Japan, South Africa, the United States, and the Soviet Union—had explored the region but made no territorial claims. These twelve countries formed the Council of Claimant States as "consultative members"; the council's authority was restricted to making recommendations by unanimous vote. Four additional nations later became consultative members—Poland in 1977, West Germany in 1981, and Brazil and India in 1983—raising the total number to sixteen. The treaty was also open to accession by other states; as of the end of 1988, twelve nations had formally become "acceding members." Uruguay became an acceding member in 1980, and in 1984 reaffirmed its possible rights over Antarctic territory. Other Southern Cone states have not participated— Peru has little interest in Antarctica and Paraguay and Bolivia have virtually ignored it.

The Antarctic Treaty made significant accomplishments after its inception. It succeeded in preventing conflict in the Antarctic, as it was designed to do. The signatory states agreed to set aside (but not renounce) their demands during the life of the treaty. The council also succeeded in its goals of internationalizing and demilitarizing Antarctica, prohibiting nuclear testing and radioactive waste disposal on the continent, and ensuring that the region was used for peaceful purposes (including, most prominently, cooperative exploration and scientific investigations). Signatory states were accorded free access to the entire region with mutual rights of inspection of all national installations. The treaty prohibits "any measures of a military nature, such as the establishment of military bases and fortifications, the carrying out of military maneuvers as well as the testing of any types of weapons." It allows military personnel and equipment to be used only for scientific and other peaceful purposes. No treaty violations have been reported.

There have been increasing pressures for changes in the Antarctic regime. At the first seven consultative meetings held under the treaty, the topic of resources was kept off the agenda (it had purposely not been addressed in the treaty), but in the 1970s concern was expressed about the future utility and continuing existence of the treaty if petroleum or natural gas should be discovered in the Antarctic or under the surrounding continental shelf. Consequently, in 1981, the consultative members agreed to establish principles for dealing with the issue of mineral resources. Events had caught up with Antarctic governance—especially the increased price of petroleum and improved technology for extracting resources in conditions of extreme cold. Marine resources, especially an amazingly abundant high-protein crustacean called krill, had also attracted attention. Japan, Poland, and the Soviet Union were the major harvesters, but other nations indicated interest in having a share.

The treaty specified that after thirty years (that is, 1991), any contracting party may request a review conference for consideration of modifications or amendments. It also allows members to withdraw from the treaty after a further four-year period. Consequently, in the 1980s several states began to maneuver to strengthen their positions in case the treaty should become ineffective. The Antarctic remained essentially a vast uninhabited frontier, with a large number of states interested in exploration, scientific investigation, mineral and marine resource exploitation, and even settlement. It was thought that certain states might reassert territorial claims. Strains were apparent by 1984. Chile began the development of a "gateway city" in the Antarctic to support future mining and tourism—and to strengthen its territorial claim. In December 1984, the United Kingdom turned over to Chile a base on Adelaide Island in an area also claimed by Argentina; Argentine nationalists vehemently protested the action.

The current status of the Antarctic Treaty was further complicated in the United Nations. Third World nations not a part of the Antarctic Treaty regime argued for globalization of the region's governance and distribution of its resources. On November 30, 1983, the United Nations General Assembly adopted a resolution calling for a thorough study of the issue. In response, the treaty nations tried to demonstrate the strength of the existing system. The Polar Research Board of the U.S. National Academy of Sciences held a workshop on the future of the Antarctic in January 1985 at Beardmore Station, a remote research camp near the South Pole. Twenty-five countries sent fifty-seven scientists, diplomats, international lawyers, environmentalists, and others to attend the workshop. The debate over whether Antarctica should be regulated by the Antarctic Treaty or by the United Nations still had not been resolved as of 1988.

LAW OF THE SEA

The Inter-American Dispute

What began as a territorial sea issue between the United States and certain South American west coast states developed into a global concern in which all Latin American states became involved to some degree. The problem first centered upon the claims of Chile, Peru, and Ecuador to a 200-mile off-shore territorial limit and the consequent political and legal conflict with the United States.

In 1947, presidential declarations emanating from Chile and Peru claimed sovereignty over the seas adjacent to their coasts extending to a distance of 200 nautical miles. In 1952 they were joined by Ecuador at the First Conference on the Exploitation and Conservation of the Maritime Resources of the South Pacific in Santiago. They signed a joint declaration establishing a 200-mile maritime zone, including both the sea and the underlying land area, over which they claimed "sole sovereignty and jurisdiction." Their rationale was that the offshore food and economic materials were essential national resources and that they had the right and duty to protect and regulate them against outside exploitation. They argued that the 200-mile boundary included the outer limits of the food-rich Humboldt Current, which formed a "natural" and specific maritime unit. The three states convened a second conference at Lima in December 1954; there they signed six supplementary agreements for joint defense and action in the event of outside violations of their sovereignty in the maritime zone. They created a standing committee, the South Pacific Commission, to hold annual consultative meetings.

Beginning in 1955, the United States sought, with no success, to negotiate its differences with the three Latin American states. The United States, along with other large maritime powers, adhered to the traditional 3-mile limit in territorial seas and a contiguous 12-mile zone reserved for exclusive fishing rights. The United States protested the South American claims as unilateral declarations at variance with generally accepted limits of territorial waters. An attempt to negotiate the dispute was made at the Santiago Negotiations on Fishery Conservation Problems (September 14–October 5, 1955) attended by Chile, Peru, Ecuador, and the United States, but the fundamental disagreement remained. In February 1967 the United States proposed that the dispute be submitted to the International Court of Justice or that another conference be held. The South American states refused both proposals, although some informal talks were continued.

In September 1951 Ecuador seized and fined U.S.-owned tuna boats, accusing them of illegally fishing in Ecuadorian waters. Peru made its first such seizure in February 1955 and Chile in December 1957. The U.S. Congress took action to protect U.S. fishermen and promulgated legislation that in effect demanded restitution from the Latin American states. The Fishermen's Protective Act of 1954, amended in 1968, provided that, in any case where a U.S. vessel was seized by a foreign country under territorial waters claims not recognized by the United States, the secretary of state should take action "to attend to the welfare of such vessel and its crew while it is held by such country and to secure the release of such vessel and crew" and to collect costs from the foreign country, and that the secretary of the treasury should reimburse the vessel's owners for any fines paid. The 1968 amendment broadened the scope of reimbursement and, more important, provided that if the foreign country did not reimburse the United States within 120 days of a claim, the secretary of state should withhold an amount equal to the claim from U.S. assistance funds programmed for the country. The Foreign Assistance Act of 1961 provided that, in determining a country's eligibility for assistance, consideration should be given to excluding those countries that had seized U.S. vessels. The Foreign Military Sales Act of 1963 provided that "no defense article or defense service shall be sold by the United States Government . . . to any country which . . . seizes or takes into custody or fines an American fishing vessel engaged in fishing more than twelve miles from the coast of that country" (Hagen, 1969). Ecuador eventually ceased seizing vessels; by then, the question of law of the sea had evolved into a global issue.

The Global Concern

By the mid-1950s, a number of nations throughout the world, including others in Latin America, began to assert claims to an extension of the territorial seas or contiguous areas. Several factors caused the increased pressures for a change in the international law of the sea, including a growth in the economic uses of the oceans, dramatic advances in the technology for exploiting ocean resources, an increased awareness of environmental problems, and a general desire of small states forming the global majority to have a voice in the shaping of international law. The scope of the issue was formidable. The oceans cover about 70 percent of the earth's surface, over which some 95 percent of world trade moves, and contain huge petroleum and other mineral reserves. Virtually all states had some interest in the rules governing the oceans. Thus, the issue posed a major challenge to procedures for international cooperation.

The United Nations first attempted to resolve some of these problems at the First United Nations Conference on the Law of the Sea in 1958 at Geneva. The conference partially codified the international law of the sea by adopting four conventions relating to the territorial sea and contiguous zone, the high seas, the continental shelf, and living resources. The Second UN Law of the Sea Conference was held in 1960 to attempt to resolve such issues as territorial sea, continental shelf, and contiguous fishing zone limits and jurisdictions, but without success.

In 1967 Malta placed its "Pardo Plan" on the UN General Assembly agenda. It addressed "the question of the reservation exclusively for peaceful purposes of the seabed and the ocean floor, and the subsoil thereof, underlying the high seas beyond the limits of national jurisdiction and the use of their resources in the interests of mankind." In response, the General Assembly created a thirty-two-nation Special Committee, which, after two years of study, produced a statement of principles but left many problems unresolved. In December 1970 the General Assembly called for a Third UN Law of the Sea Conference to deal not only with the questions remaining from the previous two conferences but also with a number of new ones that had subsequently arisen. The Special Committee was enlarged to ninety-one nations and reconstituted as the UN Committee on the Peaceful Uses of the Seabed and the Ocean Floor Beyond the Limits of National Jurisdiction (Seabed Committee). It engaged in almost three years of preparatory work for a comprehensive conference.

The Third United Nations Conference on the Law of the Sea (UNCLOS III) convened in December 1973. After nine years of intense negotiations among various nations of the world, it produced in 1982 a comprehensive treaty for a global law of the sea regime. Some 156 states participated, about 120 of which were coastal states.

Latin American Positions

During the years of negotiations for a modern and comprehensive law of the sea, different approaches developed to several of the related issues. Some coastal states viewed the decision to extend their national jurisdiction seaward as a sovereign right, considering contiguous oceans as vital national resources subject to territorial state sovereignty. Chile, Peru, and Ecuador were later joined by Brazil claiming a 200-mile territorial sea.

Most Caribbean states held a different view. It was expressed in the Declaration of Santo Domingo, formulated at the Specialized Conference of Caribbean Countries Concerning the Problems of the Sea, attended by fifteen states in 1972. The declaration was signed by Colombia, Costa Rica, the Dominican Republic, Guatemala, Haiti, Honduras, Mexico, Nicaragua, Trinidad-Tobago, and Venezuela. Five delegations declined to sign: Barbados, El Salvador, Guyana, Jamaica, and Panama. The declaration favored state sovereignty extending only to a limit of twelve nautical miles seaward, with ships afforded innocent (nonbelligerent) passage through the territorial sea on a nondiscriminatory basis. The Santo Domingo Declaration also proposed the concept of the "patrimonial sea," an area, including the territorial sea, not to exceed 200 nautical miles, within which a state exercised rights over resources but not sovereignty. Thus a state could not regulate navigation through the area, but it could manage the living and nonliving resources of the ocean, seabed, and subsoil. The concept was used during UNCLOS III to bring about a compromise among positions regarding sovereignty and resource allocation.

The negotiations also proceeded in a North-South context. The Pardo Plan had first formulated the idea of the "common heritage of mankind"; it quickly became a Third World rallying point. (The Third World later applied it to the future of the Antarctic Treaty.) On April 30, 1982, the bulk of the Latin American states, like nearly all Third World states, voted in favor of the UN Convention on the Law of the Sea. The United States voted against it, and a number of developed states abstained. The vote was 130 states for the treaty, four opposed (United States, Israel, Turkey, and Venezuela), and seventeen abstentions (mostly the Soviet bloc, except for Rumania, and the European states). The chief Third World negotiator was Alvaro de Soto of Peru. The voting pattern, partially along North-South lines, put off but apparently did not eliminate a new ocean order, and threatened a new source of North-South discord.

The Law of the Sea Convention

The Law of the Sea Convention was opened for signature in December 1982. As of June 1986, 159 states had signed and twenty-six states plus the UN Council for Namibia had ratified it. The treaty will enter into force one year from the date of the sixtieth ratification or accession. It sets a twelve-mile territorial waters limit, establishes a 200-mile exclusive "economic zone" for coastal nations (with a definition of oil-drilling rights), regulates shipping lanes and provides for rights of passage for civilian and military ships through narrow straits, guarantees free navigation for naval forces, regulates scientific exploration and fisheries, requires environmental protection and pollution controls, controls mining under the deep sea, and establishes a system of international courts to arbitrate disputes at sea. Most of the provisions have become the de facto source of the international law of the sea for both signatories and nonsignatories.

From the start of the negotiations, provisions regulating the mining of the profuse mineral nodules that lie in the seabed were the focus of differences that finally could not be resolved. A compromise was struck with the establishment of a dual authority, one that would mine on behalf of the less developed countries and another that would license private enterprise to have access to mining sites. But the Reagan administration, while acknowledging that the United States strongly desired almost all other treaty provisions, decided that Article 11 did not adequately protect the U.S. firms that were exploring and developing technology to mine the seabed.

THE NEW INTERNATIONAL ECONOMIC ORDER

The origins of the New International Economic Order (NIEO) may be traced to the first United Nations Conference on Trade and Development (UNCTAD) held in Geneva in 1961. UNCTAD began as an ad hoc body, but, guided by its first secretary general, Raúl Prebisch of Argentina, the General Assembly converted it to a permanent organ in the United Nations System in December 1964. At UNCTAD I, Third World states had formed the Group of 77, a coalition to unify and articulate their objections to the global trade, aid, and development practices of the mid-1960s. The Group of 77, led by Algeria, then used its numerical majority to convene the Sixth Special Session of the General Assembly in 1974 and adopt a Declaration on the Establishment of a New International Economic Order. It also approved the Charter of Economic Rights and Duties of States sponsored by Mexican President Luís Echeverría. Thus, the formal establishment of the NIEO occurred in 1974, but it had grown out of earlier precedents and concerns.

The NIEO operates primarily through the Group of 77, which retains its original name, although it has grown in membership to about 120 Third World countries. They meet before sessions of the General Assembly and other gatherings (such as UNCTAD) to try to decide on a common course of action.

The NIEO views the world in terms of a North-South division between the industrialized rich nations (found mostly in the Northern Hemisphere of the globe) and the poor, developing nations (clustered in the Southern Hemisphere). In this sense, the Third World is equated with the South and has essentially developmentalist goals. These nations seek to restructure the existing world economic system in a variety of ways, mainly through obtaining trade concessions from the buyers of their commodities and increasing their sources of development capital. The 1974 declaration demanded a change in the international economic system from one dominated by the rich and powerful states to one that would offer benefits to all and contribute effectively to the development and modernization of the developing states. The associated charter spelled out in some detail the principles and practices needed to implement the NIEO.

The Group of 77 has had some success in its endeavors. It played a major role in the evolution of UNCTAD and was instrumental in the creation of the Special United Nations Fund for Economic Development (SUNFED), the United Nations Capital Development Fund (UNCDF), and the International Development Association (IDA) as an affiliate of the World Bank; it also made an effort to use the International Monetary Fund (IMF) to promote developmental goals. The Group of 77 has also organized a series of special UN conferences to address a wide range of other issues they consider crucial to their interests: on the environment, population, food, the law of the sea, disarmament, women, industrialization, desertification, technology transfer, rural development, and the role of science and technology in development. These conferences, however, have rarely led to concrete results. The Group of 77 represents a majority of the UN membership and can pass any action that it chooses in the General Assembly—if it maintains its cohesiveness. It has not, however, been able to persuade or compel the North to accept its tenets or adopt its prescriptions.

For most of Latin America most of the time, the "Third World" has been synonymous with the "developing world." The regional actors, including members of the Nonaligned Movement, seem to have concluded that they share special economic problems with other developing nations, particularly in their relations with the developed world. In fact, the Latin American region took the lead in addressing a wide range of issues beginning in the early 1960s. The important issues, from their points of view, involved development and the world economy, especially world trade, public assistance, and private investment. At the same time, Latin America approached the NIEO as a regional bloc. CECLA was established in 1964 and was superseded by SELA in 1975 (see Chapter 7). Both were concerned, among other things, with attempting to form a united Latin American front prior to interacting not only with the North but also with the rest of the South in the General Assembly, UNCTAD, IMF, the World Bank Group, and other forums. They also pursued subregional economic integration schemes to achieve restructured trading relationships. Latin Americans seemed to place as much reliance on regional IGOs as on the NIEO in approaching the problems that beset them.

BIBLIOGRAPHIC COMMENT

Vaky (1983) edited a collection of essays discussing a broad range of Latin American international relations under the concept of governance. General studies regarding the Panama Canal are provided by Ealy (1971), Liss (1969), Mack (1944), Miner (1940), and Williams (1915). Interests in a Nicaraguan canal are described by Rodríguez Serrano (1968). Hearings on the revised canal treaties are published in U.S. Senate, Committee on Foreign Relations (1977/1978); U.S. Library of Congress (1977) presents a lengthy compendium of documents. Crane (1978) puts forth the case against the treaties by a conservative congressional opponent, with an introduction by then Governor Ronald Reagan. Moffett (1985) analyzes the uninspiring U.S. ratification process.

On Mexican-U.S. riverine questions, see Eaton (1987), Enríquez Coyro (1975–1976), Gregg (1958), Hundley (1966), Jessup (1973), and Liss (1969). Tamayo (1983) gives a detailed analysis of U.S.-Mexican border relations from a Mexican perspective. Mexico (1975) presents the official position on U.S.-Mexican negotiations over the Colorado River salinity issue.

Vargas Silva (1979), a law of the sea handbook of definitions and chronology (1492–1979), takes a particular interest in Latin American positions. For a variety of particulars concerning Latin America, territorial waters and fishing rights controversies, and an international oceans regime, see Alvarado Garaicoa (1968), Hagen (1969), Morris (1979), Orrego Vicuña (1976), Pontecorvo (1986), Smetherman and Smetherman (1974), and Trindade (1982).

On the problems related to arms control, see Stinson and Cochrane (1971), U.S. Arms Control and Disarmament Agency (1975), and U.S. Senate Foreign Relations Committee (1971). García Robles (1967, 1979) discusses the Tlatelolco Treaty from the perspective of a prime mover in having it adopted. Redick (1978) analyzes U.S. nuclear policy in Latin America under President Carter. Child (1988) is the best single source on the international politics of the Antarctic.

Ffrench-Davis and Tironi (1981) and Navarette et al. (1980) discuss the New International Economic Order (NIEO) with primary reference to Latin America. Beltrán and Fox de Cardona (1980) condemn the imperialist nature of the North American media.

PART FIVE

■

Conclusion

Intense debates have long taken place about the consequences of policies and interactions in the Latin American subsystem. Conflicting views have emerged concerning the effects of foreign policy instruments and international interactions concerning trade, investment, economic and military assistance programs, and diplomatic and cultural relations, as well as diplomatic and economic coercion, subversion, military and paramilitary intervention, and war. They have raised issues and questions over which serious analysts disagree, especially concerning the influence of strong external states on the policies and political systems of the regional Latin American states. Chapter 13 concludes the book with general explanations and prescriptions and provides a critique of the major theories of Latin American international relations.

CHAPTER THIRTEEN

■

Explanations and Prescriptions

A NUMBER OF THEORIES have appeared in the study of international relations that are particularly relevant to Latin America, and some have been formulated with particular reference to the region. The principal theories include the realist-idealist dichotomy, the Marxist critiques and alternatives, liberal developmentalism with its various shades of analysis, and the variants of dependency theory (especially structuralism and neo-Marxism). These theories of international relations purport to explain Latin America in the international political system and offer policy prescriptions for the various actors.

THE THEORETICAL ENTERPRISE

All of the theories mentioned above (and analyzed below) are heavily policy oriented. They are concerned both with explaining state behavior and the international system and with influencing state policies and the decisions of other actors. Prior to engaging in specific theoretical critiques, therefore, a brief review of the nature of theory and the relationship to policy is in order.

Most international relations (IR) specialists today agree on the importance of theoretical inquiry. A theory is a set of propositions designed to explain a class of phenomena, such as those analyzed in this book. Furthermore, IR specialists tend to be practical as well as scientific and philosophical. They have tended to be interested in policy prescriptions along with objective analysis and subjective understanding. Indeed, the latter two enterprises have often led to interest in policy problems.

"Theory" is often used colloquially or pejoratively to connote an untested idea or opinion in political discourse. For the purposes of this book, this meaning and practice are emphatically rejected. A mere subjective preference is not the equivalent of theoretical judgment in any critical sense. Indeed, a cardinal rule for serious political analysts (including those who wish to influence policies) is to be self-conscious about their intellectual processes— that is, to understand the nature of one's thoughts and of the thoughts of others through theoretical analysis.

The various intellectual processes that people may engage in are represented by the different kinds of statements they make. In the case of international relations and other social sciences, we should distinguish between five categories of assertions: (1) descriptive (factual), (2) explanatory, (3) predictive, (4) normative (value), and (5) prescriptive. Explanatory statements give meaning to descriptive statements, typically answering some form of the question "why?" Predictive statements are usually derived by extrapolating trends and applying explanations to presume future conditions. Political scientists are by and large modest about their predictive claims, but prediction is particularly relevant when it considers policy consequences before the fact of implementation. Normative statements express a preference in terms of right and wrong, desirable and undesirable, and other value-based objectives. Prescriptive statements go beyond assessment or contemplation to offer advice with the purpose of affecting events. Prescriptive statements usually have normative and predictive elements; that is, they are normative in the sense that purposes proceed from some image or view of a desirable state of affairs, and are predictive when stating what course of action will accomplish a given purpose.

These statements are reflected in three kinds of political theory: (1) empirical (behavioral) theory, which analyzes politics by scientific methods; (2) normative theory, which studies politics in philosophical, ethical (perhaps tied to legal), or ideological terms; and (3) policy theory, which offers advice for policy action. These theories are separate but not mutually exclusive; indeed, the theories examined here fall under the category of policy theory but include empirical and normative elements.

No matter what specific purposes one may bring to the study of IR, the beginning point is to strive to understand objectively the world in which we live. Thinking may then shift to normative evaluations. Both objective and subjective understanding may be applied to policy prescription. Normative conclusions may go beyond clarifying values about proper behavior by recommending what should be done in matters of action. Empirical theory may tell policymakers the best way to achieve a desired goal—what is possible or not—after what is desirable has already been determined. Thus, knowledge of politics may be applied to solving actual problems.

The expectation of theorists to "use" political knowledge in the policy arena raises questions about scholarship. Should theorists go beyond objective and ethical analysis about political behavior to prescribe policy? Those who answer in the affirmative (and I am among them) argue that, since all policy is ultimately based on values, a detached approach may not be particularly desirable. As Charles Lerche succinctly put it, "if the serious scholars suspend normative judgment on events, the function of assigning value to policy choices falls to political leaders, journalists, and other manipulators of the mass psyche."

Wahlke and Dragnich (1966:16–17) entered an important caveat about policy prescribing. They pointed out that disagreements arise over the identification of both problems and solutions. Political knowledge cannot tell us whose problem definition or policy prescription is right, because it cannot tell us what political ends we ought to seek or to what particular goals our factual knowledge ought to be applied. Furthermore, since prescriptive statements almost always have normative overtones, political knowledge may be used for purposes of which one may thoroughly disapprove. They note the often-cited Book V of Aristotle's *Politics*, which offers knowledge about the causes of revolution. That knowledge may serve very different purposes—those of a tyrant protecting his power against rebellious subjects, a democratic leader working for stability in an open society, an ego-gratifying agitator manipulating the revolution, and a leader using revolution as a means to human progress.

REALISM, IDEALISM, AND MARXISM

Realist and Idealist Perspectives

Plano and Olton (1988) gave useful definitions of realism and idealism as alternative approaches for formulating and evaluating foreign policy. The realist perspective, the oldest concept in IR theory and practice, is fundamentally pragmatic. In general terms, realism is a view of the world as it is, as distinguished from abstract or speculative preferences. In international relations, realists emphasize national interest as the fundamental guide to policy-making in the sense of the state's most vital needs of self-preservation, independence, territorial integrity, military security, and economic well-being. When a state bases its foreign policy strictly on national interest and power politics, it can be described as pursuing a realist, as distinguished from an idealist, policy. The realist defines interest in terms of power and emphasizes the balance of power as the principal guide to policy-making and to understanding the structure of the international system. The realist school starts with the assumption that power is the key factor in all international relationships. The wise and efficient use of power by a state in pursuit of its national interest is, says the realist, the main ingredient of a successful foreign policy.

Idealism is the pursuit of high principles, purposes, or goals; a representation of things as they might or should be rather than as they are. The idealist approach to international relations is based on principles involving international norms, legal codes, and moral-ethical values. The idealist believes that foreign policies based on moral-legal principles are more effective than power politics because they are more durable and better promote unity and cooperation among states. Political idealism involves not force and coercion but winning over the minds and allegiances of people to accept principles that ought to govern state conduct. This view assumes that foreign policies should strive to create a better world order and emphasizes international law, organization, and other regimes that regulate the system by accommodating conflict and facilitating cooperation.

Practices associated with realism—balance-of-power, strategic, and geopolitical calculations, and conflict—have been important aspects of the Latin

American subsystem from its beginnings to the present. The policy implications of conflict in the current era of Latin American international relations are especially profound for the United States as the most powerful external actor and the most willing and able to use coercive diplomacy. Nevertheless, the United States was not the first, nor is it the only, state to engage in power politics in Latin America. Power politics have characterized much of Latin America's relations with many external states as well as inter–Latin American relations, particularly by certain South American states in the Southern Cone.

The Marxist Alternatives

Marxism and the Leninist interpretation were among the earliest theoretical dissents from realism and imperialism from the mid-nineteenth century through World War I. Marxist-Leninist ideas offered alternatives to what proponents considered ineffective liberalism and idealism. A set of economic and political doctrines were formulated, characterized by the theories of dialectical materialism, surplus value, and class struggle. As developed by Karl Marx and Friedrich Engels in the middle to late nineteenth century, Marxism viewed the state as a device for exploitation of the masses by a dominant bourgeois (capitalist) class. They argued that the functioning of the international political system was rooted in social and economic factors. While Marx said little about Latin America beyond a brief tract on Mexico, some of today's theories about the region's international relations recall the earlier Marxist arguments. This has been especially true of neo-Marxist dependency theory (discussed below). Of more immediate importance, however, were Lenin's interpretations, which have also provided the basis for subsequent theorizing.

Lenin made the most influential extensions of Marx's theories. His theory of imperialism was set forth most cogently in his 1912 essay, *Imperialism— the Highest Stage of Capitalism*. To Lenin, the capitalist economic system was the driving force behind both colonization and war; economic factors dominated the capitalist states' calculations and their policies inevitably became imperialist. Lenin's influence was even greater after his seizure of power in Russia in 1917 and creation of the Soviet Union.

Initial Soviet assessments of Latin American society were heavily dependent on Marxist concepts of class struggle, with the conclusion that both "objective" and "subjective" conditions necessary for a proletarian revolution were lacking. The region was too advanced industrially to fit the Marxist precapitalist idea, but it was not describable as a mature capitalist industrial economy either. Thus, Latin America was unique in Marxian terms; it stood midway between precapitalist and mature capitalist stages. In addition, the middle and upper classes were too strong for a successful revolution by the small working class, which itself seemed too interested in achieving middle-class status. Following World War II, Soviet writers tentatively explored the notion that the region shared some common characteristics with the newly independent, precapitalist, non-Communist, underdeveloped Third World in Asia and

Africa. In particular, U.S. economic domination offered the possibility of an anti-imperialist revolution, even though Latin America continued to have unique social and economic characteristics. Since the mid-1960s they have emphasized the decline of U.S. influence in the region. At the same time, traditional Marxism-Leninism has been challenged by Latin American guerrilla groups who have advocated Trotskyism, Maoism, and especially, Fidelismo (see the discussion in Chapter 6).

The Era of European Imperialism

Imperialism and accepted balance-of-power mechanisms and policies provided a principal thrust of classic *realpolitik*. Imperialism suggests a superior-inferior relationship in which an area and its people are subordinated to the will of a foreign state.

European imperialism in Latin America during the nineteenth century took on special characteristics. From the Latin American point of view, the external powers were not effectively restrained by the balance-of-power system. The Latin American countries had a low capability level in relation to the outside world, making them subject to pressures from the more dynamic European powers and, in some instances, from the United States. Nevertheless, certain aspects of the global balance-of-power system helped protect the Latin American states.

The European states were not uninhibited and conceivably they might have been even more unheeding of Latin American sovereignty. The era of "new imperialism" in the latter half of the nineteenth century and up to World War I, involving highly competitive European great power activities in the Middle East, Africa, and Asia, also marked the height of European interest in Latin America. However, the region figured in no significant way in the worldwide imperialism-colonialism thrust, and the Latin American states managed to maintain a considerable measure of independence in comparison with much of the rest of the non–North Atlantic world. This situation was a curious one on the surface, considering that imperialism was then viewed as a normal product of international competition, that it was characterized by the development of the alliance system in Europe to divide colonial spoils, and that its causation is generally ascribed to economic motives.

The United States and Power Politics

The realist-idealist dichotomy relates particularly to the debates over the preferred approach to foreign policy-making in the United States. Many realists regard the United States as being misled by popular attitudes and moral self-righteousness into adopting idealistic guidelines in the making of foreign policy decisions. The result, according to the realists, is the inability of the United States to compete effectively with other states that base their policies on the hard realities of national self-interest. Idealists tend to reject the power-centered realist approach as Machiavellianism producing only short-term gains. For the idealist, the most successful policies have been based on values that have won both domestic and overseas support. The realist-idealist dichotomy in today's world should not be overstated, however. Realism and idealism may converge, and policy debates and decisions often attempt to reconcile the two. In practice, policies often have combined some mixture of realism and idealism. In such cases, realism specifies the means for achieving goals and idealism justifies the policies adopted.

During the twentieth century the United States has responded to what it considered to be security risks with strong coercive power and seemingly little regard for the consequences beyond the immediate situation being addressed. This approach was demonstrated by extensive interventions in several Caribbean states in the first third of the twentieth century, and more recently by rebel invasions of Cuba in the early 1960s, military interventions in the Dominican Republic in 1965 and in Grenada in 1983, and a mix of coercive instruments in Central America in the 1980s. At other times, however, the United States has been sensitive to Latin American and world opinion and to the effects its actions might have in other parts of the hemisphere and the world. This approach seems to have prevailed with the adoption of noninterventionist policies in the 1930s and restraint, off and on, in the postwar period, most clearly during the first half of the Carter presidency. Idealism has also been reflected in the vacillating efforts to promote democracy and human rights at times during the twentieth century, sometimes paralleling *realpolitik*. As noted in Chapter 5, even though U.S. policymakers often couch their Latin American policies in moral rhetoric, they almost always formulate policies in terms of the perceived realities of national interest and security.

The Caribbean became the most important extracontinental area for the United States after the turn of the century. It was clearly considered in the U.S. sphere of influence, and policies there were understandable in terms of strategic geopolitical calculations. Alfred Thayer Mahan's seapower thesis, dating from the 1890s, was the initial important geopolitical expression of U.S. interests (see Chapter 5). It has influenced the thinking of U.S. policymakers to the present day. Ironically, however, almost as soon as Mahan's theories became accepted as the foundation for U.S. policy in Latin America, events began to make them irrelevant. In previous centuries, technological changes had been absorbed in warfare without fundamental systemic changes, and the bases for national power tended to be measured, almost crudely, in terms of military and economic factors and in territorial holdings. This continuity of international political culture was seriously disrupted, however, after 1914, and even more after 1939, by awesome technological developments—the submarine, aircraft, "instant" communications, and, most profoundly, nuclear weapons. Mahan's doctrines concerning the Caribbean area, as well as his broader principles of sea power, were outdated by events and lost their validity. Nevertheless, they were highly relevant to power politics for the first half of the twentieth century in the sense that, in some form, they were accepted by U.S. strategists almost as an article of national faith. This widespread view was evidenced especially by the sacrosanctity of the

Panama Canal in statements by military men and diplomats through World War II until the dawn of the nuclear age.

The Caribbean area, with its important strategic position for the United States, most often has been the testing ground for emerging U.S. policies toward Latin America at large. There the United States first pursued military and economic intervention, "taught" democracy, and intervened against communism. Yet even the Caribbean has provided illustrations of the limits of U.S. power, even in the imperialist period during the first third of this century. U.S. actions probably deterred European interventions for the decade prior to World War I; but afterward U.S. coercion continued even though the threat of European incursions was virtually nil. The political price for U.S. interventions was high. The United States was intimately involved in the substance of Caribbean politics; it determined the appropriateness of constitutions, the eligibility of persons for election to presidencies, and the legitimacy of political parties. Furthermore, the proximate objective of enforcing democracy through intervention in order to serve long-range goals of stability was absolutely unrealized. After the U.S. withdrawal from Cuba, the Dominican Republic, Haiti, Nicaragua, and Panama, dictators arose in all of those states, several coming from police forces trained by the United States to protect constitutional government. In sum, intervention failed to meet long-range U.S. interests, aroused bitter antagonisms in many quarters, entangled the United States in daily participation in Caribbean politics, and left dictatorships behind.

U.S. policy failures since the 1960s further illustrate the generally dysfunctional character of conflict and policies of coercion by which U.S. interests are ill-served. For example, Castro was not brought down either by unilateral or by multilateral means; if anything, Cuba was moved to a closer relationship with the Soviet Union and eventually won considerable sympathy in Latin America and other parts of the world. Furthermore, inter-American cooperation was seriously eroded by the Cuban issue. In Guatemala, the Dominican Republic, and Chile, where interventions achieved short-term goals of helping to bring down regimes or groups ideologically opposed by the United States, coercion helped to interrupt social change and had a destabilizing impact on those societies. Furthermore, unilateral interventions violated inter-American law, created a general atmosphere of Latin American hostility toward the United States inimical to inter-American cooperation in general, and heightened frictions among political groups within individual Latin American states. These costs seemed to be out of proportion to the benefits gained.

Conflict in Central America in the 1980s has continued to focus attention on important questions about U.S. policies of coercion. When Ronald Reagan became president in 1981, he sought to reestablish the U.S. presence in the region. Despite considerable effort, the administration, like that of President Carter before, did not resolve the problems it set out to deal with. In fact, the problems seemed to become even more complex and intractable. Conflict in Central America, beginning in the late 1970s and accelerated in the 1980s, again focused attention on the conceptual bases for U.S. policy. The dominant calculations for U.S. actions were, paradoxically, drawn from a combination of strategic perceptions of Central America dating from the early twentieth century and more recent experiences far removed from Central America. On the one hand, official policy rationales—as well as much of the criticism put forth by policy opponents—were taken from experiential sources outside the arena to which they were applied. For example, much of the public debate about Central American conflict revolved around the "another Vietnam" syndrome, with contending positions drawing different "lessons" from the Southeast Asian experience. Strategic thinking, as revealed in Reagan administration statements and expressed in the Kissinger Commission report, derived not only from Central American policies devised more than eight decades before, but also from nineteenth-century European balance-of-power theory as shaped by perceptions of the post–World War II cold war. The principal question for U.S. policy orientation as of the end of the Reagan presidency was not one of isolationism or withdrawal—the United States as both global superpower and regional actor will be deeply involved in Latin America—but whether it would pursue its interests unilaterally or multilaterally. The new conditions of the Latin American subsystem (see Chapter 2) call for a new multilateralism toward the region, including, perhaps especially, in the Circum-Caribbean. An effective foreign policy in the contemporary world requires cooperation within alliances and associations.

Latin American Realism

Latin American leaders also formulate policies in terms of national interests based on theories of national security. More often than not, however, national security for them is synonymous with national development, especially economic. Whereas the U.S. notion of security emphasizes external challenges to its global and regional interests, Latin American thinking focuses on internal challenges to national unity, with external perceptions limited to contiguous border and territorial disputes and, in some cases, great power intervention.

In the Southern Cone and Brazil, however, important political elements have thought in conventional power political terms. Military men in particular have adopted geopolitical strategic perspectives based on the organic theory of the state, an extreme version of power politics that views conflict as natural, inevitable, and necessary if a nation is to survive and achieve its "destiny" (see Chapter 3). This kind of thinking has been responsible not only for giving impetus to conflict and arms races in the Southern Cone subsystem but for justifying domestic repression as well. Most of this geopolitical thinking cannot be taken seriously in theoretical terms, but it must be recognized as a source of action that has discredited military regimes in the subregion and made the development of fragile democracies and tenuous economies there—as well as in other parts of Latin America—an imperative for Latin America and the United States. That is, the asymmetrical security perceptions in Latin America and the United States must be reconciled.

LIBERAL DEVELOPMENTALISM

Development Theory in Comparative Politics

Comparative political analysis has purported to place Latin America in a larger than regional mold in terms of development theory and the concept of modernization. Many Latin Americanists, including myself, have long concluded that development theory failed to explain convincingly Latin American national development or to use satisfactorily Latin American data to support general assertions. Nevertheless, the theory has been the basis for important state policies and has been prominent in debates over them to the present day; moreover, some process of developmental change takes place, even if it is inadequately understood. Thus, a serious consideration of development theory in the Latin American context is in order.

With the emergence of formerly colonial peoples as new sovereign nations over much of the globe after World War II, certain scholars detected the seeming irrelevance of the West European and North American experiences to the analysis of the new "developing world." In this sense, development theory provided a necessary corrective to traditional modes of comparative analysis, which tended to be misleading when applied outside the North Atlantic area.

Development theory loosely grouped Latin America with the "emerging nations" of Asia and Africa under the rubrics of "underdeveloped" or "developing," as distinguished from the "developed" nations of Western Europe and North America. "Developed" states were equated with the notions of "modern," "industrial," and "Western"; conversely, the "underdeveloped world" was characterized as "traditional," "preindustrial," and "non-Western," with its members often referred to as "new nations." Development theory suggested further that underdeveloped states go through a "transitional" process, moving from traditional to modern societies. Some development theorists suggested that certain imperatives of change move societies inexorably through a transitional process toward modernity.

While development theory properly alerted us to the fact that Latin America is fundamentally different from Western Europe and North America, this awareness does not justify an assumption that Latin America is to be equated with Asia and Africa. Much of the Latin American region shares with other regions the challenges of change: It goes through social, economic, and political transformations; experiences frustration associated with economic dependence on the major industrial states; and desires to refrain from involvement in great power rivalries. Crucial and fundamental differences exist, however, between Latin America and the rest of the developing world as well as between the region and the developed nations and within Latin America itself.

The various classifications associated with developing states—new, non-Western, industrializing nations—were highly questionable in the Latin American context. In the first place, Latin America was not composed of "new nations." Most of the Latin American states gained their sovereign independence between 1804 and 1824, well over a century before most Asian and African nations "emerged" into nationhood. Developmental theorists eventually accommodated this obvious reality, but they still tended not to understand the importance of the established traditions of Latin American nationhood. The earlier and different colonial heritage from the rest of the developing world and longer history of independence, combined with a unique sociocultural base, produced a distinct Latin American developmental tradition.

The region is difficult to classify with certainty as either Western or non-Western. The Roman Catholic heritage, European languages, and some other cultural aspects are distinctly Western; but non-Western indigenous American Indian and imported African cultures are interwoven in important patterns. Inasmuch as Spain and Portugal imposed a large degree of their Iberian culture and politics on Latin America, then it can be described as Western; but Spain and Portugal are on the periphery of what is usually studied as Western civilization. Furthermore, the Latin American colonial heritage was different from most of the rest of the developing world.

The level of industrialization varies widely in Latin America. Some states, such as Haiti, Ecuador, Bolivia, and Grenada, might be considered preindustrial. Others, such as Mexico and Argentina, have reached high levels of industrialization, and, most notably, Brazil has constructed a well-diversified and heavily industrialized economy. Furthermore, it does not necessarily follow that every nation with a low industrial level is correspondingly low in social or political modernity, or that industrialized nations are modern in all other respects. Uruguay and Costa Rica, for example, reached modern levels of social organization within representative democratic frameworks while their traditional, agriculture-pastoral, nonindustrial economies persisted.

Some broader methodological problems are associated with development theory. Latin America fits erratically into any theory of unilinear, inexorable movement from traditionalism to modernism. The assumption that there is such a steady progression from the old to the new may be criticized as a form of historicism, the idea of inevitable deterministic "forces of history." It also implies ethnocentrism, the view that developing nations ought to become like the model equating modernism with old, Western, industrialized states. More specifically with regard to Latin America, the region's history reveals no inevitable progression along a traditional-modern continuum. Traditional Latin American political, economic, and social structures have proved remarkably resistant to change.

This view does not deny that political development is susceptible to systematic theoretical explanation, nor does it argue against inter-area comparisons of the developmental process. Rather, it suggests that extant theory is only partially useful. It is inappropriate to append uncritically Latin America onto a theory derived from other experiences. Latin America should be included in the broader perspective of the international political system, but its special place in that system must be recognized in political analysis.

Latin America is an identifiable region and a coherent international subsystem. As a practical policy as well as a theoretical matter, the region deserves attention on its own terms.

Policy Applications

Development theory has provided the basis for a significant portion of U.S. policy in Latin America. U.S. policymakers after World War II assumed that economic growth led to stable democratic societies; many held the view that democracy must be based on a free-enterprise economic system. During the Alliance for Progress period, economic planning combined with social reform was stressed. A further assumption, reflected in aid programs, was that Latin American political violence was linked to poverty and that economic development would deter such political "instability"; development came to be subordinated to "anticommunism." By 1968 and the adoption of the Nixon "low profile" policy, developmentalism was essentially abandoned. It was rediscovered (and amended) by the Reagan administration and provided the initial rationale behind the Caribbean Basin Initiative and some other actions in Central America. Developmentalism also continues to be the favored alternative to coercion in the U.S. debate over Latin American policy, as well as in the advice coming from Europe and Latin America.

A debate over the relationship between foreign economic assistance and political and social change in recipient states has been carried on in the context of development theory. These problems have important implications for U.S. policies, as well as those of other actors such as the European Community and the international lending institutions. Critics of developmentalism have charged that economic aid, either purposely or unwittingly, supports the Latin American status quo rather than stimulating reform. Other analysts suggest that economic aid may lead to violence by breaking down existing social structures. Either connection between economic development and political change seems tenuous. The United States attempted with little success to influence political forms with economic aid; the failure of social experimentation under the Alliance for Progress is primary evidence. A connection doubtless exists between economics and politics, and Latin American economic needs are susceptible to influence from external states; but economic development cannot substitute for political development or compensate for political underdevelopment. Whereas technology and investment capital can be exported to facilitate economic development, the institutions and traditions of representative or social democracy cannot; it seems that political forms must evolve according to national configurations rather than by copying foreign models.

Military Cooperation and Developmentalism

International military cooperation forms a special area of consideration for development theory and policies, particularly in the Latin American context. All Latin American states and their military establishments have depended at some time and to some extent on foreign powers for their military modernization. As with international economic consequences, the effects of international military relations are difficult to determine. It is obvious that external states gain influence when Latin American states rely on them for arms acquisitions, military organizations, and tactics based on the external models. Other areas, however, such as military philosophy and ideology and civil-military relations, are more difficult to measure and to assign causality.

A major debate among decision makers in seller states (especially the United States) and an important domestic issue among certain political groups in Latin America is the question of allocating resources for military expenditures that could be better spent for economic development (however conceived) or applied to a reduction of national expenditures. A related assumption voiced by critics of the arms trade, at least throughout the twentieth century, is that it has stimulated arms races among the regional states. The result may be that domestic political conflict in Latin American politics will intensify and that efforts to reduce those expenditures by external pressures will be futile. That arms purchases are directly related to arms races and the possibilities of armed international conflict has also been debated. A state's purported fear of an external military threat may be an excuse to buy arms for purposes of national military prestige and to maintain a military establishment by professional military men acting in their self-interest.

The political-developmental effects of both military and economic programs have been subject to much criticism. An analytical point of departure concerning foreign military influences in Latin America is the "traditionalist" versus "revisionist" debate. These positions have been equated with "idealism" and "realism," respectively, in the debate over developmentalism and military cooperation. While most of that debate has referred to U.S. influences, similar positions may be assumed regarding the European states in Latin America prior to World War II, particularly those of Germany and France.

The traditional/idealist view links international military relations to the frequent role of the Latin American armed forces as the direct arbiters of domestic politics. It maintains that Latin American military establishments are essentially defenders of the status quo and thwart political, social, and economic development. Furthermore, a number of traditionalist critics of U.S. military assistance programs see a causal relationship between military aid and conservative or reactionary Latin American militarism impeding national development. As a result, these critics claim that there is a positive correlation between military assistance and the increase in or maintenance of Latin American militarism, holding the United States responsible.

The revisionist/realist school holds, contrarily, that the fact of political involvement by Latin American military establishments is an expression, rather than a cause, of underdevelopment, and that the armed forces may be mobilized to perform useful nation-building functions. They claim that the military in Latin America is peculiarly suited to strike a balance between stability and change since they embody a combination of authority and reform-mindedness. Some military regimes themselves have claimed to have abandoned their role as defenders of the status quo and as allies of the upper class against civilian governments who sought reform. Revisionists tend to deny causal relationships between external military assistance and domestic military behavior, stressing internal rather than foreign factors influencing Latin American affairs. Others argue that U.S. military aid has played a positive role in Latin American modernization. Revisionists do not accept the idea that there is a causal relationship between military assistance and militarism.

Revisionists correctly insist that military regimes be viewed as part of the total structure and function of society. Their stress on military regimes as effective instruments of modernization, however, is at least open to question and, in view of the Latin American experience with military regimes over the past two decades, virtually discredited. The "revisionist" U.S. policy adopted in 1963, essentially unchanged until 1976, and revived in Central American policy in the 1980s, especially tends to accept a simplistic faith in the modernizing possibilities of the Latin American military. In the first place, this undifferentiated view ignores that individual officers or groups may and do act in a predatory manner. Second, the recent experience of a number of military governments challenges the assumption that even reform-minded military rule can be an effective instrument for progress; the record so far shows some achievements but mostly only partial success or outright failure. Furthermore, the blatantly repressive nature of certain military regimes flies in the face of developmentalist tenets and supports the traditionalist-idealist view. Especially in Southern Cone politics, concepts of "security" have justified military rationales for domestic intervention and repression.

A shortcoming of both theoretical perspectives, and of state policies based on them, is that they assume the institutional nature of all Latin American armed forces. They see them as organized into a cohesive military establishment and acting as a disciplined corporate entity, either for good or evil. Theories of Latin American civil-military relations must be revised to allow for the reality of "noninstitutionality" in many cases as a continuing rather than transitory state. In these instances, theory must also take into account the consequences of personalities and interpersonal relationships—that is, relations revolving around personal interactions among a chief executive, important military officers, and their key associates, rather than processes involving a bureaucratically well-organized "presidency" and "military establishment."

DEPENDENCY THEORIES

Competing Economic Theories

In the immediate aftermath of World War II, the Economic Commission for Latin America (ECLA) published a comprehensive analysis of economic development in the region. That analysis, inspired especially by the emerging theories of the Argentine economist Raúl Prebisch, marked the formal introduction of structuralist economic theory, which challenged orthodox approaches. It gained increasing favor as a basis for Latin American economic policies until it, too, was challenged and fell out of favor. Nevertheless, continuing into the late 1980s, the theory of structural economic dependency has been at the center of an ongoing debate about the economic aspects of Latin American development and related policies.

As a matter of background, competing Latin American economic development theories should be defined. The "traditional" or "classical" view dated from the middle to the late nineteenth century in most Latin American states. That was the period when Latin American elites began to lead a conscious thrust for economic modernization, usually in alliance with foreign entrepreneurs. Economic development was seen as requiring the attraction of foreign capital by means of cooperation. Modernization, in concert with foreign assistance, was actively encouraged by certain Latin American elites who sought increased wealth for themselves as well as a cultural milieu comparable to that of the world's most prestigious nations. This policy position relates to the "modernist" category of nationalism analyzed in Chapter 3. It continues in the late 1980s in modified form as a school of economic thought sometimes labeled the "neoclassical" model.

An important economic policy debate developed after World War II between "monetarists" and "structuralists." This debate was especially intense in the late 1950s and early 1960s but continues to the present day. Both schools are committed to national development, but they disagree over economic strategies. The two approaches advance different interpretations of the causes of inflation and the scope of government intervention in the economy and have different attitudes toward international trade and foreign investment. The structuralists were the intellectual offspring of Latin American economists, led by the Argentine Raúl Prebisch and including the Mexican Víctor Urquidi and the Brazilian Celso Furtado. Their theories served as the basis for the reformist approach of the United Nations Economic Commission for Latin America (ECLA). A principal spokesman for the monetarists was the Brazilian Roberto Campos; monetarist thinking was and continues to be identified with the orthodox economics championed by the International Monetary Fund, and with multinational business corporations and the governments of most industrialized nations.

The monetarist theory essentially argues that price stability is the main prerequisite for economic growth. Therefore, the major task in Latin American economic development is controlling the inflation that retards long-term investment, undermines wages, leads to labor strikes, and in general inspires social and political instability as well as economic chaos. The principal causes of inflation are expansive monetary and fiscal policies and the increased role of government as the promoter of development through public spending and deficit financing. The monetarist solution is to return to a free-market system by increasing the economic role of the private sector and reducing government intervention. Disciplined monetary policies reducing aggregate demands, such as rejecting large wage demands, restricting credit, raising taxes, and reducing government spending and employment, suffice to reduce inflation. Such austerity programs decrease the demand for consumer goods imports, and reduced domestic consumption increases export supplies, relieving balance-of-payment pressures and increasing the capacity to import capital goods for industrialization. Control of inflation attracts foreign investment, a crucial source of capital for economic development.

Prebisch's structuralist theory visualizes the world economy in terms of a "center-periphery" structure, with industrialized states forming the center and underdeveloped ones the periphery. Underdevelopment, the theory goes, was perpetuated by this structure primarily because the center sold increasingly expensive manufactured goods to the periphery in return for raw materials at increasingly unfavorable terms for underdeveloped markets. The unfair terms of trade, Prebisch said, were a form of colonialism, a dependence escapable only through the industrialization and sustained growth of the peripheral economies. Prebisch advocated prescriptions for economic development on a regional and global scale, involving convergent domestic and international reforms and measures. Internationally, Prebisch advocated that the Latin American states reduce their external dependency through the integration of their economies and that they broaden the size of their markets for local industry and join with other producers of primary exports in commodity agreements limiting supply and increasing the prices received. Prebisch appealed to the center for help in the way of public economic assistance, private investment, and trade preferences; but he emphasized that poor nations must depend primarily on themselves and not rely on external aid. "External cooperation is important," he said, "but only as a means of supplementing and stimulating internal action, not as a substitute for it" (Prebisch, 1970).

Structuralists argue that the causes of Latin American inflation are to be found in economic structural (institutional) rigidities and inelasticities; they conclude that monetary policy alone cannot reduce inflation over the long run or stimulate economic growth. They advocate structural reform of traditional institutions that prove incapable of adjusting to change. While Latin American population growth, industrialization, and urbanization increases the demand for food, the archaic land tenure system (*latifundia*) has not been able to increase the food supply significantly, with inflationary results. The structuralists argue that industrial institutions and foreign trade patterns are also structured so as to increase inflation and retard growth. When imports grew faster than the export of primary mineral and agricultural products, balance-of-payments problems were created.

Structuralists have little faith in monetary policies, saying that austerity retards growth, and they look to government to bring about basic reforms. They advocate agrarian reform and government-supplied credit to modernize agricultural methods; government policies to encourage export diversification, including industrial products; heavy taxes on imported luxury goods and inefficiently utilized land holdings; and more public investment in the capital goods industry. Structuralists recognize the need to import capital in money and kind but argue that Latin America should simultaneously industrialize so as to become less dependent on imports (i.e., pursue import-substitution industrialization policies). They also have been the strongest advocates of economic integration theory.

Neo-Marxist Dependency

A major school of dependency theory employs a generally Marxist frame of reference. In an important sense it is the "radical school" that has offered an array of theories and prescriptions for economic development over the years. Marxist theory goes far beyond the economic parameters described above, however, to construct a general sociopolitical as well as economic theory of international relations. The *dependistas*, as they came to be known, have tended to agree with structuralists that archaic institutions were at the root of underdevelopment, emphasizing that the existing "modern" social sectors exploit national productivity rather than generate it for development. They reject the moderate "reform the system" approach of the structuralists, however, and advocate a socialist revolution. Sometimes referring to themselves as the "true nationalists," radicals would eliminate the existing private agricultural system, institute state ownership of large industries, and either exclude foreign investment or allow it to operate only under the strictest controls. In the 1980s they called for renunciation of the foreign debt or for greatly reduced service payments. Radical solutions have been attempted by several different Latin American regimes, including the violent revolution by Castro in Cuba, the elected Marxist government of Salvador Allende in Chile, and the military socialist juntas in Peru and Bolivia; the Sandinista government in Nicaragua and the APRA government in Peru also advocate and in some ways are able to pursue such policies. Neo-Marxist dependency theory is also subscribed to by most Liberation Theologists.

A basic premise of the dependistas is that Latin American economic development has been determined by the interests and activities of external capitalist states and multinational corporations (MNCs) operating in the world capitalist market; Latin American economies are dependent because they are conditioned by external capitalist forces over which they have little control. Economic dependence is seen as an inevitable result of international capitalist politics. Foreign investment, a corollary to the expansionist tendencies of capitalist economies, especially in the United States, is invariably detrimental to the recipient. The dependency relationship ultimately is conflictual, according to this dependency theory, and in this sense the theory largely restates the Leninist theory of imperialism. Conflict is said to be caused by the search by industrial capitalist societies for raw materials, insufficiently supplied at home, and for outlets for manufactured products and capital, which are in an overabundance at home.

Economic dependence is said to have had a profound effect on internal Latin American economies—stagnation, unemployment, income inequality, and disequilibrium are seen as directly related to the underdeveloped state's subordinate position under the dominant capitalist states and MNCs. These economic effects in turn help shape social and political structures as well. International inequalities retard domestic economic development, consequently weakening power bases for the establishment of egalitarian social policies. Some dependency theorists speak of "internal colonialism" within Latin American nations, whereby resources are continuously transferred away from majority underdeveloped social sectors to the minority advanced sector. The latter is linked to foreign capitalists and the international capitalist economy, thus intensifying unequal internal distribution of income and social rewards. Dependistas further argue that external military relationships are responsible for Latin American militarism.

In sum, dependency theory posits a dependent condition in which Latin American states are subject to decisions made from abroad and to unfair competitive forces in international markets. This condition results in the intensification of economic monoculturalism and a widening gap between rich and poor nations and between classes within Latin American societies. It leads to national disintegration characterized by military regimes supporting oligarchic or bourgeois interests.

Structural dependency theory shares several premises with the neo-Marxist school, but they differ in fundamental respects. The structuralist solution to underdevelopment is found in policies of import substitution (encouraging local industry to produce goods replacing those purchased from external sources) and economic integration (widening markets for locally produced goods and increasing Latin American bargaining power with the rest of the world). Neo-Marxist theorists reject the structuralist assumption that Latin America can institute such a developmental process, arguing that underdevelopment is not a precapitalist condition but a consequence of capitalism and part of the global capitalist economy. They are particularly critical of import-substitution policies, arguing that such actions have not freed the periphery from the center but instead have deepened patterns of dependence.

Many other Marxist theorists implicitly reject the idea of dependencia. For example, studies over the past two decades by Marxist scholars at the Institute of Latin American Studies at the Academy of Sciences of the USSR (Moscow) emphasize the growing independence of many Latin American states from U.S. domination. This position is ideologically consistent with Leninism, as anti-imperialism must assume that independence is possible. It is also consonant with present conservative (cautious) Soviet policies that emphasize diplomacy with Latin American states rather than subversion.

Critics (myself among them) challenge the assumptions of dependency theory. Critics may acknowledge that the theory contains a large element of truth, but they argue that it contains major logical and empirical fallacies. They challenge the assertions that economic dependence is a necessary consequence of capitalist economies and that private foreign investment in Latin America invariably is exploitive. Critics point out that powerful states, whether capitalist or noncapitalist, always have imposed economic dependence on weaker ones. They further note that dependency theorists ignore the possibility of Cuba's economic dependency on the Soviet Union and confine their observations to relationships dominated by capitalist powers (Ray, 1973). We may also call attention to cleavages within Latin America, where relatively weaker states complain of domination by the stronger ones. For example, such claims were common among the majority of members of the Latin American Free Trade Association against their colleagues Mexico, Brazil, and Argentina. This position has also been taken by local buffer states in the Southern Cone balance-of-power system, which has little to do with the world capitalist economy. Within the region, the basis for dependency is not capitalism but a disparity of power in which weak actors are vulnerable to exploitation in whatever kind of markets they operate.

Another important criticism of dependency theory is that it tends to ignore or obscure alternative policies that can significantly reduce dependency. For example, they may expropriate foreign investment or regulate it more in accordance with their interests, or they may associate through economic integration, commodity agreements, and other international accords to max-imize their bargaining power. These alternatives, in fact, have increasingly characterized the main foreign policy efforts of the regional actors over the past quarter-century.

The idea of inevitable dependency through foreign investments seems to oversimplify highly complex relationships. Foreign investment has had widely varying effects on Latin American development, some detrimental and others beneficial. This position is supported by Hunter and Foley (1975), who conclude, among other things, that foreign investment has helped to transfer technology from more advanced nations to Latin America and permitted higher economic growth rates in the region than would otherwise exist. The bulk of investment, however, has been attracted to the more advanced Latin American economies rather than the poorer ones in more need of help, and investments in extractive industries, by their nature, have contributed little to Latin American economic growth.

Marxist-Leninists have viewed business enterprise as a front or agent for capitalist states or as having a symbiotic relationship working in concert with those states rather than as autonomous system actors. A different view was presented in December 1971 by Salvador Allende, then the Marxist president of Chile. At the UN General Assembly, while condemning the subversive intervention by ITT in Chilean political affairs, Allende said this: "We are witnessing a pitched battle between the great corporations and sovereign states, for the latter's fundamental political and military decisions are being interfered with by worldwide organizations which are not dependent on any single state and which are not accountable to or regulated by any parliament or institution representing the collective interest."

Dependency theory also addresses the consequences of international military cooperation. The arms trade does not necessarily involve a political function if it is viewed by the actors strictly as a commercial transaction. If Latin American industries are unable to produce equipment, arms, and munitions in sufficient quantity or to provide updated models and spare parts, the Latin American armed services may become dependent on foreign manufacturers. The relative independence in military affairs on the part of major states, especially Brazil and significantly by Argentina and Chile, indicates that dependency may be broken by local policy efforts despite the wishes of outside suppliers.

The impact of one military establishment on the institutions of another is not necessarily the most important consequence of military interaction. The professional level achieved by the regional armed forces has varied widely, as they first copied European military establishments, especially French and German ones, and later that of the United States. The various external styles were reflected in Latin American military organization, training and educational methods, strategy and tactics, and arms acquisitions. This observation is superficial, however, if the impact is not of political consequence. It is not enough to observe, for example, that one or another Latin American army adopted French, German, or U.S. training methods or organizational schemes and then conclude that an influential linkage exists. Imitation may be manifested only in appearances, with actual military behavior taking place that is alien to the external model. For example, the Prussian General Staff system was emulated by most Latin American states between 1890 and World War II. Yet it was also almost universally adopted around the globe by Germany's friends and enemies alike and even by its major rivals for influence in Latin America (France and the United States). Logically, the adoption of the German staff system did not necessarily indicate direct German political influence in Latin America (or anywhere else). Likewise, since World War II, most Latin American states have imitated the U.S. Department of Defense and armed forces organization, but differing relations have existed with the United States, and there have been varying patterns of civil-military relations within Latin America as well. The analyst must attempt to ascertain how far imitation of external military systems has led to substantive attitudes by Latin American military men toward their civil-military relations.

Established trends in external military aid and Latin American militarism—that is, the decade-and-a-half rise in military dominance of Latin America despite a sharp decrease in U.S. government assistance from the mid-1960s to the late 1970s—present an incongruity for dependency theory and the traditionalist critique. Irving Louis Horowitz (1977) concluded that if theories of dependency had been cited to explain Latin American militarism, we might well have anticipated a sharp reduction rather than a pronounced increase in militarization. Horowitz argued that Latin American militarism is not so much a function of either dependency or developmentalism as it is a response to the inner history and military dynamics of the hemisphere and specific national conditions. Although neither dependency nor developmental perspectives are entirely removed from the realities of hemispheric conditions, it is clear that Latin American militarism should not be perceived as a mechanical response to foreign pressures, especially when such pressures move counter to observable trends.

BIBLIOGRAPHIC COMMENT

Little has been written on the realist-idealist dichotomy with reference to Latin America from a theoretical point of view. Khachaturov (1982) provides a very brief Marxist comment on imperialist ideology and Latin America.

General aspects of developmentalism and dependency are treated by several authors. Fishlow (1985) gives an excellent summary of the content and status of international economic theory and political practice in Latin America since World War II. Mansilla (1985) tackles the amorphous subject of defining Latin America as part of the Third World, emphasizing the ambivalent character of dependency and other theories. Wiarda (1985) contains provocative essays on the various developmental and dependency theories with significant references to Latin America. See essays by Martz (1966), Stepan (1966), and Douglas Chalmers and Philippe Schmitter in Chalmers (1972) for early insightful critiques of political development theory by Latin American specialists. Wiarda (1982) makes a strong case for a distinct Latin American developmental tradition. See reviews of the literature and changing concepts of the role of the armed forces in Latin American politics by Atkins (1974), McAlister (1966), Rankin (1974), and Roett and Tierney (1971). On the consequences of military programs, see Kemp (1970) and Putnam (1967); Fitch (1979) is excellent on the political impact of U.S. military aid to Latin America. Heller (1978) and Remmer (1978) provide balanced assessments of U.S. military policies. For the developmental views of an important monetarist, see the works of Campos, and for the positions of influential structuralists, see the writings of Prebisch and Urquidi. Krieger Vasena and Pasos (1973) represent traditionalism.

Frank (1967, 1969, 1972) was the pioneer *dependista* to extend the theory to include sociopolitical outcomes. Other neo-Marxist dependency theory as it applies to Latin America is advocated by Bodenheimer (1971), Cardoso and Faletto (1969, 1979), Cockroft, Frank, and Johnson (1972), Santos (1970), and Szymanski (1981); Bodenheimer, Chirote, and Szymanski especially address Latin American foreign policy-making in terms of economic dependence. Some essential later corrections are made by Bollen (1983) and Thomas (1984). More general works on dependency theory, including analyses and criticism, are by Bonilla and Girling (1973), Chilcote and Edelstein (1974), and Ocampo et al. (1976). Ray (1973) and T. Smith (1979) are cogent critiques of dependency theory.

References

Acheson, Dean (1966). "Dean Acheson's Version of Robert Kennedy's Version of the Cuban Missile Affair." *Esquire,* 71 (February): 76–77.

Agee, Philip (1975). *Inside the Company: CIA Diary.* Harmondsworth, England: Penguin.

Agor, Weston H., and Andres Suárez (1972). "The Emerging Latin American Political Subsystem." *Proceedings of the Academy of Political Science,* 30 (August): 153–166.

Aguilar, Luis E. (ed.) (1968). *Marxism in Latin America.* New York: Alfred A. Knopf.

ALADI [Asociación Latinoamericana de Integración] (1980). *La Asociación Latinoamericana de Integración: Un Análisis Comparativo.* Buenos Aires: Secretaría General de ALADI.

Alba, Victor (1968). *Politics and the Labor Movement in Latin America.* Stanford, Calif.: Stanford University Press.

Alexander, Robert J. (1963). *Communism in Latin America.* New Brunswick, N.J.: Rutgers University Press.

Alexander, Robert J. (1965). *Organized Labour in Latin America.* New York: The Free Press.

Alexander, Robert J. (1973). *Trotskyism in Latin America.* Stanford, Calif.: Hoover Institution.

Allison, Graham T. (1971). *Essence of Decision: Explaining the Cuban Missile Crisis.* Boston: Little, Brown.

Alvarado Garaicoa, Teodora (1968). *El Dominio del Mar.* Guayaquil, Ecuador: Universidad de Guayaquil.

Alvarez, Alejandro (1907). *Chile ante la segunda conferencia de la Haya.* Santiago de Chile: n.p.

Alvarez, Alejandro (1922). *International Law and Related Subjects from the Point of View of the American Continent.* Washington: Carnegie Endowment for International Peace.

Alvarez, Alejandro (1924). *The Monroe Doctrine: Its Importance in the International Life of the States of the New World.* New York: Oxford University Press.

Ameringer, Charles D. (1974). *The Democratic Left in Exile: The Anti-Dictatorial Struggle in the Caribbean, 1945–1959.* Coral Gables, Fla.: University of Miami Press.

Amuchástegui Astrada, Armando (1980). *Argentina-Chile: Controversia y Mediación.* Buenos Aires: Ediciones Ghersi.

Anderson, Thomas P. (1981). *The War of the Dispossessed: Honduras and El Salvador, 1969.* Lincoln: University of Nebraska Press.

Anguiano Roch, Eugenio (1980). "China: La Política de Cooperación con el Tercer Mundo." *Estudios de Asia y Africa* (México), 15 (July-September): 515–570.

Area, Leandro (1984). *El Golfo de Venezuela: Documentación y Cronología*. Caracas: Universidad de Venezuela.

Arnáiz y Freg, Arturo, and Claude Bataillon (eds.) (1965). *La Intervención Francesa y el Império de Maximiliano*. México: Asociación Mexicana de Historiadores.

Arze Q., Eduardo et al. (1984). *Doctrina y Política Internacionales de Bolivia*. Cochabamba: Instituto de Estudios Internacionales, Universidád Mayor de San Simón.

Ashley, Timothy (1987). *The Bear in the Back Yard: Moscow's Caribbean Strategy*. Lexington: Lexington Books.

Atkins, G. Pope (1974). "The Armed Forces in Latin American Politics," in Charles Cochran (ed.), *Civil-Military Relations*. New York: The Free Press.

Atkins, G. Pope (1984). "Diplomacy in the South Atlantic Crisis," in Jack W. Hopkins (ed.), *Latin America and Caribbean Contemporary Record*, vol. 2. New York: Holmes & Meier: 22–23.

Atkins, G. Pope, and Larman C. Wilson (1972). *The United States and the Trujillo Regime*. New Brunswick, N.J.: Rutgers University Press.

Audera, Victor (1955). *La Población y la Inmigración en Hispano-América*. Madrid: Ediciones Cultura Hispánica.

Avery, William P., and James D. Cochrane (1973). "Innovation in Latin American Regionalism: The Andean Common Market." *International Organization*, 27 (Spring): 181–223.

Axline, W. Andrew (1979). *Caribbean Integration: The Politics of Regionalism*. London: Francis Pinter.

Ayearst, Morley (1960). *The British West Indies*. New York: New York University Press.

Baerresen, Donald, Martin Carnoy, and Joseph Grunwald (1965). *Latin American Trade Patterns*. Washington, D.C.: Brookings Institution.

Bagley, Bruce M. (ed.) (1987). *Contadora and the Diplomacy of Peace in Central America*, 2 vols. Boulder: Westview.

Bagley, Bruce M. (1988). "Winning Battles, Losing the War: U.S. Anti-Drug Policies in Latin America." *Hemisphere*, 1 (Fall): 31–34.

Bagú, Sergio (1961). *Argentina en el Mundo*. México: Fondo de Cultura Económica.

Bailey, Norman A. (1967). *Latin America in World Politics*. New York: Walker.

Baily, Samuel L. (ed.) (1971). *Nationalism in Latin America*. New York: Knopf.

Baily, Samuel L. (1976). *The United States and the Development of South America, 1945–1975*. New York: New Viewpoints.

Bambirra, Vania et al. (1971). *Diez Años de Insurrección en América Latina*. Santiago de Chile: Ediciones Prensa Latino-americana.

Barber, Willard F., and C. Neale Ronning (1966). *Internal Security and Military Power: Counterinsurgency and Civic Action in Latin America*. Columbus: Ohio State University Press.

Barclay, Glen St. John (1971). *Struggle for a Continent: The Diplomatic History of South America, 1917–1945*. London: Whitefriars.

Barnet, Richard S., and Ronald E. Muller (1975). *Global Reach: The Power of the Multinational Corporations*. New York: Simon & Schuster.

Barrera Valverde, Alfonso (1982). *Hombres de Paz en Lucha*, 2 vols. Quito: Ediciones J.L.I.

Baster, A.S.J. (1935). *The International Banks*. London: P. S. King.

Bastos de Avila, Fernando (1964). *La Inmigración en América Latina*. Washington, D.C.: Pan American Union.

Bates, Margaret J. (ed.) (1957). *The Migration of Peoples to Latin America*. Washington, D.C.: Catholic University of America.

Behrman, Jack N. (1972). *The Role of International Companies in Latin America*. Lexington, Mass.: Lexington Books.

Bejar, Héctor (1970). *Peru 1965: Notes on a Guerrilla Experience*. New York: Monthly Review.

Beltrán, Luís Ramiro, and Elizabeth Fox de Cardona (1980). *Comunicación Dominada: Estados Unidos en los Medios de América Latina*. México: Instituto Latinoamericano de Estudios Transnacionales.

Bemis, Samuel Flagg (1943). *The Latin American Policy of the United States*. New York: Harcourt Brace.

Bender, Lynn D. (1974). *The Politics of Hostility: Castro's Revolution and U.S. Policy*. San Juan: Inter-American University.

Bernstein, Harry (1961). *Making an Inter-American Mind*. Gainesville: University of Florida Press.

Bernstein, Marvin (ed.) (1966). *Foreign Investment in Latin America*. New York: Knopf.

Berryman, Philip (1987). *Liberation Theology: Essential Facts About the Revolutionary Religious Movement in Latin America and Beyond*. Philadelphia: Temple University Press.

Beverina, Juan (1921–1933). *La Guerra del Paraguay*, 7 vols. Buenos Aires: Estab. Graf. Ferrari Hnos.

Bhana, Surendra (1975). *The United States and the Development of the Puerto Rican Status Question, 1936–1968*. Lawrence: University Press of Kansas.

Bianchi, Andres, Robert Devlin, and Joseph Ramos (1985). *External Debt in Latin America: Adjustment Policies and Renegotiation*. Boulder: Lynne Rienner Publishers.

Blachman, Morris J., William M. Leogrande, and Kenneth E. Sharpe (eds.) (1986). *Confronting Revolution: Security Through Diplomacy in Central America*. New York: Pantheon Books.

Blakemore, Harold (1984). *Central American Crisis: Challenge to U.S. Diplomacy*; monograph supplement to *Conflict Studies* (London).

Blanco, Hugo (1972). *Land or Death: The Peasant Struggle in Peru*. Trans. N. Allen. New York: Pathfinder.

Blasier, Cole (1985). *The Hovering Giant: U.S. Responses to Revolutionary Change in Latin America*, rev. ed. Pittsburgh: University of Pittsburgh Press.

Blasier, Cole (1988). *The Giant's Rival: The USSR and Latin America*, rev. ed. Pittsburgh: University of Pittsburgh Press.

Blasier, Cole, and Carmelo Mesa-Lago (eds.) (1979). *Cuba in the World*. Pittsburgh: University of Pittsburgh Press.

Bode, William R. (1986). "The Reagan Doctrine." *Strategic Review* (Winter): 21–29.

Bodenheimer, Susanne (1971). *The Ideology of Developmentalism: The American Paradigm-Surrogate for Latin American Studies*. Beverly Hills, Calif.: Sage.

Boersner, Demetrio (1982). *Relaciones Internacionales de América Latina: Breve Historia*. Caracas: Nueva Sociedád.

Boff, Leonardo (1985). *Church Charisma and Power: Liberation Theology and the Institutional Church*. New York: Crossroad.

Bollen, K. (1983). "World System Position, Dependency, and Democracy: The Cross-National Evidence." *American Sociological Review*, 48 (August): 468–479.

Bonachea, Ramón L., and Marta San Martín (1974). *The Cuban Insurrection, 1952–1959*. New Brunswick, N.J.: Transaction.

Bonachea, Rolando E., and Nelson P. Valdes (eds.) (1972a). *Cuba in Revolution.* Garden City, N.Y.: Anchor.

Bonachea, Rolando E., and Nelson P. Valdes (eds.) (1972b). *Revolutionary Struggle, 1947–1958, by Fidel Castro.* Cambridge, Mass.: MIT Press.

Bond, Robert D. (ed.) (1977). *Contemporary Venezuela and Its Role in International Affairs.* New York: New York University Press.

Bonilla, Frank, and Robert Girling (ed.) (1973). *Structures of Dependency.* Stanford, Calif.: Stanford University Press.

Bonsal, Philip W. (1971). *Cuba, Castro, and the United States.* Pittsburgh: University of Pittsburgh Press.

Box, Pelham H. (1929). *The Origins of the Paraguayan War.* Urbana: University of Illinois Press.

Boyd, Gavin (ed.) (1984). *Regionalism and Global Security.* Lexington: Lexington Books.

Branch, Taylor, and Eugene M. Popper (1982). *Labyrinth.* New York: The Viking Press.

Braunthal, Julius (1967–1980). *History of the International,* vol. 1, 1864–1914, New York: Praeger; vol. 2, 1914–1943, New York: Praeger; vol. 3, 1943–1968, Boulder: Westview.

Braveboy-Wagner, Jacqueline Anne (1984). *The Venezuelan-Guyana Border Dispute: Britain's Colonial Legacy in Latin America.* Boulder: Westview.

Braveboy-Wagner, Jacqueline (1986). *The Caribbean in World Affairs: The Foreign Policy of the English-Speaking States.* Boulder: Westview.

Brigagão, C. (1986). "The Brazilian Arms Industry." *Journal of International Affairs,* 40 (Summer): 101–114.

Brown, Cynthia (ed.) (1985). *With Friends Like These: The Americas Watch Report on Human Rights and U.S. Policy in Latin America.* New York: Pantheon.

Bryan, Anthony T. (ed.) (1986). *The Organization of American States and the Commonwealth Caribbean: Perspectives on Security, Crisis and Reform.* St. Augustine: University of the West Indies, Institute of International Relations.

Buergenthal, Thomas, Robert E. Norris, and Dinah Shelton (1983). *Protecting Human Rights in the Americas.* San José: Editorial Juricentro.

Bulnes, Gonzalo (1955). *Guerra del Pacífico,* 2d ed., 3 vols. Santiago de Chile: Editorial del Pacífico.

Burns, E. Bradford (1987). *At War in Nicaragua: The Reagan Doctrine and the Politics of Nostalgia.* New York: Harper & Row.

Burr, Robert N. (1967a). *By Reason or Force: Chile and the Balancing of Power in South America, 1830–1905.* Berkeley: University of California Press.

Burr, Robert N. (1967b). *Our Troubled Hemisphere: Perspectives on United States–Latin American Relations.* Washington, D.C.: Brookings Institution.

Bywater, Hector C. (1925). *The Great Pacific War.* Boston: Houghton Mifflin.

Cady, John F. (1929). *Foreign Intervention in the Rio de la Plata, 1838–1850.* Philadelphia: University of Pennsylvania Press.

Caicedo Castilla, José Joaquín (1970). *El Derecho Internacional en el Sistema Interamericano.* Madrid: Ed. Cultura Hispánica.

Calder, Bruce J. (1984), *The Impact of Intervention: The Dominican Republic During the U.S. Occupation of 1916–1924.* Austin: University of Texas Press.

Cale, Edward G. (1969). *Latin American Free Trade Association.* Washington, D.C.: Department of State.

Callcott, Wilfred Hardy (1968). *The Western Hemisphere: Its Influence on United States Policies to the End of World War II.* Austin: University of Texas Press.

Campos, Roberto de Oliveira (1963). *Economia, Planejamento e Nacionalismo*. Rio de Janeiro: APEC Editora.

Campos, Roberto de Oliveira (1967). *Reflections on Latin American Development*. Austin: University of Texas Press.

Campos, Roberto de Oliveira (1976). *O Mundo que Vejo e Não Desejo*. Rio de Janeiro: Livraria José Olympio Editora.

Cantori, Louis J., and Steven L. Spiegel (eds.) (1970). *The International Politics of Regions*. Englewood Cliffs, N.J.: Prentice-Hall.

Canyes Santacana, Manuel (1963). *The Organization of American States and the United Nations*, 6th ed. Washington, D.C.: Pan American Union.

Cárcano, Ramón J. (1939–1942). *Guerra del Paraguay*, 2 vols. Buenos Aires: Ed. Domingo Viau.

Cardoso, F. H., and Enzo Faletto (1969). *Dependéncia y Desarrollo en América Latina*. México: Siglo XXI Editores. English trans. (1979). *Dependency and Development in Latin America*. Berkeley: University of California Press.

Carey, James C. (1964). *Peru and the United States, 1900–1962*. Notre Dame, Ind.: University of Notre Dame Press.

Cardenal, Ernesto (1976–1982). *The Gospel in Solentiname*. 4 vols. New York: Orbis.

Carnegie Endowment for International Peace (1931). *The International Conferences of American States, 1889–1928*. Ed. James Brown Scott. Washington, D.C.

Carnegie Endowment for International Peace (1940). *The International Conferences of American States: First Supplement, 1933–1940*. Washington, D.C.

Carnegie Endowment for International Peace (1943). *Conferencias Internacionales Americanas: Primer Suplemento, 1938–1942*. Washington, D.C.

Carneiro, David (1946). *Historia da Guerra Cisplatina*. São Paulo: Ed. Nacional.

Carvalho, Delgado de (1959). *Historia Diplomática do Brasil*. São Paulo: Companhia Editora Nacional.

Castañeda, Jorge (1956). *México y del Orden Internacional*. México: El Colégio de México.

Castillero Pimentel, Ernesto (1961). *Política Exterior de Panamá*. Panamá: Impresora Panamá.

Cavelier, Germán (1960). *La Política Internacional de Colombia*, 2d ed., 4 vols. Bogotá: Editorial Iqueima.

CEPAL [Comisión Ecónomica para América Latina] (1982). *Relaciones Económicos de América Latina con los Países Miembros del Consejo de Asistencia Mutua Económica (CAME)*. Santiago: Naciones Unidas.

Cepeda Ulloa, Fernando, y Rodrigo Pardo García-Peña (1985). *Contadora: Desafío a la Diplomacia Tradicional*. Lima: Centro de Estudios Internacionales de la Universidad de Los Andes.

Chalmers, Douglas A. (ed.) (1972). *Changing Latin America: New Interpretations of Its Politics and Society*. Philadelphia: Proceedings of the Academy of Political Science, vol. 30.

Chayes, Abram (1974). *The Cuban Missile Crisis*. New York: Oxford University Press.

Chilcote, Ronald, and Joel Edelstein (eds.) (1974). *Latin America: The Struggle with Dependency and Beyond*. New York: Halsted.

Child, John (1979a). "From 'Color' to 'Rainbow': U.S. Strategic Planning for Latin America, 1919–1945." *Journal of Inter-American Studies and World Affairs*, 21 (May): 233–260.

Child, John (1979b). "Geopolitical Thinking in Latin America." *Latin American Research Review*, 14 (no. 2): 89–111.

Child, John (1980a). "Strategic Concepts of Latin America: An Update." *Inter-American Economic Affairs* (Summer): 61–82.

Child, John (1980b). *Unequal Alliance: The Inter-American Military System 1938–1978*. Boulder: Westview.

Child, Jack (1985). *Geopolitics and Conflict in South America: Quarrels Among Neighbors*. New York: Praeger.

Child, Jack (1988). *Antarctica and South American Geopolitics: Frozen Lebensraum*. New York: Praeger.

Cisneros-Lavaller, Alberto (1982). "Old Wine in New Bottles: An Essay on the Study of Inter-American Relations." *The New Scholar*, 8: 267–288.

Clark, J. Reuben (1930). "Memorandum on the Monroe Doctrine." Washington, D.C.: Department of State.

Clark, Truman R. (1975). *Puerto Rico and the United States, 1917–1933*. Pittsburgh: University of Pittsburgh Press.

Cline, Howard F. (1963). *The United States and Mexico*, rev. ed. Cambridge, Mass.: Harvard University Press.

Clissold, Stephen (ed.) (1970). *Soviet Relations with Latin America, 1918–68: A Documentary Survey*. London: Oxford University Press.

Cochran, Charles L. (1968). "The Development of an Inter-American Policy for the Recognition of De Facto Governments." *American Journal of International Law*, 62 (April): 460–464.

Cochrane, James D. (1969). *The Politics of Regional Integration: The Central American Case*. New Orleans: Tulane University Press.

Cochrane, James D. (1972). "U.S. Policy Toward Recognition of Governments and Promotion of Democracy in Latin America Since 1963." *Journal of Latin American Studies*, 4 (November): 275–291.

Cockcroft, James D., Andre Gunder Frank, and Dale L. Johnson (1972). *Dependence and Underdevelopment: Latin America's Political Economy*. Garden City, N.Y.: Anchor.

Cohen Orantes, Isaac (1972). *Regional Integration in Central America*. Lexington, Mass.: Lexington Books.

Conil Paz, Alberto A., and Gustavo E. Ferrari (1966). *Argentina's Foreign Policy, 1930–1962*. Trans. Joseph J. Kennedy. Notre Dame: University of Notre Dame Press.

Connell-Smith, Gordon (1966). *The Inter-American System*. London: Oxford University Press.

Connell-Smith, Gordon (1974). *The United States and Latin America*. New York: Halsted.

Considine, John J. (1964). *The Church in the New Latin America*. Notre Dame: University of Notre Dame Press.

Corkran, Herbert (1972). *Patterns of International Cooperation in the Caribbean, 1942–1969*. Dallas: Southern Methodist University Press.

Corominas, Enrique V. (1954). *In the Caribbean Political Arenas*. Trans. L. C. Foresti. Cambridge: Cambridge University Press.

Council of the Americas (1973). *The Andean Pact*. New York.

Craig, Richard (1981a). "Operación Intercepción: Una Política de Presion Internacional." *Foro Internacional*, 22 (October/December): 203–230.

Craig, Richard B. (1981b). "Colombian Narcotics and United States–Colombian Relations." *Journal of Inter-American Studies and World Affairs*, 23 (August): 243–270.

Craig, Richard B. (1983). "Domestic Implications of Illicit Colombian Drug Production and Trafficking." *Journal of International Studies and World Affairs*, 25 (August): 325–350.

Craig, Richard B. (1985). "Illicit Drug Traffic and U.S.–Latin American Relations." *Washington Quarterly*, 8 (Fall): 105–124.

Crane, Philip M. (1978). *Surrender in Panama: the Case Against the Treaty*. New York: Dale Books.

Cuevas Cancino, Francisco M. (1954). *Roosevelt y la Buena Vecinidad*. Mexico: Fondo de Cultura Economica.

Cuevas Cancino, Francisco M. (1955). *Del Congreso de Panamá a la Conferencia de Caracas, 1826–1954*, 2 vols. Caracas: Ragon.

Cummins, Lejune (1958). *Quijote on a Burro: Sandino and the Marines, A Study in the Formulation of Foreign Policy*. México: Imp. Azteca.

Cunha, Pedro Penner da (1977). *A Diplomacia da Paz: Rui Barbosa em Haia*. Rio de Janeiro: Ministerio de Educacao e Cultura.

Davis, Harold E., Larman C. Wilson, and others (1975). *Latin American Foreign Policies*. Baltimore: Johns Hopkins University Press.

Davis, Harold Eugene, John J. Finan, and F. Taylor Peck (1977). *Latin American Diplomatic History: An Introduction*. Baton Rouge: Louisiana State University Press.

Davis, William C. (1950). *The Last Conquistadores: The Spanish Intervention in Peru and Chile, 1863–1866*. Athens: University of Georgia Press.

Debray, Regis (1967). *Revolution in the Revolution? Armed Struggle and Political Struggle in Latin America*. New York: Monthly Review.

Debray, Regis (1970). *Strategy for Revolution*. New York: Monthly Review.

Debray, Regis (1976). *Che's Guerrilla War*. Harmondsworth: Penguin.

Dell, Sidney (1972). *The Inter-American Bank*. New York: Praeger.

Dennis, William J. (1931). *Tacna and Arica*. New Haven, Conn.: Yale University Press.

Deutsch, Karl W. (1988). *The Analysis of International Relations*, 3d ed. Englewood Cliffs, N.J.: Prentice-Hall.

Díaz, Luís Miguel (1983). *Historia de las Relaciones Internacionales de México*. México, D.F.: Editorial Poirúa.

Díaz Albonico, Rodrigo (ed.) (1977). *Antecedentes, Balance y Perspectivas del Sistema Interamericano*. Santiago: Editorial Universitaria.

Díaz-Alejandro, C. (1977), "Foreign Investment by Latin Americans," in T. Agmon and C. P. Kindleberger (eds.), *Multinationals from Small Countries*. Cambridge: MIT Press.

Dinerstein, Herbert S. (1967). "Soviet Policy in Latin America." *American Political Science Review*, 61 (March): 80–90.

Dinerstein, Herbert S. (1976). *The Making of a Missile Crisis: October 1962*. Baltimore: Johns Hopkins University Press.

Dinges, John, and Saul Landau (1980). *Assassination on Embassy Row*. New York: Pantheon Books.

Domínguez, Jorge I. (1978). "Consensus and Divergence: The State of the Literature on Inter-American Relations in the 1970s." *Latin American Research Review*, 13 (no. 1): 87–126.

Domínguez, Jorge (1982). *Cuba: Internal and International Affairs*. Beverly Hills: Sage.

Dozer, Donald M. (1966). "Recognition in Contemporary Inter-American Relations." *Journal of Inter-American Studies*, 8 (April): 318–335.

Draper, Theodore (1965). *Castroism: Theory and Practice*. New York: Praeger.

Draper, Theodore (1968). *The Dominican Revolt*. New York: Commentary.

Draper, Theodore (1971). "The Dominican Intervention Reconsidered." *Political Science Quarterly*, 86 (March): 136.

Drekonja K., Gerhard and Juan G. Tokatlian (eds.) (1983). *Teoría y Práctica de la Política Exterior Latinoamericana*. Bogotá: Universidad de los Andes.

Duff, Ernest, and John McCamant (1976). *Violence and Repression in Latin America*. New York: The Free Press.

Duncan, W. Raymond (1985). *The Soviet Union and Cuba: Interests and Influence*. New York: Praeger.

Duran, Esperanza (1985). *European Interests in Latin America*. London: Routledge and Kegan Paul for the Royal Institute of International Affairs.

Ealy, Lawrence O. (1971). *Yanqui Politics and the Isthmian Canal*. University Park: Pennsylvania State University Press.

Eaton, David J. (1987). *The State of the Rio Grande/Rio Bravo: A Study of Water Resource Issues Along the Texas/Mexico Border*. Tucson: University of Arizona Press.

Economic Commission for Latin America and the Caribbean (ECLAC) (1985). *External Debt in Latin America: Adjustment Policies and Renegotiation*. Boulder: Lynne Rienner Publishers.

Economic Commission for Latin America and the Caribbean (ECLAC) (1986). *Debt, Adjustment, and Renegotiation in Latin America: Orthodox and Alternative Approaches*. Boulder: Lynne Rienner Publishers.

Edwards, Augustín (1937). *La América Latina y la Liga de las Naciones*. Santiago de Chile: Editorial Universitaria.

Eells, Richard (1976). *Global Corporations: The Emerging System of World Economic Power*, rev. ed. New York: The Free Press.

Enríquez Coyro, Ernesto (1975/1976). *El Tratado entre México y los Estados Unidos de América sobre Ríos Internacionales*, 2 vols. México: Universidad Nacional Autónoma.

Epstein, Fritz T. (1941). *European Military Influences in Latin America*. Microfilm. Washington, D.C.: Library of Congress.

Erisman, H. Michael (1985). *Cuba's International Relations: The Anatomy of a Nationalistic Foreign Policy*. Boulder: Westview.

Erisman, Michael, and John D. Martz (eds.) (1982). *Colossus Challenged: The Struggle for Caribbean Influence*. Boulder: Westview.

Escobari Cusicanqui, Jorge (1975). *Historia Diplomática de Bolivia: Política Internacional*, 2d ed. La Paz: Litografías e Imprentas Unidas.

Estigarribia, José Felix (1950). *The Epic of the Chaco: Marshal Estigarribia's Memoirs of the Chaco War, 1932–1935*. Ed. Pablo Max Ynsfran. Austin: University of Texas Press.

Etheredge, Lloyd S. (1985). *Can Governments Learn? American Foreign Policy and Central American Revolutions*. New York: Pergamon Press.

Evanson, Robert K. (1985). "Soviet Political Uses of Trade with Latin America." *Journal of Inter-American Studies and World Affairs*, 27 (no. 2): 99–127.

Falcoff, Mark, and Robert Royal (eds.) (1987). *The Continuing Crisis: U.S. Policy in Central America and the Caribbean*. Washington, D.C.: The Ethics and Public Policy Center.

Falk, Richard A., and Saul H. Mendlovitz (eds.) (1973). *Regional Politics and World Order*. San Francisco: W. H. Freeman.

Farer, Tom J. (1981). "Reagan's Latin American Policy." *The New York Review of Books*, 28 (March 19): 10–15.

Feinberg, Richard E. (ed.) (1982). *Central America: International Dimensions of the Crisis*. New York: Holmes & Meier.

Feis, Herbert (1950). *The Diplomacy of the Dollar: First Era, 1919–1932*. Baltimore: Johns Hopkins University Press.

Feld, Werner, and Gavin Boyd (1980). *Comparative Regional Systems*. New York: Pergamon.

Fenwick, Charles G. (1963). *The Organization of American States: The Inter-American Regional System*. Washington, D.C.: Kaufman.

Ferllini S., Héctor, Miguel Díaz S., and Oscar Castillo R. (eds.) (1983). *Un Viaje Histórico: El Papa en una Región de Conflicto*. San José: Uruk Editores.

Fernández, Carlos José (1955–1967). *La Guerra del Chaco*, 4 vols. Buenos Aires and Asunción: n.p.

Fernández, Damián J. (1988). *Cuba's Foreign Policy in the Middle East*. Boulder: Westview.

Fernández-Shaw, Felix (1963). *La Organización de los Estados Americanos (O.E.A.)*, 2d ed. Madrid: Ediciones Cultura Hispánica.

Ferrari, Gustavo (1981). *Esquema de la Política Exterior Argentina*. Buenos Aires: Editorial Universitaria de Buenos Aires.

Ferrer, Aldo (1973). "Relaciones Económicas entre la Comunidad Económica Europa y América Latina." *Estudios Internacionales*, 6 (October-December): 3–42.

Ferris, Elizabeth G. (1987). *The Central American Refugees*. New York: Praeger.

Ffrench-Davis, Ricardo, and Ernesto Tironi (eds.) (1981). *Hacia un Nuevo Orden Económico Internacional: Temas Prioritários para América Latina*. México: Fondo de Cultura Económica.

Findling, John E. (1987). *Close Neighbors, Distant Friends: United States–Central American Relations*. New York: Greenwood Press.

Fisher, Bart S. (1972). *The International Coffee Agreement*. New York: Praeger.

Fishlow, Albert (1985). "The State of Latin American Economics," Chapter 5 in Inter-American Development Bank, *Economic and Social Progress in Latin America, 1985 Report*. Washington, D.C.

Fishlow, Albert, and Carlos Díaz Alejandro (1984). *Rich and Poor Nations in a World Economy*. New York: McGraw-Hill.

Fitch, John Samuel (1979). "The Political Impact of U.S. Military Aid to Latin America: Institutional and Individual Effects." *Armed Forces and Society*, 5 (Spring): 360–386.

Foner, Philip S. (1972). *The Spanish-Cuban-American War and the Birth of American Imperialism*. New York: Monthly Review.

Fontaine, Roger W., and James D. Theberge (eds.) (1976). *Latin America's New Internationalism: The End of Hemispheric Isolation*. New York: Praeger.

Franco Filho, Georgenor de Sousa (1979). *O Pacto Amazônico: Idéis e Conceitos*. Belém: Falangola.

Frank, André Gunder (1967). *Capitalism and Underdevelopment in Latin America: Historical Studies of Chile and Brazil*. New York: Monthly Review.

Frank, André Gunder (1969). *Latin America: Underdevelopment or Revolution*. New York: Monthly Review.

Frank, André Gunder (1972). *Lumpenbourgeoise-Lumpendevelopment: Dependence, Class, and Politics in Latin America*. New York: Monthly Review.

García Robles, Alfonso (1967). *The Denuclearization of Latin America*. New York: Carnegie Endowment for International Peace.

García Robles, Alfonso (1979). *The Latin American Nuclear-Weapon-Free Zone*. Muscatine, Iowa: Stanley Foundation.

Gauhar, Altaf (ed.) (1985). *Regional Integration: The Latin American Experience*. Boulder: Westview.

Gerassi, John (ed.) (1968). *Venceremos! The Speeches and Writings of Che Guevara*. New York: Macmillan.

Gil, Federico G. (1985). "Latin American Studies and Political Science: A Historical Sketch." *LASA Forum*, 16 (Summer).

Gilio, Maria Esther (1972). *The Tupamaro Guerrillas*. New York: Saturday Review.

Glade, William P. (1969). *The Latin American Economies*. New York: American Book.

Gleijeses, Piero (1978). *The Dominican Crisis: The 1965 Constitutionalist Revolt and American Intervention*. Baltimore: Johns Hopkins University Press.

Goebel, Julius (1915). *The Recognition Policy of the United States*. New York: Columbia University Press.

Goldhamer, Herbert (1972). *The Foreign Powers in Latin America*. Princeton, N.J.: Princeton University Press.

Goldman, Marshall (1966). *Soviet Foreign Aid*. New York: Praeger.

Gómez Robledo, Antonio (1959). *La Seguridad Colectiva en el Continente Americano*. México: Universidád Nacional Autonoma.

Gómez-Robledo Verduzco, Alonso (ed.) (1981). *Relaciones México-Estados Unidos: Una Visión Interdisciplinaria*. México: Universidad Nacional Autonoma.

Goñi Garrido, Carlos M. (1984). *Cronica del Conflicto Chileno Argentino*. Buenos Aires: Ediar Editores.

González Hernández, Juan Carlos, and Enrique Alvarez Conde (1984). *Argentina en el Sistema Internacional*. Madrid: Instituto de Cuestiones Internacionales.

González, Luis J., and A. Sánchez S. (1969). *The Great Rebel: Che Guevara in Bolivia*. New York: Grove.

Gordon, Wendell C. (1941). *The Expropriation of Foreign-Owned Property in Mexico*. Washington, D.C.: American Council on Public Affairs.

Gott, Richard (1970). *Guerrilla Movements in Latin America*. London: Nelson.

Gouré, Leon, and Morris Rothenberg (1975). *Soviet Penetration of Latin America*. Miami, Fla.: University of Miami Press.

Grabendorff, Wolf (1982). "Interstate Conflict Behavior and Regional Potential for Conflict in Latin America." *Journal of Inter-American Studies and World Affairs*, 24 (August): 267–294.

Grabendorff, Wolf, and Riordan Roett (eds.) (1985). *Latin America, Western Europe, and the U.S.: Reevaluating the Atlantic Triangle*. New York: Praeger.

Grayson, George W. (1984). *The United States and Mexico: Patterns of Influence*. New York: Praeger.

Gregg, R. D. (1958). *The Influence of Border Troubles on Relations Between the United States and Mexico*. Baltimore: Johns Hopkins University Press.

Greño Velasco, José Enrique (1972). "Las Políticas Nacionales en el Marco del Tratado de la Cuenca del Plata." *Revista de Política Internacional* (Madrid), no. 121 (May-June), pp. 99–122.

Gromyko, Andrei (1972). "Some Implications of the Cuban Missile Crisis," in Alvin Z. Rubinstein (ed.), *The Foreign Policy of the Soviet Union*, 3d ed. New York: Random House.

Grunwald, Joseph (ed.) (1978). *Latin America and World Economy: A Changing International Order*. Beverly Hills, Calif.: Sage.

Grunwald, Joseph, Miguel S. Wionczek, and Martin Carnoy (1972). *Latin American Economic Integration and U.S. Policy*. Washington, D.C.: Brookings Institution.

Guevara, Ernesto "Che" (1961). *Guerrilla Warfare*. New York: Monthly Review.

Guevara, Ernesto "Che" (1973–1974). *Obras Completas*, 5 vols. Buenos Aires: Ed. Cepe.

Guevara, Ernesto (1985). *Guerrilla Warfare*. Introduction and Case Studies by Brian Loveman and Thomas M. Davies, Jr. Lincoln: University of Nebraska Press.

Guimaraes, Irineu (1979). *Puebla, O Papa no Continente dos Indios.* Rio de Janeiro: Expressão e Cultura.

Gutiérrez, Gustavo (1973). *Theology of Liberation: History, Politics, and Salvation:* Maryknoll, N.Y.: Orbis.

Hagen, Virginia M. (1969). *The Latin American–United States Fishing Rights Controversy with Specific Reference to Chile, Ecuador, and Peru.* Washington, D.C.: Library of Congress.

Hartlyn, Jonathan, and Samuel A. Morley (eds.) (1986). *Latin American Political Economy: Financial Crisis and Political Change.* Boulder: Westview.

Hayes, Margaret Daly (1984). *Latin America and the U.S. National Interest: A Basis for U.S. Foreign Policy.* Boulder: Westview.

Heare, Gertrude (1971). *Trends in Latin American Military Expenditures.* Washington, D.C.: Department of State.

Hebblethwaite, Peter (1985). *Pope John XXIII: Shepherds of the Modern World.* New York: Doubleday.

Heilman, John G. (1973). *Ideological Conflict and Institutional Differentiation in West German Relations with Latin America.* Ph.D. dissertation, New York University.

Heine, Jorge, and Juan M. García-Passalacqua (1983). *The Puerto Rican Question.* New York: Foreign Policy Association.

Heine, Jorge, and Leslie F. Manigat (eds.) (1986). *The Caribbean and World Politics: Cross-Currents and Cleavages.* New York: Holmes & Meier.

Heller, Claude (1978). "La Asistencia Militar Norteamericano a América Latina: Una Perspectiva Política." *Estados Unidos: Perspectiva Latinoamericana* (México), 4 (no. 2): 137–166.

Herman, Donald L. (ed.) (1973). *The Communist Tide in Latin America.* Austin: University of Texas Press.

Hermann, Charles F., Charles W. Kegley, Jr., and James N. Rosenau (eds.) (1987). *New Directions in the Study of Foreign Policy.* Boston: Allen & Unwin.

Herrera, Felipe (1970). *Nacionalismo, Regionalismo, Internacionalismo: América Latina en el Contexto Internacional.* Buenos Aires: Banco Interamericano de Desarrollo.

Herrera, Felipe (1986). *Desarrollo e Integración.* Santiago de Chile: Editorial Emision.

Hilton, Ronald (ed.) (1969). *The Movement Toward Latin American Unity.* New York: Praeger.

Hirschman, Albert O. (1963). *Journeys Toward Progress: Studies of Economic Policy Making in Latin America.* New York: Twentieth Century Fund.

Hirschman, Albert O. (1972). *A Bias for Hope: Essays on Development in Latin America.* New Haven, Conn.: Yale University Press.

Hirst, Monica, and Roberto Russell (1987). *Democracía y Política Exterior: Los Casos de Argentina y Brazil.* Buenos Aires: FLACSO Facultad Latinoamericana de Ciencias Sociales Programa Buenos Aires.

Hodges, Donald C. (trans. and ed.) (1973). *Philosophy of the Urban Guerrilla: The Revolutionary Writings of Abraham Guillen.* New York: William Morrow.

Holbrik, Karel, and Philip L. Swan (1972). *Trade and Industrialization in the Central American Common Market: The First Decade.* Austin: University of Texas Press.

Holsti, K. J. (1988). *International Politics,* 5th ed. Englewood Cliffs, N.J.: Prentice-Hall.

Horelick, Arnold L. (1964). "The Cuban Missile Crisis: An Analysis of Soviet Calculations and Behavior." *World Politics,* 16 (April): 263–280.

Horowitz, Irving Louis (1977). "From Dependency to Determinism: The New Structure of Latin American Militarism." *Journal of Political and Military Sociology,* 5 (Fall): 217–238.

Houston, John A. (1956). *Latin America in the United Nations*. New York: Carnegie Endowment for International Peace.

Hovet, Thomas (1960). *Bloc Politics in the United Nations*. Cambridge, Mass.: Harvard University Press.

Hundley, Norris (1966). *Dividing the Waters: A Century of Controversy Between the United States and Mexico*. Berkeley: University of California Press.

Hunter, John M., and James W. Foley (1975). *Economic Problems of Latin America*. Boston: Houghton Mifflin.

Huntington, Samuel P. (1974). "Civil Violence and the Process of Development," in *Civil Violence and the International System*, Part 2. London: International Institute for Strategic Studies.

Immerman, Richard H. (1982). *The CIA in Guatemala: The Foreign Policy of Intervention*. Austin: University of Texas Press.

Ince, Basil A. (ed.) (1979). *Contemporary International Relations of the Caribbean*. St. Augustine: Institute of International Relations, University of the West Indies.

Ingram, G. N. (1974). *Expropriation of U.S. Property in South America*. New York: Praeger.

Institute of International Studies (1965). *Trends in Social Science Research in Latin American Studies: A Conference Report*. Berkeley: University of California Press.

Inter-American Development Bank (1966). *The Inter-American Development Bank and Economic Integration of Latin America*. Washington, D.C.

Inter-American Development Bank (1974). *Fifteen Years of Activities*. Washington, D.C.

Inter-American Development Bank (1984). *External Debt and Economic Development in Latin America: Background and Prospects*. Washington, D.C.

Inter-American Development Bank (1985). *Economics and Social Progress in Latin America: External Debt, Crisis and Adjustment: 1985 Report*. Washington, D.C.

Inter-American Institute for International Legal Studies (1966). *The Inter-American System*. Dobbs Ferry, N.Y.: Oceana.

Inter-American Institute for International Legal Studies (1968). *Instruments Relating to the Economic Integration of Latin America*. Dobbs Ferry, N.Y.: Oceana.

Ireland, Gordon (1938). *Boundaries, Possessions, and Conflicts in South America*. Cambridge, Mass.: Harvard University Press.

Ireland, Gordon (1941). *Boundaries, Possessions, and Conflicts in Central and North America, and the Caribbean*. Cambridge, Mass.: Harvard University Press.

Irish, Donald P. (ed.) (1978). *Multinational Corporations in Latin America*. Athens: Ohio University.

Jackson, D. Bruce (1969). *Castro, the Kremlin, and Communism in Latin America*. Baltimore: Johns Hopkins University Press.

Jacobini, H. B. (1954). *A Study of the Philosophy of International Law as Seen in Works of Latin American Writers*. The Hague: Martimes Nijhoff.

Jaguaribe, Hélio (1973). *Political Development: A General Theory and a Latin American Case Study*. New York: Harper & Row.

Jaguaribe, Hélio (1985). *El Nuevo Escenario Internacional*. México: Fondo de Cultura Económica.

James, Daniel (ed.) (1968). *The Complete Bolivian Diaries of Che Guevara and Other Captured Documents*. New York: Stein & Day.

Jameson [sic], Edward A. (1950). "Keeping Peace in the Caribbean Area." Washington, D.C.: Department of State.

Jamison, Edward Alden (1980). "Cuba and the Inter-American System: Exclusion of the Castro Regime from the Organization of American States." *The Americas*, 36 (January): 317–346.

Jessup, Philip C. (1973). "El Chamizal." *American Journal of International Law*, 67 (July): 423–445.

Johnson, Cecil (1970). *Communist China and Latin America, 1959–1967*. New York: Columbia University Press.

Johnson, Haynes B. et al. (1964). *The Bay of Pigs*. New York: W. W. Norton.

Kane, William E. (1972). *Civil Strife in Latin America: A Legal History of U.S. Involvement*. Baltimore: Johns Hopkins University Press.

Karnes, Thomas L. (1961). *The Failure of Union: Central America, 1824–1960*. Chapel Hill: University of North Carolina Press.

Karol, K. S. (1970). *Guerrillas in Power: The Course of the Cuban Revolution*. New York: Hill & Wang.

Kaufman, Edy (1976). *The Superpowers and Their Spheres of Influence: The United States and the Soviet Union in Eastern Europe and Latin America*. London: Croom Helm.

Kaufman, Edy, Yoram Shapira, and Joel Barromi (1979). *Israeli–Latin American Relations*. New Brunswick: Transaction Books.

Kearns, Kevin C. (1972). "The Andean Common Market." *Journal of Inter-American Studies and World Affairs*, 14 (May): 225–249.

Kegley, Charles W., and Eugene R. Wittkopf (1988). *The Global Agenda: Issues and Perspectives*, 2d ed. New York: Random House.

Kelchner, Warren H. (1929). *Latin American Relations with the League of Nations*. Boston: World Peace Foundation.

Kelly, Philip L. (1971). *The Consistency of Voting by the Latin American States in the United Nations General Assembly*. Ph.D. dissertation. University of Nebraska.

Kemp, Geoffrey (1970). *Some Relationships Between U.S. Military Training in Latin America and Weapons Acquisition Patterns, 1959–1969*. Cambridge, Mass.: MIT Press.

Kennedy, Robert F. (1969). *Thirteen Days: A Memoir of the Cuban Missile Crisis*. New York: Norton.

Keogh, Dermot (ed.) (1985). *Central America, Human Rights and U.S. Foreign Policy*. Cork, Ireland: Cork University Press.

Keohane, Robert, and Joseph Nye (1977). *Power and Independence*. Boston: Little, Brown.

Khachaturov, K. (1982). "Latin America and Imperialist Ideology." *International Affairs* (Moscow), 12 (December): 92–100.

Khrushchev, Nikita S. (1971). *Khrushchev Remembers*. Boston: Little, Brown.

Kirkpatrick, Jeane (1979). "Dictatorships and Double Standards." *Commentary* (November): 34–45.

Kirkpatrick, Jeane (1981). "U.S. Security and Latin America." *Commentary* (January): 29–40.

Kolinski, Charles J. (1965). *Independence or Death! The Story of the Paraguayan War*. Gainesville: University of Florida Press.

Krause, Walter, and F. John Mathis (1970). *Latin America and Economic Integration*. Iowa City: University of Iowa Press.

Krieger Vasena, Adalbert, and Javier Pazos (1973). *Latin America*. London: E. Benn.

Kryzanek, Michael J. (1985). *U.S.–Latin American Relations*. New York: Praeger.

Lafer, Celso (1982). "A Nova Ordem Mundial num Sistema Internacional em Transformacão." *Revista Brasileira de Estudios Políticos*, 55 (July): 7–63.

Lafer, Celso (1984). *O Brasil e a Crise Mundial: Paz, Poder e Política Externa*. São Paulo: Editora Perspectiva.

Lagos Matus, Gustavo (ed.) (1979). *Las Relaciones entre América Latina, Estados Unidos y Europa Occidental*. Santiago: Instituto de Estudios Internacionales de la Universidád de Chile.

Langley, Lester D. (1968). *The Cuban Policy of the United States*. New York: John Wiley & Sons.

Langley, Lester (1976). *Struggle for the American Mediterranean: United States–European Rivalry in the Gulf-Caribbean, 1776–1904*. Athens: University of Georgia Press.

Langley, Lester D. (1980). *The United States and the Caribbean, 1900–1970*. Athens: University of Georgia Press.

Langley, Lester D. (1982). *The United States and the Caribbean in the Twentieth Century*. Athens: University of Georgia Press.

Lanús, Juan Archibaldo (1984). *De Chapultepéc al Beagle: Política Exterior Argentina, 1945–1980*. Buenos Aires: Emecé.

Latané, John H. (1920). *The United States and Latin America*, rev. and retitled ed. Garden City, N.J.: Doubleday, Page. Original ed.: (1900). *The Diplomatic Relations of the United States and Spanish America*. Baltimore: Johns Hopkins University Press.

Leiken, Robert S. (ed.) (1984). *Central America: Anatomy of a Conflict*. New York: Pergamon Press.

Leiken, Robert S., and Barry Rubin (eds.) (1987). *The Central American Crisis Reader*. New York: Summit Books.

Levenstein, Harvey A. (1971). *Labor Organizations in the United States and Mexico*. Westport: Greenwood.

Levin, Peter J. (1972). "The Development Program of the Rio de la Plata Basin." *Journal of Developing Areas*, 6 (July): 493–522.

Levine, Daniel H. (1986). *Religion and Political Conflict in Latin America*. Chapel Hill: University of North Carolina Press.

Lewis, Gordon K. (1972). *The Virgin Islands*. Evanston: Northwestern University Press.

Lewis, Sybil Farrell, and Dale T. Mathews (comps.) (1984). *Documents on the Invasion of Grenada, October 1983*. Rio Piedras, P.R.: Institute of Caribbean Studies, University of Puerto Rico.

Lincoln, Jennie K., and Elizabeth G. Ferris (eds.) (1984). *The Dynamics of Latin American Foreign Policies*. Boulder: Westview.

Liss, Sheldon (1965). *A Century of Disagreement: The Chamizal Conflict, 1864–1964*. Washington, D.C.: University Press.

Liss, Sheldon (1969). *The Canal: Aspects of United States–Panamanian Relations*. Notre Dame: University of Notre Dame Press.

Lockey, Joseph B. (1920). *Pan Americanism: Its Beginnings*. New York: Macmillan.

Logan, John A. (1961). *No Transfer: An American Security Principle*. New Haven: Yale University Press.

Los Obispos Latinoamericanos entre Medellín y Puebla: Documentos Episcopales 1968–1978 (n.d.). San Salvador: UCA Editores.

Lowenfeld, Andreas F. (ed.) (1971). *Expropriation in the Americas*. Port Washington, N.Y.: Kennekat.

Lowenthal, Abraham F. (1972). *The Dominican Intervention*. Cambridge: Harvard University Press.

Lowenthal, Abraham F. (1976). "The United States and Latin America: Ending the Hegemonic Presumption." *Foreign Affairs*, 55 (October): 199–213.

Lowenthal, Abraham F. (1983). "Ronald Reagan and Latin America: Coping with Hegemony in Decline," in Kenneth A. Oye, Robert J. Lieber, and Donald Rothchild (eds.), *Eagle Defiant: United States Foreign Policy*. Boston: Little, Brown & Co.

Lowenthal, Abraham F. (1987). *Partners in Conflict: The United States and Latin America*. Baltimore: Johns Hopkins University Press.

Lowenthal, David (1961). *The West Indies Federation*. New York: Columbia University Press.

Lozano de Rey, Ester, and Pilar Marulanda de Galofre (1982). *Como se Hace la Política Exterior en Colombia*. Bogotá: Ediciones Tercer Mundo.

Lupsha, Peter A. (1981). "Drug Trafficking: Mexico and Colombia in Comparative Perspective." *Journal of International Affairs*, 35 (Spring/Summer): 95–115.

Mack, Gerstle (1944). *The Land Divided: A History of Panama and Other Isthmian Canal Projects*. New York: Knopf.

Maeztu, Ramiro de (1941). *Defensa de la Hispanidad*, 4th ed. Madrid: Cultura Española.

Mahan, Alfred Thayer (1918). *The Interest of America in Sea Power, Present and Future*. Boston: Little, Brown.

Maira, Luis (ed.) (1986). *El Sistema Internacional y América Latina: Una Nueva Era de Hegemonía Norteamericana?* Buenos Aires: RIAL, Grupo Editor Latinoamericano.

Manhattan, Avro (1946). *Latin America and the Vatican*. London: Watts.

Mansbach, Richard W., Yale H. Ferguson, and Donald E. Lampert (1975). *The Web of World Politics: Nonstate Actors in the Global Political System*. Englewood Cliffs, N.J.: Prentice-Hall.

Mansilla, H.C.F. (1985). "Latin America Within the Third World: The Search for a New Identity, the Acceptance of Old Contents." *Ibero-Amerikanisches Archiv*, 11 (no. 2): 171–191.

Marighella, Carlos (1970). "Mini-Manual of the Urban Guerrilla." *Tricontinental* (Cuba) (January-February).

Marighella, Carlos (1971). *For the Liberation of Brazil*. Harmondsworth: Penguin.

Maritano, Nino (1970). *A Latin American Economic Community*. Notre Dame, Ind.: University of Notre Dame Press.

Marshall, Jonathan et al. (1987). *The Iran-Contra Connection: Secret Teams and Covert Operations in the Reagan Era*. Boston: South End Press.

Martz, John D. (1966). "The Place of Latin America in the Study of Comparative Politics." *Journal of Politics*, 28 (February): 57–80.

Martz, John D. (1970). "Guerrilla Warfare and Violence in Contemporary Latin America." *Annals of the Southeastern Conference on Latin American Studies*, 1 (March): 141–165.

Martz, John D., and Lars Schoultz (eds.) (1980). *Latin America, the United States, and the Inter-American System*. Boulder: Westview.

Martz, Mary Jeanne Reid (1978). *The Central American Soccer War: Historical Patterns and Internal Dynamics of OAS Settlement Procedures*. Athens: Ohio University.

Martz, Mary Jeanne Reid (1979). "SELA: The Latin American Economic System: 'Ploughing the Seas?'" *Inter-American Economic Affairs*, 32 (Spring): 33–64.

Matthews, Herbert (1961). *The Cuban Story*. New York: Braziller.

May, Ernest R. (1975). *The Making of the Monroe Doctrine*. Cambridge: Harvard University Press.

May, Herbert K. (1968). *Problems and Prospects of the Alliance for Progress*. New York: Praeger.

McBride, Robert J. (ed.) (1981). *Mexico and the United States: Energy, Trade, Investment, Tourism*. Englewood Cliffs, N.J.: Prentice-Hall, for the American Assembly.

McClelland, Donald H. (1972). *The Central American Common Market*. New York: Praeger.

McClintock, Cynthia (1984). "Why Peasants Rebel: The Case of Peru's Sendero Luminoso." *World Politics*. 37: 1.

Mecham, J. Lloyd (1961). *The United States and Inter-American Security, 1889–1960*. Austin: University of Texas Press.

Mecham, J. Lloyd (1965). *A Survey of United States–Latin American Relations*. Boston: Houghton Mifflin.

Mecham, J. Lloyd (1966). *Church and State in Latin America*, rev. ed. Chapel Hill: University of North Carolina Press.

Meira Penna, J. O. de (1967). *Política Externa*. Rio de Janeiro: Livraria Agir Editora.

Melo, Artemio Luis (1979). *La Cuestión Internacional del Canal de Beagle*. Buenos Aires: Ediciones Depalma.

Mercado, R. (1982). *El Partido Comunista del Perú: Sendero Luminoso*. Lima: Ediciones de Cultura Popular.

Mercier Vega, Luis (1969). *Guerrillas in Latin America*. New York: Praeger.

Mesa-Lago, Carmelo, and June Belkin (eds.) (1981). *Cuba in Africa*. Pittsburgh: University of Pittsburgh Press.

México. Secretaria de Relaciones Exteriores (1975). *La Salinidad del Río Colorado: Una Diferencia Internacional*. México: Col. del Archivo Histórico Diplomático Mexicana, Serie Documental 13.

México (1985). *Política Exterior de México: 175 Años de Historia*, 4 vols. México: Secretaria de Relaciones Exteriores.

Middlebrook, Kevin, and Carlos Rico (eds.) (1986). *The United States and Latin America in the 1980s: Contending Perspectives on a Decade of Crisis*. Pittsburgh: University of Pittsburgh Press.

Milenky, Edward S. (1973a). "Developmental Nationalism in Practice: The Problems and Progress of the Andean Group." *Inter-American Economic Affairs*, 26 (Spring): 49–68.

Milenky, Edward S. (1973b). *The Politics of Regional Organization in Latin America: The Latin American Free Trade Association*. New York: Praeger.

Milenky, Edward S. (1978). *Argentina's Foreign Policies*. Boulder: Westview.

Millett, Richard, and W. Marvin Will (eds.) (1979). *The Restless Caribbean: Changing Patterns in International Relations*. New York: Praeger.

Mock, James R. (1942). "The Creel Committee in Latin America." *Hispanic American Historical Review*, 22 (May): 262–279.

Moffett, George D., III (1985). *The Limits of Victory: Ratification of the Panama Canal Treaties*. Ithaca: Cornell University Press.

Molineu, Harold (1986). *U.S. Policy Toward Latin America: From Regionalism to Globalism*. Boulder: Westview.

Mordecai, John (1968). *Federation of the West Indies*. Evanston, Ill.: Northwestern University Press.

Morris, Michael A. (1979). *International Politics and the Sea: The Case of Brazil*. Boulder: Westview.

Morse, Richard (1964). "The Strange Career of 'Latin American Studies.'" *The Annals*, 356 (November): 106–112.

Moss, Robert (1972). *Urban Guerrillas*. London: Temple Smith.

Movimiento de Liberación Nacional (1971). *Actas Tupamaras*. Buenos Aires: Schapire Editor.

Mower, Alfred Glenn, Jr. (1982). *The European Community and Latin America: A Case Study in Global Role Expansion*. Westport: Greenwood.

Mujal-Leon, Eusebio (1983). "El Socialismo Europeo y la Crisis en Centroamérica." *Foro Internacional*, 24 (October/December): 155-198.

Muñoz, Heraldo (1987). "The Dominant Themes in the Study of Latin American Foreign Relations." Paper, International Studies Association, Washington, D.C., January 1987.

Muñoz, Heraldo, and Joseph S. Tulchin (eds.) (1984). *Latin American Nations in World Politics*. Boulder: Westview.

Munro, Dana G. (1964). *Intervention and Dollar Diplomacy in the Caribbean, 1900-1921*. Princeton, N.J.: Princeton University Press.

Munro, Dana G. (1974). *The United States and the Caribbean Republics, 1921-1933*. Princeton, N.J.: Princeton University Press.

Murillo-Castaño, Gabriel (1984). *Migrant Workers in the Americas: A Comparative Study of Migration Between Colombia and Venezuela and Between Mexico and the United States*. La Jolla: Center for U.S.-Mexican Studies, University of California at San Diego.

Mutchler, David E. (1971). *The Church as a Political Factor in Latin America*. New York: Praeger.

Myrdal, Gunnar (1957). *Economic Theory and Underdeveloped Nations*. London: G. Duckworth.

Nakagawa, Fumio (1983). "Japanese–Latin American Relations since the 1960s: An Overview." *Latin American Studies* (Japan), 6: 63-74.

Navarette, Jorge Eduardo et al. (1980). *Alcances y Perspectivas del Nuevo Orden Internacional: Mesas Redondas*. México: Universidad Autónoma.

Newfarmer, Richard (ed.) (1984). *From Gunboats to Diplomacy: New U.S. Policies for Latin America*. Baltimore: Johns Hopkins University Press.

Novak, Michael (1987). *Will It Liberate? Questions About Liberation Theology*. New York: Paulist Press.

Nuñez del Arco, José, Eduardo Margaín, and Rachells Cherol (eds.) (1984). *The Economic Integration Process of Latin America in the 1980s*. Washington, D.C.: Inter-American Development Bank.

O'Neill, Edward A. (1972). *Rape of the American Virgins*. New York: Praeger.

Ocampo, José et al. (1976). *Dependency Theory*. Riverside, Calif.: Latin American Perspectives.

Ojeda, Mario (1976). *Alcances y Límites de la Política Exterior de México*. México: El Colegio de México.

Oliver, Covey (1964). *The Inter-American Security System and the Cuban Crisis*. New York: Oceana.

Orrego Vicuña, Francisco (1976). *Los Fondos Marinos y Oceánicos: Jurisdicción Nacional y Régimen Internacional*. Santiago de Chile: Editorial Andres Bello.

Oswald, J. Gregory (comp. and trans.) (1970). *Soviet Image of Contemporary Latin America*. Austin: University of Texas Press.

Palmer, David Scott (1986). "Rebellion in Rural Peru: The Origins and Evolution of Sendero Luminoso." *Comparative Politics*, 18: 2.

Pan American Union/General Secretariat of the Organization of American States (1968). *Study of the Diary of 'Che' Guevara in Bolivia*. Prepared by the OAS Special Consultative Committee on Security at its Eleventh Regular Meeting.

Pan American Union/General Secretariat of the Organization of American States (1973). *Applications of the Inter-American Treaty of Reciprocal Assistance, 1948-1972*, 2 vols.

Pan American Union/General Secretariat of the Organization of American States (1973-1975). *Documents Prepared by the OAS Special Committee to Study the Inter-American System and to Propose Measures for Restructuring It (CEESI)*, 12 vols.

Pan American Union/General Secretariat of the Organization of American States (1981). *Basic Instruments of the Organization of American States*. Treaty Series No. 61, OEA/Ser. X/II (English). Washington, D.C.

Papp, Daniel S. (1988). *Contemporary International Relations: Frameworks for Understanding*, 2d ed. New York: Macmillan.

Parkinson, F. (1974). *Latin America, the Cold War, and the World Powers, 1945–1973*. Beverly Hills, Calif.: Sage.

Parkinson, F. (1987). "Some Legal and Institutional Aspects of the Debt Crisis." *Coexistence* (Netherlands), 24: 155–168.

Pastor, Robert A. (1984). "U.S. Immigration Policy and Latin America: In Search of the 'Special Relationship.'" *Latin American Research Review*, 19 (no. 3): 35–56.

Pastor, Robert A. (1987a). *Condemned to Repetition: The United States and Nicaragua*. Princeton: Princeton University Press.

Pastor, Robert A. (ed.) (1987b). *Latin America's Debt Crisis: Adjusting to the Past or Planning for the Future?* Boulder: Lynne Rienner Publishers.

Pearson, Frederic S., and J. Martin Rochester (1988). *International Relations: The Global Condition in the Late Twentieth Century*, 2d ed. New York: Random House.

Pellicer, Olga (ed.) (1983). *La Política Exterior de México en los Ochenta*. México, D.F.: Centro de Investigación y Docencia Económicas.

Pérez Concha, Jorge (1961–1964). *Ensayo Histórico-Crítico de las Relaciones Diplomáticas del Ecuador con los Estados Limítrofes*, 2 vols. Quito: Editorial Casa de la Cultura Ecuatoriana.

Perina, Rubén (ed.) (1985). *El Estudio de las Relaciones Internacionales en América Latina y el Caribe*. Buenos Aires: Grupo Editor Latinoamericano.

Perkins, Dexter (1927). *The Monroe Doctrine, 1823–1826*. Cambridge: Harvard University Press.

Perkins, Dexter (1933). *The Monroe Doctrine, 1826–1867*. Baltimore: Johns Hopkins University Press.

Perkins, Dexter (1937). *The Monroe Doctrine, 1867–1907*. Baltimore: Johns Hopkins University Press.

Perkins, Dexter (1963). *A History of the Monroe Doctrine*. Boston: Little, Brown.

Perkins, Dexter (1966). *The United States and the Caribbean*, rev. ed. Cambridge: Harvard University Press.

Perkins, Whitney T. (1981). *Constraint of Empire: The United States and Caribbean Interventions*. Westport: Greenwood.

Perry, William, and Peter Wehner (eds.) (1985). *The Latin American Policies of U.S. Allies: Balancing Global Interests and Regional Concerns*. New York: Praeger.

Peterson, Harold F. (1964). *Argentina and the United States, 1810–1960*. Albany: State University of New York.

Petras, James, and Morris Morley (1975). *The United States and Chile: Imperialism and the Overthrow of the Allende Government*. New York: Monthly Review.

Pike, Frederick B. (1963). *Chile and the United States, 1880–1962*. Notre Dame: University of Notre Dame Press.

Pike, Frederick B. (1971). *Hispanismo, 1898–1936: Spanish Conservatives and Liberals and Their Relations with Spanish America*. Notre Dame: University of Notre Dame Press.

Pike, Fredrick B. (1977). *The United States and the Andean Republics: Peru, Bolivia, and Ecuador*. Cambridge: Harvard University Press.

Pittman, Howard T. (1981). *Geopolitics in the ABC Countries: A Comparison*, 5 vols. Ph.D. dissertation, The American University.

Plano, Jack C., and Roy Olton (1988). *The International Relations Dictionary*, 4th ed. New York: Holt, Rinehart and Winston.

Platt, D.C.M. (1973). *Latin America and British Trade, 1806–1914*. New York: Barnes & Noble.

Poblete Troncoso, Moises, and Ben G. Burnett (1960). *The Rise of the Latin American Labor Movement*. New York: Bookman.

Política Internacional de la Revolución Cubana (1966), 2 vols. La Habana: Editora Politica.

Pontecorvo, Giulio (ed.) (1986). *The New Order of the Oceans*. New York: Columbia University Press.

Poppino, Rollie E. (1964). *International Communism in Latin America*. New York: The Free Press.

Porzecanski, Arturo C. (1973). *Uruguay's Tupamaros*. New York: Praeger.

Prados, John (1986). *Presidents' Secret Wars: CIA and Pentagon Covert Operations Since World War II*. New York: William Morrow.

Prebisch, Raúl (1964). *Nueva Política Comercial para el Desarrollo*. México: Fondo de Cultura Económica.

Prebisch, Raúl (1970). *Change and Development: Latin America's Great Task*. Washington, D.C.: Inter-American Development Bank.

Price, Glen (1967). *Origins of the War with Mexico*. Austin: University of Texas Press.

Puig, Juan Carlos (ed.) (1984). *América Latina: Políticas Exteriores Comparadas*. Buenos Aires: Grupo Editor Latinoamericano.

Purcell, John F. H. (1982). *Trade Conflicts and U.S.-Mexican Relations*. La Jolla: Program in US-Mexican Studies, University of California at San Diego.

Purcell, Susan Kaufman (ed.) (1981). *Mexico–United States Relations*. New York: Academy of Political Science.

Putnam, Robert D. (1967). "Toward Explaining Military Intervention in Latin American Politics." *World Politics*, 20 (October): 83–110.

Quesada, Vicente G. (1918–1920). *Historia Diplomática Hispanoamericana*, 3 vols. Buenos Aires: La Cultura Argentina.

Radu, Michael S. (1984). "Terror, Terrorism, and Insurgency in Latin America." *Orbis*, 18 (Spring): 27–40.

Radu, Michael, and Vladimir Tismaneanu (1986). *Revolutionary Organizations in Latin America*. Boulder: Westview.

Rankin, Richard C. (1974). "The Expanding Institutional Concerns of the Latin American Military Establishments." *Latin American Research Review*, 9 (Spring): 81–108.

Ravines, Eudocio (1951). *The Yenan Way: The Kremlin's Penetration of South America*. New York: Scribner's.

Ray, David (1973). "The Dependency Model of Latin American Underdevelopment: Three Basic Fallacies." *Journal of Inter-American Studies*, 15 (February): 4–20.

Redick, John R. (1978). "Regional Restraint: U.S. Nuclear Policy and Latin America." *Orbis*, 22 (Spring): 161–200.

Remmer, Karen L. (1978). "Evaluating the Policy Impact of Military Regimes in Latin America." *Latin American Research Review*, 13 (no. 2): 39–54.

Rens, Jef (1959). "América Latina y la Organización Internacional del Trabajo." *Revista Internacional del Trabajo* (Geneva), 60 (July): 1–29.

The Report of the President's National Bipartisan Commission on Central America [Kissinger Commission Report] (1983). New York: Macmillan.

Rippy, J. Fred (1938). *Latin America in World Politics*, 3d ed. New York: F. S. Crofts.

Rippy, J. Fred (1958). *Globe and Hemisphere*. Chicago: Henry Regnery.

Rippy, J. Fred (1959). *British Investments in Latin America, 1822–1949*. Minneapolis: University of Minnesota Press.

Robertson, William Spence (1923). *Hispanic Relations with the United States*. New York: Oxford University Press.

Rodley, N. S., and C. Neale Ronning (eds.) (1974). *International Law in the Western Hemisphere*. The Hague: Nijhoff.

Rodrígues, José Honorio (1966). *Interesse Nacional e Política Externa*. Rio de Janeiro: Editora Civilização Brasileira.

Rodríguez Larretta, A. (1938). *Orientación de la Política Internacional en América Latina*, 2 vols. Montevideo: Peña.

Rodríguez Serrano, Felipe (1968). *El Canal por Nicaragua*. Managua: Editorial Alemana.

Roett, Riordan (1984). "Democracy and Debt in South America: A Continent's Dilemma." *Foreign Affairs*, 62: 695–720.

Roett, Riordan, and James F. Tierney (eds.) (1971). "The Military in Latin America." *International Journal of Politics*, vol. 1 (Summer-Fall), entire issue.

Romualdi, Serafino (1967). *Presidents and Peons: Recollections of a Labor Ambassador in Latin America*. New York: Funk & Wagnalls.

Ronning, C. Neale (ed.) (1970). *Intervention in Latin America*. New York: Knopf.

Ropp, Steve C., and James A. Morris (1986). *Central America: Crisis and Adaptation*. Albuquerque: University of New Mexico Press.

Rosenau, James N. (ed.) (1961, 1969). *International Politics and Foreign Policy*. New York: The Free Press.

Rosenau, James N., Kenneth W. Thompson, and Gavin Boyd (eds.) (1976). *World Politics*. New York: The Free Press.

Rout, Leslie B. (1970). *Politics of the Chaco Peace Conference, 1935–39*. Austin: University of Texas Press.

Ruilova, Leonardo (1978). *China Popular en América Latina*. Quito: Instituto Latinoamericano de Investigaciones Sociales.

Ruíz Moreno, Isidro (1961). *Historia del las Relaciones Exteriores Argentinas, 1810–1955*. Buenos Aires: Editorial Perrot.

Russett, Bruce M. (1967). *International Regions and the International System*. Chicago: Rand McNally.

Sabaté Lichtschein, Domingo (1985). *Problemas Argentinos de Soberanía Territorial*, 3d ed. Buenos Aires: Abeledo-Perrot.

Sampson, Anthony (1973). *The Sovereign State of ITT*. New York: Stein & Day.

Sampson, Anthony (1975). *The Seven Sisters: The Great Oil Companies and the World They Made*. New York: Viking.

Sanchez, Nestor D. (1983). "The Communist Threat." *Foreign Policy*, 52 (Fall): 43–50.

Sánchez G., Walter, and Teresa Pereira L. (eds.) (1977). *Cientocincuenta Años de Política Exterior Chilena*. Santiago de Chile: Instituto de Estudios Internacionales de la Universidad de Chile.

Sanders, Thomas G. (1970). "The Church in Latin America." *Foreign Affairs*, 48 (January): 285–299.

Sandifer, Durward V., and Ronald L. Scheman (1966). *The Foundations of Freedom: The Interrelationship Between Democracy and Human Rights*. New York: Praeger.

Santos, Theotonio dos (1970). *Dependencia Económica y Cambio Revolucionario en América Latina*. Caracas: Ed. Nueva Izquierda.

Saunders, John (ed.) (1986). *Population Growth in Latin American and U.S. Security*. Winchester: Allen & Unwin.

Scheer, Robert (ed.) (1968). *The Diary of Che Guevara-Bolivia: November 7, 1966–October 7, 1967*. New York: Bantam.

Scheman, L. Ronald (1987). "Rhetoric and Reality: The Inter-American System's Second Century." *Journal of Interamerican Studies and World Affairs*, 29 (Fall): 1–31.

Schlesinger, Arthur M. (1965). *A Thousand Days*. Boston: Houghton Mifflin.

Schmidt, Hans (1971). *The United States Occupation of Haiti, 1915–1934*. New Brunswick: Rutgers University Press.

Schmitt, Karl M. (ed.) (1972). *The Roman Catholic Church in Modern Latin America*. New York: Knopf.

Schmitt, Karl M. (1974). *Mexico and the United States, 1821–1973*. New York: Wiley.

Schmitter, Philippe C. (1972). *Autonomy or Dependence as Regional Integration Outcomes: Central America*. Berkeley: University of California Press.

Schneider, Ronald M. (1976). *Brazil: Foreign Policy of a Future World Power*. Boulder: Westview.

Schoultz, Lars (1981). *Human Rights and United States Policy Toward Latin America*. Princeton: Princeton University Press.

Schoultz, Lars (1987). *National Security and United States Policy Toward Latin America*. Princeton: Princeton University Press.

Schump, Walter (1971). *Las Guerrillas en América Latina*. Buenos Aires: Punto Crítico.

Scott, James Brown (1909). *The Hague Peace Conferences of 1899 and 1907*, 2 vols. Baltimore: Johns Hopkins University Press.

Seabury, Paul, and Walter A. McDougall (eds.) (1984). *The Grenada Papers*. San Francisco: Institute for Contemporary Studies.

Seara Vázquez, Modesto (1985). *Política Exterior de México*, 3d ed. México: Harla—Harper & Row Latinoamericana.

Segal, Aaron (1968). *The Politics of Caribbean Economic Integration*. Rio Piedras: University of Puerto Rico Press.

Selcher, Wayne A. (1978). *Brazil's Multilateral Relations Between First and Third Worlds*. Boulder: Westview.

Selcher, Wayne A. (ed.) (1981). *Brazil in the International System: The Rise of a Middle Power*. Boulder: Westview.

Sepúlveda, César (1973). *El Sistema Interamericano*. Valladolid: Universidad.

Sepúlveda, César (1975). *Las Fuentes del Derecho Internacional Americano: una Encuesta sobre los Métodos de Creación de Reglas Internacionales en el Hemisferio Occidental*, 2d ed. México: Editorial Porrúa.

Shapiro, Samuel (ed.) (1968). *Cultural Factors in Inter-American Relations*. Notre Dame: University of Notre Dame Press.

Sharp, Daniel A. (ed.) (1972). *U.S. Foreign Policy and Peru*. Austin: University of Texas Press.

Shaw, Royce Q. (1979). *Central America: Regional Integration and National Political Development*. Boulder: Westview.

Sigmund, Paul E. (1980). *Multinationals in Latin America: The Politics of Nationalization*. Madison: University of Wisconsin Press.

Sigmund, Paul E. (1982). "Latin America: Change or Continuity?" *Foreign Affairs*, 60: 629–657.

Singletary, Otis A. (1960). *The Mexican War*. Chicago: University of Chicago Press.

Slater, Jerome (1967). *The OAS and United States Foreign Policy*. Columbus: Ohio State University Press.

Slater, Jerome (1969). "The Decline of the OAS." *International Journal*, 24 (Summer): 497–506.

Slater, Jerome (1970). *Intervention and Negotiation: The United States and the Dominican Revolution*. New York: Harper & Row.

Smetherman, Bobbie B., and Robert M. Smetherman (1974). *Territorial Seas and Inter-American Relations*. New York: Praeger.

Smith, Robert Freeman (1960). *The United States and Cuba: Business and Diplomacy, 1917–1960*. New York: Bookman.

Smith, Robert Freeman (ed.) (1981). *The Era of Caribbean Intervention, 1898–1930*. Malabar: Krieger Publishing.

Smith, Tony (1979). "The Underdevelopment of Development Literature: The Case of Dependency Theory." *World Politics*, 31 (January): 247–288.

Solís-Rivera, Luís G. (1987). "Peace and the Future of Central America: A Costa Rican Viewpoint." Washington, D.C.: Friedrich Ebert Stiftung, Washington Office.

Sorenson, Theodore C. (1965). *Kennedy*. New York: Bantam.

Springer, Hugh W. (1962). *Reflections on the Failure of the First West Indian Federation*. Cambridge, Mass.: Harvard University Press.

Stepan, Alfred (1966). "Political Development Theory: The Latin American Experience." *Journal of International Affairs*, 20 (no. 2): 63–74.

Stewart, Watt (1946). *Henry Meiggs*. Durham, N.C.: Duke University Press.

Stewart, Watt (1964). *Keith and Costa Rica*. Albuquerque: University of New Mexico Press.

Stinson, Hugh B., and James D. Cochrane (1971). "The Movement for Regional Arms Control in Latin America." *Journal of Inter-American Studies*, 13 (January): 1–17.

Stuart, Graham H., and James Tigner (1975). *Latin America and the United States*, 6th ed. Englewood Cliffs: Prentice-Hall.

Suárez, Andrés (1967). *Cuba, Castro, and Communism*. Cambridge: MIT Press.

The Sunday Times of London Insight Team (1982). *War in the Falklands: The Full Story*. New York: Harper & Row.

Switzer, Kenneth A. (1973). "The Andean Group." *Inter-American Economic Affairs*, 26 (Spring): 69–81.

Syzmanski, A. (1981). *The Logic of Imperialism*. New York: Praeger.

Tamayo, Jesús (1983). *Zonas Fronterizas*. México: D.F.: CIDE.

Taylor, Philip B. (1963). *Law and Politics in Inter-American Diplomacy*. New York: John Wiley & Sons.

Teitelbaum, Michael S. (1984). *Latin Migration North: The Problem for U.S. Foreign Policy*. New York: Council on Foreign Relations.

Theberge, James D. (ed.) (1972). *Soviet Seapower in the Caribbean*. New York: Praeger.

Theberge, James D. (ed.) (1973). *Russia in the Caribbean*, 2 Parts. Washington, D.C.: Georgetown University Press.

Theberge, James D. (1974). *The Soviet Presence in Latin America*. New York: Crane, Russak.

Thomas, Ann Van Wynen, and A. J. Thomas (1963). *The Organization of American States*. Dallas: Southern Methodist University Press.

Thomas, C. (1984). *The Rise of the Authoritarian State in Peripheral Societies*. New York: Monthly Review Press.

Thompson, William R. (1973). "The Regional Subsystem." *International Studies Quarterly*, 17 (March): 89–117.

Thorp, Rosemary, and Laurence Whitehead (eds.) (1987). *Latin American Debt and the Adjustment Crisis*. Pittsburgh: University of Pittsburgh Press.

Tokatlian, Juan, and Klaus Schubert (1982). *Relaciones Internacionales en la Cuenca del Caribe y la Political de Colombia*. Bogotá: Camara de Comercio de Bogotá.

Tomassini, Luciano (ed.) (1981). *Relaciones Internacionales de la América Latina*. México: Fondo de Cultura Económica.

Trindade, Antônio Augusto Cançado (1981). "Posicoes Internacionais do Brasil no Plano Multilateral." *Revista Brasileira de Estudios Políticos*, 52 (Janeiro): 147–218.

Trindade, Antônio Augusto Cançado (1982). "Direito do Mar: Indicacoes para a Fixacao dos Limites Laterais Matimos." *Revista Brasileira de Estudos Politicos*.

Trindade, Antônio Augusto Cançado (1985). "A Evolução das Competencias dos Orgãos Politicos Internacionais: Os Casos da ONU e da OEA." *Revista Brasileria de Politica Internacional*.

Tulchin, Joseph S. (1983). "Emerging Patterns of Research in the Study of Latin America." *Latin American Research Review*, 18 (no. 1): 85–94.

U.S. Arms Control and Disarmament Agency (1975). *Arms Control and Disarmament Agreements: Texts and History of Negotiations*.

U.S. Department of Commerce (1951). *Foreign Aid by the United States Government, 1940–1951*.

U.S. Department of State (1962). *Inter-American Efforts to Relieve International Tensions in the Western Hemisphere*.

U.S. Department of State (1973). *Arms Sales in Latin America*.

U.S. Department of State (1975). *U.S. Policy Toward Latin America: Recognition and Non-Recognition of Governments and Interruptions in Diplomatic Relations, 1933–1974*.

U.S. Department of State (1987a). "The Holy See." *Background Notes* (March).

U.S. Department of State (1987b). *International Narcotics Control Strategy Report* (March).

U.S. House of Representatives, Committee on Foreign Affairs (1946, 1947). *Inter-American Military Cooperation Act: Hearings*.

U.S. House of Representatives, Committee on Foreign Affairs (1950). *Twenty-ninth Report to Congress on Lend-Lease Operations*.

U.S. House of Representatives, Committee on Foreign Affairs (1975). *The United States and Chile during the Allende Years: Hearings*.

U.S. House of Representatives, Committee on Foreign Affairs (1981). *The Caribbean Basin Policy: Hearings*.

U.S. Library of Congress (1936–1985). *Handbook of Latin American Studies*, 45 vols. Austin: University of Texas Press.

U.S. Library of Congress, Congressional Research Service (1977). *Background Documents Relating to the Panama Canal*. Prepared for the United States Senate Committee on Foreign Relations.

U.S. Senate, Committee on Foreign Relations (1960). *United States–Latin American Relations: Compilation of Studies*.

U.S. Senate, Committee on Foreign Relations (1971). *Additional Protocol II to the Latin American Nuclear Free Zone Treaty*.

U.S. Senate, Committee on Foreign Relations (1977/1978), 5 vols. *Hearings on the Panama Canal Treaty and the Treaty Concerning the Permanent Neutrality and Operation of the Panama Canal*.

U.S. Senate, Select Committee on Secret Military Assistance to Iran and the Nicaraguan Opposition and U.S. House of Representatives Select Committee to Investigate Covert Arms Transactions with Iran (November 1987). *Report of the Congressional Committees Investigating the Iran-Contra Affair with Supplemental, Minority, and Additional Views*. S. Rept. No. 100-216; H. Rept. No. 100-433.

U.S. Senate, Select Committee to Study Government Operations with Respect to Intelligence Activities (1975a). *Alleged Assassination Plots Involving Foreign Leaders: An Interim Report.*

U.S. Senate, Select Committee to Study Government Operations with Respect to Intelligence Activies (1975b). *Covert Action in Chile, 1963–1973: Staff Report.*

U.S. Senate, Select Committee to Study Government Operations with Respect to Intelligence Activities (1976). *Final Report.*

United Kingdom (1982). *The Disputed Islands: The Falklands Crisis: A History and Background.* London: H.M.S.

United Nations (1961). *The United Nations and Latin America: A Collection of Basic Information Material.* New York.

United Nations (1972). *Recopilación de Documentos Básicos de la Comisión Especial de Coordinación Latinoamericana.* New York.

U.N. Economic Commission for Latin America (1956). *La Integración Económica de Centroamérica.* New York.

U.N. Economic Commission for Latin America (1959). *The Latin American Common Market.* New York.

Urquidi, Víctor L. (1962). *Free Trade and Economic Integration in Latin America.* Berkeley: University of California Press.

Urquidi, Víctor L. (1964). *The Challenge of Development in Latin America.* New York: Praeger.

Urquidi, Víctor L., and Rosemary Thorp (eds.) (1973). *Latin America in the International Economy.* New York: Wiley.

Vacs, Aldo César (1987). *Discreet Partners: Argentina and the USSR Since 1917.* Pittsburgh: University of Pittsburgh Press.

Vaky, Viron P. (ed.) (1983). *Governance in the Western Hemisphere.* New York: Praeger, for Aspen Institute for Humanistic Studies.

Valenta, Jiri, and Esperanza Duran (eds.) (1987). *Conflict in Nicaragua: A Multidimensional Perspective.* Boston: Allen & Unwin.

Valois Arce, Daniel (1970). *Reseña Historia sobre los Limites de Colombia y Venezuela.* Medellin: Editorial Bedout.

Van Alstyne, Richard W. (1955). "Britain in Latin America After 1865." *Current History,* 28 (March): 148–153.

Vanderlaan, Mary B. (1986). *Revolution and Foreign Policy in Nicaragua.* Boulder: Westview.

Varas, Augusto (ed.) (1987). *Soviet–Latin American Relations in the 1980s.* Boulder: Westview.

Vargas Silva, Jorge A. (1979). *Terminología sobre Derecho del Mar.* México: Centro de Estudios Económicos y Sociales del Tercer Mundo.

Vázquez, Josefina Zoraida, and Lorenzo Meyer (1985). *The United States and Mexico.* Chicago: University of Chicago Press.

Vázquez Carrizosa, Alfredo (1983). *Las Relaciones de Colombia y Venezuela: La Historia Atormentada de dos Naciones.* Bogotá: Ediciones Tercer Mundo.

Venezuela, Ministerio de Relaciones Exteriores (1983). *Documentos Relativos a los Limites entre Venezuela y Colombia.* Caracas.

Venezuela, Ministerio de Relaciones Exteriores (1984). *Historia Oficial en la Discusión entre Venezuela y la Gran Bretaña sobre sus Limites en la Guayana.* Caracas.

Vernon, Raymond (1971a). *Multinational Enterprise and National Security.* London: Institute for Strategic Studies.

Vernon, Raymond (1971b). *Sovereignty at Bay: The Multinational Spread of U.S. Enterprises.* New York: Basic Books.

Wahlke, John C., and Alex N. Dragnich (eds.) (1966). *Government and Politics*. New York: Random House.

Walker, Thomas W. (ed.) (1987). *Reagan Versus the Sandinistas: The Undeclared War on Nicaragua*. Boulder: Westview.

Ware, David (1980). "The Amazon Treaty: A Turning Point in Latin American Cooperation?" *Texas International Law Journal*, 15 (Winter): 117–137.

Weinberg, Albert K. (1935). *Manifest Destiny*. Baltimore: Johns Hopkins University Press.

Wells, Henry (1969). *The Modernization of Puerto Rico*. Cambridge, Mass.: Harvard University Press.

Wesson, Robert G. (1981). *The United States and Brazil: Limits of Influence*. New York: Praeger.

Wesson, Robert (ed.) (1982). *U.S. Influence in Latin America in the 1980s*. New York: Praeger.

Wesson, Robert, and Heraldo Muñoz (eds.) (1986). *Latin American Views of U.S. Policy*. New York: Praeger.

Whitaker, Arthur P. (1954). *The United States and Argentina*. Cambridge: Harvard University Press.

Whitaker, Arthur P. (1954). *The Western Hemisphere Idea*. Ithaca: Cornell University Press.

Whitaker, Arthur P. (1973). "The New Nationalism in Latin America." *Review of Politics*, 35 (January): 77–90.

Whitaker, Arthur P., and David C. Jordan (1966). *Nationalism in Contemporary Latin America*. New York: The Free Press.

White, E. (1981). "The International Projection of Latin American Firms," in K. Kumar and M. McLeod (eds.), *Multinationals from Developing Countries*. Lexington: D. C. Heath.

Wiarda, Howard J. (ed.) (1982). *Politics and Social Change in Latin America: The Distinct Tradition*, 2d ed. Amherst: University of Massachusetts Press.

Wiarda, Howard J. (ed.) (1985). *New Directions in Comparative Politics*. Boulder: Westview.

Wiarda, Howard J. (ed.) (1986a). *Iberian–Latin American Connection: Implications for U.S. Foreign Policy*. Boulder: Westview.

Wiarda, Howard J. (1986b). *Latin America at the Crossroads: Debt and Development Strategies for the 1990s*. Boulder: Westview.

Wilkins, Mira (1970). *The Emergence of Multinational Enterprise*. Cambridge: Harvard University Press.

Wilkins, Mira (1974). *The Maturing of Multinational Enterprise*. Cambridge: Harvard University Press.

Willetts, Peter (1984). "Latin America, the United Nations, and the Non-Aligned Movement," in J. W. Hopkins (ed.), *Latin America and Caribbean Contemporary Record*. New York: Holmes & Meier.

Williams, Felicity (1984). *La Internacional Socialista y América Latina: Una Visión Crítica*. México: Universidad Autónoma Metropolitana.

Williams, Mary W. (1915). *Anglo-American Isthmian Diplomacy, 1815–1915*. Washington, D.C.: American Historical Association.

Wilson, Larman C. (1964). *The Principle of Non-Intervention in Recent Inter-American Relations: The Challenge of Anti-Democratic Regimes*. Ph.D. dissertation, University of Maryland.

Wilson, Larman C. (1986). "The Contemporary Practice of International Law in Central America: Intervention and Non-Intervention." *Towson State Journal of International Affairs*, 20 (Spring): 85–105.

Wood, Bryce (1961). *The Making of the Good Neighbor Policy*. New York: Columbia University Press.

Wood, Bryce (1966). *The United States and Latin American Wars, 1932–1942*. New York: Columbia University Press.

Wood, Bryce (1972). "Scholarly Exchange Between Latin America and the United States." *Proceedings of the Academy of Political Science*, 30, No. 4: 123–140.

Wood, Bryce (1985). *The Dismantling of the Good Neighbor Policy*. Austin: University of Texas Press.

Wood, Bryce, and Minerva Morales M. (1965). "Latin America and the United Nations." *International Organization*, 19 (Summer): 714–724.

World Bank Group (1972). *The World Bank Group in the Americas*. Washington, D.C.

Wyden, Peter (1979). *Bay of Pigs: The Untold Story*. New York: Simon and Schuster.

Yalem, Ronald (1970). *Regional Subsystems and World Politics*. Tucson: University of Arizona Press.

Zea, Leopoldo (1960). *Latin America and the World*. Norman: University of Oklahoma Press.

Zook, David H. (1960). *The Conduct of the Chaco War*. New Haven: Bookman Associates.

Zook, David H. (1964). *Zarumilla-Marañon: The Ecuador-Peru Dispute*. New York: Bookman Associates.

Acronyms

ACAT	Continental Association of American Workers
AFL-CIO	American Federation of Labor–Congress of Industrial Organizations
ALADI	Latin American Integration Association
ALN	National Liberation Action
ATLAS	Unionized Latin American Workers' Group
BIS	Bank for International Settlements
CACM	Central American Common Market
CARICOM	Caribbean Common Market, Caribbean Community
CARIFTA	Caribbean Free Trade Association
CBI	Caribbean Basin Initiative
CCD	United Nations Committee on Disarmament
CECLA	Special Latin American Coordinating Committee
CELAM	Conference of Latin American Bishops
CIA	Central Intelligence Agency
CIPIC	Intergovernmental Council of Copper Exporting Countries
CIT	Inter-American Federation of Labor
CLASC	Latin American Confederation of Christian Trade Unionists
CODECA	Caribbean Economic Development Corporation
CROM	Regional Confederation of Mexican Labor
CTAL	Confederation of Latin American Workers
CUTAL	Single Central Association of Latin American Workers
EC	European Community
ECLA	United Nations Economic Commission for Latin America
ECLAC	United Nations Economic Commission for Latin America and the Caribbean
ECOSOC	United Nations Economic and Social Council
ELN	National Liberation Army
EPL	Popular Liberation party
ERP	Revolutionary Army of the People
EXIM	Export-Import Bank of Washington
FALN	Armed Forces of National Liberation
FAP	Peronist Armed Forces
FAR	Revolutionary Armed Forces

FARC	Armed Forces of Colombia
FARN	Armed Forces of National Resistance
FDN	National Democratic Front
FDR	Democratic Revolutionary Front
FIR	Revolutionary Leftist Front
FLN	National Liberation Front
FMLN	Farabundo Martí National Liberation Front
FPL	Farabundo Martí Popular Forces of Liberation
FSLN	Sandinist National Liberation Front
GATT	General Agreement on Tariffs and Trade
IAEA	International Atomic Energy Agency
ICAITI	Central American Institute of Industrial Research
ICFTU	International Confederation of Free Trade Unions
ICJ	International Court of Justice
IDB	Inter-American Development Bank
IMF	International Monetary Fund
INTAL	Institute for the Integration of Latin America
IOEC	Organization of Iron Ore Exporting Countries
IPEB	International Organization of Banana Exporters
IRELA	Institute for European–Latin American Relations
ITT	International Telephone and Telegraph
JCR	Revolutionary Coordinating Committee
LAFTA	Latin American Free Trade Association
M-19	19th of April Movement
MIR	Movement of the Revolutionary Left
MNC	Multinational corporation
MPSC	Popular Social Christian Movement
MR-13	13th of November Revolutionary Movement
NATO	North Atlantic Treaty Organization
NIEO	New International Economic Order
NPT	Non-Proliferation Treaty
NSC	National Security Council
OAS	Organization of American States
ODECA	Organization of Central American States
OECS	Organization of Eastern Caribbean States
OIR	Revolutionary Integration Organization
OLADE	Latin American Energy Organization
OLAS	Organization of Latin American Solidarity
OPANAL	Organization for the Prohibition of Nuclear Weapons in Latin America
OPEC	Organization of Petroleum Exporting Countries
ORIT	Inter-American Regional Organization of Workers
PAFL	Pan American Federation of Labor
PRTC	Central American Workers' Revolutionary party
SELA	Latin American Economic System

UNCLOS	United Nations Conference on Law of the Sea
UNCTAD	United Nations Conference on Trade and Development
UNO	United Nicaraguan Opposition
VPR	Popular Revolutionary Vanguard
WFTU	World Federation of Trade Unions

Index

Organizations are alphabetized under their full names rather than their acronyms. See List of Acronyms on page 397.

Acheson, Dean, 122
Act for International Development
  (1950), 267
Adams-Onís Treaty (1821), 115, 289
Agee, Philip, 307
Agricultural Trade Development and
  Assistance Act (1954), 267
Alberdi, Juan Bautista, 228
Alfonsín, Raúl, 252, 287, 316
Allende, Salvador, 69, 101, 127, 128,
  148, 163, 310, 366, 368
Alliance for Progress, 41, 121, 123–
  125, 126, 127, 182, 183, 215,
  234, 268–269, 284–285, 361
Altamira, Rafael, 290
Alvarez, Alejandro, 203
Amazon Basin, River, countries, 33,
  55, 198, 305, 306
Amazon Cooperation Treaty, Amazon
  Pact, 33
American Committee on Public
  Information (Creel Committee),
  292
American Congress (1847), 178
American Convention on Human
  Rights (1969) (Pact of San José),
  208, 231
American Declaration on the Rights
  and Duties of Man (1948), 208
American Federation of Labor–Congress
  of Industrial Organizations (AFL-
  CIO), 151, 152, 153–154

American Institute for Free Labor
  Development, 153
Americanismo, 66, 175–176, 177–180
Anaya, Mélida, 166
Ancón Treaty (1883), 301
Andean Common Market, Andean
  Group, 33, 183, 184, 194, 196
Andean Pact (Agreement of Cartagena),
  194, 195
Andean region, Andean mountains, 22,
  55
Anglo-American Caribbean
  Commission, 188
Anglo-Argentine War, 46, 95, 97, 132,
  225–226, 227, 243–244, 287,
  297, 314–317, 321
Anguilla, 189–190
Antarctic Treaty (1959), Antarctica, 33,
  46, 54, 83, 297, 317, 335, 336,
  340–342, 345
Antigua-Barbuda, 28, 56, 82, 189, 191,
  192, 213, 232, 269, 340
Anti-War Treaty of Non-Aggression and
  Conciliation (1933), 227
APRA Rebelde, 161
Aprista party, 152, 161
Arbenz Guzmán, Jacobo, 81, 122, 308
Arévalo, Juan, 308
Argentina, 28
  Antarctica and, 340–342
  arms control, 238, 336, 338, 339,
    340

balance of power, 38–39, 40, 77, 79, 299–300
Brazil and, 38, 46, 299–300, 316
capability analysis of, 54, 55, 56, 59, 61, 62, 63
Central America and, 321
Chile and, 39, 46, 299–300, 317–318
Communist party, 156
cultural relations, 292, 293
decision making in, 71, 72, 76
diplomatic relations, 75, 289
economic integration and association, 192, 193, 196, 197, 198, 199
economic relations, 257, 258, 259, 261–262, 264, 265, 266, 271, 273, 360
France and, 8
geography, 32, 33
geopolitics, 82–83
Germany and, 89, 91, 92, 93, 94
guerrilla groups, 163
Hague System, 238
Inter-American System, 204, 213, 218, 219, 220, 225–226, 233, 306
Israel and, 105, 106
Italy and, 89, 96
Japan and, 104
leadership aspirations, 29, 77, 79
League of Nations and, 239
military relations, 166, 277, 278, 280, 281, 282, 286, 287, 369
narcotics traffic and, 274
nationalism, 67
Nonaligned Movement, nonalignment, 80, 81, 252
People's Republic of China and, 106, 107
Soviet Union and, 33, 46, 304, 314
Spain and, 97
Spanish American union and, 176, 177, 178, 179
United Kingdom and, 86, 87, 89–90, 92, 95, 299–300, 310, 313–317
United Nations and, 249
United States and, 33, 123, 129, 132

Arias, Oscar, 45, 324
Arias plan. *See* Procedure for the Establishment of a Firm and Lasting Peace in Central America
Armed Forces of Colombia (FARC), 162
Armed Forces of National Liberation (FALN), 162
Armed Forces of National Resistance (FARN), 162
Arms control, 19, 237, 239, 335–340
Arms industry, 278
Aruba, 269
Asturias, Miguel Angel, 164
Asturias, Rodrigo (pseud. Ilmo, Gaspar), 164
Atlantic Community Development Group for Latin America, 147, 148
Australia, 286, 341
Austria, 213
Automotive companies, 144, 147

Baena Soares, João Clemente, 212
Bahamas, 28, 56, 82, 191, 264, 265, 266, 269, 274, 282, 340
Baker Initiative, 262
Baker, James A., 248, 262
Balance of power, 6, 13–15, 23, 296
bipolar system, 14, 40, 48
multiple balance, 14, 89, 355
spheres of influence, 14–15, 21
subsystem change and, 33, 34–47
Bank for International Settlements (BIS), 262
Banking, banks, 64, 146–147, 260, 262. *See also* Debt
Barbados, 28, 56, 59, 70, 81, 189, 190, 191, 212, 253, 264, 265, 266, 269, 273, 282, 340, 345
Barbosa, Ruy, 238
Bateman Cayón, Jaime, 163
Batista, Fulgencio, 124, 161, 311
Bautista, Nicolás, 162
Beagle Channel, 46, 140, 287, 317–318
Behn, Sosthenes, 147
Bejar, Héctor, 161
Belgium, 213, 285, 341

Belgrade Conference (1961), 252
Belize, 28, 56, 70, 81, 191, 212, 243,
    253, 264, 265, 266, 269, 274,
    282, 312–313, 328, 338, 340
Bermudez, Enrique V., 165, 166
Betancourt, Rómulo, 230
Betancur, Belisario, 163
Big stick policy. See Roosevelt
    Corollary
Biological Weapons Convention (1975),
    336
Blanco, Hugo, 161
Boff, Leonardo, 142, 143
Bolívar, Simón, 66, 176, 177
Bolivarian Congress (1833), 179
Bolivia, 28
    Antarctica and, 341
    arms control, 337, 340
    capability analysis of, 54, 55, 56, 59,
        64
    Chile and, 30, 38, 55, 301
    Communist party, 169
    decision making in, 71, 72
    economic integration and association,
        192, 194, 195, 196, 197, 198
    economic relations, 259, 261–262,
        264, 265, 266
    geography, 32, 33, 38
    Germany and, 89, 92, 93
    guerrilla groups, 163–164, 311–312
    Inter-American System and, 233
    International Tin Agreement
        membership, 251
    Japan and, 104
    League of Nations and, 240
    military relations, 277, 280, 282
    narcotics traffic and, 274, 275, 276
    nationalism, 69, 168
    nonalignment, Nonaligned Movement
        and, 81, 274, 275, 276
    Paraguay and, 240, 279, 280, 301,
        305
    Peru and, 38, 55, 300–301
    Spain and, 90
    Spanish American union, 176, 178,
        179
    United States and, 132

Bolivian Movement of the
    Revolutionary Left, 164
Bolshevik Revolution, Russian
    Revolution, 98, 99, 155, 279, 289,
    304
Bosch, Juan, 309
Braganza family, 65
Brandt, Willy, 158, 159
Brandt Commission, 159
Bravo, Douglas, 162
Brazil, 28, 29
    Africa/Middle East and, 46, 47
    Antarctica and, 341
    Argentina and, 38, 46, 299–300, 316
    arms control, 47, 337, 338, 339,
        340
    balance of power, 38–39, 77, 79,
        299–300
    capability analysis of, 54, 55, 56, 59,
        61, 62, 63
    Chile and, 299–300
    coffee agreement and, 250
    cultural relations, 292, 293
    debt, 47
    decision making in, 72, 74, 75, 76
    economic integration and association,
        192, 193, 196, 197, 198, 199
    economic relations, 257, 258, 259,
        261–262, 263, 264, 265, 266,
        271, 273
    France and, 89
    geography, 32, 33, 34
    geopolitics, 82–83
    Germany and, 91, 92, 94
    guerrilla groups, 163
    Hague System and, 237, 238
    Holy See and, 138, 139
    Inter-American System and, 204,
        219, 220, 224, 227, 232, 306, 310
    Israel and, 105
    Japan and, 47, 104
    law of the sea and, 345
    leadership aspirations, 77, 79
    League of Nations and, 239
    military relations, 277, 278, 280,
        281, 282, 286, 369
    narcotics traffic and, 274

nationalism, 65–66, 67, 175
nonalignment, Nonaligned Movement
    and, 80, 81, 252
Organization of Iron Ore Exporting
    Countries membership, 251
People's Republic of China and, 106,
    107
Portugal and, 87–88, 95, 96
Soviet Union and, 304
Spanish American union and, 177,
    178, 179
United Kingdom and, 40, 86, 90,
    92, 299–300
United Nations and, 249
United States and, 34, 47, 110–111,
    126, 129, 132, 133
Uruguay and, 300
British Commonwealth. *See*
    Commonwealth of Nations
British Guiana. *See* Guyana
British Honduras. *See* Belize
British Virgin Islands, 246, 269
Brum, Baltasar, 219
Brum Doctrine, 219
Bryan-Chamorro Treaty, 185
Bunau-Varilla, Philippe, 330, 331
Bunke, Tamara "Tania," 164
Bunker, Ellsworth, 332
Burnham, L.F.S., 190
Business enterprise, 143–150

Caamaño, Francisco, 309
Calero, Adolfo, 165, 166
Calvo, Carlos, 215
Calvo Doctrine, 215–216, 217
Camdessus, Michael, 249
Campos, Roberto, 364
Canada, 190–191, 213, 221, 234, 246,
    270, 272, 286
Capability analysis, 10–11, 17
Cardenal, Ernesto, 143
Caribbean Basin. *See* Circum-Caribbean
Caribbean Basin Initiative (CBI), 132,
    269–270, 272, 321, 361
Caribbean Commission, 188

Caribbean Common Market, Caribbean
    Community (CARICOM), 183,
    191–192, 273
Caribbean Council, 188
Caribbean Economic Development
    Corporation, 189
Caribbean Free Trade Association
    (CARIFTA), 183, 190–191
Caribbean integration, 188–192
Caribbean Legion, 318–319
Caribbean Regional Conference on
    Drug Abuse (1987), 275
Cartagena Group, 261, 262
Carter, Jimmy, 103, 128–130, 288,
    320, 332, 357
Castañeda, Eduardo Sancho (pseud.
    Cienfuegos, Ferman), 166
Castillo Armas, Carlos, 308
Castro, Cipriano, 302
Castro, Fidel, 69, 74, 125, 161, 162,
    164, 167, 168, 252, 253–254,
    262, 307, 311, 357, 366
Castro revolution. *See* Cuban
    Revolution
Caudillismo, caudillos, 62, 74
Cayetano Carpio, Salvador, 166
Central America, 31–32, 184–188,
    269, 320–326, 357. *See also*
    Circum-Caribbean
Central American Common Market
    (CACM), 181, 182, 184, 186–188
Central American Court of Justice, 185
Central American Economic
    Cooperation Committee, 186
Central American Federation, 177, 185
Central American Institute of
    Industrial Research (ICAITI), 186
Central American Workers'
    Revolutionary party (PRTC), 166
Central Intelligence Agency (CIA), 128,
    166, 306–307, 309, 310
Cerro de Pasco, 145
César, Alfredo, 165
Chaco War, 240, 279, 280, 301, 305
Chamizal dispute, 335
Charter of Economic Rights and Duties
    of States (1974), 346

Charter of Punta del Este, 124, 234, 268
Chile, 28
  Antarctica and, 341, 342
  Argentina and, 39, 46, 299–300, 317–318
  arms control, 238, 337, 342
  balance of power, 38–39, 77, 299
  Bolivia and, 30, 38, 55, 301
  Brazil and, 299–300
  capability analysis of, 54, 55, 56, 59, 61, 62, 63, 64
  CIPIC membership, 251
  cultural relations, 293
  decision making in, 69, 71, 73
  economic integration and association, 192, 193, 194, 195
  economic relations, 258, 259, 261–262, 264, 265, 266, 271
  geography, 32, 33
  geopolitics, 82, 83
  Germany and, 89, 92, 93
  guerrilla groups, 312
  Hague System, 238
  Holy See and, 140, 141
  Inter-American System and, 218, 219, 220, 224, 226, 232, 235
  IOEC membership, 251
  Israel and, 105
  law of the sea and, 342, 343, 344
  leadership aspirations, 29, 77, 79
  League of Nations and, 239, 240
  military relations, 277, 278, 279, 281, 282, 285, 286, 287, 369
  nationalism, 67
  nonalignment, Nonaligned Movement and, 80, 81, 253
  People's Republic of China and, 107
  Peru and, 38, 300, 301
  Soviet Union and, 101, 304
  Spain and, 90, 292
  Spanish American union, 176, 178, 179, 180
  United Kingdom and, 92
  United Nations and, 249
  United States and, 127, 128, 129, 132, 327, 357

China. See People's Republic of China
Christian Democratic parties, 95, 137, 141, 153, 155, 156
Christian Democratic World Union, 95, 155, 156
Chrysler, 144, 147
Churchill, Winston, 189
Cienfuegos, Ferman. See Castañeda, Eduardo Sancho
Circum-Caribbean, 31–32, 45–46, 53, 296–297, 318–326
Clark, J. Reuben, 120
Clayton-Bulwer Treaty (1850), 37, 87, 90, 91, 329
Cleveland, Grover, 117
Coffee agreement (1962), 250
Cold war, 9, 40, 48, 81, 121, 123, 124, 157, 240, 251, 267, 289, 306, 358
Colombia, 28, 185
  arms control, 340
  balance of power, 39
  capability analysis of, 55, 56, 59, 61, 62, 63, 64
  coffee agreement and, 250
  Contadora and, 45, 55, 323
  decision making in, 71, 72, 73
  diplomatic relations, 78–79, 289
  economic integration and association, 191, 192, 193, 194, 198
  economic relations, 258, 259, 261–262, 264, 265, 266, 270, 271, 272
  geography, 31, 32, 33
  guerrilla groups, 162–163, 311, 312
  Holy See and, 139, 141, 142
  Inter-American System and, 219, 232
  law of the sea and, 345
  leadership aspirations, 29, 79
  League of Nations and, 240
  military relations, 277, 279, 280, 282, 286
  narcotics traffic and, 274, 275, 276
  nonalignment, Nonaligned Movement and, 80, 81, 253, 254
  Peru and, 300

Spanish American union, 176, 177, 178, 179
United Kingdom and, 90
United States and, 131, 328–330
Colorado River problem, 127, 335
Commercial Bureau of the American Republics, 205
Commodity agreements, 250–251
Commonwealth Caribbean Countries, 28, 31, 69–70, 96, 271–272
Commonwealth of Nations, 49, 189
Communist International, Comintern, 99, 155, 156–157, 289
Communist parties, 98, 99, 154–155, 156–157, 289, 304, 311
Conable, Barber B., 248
Confederation of Latin American Workers (CTAL), 151–152, 153
Conference of Latin American Bishops (CELAM), 137–141
Conflict, 17–18, 295–326
Congress of Jurists (1877–1879), 179
Congress of Panama (1826), 177, 178
Conservative parties, 139
Contadora Group, Contadora process, 45, 46, 55, 140, 323, 324, 325
Contadora Support Group, 45, 323, 324, 325
Continental Association of American Workers (ACAT), 151
Continental Congress, Continental Treaty (1856), 178–179
Contras, 164–166, 323
Convention Chartering the Central American Bank for Economic Integration (1960), 186
Convention for the Maintenance, Preservation, and Re-establishment of Peace (1936), 219
Convention on the Rights and Duties of States (1933), Additional Protocol (1936), 217
Coolidge, Calvin, 118, 304
Costa Rica, 28, 31
    arms control, 340
    capability analysis of, 52, 59, 61
    decision making in, 73

economic relations, 264, 265, 266, 269, 273
guerrilla groups, 165
Hague System, 238
Holy See and, 141
integration, 185, 186, 187, 188
Inter-American System and, 222, 227, 231
law of the sea and, 345
League of Nations and, 239, 240
military relations, 282
nonalignment, 81
Council of the Americas, 147
Council on Foreign Relations, 149
Creel, George, 292
Creole Oil Company, 146, 149
Cruz, Arturo, 165, 166
Cuba, 28, 49
    Africa and, 62, 129
    arms control, 337, 338, 340
    capability analysis of, 56, 59, 63
    cultural relations, 293
    diplomatic relations, 289
    economic relations, 258, 259, 264, 265, 266, 269, 272–273
    guerrilla groups, guerrilla warfare, 311–312
    Inter-American System and, 204, 209, 212, 213, 218, 222, 223-224, 231
    Japan and, 272
    military relations, 282, 285
    nationalism, 69
    nationalization, 71
    Nicaragua and, 322
    nonalignment, Nonaligned Movement and, 81, 252, 253–254, 259
    People's Republic of China and, 106, 107
    Soviet Union and, 31, 40, 41, 42, 43, 45, 71, 81, 85, 98, 100, 101, 304, 367
    Spain and, 90, 95
    United Nations and, 241, 243
    United States and, 37, 41, 45, 112, 113, 117, 120–122, 124–128, 130,

131, 302, 303–304, 308–311, 320, 356, 357
Cuban missile crisis (1962), 41–42, 98, 100, 125–126, 222, 224, 337
Cuban Revolution, 40, 69, 121, 122, 157, 161, 268, 289
Cuenca del Plata accord (1969), 33, 197–198
Cultural relations, 290–293

Danish West Indies, 35, 37, 39, 86, 89, 113, 118
Dávila, Carlos, 210
Death squads, 160
Debray, Régis, 168
Debt, 42, 43–44, 47, 64, 110, 132, 133, 248, 249, 257–258, 259–263
Decision making, decision theory, 11–12
Declaration on the Establishment of a New Economic Order, 346
de la Puente Uceda, Luís F., 161
de Larosiere, Jacques, 249
de Lesseps, Ferdinand, 329
de Maeztu, Ramiro, 291
de Soto, Alvaro, 345
de Unamuno, Miguel, 290
Democratic Action party, 162
Democratic Movement, 165
Democratic party, 155
Democratic Revolutionary Front (FDR), 166
Denmark, 213. See also Danish West Indies
Dependency, dependency theory, 47, 363–369
  neo-Marxist, 366–369
  structural, 364, 365–366, 367
D'Escoto, Miguel, 143
Development theory, developmentalism, 48, 359–363
Diplomacy, diplomatic relations, 18, 257, 288–290
Disarmament. See Arms control
Doctrine of the Two Spheres, 113
Dollar diplomacy, 303

Dominica, 28, 56, 81, 189, 191, 192, 213, 253, 269, 338, 340
Dominican Republic, 28
  arms control and, 340
  capability analysis of, 57, 62
  economic integration, 187, 191
  economic relations, 262, 264, 265, 266, 269, 273
  Haiti and, 305
  Holy See and, 140, 141
  Inter-American System and, 62, 218, 222, 227, 230
  law of the sea and, 345
  League of Nations and, 239
  military relations, 282
  narcotics traffic and, 274–275
  nonalignment, 82
  Spain and, 36, 90, 179
  United Nations and, 243
  United States and, 37, 113, 118, 120, 126, 302, 303, 304, 309, 356
Dominican Revolutionary party (PRD), 158
Drabble, George, 145
Drago, Luis M., 216, 238
Drago Doctrine, 216, 238
Dulles, John Foster, 122, 308
Dutch Guiana. See Suriname
Dutch West Indies Company, 144

Easter Island, 33
East-West conflict. See Cold war
Echevarría, Luís, 200, 346
Economic relations, 79–80, 257–276
Economic integration, 21, 180–184, 366
Ecuador, 28, 176
  arms control and, 337, 340
  balance of power, 39
  capability analysis of, 54, 57, 64
  coffee agreement and, 250
  economic relations, 262, 264, 265, 266
  economic integration and association, 192, 193, 194, 197, 198
  geography, 32

guerrillas and, 312
Holy See and, 141
Inter-American System and, 209, 223
labor unions, 72
law of the sea and, 342, 343, 344,
    345
League of Nations and, 239
military relations, 277, 279, 280,
    282
narcotics traffic and, 274
nonalignment, Nonaligned Movement
    and, 81, 252
OPEC membership, 49, 250
Peru and, 305–306
Spanish American union, 178, 179
United States and, 128, 306, 307
Ecuadorian Democratic Left, 158
Egypt, 213
Eisenhower, Dwight D., 122, 124, 125,
    309
Eisenhower, Milton, 122, 123
Eisenhower Plan, 123, 234, 268
Eisenhower-Remón Treaty (1955), 331
El Salvador, 28
    arms control and, 340
    capability analysis of, 57, 59, 60
    Communist party, 166
    Contadora and, 323
    diplomatic relations, 76
    economic relations, 264, 265, 266,
        269, 273
    guerrilla groups, 166–167
    Holy See and, 140
    Honduras and, 62, 319
    integration, 185, 186, 187, 188
    Inter-American System and, 222,
        227, 231, 232, 233
    law of the sea and, 345
    military relations, 279, 282, 287,
        288
    Nicaragua and, 320
    nonalignment, 81
    Social Democratic party, 166
    Soviet Union and, 304
    Spanish American union, 179
    United States and, 71, 129, 131,
        320, 321

Electronics industry, 144
Emergency Advisory Committee for
    Political Defense, 220
Ends-means analysis, 9, 77–80
Engels, Friedrich, 354
England. See United Kingdom
Enríquez, Miguel, 163
Esquipulus II accords. See Procedure
    for the Establishment of a Firm
    and Lasting Peace in Central
    America
Estrada, Genaro, 228
Estrada Doctrine, 228, 229, 290
Europe. See individual countries
European Community (EC), 96–97,
    199, 213, 225–226, 271–272, 315,
    316, 323, 325, 361
Executive Committee of the National
    Security Council, 125
Expansionists of 1898, 117
Export-Import Bank of Washington
    (EXIM), 263, 264, 267–268, 315
External debt. See Debt

Falangism, 93, 291, 292
Falkland/Malvinas islands, 87, 95, 97,
    189, 225–226, 301–302, 313–317
Farabundo Martí National Liberation
    Front (FMLN), 166
Farabundo Martí Popular Forces of
    Liberation (FPL), 166
Fascism (Italian), 157
Febrerista Revolutionary party, 158
Ferdinand VII, 289
Fidelismo, 74, 355
Finland, 213
Firmenich, Mario, 163
First South American Congress (1888–
    1889), 179–180
Fishermen's Protective Act (1954), 343
Foco theory, 167–168
Fonseca Amador, Carlos, 164
Ford, Gerald, 126, 127–128, 307
Foreign debt. See Debt
Foreign policy orientations, 8–10, 77–
    83
France, 7, 28, 96, 177

arms control and, 338, 339, 340, 341
balance of power, 35, 39–40, 88, 89, 91
Caribbean territories, 31, 35, 39, 85, 86, 95, 188–189
cultural relations, 290, 292, 293
diplomatic relations, 289
economic relations, 191, 257, 258, 259, 270
Inter-American System and, 213
military relations, 277, 278, 279, 280, 285, 286
Panama Canal and, 91, 328–329, 330
United Nations and, 246
See also individual countries
Franco, Francisco, 93, 95, 96, 290, 291
Free trade theory, 181, 184
Freedom of Action Resolution (1975), 224
Furtado, Celso, 364

Gadsden, James, 298
Gadsden Purchase (1853), 298
Galapagos Islands, 33
Galtieri, Leopoldo, 314
García, Alan, 262
García Robles, Alfonso, 337
General Agreement on Tariffs and Trade (GATT), 199
General Confederation of Labor, 152
General Treaty of Central American Economic Integration (1960), 186
Geneva protocol (1925), 336–337
Geopolitics, 54, 82–83, 299
Georgetown Treaty (1972), 191
Germany, 7, 96
  Antarctica and, 341
  balance of power, 36, 37, 40, 89, 92
  cultural relations, 292, 293
  diplomatic relations, 95
  economic relations, 191, 257, 258, 259, 270
  Inter-American System and, 213, 220

military relations, 92, 277, 278, 279, 280, 285, 286
Gómez, José F., 290
Gondra, Manuel, 226
González, Norberto, 246
Gonzáles Posada, Adolfo, 290
Good Neighbor Policy, 99, 119–121, 292, 304, 330
Goulart, João, 337
Grace, William Russell, 146
Gran Colombia, 176
Great Britain. See United Kingdom
Great War (1836), 299
Greece, 213
Greenland, 221
Grenada, 28, 46, 57, 59, 62, 63, 81, 131, 189, 191, 192, 213, 218, 252, 264, 265, 266, 269, 282, 297, 321, 322, 340, 356
Group of 77, 48, 346, 347
Guatemala, 28
  arms control and, 338, 340
  Belize and, 70
  capability analysis of, 57, 59–60
  economic relations, 264, 265, 266, 269, 273
  Germany and, 92
  guerrilla groups, 164, 311
  integration, 185, 186, 187, 188
  Inter-American System and, 212, 213, 218, 222, 223, 231, 232, 233
  law of the sea and, 345
  Mexico and, 313
  military relations, 277, 280, 282, 287, 288
  nonalignment, 82
  Soviet Union and, 99
  Spanish American union, 179
  United Kingdom and, 87, 95, 312–313
  United Nations and, 243
  United States and, 41, 129, 302, 303, 308, 313, 320, 321, 322
Guatemalan National Revolutionary Union, 164
Guerrilla groups, guerrilla warfare, 29, 159–169, 296, 311–312, 318–319

Guevara, Ernesto "Che," 101, 142, 163–164, 167–169, 308, 311
Gutiérrez, Gustavo, 142
Guyana, 28, 32, 33, 57, 70, 81, 191, 198, 212, 213, 253, 264, 265, 266, 274, 282, 312, 338, 340, 345
Guzmán Reynoso, Abimael, 162

Hague Court of Arbitration, Permanent Court of Arbitration, 118, 237
Hague Peace Conferences, Hague System, 40, 180, 203, 237–238
Haig, Alexander, 233–315
Haiti, 28
    arms control and, 340
    capability analysis of, 57, 59, 60, 63
    Dominican Republic and, 305
    economic integration, 191
    economic relations, 258, 264, 265, 266, 269
    France and, 88
    Holy See and, 140
    Inter-American System and, 222, 227, 231
    law of the sea and, 345
    military relations, 282
    nonalignment, 82
    United States and, 131, 302, 303, 304
Handel, Shafick Jorge, 166
Harding, Warren G., 304
Hay, John, 329
Hay-Bunau-Varilla Treaty (1903), 330
Hay-Herrán Treaty (1903), 330
Hay-Pauncefote Treaty (1901), 90, 329
Hepburn bill (1902), 330
Hernández, José, 67
Herrera, Felipe, 234, 235
Hispanidad, 93, 95, 291, 292
Hispanismo, 90, 93, 290–291
Hitler, Adolf, 93
Ho Chi Minh, 167, 168
Holland. See Netherlands
Holy Alliance, 177
Holy See. See Roman Catholic Church
Honduras, 28

    arms control and, 340
    capability analysis of, 57, 58–60
    economic relations, 258, 264, 265, 266, 269, 273
    El Salvador and, 62, 319
    Hague System and, 238
    integration, 185, 186, 187
    Inter-American System and, 222, 227, 231, 233
    law of the sea and, 345
    military relations, 282, 288
    nonalignment, 82
    United Nations and, 243
    United States and, 302, 303, 308, 321, 322, 329
Hoover, Herbert, 120, 304
Hotel industry, 147
Hull, Cordell, 120, 122, 242
Hull-Alfaro Treaty (1939), 331

Ibero-America, 28
Idealism, theory of, 353, 354, 355–356, 362
Iglesias, Enrique, 234, 246, 247
Ilmo, Gaspar. See Asturias, Rodrigo
Imbert, Antonio, 309
India, 341
Institute for European–Latin American Relations (IRELA), 96–97
Institute for the Integration of Latin America (INTAL), 182
Institute of Latin American Studies of the Academy of Sciences of the USSR, 98, 367
Insurgency. See Guerrilla groups
Inter-American Children's Institute, 207
Inter-American Commission of Women, 207
Inter-American Commission on Human Rights, 208, 210, 211, 231–233
Inter-American Committee on Peaceful Settlement, 211
Inter-American Conferences, 209, 212, 215, 216, 223, 226
Inter-American Council for Commerce and Production, 147

Inter-American Council for Education, Science, and Culture, 211
Inter-American Council of Jurists, 209–210
Inter-American Court of Human Rights, 208
Inter-American Cultural Council, 210, 211
Inter-American Defense Board, 207, 210, 220
Inter-American Defense College, 210
Inter-American Development Bank (IDB), 182, 198, 213, 234, 268, 272, 273
Inter-American Development Commission, 233
Inter-American Drug Abuse Control Commission, 275
Inter-American Economic and Social Council, 199, 209, 211
Inter-American Federation of Labor (CIT), 152, 153
Inter-American Financial and Advisory Committee, 233
Inter-American Indian Institute, 207
Inter-American Institute of Agricultural Sciences, 207
Inter-American Juridical Committee, 210, 220
Inter-American Neutrality Committee, 220
Inter-American Nuclear Energy Commission, 210
Inter-American Peace Committee, 210, 211
Inter-American Peace Force, 62
Inter-American Regional Organization of Workers (ORIT), 152, 153
Inter-American Specialized Conference on Human Rights, 208
Inter-American Statistical Institute, 207
Inter-American System, 40, 41, 43, 45, 49, 202–235, 331
  anti-communist alliance, 122, 124, 215, 222, 223–225, 308
  constitutional bases, 207–209
  democracy and human rights, 228–233
  economic cooperation, 233–235
  economic integration and, 180, 182, 183
  ideological pluralism, 225
  institutional development, 205–207
  mutual security, 218–226, 314, 315, 316, 323
  nonintervention, 120, 215–218
  Pan Americanism and, 202–203, 212, 214
  peaceful settlement, 226–228, 240, 305, 306, 308, 319
  peacekeeping force, 310
  policy instrument, 203–204
Inter-American Treaty of Good Offices and Mediation (1935), 227
Inter-American Treaty of Pacific Settlement (1948), Pact of Bogotá, 208, 227
Inter-American Treaty of Reciprocal Assistance (1947), Rio Treaty, 40, 81, 192, 207, 208, 209, 212, 218, 221, 222–226, 229, 315
Intergovernmental Council of Copper Exporting Countries (CIPIC), 251
International Atomic Energy Agency (IAEA), 338–339
International Bank for Reconstruction and Development. See World Bank Group
International Basic Economy Corporation, 147
International Bauxite Association, 251
International Bureau of the American Republics, 205
International Coffee Agreement (1962), 250–251
International Confederation of Free Trade Unions (ICFTU), 152
International Conferences of American States, 205, 209, 214, 238. See also Inter-American Conferences
International Court of Justice (ICJ), 245–246, 312, 317
International Development Agency, 248

International Federation of Christian Trade Unions, 153
International Finance Corporation, 248
International governmental organizations, 6, 13, 15–16, 19, 237–254
International Ladies Garment Workers Union, 153
International law, 6, 15
International Monetary Fund (IMF), 64, 199, 248–249, 262, 267, 347, 364, 368
International Organization of Banana Exporters (IPEB), 251
International political analysis, 4–5
International regimes, 6, 19, 328–347
International subsystems, regional subsystems, 20–21, 23–49
International Telephone and Telegraph (ITT), 144, 147, 310
International Union of American States, 205
Iran, 293
Iran-contra affair, 166, 308, 326
Isolationism, 80–81
Israel, 104–106, 213, 345. See also individual countries
Italy, 7, 36, 37, 89, 191
    cultural relations, 292, 293
    Inter-American System and, 213, 220
    military relations, 279, 280, 281, 285
    See also individual countries

Jamaica, 28, 57, 81, 189, 190, 191, 212, 251, 253, 264, 265, 266, 269, 272, 273, 274, 282, 340, 345
Jamaica letter, 176
Jamaican People's National party, 158
Japan, 7, 43, 46, 103–104
    Antarctica and, 341–342
    economic relations, 259, 260, 270, 271, 272
    Inter-American System and, 213, 220
    military relations, 279
    Panama Canal and, 334

Jefferson, Thomas, 116
Johnson, Lyndon B., 123, 126, 182
Jovel, Ernesto, 166
Juárez, Benito, 91, 298

Keith, Miner Cooper, 146
Kennedy, John F., 123–126, 268, 309
Khrushchev, Nikita, 309
Kissinger, Henry, 127, 128, 131, 321, 332
Kissinger Commission. See Report of the President's National Bipartisan Commission on Central America
Knights of Malta, 137–138
Knox, Philander C., 303
Kubitschek, Juscelino, 223, 268, 340

Labor unions, international labor movements, 29, 72, 150–154
Latin American Confederation of Christian Trade Unionists (CLASC), 153
Latin American Economic System (SELA), 82, 180, 199–200, 248, 252, 261, 347
Latin American Energy Organization (OLADE), 82, 252
Latin American Free Trade Association (LAFTA), 181, 182, 183, 184, 192–194, 197, 368
Latin American Integration Association (ALADI), 183, 184, 196–197
Latin American Nuclear Free Zone. See Treaty for the Prohibition of Nuclear Weapons in Latin America
Law of the sea, 19, 342–346
League of Nations, 40, 180, 238–241, 301, 305, 306. See also individual countries
Lehder, Carlos, 275–276
Lend-Lease Act (1941), Lend-Lease programs, 281
Lenin, V. I., 155, 355
Leninism. See Marxism-Leninism
Letelier, Orlando, 287
Leticia conflict, 240–241, 306
Liberal parties, 139

Liberation Theology, 142–143, 366
Limited Test Ban Treaty (1963), 336
Lleras Camargo, Alberto, 210, 242
Lobaton, Guillermo, 161
Lodge, Henry Cabot, 117
Lombardo Toldedano, Vicente, 151–152
Lomé convention, 96, 271–272
London Club, 261
"Low profile" policy, 127, 268
Lucas García, Roméo, 288, 320

McCone, John A., 310
Magdalena-Cauca river system, 55
Mahan, Alfred Thayer, 117, 356–357
Malvinas islands. See Falkland/Malvinas islands
Manifest Destiny, 115, 297
Mao Tse-Tung, Maoism, 162, 167–168, 355
Marighella, Carlos, 163, 169
Marín, Pedro Antonio (pseud. Vélez, Manuel Marulanda), 162
Maritain, Jacques, 137
Marshall, George C., 122
Martí, José, 69
Marx, Karl, 354
Marxism, Marxist, 69, 74, 97, 98, 156, 354–355
Marxism-Leninism, 354–355, 366, 367, 368
Maximilian, Archduke of Austria, 91, 298
Meatpacking companies, 145
Medellin cartel, 274, 275, 276
Meeting of Consultation of Ministers of Foreign Affairs, 207, 208, 209, 211, 219–220, 223, 224, 225, 230, 233
Meiggs, Henry, 146
Mexican Revolution (1910), 299
Mexican-U.S. riverine agreements, 335
Mexican-U.S. war, 298
Mexico, 28, 30–31
    aid to Latin American states, 191
    arms control, 337, 340

capability analysis of, 44, 53, 55, 57, 59, 61, 62, 63, 64, 77
Central America and, 185, 187, 322
Contadora and, 323
cultural relations, 293
debt, 44
decision making in, 71, 72, 73, 75, 76
diplomatic relations, 289, 290
economic integration and association, 192, 193, 196
economic relations, 44, 258, 259, 261, 262, 264, 265, 266, 270, 271, 273
economy, 63, 64
expropriations, 120
France and, 36, 88, 91, 179, 297, 298
geography, 31
Germany and, 92
Guatemala and, 313
guerrilla groups, 166
Hague System and, 237, 238
Holy See and, 139, 141
Inter-American System and, 219, 220, 227
Israel and, 105
law of the sea and, 345
leadership aspirations, 29, 77, 79
League of Nations and, 239
military relations, 281, 282
narcotics traffic and, 274, 275
nationalism, 44, 67
nonalignment, Nonaligned Movement and, 80, 81, 253, 254
People's Republic of China and, 106, 107
Soviet Union and, 98, 304
Spain and, 90, 95, 297
Spanish American union, 176, 177, 178, 179
United Kingdom and, 86, 87, 90, 298
United States and, 30–31, 37, 38, 44, 110–111, 113–114, 115, 117–118, 120, 127, 129, 130, 131, 296–298, 307, 335

Military cooperation, 276–288, 361–363
Military establishments, 29, 62, 68–69, 76
Mining companies, 145
Moncayo García, Jaime, 200
Monetarists, 364–365
Monroe, James, 113
Monroe Doctrine, 37, 113, 114–115, 116, 117, 120, 216, 218, 219, 220, 240, 303
Montoneros, 163
Montserrat, 189, 190, 191, 192, 246, 269
Mora, José A., 210, 212
Morocco, 213
Movement of the Revolutionary Left (MIR), 161, 162, 163
Multinational corporations (MNCs), 13, 29, 143–144, 154, 195, 366. *See also* Business enterprise
Mutual Defense Act (1949), 281
Mutual Defense Assistance pacts, 283
Mutual Security Act (1951), 267, 283

Napoleon III, 298
Napoleonic Wars, 88
Narcotics traffic, 110, 132, 133, 274–276, 296
National Democratic Front (FDN), 165, 166
National Liberation Action (ALN), 163
National Liberation Army (ELN), 161, 162, 164
National Liberation Front (FLN) (Tupumaros), 162
National Revolutionary Movement, 166
National Security Council (NSC), 125, 166, 307–308
Nationalism, Latin American, 64–70
Nation-state, 6–8
Netherlands, 7, 28, 177
  arms control and, 338
  balance of power, 35
  Caribbean and, 31, 35, 39, 85, 86, 89, 95, 188
  economic relations, 191, 270, 271

Inter-American System and, 213
United Nations and, 246
See also individual countries
Netherlands Antilles, 240, 269
Neutralism, neutrality. *See* Nonalignment
New Dialogue, 127–128
New International Economic Order (NIEO), 48, 158–159, 248, 346–347
New Jewel Movement, 130
New Zealand, 341
Nicaragua, 28, 46
  arms control and, 340
  capability analysis of, 57, 59–60
  diplomatic relations, 76
  economic relations, 264, 265, 266, 269, 273
  guerrilla groups, 164–166
  Holy See and, 140
  integration, 186, 187, 188
  Inter-American System and, 218, 222, 224, 227, 230–231, 233, 235
  International Court of Justice and, 245–246
  law of the sea and, 345
  military relations, 279, 282, 287
  nationalization, 71
  nonalignment, Nonaligned Movement, 81, 253
  Soviet Union and, 31, 45, 71, 81, 85
  United Nations and, 243, 244
  United States and, 112, 120, 129, 130, 131–132, 185, 303, 304, 308, 320–321
Nicaraguan Resistance. *See* Contras
Nicaraguan Revolution (1979), 45, 46, 69, 161, 163, 164–165, 166, 215, 223, 312, 320
19th of April Movement (M-19), 163
Nixon, Richard M., 122, 126–128, 268, 285
Nonalignment, Nonaligned Movement, 9, 47–49, 80–81, 251–254, 347
Non-Proliferation Treaty (1968) (NPT), 336, 339–340
Nonstate actors, 12–13, 29, 135–169

Noriega, Manuel, 276
North Atlantic Treaty Organization (NATO), 94
Norway, 341
No-Transfer Resolution (1811), 113, 114
Nuclear capability, 63, 83, 297

Oduber, Daniel, 158
Oil industry. See Petroleum industry
Olney, Richard, 117
Olney Corollary, 117
Operation Blast Furnace (1986), 275
Operation Pan America, 233, 268
Operation Snowcap (1988), 275
Orfila, Alejandro, 212
Organization for the Prohibition of Nuclear Weapons in Latin America (OPANAL), 338
Organization of American States (OAS), 70, 199
    Charter of, 40, 192, 207, 208, 209, 210–211, 218, 225, 229
    establishment of, 213
    membership, 212–213
    organizational structure, 208, 209–212
    See also Inter-American System
Organization of Central American States (ODECA), 185–186
Organization of Eastern Caribbean States (OECS), 192
Organization of Iron Ore Exporting Countries (IOEC), 251
Organization of Latin American Solidarity (OLAS), 161
Organization of Petroleum Exporting Countries (OPEC), 49, 250, 251
Organization of the Armed People, 164
Orinoco River, 55
Ortega y Gasset, José, 290
Ortiz Meña, Antonio, 234
Outer Space Treaty (1967), 336

Paline Commission, 158
Palme, Olaf, 158

Pan American Federation of Labor (PAFL), 151, 153
Pan American Health Organization, 207
Pan American Institute of Geography and History, 207
Pan American Union, 205, 207, 209, 210
Pan Hispanism, 49, 292
Panama, 28, 39, 177
    arms control and, 340
    capability analysis of, 57, 345
    Contadora and, 45, 55, 340
    diplomatic relations, 76
    economic integration, 187
    economic relations, 264, 265, 266, 269, 273
    Inter-American System and, 204, 212, 222
    Japan and, 334
    law of the sea and, 345
    League of Nations and, 240
    military relations, 281, 282, 283
    narcotics traffic, 274, 276
    nonalignment, 81
    United Nations and, 243
    United States and, 43, 120, 126, 127, 129, 222, 302, 304, 328–334, 357
Panama Canal, 37, 39–40, 114, 118, 119, 127, 129, 131, 302, 303, 306, 328–334, 337, 357
Panama Canal Act (1979), 334
Panama Canal Treaties (1979), 332, 333–334
Papacy. See Roman Catholic Church
Paraguay, 28, 74
    Antarctica and, 341
    arms control and, 340
    balance of power, 39, 54, 79
    Bolivia and, 240, 279, 280, 301, 305
    capability analysis of, 54, 58
    economic integration, 192, 193
    economic relations, 264, 265, 266, 271
    France and, 89

geography, 32, 33, 38
Inter-American System and, 224,
    227, 233
League of Nations and, 240
military relations, 277, 279, 282,
    287
narcotics traffic and, 274
nationalism, 68
Spanish American union, 176, 180
Paraguayan War (1865–1870), 300
Pardo plan, 344, 345
Paris Club, 261
Partial Test Ban Treaty (1963), 339
Pascal Allende, Andres, 163
Pastora, Eden, 165, 166
Pauncefote, Lord, 329
Paz Zamora, Jaime, 164
Peace of Westphalia, 7, 136
People's Republic of China, 7
    arms control and, 338, 339–340
    cultural relations, 293
    economic relations, 259
    guerrilla warfare and, 311
    See also individual countries
Pérez, Carlos Andrés, 158, 200
Pérez Alfonso, Juan Pablo, 250
Pérez de Cuellar, Javier, 244, 316
Pérez-Guerrero, Manuel, 248
Pérez Triana, Santiago, 238
Perón, Juan Domingo, 80, 92, 123,
    152, 252
Peronist Armed Forces (FAP), 163
Pershing, John Joseph, 299
Peru, 28
    Antarctica and, 341
    arms control, 340
    balance of power, 39, 54
    Bolivia and, 38, 55, 300–301
    capability analysis of, 54, 55, 58, 59,
        63, 64
    Chile and, 38, 300, 301
    Colombia and, 300
    Communist party, 161
    cultural relations, 292
    economic integration and association,
        192, 193, 195, 196, 197, 198

economic relations, 258, 259, 261,
    262, 264, 265, 266, 271
Ecuador and, 305–306
France and, 89
geography, 32, 33, 38
Germany and, 92, 93
guerrilla groups, 161, 311
Holy See and, 141
Inter-American System and, 209,
    223, 227, 235
IOEC membership, 251
Japan and, 104
labor unions, 72
law of the sea and, 342, 343, 345
leadership aspirations, 29, 79
League of Nations and, 240
military relations, 277, 278, 279,
    280, 281, 282, 285, 286
narcotics traffic, 274, 275
nationalism, 68, 69
nationalization, 69, 71
nonalignment, Nonaligned Movement,
    81, 253
People's Republic of China and, 107
Soviet Union and, 286
Spain and, 90, 179
Spanish American union, 176, 177,
    178, 179, 180
United States and, 122, 126, 127,
    132, 306
Petroleum industry, 69, 144, 146, 148
Philippines, 220
Pinochet, Augusto, 74, 132, 288
Plaza Lasso, Galo, 212
Poland, 341
Political integration, 21, 175–180
Political parties, transnational political
    parties, 29, 66, 94–95, 154–159
Pope John XXIII, 141, 143
Pope John Paul II, 141, 142, 143, 325
Pope Paul VI, 141, 142, 273
Popular Liberation party (EPL), 163
Popular Revolutionary Vanguard
    (VPR), 163
Popular Social Christian Movement
    (MPSC), 167
Porter, Horace, 238

Porter Doctrine, 238
Portugal
  balance of power, 35–36, 85
  economic relations, 257
  Inter-American System and, 213
  United Nations and, 246
  See also individual countries
Prebisch, Raúl, 68, 246, 247, 248,
  346, 363, 364, 365
Procedure for the Establishment of a
  Firm and Lasting Peace in Central
  America (1987), 45, 46, 324–326
Puerto Rico, 118, 155, 188, 189, 270,
  302, 337, 338

Quadros, Jânio, 81

Rangel, Domingo Alberto, 162
Reagan, Ronald, 103, 130–133, 275,
  287, 288, 316, 332, 357
Reagan Doctrine, 130
Realism, theory of, 353–354, 355–356,
  358, 362
Regional Confederation of Mexican
  Labor (CROM), 151
Regional consciousness, 29–30
Regional organizations, 16, 21
Regional subsystems. See International
  subsystems
Regionalism, 21
Report of the President's National
  Bipartisan Commission on Central
  America, 101–102, 131, 321, 323,
  358
Republican party, 122, 155
Revisionist orientation, 10
Revolutionary Armed Forces (FAR),
  163, 164
Revolutionary Army of the People
  (ERP), 166
Revolutionary Coordinating Committee
  (JCR), 161
Revolutionary Integration Organization
  (OIR), 162
Revolutionary Leftist Front (FIR), 161
Rio de la Plata region, river system,
  33, 39, 55, 197

Rio Commission of Jurists, 203
Rio Grande, 297, 298
Rio Treaty. See Inter-American Treaty
  of Reciprocal Assistance
Robelo, Alfonso, 165
Roca, Roberto, 166
Rockefeller, Nelson A., 126, 263
Rockefeller Report (1969), 126–127
Rodríguez Larretta, Eduardo, 229, 230
Rojas, Ricardo, 67
Rojas Pinilla, Gustavo, 163
Roman Catholic Church, 7, 29, 73,
  135–143
  anticlericalism, 139–140
  Central America and, 140, 141
  Council of Europe and, 136
  economic relations, 273
  Inter-American System and, 136,
    140, 213, 317
  international actor, 12–13, 135–137
  Non-Proliferation Treaty and, 136
  papal relations with Latin America,
    137–141, 317–318
  social change and, 141–143
  Southern Cone and, 141
  Spanish America and, 138
  United Nations, 136
Romualdi, Serafino, 153
Roosevelt, Franklin D., 120, 263, 304
Roosevelt, Theodore, 117
Roosevelt Corollary, 118, 120, 214,
  216, 217, 303
Rosas, Juan Manuel de, 299
Rowe, Leo S., 238

Saavedra Lamas, Carlos, 227
St. Christopher-Nevis, 28, 58, 59, 82,
  189, 190, 191, 192, 213, 269,
  338, 340
St. Kitts. See St. Christopher-Nevis
St. Lucia, 28, 58, 81, 189, 191, 192,
  213, 253, 269
St. Vincent-Grenadines, 28, 58, 82,
  189, 191, 192, 213, 269
San Martín, José de, 66
Sandinist National Liberation Front
  (FSLN), 69, 164–165, 196, 231

Sandinista Revolutionary Front, 165
Sandinista Unity of Miskito, Sumas,
    and Ramas (MISURASATA), 165
Santa Cruz, Andrés, 300
Saudi Arabia, 213
Schneider, René, 310
Schweitzer, Pierre-Paul, 249
Scott, James Brown, 203
Seabed Arms Control Treaty (1972),
    336
Second Lima Conference (1864–1865),
    179
Sendero Luminoso, 162
Seward, William H., 116
Single Central Association of Latin
    American Workers (CUTAL), 152,
    153
Soccer war, 319
Social Democratic parties, 95, 155,
    156, 157–159
Social Progress Trust Fund, 234
Socialist International, 95, 155, 156,
    157–159
Solano López, Francisco, 300
Somoza family, regime, 76, 164, 196,
    231, 319, 320
South Africa, 341
South America, defined, 31, 32–33
South Atlantic, 33, 46, 54, 83
South Korea, 213, 293
Southern Cone, Southern Cone
    subsystem, 32–33, 34, 38–39, 42,
    43, 46–47, 54, 63, 78, 82, 297,
    299–301, 340, 358, 363, 368
Southern Opposition Bloc, 165
Soviet Union, 93, 95, 97–103
    Antarctica and, 341, 342
    arms control and, 338, 339
    balance of power, 41, 42, 54, 85, 98
    Central America and, 101–103
    Comintern and, 155, 156–157
    cultural relations, 293
    diplomatic relations, 289
    economic relations, 259, 272–273
    military relations, 283, 285, 286
    subversive activities, 304
    See also individual countries

Spain, 96, 177
    balance of power, 35–36, 85, 87
    cultural relations, 290, 291–292, 293
    diplomatic relations, 289, 290
    economic relations, 257
    Inter-American System and, 213
    military relations, 279, 285
    United Nations and, 246
    See also individual countries
Spanish America, defined, 28, 29
Spanish American union, congresses,
    176–179
Special Conference of Caribbean
    Countries Concerning the Problems
    of the Sea (1972), 345
Special Latin American Coordinating
    Committee (CECLA), 198–199,
    248, 347
Spooner Amendment (1902), 330
Stalin, Josef, 98, 157
Stroessner, Alfredo, 74, 132, 288
Suriname, 28, 32, 33, 58, 69, 81, 191,
    198, 253, 264, 265, 266, 271,
    274, 282
Sweden, 191, 213
Switzerland, 213, 279, 316
Systems theory, as analytic framework,
    3–6

Tack, Juan, 332
Tacna-Arica dispute, 240
Taft, William Howard, 118, 119
Terrorism, terrorist, 160–161
Texas, 37, 297–298
Thatcher, Margaret, 314, 316
Third World, 9, 47–49, 159, 314, 315,
    342
13th of November Revolutionary
    Movement (MR-13), 164
Tito, 254
Tobar, Carlos R., 228
Tobar Doctrine, 228
Torres Restrepo, Camilo, 142, 162
Torrijos, Omar, 332
Transisthmian canal. See Panama Canal
Treaty for the Prohibition of Nuclear
    Weapons in Latin America (1968)

(Treaty of Tlatelolco), 336, 337–339
Treaty of Confederation, 178
Treaty of Guadalupe Hidalgo (1848), 115
Treaty of Montevideo (1828), 299
Treaty of Montevideo (1960), 192, 193, 194
Treaty of Montevideo (1980), 196
Treaty of Perpetual Union, League, and Confederation, 177
Treaty of Union and Defensive Alliance (1865), 179
Treaty to Avoid or Prevent Conflicts Between the American States (1923), 226–227
Trinidad-Tobago, 28, 58, 63, 70, 81, 189, 190, 191, 212, 226, 253, 264, 265, 266, 269, 282, 340, 345
Trotskyism, 355
Trujillo, Ciro, 162
Trujillo, Rafael, 76, 305, 319
Truman, Harry S, 122
Turkey, 345
26th of July Movement, 161, 308

U Thant, 337
Ubico, Jorge, 308
Ungo, Guillermo Manuel, 166–167
Union of American Republics, Union of American States, 205
Unionized Latin American Workers' Group (ATLAS), 152–153
United Arab Republic, 293
United Brands, 146, 148
United Fruit Company, 146, 148, 308
United Kingdom, 7, 28, 177
    Antarctica and, 341, 342
    arms control and, 338, 339
    balance of power, 35, 36, 37, 39, 40, 86–87, 88–90, 92
    Caribbean and, 31, 35, 38, 39, 86, 70, 90, 95, 96, 188, 191
    cultural relations, 292, 293
    diplomatic relations, 300
    economic relations, 257, 258, 259, 270, 271
    Inter-American System and, 213, 225–226
    military relations, 86, 277, 279, 285, 286
    transisthmian canal, 37, 86, 90, 328–329
    United Nations and, 243, 246
    See also individual countries
United Nations (UN), 95, 241–249
    Antarctica and, 342
    arms control, 336–337
    economic and financial institutions, 246–249
    Latin American participation in, 49, 79, 180, 241–242
    relationship to Inter-American System, 207, 213, 225–226, 242–246
    See also individual countries
United Nations Committee on Disarmament (CCD), 336, 340
United Nations Conference on Law of the Sea (UNCLOS), 344, 345
United Nations Conference on Trade and Development (UNCTAD), 48, 68
United Nations Convention on Law of the Sea (1982), 345–346
United Nations Development Program, 248
United Nations Economic and Social Council (ECOSOC), 241, 246
United Nations Economic Commission for Latin America (ECLA), 68, 82, 234, 246–247, 252, 261, 363, 364
United Nations Economic Commission for Latin America and the Caribbean (ECLAC). See United Nations Economic Commission for Latin America (ECLA)
United Nations General Assembly, 48, 243, 316–317, 337, 346
United Nations Security Council, 243, 244, 308, 312, 314, 315, 316, 331, 332

United Nicaraguan Opposition (UNO).
    See Contras
United States of America, 7, 28, 108–
    133
  arms control and, 338, 339, 341
  balance of power, 36, 37–38, 39–47,
    121, 124, 128, 131, 354–358
  Circum-Caribbean and, 31, 38, 40,
    42–43, 45–46, 110–111, 112, 113–
    114, 115, 117, 119–121, 123, 129–
    132, 188, 191
  communism and, 112, 121–124, 128,
    129, 130–132
  cultural relations, 292, 293
  democracy and human rights, 111–
    112, 115–116, 119, 121, 123, 124,
    126, 128–130
  diplomatic relations, 119
  economic relations, 257, 258, 259,
    260, 263–270
  imperialism, 116–119, 302–304
  Inter-American System and, 209,
    222, 226, 232, 235
  isolationism, 112–114, 116
  law of the sea and, 342, 343, 345
  migration, 110, 129, 131, 133
  military relations, 277, 279, 280–
    285, 286, 288
  narcotics traffic and, 110, 132, 133,
    275, 276
  nonproliferation, 129
  Southern Cone and, 46–47, 110–111,
    117, 129, 132
  Spain and, 115, 117, 118
  Spanish American congresses, 177,
    178, 179
  United Kingdom and, 117
  United Nations and, 243, 244, 246
  See also individual countries
Urquidi, Víctor, 68, 246, 247, 364
Uruguay, 28
  Antarctica and, 341
  Argentina and, 300
  arms control and, 340
  balance of power, 79, 299
  Brazil and, 300
  capability analysis of, 54, 58, 59, 61

  decision making in, 73
  diplomatic relations, 289
  economic integration and association,
    192, 193
  economic relations, 262, 264, 265,
    266, 271
  France and, 89
  geography, 32, 33, 38
  guerrilla groups, 162, 312
  Inter-American System and, 224,
    227, 232, 233
  military relations, 277, 282, 287,
    288
  nationalism, 67
  nonalignment, 82
  Paraguay and, 300
  Soviet Union and, 98, 304
  Spanish American union, 176, 180
  United Kingdom and, 86, 90
  United States and, 129, 132, 307
U.S. Virgin Islands, 118, 188, 246,
    270, 338

Vance, Cyrus, 231, 232
Vargas, Getulio, 292
Vásquez Caastaño, Fabio, 162
Vatican. *See* Roman Catholic Church
Vatican Development Fund, 273
Vatican II, 141
Vélez, Manuel Marulanda. *See* Marín,
    Pedro Antonio
Venezuela, 28
  arms control and, 337, 338, 340
  balance of power, 77
  capability analysis of, 55, 58, 59, 61,
    63, 64
  Communist party, 162
  Contadora and, 45, 55, 323
  decision making in, 61, 70, 71, 72,
    73
  economic integration and association,
    192, 198
  economic relations, 191, 258, 259,
    261, 262, 263, 264, 265, 266,
    270, 271, 273
  geography, 31, 32, 33
  Germany and, 92, 302–303

guerrilla groups, 162, 311
Guyana and, 70
Holy See and, 141
IOEC membership, 251
Inter-American System and, 212, 216,
    222, 224, 230, 231
Israel and, 105
Italy and, 302–303
law of the sea and, 345
leadership aspirations, 29, 77, 79
military relations, 277, 280, 282,
    286, 288
narcotics traffic, 274
nonalignment, Nonaligned Movement,
    82, 253
OPEC membership, 49
Spanish American union, 176, 178,
    179
United Kingdom and, 87, 90, 95,
    302–303, 312
United Nations and, 243
United States and, 122, 128, 131,
    302–303
Vergara Navarro, Rafael, 163
Versailles Peace Conference, Versailles
    treaty, 238–239, 279
Vicuña, Pedro Felix, 228
Villa, Francisco (Pancho), 299
Villalobos, Joaquín, 166

Violence, 18–19, 295–326
Virgin Islands. *See* British Virgin
    Islands; U.S. Virgin Islands

Walker, William, 179
Walker Commission, 329
War of the Pacific, 301
War of the Triple Alliance. *See*
    Paraguayan War
Washington Protocol (1929), 301
Welles, Sumner, 120
West Indies Federation, 69–70, 189–
    190, 313
Western Hemisphere Idea, 32, 49, 112–
    114, 116, 121, 202, 203
Wilson, Woodrow, 116, 118, 119, 239,
    292, 304
World Bank Group, World Bank, 191,
    199, 248, 262, 267, 273, 347
World Court. *See* International Court
    of Justice
World Eucharistic Congress, 141
World Federation of Trade Unions
    (WFTU), 152

Yugoslavia, 213

Zamorra, Rubén, 167
Zuazo, Siles, 164